WOMEN, POLITICS, AND CHANGE

WOMEN, POLITICS, AND CHANGE

Louise A. Tilly
AND
Patricia Gurin
EDITORS

RUSSELL SAGE FOUNDATION   NEW YORK

The Russell Sage Foundation

The Russell Sage Foundation, one of the oldest of America's general purpose foundations, was established in 1907 by Mrs. Margaret Olivia Sage for "the improvement of social and living conditions in the United States." The Foundation seeks to fulfill this mandate by fostering the development and dissemination of knowledge about the political, social, and economic problems of America. It conducts research in the social sciences and public policy, and publishes books and pamphlets that derive from this research.

The Board of Trustees is responsible for oversight and the general policies of the Foundation, while administrative direction of the program and staff is vested in the President, assisted by the officers and staff. The President bears final responsibility for the decision to publish a manuscript as a Russell Sage Foundation book. In reaching a judgment on the competence, accuracy, and objectivity of each study, the President is advised by the staff and selected expert readers. The conclusions and interpretations in Russell Sage Foundation publications are those of the authors and not of the Foundation, its Trustees, or its staff. Publication by the Foundation, therefore, does not imply endorsement of the contents of the study.

Library of Congress Cataloging-in-Publication Data

Women, politics, and change / Louise A. Tilly and Patricia Gurin,
    editors.
        p.   cm.
    Includes bibliographical references.
    ISBN 0-87154-884-4
    1. Women in politics—United States.   2. Women's rights—United
States.   I. Tilly, Louise.   II. Gurin, Patricia.
HQ1236.5.U6W667   1990
305.42'0973—dc20

90-8381
CIP

Acknowledgments

Many people contributed to the process of producing this volume. We are grateful for valuable advice from Alice Kessler-Harris and the thoughtful contributions of William Chafe, Barbara Farah, Joan Hoff-Wilson, Kristin Luker, and Virginia Sapiro to our workshops. We thank the book's anonymous reviewers for their perceptive and helpful comments and our co-authors for their important contributions to each other and to us about substance and style. Meticulous editing, checking and typing were done by Kathleen Donleavy, Charlott Neuhauser, Diane Poland (who also arranged the workshops), Charlotte Shelby, Maria Springer, Sarah Tilly and Ann Watson: we are grateful to one and all of them. Finally, our thanks to the Russell Sage Foundation for supporting the workshops and publications of this book, and special thanks to Peter de Janosi, Vice-President of the Foundation, and Priscilla Lewis, Director of Publications, who supported and guided this project from inception to publication.

Contributors

Kristi Andersen is associate professor of political science at the Maxwell School of Citizenship, Syracuse University. She is author of many papers on women in American politics and *The Creation of a Democratic Majority, 1928–1936* (1979).

Alida Brill, formerly the Program Officer at the Russell Sage Foundation, is the co-author of *Dimensions of Tolerance* (1983). Prior to moving to New York City, she was a researcher at the Survey Research Center, University of California-Berkeley. She is the co-convener of the Women's Dialogue—US/USSR.

Nancy F. Cott is professor of history and American studies at Yale University. She is author of *The Bonds of Womanhood: 'Woman's Sphere' in New England, 1780–1835* (1977) and *The Grounding of Modern Feminism* (1987).

Elizabeth Faue holds the Susan B. Anthony Post-Doctoral Fellowship in History and Women's Studies at the University of Rochester in 1988–1990. She is the author of a forthcoming book, *Community of Suffering and Struggle: Gender, Labor and Relief in Minneapolis, 1915–1945* and currently is working on a study of gender and the political culture of labor in the United States.

M. Patricia Fernández-Kelly is a research scientist at the Johns Hopkins University Institute for Policy Studies and an associate professor of sociology at the same institution. She is the author of *For We are Sold, I and My People: Women and Industry in Mexico's Frontier* (1983) and of articles on immigration, international economic restructuring, and the employment of Hispanic women in garment and electronics industries in Southern California and Southern Florida. With June Nash she co-edited *Women, Men, and the International Division of Labor* (1983), and with filmmaker Lorraine Gray she co-produced *The Global Assembly Line*, an Emmy-winning documentary exploring the effects of economic internationalization.

Jo Freeman has a Ph.D. in Political Science from the University of Chicago and a J. D. from the New York University School of Law. She is the author of *The Politics of Women's Liberation* (1975), which won a prize for the best scholarly work on women and politics of the American Political Science Association (1976). She is also editor of *Women: A Feminist Perspective* (most recent edition, 1989), and *Social Movements of the Sixties and Seventies* (1983).

Anna M. García is a research associate at the Center for U.S.-Mexican Studies at the University of California-San Diego. She has participated in numerous projects focusing on health, migration, the access to public services on the part of Mexican immigrants, and Hispanic women's employment. With M. Patricia Fernández-Kelly, she is the co-author of "Informalization at the Core: Hispanic Women, Homework, and the Advanced Capitalist State," in *The Informal Economy: Studies in Advanced and Less Developed Countries* (1989).

Patricia Gurin is professor of psychology and women's studies and a faculty associate of the Institute for Social Research at the University of Michigan. She is co-author of *Black Consciousness, Identity, and Achievement* (1975); *Hope and Independence: Blacks' Reactions to Electoral and Party Politics* (1989); *Gender and Racial Socialization in the Classroom* (1982), and co-editor of *Race and the Social Sciences* (1969). She organized the project on which *Women, Politics, and Change* is based while she was a Resident Scholar at the Russell Sage Foundation.

Nancy A. Hewitt is associate professor of history at the University of South Florida. Her publications include *Women's Activism and Social Change: Rochester, New York, 1822–1872* (1984), "Feminist Friends: Agrarian Quakers and the Emergence of Women's Rights" (1986), and "Beyond the Search for Sisterhood: American Women's History in the 1980's" (1985). She is currently working on a comparative study of

Anglo, black and Latin women in Tampa, Florida, 1885–1945, and is the American editor for *Gender & History*.

Evelyn Brooks Higginbotham is assistant professor of American history at the University of Pennsylvania. She is author of *Righteous Discontent: The Women's Movement in the Black Baptist Church, 1880–1925* (forthcoming) and is currently writing a book on black women and politics in the twentieth century.

Leonie Huddy is assistant professor of political science at the State University of New York at Stony Brook. Her main research interests are in political psychology, particularly the politics of intergroup relations. She is the author and co-author of various articles, book chapters, and manuscripts on women and politics, bilingual education, and the politics of aging.

Herbert Jacob is professor of political science at Northwestern University. He has written extensively on law and politics in the United States. His most recent book is *Silent Revolution: The Transformation of Divorce Law in the United States* (1988). He is currently investigating the ways in which men and women use their understandings of the law to negotiate child support and custody settlements.

Jacqueline Jones is professor of history at Wellesley College. Her book, *Labor of Love, Labor of Sorrow: Black Women, Work and the Family from Slavery to the Present* (1985), won the Bancroft Prize. She is currently working on a study of the Southern origins of the Northern underclass.

M. Kent Jennings is currently professor of political science and a program director at the Center for Political Studies, University of Michigan, and professor of political science at the University of California-Santa Barbara. He is the author or co-author of *Community Influentials* (1964), *The Political Character of Adolescents* (1974), *Governing American Schools*, (1974), *Generations and Politics* (1981), and *Parties in Transition* (1986).

Rebecca Klatch received her Ph.D. from Harvard University in 1984. She is currently assistant professor of sociology at University of California-Santa Cruz. In 1989–1990, she is a fellow at the Stanford Humanities Center. She is currently researching the 1960s generation by comparing women and men active in Students for a Democratic Society and Young Americans for Freedom.

David Knoke is professor and chair, department of sociology, University of Minnesota. He received his Ph.D. from the University of Michigan in 1972 and specializes in the study of organizations and political sociology. Recent books include *The Organizational State* (with Edward O. Laumann) (1987), *Organized for Action: Commitment in Voluntary Associations* (1981), and *Structural Politics: The Network Perspective*. In 1989 he was a Fulbright Senior Research Scholar in West Germany, working with Franz Urban Pappi on a comparative study of American and German national labor policy domains.

Suzanne Lebsock received her doctorate in history from the University of Virginia in 1977. She is author of *The Free Women of Petersburg: Status and Culture in a Southern Town, 1784–1860* (1984), which won the Bancroft Prize and the Berkshire Conference prize in 1985, and of *Virginia Women, 1600–1945: 'A Share of Honour.'* (1984) She is professor of history, Rutgers University.

William Lehrman, assistant professor at Virginia Polytechnic Institute, is writing a book on the social history of the life insurance industry.

Jane Mansbridge is professor in political science and sociology and a member of the research faculty of the Center for Urban affairs and Policy Research at Northwestern University. She is the author of *Why We Lost the ERA* (1986), the co-winner of the American Political Science Association's Kammerer award in 1987 and Schuck award in 1988, and *Beyond Adversary Democracy* (1980) and editor of *Beyond Self-Interest* (1990). She has held fellowships from the Woodrow Wilson Foundation, the National Science Foundation, the Rockefeller Foundation, and the Institute for Advanced Study in Princeton.

Ruth Milkman is associate professor of sociology at University of California-Los Angeles. She has written many scholarly articles on women's work, is the editor of *Women, Work and Protest: A Century of Women's Labor History* (1985) and author of *Gender at Work: The Dynamics of Job Segregation By Sex During World War II* (1987), which was awarded the Joan Kelly Prize in Women's History by the American Historical Association. Her current research interests include, in addition to women's labor history, changing industrial relations and new technology in the U.S. auto industry.

Barbara J. Nelson, a political scientist, is professor of public affairs and planning and co-director of the Center on Women and Public Policy at the Humphrey Institute, University of Minnesota. She is the author of *Making an Issue of Child Abuse: Political Agenda Setting for Social Problems* (1984), *American Women in Politics: A Selected Bibliography and Resource Guide* (1984), and co-author with Sara M. Evans of *Wage Justice: Comparable Worth and the Paradox of Technocratic Reform* (1989).

David O. Sears is professor of psychology and political science and Dean of Social Sciences at the University of California-Los Angeles. He received his B.A. in history from Stanford University, and his Ph.D. in psychology from Yale University in 1962, and has taught at UCLA since then. His books include *Public Opinion* (with Robert E. Lane) (1964), *The Politics of Violence: The New Urban Blacks and the Watts Riot* (with John B. McConahay) (1973), *Tax Revolt: Something for Nothing in California* (with Jack Citrin) (1982), and *Political Cognition: The 19th Annual Carnegie Symposium on Cognition* (edited with Richard R. Lau) (1986). He has published articles and book chapters on a wide variety of topics in social and political psychology, including attitude change, mass communications, ghetto riots, political socialization, voting behavior, and racism.

Kay Lehman Schlozman is professor of political science at Boston College where she teaches, among other topics in American politics, a course on Women and Politics. She is co-author of *Injury to Insult: Unemployment, Class, and Political Response* (with Sidney Verba) (1979) and *Organized Interests and American Democracy* (with John Tierney) (1985) and editor of *Elections in America* (1987). Her current research focuses upon voluntary participation in political and community life in America.

Louise A. Tilly is professor of history and sociology at the New School for Social Research and chair of its Committee on Historical Studies. She is author, with Joan Scott, of *Women, Work and Family* (1978, revised edition 1987), *Politics and Class in Milan, 1880–1902* (forthcoming) and co-authored (with Heidi Hartmann and Robert Kraut) the report of the Panel on Technology and Women's Employment of the National Research Council (1986). She is currently working on a study of contrasting groups of women workers in turn-of-the-century France.

Sidney Verba is the Carl H. Pforzheimer University Professor at Harvard University. He has written extensively on citizen participation in the United States and elsewhere. He is the author or co-author of a number of books in the field, including *The Civic Culture* (1963), *Participation in America* (1972), *Participation and Political Equality* (1978), *Injury to Insult* (1979), and *Equality in America* (1985).

Susan Ware teaches in the history department at New York University, where she also coordinates the Women's History program. She is the author of several books on women in public life, including *Beyond Suffrage: Women in the New Deal* (1981) and *Partner and I: Molly Dewson, Feminism, and New Deal Politics* (1987). She is currently writing a book about popular heroines of the 1930s, which focuses on Amelia Earhart.

Robert Wuthnow is professor of sociology at Princeton University. His recent books include *Communities of Discourse: Ideology and Social Structure in the Reformation* (1989) and *The Restructuring of American Religion: Society and Faith Since World War II* (1988).

Contents

WOMEN, POLITICS, AND CHANGE

PART **I**

Introduction

1

Women, Politics, and Change

Louise A. Tilly / Patricia Gurin

In discussing the rights of women, we are to consider, first, what belongs to her as an individual, in a world of her own, the arbiter of her own destiny, . . . Secondly, if we consider her as a citizen, as a member of a great nation, she must have the same rights as all other members, according to the fundamental principles of our Government. . . . Thirdly, viewed as a woman, an equal factor in civilization, her rights and duties are still the same—individual happiness and development. Fourthly, it is only the incidental relations of life, such as mother, wife, sister, daughter, which may involve some special duties and training. The isolation of every human should and the necessity of self-dependence must give each individual the right to choose his own surroundings. The strongest reason for giving woman all the opportunities for higher education, for the full development of her faculties, her forces of mind and body; for giving her the most enlarged freedom of thought and action; a complete emancipation from all forms of bondage, of custom, dependence, superstition; from all the crippling influences of fear—is the solitude and personal responsibility of her own individual life.[1]

So spoke Elizabeth Cady Stanton, feminist and suffragist, in her statement to the U.S. Senate Committee on Woman Suffrage, February 20, 1892. Her words are striking in their contemporary tone, in their inclusion of familial as well as formal political and civic equality. At the same time they echo eighteenth century Enlightenment ideas about individual rights and responsibilities, a long-lasting political model in the United States. Our view of women's politics includes more than feminist poli-

3

tics, and we are more interested in collective action than in individual action: We begin here, however, because this quotation raises an important contextual theme of this book, that of historical continuity and change. Other major themes are the meaning of politics and the place of women's politics in the context of large-scale structural change.

Three intellectual opportunities shape this project. The first is theoretical: the opportunity to apply the suggestion of feminist scholars that to understand women and politics we must broaden and expand our definition of politics—past and present.[2] The second is sociological: the opportunity to bring a structural perspective to the problem of women's politics. The third is historical: the opportunity to look in detail at the "long" twentieth century, starting in the 1880s and coming up to the present, to compare not only the first and second great waves of women's feminist activism—two periods of women challenging the state and other institutions—but also the context and content of more routine politics in other periods.

What Is Politics?

In the late nineteenth century, middle-class American women wrote tracts, marched, petitioned, and demonstrated to support temperance, demanding government intervention to prohibit the sale of liquor; in 1901 Cuban and Italian immigrant women in Tampa, Florida—some workers themselves and others simply Latin community members—joined male workers in a hard-fought strike of cigar makers for improved working conditions and the right to organize (Lebsock and Hewitt, this volume). In the late twentieth century, women, young and old, but primarily middle class, marched, lobbied, and campaigned for the Equal Rights Amendment; women hospital workers—many of them black and Hispanic—led their union in struggles for recognition, better wages, and improved working conditions (Mansbridge and Milkman, this volume). Through these actions, women were collectively and individually attempting to affect the distribution of power and/or resources in a state or community. In short, they were engaged in politics.

Any study of politics must define its terrain: What is politics? One answer is the "authoritative allocation of values for a society"; the mellifluous phrase is David Easton's.[3] Easton rejects definitions that simply concern relations between citizens and their government within states as too narrow and rejects as well definitions that are so broad that they encompass the power component in personal relations. For us, the problem with his definition (although he would disagree) is that it seems both to require that all actors be members of the polity and to suggest too consensual a process.

Sidney Verba and Norman H. Nie define political participation in a way "narrower [than some] in that [they] consider as acts of participation only those activities aimed at influencing the government in some way . . . they have a broad view of the ways one can influence the government—both inside and outside the electoral sphere."[4] Yet Verba and Nie's classification of the political acts that interest them—voting, campaigning, initiating contact with officials, and group or organizational activities—has an important limitation for our purposes: their "concern is with activities 'within the system'—ways of influencing politics that are generally recognized as legal and legitimate."[5]

This highly contemporary definition is inappropriate for historical investigation, for it assumes both a particular type of state and political system and a broadly inclusive polity. These conditions did not obtain in the past. Women were not members of the polity when they had no right to vote, hold office, or sit on juries; even after they received the vote through the Nineteenth Amendment to the U.S. Constitution, their rights as citizens were not clear (Andersen, this volume). Susan B. Anthony had pointed out the implications of this anomaly much earlier, when she argued her case at her 1873 trial for voting:

> Your denial of my citizen's right to vote is the denial of my right to consent as one of the governed, the denial of my right of representation as one of the taxed, the denial to a trial by a jury of my peers as an offender against law. . . . All of my prosecutors, from the eighth ward corner grocery politician, who entered the complaint, to the United States Marshal, Commissioner, District Attorney, District Judge, your honor on the bench, not one is my peer.\ . . .[6]

Women received suffrage in all states only in 1920. (A similar argument could be made by southern blacks, progressively disfranchised in the period starting in 1877, but accelerating in the 1890s.) In order to give women's politics a single definition before and after suffrage we need a broader definition.

Resource Mobilization

Recent theories of political mobilization that emphasize the role of organizational resources in fostering all types of collective action provide the needed breadth.[7] Critical of the crowd metaphor and of social breakdown and individual frustration as sources of collective movements, the resource mobilization theorists stress the importance of previously existing organizations and resources. Organized collectivities are able to marshal participants for specific events and activities, recruit new members, formulate strategies, garner support from potential allies, and sustain action even in the face of failure. Resource mobilization theories treat both orderly and disorderly collective action as politics, and as instrumental and rational modes of pursuing group ends. They use the term "collective action" for coordinated action on behalf of shared interests or for action in which sets of people commit pooled resources, including their own efforts, to common ends.[8] For William Gamson, the basic unit of analysis is the challenging group, whose members are "seeking the mobilization of an unmobilized constituency and [whose] antagonist or target influence lies outside of this constituency."[9] In his view, mobilizations to defeat or elect a candidate, or to advance a social policy outside party politics, are simply different forms of political behavior: "In the place of the old duality of extremist politics and pluralistic politics, there is simply politics. The American Medical Association and Students for a Democratic Society are not different species but members of the same species faced with different political environments."[10]

We take account of collective action in addition to conventional definitions of politics. When we define politics (as efforts to affect the distribution of power and resources in a state community) in this way, we can bring in the entire spectrum of women's politics, that of both disfranchised and franchised women, and we can compare periods before and after females had the vote. In terms of our definition, very little collective action is not also politics. One example that might qualify as nonpolitical is a large gathering of collective cultural expression, like a rock festival, say, Woodstock. Such events, although collective, are not directed toward power or redistributive issues, hence are excluded from our definition of politics. (It should be noted, however, that in practice it is state or community official responses that label collective acts political or not, independently of the participants' intentions, and it is difficult to imagine large collective acts that do not take on some political coloration, as indeed Woodstock did in 1969.) For the purposes of this volume, power struggles in the family are also excluded from our definition of politics, which is limited to the arena of the state or collective units within it. Outside collective action are political acts that are individual, like voting (although when it is deliberate bloc voting, voting is collective action), or individual refusals by southern blacks to perform certain types of work that had political import in the Reconstruction South and the succeeding period with its Jim Crow laws (Jones, this volume). Both of these types of acts fall under our rubric of politics even if they are not collective because they are motivated by political purposes or had political consequences. Our broad definition of politics thus includes claims not only by those "outside the system," but also by citizens whose ability to influence the system through voting and other types of participation is limited, either structurally or because of historical patterns of discrimination.

Dimensions of Women's Politics

Within the bounds of our definition of politics, there are three major dimensions along which women's politics can be situated: forms, bases, and issues. Women's participation takes two *forms:* (1) "politics" in the conventional sense, which includes social movements or other types of "claiming" politics;[11] pressure group politics, electoral politics, and leader-initiated (both legislative and executive leaders are included here) action for change in the distribution of power and resources; (2) "protopolitical" activities, which include direct collective appeals to authorities (unmediated by organization), often in defense of customary rights or statuses, and membership and action in organizations that work outside the formal political arena. Through such activities women may acquire organizational skills or networks of relationships, accumulate resources, and define their interests and/or acquire consciousness of their collective situation.

The two major forms of political activity have different *bases.* Protopolitics, even when organizations mediate the relationship, is based on solidarities formed in everyday life (those of family, community, and collective experience). Conventionally defined political activities, social movements, and other forms of claiming politics are normally based on voluntary organizations formed explicitly for political purposes. With the targets of politics becoming increasingly national at the end of the nineteenth century, and with the granting of suffrage, women's activity in electoral and pressure group politics based on organizations with explicit political goals gradually increased. Nevertheless, neither protopolitics nor social movements in which women were central actors disappeared.

The *issues* of women's politics run along a continuum ranging from those in which being female is irrelevant (and communal, familial, racial, class, or national issues dominate) and those in which women's interests *as women* (either the interests of all women or those of particular subsets) are foremost.

A Historical Overview of Women's Politics

Let us look at greater length at the three dimensions of women's politics chronologically in the United States.

There are two types of protopolitical activities. The first is direct appeals to authorities via protest or symbolic, ritualized demands, unmediated by organization. Jacqueline Jones (this volume) offers an example in the acts of resistance in which southern free black women refused to work in the fields for planters or worked only slowly and erratically for white women in their homes. Another example is the setting of food prices in the era of the American Revolution by women who insisted that merchants sell commodities at a "fair price" determined by their customers.[12] In its pure form, such price setting occurred primarily before our period. However, boycotts against certain "overpriced" products by Jewish women on the lower east side of New York between 1902 and 1917 share, in their early phases at least, the community base and lack of organization that characterized earlier price setting.[13] The southern black women resisted what they saw as unjust demands on them; the women who took part in price setting or boycotts resisted by their action food prices they perceived as iniquitous. These acts tended to be reactive rather than proactive, defending a vision of a just society that had, or should have, existed.

This type of protopolitics is generally associated with specific bases for action. In decentralized nineteenth century America, women, like men, acted politically and collectively within groups in which bonds grew out of common everyday experience. Solidarities of household or community, for example, were based on shared status, shared rights or privileges, shared oppression, or more banal daily factors like the household division of labor. These were the solidarities of everyday life. Women going about their tasks could easily join food protests and other popular politics—collective action that grew out of the quotidian.

Women also acquired skills and resources in a second type of protopolitical activity—participation in voluntary organizations with no explicit political goals. In these organizations they could develop as well a consciousness of their interests essential for any future political mobilization. Resources and skills garnered in nonpolitical organizations are often transferred from one organization to another, and by this means provide a route to formal political activity.

Alexis de Tocqueville laid Americans' propensity to voluntary association to their early experience with political organizations. He wrote:

> There is only one country on the face of the earth where the citizens enjoy unlimited freedom of association for political purposes. This same country

is the only one in the world where the continued exercise of the right of association has been introduced into civil life, and where all the advantages that civilization can confer are procured by means of it. . . . In their political associations, the Americans of all conditions, minds, and ages daily acquire a general taste for association, and grow accustomed to the use of it. There they meet together in large numbers, they converse, they listen to each other, and they are mutually stimulated to all sorts of undertakings. They afterward transfer to civil life the notions they have thus acquired, and make them subservient to a thousand purposes. Thus it is by the enjoyment of a dangerous freedom that the Americans learn the art of rendering the dangers of freedom less formidable.[14]

The American Revolution, a period of intense political contention and challenge, had indeed witnessed an upsurge of revolutionary committees or clubs, examples of political organizations. However, Tocqueville's model, in which political organization served as a prototype for other associations, considered only men; most women experienced voluntary association first in organzations not explicitly directed to politics. Mary Ryan's study of Oneida County, New York, in the antebellum period reveals a "remarkable variety and vivacity of voluntary associations." Moreover, one third of the twenty-six religious and charitable associations listed in the 1832 Utica City Directory were exclusively female.[15]

By no means, however, were all antebellum women's organizations nonpolitical. Nancy Hewitt's study of Quaker women's politics in Rochester, New York, demonstrates that these women mounted radical challenges to the distribution of power and resources in both their community and the nation around the issues of the abolition of slavery, temperance, and women's rights. Elizabeth Cady Stanton developed a radical critique of marriage which she later had to temper when she sought supporters for her and Anthony's position calling for universal (rather than simply black male) suffrage in 1869.[16]

Later in the nineteenth century, women's associational propensity continued, but the scope of their associations broadened. Many organized women were concerned with the distribution of resources in their communities, but did not struggle for power in a broader sense. "After 1870 clubs of all kinds proliferated . . . ," write Anne Firor Scott and Andrew Scott. "Their purposes were various: literary studies, community action, civic reform; but whatever the purpose they represented also an effort at self-improvement and self-education."[17]

Another type of associational activity was the systematic examination or thoughtful reflection on problems in a study club or prayer group, a long-held American tradition. This kind of activity could awaken women to matters that demanded solutions and sometimes could lead to action. Consciousness-raising groups, in this perspective, may be understood as a latter-day iteration of a cluster of longstanding women's activities through which collective definitions develop.

In both the nineteenth and early twentieth centuries, women gained organizational experience most often in voluntary associations, often religious or philanthropic in purpose, which provided services for the community or specific groups within it. Without the vote, women could not translate the politics of associational activism and the resources gained thereby into electoral politics. This does not mean, however, that reform-minded women did not also act collectively to sway politically powerful men.

Both philanthropic organizational and civic reform activities remained characteristic of American women even after they gained the suffrage, at least partly *because* of their experience when their direct entry into electoral politics was blocked and partly because the local community arena continued to be the arena of so many of their socially constructed self-defined interests.

In the 1880s and 1890s the rich and dense network of women's associations concerned with nonelectoral ends was joined by suffrage organizations and others, such as temperance groups, with local *and* national political goals (Lebsock, this volume). This change signaled renewed movement from a politics concerned with the distribution of social resources to one concerned with the redistribution of power. (The antebellum women's coalition for abolition, temperance, and women's rights had earlier worked for a radical redistribution of power.) A high point of women's social movement activity ensued, continuing until national suffrage was gained in 1920 and the Prohibition Amendment passed. These social movement organizations adopted the forms of electoral politics—meetings, demonstrations, petitions—even before women gained the vote. With the contemporaneous growth of an industrial capitalist economy and a vigorous labor movement, unions came to serve a function similar to that of civic or national associations. They represented workers' interests, and, to a degree that varied systematically in different types of unions (Milkman, this volume), sometimes acted explicitly on behalf of women workers. Early unions shared the social movement form with reform organizations and developed the strike as their typical form of protest. Unions, and the temperance and suffrage associations that acted on behalf of unrepresented constituencies, often displayed a more confrontational style than mainstream political organizations (including women's civic reform organizations), but they shared much of the latter's repertoire of collective action.[18]

Only after 1920 was women's politics able to expand to include electoral efforts to shape government policies. Nevertheless, as Nancy Cott shows in this volume, women continued to favor organizations other than political parties through the decade of the 1920s. No "women's bloc" emerged despite a high level of participation in organizations. The twenties also saw a slow expansion of women voting (Andersen, this volume) and new party activism by black women (Higginbotham, this volume). In the thirties, there came greater participation in parties and unions (Faue and Milkman, this volume) as family and domestic matters such as jobs and mortgages became political issues in the Depression. The fifties saw women still pursuing politics in nonpartisan pressure groups such as the League of Women Voters (Ware, this volume).

According to Jo Freeman, the contemporary women's movement in its early years took two distinct forms, neither of them electoral. The bases, Freeman continues, were two different cohorts of women. The first was the women connected to the national and state commissions on the status of women (originally appointed in 1961 by President Kennedy) who formed the National Organization for Women (NOW) in 1966. The second was a loose coalition of small groups of younger women, many of whom had been involved in the civil rights or anti–Vietnam War movements. "The two branches . . . are structured in distinctly different ways," Freeman writes:

> The "older branch" possesses several prominent and numerous minor core organizations. The structure of such groups as NOW, the Women's Equity Action League (WEAL), Federally Employed Women (FEW), and some fifty different organizations and caucuses of professional women has tended to be traditionally formal, usually containing local chapters and national governing bodies. . . . All started as top-down national organizations lacking a mass base. . . .
>
> The structure of the "younger branch," on the other hand, can best be thought of as a decentralized, segmented network of autonomous groups. Its basic unit is the small group of from five to thirty women held together by an often tenuous network of personal contacts and feminist publications. . . . With time and growth, the informal communications networks have partially stratified along functional lines, so that, within a single city, participants in, say, a feminist health clinic will know less of different groups in their own area than of other health clinics in different cities. . . .
>
> [Their] conscious lack of hierarchy means that the groups share a common culture but are politically autonomous. . . .[19]

In some respects, the contemporary "younger branch" harked back to the antebellum movement with its lack of formal organizations for women's rights and its dependence on informal networks ready to make radical demands.

The two cohorts were women in different contexts. The context of the "older branch" of the 1960s was the federal government-sponsored commission on women and its state offshoots. The context of the "younger branch" was the civil rights and student movements, both committed to nonhierarchical process and direct, unmediated forms of politics concerned with social and cultural issues as well as with more narrowly political issues. The formula of the "younger branch" had more in common with a protopolitics, consciously chosen, than with the organizational forms that had predominated at the turn of the century.

In the 1980s feminist politics again became characterized by formal organizations—primarily pressure groups. Many New Right groups, pursuing antifeminist goals—in which women played an important role as members—organized in pressure groups that paralleled those of their rivals (Klatch, this volume).

The Context of Large-Scale Structural Change

Two large-scale processes of structural change shaped the protopolitics and politics described here. First was the growth of a relatively centralized, strong state apparatus. Second was the growth of a capitalist industrial economy.

The beginning of the twentieth century saw a transition, according to Stephen Skowronek, from the nineteenth century state of courts and parties to a more bureaucratic, administrative state. According to Skowronek's analysis, the American Revolution rejected "the organizational qualities of the state . . . evolving in Europe over the eighteenth century."[20] The authors of the Constitution concentrated authority in the central government, but left most political institutions to the control of the states. The result was a state of parties (locally based organizations that distributed patronage) and courts (which defined the rights and duties of the various political actors).

The combined effects of industrialization, with the great growth in scale of the economy and the rise of a labor movement, and urbanization, with both rural-to-urban migration and the settlement of overseas immigrants in cities, undermined this nineteenth century state; in the early years of the twentieth century, a new administrative state was born. In it the President and agents of the administrative apparatus gained enormous responsibilities. This state took on new functions, including some regulation of the economy—for example, antitrust policies in response to abuses accompanying the unbridled economic competition at the end of the nineteenth century. Intervention did not include general regulation of working conditions, however. The Supreme Court viewed such efforts as violations of the right to free contract. Reformers turned instead to legislation that would protect women only, on the grounds of their physical weakness and maternal responsibilities, creating a legal and political precedent that would affect women's politics throughout the twentieth century (Freeman, this volume).

"Progressive" reforms proliferated at the turn of the century and up to World War I. These included, in the matter of elections, innovations that brought officials closer to voters: direct election of senators, direct primaries, and the initiative, referendum, and recall. At the same time, however, blacks and poor whites were being disfranchised in the South through poll taxes and literacy tests, while voting requirements that similarly disfranchised immigrants in northern cities were introduced. The Progressive credo emphasized the value of expert civil servants in the place of potentially corrupt members of patron-client networks.[21] Women Progressives focused especially on the hardships of women and children in urban life and in the workplace. They were advocates for these powerless groups with urban and national politicians, and served them in settlement houses and other social agencies.

Growth of the government bureaucracy at national, state, and local levels, and its increasing specialization, was paralleled by the growth of the service and clerical sectors of the economy. Employment in these sectors expanded, and with it a new area for women's employment. Only in the 1910 population census, however, did a clerical occupation ("stenographers and typists") make the list (it was number eight) of the ten leading occupations for women. Servant was the leading female occupation through 1940, with agricultural laborer second through 1910 (the latter occupation dropped to tenth in 1920 and disappeared only in 1940). Clerical occupations came to dominate women's employment in the 1950 census. There were women's professions, such as teaching, nursing, and social work, that also expanded in the period, but the women employed in them were far less numerous than those in clerical occupations. Overall, there was a slow increase in women's labor force participation, but it continued to be concentrated in a few occupations, mostly in the service sector.

World War I, like the Civil War in an earlier period, saw further expansion of government functions, including a military draft, greater direct taxing power, aid to agriculture, and new social programs (for families of soldiers, for example). Although the war induced an economic boom, solutions to the longer-range problems of poverty, immigration, the national economy, and labor relations were not advanced. At the end of the war, national woman's suffrage was achieved through the passage of the Nineteenth Amendment. Suffrage movement organizations were dismantled and women demobilized from their effective mass political movement, its ends realized. Yet women received the vote in a period in which parties were becoming less important as distributors of patronage, as a consequence of progressive good government reform and increasing delegation of government to experts. Elections were becoming less central to American politics. As the trend of voter turnout moved downward between 1896 and the 1920s, pressure group politics became increasingly important. (Lebsock, this volume, suggests that women, with their rich organizational history, made an important contribution to this shift.) Suzanne La Follette, feminist and pacifist, declared in 1926, "It is a misfortune for the woman's movement that it has succeeded in securing political rights for women at the very period when political rights are worth less than they have been at any time since the eighteenth century."[22]

New women voters also confronted a rising conservatism, as three Republican presidents, from 1920 to 1932, supported business/government corporatism and rejected federal government responsibility for poverty or labor relations. Even these conservative administrations, however, did not undo the reforms of the Progressive period. Indeed, some additional Progressive programs were adopted in these years, although usually in somewhat attenuated form. Among these were two acts which directly affected women: the Sheppard-Towner Act (1921) and the Cable Act (1922). Sheppard-Towner, pushed by the Women's Joint Congressional Committee (WJCC, an umbrella pressure group for women's organizations), passed the Congress with huge majorities. It provided funds for locally administered maternal and infant care, conferences on childcare, and public education on these problems. The WJCC also actively supported passage of the Cable Act, which gave American women married to foreigners (except for Chinese who were themselves ineligible for citizenship by naturalization) the rights of naturalized citizens. Earlier laws had linked a married woman's citizenship automatically to that of her husband. (The act was amended only in 1930–1931, to make wives' citizenship fully independent of their husbands' status.) As Nancy Cott writes, these two acts "neatly illustrate the dual legacy of the suffrage campaign, for as profoundly as Sheppard-Towner declared that women, as mothers, differed from men in their relation to the state, the Cable Act declared that women as people required the same relation to the state as men—or almost."[23]

By 1930 three fourths of the states had passed laws which provided for mothers' pensions; nine had passed general old age pension laws. The provisions of the state mothers' pension and workmen's compensation laws passed in the 1920s and 1930s reflected their supporters' gender assumptions (Nelson, this volume): Women could claim state aid as mothers if they lost their husbands' support through death or disability. Men's entitlement to state aid went via their economic role as workers. Congress did not renew the Sheppard-Towner Act in 1929, when its original authorization expired. Although Harding declared economic "normalcy," and overall there was economic growth, the international picture was not so bright. Trade protectionism and agricultural distress increased across the globe. The twenties were a period of great rural to urban migration, of both blacks and whites, as crisis spread in the agricultural economy.

The crash of 1929 occurred in an economy whose financial sector was overexpanded speculatively, whose agricultural sector was in a deep depression, and whose income was distributed in a polarized and inequitable manner. Banks and businesses failed, and unemployment rose rapidly. The Republican administration of Herbert Hoover regularly announced, against strong evidence to the contrary, that things were getting better.

Franklin Delano Roosevelt's election in 1932 changed matters. Although the Democrats had customarily opposed government intervention, and indeed had offered no systematic programs in the electoral campaign, Roosevelt hastened to sponsor a large array of legislation designed to reassure Americans, to attack the most urgent problems, and to lay the basis for longer-term solutions. Unemployment was addressed by federal relief and several types of work assistance. A National Industrial Recovery Act (NIRA) prohibited most child labor, as well as interference with labor organizing. When the Supreme Court found the NIRA unconstitutional, Congress reenacted several of its functions; most important here was the Wagner Act, which guaranteed unions the right to organize and bargain collectively. Even in the fervor of reform and expansion of the economic role of government one matter was left unchanged: Protective legislation continued to be gender specific (Faue, this volume). It operated as a legal constraint on women's labor force participation. In 1935 Congress approved the Social Security Act, the most far-reaching program passed by the New Deal. The act established a national system of old age pensions, paid for by a payroll tax. It also included provisions for an unemployment compensation system and joint federal-state assistance to the elderly, the handicapped, and dependent mothers and children living in poverty.

The postwar years were a prosperous time in which growth rates returned to and surpassed 1929 levels. Real GNP per capita in 1971 was roughly double that of 1929. The distribution of income among households also was leveled to some degree, with a substantial reduction in the share going to the top 5 percent of wealthiest families. Population grew much more rapidly in the baby boom of the 1950s and 1960s than it had in the 1930s. Government intervention in the economy increased in the Kennedy and Johnson years, as the American version of the welfare state was constructed. Minimum wages were increased, and social security was first extended and then indexed to the cost of living. The first budget which increased spending without raising taxes was the Kennedy budget of 1963, proposed in a period of threatened recession. Lyndon Johnson's progressive Great Society policy included direct federal aid to schools and Medicare for the elderly who were eligible for social security (that is, those who had earned entitlement through wage work in covered industry or through marriage to such an individual).

The 1960s and 1970s were also a period of social movements. The background of the civil rights movement lies in changes in the political economy of the South, in particular the end of the cotton-based economy and the accompanying phenomenon of black migration to the cities of the South and the North. Blacks' battles for restoration of their civil rights began in the South but eventually swept the North. They were soon followed by the student and anti–Vietnam War movements. A feminist movement gathered momentum in the late 1960s, organized in the two branches described by Freeman and discussed below.

Women's labor force participation increased steadily in the postwar period, despite the baby boom, to reach a level of 51.4 percent in 1981 compared with 31.8 percent in 1947. In the 1970s and 1980s fertility plummeted, and age at first marriage and divorce rates increased rapidly. The new higher rates of female labor force participation included for the first time many married women, even those with children under age 6. A concomitant of the new labor force and divorce patterns was an increase of female-headed households and of women as the chief wage-earner in households. Recently, the proportion of women has increased greatly in professions such as medicine, the law, and accounting, and in upper management positions in business. Although labor force participation patterns have changed, and some occupations have become more female, sex segregation in occupations continues; the index of segregation by sex among white workers fell from 46 in 1940 to 41 in 1981, a modest decline concentrated mostly in the decade of the 1970s. The decline was arguably due to civil rights legislation (Title VII of the Civil Rights Act of 1964) forbidding discrimination in hiring and the affirmative action programs which were mandated in the enforcement process. Persistent wage inequality between the sexes continues to accompany occupational segregation.

Progressive legislation, increasing government participation in the economy, the growth of bureaucracy and services in government and in the private sector, and persistent inflation slowed dramatically with the recession of 1979–1982 and the election of Ronald Reagan in 1980. Social programs were cut and a generally conservative outlook on the economy and society prevailed.

How did these large-scale political and economic changes affect the forms, bases, and issues of women's politics?

Large-scale political change—the expansion of government functions accompanying the development of the welfare state—and similar expansion on the state and local level (where education was especially important) opened up new employment for women in government. Women's employment in this area has served as a bridge to and base for interest group and party political participation. Women in teaching and women in clerical and management positions in government, as members of either unions or pressure group organizations, are especially visible (Knoke, Schlozman, and Jennings, this volume). Increased women's labor force participation in the private service sector, especially in those industries that are at least partially unionized—here hospitals and social work are important—has also led women to pressure group and party politics. These are new bases for women's politics, although the voluntary association (including unions) continues to serve as a central institution for women's activism. Over the twentieth century, then, but especially after 1960, the political party became a new form of women's politics.

Urbanization—with its concentration of population and its economic and social problems—has been accompanied by greater integration of women and men in local reform and social movement politics. (There was an early example of this type of integration in the antebellum period, when women and men worked together in abolitionist, temperance, pacifist, and women's rights organizations.) In the late nineteenth and early twentieth centuries, women and men worked together on issues of child welfare, educational reform, and housing. They promoted protective legislation for women and children and laws that curbed homework and child labor. Women were commonly more active on these issues than they were on reforms to encourage good government or improvement of urban services—getting rid of political machines and corruption, improving urban transportation and sanitation, and so on. They brought expertise gained in women-only voluntary associations to the issues of health, education, and welfare, reformulated as government responsibilities. Women and men also worked together in national social movements such as black rights, socialism, and labor, where issues of race and class dominated. Turn-of-the-century and Progressive-era politics saw thus both an increase in gender-integrated reform politics and the continued importance of women-only organizations such as women's clubs, settlement houses, and the National American Woman Suffrage Association. Later twentieth century social movements such as civil and welfare rights and women's liberation furthered the integration of women into party politics as voters and candidates. Historically, women-only organizations seem to have opened new paths for women's politics; as they achieved their goals, or at least some of them, they were supplemented but not supplanted by organizations in which women and men worked together.

To sum up, the nineteenth and twentieth centuries have seen great growth in the domain of women's politics, along with growth in the domain of government. New bases for women's politics have emerged with changing employment patterns. Women have continued to work politically in voluntary associations and at the local level; but through their labor market involvement as workers providing state services and as union members, they have moved into the national political arena in both party and pressure group politics. Correspondingly, the bases and forms of women in politics have become more similar to those of men. New issues—for example, maternity leave and daycare—have emerged as women's relationship to the family and workplace has changed.

The contemporary women's movement has gone beyond work-related issues, moreover, and has brought issues of sexuality and private life (such as abortion, homosexuality and gay and lesbian rights, wife abuse and other forms of family violence, displaced homemakers and the poverty of female-headed households) into the legislative arena. Are these new issues related to the patterns of structural change reviewed above? To the extent that women's increased labor force participation both increased their potential autonomy and increased pressures on married couples, yes. Also, the greater integration of men and women in political and economic institutions has to some extent delegated these issues (except gay rights) to women-only or primarily female organizations—to which, of course, many women who are also members of gender-integrated institutions belong. Why did these issues become so important in the contemporary women's movement compared with that of the earlier twentieth century? The woman suffrage movement's avoidance of these issues, or similar ones, was a deliberate strategy. Most of its leaders felt that it was vital to avoid the divisiveness of such issues as divorce and "free love" in order to focus on suffrage first and foremost. (As Ellen DuBois points out, Elizabeth Cady Stanton's radical position on marriage and divorce in the late 1860s was played down by her colleagues.)[24] The social movement climate of the second half of the twentieth century, which the later women's movement shared, made cultural and personal issues political. As structural change both increased women's labor force participation and increased the fragility of married life, the contemporary women's movement embraced rather than avoided cultural and sexuality issues. (Here, however, the avoidance of discussion of lesbianism by the older branch of the movement should be noted. Also, as Jacob, this volume, shows, divorce reform was an issue not greatly influenced by feminist organizations in the 1960s and 1970s.)

Continuity and Change

Many aspects of political life have changed for women since 1890, yet many continue in much the same form. The historical themes of continuity and change run throughout the chapters assembled here. Overall, disparate goals and cleavages in ideology, class, and ethnic/racial background have prevented women from acting as a single interest group. This very divisiveness, moreover, is a form of continuity. Two conflicting ideologies in particular have divided women politically across time. (We simplify here; there was ideological overlap in some groups' or individuals' positions, and many variants within each ideology.) One ideology emphasizes equal rights and the similarities between men and women; the other emphasizes gender differences and the belief that women have a special capacity for humanizing the public world. Both ideologies have been present across the long sweep of the nineteenth and twentieth centuries; indeed, individuals and organizations sometimes drew on both in their attitudes and tactics. And sometimes one ideology has been dominant, depending on the state of the economy and the political system at the time.

Ideological and Structural Cleavages

In order to trace these ideological changes and divisions, we must begin with the broad equal-rights movement in the mid nineteenth century—an earlier starting point than that taken by our authors. A *humanist* or *egalitarian* ideology, which grew out of the antislavery crusade in the 1830s and 1840s, dominated the first woman's rights movement. Alice

Kessler-Harris describes its central belief: "Women, by virtue of their common humanity with men, are entitled to all the same rights and privileges. They share with men . . . a set of human rights that transcend biological/gender differences."[25] The organizers of the first woman's rights convention held in 1848 in Seneca Falls, New York, emphasized common humanity and the same rights for men and women. Quaker women, in particular, worked together with men to analyze critically the condition of women and men and contributed to the progressive abolitionist, pacifist, and temperance movements in which they participated.[26] The language of these movements encouraged these radical egalitarians in this direction, and their experience as abolitionists taught them that men and women were more alike than different. This belief was reinforced by men's and women's joint membership and participation in many antislavery societies. Breaking the taboo against women speaking in public, the great antislavery female orators—Angelina Grimke, Sojourner Truth, Lucretia Mott, Abby Kelley Foster, Maria W. Stewart, and later Susan B. Anthony—demonstrated, for example, that rhetorical skill was as natural for women as for men. Aware of the many restrictions on women's participation in public institutions, these women activists argued for social and cultural changes to lift these restrictions as well as for strictly legal and political rights.

Following the Civil War and the bitter break between feminist advocates of universal suffrage, in particular Elizabeth Cady Stanton and Susan B. Anthony, and former abolitionists who put black suffrage before that of women, women's politics increasingly reflected a second ideology. Variously termed domestic or *woman-centered*, this view accepted and extended the prevailing ideology of separate spheres for men and women to provide a rationale for women to bring their domestic roles into public activities. Women who subscribed to this ideology were less militant about rights for women than about their roles as wives and mothers with a special obligation to family and community. Stressing biological differences between men and women, these women emphasized the compassionate and moral nature of women and their duty to curb the natural aggressiveness and competitiveness of men. They believed that a place for women in the public sphere was warranted by their unique obligation rather than by equality itself.

In the 1890s and early 1900s the woman-centered ideology was upheld also by service and reform activists who championed legislation and social programs to protect and help women and children. By that time some advocates of woman suffrage had also accepted aspects of the woman-centered ideology. To appeal to a wide range of suffrage supporters, Susan B. Anthony had de-emphasized her earlier goals of transforming society to achieve equal rights and stressed the single goal of winning equal *political* rights. The vision of social and cultural changes that would be required to achieve equality in other areas did not disappear, however. Some female reformers—especially the settlement house workers and the activists in the Women's Trade Union League— and some suffrage activists maintained commitment to a broader definition of equality. Nancy Cott describes the spectrum of ideology in the woman's movement at the close of the century as having a seesaw quality:

> . . . at one end, the intention to eliminate sex-specific limitations; at the other, the desire to recognize rather than quash the qualities and habits called female, to protect the interests women had already defined as theirs and give those much greater public scope. A tension stretched between emphasis on the rights that women (like men) deserved and emphasis on the particular duties or services that women (unlike men) could offer society. No collective resolution of these tensions occurred and seldom even did individuals permanently resolve them in their own minds.[27]

Ideological tension persisted in the final drive for woman suffrage in the first two decades of the twentieth century. Carrie Chapman Catt put together a broad coalition of women, some of whom argued for suffrage based on a belief that the electoral system would benefit from women's special nature; others on a belief that political equality was required to achieve general equality. The coalition proved unstable, however. In 1913 Alice Paul and others formed the Congressional Union (CU), a separate organization to fight for suffrage and for a broad program demanding equal rights and equal treatment. After suffrage was won, the CU became the National Woman's Party, sponsor of the Equal Rights Amendment (ERA) that was introduced into Congress for the first time in 1923.

This ideological dualism continued to influence women's politics in the decades between 1920 and the emergence of the modern women's movement in the late 1960s. It affected the stance that women took in partisan politics (Andersen and Cott, this volume), fueled political disagreement about the ERA and protective legislation in the 1920s and 1930s (Freeman, this volume),[28] and was the basis of cleavage between older and younger women in the Farmer-Labor party in the 1930s (Faue, this volume). For the most part, however, an ideology emphasizing women's vulnerability in the labor market and in the marriage bargain was dominant in women's politics and their treatment by the law until the late 1960s (Freeman).

The balance shifted in the 1960s and 1970s, producing a revolution in women's legal status. Freeman describes these developments. Congress led the way by passing the 1963 Equal Pay Law, which committed the federal government to improving women's economic position, and the 1964 Civil Rights Act, which prohibited sex discrimination in employment, and in the 1970s by sending the ERA to the states and passing laws that encouraged equal opportunity for women. The Supreme Court fundamentally altered its interpretation of women's position. Until 1971 "virtually all laws that classified by sex were constitutional; their purpose was to protect a dependent group. Today most such laws have been found unconstitutional."[29] Equality and women's rights became increasingly important political issues within the parties (see Jennings, this volume) and legislative bodies.[30] The older branch of the contemporary women's movement primarily sought equal rights. The rights agenda was most prominent in the drive to get the ERA ratified by the state legislatures. Indeed, ideological division about gender difference and similarity was an important basis of the bitter fight between women who supported the ERA and those who opposed it. Even among supporters, however, some women continued to question the extent to which women and men differ, and whether womanliness and motherhood can form a basis of feminism.

Contemporary exponents of the woman-centered ideology, now called maternal feminists and represented best by Jean Bethke Elshtain,[31] do not subscribe to biological differences between men and women. In the view of some,[32] they are less moralistic than were earlier activists who stressed women's differences from men. According to maternal feminists, differences in the early socialization of boys and girls and women's adult experiences as mothers are significant in forming women's identities and values. Boys are pushed to separate from their mothers at an early age, they argue, and hence develop an ethic of justice revolving around individual rights and universal standards of morality. Girls, held by their mothers in a closer bond, are believed to develop an ethic of care revolving more around relationships than rights; females furthermore come to value particularities in determining moral behavior.[33] Motherhood is thought to strengthen the ethic of care. Carol Dietz points out that the maternal feminists politicize these social psychological differences and describes the maternal feminists' conception of a woman citizen as a loving being devoted to the protection of vulnerable human life and to making the virtues of mothering the template for a new, more humane public world.[34]

If this ideological cleavage were restricted to today's feminists, it would hardly bear mention. But our authors show that disagreement about the nature of male and female produces strange political coalitions among contemporary women. In debates about pornography, maternity leave, and custody of children, feminists who emphasize gender differences and social conservatives of the New Right take similar positions, although they disagree on the appropriate sphere for women's activities. Egalitarian feminists and New Right economic conservatives are aligned on equal rights and personal choice, even though they disagree about the appropriate role for government (Klatch, this volume).

Not surprisingly, given these ideological disagreements as well as important differences in class, region, and ethnicity, women have rarely voted as a bloc, supported female candidates in proportions greater than men, or pushed a consensual women's agenda (Cott and Sears and Huddy, this volume). *Particular* groupings of women have acted collectively to advance goals they have defined as their interests as women. The woman suffrage movement is the most spectacular example (but even it included large organizations—the NAWSA and the CU—which disagreed deeply about method and distrusted and sometimes dismissed each other's actions). Others include the Women's Joint Congressional Committee's support for the Sheppard-Towner and Cable Acts, the broad coalition supporting ratification of the ERA in the 1970s and 1980s, and the coalition of feminists and antifeminist social conservatives in Women Against Pornography. But overall, women have never been a single interest group.

At first glance, alternation appears to characterize the relationship between the ideologies emphasizing gender differences and similarities. However, history does not repeat itself in a simple fashion. The dominance of one ideology over the other has changed with demographic, economic, and political transformations.

The nineteenth century consolidation of industrial capitalism and greater separation of home and of work fostered a domestic culture for middle-class women. Less advantaged women worked outside the home, but their jobs were generally segregated from those of men. The rising influence of political parties between 1840 and the end of the century furthered separation between men and women (Lebsock, this volume). Increasingly, powerful parties became the political channel for white men. Disfranchised women generally invested their energies in a range of voluntary activities. Middle-class women, in particular, found an outlet for their newly acquired advanced education and greater leisure in voluntarism. (Black men's hard-won enfranchisement was essentially destroyed by laws passed in southern legislatures in the 1880s and 1890s. From that period into the twentieth century, black men and women formed independent political organizations, protested against lynching, and worked for political rights.) At the end of the nineteenth century, an ideology emphasizing biological differences fit the nation's overall political conservatism. For some of its supporters, this ideology reflected and justified the structural separation of men and women, of blacks and whites, and of immigrants and native-born persons in the late nineteenth century economy and political system. Some adherents of a woman-centered ideology were not simply conservative, however. Progressive social reformers also stressed gender differences and advocated protective legislation for women and children because they believed that these groups in particular were vulnerable victims of capitalism.

The balance shifted after the middle of the twentieth century as a consequence of demographic, political, and economic changes: lowered fertility rates; increased employment of women; growth in number of households, especially those headed by women; and increased integration of women and men in political institutions. The political and social unrest associated with the civil rights, antiwar, and women's movements in the 1960s and 1970s led many Americans to question the justice of social constraints on individuals, including rigid gender roles and presumed differences between men and women. *Separate* spheres for men and women had been characteristic of the nineteenth century social structure and *integrated* spheres more characteristic of the second half of the twentieth century social structure.[35] The reemergence of woman-centered feminist theories and reassertion of customary gender roles and family values among social conservatives in the 1980s, however, demonstrate a continuing vacillation between the ideologies that divide women politically. Nonetheless, equality of rights is now broadly institutionalized and buttressed by law. It is unlikely that the ideology of difference will again dominate women's politics in the form that it did at the turn of the century because men and women are now much more integrated in the economy and in political institutions.

Other ideological disagreements also separate women. Some are loyal Republicans; others are loyal Democrats or Independents. Some define themselves as conservatives and subscribe to an individualistic, antigovernment ideology; others call themselves liberals and favor redistributive policies and a strong national government. Our authors who analyze *contemporary* party and electoral politics find that (1) the distribution of liberal and conservative beliefs among women is nearly identical to the distribution among men; (2) partisanship and liberal-conservative identification are the best predictors of the policy positions preferred by both men and women; (3) male and female delegates to each party's presidential nominating conventions have more in common politically than do female Republican and Democratic delegates (Jennings, this volume); and (4) men and women hold remarkably similar attitudes about gender roles (Sears and Huddy, this volume). There have been deep-seated historical attitudinal changes, but men and women have changed together.[36] With the exception of attitudes toward war and violence, they have held similar political attitudes ever since the polls began monitoring public attitudes in the 1930s, and on most issues they agree now even more than they did earlier.[37] Historical and structural factors undergird the ideological similarities between men and women. Men and women have become more integrated into political and economic life. Both groups are also more educated now than they were earlier. Women have achieved virtual equality with men in access to education, and this has been accompanied by a shared shift in attitudes. With similar attitudes and similar relationships to the economy and polity, it is no wonder that men in the public at large support women's issues in proportions not dissimilar to women. Women predominate, however, among the activists for gender equality. Finally, ideological similarity between men and women has been preserved because the structure of gender relations has changed little. The interdependence of married men and women and parents and children of both sexes within the family has remained strong even as divorce has increased. Men and women have reacted similarly to the economic, political, and cultural changes in the twentieth century because they are still so closely connected and in many ways share similar structural situations.

Three factors then have created and maintained divisions among women: (1) increasing structural integration of men and women; (2) continuing embeddedness of families within ethnic groups, social classes, and religious communities; and (3) the physical segregation of blacks and whites, different ethnic groups, and social classes. Husbands and wives and parents and children share gains and losses as members of racial, ethnic, and regional groups and social classes. Because women rarely interact as equals with women of different social groups, they have difficulty making their gender and common experiences as wives, mothers, and daughters a basis for political solidarity. (Nor do men often interact as equals across class lines.) Not surprisingly, our authors and other historians have documented class, ethnic, and racial divisions in many different forms of women's politics: the woman suffrage movement and the club movement (Lebsock, Cott, and Higginbotham, this volume); the Socialist movement, in which immigrant women accepted women's customary family roles and native-born women pressed Socialist organizations to work for gender equality;[38] political parties in which black women encountered racism from white women and white men (Higginbotham, this volume); nonpartisan political organizations (Ware, this volume); and labor organizations (Lebsock, Hewitt, Jones, and Milkman, this volume). The National Women's Trade Union League, active at the turn of the century, was eventually weakened by class and ethnic disagreements, and racism broke the fleeting class solidarity of women in the Southern Tenant Farmers' Union in the 1930s. However, our authors also highlight moments of interracial, cross-class, and inter-ethnic cooperation. Particular chapters of the NAWSA purposely de-signed different instrumental appeals to black and white women and other distinct groups of women. The Commission on Interracial Cooper-ation and the YWCA attained sporadic cooperation across racial lines (Cott and Lebsock, this volume). These historical examples demonstrate that women *can* achieve political solidarity when their organizations and leaders deliberately pursue strategies to reach women in different social circumstances.

The structural integration of men and women is thus a potential political liability for gender-solidarity–based politics. Women have been less able than blacks and some ethnic groups to mobilize group bonds in social movements and in collective action within electoral and party politics. Nevertheless, gender integration can be a political asset for women in forging alliances and exacting support from powerful men in government and in the private sector. Thus, while the structure of gen-der relations may inhibit the development of female solidarity, at the same time it provides a political mechanism (less available to blacks and most ethnic minorities) that capitalizes on coalitions and consensus be-tween the sexes.

Forms of Women's Politics

Another apparent continuity in women's politics is the importance of voluntary group involvement outside parties. From the early nineteenth century to the present, women have joined and worked for change through voluntary associations, most often without explicitly partisan goals. In this activity, they pioneered the typically twentieth century political strategy of interest group politics (Lebsock and Cott, this vol-ume). A less salutary continuity that accompanies this type of associa-tionism is the pattern of lesser resources in women's organizations. Cott concludes that in the 1920s men's lobbying organizations had economic clout that women's organizations lacked; Schlozman shows that wom-en's pressure groups still have fewer economic resources than others;

and Jennings demonstrates that even among party elites, a gender disparity in access to political resources continues.

Nonpartisan organizations have continued to be a vehicle for wom-
en's politics, but the degree of organization, links with other groups,
and cooperation have increased (Cott, Ware, and Schlozman, this volume). The Women's Joint Congressional Committee was promptly established as a Capitol Hill clearinghouse and lobby once women gained
the suffrage (Cott, this volume). Women are now part of the professional lobbying community (Schlozman, this volume). They are sufficiently integrated in party structures that they can press women's issues
in that context (Jennings and Mansbridge, this volume). Further, Jennings shows that women convention delegates, although still more
likely to be in women's organizations (especially school and teacher-
related ones), are increasingly affiliated with gender-integrated labor
organizations, service clubs, and professional groups.

Other changes in the forms of women's politics are also noted by our
authors. The distinctiveness of women's politics has waned with their
integration in political and economic life, although Knoke (this volume)
finds that contemporary women's pressure groups are much more democratic and their members more active than are other groups lobbying in
Washington. Although women continue to be active in nonpartisan organizations, these organizations are themselves transformed. They now
move in the channels of conventional politics, at least that part of it
represented by interest groups. Subsets of women still pursue their
perceived interests, but their method is now subsumed in that of others.
Some of the new forms of political action have been built on more
complex networks and coalitions (Hewitt, this volume); others have
involved new types of organizations and militance as workers (Milkman, this volume). In the 1970s and 1980s women's access to political
power increased. Relations between feminist organizations and congressional staffs have moved closer, and women lawyers have developed
the skills to advocate feminist issues in the legal system (Schlozman and
Freeman, this volume). Schlozman also demonstrates that the women's
voluntary organizations of the 1980s are more likely to work through a
professionally staffed pressure group organization than by mass mobilization of their members.

Women's participation in electoral politics has increased dramatically.
The increase has come in voting and officeholding (Andersen and Ware,
this volume) and within political parties (Jennings, this volume). Although Higginbotham (this volume) examines black women's politics
primarily in the 1920s, she looks also to the great change in party allegiance in the 1930s which brought black women into a much more

active position in political movements seeking the economic and social improvement of blacks. Jones (this volume) discerns many precedents for black women's resistance to southern white supremacy in earlier activism; hence she interprets their militancy in civil rights as a change in degree, not in kind.

Women's organizations have become part of the Washington pressure group community. Although the ratification of the ERA failed, women were an effective political force on this issue in a large majority of the states. Although separate women's institutions had a major effect in nineteenth century women's politics on issues like temperance and suffrage, integrated organizations have become more common in the twentieth century (Lebsock, Andersen, and Faue, this volume). The proportions of women who participate in politics through gender-integrated institutions have grown enormously. Further, women's authority and power in integrated institutions (the cases discussed in this volume are unions and political parties) have increased (Milkman and Jennings, this volume).

In brief, in the areas of ideology, interests, and organizations a combination of continuity and change best describes the course of women's politics in the twentieth century.

Women's Politics in the United States, 1890–1980

The chapters in this volume cover a wide range of topics and a long arc of time. Part II illustrates the fluid boundaries between protopolitics and politics, as well as the continuing pattern of voluntarism in women's politics. Electoral politics, broadly conceived, is the topic of Part III. Part IV examines continuities and discontinuities in women's voluntarism, and Part V examines the politicization of gender. Part VI constitutes an epilogue to the volume.

These chapters emerged from three workshops that provided social historians, political scientists, sociologists, and a psychologist and anthropologist or two with a cross-disciplinary opportunity to consider problems and issues in women's relationship to politics. Despite lively interchange and commitment to the value of integrating perspectives found in the different social sciences, with few exceptions the participants produced chapters that follow the methodologies and assumptions of their own disciplines. Particular chapters in the collection will, therefore, appeal more to one audience than another. The case studies will be more attractive to social historians and anthropologists and the quantitative and survey studies to political scientists and other social scientists. We hope that the presence of widely ranging approaches and topics within a single volume, however, will entice some readers to cross boundaries and sample the unfamiliar.

This book should be viewed as a set of case examples of how twentieth century American women have participated in politics. These cases are not organized by periods, however, because continuities and changes do not fit into distinct periods. Nor is there one chapter that delineates the many ideological controversies within contemporary feminism or one that focuses exclusively on the modern women's movement. Instead, these topics are covered by several of our authors as they focus on voluntarism, electoral politics, or the politicization of gender. Readers will find that our authors are not of one mind about the meaning of feminism or the significance of the women's movement, and especially about the broad definition of politics that we, the editors, have taken. And one or two authors stretch the definition further than we do. This is a book that permits, indeed sets out to include, many points of view. The selection of the workshop participants, of course, shaped the content of the book and resulted in omissions that in hindsight we regret. In particular, no chapter examines women in the national government bureaucracy that grew substantially over the twentieth century, and there is only limited coverage of women in political movements on the left. The book's emphasis on the increasing integration of men and women in political institutions may also partially reflect the authors who were selected for this project. Some scholars would stress more than our authors the importance of separate institutions, although separate women's organizations are fewer in number and appeal to proportionately fewer women than was true at the turn of the century. As with any set of case examples, these chapters do not exhaust either the topics or theoretical approaches that could be incorporated in a study of women, politics, and change. We believe, however, that their emphasis upon structural and historical factors and their attention to the construction of gender are unique in the growing literature on women and politics.

Collectively these chapters demonstrate that women's political history is not an evolutionary phenomenon in which one model supplants another in stages. Our authors do not argue that older forms of women's politics were supplanted by newer or more modern forms after woman suffrage was won. Instead, protopolitical forms persisted as the range of political acts widened and became increasingly formalized in organizations after suffrage opened party and electoral politics to women. Similarity to turn-of-the-century bases and forms is apparent, for example, in the nonhierarchical, democratic structure and consciousness-raising techniques of one branch of the contemporary women's movement. To this day, women's lobbying organizations are less hierarchical in structure and offer a broader range of incentives than do other pressure groups (Knoke, this volume).

Similar patterns observed in women's political history are not evidence that history repeats itself. Even when circumstances in a general way are similar, as in the case of the nineteenth century (1840s–1860s), the early twentieth century (1890s–1920s), and the contemporary women's movements—all three cases came in a period in which there were other movements and groups challenging and making claims on the state and other institutions—the relationship of past and present is complex. Each historical moment is unique, but it is also the product of short- and longer-term processes of change. The past shapes and limits the present; it also structures the circumstances that offer possibilities to historical actors at any moment. To protopolitical forms have been added more institutionalized forms, as parts of an expanded repertoire of activities and of national and local organizations.

Change, then, also characterizes the "long" twentieth century examined by our authors. Three broad changes are demonstrated in the chapters in this book: (1) economic opportunities for women have increased greatly; (2) equality in men's and women's legal status is greater now than ever before; and (3) women and men are now more fully, though not completely, integrated in politics and the economy. There has been a distinctive women's politics, as women have fought for political incorporation over the twentieth century. Nevertheless, women's politics is now less different from men's politics than it was at the turn of the century. Women's politics is now characterized by *general* patterns of citizenship and participation.

Notes

1. Quoted in Buhle and Buhle (1978), pp. 325–326.
2. For contemporary critiques, see Bourque and Grossholtz (1974); Goot and Reid (1975); Keohane (1981); Sapiro (1979). For a historical critique, see Baker (1984).
3. Easton (1971), p. 129.
4. Verba and Nie (1972), p. 29.
5. Verba and Nie (1972), p. 3.
6. Quoted in Peattie and Rein (1983), p. 80.
7. Gamson (1975), p. 19.

8. Tilly (1981), p. 17.
9. Gamson (1975), p. 19.
10. Gamson (1975), p. 19.
11. See Peattie and Rein (1983). Charles Tilly (1986) defines a social movement as a "sustained challenge on behalf of an unrepresented constituency" (p. 174).
12. Countryman (1981), pp. 182–183.
13. Frank (1985).
14. Tocqueville (1947), pt. 2, p. 331.
15. Ryan (1981), pp. 106, 105–144.
16. Hewlett (1986); DuBois (1978), p. 184.
17. Scott and Scott (1982), pp. 20–21.
18. On repertoires, see C. Tilly (1986).
19. Freeman (1979), pp. 168–179.
20. Skowronek (1982), p. 27.
21. Cott (1987), pp. 101–102.
22. Quoted in Cott (1987), p. 102.
23. Cott (1987), p. 98.
24. DuBois (1978), pp. 184–185.
25. Kessler-Harris (1985a), p. 145.
26. Hewitt (1986).
27. Cott (1987), pp. 19–20.
28. Also see Kessler-Harris (1985b).
29. Also see Mansbridge (1986).
30. Gertzog (1984).
31. Elshtain (1982). For another maternalist view, see Ruddick (1980).
32. Kessler-Harris (1985a), p. 157.
33. The maternal feminists draw heavily upon the psychoanalytic object-relations theory of Chodorow (1978) and the moral development theory of Gilligan (1982). The contemporary expression of the other side of the controversy draws from sociological theory and from a different school of psychoanalysis associated with the French theorist Jacques Lacan. In this view, gender identity is continually redefined and socially constructed in different contexts. See Conway, Bourque, and Scott (1987), p. xxiv; Epstein (1988).
34. Dietz (1987), p. 11. For an earlier statement of the maternal view, see Charlotte Perkins Gilman Stetson (1979).
35. See Freedman (1979) for a historical analysis of separatism in women's politics. She credits the strength of separate female institutions with political gains won up to suffrage and the subsequent decline of feminism to integration (p. 254).

36. These structural changes that produced the shift in role attitudes were not distributed evenly across all Americans. Their impact was felt less by members of conservative than of liberal organizations and less by older than younger people, but this was true among both men and women. See Wuthnow, this volume; Thornton and Freedman (1979); Thornton, Alwin, and Camburn (1983).

37. Sears and Huddy (this volume); Shapiro and Mahajan (1986); Gurin (1985); Thornton and Freedman (1979); Thornton, Alwin, and Camburn (1983).

38. Buhle (1981).

Protopolitics and Fluid Boundaries

Part II focuses on protopolitics, which includes both action in organizations that work outside the formal political arena and direct collective appeals to authorities, unmediated by organization. Lebsock, Hewitt, and Milkman examine women's activity in organizations conventionally considered to be outside politics, activity which we believe is at bottom concerned with the distribution of power and resources in state or community, hence political. Jones and Fernández-Kelly and García explore the direct-appeal aspect of protopolitics. Taken together, these chapters begin to expand our definition of politics.

Suzanne Lebsock opens by examining late nineteenth century and early twentieth century patterns of women's politics. She emphasizes the nationalization of formerly local issues and the growth of such national organizations as the Woman's Christian Temperance Union and the National American Woman Suffrage Association. Women were also active in women's clubs (black women's clubs played an especially important role in the face of black disfranchisement in the South), in settlement houses, and in pacifist organizations. Women activists tended to disparage partisanship; suffrage groups argued that women would bring moral qualities into the national political scene. Not all women were feminists or even supporters of suffrage: "Antis" were part of the scene in the same period.

Nancy A. Hewitt's chapter offers a local case study of Tampa, a multiethnic city with clear class cleavages, at the turn of the century. She compares activist women in Tampa with the activist women she and others have studied in northern cities in the antebellum period. Women's benevolent and reform associations led by well-to-do native-born women in Tampa, for example, resembled those of the earlier period. These prosperous women were joined by upper-class Latin women during the Spanish-American War. In contrast, the more explicitly political activities surrounding union mobilization brought forth no gender coalitions across class lines. There the basic unit for resistance was the working-class community around the cigar factories, a community whose solidarity was based on relations both on and off the job.

The relationship of women to the union movement is also explored by Ruth Milkman. She employs an institutional perspective in a study of four types of unions designed to explain the extent to which these unions organize women or fight for women's issues. The four types are craft unions, "new" unions (here the International Ladies' Garment Workers' Union is the key example), industrial unions, and service unions; they are roughly cohorts—the first founded in the late nineteenth century, the second in the early twentieth, the third in the 1930s, and the fourth in the period after World War II. With the rise of service unions women have been actively organized and their interests supported on a much larger scale.

Jacqueline Jones looks at both black and white women in the South between 1890 and 1965. In terms of working for women's political rights, voting, and officeholding, women of both races look apolitical. In terms of a broader definition of politics, middle-class women of both races were active in social welfare organizations, in which, however, interracial cooperation never emerged. Although at the national level the National American Woman Suffrage Association's "southern strategy" carefully separated woman suffrage and black civil rights (denying the latter), black women linked the two. Working-class women of both races took part in collective action (strikes, for instance), in tenant farmers' and sharecroppers' organizations, and in individual expressions of resistance. The civil rights movement from the mid 1950s on adopted tactics already tested by black women in the 1940s and even earlier.

M. Patricia Fernández-Kelly and Anna M. García provide a contemporary analysis of patriarchal family solidarity as a basis for Hispanic women's relationship to work and politics. Both Cuban and Mexican women accept patriarchal norms, but their contrasting class backgrounds and modes of incorporation into the apparel industries of Florida and California affect how well these norms work for the two groups. For Cuban women, patriarchal reciprocity is realistic; it allows women a marginal labor market advantage and provides an ideological basis for ethnic political solidarity. For Mexican women, the absence of economic underpinnings for the implementation of patriarchal norms produces economic vulnerability which inhibits both ethnically based and feminist politics.

2

Women and American Politics, 1880–1920

Suzanne Lebsock

The Cesspool and the Broom

Long before they were voters, American women were important political actors. The four decades preceding the passage of the Nineteenth Amendment, in fact, were a great age for women in politics—certainly greater than anything that had been seen before and arguably greater than anything seen again until after the rebirth of feminism in the late 1960s. In the context of centuries of exclusion from formal politics, the rising of American women between about 1880 and 1920 was nothing less than phenomenal.

Most men would not have used the word "politics" to describe what the women were doing. Instead they called it "philanthropy" or "service" or, in a few cases, "disorderly conduct." Politics was by definition something men did; and as feminists intensified their demands for admission into the formal political community of voters, some men and some women intensified their insistence that politics was no business for ladies. Metaphors of filth abounded: Politics was a sewer, a cesspool, a slimepit. To this feminists gave various replies, but here metaphors tended toward the spick and span. However slimy politics might be (a point of considerable controversy), who better than the nation's housekeepers to clean it up? Who better to transform mere politics into public service? Besides, homemakers were already involved in politics whether they liked it or not: "Politics comes in through the water pipes, gas jets and almost every other way."[1]

The turn of the century, in other words, was a time of urgent contention over the definition of politics: What was its nature? Who participated in politics and who ought to participate? These questions were not settled before 1920, not for good, anyhow. Like our activist progenitors of eighty years ago, many of the authors of this book are engaged in an attempt to redefine politics, both in the present and for the past. As was also the case eighty years ago, the entire debate is given energy and substance by women's demands for knowledge, recognition, and power.

In the present debate, brooms and mops do not rank high among our metaphors. But we have a good deal else to take from the remarkable activist women who helped change the political landscape in the forty years surrounding the turn of the century. This chapter is intended as a primer on their history and as a guide to questions which scholars are, or ought to be, asking. It is offered in a provisional spirit, partly because our knowledge is patchy and partly because it is growing fast; our present perspectives on the period may soon be radically changed by work now in progress.

Most American women could not vote in general elections until sometime between 1910 and 1920 (it varied from state to state), nor were they welcome in the major political parties, nor could they hold most public offices. We begin, then, with the recognition that women's politics took institutional forms different from those with which political history has ordinarily been concerned. The present consensus is that for women the standard form of political participation was the voluntary association. The pages that follow outline in more or less chronological order the rich associational history of women in the forty years after 1880, beginning with the Woman's Christian Temperance Union and ending with the triumphant, if ironic, final decade of the woman suffrage crusade. While there were always variations and exceptions, there were also some common themes: These were single-sex organizations, or, as in the case of the settlement movement, they were dominated by women; they insisted on the urgency and importance of the interests of women (which included but were not identical to the interests of children); and they consistently promoted an interventionist state—a common enough concept now, but at the time a significant innovation.

How might all this bear on questions of longstanding interest to political historians and political scientists? First, the United States in the period under study experienced one of its great periodic adventures in reform, generally referred to as Progressivism. The study of women's politics suggests that Progressivism, to a degree never before appreciated, was a women's movement. Second, in this period the political system underwent a major shift, in the shorthand of political science, from mass politics to interest group politics. This shift had many components, but perhaps the central one was the relative decline of the vote and of partisanship as centers of (male) political activity, to be largely replaced by organized interest groups. Women may have contributed a great deal to this shift, having (except in a few states in the West) no tradition of voting, having good reason to suspect political parties, and having for decades been organized on an interest group basis.

Of course it would be a great irony if women got the vote just as the vote itself was becoming less important, but this indeed appears to have been the case, and this is one example of how a political analysis can give us a new perspective on a point of common knowledge in the history of women. Closer attention to politics should also help advance our thinking on some of the major areas of controversy among historians of women. One such area encompasses questions about the nature and significance of gender differences, including the question of whether there was such a thing as a women's culture. The pages that follow suggest that although there was a great deal of conflict among organized women's groups, a case can nevertheless be made for a women's political culture. And if that is the case, then the notion of what constituted *the* political system needs to be made very much more inclusive than it previously has been.

We also need answers to questions not fully articulated by either historians of women or historians of politics: What, for example, was the significance of the fact that the greatest political age for women (including black women) was for black people as a group an age of disfranchisement and increasing legal discrimination? To take a metaphor from the suffragists, we may be in for some sweeping reinterpretations.

Varieties of Women's Politics: The Nineteenth Century

For nineteenth century women, the characteristic form of political activism was participation in a voluntary association. Whether women would have chosen this path had they had the option of voting we will never know. The vote, in any case, came late and by fits and starts. The women of Wyoming came into the union voting in 1890, and by 1896 they were joined by the women of Utah, Colorado, and Idaho. But the movement stalled there. While women in several states were granted partial suffrage—most often in school or municipal elections—not until 1910 was another state added to the full suffrage column.[2] In the meantime, most American women, if they wanted influence, had no choice but to work through nonelectoral politics.

By the beginning of the twentieth century, they had had over a hundred years of practice. Women organized societies for the relief of the poor as early as the 1790s; and in the antebellum period the causes multiplied to include temperance, women's rights, the abolition of slavery, prison reform, education, the rescue of "fallen" women, better conditions for workers, historic preservation, and every sort of scheme to spread and entrench evangelical Christianity. These women activists were typically middle or upper class and they usually worked through membership organizations.[3] But as Hewitt makes plain in this volume, there were other patterns as well. At one extreme were women whose collective activity lasted only a few days or even less, like the bread rioters of 1863 who forced the Confederacy to provide relief from inflation and profiteering. At the other extreme were women who lived entirely inside an organization: The Shakers, for example, created new communities in which women lived separately from men and governed equally with them.[4]

As might be expected, tactics varied as widely as organizational forms.[5] The bread rioters smashed store windows and "impressed" merchandise. Operatives in the New England textile mills organized "turnouts" and in Massachusetts inspired the first legislative investigation into working conditions. Women everywhere exercised their one formal political right by circulating petitions, in some campaigns collecting thousands of signatures. Some spoke in public, a highly controversial and symbolically loaded act. Others pamphleteered, wrote letters to editors, and in a few cases published newspapers of their own. A few wrote political novels. In almost every community women's organizations built charitable institutions and to keep them functioning sponsored countless fundraising events. Last—whether least is at present impossible to say—were the accumulated actions of individual women who lived intimately with powerful men.

"Do Everything":
The Woman's Christian Temperance Union

Not until we know more about these nineteenth century manifestations of women's politics will we have the full context for measuring the significance of the Woman's Christian Temperance Union (WCTU). This chapter begins with the WCTU because it appears to have been the first nationally organized mass movement of American women. The chapter correspondingly ends in 1920, when, as conventional wisdom has it, the triumph of the woman suffrage movement left American women without a center for further mass action organized on a national scale. (Please note, however, Cott's challenge to that wisdom in this volume.) The WCTU was born in direct action in the "Crusade" of 1873–1874. Employing prayer, hymns, and the occasional axe or hatchet, women shut down saloons in 250 towns in Ohio and elsewhere. By the fall of 1874 the crusaders had formed a national organization. By the 1880s their organization had made legislative action a top priority and had become the dominant force in the American temperance movement. It was also a major force in the lives of American women. With a paid membership of 150,000 by 1892, the WCTU claimed to be the nation's largest women's organization.[6]

Both the WCTU's remarkable growth and its penchant for legislation have been attributed largely to the shrewd and charismatic leadership of Frances E. Willard. President of the WCTU from 1879 to 1898, Willard had a knack for inciting previously apolitical women to collective action and for advancing outrageous propositions by wrapping them in sentimental and patriotic slogans. "Home Protection" was what she wanted, said Willard, "For God and Home and Native Land." Under these labels, the WCTU undertook an extraordinary range of reforms, marshaling an impressive array of tactics.

Willard called this the "Do Everything" policy; historians have since interpreted it as organizational genius at work.[7] In the WCTU there was a tactic for every taste. A timid newcomer might begin her temperance career by attending mothers' meetings to discuss methods of rearing pure children in an impure world. She need never go further, but she might proceed to prison visiting or attending sexual assault trials to make sure the all-male juries took the charges seriously. If she moved into the leadership, she might find herself organizing a convention or a petition drive, running a campaign for local option, making speeches, drafting bills, or buttonholing legislators.

All these excursions beyond the home were made in the name of Home Protection, which meant different things in different places. One of Willard's cannier policies was to insist that local and state unions reserve the right to endorse, rebut, or ignore positions taken by the national organization, a rule that made it possible to retain and even expand membership among relatively conservative women while the national organization and Willard herself took increasingly adventurous stances on all kinds of issues.[8]

From the beginning, the WCTU's central purpose was to combat the evils of alcohol. This remained an important source of recruits, not only because women were frequently the victims of male alcoholism and because temperance was considered a respectable cause for women, but also because the drunkard and his long-suffering wife were powerful symbols of what was wrong between the sexes. The WCTU tapped a wellspring of female resentment of male irresponsibility and self-indulgence in all its forms. This resentment found an explicitly political target when early attempts to secure temperance legislation failed, defeated in part because women lacked the power to hold legislators accountable.[9] Small wonder that the national WCTU was showing overtly feminist colors by 1881, endorsing woman suffrage in that year and going on to advocate dress reform, guardianship rights for mothers, greater authority for women in the churches, improved treatment of female prison inmates, better wages and conditions for women workers, and a host of measures to combat prostitution, including tougher statutory rape laws and the establishment of a single (lofty) standard of sexual morality for women and men.[10]

This roster of feminist reforms only began the list of causes championed by the WCTU, and the list grew as the national leadership shifted its vision of the relationship between alcohol and social problems. At first, WCTU literature portrayed drink as the root of nearly all evil. By the late 1880s, some temperance women were instead casting alcoholism as a symptom, the result more than the cause of poverty and other social ills. Here, if it was needed, was a mandate for action on all fronts. By 1893 Willard had converted to a form of socialism. The organization never went so far, but WCTU programs did show increasing attention to economic injustice. This meant social service as well as education and legislation. In Chicago, the hub of WCTU activity, the WCTU in 1889 "was sponsoring two day nurseries, two Sunday schools, an industrial school, a mission that sheltered four thousand homeless or destitute women in a four-month period, a free medical dispensary that treated over sixteen hundred patients a year, a lodging house for men that had to date provided temporary housing for over fifty thousand men, and a low-cost restaurant."[11]

By the time of Willard's death in 1898, the Anti-Saloon League had replaced the WCTU as the major force behind American temperance, and the WCTU itself narrowed its program, concentrating mainly on the liquor traffic.[12] Plenty of other organizations were available to take up work on social issues, however, and these organizations in many ways followed the WCTU's lead. First, they were single-sex or female-dominant organizations and as such made sure that the interests of women (or at least of selected groups of women) were defined, articulated, and pushed on to legislative agendas. Second, these organizations promoted an activist (we might say coercive) state. By the 1880s the WCTU had committed itself to state-level prohibition, and its legislative program expanded from there. Organized women would continue to call for government action, largely because they saw the problems of modern society as too complex and pervasive to be solved by volunteers. It may have been, too, that women's experience of sheer physical vulnerability inclined them to believe that government interposition was positive. What sort of voluntary action could stop hundreds of drunken husbands from beating or raping their wives? Better to charge the state with the responsibility of cutting off the liquor supply. Like the WCTU, the more the women's organizations engaged in formal politics, the more converts they gathered for the woman suffrage movement.

Third, most women's organizations would to one degree or another preach the "Politics of the Mother Heart" (another Willardism). They would argue that women were especially well equipped, and men ill equipped, to understand and deal with certain public issues. They would justify their own political activity as a contribution to the welfare of family and home. They would explain that modern life merged the domestic sphere of women with the public sphere of men and that forging a new public role for women could thus be the only responsible course. In the case of the social settlement workers, they would confound the spheres by living collectively in large homes that were centers for public agitation.

By the turn of the century, women were organizing everywhere. Kin to the WCTU, though much less well studied, was the Young Women's Christian Association (YWCA). Concentrating on advocacy and social services for working women, the YWCA by 1891 was organized in 225 cities.[13] Another flourishing Protestant crusade was carried forward through the home mission movement of the various denominations. White southern Methodist women, for example, organized in 1886 and were at first confined by their male governors to building and maintaining parsonages. They soon expanded their mandate to include the establishment of a full range of institutions to serve and evangelize the poor—whites, blacks, and immigrants. They also threw their collective weight into legislative battles for prohibition, better public schools, and the abolition of child labor. As one leader phrased it, "The state is God's ministry of organization, through which he must work."[14]

The Club Movement and the Crises of the 1890s

Many of the causes championed by these self-consciously Christian women's organizations gained adherents as the women's club movement picked up steam.[15] Almost every town had at least one women's club. The club movement had begun in the 1860s; what was special about the nineties was national organization. In 1890 a substantial portion of the (mainly) white women's clubs came together from across the country to found the General Federation of Women's Clubs, which claimed an initial membership of over 100,000. Black women formed their own federation, the National Association of Colored Women, in 1896. The National Council of Jewish Women was created in 1893 and the National Congress of Mothers (later the PTA) in 1897. College-educated women, hungry for continued fellowship with their educated sisters, organized the National Association of Collegiate Women in 1896. The 1890s also witnessed the rise of hereditary patriotic societies: the Daughters of the American Revolution, the Colonial Dames, and the United Daughters of the Confederacy, to name three.[16]

This organizational explosion—and men were organizing, too—was part of what Robert H. Wiebe has called the "search for order" that characterized American society in the late nineteenth and early twentieth centuries.[17] For women, there was also a search for meaningful endeavor beyond the home. Most of the women who ventured to meetings, paid their dues, and learned Robert's Rules were members of the middle class and, in a few cases, the upper class. In only rare instances were they truly leisured, but several factors combined to allow them to make time for commitments beyond their homes. Many of them could afford a servant (usually only one). While new household technology raised the standards of housekeeping, it also had the potential to free housewives from round-the-clock chores. Most important, women were giving birth to fewer babies—typically three children or four, rather than the seven or eight borne by the average American woman at the beginning of the nineteenth century. Late nineteenth century women were living longer as well, ordinarily long enough to see their last child leave home.

Opportunities for occasional escapes from domesticity had never before been so widespread,[18] nor had women's opportunities for education. And there, it seems, lay much of the impetus behind the organizational drive of the late nineteenth century. Although only a small proportion of Americans of high-school age actually attended school, the majority of graduates by 1890 were female. An increasing proportion of college students (one third in 1880, two fifths by 1910) were women, too. College students constituted only a tiny proportion of the female population (in 1890, 2.2 percent of females 18 to 21 years of age), but the experimental, sometimes embattled course of higher education for women gave them influence out of proportion to their numbers.[19] Higher learning for women was new, and the young women who emerged from the colleges and universities were determined to prove that education had not been wasted on them. They were energetic and idealistic, charged with a sense of mission (Christian or otherwise)—and they had practically no place to go. Although a small number pioneered in the professions, the majority had no more options than had their grandmothers: They could marry or they could teach school.[20]

And they could join a women's club. The club movement, among white women especially, was fueled by educated homemakers who wanted to recapture the intellectual liveliness of their college years and, even more, by less well educated women who wanted some structure for partaking of the life of the mind. Most of the early clubs were dedicated to the study of more or less high culture. Increasingly, however, women's clubs turned to social action. This was not so much a rejection of academic study as it was a sign that intellectual culture itself was increasingly concerned with analyzing American society and with proposing solutions to its manifest problems.[21]

The 1890s were a time of searching and crisis, of industrial capitalism run amok. The new corporations, and combinations of corporations, were relentless in the pursuit of their interests. While the big companies were hardly unified, they were nevertheless better organized and more powerful than any countervailing force, and the fallout was visible everywhere. Those who collected the profits became wealthy beyond comprehension, and they displayed their wealth in dazzling ways. The typical industrial worker, on the other hand, did not earn enough to support a family, even at the subsistence level. Many of these workers were immigrants who arrived by the hundreds of thousands, bringing strange (to the native-born) cultures and religions and packing into city slums. The contrast between rich and poor, stark enough in flush times, was aggravated further in the depression of 1893–1896—perhaps the worst in our history—when thousands of workers were laid off with no benefits and small prospect of government assistance. Since the middle 1880s a series of major strikes, some meeting with violence, called up visions of class warfare. Indebted farmers in the South and West made it a double threat with a Populist revolt of their own.

Government responses to all this were confused and for the most part faltering. For decades government at the national and state levels had been dedicated primarily to the happy task of promoting economic development and distributing resources (credit, public lands, and transportation subsidies, for instance) among a wide variety of competing groups and locales. As for social policy, it was sink or swim, with the national government taking next to no responsibility for basic human welfare. State and local governments dealt with poverty begrudgingly and on the cheap, maintaining a few institutions for paupers and the disabled and otherwise leaving social welfare action to a variety of charitable associations, many of them run by women.[22]

The multiple crises of the 1890s drew mixed reactions from the formal political system. Ever since the waning of Reconstruction in the early 1870s, the top leaders of the two major political parties had clung to tradition with an ardor that by hindsight seems almost perverse. Democrats and Republicans alike devoted themselves primarily to maintaining party loyalty through flashy campaigns and high-flying rhetoric. In the 1890s the Populist challenge and the economic depression demanded that the parties respond. The Democrats changed directions the most by absorbing the Populists and championing the farmer; as a result they lost badly in 1896 and remained the minority party for a generation. The Republicans changed much less, updating their old tariff rhetoric, waving the flag, and painting their opponents as dangerous radicals. The Republicans won, but they had learned little about how to address the country's problems. As for government, local officials struggled to provide stopgap relief to the destitute. The states experimented with regulation, rather than promotion, of big business. So, significantly, did Congress, although the new laws were mainly symbolic gestures and by no means indicated a general hostility in Washington to the interests of capital. In 1894 President Grover Cleveland crushed a railroad strike by sending in federal troops and arresting the leaders.[23]

Legislatures also responded to the dislocations of the 1890s by trying to reshape the electorate and the election process. Electoral reform was a complex phenomenon generated by people with various, indeed contradictory, motives. Some proponents sought a more democratic system. Others argued for a radically reduced electorate—by their lights, a better citizenry—that would prove friendlier to embattled elites. Most promised that their particular reform would reduce political corruption and create a purer, more enlightened electorate. This was a promise that could bring about a more democratic polity, as in the case of woman suffrage.[24] In the 1890s, however, and especially in the South, the argument was put to purposes tragically undemocratic.

Beginning in 1890 the great majority of southern black men were systematically disfranchised, mainly by legal and constitutional means. In state after state, white elites reacted to an interracial populist uprising by making it well-nigh impossible for blacks to vote. White men, too, were disfranchised in large numbers, but they were only secondary targets of the new electoral laws, and they were allowed to participate in the further persecution of blacks. The 1890s saw a vast increase in legally mandated racial segregation in every imaginable public place and circumstance.[25] And the 1890s set a record for racial terrorism; from 1889 to 1898 more than 1,100 blacks were lynched.[26] In all this the North and West proved willing accomplices. While the Supreme Court gave its blessing to segregation and disfranchisement, racism became respectable among all classes and was visited on all non-Anglo ethnic groups, including immigrants from Asia and from southern and eastern Europe. In the dismal history of race relations in America, the period from about 1890 to the 1920s ranks among the worst.

It may also have been among the worst for the sexual exploitation of black women and girls—a variety of racial terrorism that historians have scarcely recognized. When black clubwomen federated in the middle 1890s, their single greatest stated concern was sexual respectability. They sought to protect their daughters from white men in all events and from black men when necessary, to combat the stereotype of the loose black woman, to expose white notions about connections between rape and lynching, and to uplift the race by doing everything they could to promote the home.[27] Still unexplored, for whites as well as blacks, is how this concern for the integrity of the body related to more conventional notions of civil and political rights. Black clubwomen did, in any case, fight for civil and political rights—another topic much in need of research. In Richmond, Virginia, for example, black clubwomen forged a city-wide coalition to raise money for the defense of three black women who had been charged with murdering a white woman.[28] Confronting the formal political system became more difficult, however, as the numbers of black voters steadily diminished.

There were fewer barriers to establishing institutions. All over the country black women founded clinics, kindergartens, playgrounds, old folks' homes, settlement houses, and homes for juvenile offenders and for young women recently arrived in the city. They also gave crucial support to educational institutions, many of which had been founded by the previous generation of black activists.[29]

White clubwomen, unfortunately, were part of the problem. The formation of the General Federation made it necessary to decide who would be allowed to federate; early in the twentieth century the question was settled in a manner that made the admission of black clubs a virtual impossibility.[30] As was generally the case in this period, however, increasingly obvious bigotry on the part of whites coincided with increasing political activism on the part of women. While federation brought racism to the fore, it also generated national and state leaders who pushed the local clubs to set aside some of their literary studies and tackle more of the needs of their communities. In the 1890s white clubwomen became a major force behind public school reform, public health, environmental protection, protective legislation for women workers, the campaign against child labor, and greater rights and opportunities for women. Some clubs, it is true, remained resolutely literary; one chastened member recalled having introduced a political topic, only to be silenced by thumping umbrellas. But the total contribution of women's clubs to public institutions and public policy—a phenomenon that has yet to be fully gauged and appreciated by historians—was impressive.[31]

Progressivism and the Social Settlements

By 1910 or so, many of these reform-minded clubwomen were calling themselves Progressives, the name increasingly adopted by reformers of many stripes, and the root of the word historians have superimposed on (roughly) the first two decades of the twentieth century.[32] In the short run, reform in the Progressive era was a response to the upheavals of the 1890s; in the longer run, Progressivism can be seen as America's first collective attempt to cope with the consequences of industrial capitalism. The reforms took several major directions. First was a congeries of movements to alter the structure of government and the electoral process. Here the watchwords were efficiency and democracy—goals sufficiently incompatible with one another to make for some fascinating quarrels, both among the reformers themselves and among the historians who have tried to unravel the reformers' motives and their achievements. Second was the battle against "corporate arrogance."[33] Cast at the time as a struggle of "the people" versus "the interests," the assault on the corporations took two forms: In one, reformers attempted to dismantle the largest companies; in the other, the reformers accepted the bigness of big business and opted instead for government regulation of business practices. As businessmen themselves occupied strategic positions in some of these battles, latitude for historical interpretation is once again wide. Third was "social Progressivism," the branch of reform in which women starred. Social Progressives attempted to deal with the human wreckage of industrial capitalism and, more positively, to exploit possibilities the new order seemed to promise for social justice. Centered on the welfare of the family, the child, and the neighborhood, social Progressivism had a rural wing (the Country Life movement) as well as a much better known urban one;[34] and like other Progressives, the social Progressives left themselves open to charges by historians that their motives were less democratic than their rhetoric.

So complex was all this that one historian in 1970 proposed that the entire concept of a Progressive movement be allowed to die a merciful death.[35] But other historians have stubbornly continued to use the term and to debate the period's central themes. The new research on women will probably add weight to the conviction that Progressivism was real in some sense, and not badly named. It is clear in any case that women deserve a great deal more attention than they have yet received.

While historians have had difficulty defining the essence of Progressive reform, the leaders of the social settlement movement, Jane Addams especially, had no such problem. This was partly because they felt comfortable with keeping their own definitions open-ended. "In time," Addams wrote, "we came to define a settlement as an institution attempting to learn from life itself. . . ."[36] From the 1890s to the 1920s settlement houses were urban America's preeminent centers for reform. Products of late nineteenth century voluntarism, they had much in common with women's clubs and the WCTU. The settlement houses were dominated by women (the movement drew male residents and volunteers, but career residents ordinarily were women), and they consistently championed the interests of women and of children. Settlement workers also turned quickly to government, as they realized that solutions to their neighborhoods' problems often lay outside their neighborhoods. When Addams and Ellen Gates Starr founded Hull-House in 1889, their initial mission was to relieve the bleak life of an immigrant slum by organizing recreation and importing high culture. By 1893 Hull-House residents, working in coalition with other women's groups, had succeeded in pressuring the Illinois legislature into enacting a landmark factory inspection law.[37]

Florence Kelley, a Hull-House resident and a major force behind the law's passage, soon became the law's primary enforcer, as the governor appointed her chief factory inspector. Kelley, already the holder of a bachelor's degree from Cornell and a veteran of graduate study in Europe, subsequently completed a law degree, the better to prosecute violators.[38] Kelley's transformation into a professional expert (or expert professional) symbolized a larger transition in American reform and in women's politics: Drawing on the nascent social sciences, a new generation of reformers sought to bring empirical data, efficiency, and professional training to bear on the problems of industrial America.[39] Like Kelley, many of these new reformers were women, and many of these women lived in settlement houses.

This is not to suggest that the high moral dudgeon of late Victorian women's politics was suddenly supplanted by a cool professionalism. The intriguing quality of these Progressive era reformers was their capacity to combine and contain many seeming opposites. Addams, for example, could render a dispassionate account of all the sociological factors that caused girls to turn to prostitution, and this prevented her from personally condemning the prostitute. But Addams never doubted for an instant that the practice of prostitution was an evil.[40] Settlement workers put "neutral" science at the service of Victorian moral ends and saw no contradiction.

In similar fashion, settlement workers took the domestic and the public—spheres that in the nineteenth century were cast as mutually exclusive—and rolled them into one: Settlements were places to live, to work, and to agitate for change. Both for the residents and for reform, it was apparently a powerful combination. In creating the settlement houses, women invented a way of living in community, a community that encouraged the intense female friendships common to the nineteenth century and that provided single women with an alternative to living in eternal service to siblings and aging parents. Sprung from the claims of their families, settlement workers generated immense energy for reform. They fought for children—for playgrounds, uncontaminated milk, compulsory education, pensions for widowed mothers, a separate system for juvenile justice, and an end to child labor. They fought for women workers—for unions, a minimum wage, shorter hours, and safer conditions. They argued for workmen's compensation. They combatted the exploitation of newly arrived immigrants. They agitated for better sanitation, tougher building codes, and medical services for the poor. They campaigned for reforms in municipal and state government. Altogether they invented numerous social services, many of which they turned over to government agencies.[41]

The goal of all this, Addams would have said, was to socialize democracy. Perhaps the premier interpreter of social Progressivism, she tried to persuade a nervous middle class that the turbulence of their time was a symptom of an essentially positive evolution toward a new form of democracy. The founding fathers had seen democracy as a question of political structures, leaving a great deal to the initiative of individuals. Under modern conditions, however, individualism would no longer do, as people no longer had any choice but to depend upon and work with one another. In the coming form of democracy, which was not yet fully visible, the central spirit was one of association, cooperation, and service. Addams saw that spirit at work largely among the working classes—in unions, in the generosity of the poor to one another, even in the relationship between the ward boss and his constituents.[42]

Until World War I, when she was pilloried for her pacifism, Addams was the most celebrated woman in America. Like Willard, she had a gift for making capital of behavior that in others might seem outrageous.

Unlike Willard, she avoided sentimental slogans and instead relied on a certain well-placed vagueness to mollify the fears of the "haves" while acknowledging the aspirations of the "have-nots": According to Addams, the factory owner need not turn over the machines to the workers; he need only act *as though* the machines were owned by everyone.[43] Still, amid the mystical qualities of her program, Addams displayed a genuine curiosity about working-class people and a genuine desire to serve their interests; the same was true of many leading settlement workers. As a group, settlement workers occupied the left wing of mainstream reform.

Radicals and Direct Action

A number of unmistakably radical women, meanwhile, made the settlement workers look like the picture of respectability. The Progressive era, with its questioning spirit and its infusion of socialists and anarchists from Europe, was a high-water mark for radical politics in America. Emma Goldman crisscrossed the nation preaching the abolition of private property, the dismantling of the state and the church, and an end to marriage. Elizabeth Gurley Flynn, who got on her first soapbox at age 16, stumped the country for the self-consciously revolutionary International Workers of the World. Of particular importance for the future of women was the willingness of some radicals to agitate the issue of contraception, which no one else would touch. Goldman was among the first to raise it, and a few years later Margaret Sanger made birth control the central crusade of her long and controversial life. In the 1920s Sanger would go the way of mainstream political women, working to legalize contraceptive devices and information through a voluntary association with a middle-class membership. She began, however, as an ideological and tactical radical. Working-class women needed contraception, she argued, not only to safeguard their health, but to reduce the capitalists' supply of wage slaves. Sanger also proved a master of direct action: In 1916 she and her sister-in-law Ethel Byrne simply opened a birth control clinic. Ten days later they were raided, arrested, and sentenced to thirty days. At every turn—Sanger's refusal to be fingerprinted, Byrne's hunger strike, Sanger's triumphant emergence from jail—they generated massive, mainly sympathetic publicity.[44]

High-visibility protest took yet another form early in 1917 when women in several American cities launched passionate, at times violent, consumer protests. Best known are the "riots" of Jewish immigrant women in New York City. Pressed to the limit by the zooming inflation of World War I, thousands of rowdy housewives upended pushcarts, boycotted grocers and butchers, scared off would-be purchasers of targeted items, organized mass meetings, and marched with their children on city hall to demand fair prices. After a few weeks, the boycott came to an end. Prices had dropped about 30 percent, and the protesters had succeeded in getting public officials talking, investigating, and proposing action.[45]

These working-class demonstrators echoed some of the same themes struck by activists of the middle class (who were themselves becoming rowdier in this period): Like many middle-class reformers, the food protesters took action in the name of motherhood, taking to the streets in order to feed their children; and like most voluntary associations, they demanded positive action from government. At the same time, the food protesters were clearly mindful of the trade union tradition, for they called their actions "strikes."[46] The boycotts of 1917, and indeed a whole series of food protests and rent strikes stretching back to at least 1902, need to be seen as part of a larger struggle of working-class women for economic justice, a struggle carried on in large part by wage-earning women.

The Trade Union Movement

Compared with women of the middle class, women wage-earners were badly disadvantaged in the drive to organize. To begin, their goals were directly antagonistic to those of capital. Of leisure, they had little or none, as their workweeks were long in the factories and unlimited in the sweatshops. They were poor, making wages of one third to one half of the miserable earnings made by men of comparable skill. Women were generally restricted to unskilled and semiskilled jobs; and thus when they went out on strike, employers found them relatively easy to replace. And like male workers, the women were divided among numerous ethnic groups whose differing languages and cultures could form barriers to joint action.[47]

Wage-earning women, in other words, needed allies, and much of their history in this period is one of tricky alliances. Working-class women attempted alliances with both working-class men and upper-class women, and neither in the end lived up to their leaders' hopes. By 1920 less than 7 percent of women wage-earners belonged to trade unions compared with 20 percent of all wage-earners—both figures testimony to the overwhelming power of employers. Yet there had been moments of glorious success, and the numbers, though small by present standards, represented an enormous increase in female union membership. Compared with the hard times of the 1920s, the first twenty years of the twentieth century were upbeat decades for unionization among women workers.[48]

That working women of all descriptions could eagerly take up organization was demonstrated in the 1880s when the Knights of Labor dominated the American labor movement. Open to all, the Knights enlisted domestics as well as factory operatives, blacks and whites, and they even welcomed the wives of wage-earning men, recognizing housework as important work.[49] The Knights were in irreversible decline by the 1890s, however, and their successors in the American Federation of Labor (AFL) proved far less enthusiastic about organizing women. Although women made up a full fifth of the labor force, the AFL concentrated on those they deemed most organizable—on white, highly skilled men. While the AFL gave some lip service and occasional tangible support to women's unions, the typical AFL response to the women unionists' endeavors ranged somewhere between indifference and sabotage.[50]

This remained true well into the twentieth century, and it was a persistent problem for the women who forged a new alliance in 1903. Composed of working women and well-to-do (indeed, often rich) "allies," the National Women's Trade Union League (NWTUL) represented a conscious effort to stretch the bonds of sisterhood across class lines. Workers and allies together attempted to organize women's unions and to integrate those unions into the larger American labor movement through federation with the AFL. At times their cause looked hopeful. In 1909, for example, the New York WTUL played a major role in the greatest women's strike in history. Thirty thousand shirtwaist workers, 85 percent of them women and 80 percent of the women Jewish, walked off their jobs. To the degree that union organizers succeeded in building female membership, they did so by appealing to values with special meaning for women. As Alice Kessler-Harris argues, the core of solidarity among women workers was a shared sense of moral outrage at "the discrepancy between what society thought women ought to be and what working life made possible for them."[51]

It was an uphill struggle. Given the power of the employers, the procapital stance of government, and the disadvantages suffered by the workers, organizing women was bound to be a difficult task. Added to this was the continued noncooperation of the AFL. Finally, the WTULs themselves suffered from tensions between allies and workers. The allies in particular found it hard to transcend ethnic prejudice, the world view of their class, and the habit of telling other people what to do.

Increasingly, the National WTUL pulled its resources out of trade union organizing and began instead to campaign for protective legislation and woman suffrage. In 1909 Clara Lemlich, an immigrant seamstress, had galvanized thousands of shirtwaist workers by calling for an immediate strike. By 1915 she was on the New York WTUL payroll, making speeches to working-class women on the need for woman suffrage.[52]

The Woman Suffrage Campaign

Whatever that shift may have cost the cause of union women, in the short run it was so much clear gain for the woman suffrage movement.[53] In the years after about 1910, woman suffrage became a genuine mass movement; in 1917 the National American Woman Suffrage Association (NAWSA) claimed a membership of 2 million. It was a venerable movement by this time; historians generally date its beginnings from 1848, when a women's rights convention held in Seneca Falls, New York—the first such convention ever held—passed a controversial resolution calling for the enfranchisement of women. Over the next several decades the movement survived persistent ridicule, a civil war, a chastening alliance with the sensational free-love advocate Victoria Woodhull, and its own internal divisions over philosophy and tactics, divisions that split the movement into two rival organizations. By 1890, however, leaders of both organizations were ready to bury the hatchet, and NAWSA was formed. The movement celebrated its first major victory in 1890 when the women of Wyoming came into the union with full voting rights. By 1896 three more western states were added to the suffrage column.

Then came the "doldrums," fourteen years in which no state enfranchised its women. Behind the apparent stalling of the movement, however, there was progress. With each passing year, the suffrage cause shed a little more of its disreputability. A patchwork of partial suffrage statutes empowered increasing numbers of women to vote in school and municipal elections. NAWSA's membership grew, and for the first time the opposition got organized on a national scale, a phenomenon the suffragists chose to read as a sign of their own growing strength.

It was also one sign of divisions among American women. The last decade of the suffrage drive was notable for two seemingly contradictory trends. Never before had suffragists worked so effectively together: The ratification of the Nineteenth Amendment in 1920 was the result of a massive and highly disciplined national campaign, one which encompassed working-class women and upper-class women as well as the traditionally reform-minded middle class.[54] At the same time, it was the suffrage movement more than any other that brought out divisions among American women.

Credit for the discipline and effectiveness of the latter-day suffrage movement usually goes to Carrie Chapman Catt, who assumed the presidency of NAWSA in 1915.[55] In order to place maximum pressure on elected officials, state suffrage associations were reorganized to parallel congressional and legislative districts. Resources were systematically channeled from states where suffrage stood little chance to those with a reasonable prospect of victory. From the militant British suffrage movement, American suffragists adopted headline-grabbing tactics, speaking from automobiles and soapboxes, organizing massive parades, and heckling (or at least questioning) candidates for office.[56]

The scale of the suffrage campaigns became simply staggering. In the New Jersey campaign of 1915, suffragists "distributed over 1.5 million pieces of literature (approximately three per voter) and over half a million other promotional pieces, held 2500 outdoor and 250 indoor meetings, and sent 'flying squadrons' of speakers throughout the state." The New Jerseyans also supplied suffrage news to more than 200 newspapers. In metropolitan New York in the same year, "396,698 voters were canvassed; 2,883,264 leaflets were printed and distributed; 5,984 meetings were held and 80 newspapers were provided with suffrage news on a regular basis."[57]

With such impressive and determined organization—and an increasing number of states entering the suffrage column—nationwide victory began to look inevitable, and the cause won more friends in high places; President Woodrow Wilson endorsed the federal amendment in 1918 as a war measure. The mobilization of millions of American women on behalf of the war effort probably helped as well. Food preservation campaigns in particular underscored what suffragists had been arguing all along: There was political significance to what women did at home.

A number of prominent suffragists and reformers opposed the war first to last—among them Jane Addams and Jeanette Rankin, the first elected woman member of Congress. Their activities led to a whole new dimension of women's politics—national and global organization to stop the Great War and to prevent further wars. NAWSA, however, took the path of least resistance when the United States actually entered the war. Catt resigned from the Woman's Peace party (which she had helped found in 1915), and NAWSA engaged the organized antisuffrage movement in a contest to see who could manifest the greater patriotism.[58] The federal woman suffrage amendment was ratified just in time for the 1920 elections.

The triumph of the suffrage movement momentarily obscured the divisions among American women that had appeared in the course of the suffrage debate. As Cott points out in this volume, division was endemic to the suffrage movement. First, there were the losers, the female "antis" whose highly publicized and well-financed campaigns made it clear that not all women wanted the vote.[59] Equally troublesome to the suffragists—and to the historians who have written about them—was dissension within their own camp. Racism was a persistent problem. It is difficult to say how much the white suffragists were expressing their own prejudice and how much they were merely caving in under the bigotry they accurately perceived among men, especially southern congressmen. And it should be said that the suffragists were far better behaved than the antis, who stooped to racial demagoguery without a second thought. Nevertheless, it is clear that white suffragists feared the consequences of association with black suffragists and that most white women were unwilling to support a truly universal suffrage if such support appeared to endanger their cause. The history of the latter-day suffrage movement is riddled with racist incidents. In 1913, for example, the organizers of a massive suffrage parade in Washington, D.C., asked Ida Wells Barnett to march at the parade's end instead of marching with the other delegates from Chicago. After the parade was well under way, Wells Barnett simply slipped in among the white Chicagoans and finished out the parade. It was all a fitting symbol of the grit required of black suffragists and the faintheartedness of their white counterparts.[60]

NAWSA's quest for respectability was equally obvious in its running battle with Alice Paul and her Congressional Union (CU; later, the National Woman's Party). Taking up militant suffragism on the British plan, the CU opted for punishing the party in power, a plan that included embarrassing the President with pickets at the White House. "MR. PRESIDENT!" their placards read, "HOW LONG MUST WOMEN WAIT FOR LIBERTY?" The pickets were page-one news, especially in the summer of 1917 when some of the demonstrators were jailed and went on a hunger strike. Historians have generally concluded that such tactics were healthy for the suffrage movement as a whole: Together the CU and NAWSA combined for a "one-two punch."[61] NAWSA leaders, of course, did not see it that way. Decorous at all times and painstakingly nonpartisan, NAWSA officials disavowed the CU's every action.

The issue of partisanship was important, as a matter of both tactics and principle. As for tactics, NAWSA leaders insisted that it was foolish to favor one party over another when both could boast key advocates of woman suffrage. "Like the man who didn't care where he went after he died," as one suffragist wrote to another, "we have friends in both places."[62] There was also a long history of disappointment in the results of attempted cooperation with political parties. Neither the Republicans nor the Democrats could claim a sterling record on suffrage; neither party put a suffrage plank in its national platform until 1916.[63]

Women's experience with third parties was somewhat better, since fledgling parties tended to be eager for reform and to take allies where they could find them. In the 1890s thousands of western farm women joined the Populist party, participating in campaigns at all levels and sending forth some formidable orators, most notably Mary Elizabeth Lease (of "less corn, more hell" fame). Populism provided a ready-made rationale for such participation: Who more than woman, the central figure in family life, had a greater duty to promote the party pledged to save the family farm? The Populists fused with the Democrats in 1896, however, and abandoned their broad platform in favor of the single issue of the free coinage of silver. Their interests shunted aside, Populist women for the most part lost faith in partisan politics.[64]

A few years later, socialism seemed to offer women a new opportunity in partisan politics. Women were present as official delegates at the formation of the Socialist Party of America in 1901, and within a few years feminist socialists had pushed their confreres to grant money and organizational support for reaching women and agitating questions of special relevance to women. "As a group," writes Mari Jo Buhle, "the socialists would more than any other sector of the nation's population affirm the ultimate equality of women and the viciousness of their exploitation under capitalism." But even the socialists failed to sustain a coherent feminist program. By 1914 Socialist party feminism was visibly declining, the decline brought on by several factors, not the least of which was resistance to "special" struggles.[65] All in all, feminists seem to have found partisan politics frustrating and fundamentally unresponsive to the desires of voteless women. "Parties," as Frances Willard once said, ". . . are of no more value than so many tin cans."[66]

Some Speculations on Difference

Willard's remark was not just a case of sour grapes. Women tended to disparage partisanship, not only because they were excluded from the parties' inner councils, but because partisanship was at the center of the male system of politics. We arrive at the question of difference. Was women's political behavior different from men's? What about their values? Did women make a difference in American politics and public policy?

Until recently such questions have been given two main answers, both far too simple. The first was advanced by suffragists long before women got the vote: Women needed to be citizens so that they would apply their superior (or merely different) moral vision to the problems of their time. The promises were many and varied, although in the final years of the suffrage campaign not as cosmic as many historians have suggested. Women voters would help raise the wages of women workers above starvation level; they would clean up political corruption; they would make it more difficult for nations to go to war. (And antis often agreed—not on the need for the vote, but on women's special propensity for reform.)[67] In the twenties, however, newly enfranchised women failed to live up to the suffragists' rhetoric, and this led many observers to a second and very different perspective on the question of difference. Women evidently did not vote as a bloc in the twenties. Indeed, by some standards they did not vote very much at all. Thus the feminists' claims that women's politics would be different seemed to be laid to rest.[68]

Somewhere between the rhetorical flourishes of the suffragists and the show-me attitude of their detractors lurk possibilities for more imaginative ways of posing and answering the questions. New analyses of electoral returns suggest that women's voting patterns after 1920 were more complex than has ordinarily been appreciated. (See Andersen, this volume.) Moreover, given the conservative backlash of the twenties, it is hardly surprising that feminists failed to bring on the millennium. And given the decline in turnout among male voters—above all, given the fact that voting was *never* the primary mode of women's political activism—it seems particularly misleading to judge the character of women's politics strictly by stereotyped accounts of how they voted.[69]

Recent scholarship has refocused us on the years before 1920 and is moving rapidly along to a more interesting analysis. In an essay that aims to account for the apparent decline of feminism in the 1920s, Estelle Freedman takes an institutional approach. Women's priorities were different from those of men (different because of their history and their social position, not their anatomy), but these differences could fuel an effective political movement only when feminists created a secure and separate institutional base. The settlement houses, the women's colleges, the professional networks, the homosocial bonds that sustained women in the Progressive era all helped make a highly politicized feminist movement possible. In the twenties, by contrast, these institutions became relatively unimportant, and more and more women took their chances in male-dominated institutions. As Freedman sees it, it was a poor trade: "Women gave up many of the strengths of the female sphere without gaining equally from the man's world they entered."[70]

Case studies of states where women voted before 1920 appear to bear Freedman out, at least to the extent that they reveal the occasional existence of effective, woman-centered politics. In San Francisco, for example, newly enfranchised clubwomen targeted a judge who in their opinion had been too lenient with accused rapists. In 1913 they succeeded in having him recalled.[71] The meaning and representativeness of this case will only become clear with further study; we especially need studies—like that of Nancy Hewitt in this volume—that encompass the whole range of women's and men's politics in a given location.

In the meantime, Paula Baker's recent study of political culture in rural New York offers the most powerful argument to date on difference.[72] Baker proposes that political culture in the late nineteenth century was the sum of two strikingly different political cultures—one invented and carried on by men, the other by women. For men, voting was the characteristic form of political action, and voter turnout was high. A man might also march in a torchlight parade; this was the era of the spectacular campaign, where the chief object was to arouse the party faithful. Loyalty to party was the primary virtue—"friendship," it was called. Candidates were evaluated mainly according to character and how hard they worked for their friends; issues and programs counted for relatively little. This was partly because government was expected to do very little. The less the government did, and spent, the better.

So far, this is a fairly familiar description.[73] Baker, however, carries the story further in several ways, two of them of prime importance for us. First, she sees political participation as a primary source of male gender identity. Second, she sees in women's public activity evidence of an alternative political culture, one which men would not have dignified with the name of "politics." Women's characteristic form of political activity was participation in a voluntary association. These associations were nonpartisan and highly programmatic: Organized women wanted the government to do things, and they trusted the government to do things in part because they tended to look on government as it was portrayed in civics books. They valued intelligence and the Christian virtues. For "friendship" in the male sense of the term, they had little use.

While Baker makes an arresting case for difference, she does not see the differences as inevitable or immutable. In an earlier work, in fact, Baker has suggested that the early twentieth century brought about a sort of merger between the two political cultures. Calling it the "domestication of American politics," Baker suggests that women's politics became more like men's even as men's politics became more like women's. Women got the vote and to some degree began participating in party affairs. Men began to fall away from their rabid partisan enthusiasms; turnout declined, and men increasingly tried to exert their influence through voluntary associations, many of them organized on a national scale.[74]

This was a sea change in the American political system, the transition generally identified by historians and political scientists as the shift from mass politics to interest group politics.[75] Baker is the first scholar to make systematic connections between gender and the changing political system, and a great deal more needs to be explored. What, for example, is the significance of the fact that women got the vote just as the vote was declining in importance? And what about gender identity? When women got the vote, it would seem that voting, campaigning, and partisanship could no longer serve as a major source of male gender identity (except perhaps for the men in the proverbial smoke-filled rooms). Here is an additional explanation for declining turnout among men. At the same time, we might well ask whether any form of political behavior ever became an important part of female identity for the mass of American women. It seems probable that domesticity remained at the center of adult female identity. Domesticity, however, divides into several parts. The idea of motherhood, with its strong current of responsibility, had enormous potential for fueling political action.[76] Marriage, with its strong undercurrent of female subordination, did not. While it is not easy to distinguish cause from effect, it would seem to be no coincidence that women's political effectiveness appears to have declined in the decade that also witnessed a new enthusiasm for marriage and heterosexual expression.[77]

Another area for continued study is the development of interest group politics. Gerda Lerner once suggested that nineteenth century women, being voteless, invented or elaborated all sorts of tactics— petitioning, direct action, legislative investigations—in order to secure government action.[78] We now know that women's organizations were extremely active in the late nineteenth and early twentieth centuries. Is it possible that interest group politics, the characteristic politics of the twentieth century, was invented mainly by women?

Only research will tell. On specific public policies we already know more, and a good many studies of women in public life are slated to appear soon. This new work is likely to suggest that much of what was progressive about the Progressive era can be credited to women—as can much of what was repressive.[79] Especially noteworthy were the beginnings of the modern welfare state, forged through the interaction of social settlement workers and their "clients."[80] Scores of programs were invented by women and then handed over to the state. It would be instructive in the extreme to know why these programs were so readily transferred, what was lost in the transition, and what was gained.

Finally, all of this took place during a period of galloping racial and ethnic bigotry, perhaps the worst in our history. What does it signify that our greatest age for women in politics, black women included, was among the worst for black Americans as a group? A host of interpretations are possible. It may be argued that the two phenomena were mainly coincidental, occurring at the same time but having little connection with each other. It might also be argued that the two were very much connected, for good (*some* black women got the vote) or for ill: White women, it may ultimately appear, got the vote on the backs of black people. Agitating the question is in any case certain to result in a more subtle appreciation of the historical relationship between race and gender.

No matter how these particular questions may fare, it seems safe to predict that scholars will be paying more attention to integrating what we know about women and gender with what we know (or thought we knew) about formal politics and changing political systems.[81] It will not be clear for some time how much intellectual—or political—value this integrative approach may hold. But at the very least, it ought to help ensure that this time, the politics of Progressive era women will not be so easily forgotten.

Notes

1. Eudora Ramsay, quoted in the *Richmond* (Virginia) *Times-Dispatch*, February 1, 1916.
2. For a chart on the progress of woman suffrage in the states, see Scott and Scott (1975), pp. 166–168. The significance of partial suffrage has yet to be appreciated.
3. Cott (1977), pp. 132–159; Ginzberg (1986); Hewitt (1984); Lebsock (1984), pp. 195–236; McCarthy (1982), pp. 3–24; Ryan (1979); Ryan (1981), pp. 53–54, 83–144, 210–218; Smith-Rosenberg (1971a).
4. Chesson (1984); Campbell (1978).
5. Lerner (1977), pp. 317–322.
6. Bordin (1981).
7. Bordin (1981), pp. 13–14, 53–55, 95–116; Bordin (1986), pp. 129–154.
8. Bordin (1981), pp. 97–98. Bordin (1986), pp. 131–133, however, points out instances in which the WCTU membership was ahead of Willard.
9. Scott (1970), p. 148.

10. Bordin (1981), pp. 110–116. See Rosenthal et al. (1985), however, for a critique of the idea that the WCTU had strong ties to the suffrage movement.

11. Bordin (1981), p. 98 (quotation).

12. Bordin (1981), pp. xviii, 151–155.

13. Wilson (1979), p. 99.

14. Quoted in McDowell (1982), p. 58. See also Sims (1982).

15. The classification of organizations according to religious versus secular origins is Anne Firor Scott's. I am grateful for having had the opportunity to read parts of her forthcoming history of American women's voluntarism.

16. Woloch (1984), p. 299; Degler (1980), pp. 323–324. On the urban character of women's organizations, see Wilson (1979), pp. 91–110.

17. Wiebe (1967).

18. Woloch (1984), pp. 269–276.

19. Solomon (1985), pp. 62–64.

20. Kessler-Harris (1982), pp. 116–119; Solomon (1985), pp. 115–140; Woloch (1984), pp. 276–283.

21. This is Joseph F. Kett's idea.

22. McCormick (1979).

23. Burnham (1965); Jensen (1971), pp. 269–308; McGerr (1986).

24. Link and McCormick (1983), pp. 47–58.

25. Kousser (1974); Williamson (1984), pp. 224–258; Woodward (1974).

26. Hall (1979), p. 134; Williamson (1984), pp. 183–189.

27. Hamilton (1978), pp. 15–16.

28. Lebsock (1984b), p. 125.

29. Berkeley (1985); Lerner (1979), pp. 83–93; Neverdon-Morton (1978).

30. Blair (1980), pp. 108–110; Giddings (1984), p. 125

31. Beard (1915); Blair (1980), pp. 73–119; Scott (1984a), pp. 13–19; Bowie (1942), p. 49.

32. The literature on Progressivism is enormous. Useful introductions include Chambers (1980); Link and McCormick (1983); O'Neill (1975); and Painter (1987).

33. The term is David P. Thelen's. See Thelen (1969), p. 338.

34. On women in the Country Life movement and in the Progressivism of the rural South, see Jensen (1981b), pp. 148–152; and Kett (1985).

35. Filene (1970).

36. Addams (1930), p. 408.

37. Addams (1910), pp. 198–213; Davis (1967a); Sklar (1985), pp. 665–672; Tax (1980), pp. 65–89.

38. Sklar (1985), p. 672.

39. Lubove (1965); McCarthy (1982), pp. 125–171; Wiebe (1967). Morantz-Sanchez (1985), pp. 280–311, describes the reform activism of female physi-

cians and analyzes the double-edged consequences of that activism for the status of women in medicine. According to Leach (1980), Progressive-era empiricism was prefigured by the promotion of scientific thought among nineteenth century feminists.

40. Addams (1912).

41. Addams (1910), pp. 89–453; Cook (1979); Costin (1983), pp. 35–99; Davis (1967a); Sklar (1985), pp. 659–664; Woloch (1984), pp. 299–303.

42. Addams (1907), pp. 31–52; Addams (1964), pp. 19–22, 137–177, 270.

43. Addams (1907), pp. 148–149.

44. Buhle (1981), pp. 268–280; Gordon (1976), pp. 186–245; Kennedy (1970), pp. 72–107; Reed (1984), pp. 106–108; Tax (1980), pp. 125–163.

45. Frank (1985); Igra (1986).

46. Igra (1986), pp. 80–81. See also Hyman (1980).

47. Kessler-Harris (1975b), pp. 92–93; Kessler-Harris (1982), pp. 153, 161–162; Tax (1980), pp. 25–32.

48. Kessler-Harris (1982), p. 152.

49. Foner (1979), pp. 185–212; Levine (1983).

50. Dye (1975), pp. 113–123; Dye (1980), pp. 6–7, 13–17, 80–87, 102–109; Foner (1979), pp. 213–255, 317–323; Kessler-Harris (1975), pp. 95–101; Kessler-Harris (1982), pp. 152–159; Tax (1980), pp. 31–37.

51. Foner (1979), pp. 290–345; Kessler-Harris (1985b), p. 115; Dye (1980), pp. 88–94; Tax (1980), pp. 205–240. The Consumers' League was another important organization that tried to reach across class lines to improve the lot of wage-earning women. See Wolfe (1975).

52. Dye (1980), pp. 110–161; Foner (1979), pp. 479–486; Kessler-Harris (1982), pp. 95, 166–171; Jacoby (1975); Tax (1980), pp. 95–124.

53. Flexner (1968) [1959] is still the standard work on the suffrage movement. The narrative that follows is derived from Flexner and from several other important works, including Buechler (1986); Buhle and Buhle (1978); DuBois (1978); Kraditor (1965); O'Neill (1969); and Scott and Scott (1982).

54. DuBois (1986), p. 35.

55. Buhle and Buhle (1978), pp. 32–33, 38–39; Flexner (1968), pp. 235–237, 271–275; Fowler (1986), pp. xix, 17–18, 105–154; Scott and Scott (1982), pp. 32–33. Buechler (1986), Buhle and Buhle (1978), and Kraditor (1965) emphasize the narrowing of vision that accompanied this growing effectiveness. It should be pointed out, however, that there is no full-scale study of the ideology of the movement before 1890, and thus efforts to assess ideological changes over the long haul are handicapped.

56. DuBois (1986), pp. 52–58; Strom (1975).

57. Mahoney (1969), p. 155; Daniels (1979), p. 62.

58. Steinson (1982).

59. Degler (1980), pp. 349–355; Flexner (1971), pp. 294–305; Kraditor (1965), pp. 14–42; Stevenson (1979).

60. Giddings (1984), pp. 119–131, 159–165; Kraditor (1965), pp. 163–218; Terborg-Penn (1977, 1978).

61. Cott (1984), p. 46; Scott and Scott (1982), p. 33 (quotation).

62. Adele Clark to Roberta Wellford, September 26, 1920; Roberta Wellford Papers, University of Virginia.

63. Johnson (1978), vol. 1, pp. 199, 207.

64. Wagner (1986), pp. 364–365. See also Jensen (1981b), pp. 144–148, 154–160; Myres (1982), pp. 228–230, 233. Many women came to Populism through the Farmers' Alliance, which enrolled massive numbers of female members in the 1880s and 1890s in the West and the South. The success of the alliance in recruiting women raises questions about the relation of women's productive roles and the formation of mixed-sex versus single-sex voluntary associations: Where women were engaged in production with men in the family unit, were mixed organizations more commonplace than single-sex ones?

65. Buhle (1970), pp. 53–54. See also Buhle (1981).

66. Bordin (1981), p. 133.

67. Kraditor (1965), pp. 63–71; Stevenson (1979), p. 88.

68. Alpern and Baum (1985), pp. 47, 57–59.

69. Alpern and Baum (1985); Kleppner (1982).

70. Freedman (1979), p. 524. Sklar (1985) and Kessler-Harris (1985a) build on and revise Freedman's argument.

71. Which is not to say that all women agreed on all things. Gullett points out that on a second issue, that of shutting down dance halls, middle-class reformers clashed with working-class employees. Gullett (1984). See Sumner (1909) for a low-key assessment of the effects of woman suffrage in Colorado.

72. Baker (1987), chaps. 3 and 4.

73. Baker's treatment of men's politics is also distinctive in its insistence that men's politics was carried out within a distinct moral framework and that cynicism and suspicion of government, along with intense partisanship, were part of that framework.

74. Baker (1984).

75. Hays (1975); McCormick (1981).

76. See Kaplan (1982) for some suggestions, based on Spanish cases, about the relation between traditional female roles and political action.

77. But again, see Cott, this volume, for questions on the significance of 1920 and the alleged decline of feminism.

78. Lerner (1977), pp. 317–322.

79. For a bibliography, see Papachristou (1985). DuBois (1986), pp. 45–46, discusses women and municipal reform, an area in special need of investigation.

80. See, for example, Gordon (1985).

81. For a more general research agenda, see Scott (1986).

3

Varieties of Voluntarism: Class, Ethnicity, and Women's Activism in Tampa

Nancy A. Hewitt

In August 1901 female tobacco strippers in Tampa, Florida, having been on strike for two months, circulated an appeal in Spanish "to the American Women," asking them to help stop abductions of Cuban strike leaders by local "vigilantes."[1] During the previous fifteen years, native-born women in the city had not hesitated to step into the public arena or to chastize their male kin and neighbors for immoral or improper conduct. As Tampa grew from a rural outpost to an urban center, these women had founded an astonishing array of voluntary associations, the most prominent of which was the local Woman's Christian Temperance Union (WCTU). Women had also ventured into the electoral arena; in 1900 the month-old Tampa Woman's Club hosted a campaign speech by Democratic presidential hopeful William Jennings Bryan. Still, the moral and political as well as economic implications of supporting striking cigar makers kept these same women from responding to the pleas of their Cuban "sisters."

Most historical studies of female voluntarism have focused on middle-class, Anglo-Saxon, Protestant women who were involved in public associations, mostly in the North, in the years before woman suffrage was attained. They have thus embraced only a specific segment of voluntary societies, excluding both working-class organizations, such as unions, and partisan associations, such as political parties. In addition, sex-segregated societies have received far greater attention than mixed-sex organizations. Scholars have further defined voluntarism in terms of associations rather than activities, thus concealing the importance of collective actions that did not result in the formation of formal and relatively permanent organizations. Finally, they have suggested that female voluntarism was inspired more by spiritual and moral, than by material, concerns. The Spanish-language circular of 1901 reveals a co-existent world of female activism beyond the boundaries of the northern middle class and suggests several unexplored questions about women's voluntary activities.[2]

In Tampa, immigrant working-class women, both inside and outside the workplace, were inspired by economic necessity to enter the public arena in support of a short-lived, male-led union, *La Resistencia*. These women sought to establish bonds of sisterhood across ethnic and economic boundaries. Yet their inability to communicate with native-born women activists both literally and figuratively demonstrated the difficulty of bridging such barriers. Although support was not forthcoming, Cuban women, alongside male kin and neighbors, continued to challenge the political, social, and economic power of city fathers and mothers. The associational activity of these immigrants was inspired by specific and immediate material concerns. The immediacy of their grievances as well as the repressive responses of community leaders inhibited the formation of long-term, formal organizations. Still, the patterns of collective mobilization visible in 1901 reemerged in the immigrant community during political and economic crises throughout the first half of the twentieth century, creating continuity if not permanence over half a century of history.

Differences in form between working-class and middle-class female voluntarism have often obscured the former from historians' view. To understand female voluntarism fully, then, we must focus on women's activities rather than their associations, and on periodic mobilization as well as permanent organization. This chapter examines the relations among female voluntarists in the public arena by seeking to reveal the critical cleavages and coalitions among them within particular communities and within the larger society. It begins with a summary of my earlier assessment of women's social activism based on the study of Rochester, New York, in the years 1822–1872. It then details the dynamics of women's activism in one turn-of-the-century city—Tampa, Florida—broadening the framework of historical analysis to include the collective action of working-class and immigrant women. Within such a framework, we can ask to what extent class and ethnicity fostered different forms of female voluntarism; to what degree particular forms of female voluntarism affected the larger community; and, finally, under what conditions coalitions among women across class and ethnic boundaries were possible.[3]

Existing Studies of Women's Voluntarism

Local studies have proven particularly valuable for analyzing women's voluntarism and collective action in the nineteenth century when "the community constituted the main arena of intellectual, social and political life."[4] In pre–Civil War communities, scholars have uncovered dense networks of female activists that were central to the formation of welfare programs and the success of reform movements. Since research in these communities concerns mainly white, middle-class, Protestant women, the patterns revealed are not universal; still, it does illustrate three important points. First, even within the seemingly cohesive middle class, women disagreed about the proper definition of social order and the preferred direction of social change. Second, each network was defined by a convergence of factors—relative status within the broadly defined middle class, kinship, nativity, religious affiliation—no one of which was sufficient to assure a woman activist's identity with one cluster or another. Thus, allegiances shifted and overlapped amid rapid economic, social, and political change, while the networks themselves remained distinct for long periods. Third, despite the distinctive character of each network, female activists in general utilized domestic rhetoric and skills in justifying and carrying out their labors, engaged in sex-specific public tasks, and forged temporary alliances with other groups of women in pursuit of specific goals.

In Rochester, New York, for instance, three activist networks emerged over the second quarter of the nineteenth century—embracing advocates of benevolence, reform, and radicalism, respectively.[5] Proximity to power was particularly important in shaping the goals and styles of these three voluntarist circles. "Benevolent" ladies, members of Rochester's elite, promoted social control through philanthropy while alleviating the worst consequences of the urban and commercial development that had enriched their families. They labored unobtrusively, adhering to cultural dictates governing feminine behavior by joining only all-female societies directed toward helping the less advantaged. "Reformers" hoped to gain entry into the city's elite circles but also were motivated by evangelical religious admonitions that aimed at the perfection of society. They sought simultaneously to expand opportunities for the less fortunate, institute a single standard of moral behavior, and sustain existing social, economic, and political institutions. Women "reformers" were eager adherents to the ideals of "true womanhood"—piety, purity, domesticity, and submissiveness—and therefore worked only within sex-segregated societies and devoted themselves largely to altruistic efforts. They were more vocal and visible than their "benevolent" counterparts, however, and in their search for perfection and for resources, they forged temporary alliances with both more conservative and more radical women activists.

Rochester's "radical" women were the most distant from centers of power, the most critical of the existing order, and the most vociferous in their advocacy of a redistribution of resources and a reconstruction of class, race, and gender relations. "Radicals" also diverged in style from their "benevolent" and "reform" counterparts. They purposefully challenged decorum by wearing Turkish trousers instead of skirts, socializing in mixed racial company, speaking from public platforms, and joining "promiscuous" (sexually integrated) societies. While working on behalf of slaves, Indians, and the laboring classes, these women argued that they needed to emancipate themselves as a first step toward liberating others.

These three networks remained distinct at least through the middle decades of the century, but this did not preclude attempts at forging coalitions to advance specific causes. "Benevolent" ladies and evangelical "reformers" cooperated in founding the local orphan asylum and the Home for Friendless Women. "Reformers" and "radicals" joined forces briefly in antislavery and woman suffrage campaigns; all three groups supported temperance. Yet their styles of activism, their tactics, and their long-term goals differed sufficiently to preclude the formation of any but the most temporary alliances. Ultimately, Rochester women refused to merge their identities, their efforts, or their associations. Support for this distinctiveness and autonomy came not only from other women but also from the male kin and coworkers of women in each network.[6]

More recent and more fragmentary evidence on black, immigrant, and/or working-class women's voluntarism in the United States further confirms that female activists formed distinct networks rooted in economic, social, and familial circumstances and that as women in these networks vied for power, they sought support from similarly situated men as well as women.[7] The formation of additional networks and an increase in competition for resources occurred whenever new groups of women activists took to the public stage. Even among ethnic and racial minorities, other factors, such as class and kinship, channeled women into distinct and sometimes competing associations and movements. Middle-class black, Jewish, and Cuban women, for instance, often formed associations that paralleled those of their middle-class, Anglo-Saxon, Protestant counterparts, while their working-class "sisters" forged new forms of collective action. Certain tasks, most notably fundraising, consistently fell to women, regardless of cause or affiliation. Yet even while pursuing sex-specific forms of activity, female activists in both single-sex and mixed-sex organizations most often shared their goals and strategies and the control of their funds with kin and neighbors, including men.[8]

The complexity of voluntary networks increased not only with the addition of new circles of female activists, but also with the overall expansion of women's public efforts in the post–Civil War era. By the turn of the twentieth century, new forms of collective action appeared. Women in all groups forged more complex networks and more frequent (if not more durable) coalitions. To begin constructing a framework for analyzing this greater breadth of activity, a community study is necessary. To ensure the inclusion of the widest range of previously unstudied groups, I have chosen a particularly heterogeneous locale: Tampa, Florida, a southern community with a large black and immigrant population, characterized by a host of female voluntary associations and activities.

The Tampa Context

In the immediate post–Civil War years, Tampa was inhabited by ex-slaves and ex-slaveholders, free blacks, fishermen, cattle barons, and soldiers. In 1886 the construction of a company town built by Spanish entrepreneurs and peopled by highly skilled Afro-Cuban and white Cuban laborers turned Tampa into an industrial city. By 1910 the immigrant population—including large numbers of Italians as well as Spaniards and Cubans—numbered over 12,000 of the Tampa area's 56,000 residents. The cigar centers of Ybor City and later West Tampa were incorporated into the city proper, but they remained distinctly working class and Latin.[9] In this pioneer setting, women sought to shape the moral and material landscape to benefit themselves and their families.

In early nineteenth century cities, competing networks of female voluntarists had developed diachronically as middle-class women expanded the range and forms of their activities. In cities founded later in the century, "benevolent" associations, "reform" societies, and "radical" movements often emerged simultaneously. The various forms continued to appeal, however, to women of different social and economic circumstances. In Tampa's formative years, from 1886 to 1901, native-born, middle- and upper-class women emphasized "benevolent" and "reform" activity, while "radical" political and economic campaigns dominated working-class immigrant women's activities. Although in other cities the latter group might also be active in more conservative campaigns, such as those related to ethnic churches, anti-colonial and anti-Catholic sentiments rooted in Cubans' struggle against Spanish domination in their homeland nurtured a more radical vision.

The first boatload of Cuban workers and their families arrived in Port Tampa in the spring of 1886 to begin work in the soon-to-open cigar factories of Ybor City. At roughly the same time, a group of native-born women in Tampa proper formed a local branch of the WCTU, the first recorded female voluntary association in the town. The founders of this "reform" society included the wives and daughters of both affluent and middle-class men (bankers, merchants, judges, newspaper editors, and lawyers as well as ministers, restaurateurs, salesmen, saddlers, carpenters, and carriage-makers). A few widows of modest means, one of whom ran a "dry" boardinghouse, also joined. In the first year, members established a public reading room, a temperance Saturday school, and a full treasury.[10] By spring of 1887, WCTU members had considerably broadened the scope of their activities—forming an auxiliary branch in Ybor City, appointing a superintendent for "colored" work, petitioning federal legislators to enact statutes to punish "crimes against women and girls," and campaigning for county-wide prohibition.[11]

"Benevolent" and "Reform" Organizations in Tampa

The WCTU served as the core "reform" organization in Tampa's voluntarist networks, expanding into neighborhood and juvenile auxiliaries and spawning the public library movement, the Door of Hope Rescue Home, and the Working Woman's Mission. The most active women in these "reform" projects were wives, daughters, or widows of local entrepreneurs and professionals. Their male relatives were prominent though not powerful, well-to-do though not wealthy. Most of these families had arrived in the Tampa area in the 1880s, and their rising status in the community was dependent on industry and sobriety and on the public image of respectability projected by wives as well as husbands. As early as 1888, the *Tampa Journal* accorded the WCTU a prominence unusual for a women's organization by listing its officers in the weekly *business* directory section of the paper.[12]

Still, not all of Tampa's activist-minded women felt as comfortable with the WCTU's style and goals as did this local male editor. Some women preferred to pursue "benevolent" projects in quiet but effective ways. The members of the Ladies' Improvement Society, for example, were apparently at work for several months before announcing their plans to the press. In April 1888 work began on the Court House square "to have the depressions in the square filled with dirt and the surface then water-graded." A landscape design had already been completed by the ladies, in consultation with experts, that included a bandstand, fountain, grass plats, curved walks, and seats, the whole to be surrounded by a chain-link fence. Rarely were members of this association identified individually in the paper, though they were praised collectively. One local businessman was heard to exclaim that this was "one of the best movements ever originated in Tampa."[13]

Female members of the local elite established other charitable associations and institutions as well. The Children's Home, founded in 1892, began as an urban mission by the First Methodist Church's Woman's Home Missionary Society and soon attracted interdenominational support from many of the city's "first" families. Other projects— kindergarten associations, the Old Ladies' Home, the City Mission Board—were organized by the same circle of "benevolent" leaders. These elite Tampa families often intermarried; thus by the end of the century "benevolent" associations were composed of dense webs of women relatives.[14]

The affluent women who promoted these "benevolent" ventures are less visible to the historian's eye than their "reform"-minded counterparts in the WCTU. Yet they were undoubtedly well known to their neighbors, and much of their appeal probably rested on the altruistic and unobtrusive character of their endeavors. Willing to care for small "families" of orphans or the elderly in homelike institutions, they did not seek or need the public attention demanded by those who sought to eradicate intemperance and immorality throughout the community as a whole.

Despite differences in background, style, and purpose, these two networks of female activists sometimes joined forces to meet the demand for social services created by frontier life. The yellow fever epidemic of 1887 was such an occasion. Before any official (male) Citizens' Relief Committee was appointed by the city council, women had already donated their nursing services to the "sick poor" through the Ladies' Relief Society, a coalition of individuals from both "benevolent" and "reform" organizations. In the society's efforts, Mrs. Friebele, one of the few publicly identified organizers of the Ladies' Improvement Society, served alongside Miss Josie Weissbrod, secretary of the WCTU. "Reformer" Mary Cuscaden of the Ybor City WCTU and "benevolent" leader Mrs. Jennie Copeland of the First Methodist Woman's Home Missionary Society both perished in the effort to vanquish yellow fever.[15] When the Citizens' Committee was formed, one of its first monetary donations came from the Ladies' Relief Society.[16]

In the epidemic's aftermath, members of the Relief Society, including both WCTU campaigners and charitable ladies, turned their energies to the founding of an Emergency Hospital. This first attempt at a formal coalition between "benevolent" and "reform" networks lasted seven years. "Benevolent" women controlled the highest offices—president, secretary, and treasurer—but "reform" leaders were active on the Board of Lady Managers. Successful in establishing and furnishing a hospital, hiring a staff, and managing day-to-day operations, the coalition that founded the Emergency Hospital was destroyed, but not by conflicts among women.

Rather, in 1895 the Tampa Physicians' Protective Association, which was composed of so-called regular physicians, took issue with the women's management and refused to work alongside "irregular" practitioners employing homeopathic cures. Claiming they were "daily humiliated by being thrown into intimate contact with these [irregulars]" because of the unprofessional management of the women, the "regulars" demanded that the hospital be placed under their control. The county commission, which had contributed little to the hospital's maintenance, sided with the "regulars" as did the Hillsborough County Medical Association, demanding that the women relinquish control. Asked to stay on as a Ladies' Auxiliary Hospital Board under the supervision of male physicians, the nine lady managers angrily refused. Within a few weeks an entirely new Women's Auxiliary Board was formed, composed of the wives of the Emergency Hospital's "regular" medical staff.[17]

In the woman's club movement, "benevolent" and "reform" activists forged a successful coalition that was not taken over by men. The impetus for the original Tampa Woman's Club came from an individual who stood outside local voluntarist networks, Mrs. Helen C. Dick, a Massachusetts native "wintering" in Florida in 1900. Club membership cut across existing voluntarist networks owing in part to political-party loyalties. Overtly engaged with the political issues of the day, the Tampa Woman's Club supported local and national Democratic candidates. Mrs. Dick proclaimed that the "justification of the existence of [the] organization" was evidenced in the society's "first public meeting" at which the club gave William Jennings Bryan a platform.[18] For a dozen years the Tampa Woman's Club remained the national Federation of Woman's Clubs' lone affiliate in the city, attracting members from the WCTU, the Children's Home, the Working Woman's Mission, and other female voluntary associations.

Initially the club described itself as promoting "literary work and self-culture," and it aided in the work of the Children's Home and the Old

People's Home. From the beginning, members were interested in electoral issues; and they increasingly became concerned with "reform" projects, helping to found the Associated Charities and the new Woman's Home and Hospital, supporting the emerging home economics movement, and petitioning for improved treatment of the Seminole Indians. Members also made a concerted and eventually successful effort to secure a Carnegie Library for the city.[19] By 1912 some more "benevolent"-oriented activists formed the Tampa Civic Association, an "outdoor organization" that harked back to the Ladies' Improvement Society. More of a civic improvement than a "benevolent" society, this club promoted city sanitation and beautification projects, flower shows, a May Day festival, and fundraisers for playground equipment. At the same time, a third association, the Woman's City Club, was founded. Like the original Tampa Woman's Club, its members emphasized "reform" projects, but they focused on the needs of working women and working-class families. They constructed playgrounds in working-class neighborhoods, established a Woman's Exchange and Employment Bureau for working girls, and provided hot lunches in the public schools for workers' children.[20]

All three Tampa women's clubs, being affiliated with the national federation, were called together for an official visit by the state president in 1915. The state and national federations supported a legislative agenda that included women's suffrage. There is little evidence, however, that any of the Tampa clubs worked directly for political power. Instead, they continued to employ their funds and their influence in ways that would shape local policies and provide local services for women and workers without seeking recourse to the voting booth. Thus, the City Club's primary goal in 1915 was to establish a lace industry in Tampa, while the Civic Association raised funds for the Associated Charities, and the original Woman's Club focused on establishing a Carnegie Library.[21]

"Benevolent" leaders also concerned themselves with the plight of immigrants in Ybor City and West Tampa. In 1898 representatives of the various cigar factories donated funds to the Children's Home for repairs, suggesting that immigrant as well as native-born children were served by the institution.[22] A Day Nursery Association formed in 1902 located its first nursery in Ybor City. Eventually it hoped to open a sewing school in the same building "for the benefit of young girls who work for their living." Apparently concerned with gaining the support of affluent immigrant women, the association emphasized that it was "entirely undenominational, and it [was] the earnest desire of its promoters that all good ladies, without regard to creed or language, may co-operate and share in the privilege of contributing to the success of the work in hand." Clearly, however, the project's developers believed that Anglo-American superiority could not be denied, assuring their supporters that "it is work of this kind which is necessary if the foreigners who come to our shores are ever to understand American ideals."[23]

All of the associations, "reform" and "benevolent," that established branches or programs in Ybor City followed the model offered by the WCTU in 1887. Organizations or institutional boards were headed by native-born women, with a few wives and daughters of wealthy Spaniards and Cubans added to the bottom of the roster. Indeed, the president of the original Ybor City branch of the WCTU was the same woman, Mrs. Dr. Linton, who headed the Tampa branch. The highest-ranking resident of Ybor City, moreover, was Miss Mary Cuscaden, a member of one of the few native-born families residing in that section of the city. The only Latin women elected to office were Miss Bueno and Miss Castello, whose names were listed last on the visiting committee, which was the last committee listed on the roster.[24]

Women's Coalitions
During the Cuban–Spanish-American War

It was international politics that increased native-born women's concern with their immigrant neighbors during the 1890s. Cubans had been actively seeking independence from Spain since the Ten Years' War (1868–1878). The United States had been seeking dominion over the island for considerably longer. In 1895 the Cuban War for Independence was launched with the full economic and political support of émigré communities in New York City, Key West, and Tampa. By 1898 the success of the Cuban insurgency gave the United States its first opportunity to gain control of the island's economic resources with little danger of precipitating an international crisis with Spain. At the urging of North American investors and justified by the romantic rhetoric of national self-determination, the United States entered the war, participating in the final victorious battles. In 1898 Cuba was proclaimed a protectorate of the United States. During these years, as the Cuban War for Independence was transformed into the Spanish-American War, Tampa's native-born residents increased their interest in and interaction with the city's Cuban population.[25]

When the U.S. Army chose Tampa as its disembarkation point in 1898, war fever intensified throughout the city. Food, drink, and entertainment were provided by native-born and Cuban women along with clothing, bedding, and medical services. That same year, native-born women first became concerned with the plight of the hundreds of Cuban refugees who had fled to Tampa during the previous three years of war and of the thousands of local families left destitute by the war effort. "Benevolent" leaders then joined in the work of the Cuban-led Central Relief Committee, opening soup kitchens in Ybor City and West Tampa. At the same time, Mrs. Kate P. Stewart, a Tampa WCTU member, moved to Havana to open a new reading room, appealing to her sisters at home to supply the clothing, medicine, bedding, and books necessary to provide a safe haven for weary soldiers.[26]

Tampa Cubans did not wait for either the U.S. Army or native-born women activists to launch plans for military victory and civilian relief. José Martí, the "father of Cuban independence," visited Ybor City in November 1891, speaking at the Liceo Cubano where "women stood upon chairs, waving hats and handkerchiefs, men shoved to the stage to shake his hand, and the room filled with shouts of 'viva.' "[27] Within three days, local cigar makers had helped to form the Cuban Revolutionary Party, the purpose of which was to direct efforts in behalf of *Cuba Libre* within émigré communities. On November 28, as Martí left Ybor City, a young girl, Candelaria Carbonell, "came forth representing all the immigrants" and presented the Cuban hero with a pen and inkstand "paid for by public subscription."[28] Tampa's patriotic clubs, formed by both women and men, provided political, moral, and financial support for the cause. Martí himself proclaimed Ybor City the "civilian camp of the revolution."[29] After three and a half years of preparation, the signal to begin the military struggle was sent handrolled in a cigar wrapper from Tampa to the insurgent forces in Cuba. News of the war's eruption reached Ybor City on February 26, 1895, two days after the cigar-encased message reached Cuba, and ignited a huge celebration near the O'Halloran factory in West Tampa. The highlight of the evening was a twenty-minute "spontaneous oration" by 10-year-old Pennsylvania Herrera, daughter of one of the revolution's émigré organizers.[30] Throughout the war, Tampa's Cuban community would provide critical economic and military resources for the independence movement.[31]

Women's previous participation in revolutionary struggle in Cuba provided role models and leadership for the development of women's patriotic clubs in Ybor City and West Tampa.[32] In the latter community, Carolina Rodriguez, who braved death to carry information between separated insurgent forces in the Ten Years' War, provided living proof of women's heroism. She inspired younger women to dedicate themselves to the independence movement and to form the first female voluntary associations among Tampa's Cuban residents.[33]

Girls were socialized early into the impassioned campaign for Cuban independence. As small children, the daughters of Tampa's leading patriots presented flowers and gifts to visiting revolutionary heroes and by the age of 10 or 12 were presenting brief speeches to mass meetings.[34] The participation of women and children in patriotic demonstrations attracted the attention of local reporters. In April 1895, for instance, thousands gathered to celebrate the twenty-sixth anniversary of the first Cuban constitution. The *Tampa Tribune*'s front-page story noted that "the hall and every possible space was packed with an eager anxious throng of patriot Cubans, including several hundred ladies."[35]

Yet women's roles were never equal to those of men and were often symbolic rather than substantive in the years prior to the resumption of war in Cuba. After the eruption of hostilities, however, the mobilization of women advanced quickly, and women began to appear as prominent speakers at public rallies. At the twenty-sixth anniversary celebration, for instance, three months after war erupted, Miss Maria Luisa Sanchez was the "feature of the evening . . . her every sentence was filled with a patriotic emotion which set the whole house wild with enthusiasm."[36]

To capture that enthusiasm and galvanize it into collective action was a primary concern of Martí from his earliest visits to the Tampa area. In November 1892 he and several male compatriots traveled to a Cuban neighborhood where a "woman's club was formed"; "at its inauguration all of the men in the group spoke."[37] After February 1895 Tampa's Cuban women began forming their own revolutionary organizations in support of Martí's vision. On November 24, Anita Merchan, a young émigré, called together a circle of friends to form the *Discipulas de Martí*. Named for the "love of our great Teacher," the *Discipulas* were motivated by "the duty to help conquer our independence," believing that "we will be able, the young señoritas of Tampa, to work together to this end."[38] In the next two years, numerous other women's clubs— including *Cuba Libre, 24 de Febrero, Estrella Solitaria*—formed in West Tampa and Ybor City, contributing to Tampa's reputation within revolutionary circles.

The chief responsibility of the women's clubs was fundraising. Initially, most money raised for Cuban independence came from subscriptions among cigar workers, both male and female, who donated as much as one day's wages per week to the cause. The other important sources of funds—evening entertainments, fiestas, picnics, bazaars, and door-to-door solicitations—were organized primarily by the women's clubs. At least one such event was held almost weekly between 1895 and 1898, raising from under $100 to over $1,000 each.[39]

Kinship as well as ethnicity bound members of the women's clubs to each other and to the larger cause. Sisters Maria Luisa and Fredesvinda Sanchez helped found *Discipulas,* of which Mary Echemendia served as treasurer. Mary Echemendia's mother, Susan, founded a club for married women, *Estrella Solitaria,* modeled on the *Discipulas.* All of these women were related to leading male patriots and soldiers as were club founders America Herrera, Maria Louisa Somiellan, and Mrs. Joaquin Dueña, among others.

Neither class nor race differences impaired Cuban solidarity. From cigar makers to factory owners, female tobacco strippers to wives and daughters of Cuban capitalists, the residents of the "cigar cities" supported *Cuba Libre.* Black Cubans contributed funds and soldiers as well, inspired by the egalitarian vision of Martí and the military heroism of Afro-Cuban Antonio Maceo. Paulina Pedroso, one of the leading Afro-Cuban patriots, hosted Martí whenever he visited Tampa.[40]

Differences did emerge, however, in the forms of assistance that various classes of Cubans could provide. While America Herrera donated "her silver table service . . . and her elegant parlor set" to be auctioned for the cause, Paulina and Rupert Pedroso sold their home to provide additional funds to the party.[41] Factory laborers contributed part of their wages; working-class women donated home-made goods to fiestas and bazaars; wealthier women organized fundraising events to which they contributed their finery.

The war was not the only project that required women's services. By April 1898 nearly 3,000 Cuban refugees "were 'in great destitution in and around Tampa' and a continuous flow of new arrivals augmented that number." The refugees were originally taken into existing households and provided with food and shelter until work could be found. Women formed the *Sociedad de Beneficéncias,* modeled on mutual aid societies in Cuba, to coordinate relief efforts and donated labor, goods, or money according to their circumstances. By 1898, however, Cubans could no longer fund the war in Cuba and relief efforts at home alone. In the final year of the war, strikes and recessions hampered cigar production, and more male cigar workers left Tampa to fight in Cuba. As the profits from public benefits run by women became the primary means of filling Cuban Revolutionary party coffers, the need for new donation sources led Cuban women to seek support in the city at large. The *Discipulas* offered to teach Spanish to native-born Tampa girls whom they also invited to participate in their monthly theatrical performances. Cuban foods and costumes were presented at fiestas to attract curious native-born residents, but traditional American dishes were also served. Maud Madison, a "skirt and fancy dancer of New York," was featured at one fundraising event because of her appeal to Anglo-Americans.[42] In addition, the Central Relief Committee began to receive donations from factory owners and their wives, including Mrs. Vincente Ybor, and from "benevolent" leaders, such as Children's Home president Mrs. William B. Henderson.[43]

Yet American and Cuban visions of the independence movement diverged. Native-born women specialized in providing charity to needy refugees, while their Cuban counterparts collected arms and ammunition as well as food, clothing, and medical supplies for military expeditions. Events organized to gain native-born support involved the provision of "native" foods and music at center city hotels. Those organized within immigrant quarters were held out of doors or at the Cuban Club in Ybor City and had a more military flair. Men attended in uniform, entertainment was provided by the reenactment of insurgent victories, and women served "troop diet" on plantain leaves.[44] After U.S. troops arrived in Tampa, young Cuban women returned to "traditional" costumes to serve coffee and cake to American soldiers, to distribute cigars to the camps, and to entertain the men with Cuban songs, recitations, and dances.[45]

The patriotic images presented to native-born Tampans by Cuban women did not save their community from depredations by American soldiers who became bored, drunk, and rowdy as they awaited passage to Cuba. Once in Cuba, U.S. soldiers were offended by inhabitants of the island who did not view them as saviors and by the high proportion of Afro-Cubans integrated into insurgent forces. In Tampa itself, prejudicial publicity generated by the U.S. military, combined with local antagonism fostered by striking cigar makers and Americans' realization of the truly radical character of *Cuba Libre*, diminished the enthusiasm for Anglo-Cuban alliances at home and abroad. The U.S. government's imposition of protectorate status on Cuba in 1898 further encouraged the resurgence of paternalistic attitudes among Tampa residents toward their Ybor City and West Tampa neighbors. Simultaneously, the end of the war led to the dissolution of the women's patriotic clubs and thus to one of the most effective links between Anglo-Americans and immigrants.

Cuban Women's Collective Action Reborn

Some of the patriotic clubs became social clubs or mutual benefit societies, and the *Sociedad de Beneficéncias* continued to coordinate relief efforts for refugees at least until 1899. The resurgence of collective action in Ybor City and West Tampa did not stem directly from these associations, however, but from organizations of cigar workers. Now their target would not be Spanish tyranny in Cuba but capitalist oppression in Tampa. Strikes in 1899 and 1901 mobilized men and women of the immigrant community, but this time in the service of specific class interests. In the process, women's public coalitions were restructured, as working-class Cubans antagonized both Anglo-Americans at large and their wealthier neighbors in the Latin community. At the same time, elite Cuban and Spanish women were invited to enter Anglo-American "benevolent" and "reform" networks in ever larger numbers.

Cuban women who worked in cigar factories, and their sisters who did not, rallied to support the strike as did smaller numbers of Italian women whose families had settled in Ybor City in the 1890s.[46] The 1901 strike was waged by *La Sociedad de Torcedores de Tabaco de Tampa*, popularly known as *La Resistencia* because the society's stated purpose was "to resist the exploitation of labor by capital."[47] Modeled on a Havana-based organization, *Resistencia* sought to establish an industrial-style union that would unite laboring Cubans throughout Ybor City and West Tampa. Although their initial organizing drive was confined to cigar factories, by 1901 *Resistencia* extended its efforts into laundries, box factories, and other local industries. Counting thousands of members among skilled and unskilled workers, *Resistencia* established itself as a powerful force. In so doing, it antagonized city fathers, factory owners, and the leaders of the Cigar Makers' International Union. In July 1901 all sides braced for a long struggle.

Resistencia's strength lay in community solidarity, a solidarity that joined women and men. The most important official women's organization to participate in the strike was the *Gremio de Despalilladoras*, the tobacco strippers' branch of the union, which provided over one quarter of *Resistencia*'s membership. Its importance was reflected on the sixty-member strikes committee, on which six women served. The *Despalilladoras* was a voluntary association as well as a trade association and did not limit its activities to the workplace. Rather, its leaders worked to mobilize women throughout the community and in Key West to support the strike. At first, the tasks undertaken by striking women and their community supporters were assigned by the male leadership of *Resistencia*. As the strike dragged on, however, and with many male leaders forced out of town by a local Citizen's Committee, women initiated and led more strike-related activities.

The first task was the opening of nine *cocinas económicas*, or soup kitchens, on August 2, 1901, to provide food for strikers and their families.[48] Although the sexual division of labor in the soup kitchens is not fully documented, it appears that men directed the financial operations and bought the supplies while women generally cooked and served the food. Tampa editors reported that the food furnished at the soup kitchens was meager in quantity and poor in quality, but they also insisted that "as long as these are open, the strike will probably be maintained." Indeed, after the "forcible deportation" of sixteen *Resistencia* leaders failed to end the walkout, the *Tampa Morning Tribune* declared on the front page, "The soup houses are still in operation, and this seems to be the inspiration of prolonging the strike."[49] While Tampa's city fathers claimed to disapprove of worker-run soup kitchens on health-related grounds, the persistent attacks on them and on the harboring of evicted workers and targeted union leaders by community women suggests a more fundamental fear. City fathers appear to have interpreted women's, and especially housewives', support of the strike as reflecting a depth of community solidarity among Cubans that threatened Anglo-American dominance.[50]

Despite the negative reactions of city fathers, female tobacco strippers still hoped to gain support from city mothers. It was at this juncture that a "Committee of Strippers" circulated their Spanish-language appeal "to the American Women," asking that they "use their influence to stop abductions of strike leaders." The response of the American women was silence. The *Tribune* editors, however, demanded that the presumed author of the appeal, Altagracia Martinez, "cease making excitable speeches" and suggested that she might soon be among the deportees.[51] Latin women then petitioned Governor William Jennings, demanding an investigation of local vigilante actions.

The Citizen's Committee, unchastened by the women's appeals and petitions, continued to aid factory owners in "disciplining" strikers. The landlords in Ybor City and West Tampa were encouraged to evict strikers who were behind in rent, believing that those who "are turned out of doors . . . may be led to see the errors of their ways."[52] Taken into other homes, evicted workers and their families relied on women neighbors to stretch budgets, groceries, and accommodations. As significant numbers of men traveled to Cuba in search of glory or to other cities in search of work, some blocks became virtually all-female enclaves.

Women did more than contribute their domestic skills to strike activities. They also participated in more overtly political actions. Several traveled to Key West to organize female support committees; among them was Luisa Herrera, secretary of the *Despalilladoras*, widow of a union organizer, and frequent contributor of "inflammatory articles" to Spanish-language newspapers.[53] The success of Herrera and others depended on the existence of a network of women, skilled in collective action, that stretched from Havana through Key West to Tampa.

By mid-autumn, women in Ybor City and West Tampa took to the streets to protest actions of the Citizen's Committee and the police. Altagracia Martinez led a crowd comprised mostly of women and children who confronted a Citizen's Committee delegation as it entered Ybor City, resulting in a standoff, at least on that day.[54] This crowd and others included increasing numbers of Italian women as their male kin became subjects of employer and police harassment alongside Cuban coworkers. These women, not wage workers themselves, were moved to action by the arrests of husbands, sons, and brothers.

In October the police began arresting cigar workers on vagrancy charges, and judges assigned the men to chain gangs or jail. The afternoon of the first arrests, a large crowd, "including many women and children," assembled in Ybor City to demand an audience with the mayor. Ordered to disperse by police and fearing violence from local vigilantes, the crowd slowly dissolved. The following day, Italian and Cuban "women of the laboring community staged a march upon police headquarters" and "several delegations of women called on Mayor Wing to intercede in behalf of the strikers who [were] being run in for vagrancy by the police." The mayor rebuffed the women, but vagrancy arrests declined immediately and nearly disappeared by month's end.[55]

Self-management and militancy increased among women throughout the strike as the capacity of men to direct the strike diminished and as women adapted their organizational skills and experiences to the new cause. Community women increasingly took their lead from the *Despalilladoras* leaders, though neither the militancy of the latter nor the solidarity of the former could gain a final victory for *Resistencia*. In November cigar workers drifted back to the factories; the strike was officially declared ended on November 23, 1901. Despite defeat, Cuban women had gained a new kind of organizing experience, one based on class solidarity and interethnic cooperation with their Italian working-class neighbors, employing everyday domestic skills in public activities and extending their activities into mass demonstrations and political delegations.

As working-class Latin women pursued new forms of voluntarism in support of workers' control, their affluent neighbors were being appointed to the board of the Children's Home and were invited to join the local women's clubs by their Anglo counterparts. During this period the foundation of "sisterhood" shifted from the ethnic solidarity evidenced in the war years to the class solidarity that emerged in the strike years. As they joined city-wide "benevolent" and "reform" associations, affluent women partially withdrew from community activities in Ybor City and West Tampa, thus diminishing both the financial resources and the organizational experience available to poorer Latin activists. Their more restricted activities in the ethnic enclaves, however, permitted the emergence of new styles of activism, modeled more on working-class trade unions than on middle-class voluntary associations.[56] Repression of union activity combined with working and working-class women's limited resources to inhibit the establishment of permanent organizations, but conditions in the cigar cities nevertheless encouraged the spontaneous formation of task-oriented work groups in support of immediate and specific material concerns. In the strikes of 1910, 1920, and 1931, the lessons of 1901 would be revived and a new form of female voluntarism would take hold. In the intervening years some of these same techniques would be employed in support of mutual aid societies and other class- and community-based activities.

Conclusion

The efforts and experiences of women activists in Tampa suggest several revisions in the analytic frameworks constructed through the analysis of pre–Civil War voluntary associations. First, the notion that voluntarism emerged as a consequence of the rise of domesticity and the attendant increase in women's leisure time is not borne out by the range of working and nonworking women's collective action in Tampa. While bourgeois domesticity, the availability of servants, and the incomes of affluent or upwardly mobile husbands provided "benevolent" and "reform" leaders with additional time and money, they did not themselves inspire their voluntary labors. Nor was religious enthusiasm a sufficient guarantor of voluntary activity. Although critical to the efforts of most Anglo women, the residents of Ybor City and West Tampa were enormously active and notoriously anticlerical.[57]

The forms that women's collective action took reflected class-based interests as well as gender ideologies and ethnic heritages. The associations that "benevolent" and "reform" leaders founded provided vehicles for their ongoing if unobtrusive influence in shaping the city's social and economic order. Working and working-class women's support of strikes made their material interests more starkly visible. At the same time, the sporadic character of their organizations often concealed the larger social and moral concerns behind their activities and limited their influence on social order and social change.

Second, the meaning of the term "radical" changed between the pre– and post–Civil War periods, reflecting different patterns of activism. "Radicals" in both Rochester and Tampa were distant from centers of economic and political power; but in late nineteenth century Tampa, "radicals" were more sharply differentiated by class and often distinguished by ethnicity. When working-class Latins hailed newly formulated radical doctrines, in particular the anarchism proclaimed by some advocates of *Cuba Libre* and several leaders of *La Resistencia*, the advocacy of formerly radical issues like woman suffrage and prohibition seemed moderate.

Working-class, immigrant women's activism like that of their middle-class female and working-class male counterparts was based on solidarities that emerged from the material concerns and conditions of everyday life. Yet rarely did the first group have the resources to create the more permanent organizations forged by the latter two groups. With all the limits imposed by spontaneous action, one advantage may have been that their activities were less subject to men's influence or control than were the institutions founded by middle-class women. Still, since the resources of "radical" immigrant housewives were insufficient to sustain permanent organization, their activities may have been shaped in larger part by the alliances they forged. During the struggle for political independence in Cuba, for example, women drew cross-class support from wealthier neighbors who formed more traditional voluntary associations. During the strike of 1901, they joined forces with the male-led *La Resistencia*. The alienation of wealthy Cubans during the strike and the demise of the union after the strike meant that working and working-class women and men would have to draw more heavily on workplace and community-based solidarities to organize future collective action.

In two ways the Tampa evidence reinforces patterns first revealed in pre–Civil War communities. First, truly cross-class alliances were rare and seldom sustained. Only during the Cuban–Spanish-American War did upper-class and working-class women work side by side with mutual concern. More often, affluent women sought to aid or uplift their poorer neighbors without regard to existing social, cultural, or economic patterns. In the prohibition campaigns and in the training of young Cuban girls for domestic work rather than cigar making, upper- and middle-class voluntarists demonstrated their failure to understand the needs of those they sought to serve.

Second, class-based associations quickly gained primacy over cross-class alliances. Although the Cuban–Spanish-American War demonstrated the potential for cooperation across class and ethnic boundaries in the early years of settlement, class emerged as the more salient factor once the immigrant community achieved stability. It was only within class boundaries that interethnic cooperation increased over time. After 1900 alliances among affluent Anglo-Americans, Cubans, and Italians and between working-class Cubans and Italians were more frequent and more enduring than those between affluent and working-class members of any one ethnic group.

It is evident that in Tampa, as in Rochester, female activists more often shared their goals, strategies, and resources with men of their own families, community, and class than with men or women of other groups. Before women participated directly in electoral politics, their patterns of coalition building were particularly revealing, suggesting that relationships to power and thus to politics were perceived as emanating not from the franchise, but from the class circumstances in which they exercised the franchise. Even when women won the vote, collective action and voluntarism outside electoral politics remained primary vehicles for their expression of political views and their influence on public policy.[58]

I wish to thank Nancy Cott, Anne Scott, and Rebecca Scott for their thoughtful comments on earlier versions of this chapter and William Chafe for his good humor and good company during the workshops out of which this chapter emerged.

I would feel remiss at not acknowledging the enormous help I received on this project from these four, along with Pat Gurin and Louise Tilly, in whose debt we all find ourselves after their long hours with and close attention to each of these chapters.

Notes

1. *Tampa Morning Tribune*, August 29, 1901. Cigar workers had already been on strike for several months during 1899 and 1900. The Latin women workers printed their appeal in Spanish, but it was quoted in English in the local daily paper. For an analysis of antilabor violence by local vigilantes, see Ingalls (1987).

2. Some of these same questions have been explored in a number of other studies on southern, western, working-class, and mixed-class associations. The formative study on southern women's activism is Scott (1970). In addition, see Dye (1980); Frederickson (1981); Levine (1984); and Neverdon-Morton (1978). Much new work has also appeared on middle-class and elite women's associations between 1865 and 1920. See, for example, Blair (1980); Bordin (1981); Freedman (1981); Ginzberg (1985); Leach (1980); McCarthy (1982); and Sklar (1985). The best overview of this work and the antebellum literature is Scott (1984a, 1984b). The above studies have focused almost

exclusively on relatively stable organizations, however, and have not yet resulted in a new conceptual synthesis.

3. Race is also a significant factor in differentiating women's voluntary labors, but I have not yet collected sufficient data on black women's activities in Tampa, Florida, to allow for the analysis of racial aspects here.

4. Walkowitz (1978), p. 13. For community studies of women's pre–Civil War activism, see Smith-Rosenberg (1971a); Ryan (1981); Boylan (1984); and Hewitt (1984).

5. Hewitt (1984).

6. See also Benson (1978) and Ryan (1981). Examining activists in nineteenth century Oneida County, New York, Ryan found that men and women of the same economic, social, and familial circles supported each other in efforts to secure and solidify their middle-class status. In Rhode Island Benson found that the activities of women in the Providence Employment Society "were complementary in function" to the public activities of the men in their families (p. 302).

7. See Berkeley (1985); Cameron (1985); Janiewski (1985); Jones (1985); Levine (1984); Neverdon-Morton (1989); and Smith (1985).

8. The Women's Trade Union League (WTUL) may be an exception here, as there was no obvious male counterpart, and male kin of more affluent WTUL members may have disagreed with the WTUL's response to employer-employee problems. (See Dye 1980.) Nor would I argue that wives always followed their husbands in the advocacy of social and political programs. Nonetheless, in general, women and men of the same social and economic circumstances, particularly if bound as well by family ties, tended to share social goals and activist strategies.

9. The term "Latin" refers to the combination of immigrant groups and cultures that inhabited Ybor City and West Tampa—Cuban, Spanish, and Italian. It was the word used by immigrants themselves when referring to groups of mixed ethnic backgrounds.

10. *Tampa Journal*, January—1887. This story reported on the past few months of activity of the WCTU. No report has yet been found of the actual date and circumstances of the local WCTU's founding.

11. *Tampa Journal*, April—1887.

12. *Tampa Journal*, May 19, 1888. Despite the respectability accorded these women in local newspapers, not one of these women's husbands or fathers was listed in county histories of famous Tampans. Some members of "reform" organizations were from more prominent families, but the leaders were from an economic and social strata just below the founding families.

13. *Tampa Journal*, April 28, 1888.

14. The husbands and/or fathers of all of these women were listed in the biographical sketches of pioneer Tampans by Grismer (1950) and Robinson (1928). The Board of Trade was especially important in Tampa's develop-

ment; it oversaw the city's economic growth, including the establishment of the cigar industry. It was probably the most powerful association in the city and was as supportive of "benevolent" projects to aid the poor as it was resistant to unionization among cigar workers. "Benevolent" women's husbands were well represented on the Board of Trade throughout the early decades of the twentieth century. Although wives may not have always agreed with their husbands, there is no evidence of public disagreements between the Board of Trade and women's "benevolent" organizations.

15. *Tampa Morning Tribune*, November 3, 1887, and March 29, 1888. See also Barker (1986).

16. *Tampa Morning Tribune*, October 27 and November 10, 1887.

17. *Tampa Morning Tribune*, September 22, 25, and 26, October 3 and 17, and November 1, 1895. For a full discussion of the conflict between male professionalization and female volunteer efforts in the Emergency Hospital, see St. Julien (1986), pp. 39–47. The hospital suffered its worst economic deficits and highest death rates after the physicians' takeover and was replaced by a new county-run hospital in 1910. Another example of men taking over a successful women's voluntary association occurred with the founding of the Union City Mission. See *Tampa Morning Tribune*, October 3, 1903, November 28, 1909, and December 10, 1910.

18. *Tampa Morning Tribune*, February 21, 1900. In the post–Reconstruction South, the Democratic party was the only significant party in most communities, including Tampa.

19. St. Julien (1986), pp. 56–62.

20. *Tampa Morning Tribune*, December 7, 1912, and December 13, 1914.

21. St. Julien (1986), pp. 62–63. Other "reform"-minded voluntarists had been active in establishing the Door of Hope, which aided poor girls who had fallen into lives of vice, and the Working Woman's Mission, which provided temporary shelter and assistance in locating employment for able-bodied women. See *Tampa Journal*, April—1887; and *Tampa Morning Tribune*, August 6, 1901. The suffrage "movement" in Tampa was largely the product of one woman, Mrs. Ella C. Chamberlain, until 1917 when Tampa hosted the annual meeting of the State Equal Suffrage Association. Even after this date, suffrage was a priority for only a small circle of devoted "reformers."

22. *Tampa Morning Tribune*, November 24, 1898.

23. *Tampa Morning Tribune*, November 23, 1902, and December 6, 1903.

24. *Tampa Journal*, April 21 and May 5 and 21, 1887. For the full roster with Bueno and Castello listed last, see the May 21, 1887, issue. The symbolism of such a listing was no doubt apparent to participants and readers.

25. See Pérez, Jr. (1983), chaps. 7 and 8.

26. *Tampa Morning Tribune*, September 5, 1901. Probably most visitors to the WCTU reading room were Anglo-American rather than Cuban soldiers.

27. Steffy (1975), p. 40, derived from contemporary newspaper accounts.

28. Muñiz (1969), p. 58.

29. Martí, quoted in Steffy (1975), p. 52.

30. *Tampa Morning Tribune*, February 27, 1895.

31. See especially, Steffy (1975), p. 42; Muñiz (1969), p. 93.

32. See Parrilla Cruz (1984) and Nuez Gonzalez (1978).

33. Galvez (1897), pp. 148–150.

34. Muñiz (1969), p. 58. See also Steffy (1975), pp. 42, 73; *Tampa Morning Tribune*, February 27 and April 11, 1895.

35. *Tampa Morning Tribune*, April 11, 1895.

36. *Tampa Morning Tribune*, April 11, 1895.

37. Muñiz (1969), p. 64.

38. *Juventud Rebelde* (Havana), August 23, 1982, p. 2. This was part of a historical series on young patriots. See also Galvez (1897), who gives credit to Fredesvinda Sanchez and Mary Echemendia for founding this club.

39. Steffy (1975), pp. 72, 96.

40. Muñiz (1969), pp. 91–92; Greenbaum (1986), pp. 5–6.

41. *Tampa Morning Tribune*, April 7, 1895, p. 1; and Muñiz (1969), pp. 91–92.

42. Steffy (1975), pp. 97–98.

43. Steffy (1975), pp. 124–125.

44. Galvez (1897), pp. 104–107; Steffy (1975), p. 99.

45. Steffy (1975), pp. 104–105, 122–123.

46. Italians were sometimes used as strike breakers; but others, who had supported radical causes in Italy prior to emigration, allied themselves with radical Cubans to improve working conditions and wages in the cigar industry.

47. Quoted in Long (1965), p. 196.

48. Long (1965), p. 206; *Tampa Morning Tribune*, August 1–3, 1901.

49. *Tampa Morning Tribune*, August 7, 8, and 15, 1901.

50. There is no single statement of this view by city fathers, but the continual harangue against soup kitchens, aid to evicted tenants, and marches and demonstrations directed by women suggest that local leaders understood the depth of community support for the strike and saw breaking that support network as critical to ending the strike.

51. *Tampa Morning Tribune*, August 23 and 29, 1901. No known copy of the original Spanish-language appeal has survived.

52. *Tampa Morning Tribune*, August 18 and 23, 1901; Long (1965), p. 207.

53. *Tampa Morning Tribune*, August 23, 1901. The editors also sought the forcible deportation of this woman.

54. Del Rio (1972), pp. 64–65.

55. Long (1965), p. 210; *Tampa Morning Tribune*, October 5, 1901.

56. Affluent, middle-class, and working-class Latins would continue to pursue common goals within ethnic clubs and mutual aid societies, which were particularly important in providing health care and burial benefits for immigrants of all classes.

57. Mormino and Pozzetta (1987), chap. 7.

58. See Cott, this volume. Within electoral politics, women also achieved influence through voluntary activities. See Higginbotham and Ware, this volume.

4

Gender and Trade Unionism in Historical Perspective

Ruth Milkman

Labor unions have been the primary organizational vehicle available to represent the interests of American working women in the twentieth century and to struggle on their behalf against the twin inequalities of gender and class. Organized labor's record in relation to women is, to be sure, rather mixed. On the one hand, unions have frequently fought to improve the wages and working conditions of employed women and have often challenged sex discrimination as well. Unionized women have always earned more and had better protection against management abuses than their unorganized sisters. They have also enjoyed greater access to meaningful representation in the workplace (or "voice")[1] than their nonunionized counterparts. On the other hand, women have always been underrepresented in the ranks of organized labor relative to their numbers in the work force as a whole. Moreover, like other formal organizations, unions have frequently excluded women from positions of leadership and power and, in some historical settings, even from membership. And, all too often, unions have failed to represent the interests of women workers adequately or to do battle against gender inequality at work; in some cases they have even fought to maintain male privileges at the expense of women workers.

Studies illustrating both sides of this mixed record have proliferated in recent years, as feminist historians and social scientists have begun to explore the previously uncharted territory of women's labor history. This chapter critically evaluates the emerging literature on the relationship between women and unions and poses a question buried in that literature but rarely addressed explicitly within it—namely, *under what conditions* have unions been effective political vehicles for women workers? "Political" here is meant not in the narrow sense of formal, electoral politics, but in the broader sense of collective action and potential empowerment. While the evidence available is still too fragmentary to attempt to address this question definitively, it can be addressed in a partial way by examining the conditions that foster women's union membership, on the one hand, and women's participation and leadership in unions, on the other. The variations among individual labor organizations in regard to women's union membership, participation, and leadership, I will argue, reflect the diverse historical conditions under which particular unions were first established and their varying degrees of "maturity" as organizations.

The Debate About Women and Unions

Most of the research on women and unions is quite recent, a product of the new feminist scholarship in history and social science. The first wave of literature was largely descriptive and compensatory in nature, and its primary aim was to refute the conventional wisdom on the subject: that women workers were less militant, less easily unionized, and less active in unions than similarly situated men. Leonard Sayles and George Strauss exemplify this traditional view in their claim that "women present a major problem to the union. Not only are they hard to organize but, once organized, they are less likely to participate."[2] By reconstructing the historical record of women's efforts to unionize and their many struggles at the workplace to improve their lot, feminist scholars sought to falsify this view of women as passive, "problem" workers and demonstrated that throughout the long history of conflict between workers and employers "We Were There," as the title of one popular survey of the subject put it.[3]

This research also revealed the failure of unions to deliver their potential benefits to women workers. For example, historians documented the exclusionary practices of craft unions in the early part of the century, when many labor organizations barred women from membership or actively discouraged them from organizing, and argued that unions themselves were the "problem," not women—in effect transposing the terms of the traditional view. As Alice Kessler-Harris suggested in one of the most sophisticated treatments of this issue, "When we stop asking why women have not organized themselves, we are led to ask how women were, and are, kept out of unions." Kessler-Harris acknowledged that there were genuine obstacles to organizing women, but argued that, even in the first years of the twentieth century, these "were clearly not insurmountable barriers. Given a chance, women were devoted and successful union members, convinced that unionism would serve them as it seemed to be serving their brothers."[4] Similarly, Meredith Tax concluded that one of the main reasons women were unorganized in this early period was that "no one would organize them. And when anyone tried, women often showed that, despite all these barriers, they were raring to go."[5]

In addition to the question of why women were less often unionized than men, feminist scholars reexamined the issue of women's participation and leadership within those unions which did *not* exclude them from membership. Here, too, they documented a pattern of hostility toward women's participation on the part of male union officials, as well as a host of broader social and cultural factors discouraging women from becoming activists or leaders.[6] This new feminist perspective on unionism emerged simultaneously with and drew directly upon the critique of institutional labor history by social historians and the revisionist labor history and radical social science which constructed unions as essentially conservative institutions.

If unions have been, as the literature suggests, indifferent or even hostile to the plight of women workers, some explanation of this phenomenon is required. Although there have been few explicitly theoretical efforts to account for the apparent failure of labor unions to provide women workers with the agency to improve their lot, two dominant approaches to this problem can be distinguished, one emphasizing structural and the other cultural factors. The structural perspective explains male-dominated trade unionism in terms of gender inequality in the larger society, usually understood as structured by patriarchy. In this view, women's exclusion from and subordinate role within labor unions is critical for preserving the patriarchal order which restricts women to the home or to poorly paid jobs. Women's economic subordination, in turn, makes it difficult for them to organize or to participate actively in trade unions. Perhaps the most influential contribution here has been that of Heidi Hartmann, who argues that "men's ability to organize in labor unions . . . appears to be key in their ability to maintain job segregation and the domestic division of labor."[7] In this view, as Cynthia Cockburn states in her study of London printers, trade unions are "male power bases" that struggle "to assure patriarchal advantage."[8]

The second approach focuses attention not on the material interests of male workers, but rather on their *cultural* domination of trade union institutions. This perspective draws on the concept of "women's culture" in feminist historiography and also on historical and ethnographic accounts of women's activity in the workplace. In this view, male and female workers define their relationship to work in distinct ways, owing to their contrasting roles in society and their sex-segregated experience in the workplace.[9] Unions, the argument goes, have typically been part of male culture and are not the proper place to look for expressions of women workers' interests and struggles. Thus Susan Porter Benson's analysis of women salesworkers documents a rich female work culture which is sharply opposed to management—and yet has no relationship to unionism.[10] Even where women are union members, in this view, the union is often culturally alien to them. Not only are union meetings typically held in bars, and at night, so that women must compromise their respectability if they are to attend; but the entire discourse of unionism is built on images of masculinity. Thus Beatrix Campbell concludes that the labor movement is essentially a "men's movement," and Sallie Westwood's ethnography of a British garment shop observes that "the union seemed as far away as management, locked into an alien world of meetings and men which somehow never seemed to relate to the world of women in the department."[11]

The structural and cultural explanations of women's subordinate position within the institutions of unionism are by no means mutually exclusive. Indeed, while most commentators emphasize one or the other, some (especially in the British literature) have merged the two. Separately or in combination, what is most appealing about these theoretical perspectives is their apparent comprehensiveness: They explain not only women's underrepresentation in the ranks of union members and activists, but also their general exclusion from positions of power in labor organizations and the relatively scant attention paid to women's special concerns by most unions. Yet, despite their valuable insights into the global problem of male-dominated trade unionism, these theories are far less useful for explaining the wide range of historical *variation* in union behavior toward women that is so richly documented in recent historical and sociological research.

The concept of patriarchy, which is at the core of the structural perspective, is essentially ahistorical, as others have noted.[12] The argument that women's subordination within organized labor is an aspect of patriarchy makes it difficult to explain historical changes in the nature and extent of male domination of the labor movement. Moreover, while this perspective explains many specific cases where unions do operate as a vehicle for male workers' interests, it fails to take account of the conflicting nature of those interests in relation to women workers. As I have argued elsewhere, this view presumes that men's *gender* interest in maintaining male domination will inevitably take precedence over their *class* interest in gender equality, whereas historically there are instances of the opposite as well.[13]

Similarly, the conception of the asymmetric relationship of unions to gender-specific cultures, while usefully illuminating many specific instances of female marginality in labor unions, comes dangerously close to reifying the historically specific differences between male and female workers. It mirrors the ideology which justifies women's subordination within the labor market by reference to the assumption that women are less committed, more family-oriented workers than their male counterparts. And, ironically, like the pre-feminist literature on women and trade unions, this perspective fails to acknowledge the many historical and contemporary examples of female labor militancy that rely upon conventional forms of union behavior.

Seemingly paradoxically, there is another stream of feminist scholarship which also draws upon the concept of women's culture, but focuses on female mobilization into and within unions rather than on male domination of organized labor. For example, Temma Kaplan and Ardis Cameron have showed how women's culture and "female consciousness," rooted in traditional domestic concerns, can propel women into broad, community-based labor struggles alongside their male neighbors and kin.[14] Other recent scholarship has linked women's work culture to a distinctively female form of leadership in union organizing and to the mobilization of women workers within established union structures, suggesting that women's culture and unionism may not be incompatible after all.[15]

This work is critically important, for it begins to address the central question which is obscured by the more deterministic structural and cultural accounts of male-dominated unionism: Under what conditions have unions been effective vehicles for women workers' collective action? With the dramatic rise in women's labor force participation over the course of the twentieth century, and especially since World War II, the possibilities for female collective action and empowerment through unionism have become increasingly important. On the basis of the new scholarship reconstructing the record of women's labor struggles, we can begin to specify the conditions under which those possibilities are realizable. But this requires loosening the deterministic grip of the prevailing structural and cultural perspectives on male-dominated unionism in favor of a genuinely historicized analysis. Rather than presuming that men will always act to protect their gender interest, we must ask: Under what circumstances have they done so, and when have they instead pursued their class interest in gender equality? Similarly, rather than presuming that women's culture and unionism are inherently incompatible, we should explore the conditions under which they have and have not proved to be so.

An Organizational Perspective

Another limitation of the literature on women and unions is that, despite (or perhaps because of) the fact that it has called attention to the ways in which unions are gendered organizations, it has tended to ignore the implications of the gender-neutral organizational characteristics and dynamics of unionism for women. Although this was an understandable and necessary reaction to the long tradition of gender-blind analysis of union behavior, it may have inadvertently sacrificed valuable insights. In rescuing those insights, the growing literature on women and organizations (which, however, includes virtually no direct discussion of unions) can serve as a model. Indeed, many of the organizational factors operating to marginalize women from leadership positions in the corporations they face across the bargaining table also operate within unions, and with similar results. An obvious example is the premium on trust and loyalty which, as Rosabeth Moss Kanter has shown, leads corporate executives to be wary of recruiting women or other individuals with backgrounds different from their own (whose actions are therefore less predictable) for top positions.[16] A parallel dynamic operates within unions, where trust and loyalty are at least as important. (Unions are of course quite different from corporations in that they are not simply institutions, but also part of a social movement which mobilizes on a variety of fronts on behalf of workers' interests, including those of the unorganized. The labor movement, moreover, has a strong democratic and egalitarian tradition that is explicitly opposed to the hierarchical structure of the business world—which, after all, makes no pretense of being democratically run. Given this tradition, should the labor movement not be held to a higher standard of democracy in general, and responsiveness to the needs of women and other socially oppressed groups in particular, than corporate organizations? Perhaps it should. But there has always been a tension between the goals of unionism as part of a social movement and the tasks it is engaged in as an ongoing institution: the classic tension between union democracy and union bureaucracy.[17] And in their bureaucratic aspect, at least, unions seem to operate very much like other formal organizations—and not only in regard to women.)

Another organizational factor which fosters union leaders' distrust of women is that the very existence of labor organizations is defined by a relationship of continual conflict with a more powerful adversary: the employer upon whom union members depend for their livelihood. The unions' structurally weaker position tends to generate a siege mentality among their leaders, which in turn encourages suspicion and hostility toward any group which is perceived as making "special" demands. Union hostility toward women is often rooted in this fundamentally gender-neutral organizational dynamic (which nevertheless can and frequently does have a gender-specific outcome), rather than simply in "patriarchy" or male culture.

Organizational analysis can provide insight not only into such general dynamics, which tend to marginalize women within all labor movement institutions, but also into the factors producing variations *among* unions in their degree of openness or hostility toward women. To begin with, consider the implications for this problem of Arthur L. Stinchcombe's classic discussion of social structure and organizations, which emphasizes the persistence of organizational forms, once established, over time. Following Stinchcombe's argument that "organizational forms and types have a history, and . . . this history determines some aspects of the present structure of organizations of that type,"[18] we can hypothesize that unions that arose in different historical periods would vary systematically in their treatment of women in the present as well as the past.

In the United States, at least, the growth of unionization has occurred in readily distinguishable waves, and in each period of growth over the past century both the dominant form of unionism and the social position of women varied markedly. If, as Stinchcombe suggested, the basic goals, structures, values, and ideologies of individual unions are shaped early in their institutional life and tend to persist intact thereafter, it follows that the prevailing type of union structure (craft, industrial, and so on), the position of women in the industrial setting, and the state of gender relations more broadly in the historical period in which a particular union originates will be significant in explaining that union's behavior. Although Stinchcombe himself was not particularly concerned with gender issues, his theory of organizational inertia provides a tool with which to historicize the structural and cultural theories of women's relationship to unionism. It can incorporate into a broader framework the historical shifts in the material interests of men and women and their respective cultures, which have not remained static, but have been significantly affected by such factors as the long-term rise in female labor force participation and the strength of feminist consciousness in particular periods.

While his overall argument stressed the persistence and stability of organizational structures, Stinchcombe also discussed what he called the "liabilities of newness," arguing that in the earliest period of their existence, organizations are relatively fragile and unstable entities.[19] Other commentators have developed a similar notion and applied it to union organizations in particular. Richard A. Lester, for example, has suggested that as unions "mature," their organizational behavior changes significantly. When a labor organization first comes into existence, it is by definition on the offensive (albeit in an uphill battle); later, once it has won nominal acceptance from the employer, management increasingly takes the initiative, while the union typically settles into a reactive and often defensive role. In addition, openness to alternative ideologies and modes of organizing is generally greater in the early period of a labor union's life than in its more mature phases, when it has settled into a routine existence and has an officialdom with a stake in maintaining its established traditions.[20] This life-cycle view of organizations complicates Stinchcombe's theory and has a different emphasis, but is not necessarily inconsistent with the view that organizations once established (or "mature") tend toward structural inertia.

Extending this idea to the problem of women and trade unions, we can hypothesize that, in general, unions would be more open to demands from women and feminist approaches to organizing in their youth than in their maturity. Moreover, both bureaucratization and the development of a siege mentality among trade union leaders—which, as was already noted, tend to marginalize women within union organizations—are typically minimal in the early stages of a union's history, and both intensify as it matures. Once again, then, the gender-blind organizational logic described by theories of union maturity can help explain differences among unions that are at different life-stages at a given point in time.

Four Cohorts of American Unions

In American labor history, at least four major waves of unionization which have produced four distinct cohorts of labor organizations can be identified. The problem is simplified by the fact that each of these cohorts coincides with particular structural forms of union organization (craft, industrial, and so on), each of which recruited in specific types of occupations or industries. Each of the four union cohorts had a different historical relationship to women workers, and to a large extent the differences have persisted into the present day. Thus a historical perspective, informed by Stinchcombe's analysis of organizational inertia as well as union maturity theories, offers a potential basis for explaining the variations evident on the contemporary labor scene in women's position in unions.

The oldest group of unions, some of them with roots going back deep into the nineteenth century, are the old-line craft unions, such as the building trades "brotherhoods" or the printers. These unions today still tend to be the most hostile to women not only because of their maturity, but also because of the nature of the relationship they established to women when they were formed. Initially, their constituency of craftsmen saw women's labor as a threat to established skill and wage levels, and therefore typically excluded women from union membership (until as late as the 1940s in some cases) and generally viewed them with suspicion. Indeed, the entire logic of craft unionism was predicated on the importance of skill, and employers' reliance upon it, as the primary source of workers' power. This generated exclusionary practices directed not only against women, but against all unskilled workers. It is perhaps not accidental that craft unions have been the main focus of analysis for those scholars who argue that labor organizations serve as an instrument of patriarchy.[21] But these unions are hardly typical of the twentieth century experience, and indeed they constitute a relatively small part of the labor movement today.

A second cohort of unions emerged in the 1910s, primarily in the clothing industry. The "new unionism" of this period was at once an outgrowth of the craft union tradition and a departure from it, in some respects anticipating the industrial unionism of the 1930s. Craft exclusionism was effectively abandoned by the International Ladies' Garment Workers' Union (ILGWU) and the Amalgamated Clothing Workers (ACW) in this period, even though originally it was the skilled male cutters alone who were organized. In the wake of the militancy of women workers, most notably in the New York garment workers' strike of 1909–1910, vast numbers of unskilled and semiskilled women were incorporated into these unions' ranks. The "new unionism" recognized women workers' need for organization and also broadened the definition of unionism to encompass not only economic but also social functions, pioneering in such areas as union-sponsored health care and educational programs. Yet the leaders of these unions still viewed women as an entirely different species of worker than men. For in this period women were still typically employed for a relatively brief part of their lives, particularly in the clothing industry. Male union leaders as well as working women themselves viewed women's needs as different from those of men in the 1910s. Women's militant organizing efforts were centered not on economic demands for gender equality, but rather on moral appeals for better protection against management abuses. These appeals implicitly or explicitly invoked their special vulnerability as women.[22] Under these conditions, it was hardly surprising that the leaders of the "new unions" viewed women paternalistically, and not as equal partners; or that these unions' officialdoms remained overwhelmingly male despite the dramatic feminization of their memberships. Like the old-line craft unions, these unions today are still deeply marked by the legacy of their historical origins; their still predominantly male leaderships continue to view their majoritarian female (and now, Third World immigrant female) memberships paternalistically, as weak workers in need of protection.

A third cohort of unions took shape in the massive industrial organizing drives of the 1930s. The mass production industries in which the Congress of Industrial Organizations (CIO) unions emerged were overwhelmingly male—steel, auto, rubber, electrical manufacturing. But insofar as women were part of the production work force in these industries, the CIO organized them alongside men from the outset. And the attitude of this generation of unionists toward women workers was quite different from that of either the old craft unionists or the "new unionists" of the 1910s. In the 1920s and 1930s, in the aftermath of the suffrage victory and with growing labor force participation among married women, the claim of women to equal treatment in the public sphere gained ground.[23] The CIO opposed discrimination on the basis of sex, color, or creed in a deliberate departure from craft union traditions and practices. While older views of "woman's place" still persisted within the CIO unions, the inclusionary logic of industrial unionism and its formal commitment to the ideal of equality opened up new possibilities for women in organized labor.[24] This became particularly explicit during World War II, when women poured into the basic industries that had been organized by the CIO immediately before the war, and women's issues (such as equal pay for equal work, nondiscriminatory seniority, and female representation in labor leadership) gained a prominent position on union agendas.[25] After the war, while women once again became a minority within the work force of the basic industries, this cohort of unions retained a formal commitment to equality and antidiscrimination efforts. The United Auto Workers' Union (UAW), for example, was an early advocate of national legislation against sex discrimination and later became the first labor union in the nation to endorse the Equal Rights Amendment.[26]

Finally, a fourth group of unions emerged in the post–World War II period in the expanding service and clerical occupations, predominantly in the public sector but also in some private sector institutions (for example, hospitals). Initially, in the 1950s and 1960s these unions organized mainly blue-collar male workers, such as garbage collectors and highway workers. More recently, however, the majority of their recruits have been pink- and white-collar workers (including many professionals) in occupations where women are highly concentrated. Women were not unionized "as women" but as teachers, as hospital workers, as government clerks, and so on. However, their massive recruitment during this period of feminist resurgence and growing acceptance of the goal of gender equality ultimately led this cohort of unions to reformulate traditional labor issues in innovative ways that are especially relevant to women. For example, the American Federation of State, County and Municipal Employees (AFSCME) and the Service Employees International Union (SEIU), the two largest unions in this cohort, have led the campaign for pay equity or comparable worth in the 1980s.[27] More generally, both because of their relative youth and because they emerged in a period of feminist resurgence, these unions have been especially receptive to women's leadership and to efforts to mobilize around women's issues.

The striking differences among these four cohorts of labor organizations in regard to their relationship to women workers are traceable, at least in part, to the different historical periods in which each was ascendant. Each period was characterized by a different configuration of gender relations in the larger society, and each wave of unionism had different structural characteristics (craft, craft/industrial, industrial, service sector) and a different organizational logic. Of course, this is at best a first approximation: Many other factors—among them, economic shifts and dislocations, political and legal influences—can affect the relationship of unions to women workers. Examining the problem through a comparison of cohorts, moreover, makes it difficult to distinguish clearly between the effects of what are in fact separate variables: the organization's age, the historical period in which it originated, the type of industry, and the type of union involved. The difficulty is that all of these tend to coincide historically within each of the four cohorts. More interesting analysis might come from detailed comparative case studies of individual unions within the same cohort, which would facilitate finer distinctions. This should be an important part of the agenda for future research in this area. But in the interim, a framework that is sensitive to cohort differences among unions and to the internal process of "maturation" within labor organizations may begin to explain some of the variations in women's involvement in trade unions and in unions' effectiveness for women which remain unaccounted for in most of the existing literature.

Women's Union Membership

Consider the issue of women's union membership. Although nonmembers often benefit indirectly from the activities of unions, members benefit a great deal more. They also have direct access to political resources vis-à-vis their employers which nonmembers typically lack. The degree to which women are recruited into the ranks of organized labor, then, is one major determinant of the degree to which unions effectively represent their interests. The density of female unionization has fluctuated considerably over time, but at no point have a majority of U.S. working women been union members, and, perhaps more significantly, the male unionization rate has always been greater than the female rate. Why is this the case, and what explains the variations over time and across industries and sectors?

To address these questions, we must first note that, at least since 1935, becoming a union member in the United States was and is associated primarily with employment in a firm or industry which has been targeted by union organizers. Under the American legal and industrial relations system, whether or not an individual joins a labor union is rarely a matter of individual choice. Indeed, one can infer nothing about gender-specific preferences from the observation that a greater proportion of male workers (23 percent in 1984) than of female workers (14 percent) are union members.[28] Rather, the best predictor of union membership is one's industry or occupation, which in turn determines the likelihood that a union is present in a given workplace.

Since jobs are highly sex-segregated, women and men are not evenly distributed through industries or occupations, and in general the gender distribution of unionism is an artifact of the sexual division of labor. On the whole, throughout the century "men's jobs" have more often been unionized than women's. Yet there are also vast differences in unionization rates within both the male and female labor markets. Only 2.5 percent of the women (and 3.5 percent of the men) employed in finance, insurance, and real estate are union members, for example, while in the public sector 33 percent of the women (and 39 percent of the men) are unionized. Moreover, both survey data and analyses of union election results suggest that unorganized women today are more interested in becoming union members than their male counterparts, although this probably was not true in the early twentieth century.[29]

As theories of union maturation stress, unions (or their subdivisions) historically have tended to recruit new members for a period of time and then to stabilize in size, concentrating on serving their established members rather than on continuing to expand. For this reason, a union's gender composition at any given point in time reflects the past and present composition of the occupation, industry, or sector it targeted for unionization in earlier years. While efforts to preserve the organization over time frequently lead existing unions to undertake recruitment efforts (targeting workers employed in the same industries and occupations as their established membership), few have successfully expanded their jurisdictions to take in wholly new constituencies. (An important exception here is the Teamsters Union, which has the second largest number of female members of any union in the nation and which has diversified over a long period of time far beyond its traditional base in the trucking industry.) In recent years some industrial unions, facing severe membership losses because of reduced employment levels in their traditional jurisdictions, have launched efforts to recruit service sector workers, but so far have had limited effectiveness.

Each of the four union cohorts described above focused its original recruitment efforts on specific types of workers, and their membership composition remains broadly similar today. Each cohort of unions was guided by a distinctive and essentially gender-neutral organizational strategy, which, however, had highly gender-specific results. The early twentieth century craft unions took in primarily skilled workers. Their strategy of limiting access to skills with high market value functioned to exclude women from both craft employment and union membership in many industries—not only because of their gender but also because of their unskilled status. Whereas from one perspective this exclusionism reflected the interest of male workers in maintaining the system of patriarchy, an equally plausible account might simply stress that exclusionism—which was directed not only against women but also against immigrants, blacks, and other unskilled workers—was an organizational feature inherent in craft unionism.

Although craft unionism was the predominant form of unionism in the United States at the turn of the century, it soon gave way to new forms which lacked its structural bias toward exclusionism, first with the "new unionism" of the 1910s and later with the industrial unionism of the 1930s. Here the organizational strategy was simply to recruit everyone the employer hired within a given industrial jurisdiction. In the clothing industries that were the focus of the "new unionism," this meant organizing unprecedented numbers of women. By 1920 nearly half (43 percent) of the nation's unionized women were clothing workers.[30] The CIO, too, while recruiting many more men than women, greatly increased women's unionization level. But because the CIO's strategy centered on organizing blue-collar workers in durable goods manufacturing where relatively few women were employed, the results for women were less dramatic than in the 1910s when organization centered on the heavily female clothing trade. In both cases, though, what determined the extent of female unionization was not the union's strategy but the preexisting gender composition of the work force in the targeted industry. Where women were numerous among production workers, as in clothing in the 1910s and electrical manufacturing in the 1930s, they were recruited into unions in large numbers; where they were few, as in auto and steel, the two largest industries organized by the CIO, their numbers in the union ranks were correspondingly small. And in the 1930s there was little interest in organizing the already considerable numbers of women employed in clerical and service jobs in the tertiary sector.

While the organizational logic of craft unionism had excluded women not so much "as women" but rather because they were unskilled workers, now the inclusionary logic of industrial unionism reversed the situation—but still without any particular effort to recruit women as women. There is some fragmentary evidence that occupations and industries where women predominated in the work force were slighted because of their gender composition by CIO unions, as Sharon Strom has suggested for the case of clerical workers.[31] But in general, the targets of CIO organizing drives were selected on the basis of considerations that involved not gender, but rather the strategic importance of organizing mass-production industries to build the overall strength of the labor movement.

The same was true of the organizing drives that brought hospital workers, teachers, and a wide variety of clerical and service employees into the labor movement in the postwar period. The growth of this fourth cohort of unions (together with the decline of the third cohort due to deindustrialization) resulted in a substantial feminization of union membership in the 1970s and 1980s: By 1984, 34 percent of all unionized workers were women, a record high.[32] However, this came about not because union organizers sought to recruit women specifically, but as a by-product of their recruitment of particular categories of workers who seemed ripe for unionization. Feminization was essentially an unintended consequence of this process.[33]

On the whole, then, although throughout the century women's over-all unionization level has been lower than men's, much of the gender gap (and also its recent diminution) was the result of gender-neutral strategic and organizational factors and the preexisting segregation of women into jobs which are less likely to be unionized than those held by men. While it is reasonable to criticize the labor movement for its general failure to challenge job segregation by sex, or to target more "women's jobs" in its recruiting drives, a major part of the explanation for the general sex differential in unionization rates, and for the wide variations among unions' sex composition as well, lies in gender-neutral organizational factors operating in a sex-segregated system.

Participation and Leadership

Another crucial dimension of unions' political effectiveness for women is the extent of female participation and leadership in labor organizations. There is considerable variation among unions in this area, and while obviously the extent of women's union membership is one relevant factor, by itself it is not a satisfactory predictor of women's participation or leadership. The ILGWU, for example, is notorious for the lack of significant female representation in its leadership, despite an 85 percent female membership.[34] More generally, even in industries or occupations where women are highly unionized, their participation in labor union activities is typically less extensive than men's, although the extent to which this is the case varies considerably. Positions of union leadership, to an even greater degree than voluntary participation, have been male-dominated historically and remain so today, especially at the upper levels, although again this is more true of some unions than of others. What accounts for women's underrepresentation among labor activists and leaders? Under what conditions can the "barriers to entry" for women be overcome? And what explains the variations among unions in the extent of women's representation among participants and leaders?

Research addressing these questions has focused primarily on identifying specific personal attributes which are associated with participation and leadership and those which function as obstacles to activism. Divorced and single women, for example, are more likely than married women to be union participants and leaders, and extensive domestic responsibilities are an obstacle to activism for many women.[35] These findings help account for gender differences in union participation and leadership and also explain why some women are more likely to participate or lead than others. However, this approach provides, at best, a partial explanation. It is necessary to examine not only the attributes of women themselves, but also those of the labor organizations in which their participation and leadership is at issue.

In younger unions, which are involved primarily in recruitment of new members and organization-building, women's participation and leadership is often more extensive than in more mature unions. Most of the celebrated examples of women's militancy and leadership come from these early stages in union development, especially organizational strikes, ranging from the garment workers' "uprising" of 1909–1910 to the recent strike of Yale clerical workers.[36] But the level of women's participation and leadership tends to decline as unions become more formally organized (and bureaucratized) institutions which concentrate on collective bargaining and other means to protect and win benefits for an already established membership. Male rank-and-file union participation also tends to decline as union organizations mature, but the shift between union democracy and bureaucracy that accompanies maturation is especially complex for women.

In mature unions the problem of women's underrepresentation among activists and leaders is a specific case of the more general phenomenon of women's exclusion from leadership roles in virtually all mixed-sex formal organizations. Indeed, the record of unions in this respect is no worse than that of the corporations with which they negotiate. In both unions and corporations married women and those with heavy domestic responsibilities are less likely to become leaders than other women. And, as was already mentioned, Rosabeth Moss Kanter's organizational analysis of women's exclusion from top corporate positions is relevant to unions as well. In both cases, and perhaps even more so in the case of unions with their siege mentality, tremendous value is placed on trust and loyalty among officeholders, especially at the top levels of the organizational hierarchy. This premium on loyalty encourages the process of "homosexual reproduction," whereby males in top positions "reproduce themselves in their own image," which Kanter has described so well for corporate organizations.[37]

Conventional organizational analysis also helps explain why, when special positions are created for women within the union's organizational structure, the (presumably unintended) effect is usually to marginalize female leaders and exclude them from the centers of union power. A good example is the UAW Women's Bureau, created during World War II to cope with the sudden influx of women workers into the union's ranks. The Bureau, while doing valuable work, was then and remains to this day organizationally isolated and marginal to the union.

In contrast, those few (by definition "exceptional") women who rise through the union hierarchy on the same terms as men, and without being defined as specialists in women's concerns, seem to be taken more seriously.[38] But this route to power within the union is often blocked by the emphasis on loyalty and its attendant mechanism of "homosexual reproduction."

Another factor limiting women's access to leadership posts in mature unions is the lack of available positions. The number of vacancies narrows as membership, and with it the size of the organization, stabilizes. This reduction in the number of opportunities for advancement in the leadership structure is even more severe in unions than in other "mature" organizations, because union officialdoms are one of the few avenues of upward mobility open to workers. In a corporate or governmental organization, officeholders' careers might carry them from one organization to another (although this is actually relatively rare in the corporate world). But in the case of unions, positions of leadership, once obtained, are rarely relinquished, especially at the upper levels. Despite the formally democratic electoral machinery within unions, in practice paid officials seldom depart from their posts unless they win promotion to a higher one, retire, or die.[39] Thus in a mature labor organization, unless membership, and with it leadership, is expanding rapidly, the possibilities (for both sexes) of gaining a leadership post are relatively restricted compared with those in a young union that is actively recruiting new members and thus expanding its leadership structure.

Other critical influences on the opportunities for women to become union leaders, and especially paid officials, include the position of women in the employment structure of the jurisdiction within which the union operates, and, more broadly, the state of gender relations in the larger society during the period when the organization first develops. The more extensive women's participation in the public sphere generally, and in positions of power or importance in particular, the better are their prospects for movement into union leadership posts at a given point in time. Moreover, women's prospects will be correspondingly brighter in organizations that are relatively young or experiencing rapid growth at the time. Indeed, over the twentieth century, and particularly in the postwar period, as women's exclusion from the public sphere has diminished, female representation in the leadership of successive cohorts of unions has increased.

In the late nineteenth and early twentieth centuries, when the craft unions first emerged as a powerful force, women were still largely excluded from positions of leadership in public life. They were barred from membership in most of the craft unions, and so the question of their participation and leadership in these unions seldom arose. And while all the craft unions were forced to remove their formal bans on women's membership by the mid twentieth century, most continue to this day to view women as interlopers, and it remains almost unimaginable that women would ascend to positions of power within these unions. A recent study found that in 1985 such unions as the International Brotherhood of Electrical Workers (IBEW), the International Association of Machinists (IAM), and even the giant Teamsters Union had no female representation whatsoever among their officers or on their governing boards—despite the fact that more than one fourth of the members of both the Teamsters Union and the IBEW were female.[40]

The "new unions" created in the 1910s, despite their majoritarian female memberships, also developed as male-led organizations and still retain overwhelmingly male leaderships, with only a token female presence. Early in their history, these unions established a pattern of paternalistic (and male) leadership over an unstable (and largely female) membership, a pattern that has been preserved intact ever since. It is reinforced by the peculiar structure of the clothing industry, in which the two major unions are relatively large, impersonal institutions representing a work force scattered among a multitude of small and often unstable firms. Today, the membership of these unions is not only mostly female but also composed largely of immigrants from the Third World. The special vulnerability of these workers encourages paternalistic leadership, made up largely of men drawn from earlier immigrant generations who are now well assimilated in the larger society.

The third cohort, the CIO unions, emerged in a period when women's position in public life was quite different than it had been in the 1910s. Not only had women won the vote, but by the 1930s a generation of middle-class professional women had become well entrenched in American society, especially in the public sector.[41] While the older notion of "woman's place" remained more resilient in the working class than in the middle class, the CIO unions embraced the ideology of formal equality between the sexes. The main difficulty was that in most cases the membership of these unions was overwhelmingly male. Thus the population of potential female leaders was quite limited in the crucial, formative years. The CIO unions today, as in the past, have limited, token female representation at the upper levels of leadership—far more than in the case of the craft unions but still below the (quite modest) level of female representation among their memberships.

In the case of the fourth cohort of unions, the service and public sector organizations which emerged in the 1970s and 1980s, the pattern is quite different. These unions developed not only in a period of resurgent feminism, but also at a time when the concept of "affirmative action" had legitimacy in the liberal political culture. In addition, unions such as AFSCME, the SEIU, and the teachers' and nurses' unions and associations had a large pool of educated female members to draw from when recruiting their leadership. While even in these unions the extent of female leadership at the top levels remains far smaller than their majoritarian representation among the membership, as a group these unions have a much better record than their predecessors. They not only exhibit a growing female presence at the upper levels of leadership, but also have accumulated a large cadre of women leaders at the local, regional, and district levels. In 1985, for example, 319 of the SEIU's 820 local officers were female, as were 9 of its 61 joint council officers. Similarly, 45 percent of AFSCME's local executive board members and 33 percent of its local presidents were women in 1985.[42] The growing representation of women in secondary leadership posts not only is significant in its own right, but also augurs well for the future, since the next generation of top union officers will be drawn from this level.

Conclusion

Far from being monolithic, then, the labor movement's relationship to women workers varies significantly, both among unions and over time. Historical perspectives on the organizational logic and the particular orientation toward women of the four cohorts of labor unions help explain some of these variations, which the prevailing structural and cultural perspectives on women and unions cannot account for. As a first approximation, the political effectiveness of unions for women workers can be understood as a product of the historical conditions under which each wave of unions first developed, and of their age and maturity as organizations. In general, the older unions, both because of their advanced age *and* because of the specific historical circumstances in which they originated, seem to be less effective than their younger counterparts in regard to women's recruitment into leadership, even in cases where they have large numbers of women workers among their members. The youngest cohort of service and public sector unions has also been much more receptive to feminist concerns than the older unions. While the legacy of tradition seems to be a serious obstacle to women's advancement in many of the older unions, the experience of the newest cohort, with its large female membership and growing representation of women in leadership, offers a basis for optimism.

In the 1980s, however, organized labor is seriously embattled, losing membership and influence in the face of extremely adverse economic and political conditions. Just as women workers are beginning to secure a foothold in its ranks, the labor movement as a whole is fighting for its very survival. Significantly, however, the public and service sector unions have been the least affected by this crisis and are currently the only unions which are continuing to expand. Yet they, too, are affected by the embattled state of the labor movement as a whole. One can only hope that, as previous such crises have done, this one will ultimately give way to a revival of trade unionism. Should that occur, the prospects for continued improvement in women's relationship to unions look quite bright.

Notes

1. Freeman and Medoff (1984).
2. Sayles and Strauss (1967), p. 124.
3. Wertheimer (1977).
4. Kessler-Harris (1975b), pp. 93, 94.
5. Tax (1980), p. 32.
6. Wertheimer and Nelson (1975); Fonow (1977).
7. Hartmann (1976), p. 159.
8. Cockburn (1983), pp. 33, 35.
9. Tentler (1979).
10. Benson (1986).
11. Campbell (1984), p. 129; Westwood (1984), pp. 69–70.
12. Beechey (1979b); Rowbotham (1982); Young (1980).
13. Milkman (1987).
14. Kaplan (1982); Cameron (1985).
15. Sacks (1987); Costello (1985).
16. Kanter (1977), chap. 3.
17. See Michels (1949); Lipset (1960), chap. 12.
18. Stinchcombe (1965), p. 153.
19. Stinchcombe (1965), pp. 148–150.
20. Lester (1958).
21. For example, Hartmann (1976).
22. Kessler-Harris (1985a).
23. See the discussion in Cott, this volume.
24. Strom (1983).
25. Milkman (1987), chap. 6.

26. Gabin (1985).
27. Bell (1985).
28. Adams (1985).
29. Adams (1985); Kochan (1979); *The Wall Street Journal* (1986).
30. Wolman (1924).
31. Strom (1983), p. 372.
32. Adams (1985).
33. Bell (1985).
34. Baden (1986).
35. Wertheimer and Nelson (1975), pp. 91, 115.
36. See Tax (1980); Ladd-Taylor (1985).
37. Kanter (1977), p. 48.
38. Milkman (1987), chap. 6.
39. Lipset (1960), chap. 12, attributes this to the "one-party system" of union government.
40. Baden (1986).
41. Ware (1981).
42. Baden (1986), p. 239. Unfortunately, comparable data for earlier years are not available.

5

The Political Implications of Black and White Women's Work in the South, 1890–1965

Jacqueline Jones

Introduction

As Florence Reece and Naomi Williams both later recalled, concern for the welfare of children—their own and others'—had impelled them to take an active part in the violent labor struggles that erupted in the South during the turbulent decade of the 1930s. The wife of a United Mine Workers organizer in Harlan County, Kentucky, Reece composed the stirring labor song "Which Side Are You On?" to bolster the spirits of striking workers in 1930. "Their children live in luxury/While ours is almost wild," she wrote, contrasting the privileges afforded offspring of the mine owners with the deprivation suffered by the sons and daughters of miners. In accounting for her own fierce passions, Reece noted: "I've seen little children walking along the road down there, and their little legs would be so little and their stomachs would be so big. They didn't get anything to eat."[1] For Reece, class conflict formed the crux of the issue; in the hollow eyes of hungry children were reflected the political power and economic prerogatives of the Harlan County elite. In the end, her "womanly" concerns moved her to action in the "manly" world of labor strife and union activism.

It was Arkansas landowners who aroused the indignation of Naomi Williams, a farm wife; she traced her support for the Southern Tenant Farmers' Union to the meager compensation she received as a cotton picker, although she "done worked [herself] to death in the fields," and also to the fact that "they didn't allow no colored children to even go to

108

school but seven months, and they made them stay in the fields and the white kids was going to school all kind of every way." And so in addition to tending a garden and preserving fresh produce, raising hogs and cows, and picking cotton, she opened a school for neighborhood children and taught "everything, from the first to the eighth grade."[2] In a community stratified on the basis of race as well as class and gender, Williams's children suffered in comparison with those of local landowners, and those of her poor white neighbors as well.

Both Reece and Williams sought to fulfill their ordinary roles as wives and domestic caretakers in an extraordinary way. These women defined their place in society according to the well-being of the children for whom they felt responsible; in other words, their political agenda emerged from everyday "private" obligations. But Williams's grievances spoke to the inequities that lay at the heart of southern life, for she understood that the only honest challenge to the political hegemony of white men necessarily threatened the racial caste system as well.

This chapter seeks to explore the larger political implications embedded in various forms of southern black and white women's work from 1890 to 1965. This is a timely venture, for the old, sentimental images of southern womanhood have vanished. In the place of languishing belles, browbeaten blacks, lethargic mill operatives, and lazy sharecroppers now appear aggressive social reformers and militant agricultural and factory workers of both races. The labor (that is, production of goods and services) performed by these women encompassed not only gainful employment outside the home and domestic responsibilities within it, but also unpaid efforts to extend the nurturant impulse beyond their own families and into the larger community, state, and region. Indeed, wives' and mothers' attempts to care for their children, and the children of others, could have profound political consequences.

If political activity is defined exclusively in terms of suffrage and officeholding, then southern women appear to have been a strikingly apolitical group (compared with southern men and northerners of both sexes and races) during the first half of the twentieth century. The statistics seem compelling enough; for example, as late as 1952 one third of all southern white women and nine tenths of southern black women had never voted. The comparable figures for white men in the South, and for men and women, white and black, in the non-South, ranged from 6 to 17 percent for each racial-gender group.[3] Clearly, black southerners suffered unique liabilities in their efforts to participate in regional and national politics; the fact that they did not vote cannot be attributed to either apathy or ignorance. Between 1890 and 1915 a large proportion of all black men in the former Confederate states suffered disfranchisement through constitutional means. Most black women who registered to vote in 1920 met with a similar fate at the hands of stubborn, if startled, local southern registrars.[4] Moreover, impressionistic sources indicate that politics amounted to a form of ritualistic solidarity among southern white men in small towns and throughout the countryside; consequently, the weight of culture and tradition inhibited ordinary white women from playing a formal role in this arena of public life. Sarah Easton, the wife of a North Carolina tenant farmer, noted in the late 1930s: "I ain't never voted, but John's a Democrat. He ain't never let me vote but he thinks it's a woman's place to cut wood and stay all night in a mean neighborhood by herself."[5] She thus pinpointed the discrepancy between the physical labor she performed for her family and her relative lack of decision-making power at home and within the larger political process. In fact, then, the forces that prevented or discouraged southern women from voting persisted well after 1920, leading historian Martha Swain to suggest in her survey of those women in twentieth century politics that "the preoccupation of millions of rural and small town women of both races with domestic life to the exclusion of other interests accounts immeasurably for the widespread disinterest of women in the South in public affairs and feminist issues."[6]

Yet, in considering Swain's analysis, and in discussing the history of women and politics in general, it is useful to broaden the definition of political participation beyond the realm of narrow party affiliation and at the same time expand the definition of women's work to include not only gainful employment, but also caretaking impulses inside the home and outside the home, in local neighborhoods and communities. When the past is re-envisioned within this framework, the boundary separating public from private blurs, simply because many women chose to labor outside the home—in the marketplace or in the community—to advance their so-called private interests, identified specifically as the welfare of their children.

Here politics is defined as the system by which power, wealth, and justice are distributed within a given society. "New South" political systems included the hegemony of men over women, whites over blacks, and businessmen and landlords over the laboring poor. The period between 1890 and 1965 witnessed major transformations that affected the power wielded by white male property owners and capitalists, including the passage of the woman suffrage amendment to the constitution in 1920; the collapse of the labor-intensive plantation system and the rise of a commercial economy in its place;[7] and the persistent struggle on the part of Afro-American men and women, acting in groups and as individuals, to resist the terrorism, mass disenfranchisement, and legally sanctioned racial segregation initiated with such brutality in the late nineteenth century.[8]

It is easier to assert that women played a role in these transformations, either directly or indirectly, consciously or unconsciously, than it is to generalize about the political implications of southern women's work. This chapter considers both class and racial factors that shaped women's responses to, and efforts to influence, political change. The first part of the chapter reveals those goals and strategies shared by black and white women of a similar economic class. Middle-class women often sought to provide social services for their communities and thereby blunt the baneful effects of negligent and uncaring politicians and employers. Poor women provided labor needed to maintain southern households, factories, and plantations; their power rested mainly in their ability to deprive white housewives, factory owners, and landlords of their productive energies, since the patriarchal and racial caste sysems were preserved in order to exploit workers.

Nevertheless, the latter part of the chapter shows that analyses of women's work based only on gender and class are severely limited. For example, while middle-class white and black women labored to protect and provide for their own families, black women simultaneously challenged the racism and greed of whites of both sexes. White women could challenge their own menfolk and at the same time uphold in principle the power of whites over blacks. Similarly, although black and white women workers shared certain class interests, efforts to promote labor-union solidarity often gave way to racial prejudice in both the industrial and agricultural sectors.

In the South, then, racial conflicts undermined gender and class commonalities. The "separate spheres" inhabited by middle-class white women and men had little relevance to black women whose status was defined first and foremost (in the eyes of whites) by the labor they performed. More specifically, and more to the point, black women's work, in all its dimensions, was highly politicized within the context of the South's peculiar society. Indeed, seemingly modest acts of domesticity could have explosive consequences; sending a child to the neighborhood school was a political act when the school was a segregated white one, and cooking for a group of people was an act of defiance when the group included civil rights workers of both races. Consequently, the line dividing family and polity dissolved, highlighting the historic significance of black women's work in a time and place that denied them access to the ballot box.

This analysis raises larger theoretical issues linking politics to work. In the postbellum South, black people possessed a keen political sense, but they lacked the basic citizenship rights that would have allowed them to express their choices on a wide range of matters, including public leadership, education, and income and land distribution. What power they did possess was largely limited to the work they did, which included efforts to improve the quality of life for their own families and efforts to limit the control that whites wielded over their productive energies. In the South, all black people, regardless of age or sex, were economic actors, or potential economic actors; thus we can contrast the pervasiveness of economic relations with the more constricted formal political relations that so effectively excluded black men and women and even, in some cases, white women. The marketplace conveyed a compelling message about racial and gender relations, a message merely echoed and confirmed by the machinery of southern politics.

The Social-Welfare Work of Middle-Class Reformers and Radicals

In her account of a historic meeting between black and white middle-class women (at Tuskegee Institute, in 1920), one of the white participants later recalled the shock of recognition when she saw in "the hearts of those Negro women . . . all the aspirations for their homes and children that I have for mine."[9] Although fraught with tension and uncertainty on the part of both groups, the encounter revealed the shared concerns that characterized the volunteer efforts of privileged women of the two races, efforts that challenged the political hegemony of white men directly (as in the case of civil rights and antilynching campaigns) or indirectly (when women filled a vacuum left by the state in the provision of much-needed social services). Most of these women were married with children, and most came to social reform through their local Protestant churches and community work. Well-educated and self-conscious in their attempts to promote moral values in everyday family life, they sought public confirmation of their private roles as family members. Yet the promise of the 1920 meeting went unfulfilled, a fact foreshadowed in the mandate offered the whites by one of the black women: "Women, we can achieve nothing today unless you . . . who have met us are willing to help us find a place in American life where we can be unashamed and unafraid."[10]

Through their social-welfare work, southern women hoped to rescue the poor and unfortunate from a heartless political system, based as it was on radical economic inequalities among various groups. Organized in a variety of local societies and, in some cases, affiliated with large national groups, middle-class wives and mothers provided aid for the needy directly and, like their Progressive northern sisters, lobbied legislators in an effort to expand state and federal welfare responsibilities.[11] The integrity and stability of family life provided the common denominator for these efforts and justified fundraising and organizational activities in the areas of education; child labor; medical care; housing; personal hygiene; nutrition; temperance; care of orphans, delinquents, and the mentally ill; and industrial reform.[12] These general issues linked groups such as the women's home mission movement of the Methodist Episcopal Church, South; southern branches of the Young Women's Christian Association (YWCA); and local chapters of the National Association of Colored Women, the General Federation of Women's Clubs, and the League of Women Voters—all active in the region during the first decades of the twentieth century.

In campaigning for a new orphanage or school milk program, volunteers inevitably clashed with the fiscal and moral priorities of white male politicians and policymakers. As guardians of the home, women felt they had a special obligation to counter the laissez-faire attitude toward social welfare that prevailed in city halls and in county and state courthouses. They acted to humanize a political system based on competition and personal self-seeking, a system that worked to the detriment of women and children whose male providers had not, or in some cases had not yet, succeeded within it.

Individual women's groups thus tried to counter both the state's indifference toward social-welfare issues and the workings of a local and regional economy that left women and children vulnerable to their husbands' and fathers' participation in the marketplace. Organizations that promoted these causes and at the same time encouraged interracial cooperation went further in their critique of southern society and challenged the racial caste system itself. The YWCA and the Home Mission Society of the Methodist Episcopal Church, South, were white groups that began to solicit the support of middle-class black women in the creation of social settlements and other quasi-educational institutions during the third decade of the twentieth century. Women involved in these efforts acknowledged their common interests as wives and mothers and their common devotion to an evangelical "social gospel," southern-style.

The founding of the Commission on Interracial Cooperation (CIC) in 1920 marked the beginning of a formal attempt by southern white moderates and liberals to combat the forces of segregation and violence that had ushered in "the nadir" of black history in the South thirty years before. The Women's Committee of the CIC brought women of the two races together to address not only problems centered around women and children, but also lynching, segregation, and black suffrage.[13] Much more radical and broad-based, and ultimately more effective, were the associations initiated by blacks themselves that opened the way for the participation of all classes and both sexes and races and embraced overt political goals as well as social-welfare issues—the National Association for the Advancement of Colored People (NAACP, 1911), Congress of Racial Equality (1941), and the Student Nonviolent Coordinating Committee (SNCC, 1960), among others.[14] Although these groups included black and white men and women (with whites in the minority in all three cases), the personal interaction between white and black women held special significance in a society that held up the housewife–domestic servant relationship as the only legitimate model of interracial contact for women. Still, efforts based on black-white cooperation had a tortuous history in the South between 1890 and 1965. Some, like the white-dominated YWCA, Methodist, and CIC programs, foundered on the paternalism and condescension of their white members.[15] Others, like the Mississippi Freedom Summers Project and SNCC, in the early 1960s, collapsed under the combined weight of male-female, black-white tensions that were heightened by the physical dangers of massive, grass-roots voter registration drives in the rural South.[16]

It is clear that a gender- and class-based analysis of reform and political activism is inadequate to convey the full significance of black and white women's nonwage work outside the home. In fact, because most of this labor remained strictly segregated, a focus on cultural differences among women is imperative. Women came to these movements for reasons that were fully rooted in their individual and collective racial and class experiences, a fact that highlights their divergent interests in social-welfare programs.

The generation of southern white women that joined the ranks of Progressive reformers around the turn of the century found themselves freed from the back-breaking childrearing and homemaking tasks that had consumed all the time and energies of their mothers. These younger women embraced a proving ground for their own competence, a wider household that encompassed neighborhoods and counties, and thus reached beyond their own nuclear families.[17] The fact that they had no one strategy for improving the quality of southern life is revealed in the broad ideological range of their activities. On the right were women like Louisiana's Kate Gordon, a suffragist who asserted that white women must win the ballot in order to maintain white supremacy: "The South, true to its traditions, will trust its women, and thus placing in their hands the balance of power, the negro as a disturbing element in politics will disappear. . . ."[18] In contrast, on the left was Anne Braden, active in the Southern Conference Educational Fund (SCEF); she worked not only for political justice for blacks, but also for broad-based economic changes in the South. By Braden's own admission SCEF, founded in the mid 1950s, remained "on the fringes" of the civil rights movement, too radical for integrationist-minded groups such as the NAACP and the Southern Christian Leadership Conference.[19] However, most southern white women's associations fell between these two extremes and pursued their own interests, removed and aloof from the support proffered by blacks of both sexes. Three prime examples are the southern suffragists, the Woman's Association for the Betterment of Public School Houses in North Carolina (WABPSH), and the Association of Southern Women for the Prevention of Lynching (ASWPL).

Founded in 1890, the National American Woman Suffrage Association was dominated by northerners who eventually devised a "southern strategy" to bolster their support in a region where whites were adamant about black disenfranchisement. Southern suffragists came to the cause from the Woman's Christian Temperance Union and from late nineteenth century local study groups and literary associations. Imbued with a sense of the moral superiority of women and the need, as wives and mothers entrusted with the welfare of children, to "purify" the political process, these club members distanced themselves from the network of black women's suffrage clubs scattered throughout the urban South. White suffragists wanted to avoid "tainting" their cause with the civil rights issue, and at the same time they sought to safeguard their racial and class prerogatives.[20]

The WABPSH, which originated in North Carolina in 1902 and quickly spread to other states, had as its seemingly noncontroversial goal the improvement of school facilities for young children. But members of this group limited their efforts to white schools located within public systems that already institutionalized racial discrimination on a massive scale, and the women also sought to socialize poor white pupils into the incipient southern factory system. The pride and sense of accomplishment felt by these women reformers—their success at mitigating the effects of underfinancing on southern public education—came at the expense of black children who received nothing and at the expense of poor whites who were leaving the countryside to fuel the fires of the "New South" and its emergent industrial revolution.[21]

Perhaps most revealing of all was Jessie Daniel Ames's ASWPL. This group evolved (in the 1930s) out of its founder's work in the CIC, League of Women Voters, and Methodist Church, South, and its members decried the lynching of black men by white men claiming to protect "pure white southern womanhood." Ames herself pinpointed the "double standard of ethical and moral conduct based upon race" which routinely permitted the sexual abuse of black women by white men and at the same time subjected black men to the most barbaric forms of torture on the basis of trumped-up rape charges. Ames herself denounced the arrogance of white men as a legacy of the slave system and condemned a white South that saw "an assault by a white man as a moral lapse on his part, better ignored and forgotten, while an assault by a Negro against a white woman as a hideous crime punishable with death by law or lynching."[22]

Jessie Daniel Ames advanced a compelling critique of southern society, and she achieved real success in forging a network of concerned small-town women who defied disapproving husbands, fathers, and brothers in order to speak out against lynching and even rescue individual black men from that fate. Yet the ASWPL remained preoccupied with redeeming its own members' integrity as southern ladies and consequently eschewed formal, active contributions from black women. If the association stood in opposition to a code of morality claimed by white men of all classes, it nonetheless remained locked in the South's past, when white women were presumed superior to blacks and more religiously devout than white men. The successor to the ASWPL, the Fellowship of the Concerned (1949), was founded by Georgia's Dorothy Tilly, who exhorted its members to remain steadfast in the face of harassment from white men: "The men in the car, the uninvited guest and the editor are too *little* to intimidate praying women. Don't let them— defeat them. Don't give them that much power over your lives."[23]

Not surprisingly, then, the righteousness of suffragists and other middle-class white reformers proved inadequate to effect meaningful structural changes in the southern political economy. Indeed, viewed over the long run, the incremental everyday work of these well-to-do white women seemed to reinforce inequities and injustices throughout the region, and the accumulation of their own modest acts at home that perpetuated the caste system overshadowed their sporadic, organized efforts outside the home to combat it. The vast majority of middle-class white women, including the most liberal-minded among them, daily exploited their black domestic servants, and thus reinforced a social division of labor that had originated in slavery.[24] As long as white women remained the mistresses of black maids at home, a true harmony of political purpose would elude the two groups of women in the "public sphere."

Not unexpectedly, then, black women's unpaid work to promote family and neighborhood values reflected their unique historical experience. The "habits of mutuality"[25] that evolved out of the African past and intensified during the era of slavery gave shape to black self-help and benevolent societies in the immediate postwar years. Some of these groups, based in both rural and urban areas, enabled poverty-stricken members to provide cooperatively for expenses related to illness and burial.[26] Other associations grew out of Protestant churches, so that middle-class women could channel much-needed aid to less fortunate members of their own race.[27] In 1896 the National Association of Colored Women (NACW) was founded to coordinate a wide variety of clubs that enlisted the support of black women in rural areas and small towns to advance "the uplift of the negro race by the promotion of high ideals of home life according to religious principles."[28]

Unlike their white counterparts, black women club members could not divorce their immediate concerns with child welfare from their larger effort to resist racism in all its forms. Consequently these groups were radical by definition, as evidenced by the involvement of suffrage clubs in antilynching activism.[29] The career of Ida B. Wells Barnett, who came perilously close to physical harm herself when she exposed white-initiated terrorism in her Memphis journal, *Free Speech*, in 1892, revealed that suffrage and civil rights were inextricably linked in the minds of all black women activists. The vote was one weapon in the struggle to preserve the dignity of blacks regardless of sex, age, or class.[30] Therefore, it would be difficult to isolate the "political" from the "social-service" component of black women's club work during the early twentieth century.[31] Joining the NACW in the fight for the vote were service organizations such as Alpha Kappa Alpha and Delta Sigma Theta sororities.[32]

The Colored Women Voters' Leagues that rapidly materialized after 1920 in Alabama, Georgia, Tennessee, and Texas were designed to help newly enfranchised black women find their way through the maze of southern legislation and intimidation directed at potential voters.[33] The fact that these organizations had no specific white counterparts demonstrated that black women joined volunteer activities for reasons that were not necessarily parallel to those of white women and that black-based groups faced a host of problems that white-based groups did not. For example, local programs in the areas of health care, housing, and education sought to compensate for overt discrimination on the part of public agencies toward black neighborhoods. In Memphis a postwar black "institutional infrastructure," including women's church groups and self-help societies, provided social services which black taxpayers failed to receive from the city.[34]

The lifelong public service offered by black women like Atlanta's

Lugenia D. Burns Hope showed an inexorable progression from commitment to one's family to overt political activity on behalf of one's race. The wife of Morehouse College President John Hope, she first became involved in community issues when she helped provide a playground that black children, including her own, could use. She went on to found the Neighborhood Union of Atlanta, a group which served as an advocate for black children and adults who faced discrimination from the YMCA (in recreational facilities), the Community Chest (in aid to the poor), and the public school system, which imposed double sessions on black pupils. (The Sunset Club of Orangeburg, South Carolina, and the Women's Club of Tuskegee, Alabama, were comparable associations.) In 1932 Hope joined the Atlanta Citizenship Committee to instruct black voters about their rights. To the end of her life she remained outspoken in her impatience with white moderates who felt they knew best in the fight against Jim Crow.[35] To cite another example, the thirty-five-year career of Modjeska Monteith Simkins began with her service as Director of Negro Work for the South Carolina Tuberculosis Association (in the 1930s) and spanned work for the NAACP, Columbia (South Carolina) Women's Council, Civil Welfare League, Southern Conference for Human Welfare, and Southern Conference Educational Fund, among other civil rights groups.[36]

At times it becomes exceedingly difficult to categorize black women's efforts on behalf of their own families as either wage or salaried labor or volunteer work. Middle-class women in particular often had a professional identity that they used for political purposes—Ida Wells Barnett, the journalist, for example. Mamie Garvin Fields, a member of Charleston's black "aristocracy," attended Claflin University, and in about 1910 went on to teach at Miller Hill, an isolated South Carolina community, "a place behind God's back." Struggling to accommodate over a hundred children eager to learn, she received this response from the local (white) school trustee: "Ga'vin, whar ya fin' all these niggers? I diddin know th' was s' minny damn niggers up here on this hill. . . . Yah got too minny t'han'l? Jes' shut it *daln*, Ga'vin. Shut it *daln!*" A few years later, as a teacher on James Island, Fields had to endure the indignity of dealing with county officials who provided her with too few textbooks and made certain that the library books she did receive came from the "colored stack" distributed by the county library truck. She contained her outrage and at the same time impressed white officials with her professionalism and determination; Fields's efforts on behalf of her schoolchildren required persistence and a keen political sense. Thus, the very nature of their employment plunged black teachers into politics whether they liked it or not. Moreover, Fields would probably have had a difficult time differentiating the work she did for her job from the work she did as a member of the Charleston "Do What You Can Club" (in 1935, affiliated with the National Council of Negro Women), a volunteer group that offered help to homeless black girls.[37]

As volunteers and reformers, black women shaped the nature of political discourse in the South. Their activities helped to put white men on notice that the struggle against racism would be an insistent one. That struggle was not without its ironies; in providing services for their own communities, black women (and men) at times gave whites a justification to preserve Jim-Crow levels of funding. Atlanta municipal officials, and whites in charge of the city's Community Chest, willingly turned over their "black" budgets to Hope's Neighborhood Union.[38] And Fields felt caught between the wishes of elderly folks on James Island that children learn "good manners" to help them "come up in the world" and her own conviction that "those manners kept us 'in our place.' They conditioned us in Old South ways."[39] Such was the clash between culture and politics that white reformers rarely experienced in their world of unpaid work.

Working and Not Working in Factories, Fields, and White Households

The southern racial caste system originated in seventeenth century Virginia as a means of supplying tobacco plantation owners with a large, secure pool of agricultural labor. In the latter half of the 1600s this function had been expanded beyond its initial economic purposes to include a political dimension as well, for large landowners discovered that they could consolidate their own power if poor whites were, first, exempt from the most grueling field work, and, second, conscious of their superior status relative to blacks of both sexes and all ages.[40] Cotton emerged as the region's primary staple crop during the antebellum period and revitalized the labor-intensive southern economy; for the next century and a half, the South would depend on black labor not only for its profits, but also for its socioeconomic class structure. The outlines of the seventeenth century drama that pitted blacks against whites, and white elites against their social inferiors, persisted into the nineteenth century. By then, a fledgling industrial revolution had transformed the southern landscape and created a new class of workers: textile mill operatives who were almost exclusively white. By offering white sharecroppers cash wages, New South businessmen hoped to quench the embers of interracial protest that smoldered on the southern countryside and provide their poorer cousins with opportunities denied to black people.[41] Black factory workers remained confined to tobacco processing, a particularly disagreeable task. In essence, the manipulation of a subordinate labor force remained closely linked to attempts by well-to-do white men to maintain their monopoly on power in all its social and political manifestations.

However, efforts to mute class conflict and avoid the potential for cooperation between workers of the two races were not entirely successful. Between 1890 and 1965 resistance to the demands of landlords and factory owners assumed a variety of shapes, from radical grass-roots agrarian unions to sporadic walkouts among disaffected textile workers and major unionization drives spearheaded by textile and tobacco employees.[42] In addition to more structured forms of protest, workers of both races acted (separately, more often than not) to deprive employers of the full and unlimited use of their labor by failing to conform to industrial standards of work discipline. When they worked slowly or refused to work at all, black and white men and women reaffirmed their integrity as individuals or family members in defiance of work-discipline rules established by employers and foremen.

With its technologically backward, labor-intensive system of staple-crop agriculture, and its insatiable demand for domestic servants, the postbellum South placed a high premium on wringing every ounce of strength from black men, women, and children. Landless white men were also supposed to earn their meager bread by the sweat of their brow in the cotton and tobacco fields, but their wives were exempt from the degradation of housework outside their own homes. In essence, the economic subordination of blacks represented a continuation of market relationships established under slavery. Mechanisms of subordination were transformed after the Civil War, as terrorism and disenfranchisement replaced the slave code. Nevertheless, black people sought to exercise their relative freedom and defend themselves against rapacious white landlords and employers.

A number of factors inhibited the development of labor unions in the South, and the organization of female workers in particular: the small number of women in the industrial work force compared with the North, the significance of a family wage, the prevalence of child labor, historic racial animosities between employees (and potential employees), and the power of paternalistic mill owners.[43] Nevertheless, women played a highly visible role in instances of collective action among textile and tobacco workers, as well as among sharecroppers.

Although they managed to cooperate with one another across class lines only sporadically, women workers often shared domestic concerns that impelled them to wage an active struggle against exploitative employers. For example, in 1947 Estelle Flowers, a black North Carolina tobacco worker and single mother of four, accounted for her union militance this way: "Food takes about all my wages. . . . What do we eat? Beans, collards, cornbread. I can't afford milk for the children. My six month old baby has to have milk—one can of evaporated milk—15 cents a day. It takes $2. a week for coal and that doesn't keep the home warm. What would I do with more wages? Buy the clothes the children need— more food and I could give more to the church."[44] A white woman, wife of a United Automobile Workers official, observed of the couple's participation in a union-organizing drive in an Atlanta assembly plant during the fall of 1937: "When you see your child not having enough to eat, it is enough to put a fight in anybody."[45]

This is not to suggest that women rarely if ever shared with their menfolk a sense of the righteousness or principled fairness of their own cause. Lula Parchman's straightforward statement of her grievances toward a Madison, Arkansas, planter in the 1930s was echoed by women all over the South, in factories and fields: "They works us from sun to sun at a dollar. Conditions are pitiful with we pore folks. We get nothing scarcely. . . . I wants only a chance to make my own living and not have any other get the profit on my labor. I am tired of being denied the chance to live. I only want the po[r]tion due me."[46] Still, it is important to note that working-class women of both races often filtered their wage-work experience through the prism of family life and that the practical necessities of feeding, clothing, and schooling household members could translate into acts of resistance against employers—acts that in a fundamental way amounted to political activism.

The story of white textile-mill laborers in the South suggests the range of strategies available to both men and women in that industry. As soon as textile production began on a large scale in the region (during the 1880s), factory owners realized that they faced serious problems in subjecting rural migrants to the rigors of time-oriented labor. The operatives, fresh from farm life, brought with them a work pace which supervisors condemned as careless and lazy. Moreover, as long as mill jobs were plentiful, workers exercised their prerogative to quit whenever they wished, and perhaps return to the family homestead for a while before seeking wage employment once more.[47] However, during the Great Depression, when wages fell and desperate workers clamored for jobs, a spectacular general strike involving 400,000 Piedmont workers failed to win substantial gains. White women shared with their husbands and sons a sense of ambivalence about factory work—they preferred the cash wages over the fraudulent crop lien system practiced by cotton and tenant landlords, but felt "stretched out" in the mills—and, as union members, they played a highly visible role in organized struggles against "the bosses."[48]

The history of white workers in the South offers a curious blend of radicalism—their willingness to challenge the balance of economic power in favor of middle-class white men—and conservatism—their acquiescence in a political system that not only subordinated blacks, but also preserved the role of blacks of both sexes as potential job competitors. Consequently, racial self-interest superseded class struggle. Even when they relied on the courage and leadership of their black female coworkers, as Durham tobacco workers did in the late 1940s, white women sided with their menfolk to perpetuate discriminatory policies against blacks within their own unions. The racial-sexual division of labor peculiar to the tobacco industry reflected and reinforced larger social conflicts. Thus Velma Hopkins and Moranda Smith, two black women, won renown for their militance during the labor conflicts of the World War II era. However, union victories only encouraged employers to fire their least skilled employees (black women stemmers) and replace them with automatic stemming machines, a move which white workers failed to protest.[49]

When it came to efficiently exploiting the region's human resources, New South businessmen and industrialists were neophytes compared with the large landowners who had dominated southern political and economic life since the seventeenth century. After the Civil War, the collusion of planters, politicians, and officials of banking and credit institutions meant that landownership would continue to set the standard for power and prestige in the region;[50] although the organization of free labor (into family sharecropping and tenant farms) departed from the gang-labor system under slavery, the vast majority of black people remained effectively barred from tilling their own land. Meanwhile, increasing numbers of formerly self-sufficient white farmers found themselves drawn into a commercial economy and the quicksand of indebtedness. After 1900 large agricultural holdings became modeled after industrial corporations as landowners sought to establish tight control over their workers. By 1935, 9 million people, or 25 percent of all southerners, worked the land as wage hands, sharecroppers, and tenants; this figure included 1 million white and 700,000 black households.[51]

Regardless of race, these dependent agricultural laborers had a similarly lowly material condition. Most lived on the edge of debt peonage, caught up in the cotton lien system. They extricated themselves from debt only with the greatest difficulty, and whole families might engage in months-long, back-breaking labor and still have little or no cash, food, or clothing to show for their pains at the end of the year.[52] Gracie Turner, a North Carolina woman, in the late 1930s noted, "If I had de say half de land wold be planted in stuff to eat; nobody would have to furnish me and overcharge me when settlement time come."[53]

The "democratic promise"[54] of rural working-class solidarity, offered by small pockets of biracial Populist party activity in the early 1890s, was echoed in 1931, when a group of Alabama blacks formed the Sharecroppers Union. The rapid brutality with which white landowners responded to the union revealed the importance they attached to maintaining a servile labor force at all costs.[55] Three years later the Southern Tenant Farmers' Union (STFU) emerged in Tyronza, Arkansas, and within a few months it had attracted, by its own account, 25,000 members, many of whom joined in the general cottonpickers' strike in 1935. The opposition of local planters, New Deal bureaucrats and policy members in Washington, as well as the STFU's ill-fated decision in 1937 to join the United Cannery, Agricultural Packing and Allied Workers, rendered the group largely defunct by 1939.[56]

Women of both races contributed substantial service to the STFU, although much of that service took place on a segregated basis. For example, a group of black women in Wabbasecka, Arkansas, formed themselves into a "Blue Woman's local." Union wives considered themselves supportive of their husbands' initiatives, while women like Henrietta McGhee, Naomi Williams, and Carrie Dilworth were leaders in their own right.[57] Local meetings were often technically integrated, but many women found it difficult to work closely with someone of a different race. Asked to join a fundraising tour to New York City, McGhee and Myrtle Lawrence, an STFU activist, hardly exemplified the principle of interracial cooperation. McGhee complained of the other woman's temperamental idiosyncrasies—"don't make me stay with that ole white woman, she have fits"—as well as her proclivity to use a "spit can" while sitting on the platform before a large New York audience. H. L. Mitchell, co-founder of the STFU, noted that "Henrietta afterwards told me that she was never so embarrassed in her life as by that old white woman making everyone think the union folks were all just like those Tobacco Road people they had heard about." He concluded that "about the only thing the two sharecropper women had in common was the union."[58]

If formal unionizing efforts among rural workers failed to change the contours of the southern social landscape, white landowners nevertheless had difficulties in creating a labor force to their liking. Like textile mill workers, sharecroppers refused to live up to the expectations of their employers. Located outside the consumer society, they had few "wants" or "needs" to harden their ambition and make them work more productively. Some moved around to other plantations as often as possible, refusing to pay allegiance to a particular landlord, though failing to escape the treadmill of the staple-crop system itself.[59]

Regardless of the common duties and concerns that characterized black and white women's lives in the rural South—despite their similar fertility rates and their identical daily rounds of household chores and family obligations—they remained alienated by their different cultures and history. This fact becomes abundantly clear when we consider the political implications of free black labor in the post–Civil War era. Attempts by black husbands and wives to control their own productive energies, and to protect their families against whip-wielding employers, caused great consternation among southern whites.[60] The special strategies employed to force blacks to work in the fields—terrorist activities of the Ku Klux Klan and other vigilante groups in the 1860s; lynching and disfranchisement, especially during the 1890–1910 period—persisted well into the 1930s. During the Depression, whites down on their luck attempted to extract from black women the labor they felt was their due. A widow with seven children wrote the U.S. Department of Agriculture in 1935 that "these poor white people [in Millen, Georgia] that lives around me wants the colored people to work for them for nothing. . . ."[61] Local New Deal officials denied blacks federal aid when the nearby cotton crop was ready for harvest and conspired to keep public-works projects wages lower than the prevailing rates for laundresses and maids. As a result, when black wives decided to stay home from the fields and attend to the needs of their own families, as they did during Reconstruction, or when whole clans and villages migrated North, out of the menacing reach of creditors and convict-lease agents, as they did in great numbers from 1915 to 1970, they made a political statement of great import.[62]

Black men, women, and children toiled together in the fields; in the eyes of planters, they were all "hands," especially during the harvest season. But black mothers, wives, and daughters occupied a unique place in the southern occupational structure by virtue of their much-sought-after labor as domestic servants. Even white households of modest means depended on black female "help," and the mistress-servant relationship reduced the larger racial caste system to a particularly intimate form of exploitation. Although they possessed little in the way of formal political power, black women domestics devised ways to upset the daily routine and comfort of individual white families, ways that affected the extent and reliability of their services.[63] Taking advantage of the ubiquitous demand for domestics, these women would quit a work-place for the afternoon, or a week, or for good, without a moment's notice. On the job, they worked slowly and carelessly and appropriated food and staples for their own families, to the eternal exasperation of white housewives over the generations. Off the job, sisters and cousins and mothers and daughters shared with one another information about white women prone to speak harshly; the result was an informal system that rewarded "good" employers and punished "bad" ones. White women remained mystified by this process. In the early twentieth century they whispered darkly to one another about conspiratorial combinations of local domestics called WWTK groups (for "White Women to the Kitchen"). A generation later, in the 1930s, the daughters of these white women dubbed them "Eleanor Clubs," assuming that they were the inspiration of the egalitarian-minded First Lady.[64] In fact, the strength of kin and community ties among blacks made such formal associations unnecessary; through modest, informal means black women managed to challenge (if not undermine) the balance of power that the segregationist South struggled so desperately to preserve.

The decision among black women servants to resist their employers' demands that they "live in"—and thus remain on call twenty-four hours a day and apart from their own families—reveals how a series of individual choices could deprive whites of black labor in a dramatic way.[65] Furthermore, this attempt by black women to attend to the needs of their own families mirrored on a small scale a larger phenomenon that white southerners remarked upon with great alarm soon after the Civil War had ended. Freedwomen all over the region withdrew from the fields in order to care for children and husbands and at the same time remove themselves from abusive overseers and landowners.[66]

When a black mother decided to stay at home one day and forego the meager cash wages she might have earned as a domestic or cotton picker, so that she could patch a dress for her daughter to wear to school, she did not act in a consciously political way. But the accumulation of such decisions over the years and generations—the combined effect of servants who ruined their mistress's dinner parties by quitting at the last minute, and the field hands who lessened the landlord's margin of profit by appearing in the fields only at harvest time—sent an unmistakable message to white men and women. If the forms of resistance were not overtly political, the strategies employed by whites to counter them certainly were, including poll taxes; literacy tests; grandfather clauses; the all-white primaries, juries, and judges; and a steadfast refusal to pass antilynching legislation. Southern politicians devised these means of repression not only to counter black recalcitrance in the workplace, but also to safeguard "the southern way of life" in the midst of a myriad of protests coordinated by a new generation of black leaders in the late nineteenth century.

When the civil rights movement erupted with such force in the mid 1950s, media attention suggested to whites all over the nation that black people had decided to use new and daring tactics to secure rights long denied to them. In fact, this stage of the struggle represented a continuance of civil disobedience and court test cases that had originated in the 1940s.[67] And the family feeling that bound preachers and "mamas," brothers and sisters in the movement represented a form of racial solidarity that grew out of slavery and placed affective relationships above the crude opportunism of white employers. Black women played a special role in this process, both as "private" nurturers and as "public" leaders, for a broad spectrum of female activists, old and young, well educated and illiterate, joined forces against white policemen, voter registrars, school board members, and politicians in the 1950s and 1960s.[68] In the words of activist-folklorist Bernice Johnson Reagon:

> In most societies, it is from women that you get the most consistent concept of nationhood of any people. Women usually are very nationalistic in the way they determine what they are supposed to be doing with their lives. With Black people in the United States, we understand that one of our responsibilities is to live and struggle so that there will be another generation of people. . . . The problem of our people then was to turn around this dying recipe of slavery so that there would be a Black people. To take on that job is to be a nationalist, to be about the formation and continuance and survival of a nation. Black women as mothers have been the heart of that battle.

> We are, at the base of our identities, nationalists. We are people builders, carriers of cultural traditions, key to the formation and continuance of culture.[69]

Just as it would be difficult to separate the religious component of public protest from its political manifestations, so it would be difficult to distinguish personal from political motivations along the historical continuum of black women's labor.

Conclusion

The unique political configuration of the South—characterized by the subordination of blacks, on the one hand, and the intense rhetorical idealization of white women, on the other—had as its ultimate goal the maintenance of a social division of labor based on race, sex, and class. Black and white women worked within this socioeconomic system, with all its historical tensions and constraints, to provide for their families, kin, and neighbors. Most black and poor white wives and mothers had to seek gainful employment outside the home. Many women of the two races—especially white middle-class women and black women of all classes—joined with their peers to effect social change in the name of morality, religious devotion, and family integrity (variously defined by different groups). And finally, all women had responsibility for the care of their immediate households (though for the white middle-class housewife this care primarily involved the supervision of black domestics). As individuals and as members of a specific race and class, women placed themselves within the matrix of southern caste relationships and either bolstered, acquiesced in, or resisted the white men and ideologies that shaped the southern political structure. In the lives of black women, boundaries between private concerns and the public welfare, between family and community, between middle class and working class, between reproductive and productive labor gave way to a harmony of interests that explicitly challenged the hegemony of white property owners and housewives.

Women's work outside the realm of conventional party politics was not necessarily overtly political, but in many cases it did have political meaning. On a basic level, mothers and grandmothers played a large role in the socialization of future citizens and workers, impressing upon them certain values that would shape their behavior in the marketplace as well as at the polling place. We must be careful of course not to credit black women exclusively with the civil rights revolution in the 1950s and 1960s; nor should we hold white women responsible for the preservation of a system manipulated so successfully for so long by their husbands and fathers.

In sum, the "new social history," which encompasses the study of work, family, women, and Afro-American culture, can provide a rich view of the past, one not necessarily fragmented along public-private lines. If ballot boxes allowed southerners, or at least some southerners, to make public their choices concerning the distribution of wealth, power, and justice in their society, so, too, did volunteer groups, family relationships, and individual priorities concerning the nature and extent of gainful labor. These aspects of southern life would give women opportunities for eloquent expression of deeply held values, political views that at times reverberated through the halls of political party headquarters, court houses, and state legislatures.

Notes

1. Quoted in Lowry (1980), pp. 106–109.
2. Quoted in Wise and Thrasher (1980), p. 125.
3. Baxter and Lansing (1983), p. 78.
4. Kousser (1974); Terborg-Penn (1983), pp. 266–267.
5. Federal Writers Project (1939), p. 10. Easton added, "Two or three times I have had to defend our stuff with a shotgun when he was away, and he laughs and says that taking a man's place at home is all right but a man's place in voting is all wrong."
6. Swain (1983), p. 53.
7. Daniel (1981, 1985); Wright (1986).
8. Harding (1981).
9. Hall (1979), p. 89.
10. Hall (1979), p. 89.
11. Baker (1984).
12. See, for example, Roydhouse (1980); Roberson (1922–1923); McDowell (1979).
13. Hall (1979), pp. 94–104; Lerner (1979), pp. 109–110.
14. Sitkoff (1981); Raines (1977).
15. Hall (1979).
16. Rothschild (1982); Carson (1981).
17. Leloudis (1983); Kett (1985); Kousser (1980).
18. Kemp (1983), p. 392.
19. Braden (1981).
20. Terborg-Penn (1977, 1983).
21. Leloudis (1983).
22. Hall (1979), pp. 205–206.
23. Shankman (1981), p. 247.
24. Katzman (1978); Jones (1985), pp. 127–134.
25. Magdol (1977), pp. 35–61.
26. Blassingame (1973).
27. Lerner (1979).
28. Hamilton (1978); Reed (1920), p. 46.
29. Terborg-Penn (1983), p. 272; Neverdon-Morton (1978).
30. Barnett (1969); Aptheker (1982).
31. Nimmons (1981); Giddings (1984).
32. Terborg-Penn (1983), p. 261.
33. Terborg-Penn (1983), p. 265.
34. Berkeley (1985).

35. Rouse (1983).
36. Aba-Mecha (1978).
37. Fields (1983), pp. 126, 208–209.
38. Rouse (1983), p. 75; Harlan (1958).
39. Fields (1983), p. 221.
40. Morgan (1975).
41. See, for example, Stokes (1977).
42. McLaurin (1971); Janiewski (1985); Miller (1980); Frederickson (1982).
43. Frederickson (1985).
44. Lerner (1972), p. 267. See also Korstad (1980).
45. Quoted in Herring and Thrasher (1980), p. 182.
46. Mitchell (1979), p. 106.
47. Rodgers (1977).
48. Hall et al. (1986).
49. Janiewski (1983, 1985).
50. See, for example, Wiener (1978); Ransom and Sutch (1977).
51. McDonald and McWhiney (1980); Johnson et al. (1935).
52. Jones (1986).
53. Federal Writers Project (1939), pp. 24–25.
54. Goodwyn (1976).
55. Beecher (1934); Rosengarten (1974).
56. Grubbs (1971).
57. Wise and Thrasher (1980); Mitchell (1979), pp. 105, 112–123.
58. Mitchell (1979), p. 118.
59. Jones (1985), pp. 99–109.
60. Jones (1985), pp. 44–78.
61. Lerner (1972), p. 400.
62. Jones (1985).
63. Katzman (1978); Terborg-Penn (1985); Janiewski (1983).
64. Reed (1920), p. 46; Johnson (1943), p. 29.
65. As Janiewski (1983) points out, "Black women's not working attracted the same public scrutiny that white women's work evoked" (p. 13).
66. Jones (1985), pp. 44–78.
67. Chafe (1982).
68. Raines (1977).
69. Reagon (1982), p. 81.

6

Power Surrendered, Power Restored: The Politics of Work and Family Among Hispanic Garment Workers in California and Florida

M. Patricia Fernández-Kelly / Anna M. García

Iconoclast that I am, I would not abandon the central wisdom of natural history from its inception—that concepts without precepts are empty, and that no scientist can develop an adequate "feel" for nature (that undefinable prerequisite of true understanding) without probing deeply into minute empirical details of some well-chosen group of organisms.

Stephen Jay Gould, *The Flamingo's Smile*

Introduction

This chapter addresses a dimension of political action neglected in most writings on politics. We examine the manner in which women participate in decision-making processes affecting the access to vital resources within their own households and as part of the larger wage economy. The women in question belong to one ethnic group (Hispanic), but two different national heritages (Cuban and Mexican), and represent at least two distinct class backgrounds (workers and small business owners). All of them have been, or still are, garment workers in Los Angeles and Miami counties. Their experience accounts significantly for the boom of apparel manufacturing in southern Florida during the 1970s and for the survival and gradual expansion of the needle trade industry in southern California in the last two decades.[1] An important aspect in the life history of many of these women is their involvement in home assembly. In other words, they have been or still are part of the informal economy.

130

The theoretical focus of this chapter is on the intersection of gender, class, and ethnicity as a subject relevant to the study of political behavior.[2] Two questions guide our analysis. The first one centers on exchanges of power and authority between the sexes: To what extent do women act in their own interest as they relate to men in homes and workplaces? The second question opens up an even more elusive inquiry: How do women's personal exchanges with men interact with patterns of collective socioeconomic advancement or disadvantage?

In the case of Mexican women in southern California, employment in garment production tends to be precipitated by long-term financial need. Wives may choose to work outside the home in order to meet the survival requirements of their families in the absence of adequate earnings by their husbands or male companions. In other cases, female heads of household join the labor force after losing male support as a consequence of illness, death, or, more often, abandonment. In many of these instances, women must opt for industrial homework in order to fulfill the contradictory demands of domestic care and wage employment. Theirs is a situation of vulnerability made extreme by the proletarian status of the ethnic group to which they belong.

By contrast, Cuban women who arrived in southern Florida as exiles saw garment jobs as a transitory experience aimed at recovering or attaining middle-class standards of living. The consolidation of an economic enclave in Miami, which accounts for much of the prosperity of Cubans, was largely predicated upon the incorporation of women into the labor force. While they toiled in factories, hotels, and restaurants, their husbands formed their own businesses. Theirs was a condition of vulnerability qualified by shared objectives of upward mobility in a foreign society.

Despite their different national backgrounds, migratory histories, and class affiliations, Mexican and Cuban women share many perceptions and expectations about sexual roles: Patriarchal norms of reciprocity are considered desirable; marriage, motherhood, and dedication to family life are high priorities. Men are expected to hold authority, to be good providers, and to be loyal to their family units. However, Mexicans' and Cubans' divergent economic and social circumstances have had a differential impact upon the possibilities of upholding these values. Thus, Mexican women are often thrust into positions of financial "autonomy" as a result of men's inability to fulfill their socially assigned role, while among Cubans patriarchal mores have served to maintain group cohesion and have allowed women a marginal advantage in the labor market.

Both Cuban and Mexican women face the challenges posed by their subordination as family members and as low-skilled workers in highly competitive industries. Nevertheless, their contrasting class backgrounds and modes of incorporation into local labor markets entail different political and socioeconomic potentials. Individual and collective consciousness is implicated in this process. Our discussion below shows that among Mexican garment workers disillusion about the viability of men as economic actors can translate into greater receptivity to ideals and hopes of personal emancipation, progress, and financial independence. These ideals, however, are often distorted by poverty and the stigma attached to ethnic and gender status.

Cuban women tend to see no contradiction between personal fulfillment and a fierce commitment to patriarchal standards. Both their entrance into, and later withdrawal from, the southern Florida labor force were contingent on their adherence to hierarchical patterns of authority and a conventional division of labor between the sexes. As in the case of Mexicans in southern California, Cuban women's involvement in homework was an option mediating domestic and income-generating objectives. However, it differed in that homework among the latter was brought about by relative prosperity and expanding rather than diminishing options.

The paradoxes raised by a comparison of Mexican and Cuban garment workers are relevant to several fields of inquiry. In addition to specialized writings on Hispanics in the United States, we examine two main bodies of recent scholarly research and theory: (1) writings that claim that feminism *is* a legitimate guideline for intellectual pursuits and political practice and (2) writings that focus on the definition of politics itself. Because of the richness and complexity of both contributions, no detailed critique can be attempted here. Our purpose will be simply to raise the principal issues to which our research is relevant.

Women speaking out in their own perceived interests have been a recurrent phenomenon in the Western world for the last three centuries.[3] What makes contemporary feminism unique is an unprecedented volume of writings flowing from the pens of academic and popular authors since the late sixties.[4] In spite of historical and cultural variations, all brands of feminism share two central objectives: to gain an in-depth understanding of the specificity of women's experiences, particularly as they relate to their economic and political subordination, and to devise and implement strategies for collective change including the uplifting of women's position in society. Thus, feminism shares with Marxism the conviction that political practice should intertwine logically and intimately with a systematic inquiry into the nature of various forms of socioeconomic oppression.

From the beginning, a critique of the historical and epistemological foundations of feminism emerged from within feminism itself. This critical assessment has included a growing emphasis on class as a factor affecting levels and characteristics of female subordination, ideology, and consciousness. A second and related theme, only now being pondered by feminists, concerns the question of male privilege. Throughout the seventies, stress was placed on patriarchy, male supremacy, androcentrism, and masculine chauvinism as counterparts and cause of women's disadvantaged economic and political position.

In a path-breaking article, Heidi Hartmann presented patriarchy as an independent system of domination anteceding capitalism and based on the sexual division of labor.[5] In this scheme, women's confinement in the home was brought about through the historical coalition between working-class and capitalist men at the expense of women. Men's appropriation of women's services, partly achieved through the enactment of protective legislation and the family wage, removed women from the sphere of productive labor and, consequently, from effective political expression. The implications of this position were straightforward: Women's emancipation would depend on the elimination of the sexual division of labor and full incorporation into the productive sphere.

Hartmann's stark presentation had the advantage of underscoring peculiarities affecting women's position in capitalist societies. However, her overarching emphasis on patriarchy underestimates the extent to which women themselves have participated in political actions, some of which seem detrimental from the point of view of late twentieth century feminists. A case in point was women's participation in the struggle for the family wage and protective legislation toward the end of the nineteenth century.[6] Working-class women did not see employment outside the home as a privilege leading to self-fulfillment. Instead, they perceived the possibility of staying at home as an elusive goal worth fighting for. This perception is akin to that of many contemporary working-class and minority women. The emphasis on male privilege as the explanation for women's position in society can lead to their portrayal as puppets of history, passively succumbing to the pressures of men acting in *their* own interests.

In addition, the emphasis on patriarchy assumes that men of different class backgrounds have a similar and vested interest in the appropriation of women's sexuality and labor. This proposition should be taken as a hypothesis in need of verification rather than as a self-evident point of departure. The patriarchal family, the sexual division of labor, and the consolidation of the home as a separate realm can be seen as mechanisms to suppress women's economic and political expression. They can also be seen as tools for controlling men, particularly working-class men, by transforming them into "breadwinners" with primary responsibility for the support of women and children. The point is not to discard the idea that men benefit personally and collectively from services provided in their households. But we must investigate such benefits as outcomes of complex processes rather than as the mechanistic effect of males' universal thirst for power over women.

Finally, feminist writings often portray patriarchy as a unilateral political and economic system uniformly placing women at a disadvantage and men in a position of superiority. Research on class variations and on ethnic minorities in the United States suggests that this conclusion may be premature. Rather than as a universal system, patriarchy should be seen as a series of flexible ideologies involving norms of reciprocity for both men and women. Our discussion below suggests that patriarchal mores vary by class and that under some conditions they may represent a realistic (if not ideal) option for women and their families.

The issue of male privilege and female subordination raises political questions which are difficult to couch in conventional frameworks. In Western democratic societies politics has been seen as a specialized field of activity linking professionals to constituencies exercising civic rights. For that reason, the study of politics has emphasized such phenomena as voting patterns, government allocation of power and resources, and interest group behavior. Common to all these phenomena is that they are part of a public world which also contains wage labor. Their counterpart is the private world of the home, personal life, and unremunerated work. One of the effects of this dichotomy is to deny the political character of exchanges occurring at the level of the household.[7] Thus, the bifurcation of wage employment and unpaid domestic labor is reflected in the ideological conception of the household as a nonpolitical realm.

Marxists have provided an alternative view based upon the struggle between classes with polarized economic interests. This contribution is useful because it carries definitions of "the political" beyond the confines of interest group theory or professional politics. Instead, Marxism identifies politics as a dimension inherent in collective actions involving exchanges of power, authority, and differential access to resources.[8] Feminists have moved this idea further by stressing that the personal is political and by redefining interactions occurring within families and households. It is within those two domains that class, gender, and ethnicity mesh, creating different modes of incorporation into the labor force and different alternatives for economic and political participation outside the home.

The relationship between class and gender, the questions raised by male privilege, and a reconceptualization of the term "political" will serve as a context for our analysis of the relationship between work and home among Hispanic women. First, we provide a general overview of Hispanics in the labor force.

Hispanics and Wage Employment

There are almost 20 million persons of Hispanic ancestry living in the United States—that is, 14.6 percent of the total population. With demographic forecasts predicting that they will surpass African-Americans in number by the end of the century, Hispanics already constitute the second largest ethnic minority in this country.

Although there are many studies comparing ethnic minorities and whites in the United States, there have been few attempts to look at variations of experience *within* ethnic groups. This is true for Hispanics in general and for Hispanic women in particular. The few exceptions contrasting the employment and socioeconomic profile of Hispanic women of various national backgrounds show similarities as well as differences. For example, an in-depth examination of the 1976 Survey of Income and Education (U.S. Department of Commerce, 1978) conducted by George Borjas and Marta Tienda (1985) as well as more recent compilations based on the 1980 census (Bean and Tienda, 1987) confirms the view that socioeconomic characteristics vary significantly between Hispanic and non-Hispanic populations. These statistics also show the ample differentiation among Hispanics.

Mexicans constituted more than half of all Hispanics between ages 18 and 64 living in the United States. Of these, approximately 70 percent were born in this country. Average levels of education are quite low, with less than 50 percent having graduated from high school. About 60 percent of working-age Mexicans are under age 35 compared with less than 50 pecent of working-age non-Hispanic white workers. Cubans, on the other hand, represent about 7 percent of the Hispanic population. They are mostly foreign-born and have a mean age of 39 years. They also have a higher level of formal education than Mexicans. Fifty-eight percent of Cubans had 12 or more years of formal schooling in 1976.[9]

Cuban and Mexican marital profiles and household compositions are similar; intact marriages predominate in both groups and a low percentage of households are headed by women. Approximately 67 percent of Mexican women and 64 percent of Cuban women are married and living with their spouses. Similarly, 65 percent of Mexican men and 70 percent of Cuban men live in stable marital unions. Finally, about 74 percent of Mexican women have children under age 17 living with them. The equivalent figure for Cuban women is 62 percent.

These figures capture a general profile for comparative purposes. However, other variations are noticeable among workers in specific industries. For instance, in both southern California and southern Florida most direct production workers in the garment industry are Hispanic. Approximately 75 percent and 67 percent, respectively, of operatives in Los Angeles and Miami apparel firms are Mexican and Cuban women. Among Los Angeles garment workers, there is a high incidence of female-headed households: almost 30 percent, a figure almost double that of Mexicans living in the United States in general. By contrast, the incidence of female-headed households among Cuban garment workers is 19 percent, a figure only slightly above that of their group in general.[10]

The labor force participation rates of Mexican and Cuban women dispel the widespread notion that work outside the home is a rare experience for Hispanic women: 54.2 percent of native-born and 47.5 percent of foreign-born Mexican women were employed outside the home in 1980. The equivalent figure for the mostly foreign-born Cuban women was almost 65 percent. These figures approximate or surpass the labor force participation of non-Hispanic white women which in 1980 was 57.9 percent (Bean and Tienda, 1987).

Moreover, our review of the 1970 and 1980 Census of Population shows that while other ethnic groups in the United States have diminished their participation in blue-collar employment, Hispanic women have increased their relative share in it. This is particularly so in the production of nondurable goods. Fully 35 percent of all women employed in manufacturing in the New York Metropolitan, Greater Los Angeles, and Greater Miami areas are Hispanic. The contrast between the proportion of Hispanic and non-Hispanic women in manufacturing is striking. In Los Angeles 35.7 percent of all females in that sector are Hispanic while only 19.0 percent are Caucasian. The equivalent figures for New York and Miami are 35.1 and 17.5 percent and 28.6 and 15.4 percent, respectively.[11]

The importance of minority women's employment in assembly is readily apparent in southern California, where 67 percent of working women classified as "operators, fabricators, and laborers" belong to ethnic minority groups. Fifty-one percent of those are Hispanic. These findings run counter to the impression that Hispanic women's participation in the labor force is not significant. Moreover, census figures may underestimate the actual involvement of Hispanic women in wage labor. Many are part of the underground economy—that is, they are found in small unregulated assembly shops or doing piecework and industrial homework.

Census figures for Los Angeles County further confirm the significance of Hispanic women's employment in manufacturing: Almost 74 percent of all female "operators, fabricators, and laborers" (136,937 persons) are members of ethnic minorities. Almost 60 percent of that subgroup (105,621 persons) are Hispanic. Even more revealing is the composition of workers classified as "textile, apparel, and furnishings machine operators." Approximately 46,000 women are employed in that occupation in Los Angeles. Almost 91 percent of those are minorities; 72 percent of them are Hispanic. Equivalent data for New York and Miami (the two other areas with the fastest-growing Hispanic populations) indicate that we are looking at a substantial percentage of the manufacturing labor force.

Garment production has historically provided a locus where immigrant women, including Hispanics of various national backgrounds, have found paid employment. We now consider the features of this type of manufacturing in California and Florida.

CALIFORNIA   The history of the garment industry in southern California is closely related to changes in apparel production in New York. The latter part of the nineteenth century witnessed the preeminence of New York as a garment producer and the emergence of California as a center of manufacture of ready-made wear for mass consumption. In the 1920s the Los Angeles clothing industry expanded, stimulated in part by the arrival of runaway shops evading unionization drives in New York. From the very beginning, Mexican women were employed in nearly all positions of the industry. Accounts of the time describe the work force in the Los Angeles clothing manufacturing sector as formed mainly by Mexican females, three quarters of whom were between the ages of 16 and 23, two thirds of whom were born in the United States, and nine tenths of whom were unmarried.[12]

The Great Depression sent the Los Angeles garment industry into a period of turmoil, but the rise of the cinema in the 1930s established new guidelines for fashion and fresh opportunities for production. Los Angeles began to specialize in inexpensive women's sportswear. By 1944 the number of garment manufacturers in Los Angeles had grown to 900 with a work force of 28,000 people, 75 percent of whom were Mexican women. The value of the product was said to be in excess of $110 million. By 1975 there had been a dramatic increase of plants to an estimated 2,269 with a work force of 66,000 people.[13]

During the late 1970s and the 1980s alarm over the growing employment of undocumented Mexican women, violations of the Labor Code and Tax Law, and the expansion of homework also grew. The recent history of the apparel industry in Los Angeles has been characterized by concerns over unregulated home assembly and the negative impact of foreign imports. Throughout the 1980s there has been continued restructuring of the industry, with decreasing numbers of large firms and the proliferation of small manufacturing shops. Of 2,717 apparel and textile manufacturers in Los Angeles County in 1984, 1,695 (or 62 percent) employed between 1 and 19 workers. The total work force in the formal sector hovered around 81,400 persons, many of whom were heads of households.

Contrary to a widespread impression, garment production in Los Angeles is growing quickly. This may be due to the expansion of the so-called informal sector. Garment contractors in Los Angeles County generated approximately $3.5 billion in sales 1983. It is estimated that between 30 and 50 percent of that value may have originated in home production and unregulated shops.[14]

FLORIDA   In the early 1960s the Florida garment industry specialized in the manufacture of belts, gloves, and purses and employed fewer than 7,000 persons. This was a highly seasonal industry depending on the periodic arrival of New York entrepreneurs feeding luxury markets in Europe and the United States.

The advent of several waves of refugees as a result of the Cuban Revolution was seen by many as an opportunity for revitalizing industrial activity in southern Florida. Retired manufacturers from New York who had homes in Miami saw the advantage of opening new businesses and hiring large numbers of freshly arrived Cuban women. At the same time, New York was experiencing a resurgence of union drives. The two factors combined to create a boom in apparel manufacturing in southern Florida. By 1973 the industry employed more than 24,000 workers, of whom the vast majority were Cuban women. The same process led to the predominance of Cuban males among contractors catering to New York manufacturers. Thus, from its inception, apparel manufacturing in Miami became an illustration in gender and ethnic stratification, with 70 percent of the manufacturers being Jewish, 90 percent of the subcontractors being Cuban men, and 95 percent of the work force being Cuban women.

In 1984 the Florida apparel industry employed 35,000 workers (in the formal sector), with 716 firms located in Miami. Most of these firms employed fewer than 30 workers, and their quarterly direct payroll amounted to $64 million. The sales volume reaches approximately $1 billion yearly. Government officials estimate that at least one third of that value originates in unregulated shops and homes.

Since the late seventies there have been labor shortages in the Florida apparel industry as a result of several trends, particularly the relatively advanced age of the work force, averaging over 40 years, and the absence of a new labor supply. As we will discuss below, it is the decreasing availability of Cuban women's labor that has contributed to the expansion of industrial homework in Miami.

COMPARATIVE ASPECTS   The contrast of garment manufacture in Los Angeles and Miami raises several issues. First, the two sites differ in the timing of the industry, its evolution, maturity, and restructuring. In Los Angeles, garment production is not only older but also rooted in specific events such as the Great Depression, changing conditions for assembly in New York, emphasis on new definitions of fashion linked to casual wear, and, finally, continued reorganization during the seventies and eighties as a response to the impact of foreign imports. The apparel industry in Miami has had a shorter and more uniform history.

Second, the expansion of the Los Angeles clothing industry resulted from capitalists' ability to rely on continuing waves of Mexican immigrants, many of whom were undocumented. Mexican migration over the last century ensured a steady supply of workers for the apparel industry. By contrast, the expansion of garment production in Miami was owed to an unprecedented influx of exiles ejected by a unique political event. Cubans working in the Florida apparel industry arrived in the United States as refugees under a protected and relatively privileged status. Exile was filled with uncertainty and the possibility of dislocation but not, as in the case of undocumented Mexican aliens, with the probability of harassment, detention, and deportation.

Third, implicit in the previous point is a differentiation, on the basis of social class, between the two cases. For more than a century, the majority of Mexican immigrants have had a markedly proletarian background. Until the 1970s the majority had rural roots, although in more recent times there has been a growing number of urban immigrants.[15] In sharp contrast, Cuban waves of migration have included a larger proportion of professionals, mid-level service providers, and various types of entrepreneurs ranging from those with previous experience in large companies to those qualified to start small family enterprises. Entrepreneurial experience among Cubans and reliance on their own ethnic networks accounts, to a large extent, for their success in business formation and appropriation in Miami.[16] Thus, while Mexican migration has been characterized by relative homogeneity regarding class background, Cuban exile resulted in the transposition of an almost intact class structure containing investors and professionals as well as unskilled, semiskilled, and skilled workers.

Fourth, in addition to disparate class compositions, the two groups differ in the degree of their homogeneity by place of birth. Besides the sizable undocumented contingent mentioned earlier, the Los Angeles garment industry also employs U.S.-born citizens of Mexican heritage. Firsthand reports and anecdotal evidence indicate that the fragmentation between "Chicana" and "Mexicana" workers causes an unresolved tension and animosity within the labor force. Cubans, on the other hand, were a highly cohesive population until recently, when the arrival of the so-called Marielitos resulted in a potentially disruptive polarization of the community.

Fifth, perhaps the most important difference between Mexicans in Los Angeles and Cubans in Florida is related to their distinctive labor market insertion patterns. Historically, Mexicans have arrived in the U.S. labor market in a highly individuated and dispersed manner. As a result, they have been extremely dependent on labor market supply-and-demand forces entirely beyond their control. Their working-class background and stigma attached to their frequent undocumented status have accentuated even further their vulnerability vis-à-vis employers. By contrast, Cubans have been able to consolidate an economic enclave containing immigrant businesses that hire workers of a common cultural and national background. According to Alejandro Portes and Robert Bach (1985), the economic enclave is characterized by ". . . first, the growth and visible presence of immigrant enterprises and, second, the fact that the average immigrant does not need to go beyond the physical and social limits of the enclave to carry out many routine activities."[17]

Thus, the economic enclave partly operates as a buffer zone separating and often shielding members of the same ethnic group from the market forces at work in the larger society. The existence of an economic enclave does not preclude exploitation on the basis of class; indeed, it is predicated upon the existence of a highly diversified immigrant class structure. However, the commonalities of culture, national background, and language between immigrant employers and workers can become a mechanism for collective improvement of income levels and standards of living. As a result, differences in labor market insertion patterns among Mexicans and Cubans have led to varying social profiles and a dissimilar potential for socioeconomic attainment.

Finally, the two paths of labor market incorporation are significantly related to household composition and household strategies for gaining access to employment. It is to this point that we now turn.

Household Organization and the Politics of Home and Work

Neither proletarian atomization among Mexicans nor participation in an economic enclave among Cubans can be explained without giving attention to the role played by households and families in the allocation of workers to different segments of the labor market. Some conceptual clarification is needed at this point.

First, a distinction between "family" and "household" must be established. Family can be seen as a normative, that is, ideological notion that frequently transcends class barriers. Rayna Rapp (1984) notes the prevalence of a family ideal shared among working- and middle-class people in the United States. Such an ideal includes marriage and fidelity, the role of men as main providers and of women as primary caretakers of children, and, finally, the expectation that families so formed will reside in the same home. In other words, while changes have taken place over time, the patriarchal family as a prescriptive model continues to prevail.

While "family" designates the way things *should be*, "household" refers to the manner in which men, women, and children *actually* come together as part of observable domestic units. Households represent mechanisms for the pooling of time, labor, and other resources in a shared space. The concept of the family appears natural and unchangeable, but households constantly adjust to the pressures of the surrounding environment; they frequently stand in sharp, even painful, contrast to widespread ideals regarding the family.

Second, class accounts largely for the extent to which notions about the family can be upheld or not. Anthropological writings note that the conditions necessary for the maintenance of long-term stable unions where men act as main providers and women as principal caretakers of children have been available among the middle and upper classes but woefully absent among the poor. Nuclear households are destabilized by high levels of unemployment and underemployment or by public policy making it more advantageous for women with children to accept welfare payments than to remain dependent upon an irregularly employed man. Thus, the poor often live in highly flexible households where resources and services flow constantly but where adherence to the norms of the patriarchal family are unattainable.

These differences are apparent in the circumstances surrounding industrial homework. Homework has been an alternative sought by both Mexican and Cuban women to reconcile the responsibilities of domestic care with the need to earn a wage. Homework has also been a means for employers to lower the wage bill, evade government regulations, and maintain competitiveness in the market.

Some of the conditions surrounding Mexican homeworkers in southern California are illustrated by the experience of Amelia Ruíz. She was born into a family of six children in El Cerrito, Los Angeles County. Her mother, a descendant of Native American Indians, married at a young age the son of Mexican immigrants. Among Ruíz's memories are the fragmentary stories of her paternal grandparents working in the fields and, occasionally, in canneries. Her father, on the other hand, was not a stoop laborer but a trained upholsterer. Her mother was always a homemaker. Ruíz grew up with a distinct sense of the contradictions that plague the relationships between men and women:

> All the while I was a child, I had this feeling that my parents weren't happy. My mother was smart but she could never make much of herself. Her parents taught her that the fate of woman is to be a wife and mother; they advised her to find a good man and marry him. And that she did. My father was reliable and I think he was faithful but he was also distant; he lived in his own world. He would come home and expect to be served hand on foot. My mother would wait on him but she was always angry about it. I never took marriage for granted.

After getting her high school diploma, Ruíz found odd jobs in all the predictable places: as a counter clerk in a dress shop, as a cashier in a fast food establishment, and as a waitress in two restaurants. When she was 20, she met Miguel—Mike as he was known outside the barrio. He was a consummate survivor, having worked in the construction field, as a truck driver, and even as an ESL (English as a Second Language) instructor. Despite her misgivings about marriage, she was struck by his penchant for adventure:

> He was different from the men in my family. He loved fun and was said to have had many women. He was a challenge. We were married when I was twenty-one and he twenty-five. For a while I kept my job but when I became pregnant, Miguel didn't want me to work anymore. Two more children followed and then, little by little, Miguel became abusive. He wanted to have total authority over me and the children. He said a man should know how to take care of a family and get respect, but it was hard to take him seriously when he kept changing jobs and when the money he brought home was barely enough to keep ends together.

After the birth of her third child, Ruíz started work at Shirley's, a women's wear factory in the area. Her husband was opposed to the idea. For her, work outside the home was an evident need prompted by financial stress. At first, it was also a means to escape growing disillusion:

> I saw myself turning into my mother and I started thinking that to be free of men was best for women. Maybe if Miguel had had a better job, maybe if he had kept the one he had, things would have been different. . . . We started drifting apart.

Tension at home mounted over the following months. Ruíz had worked at Shirley's for almost a year when one late afternoon, after collecting the three children from her parents' house, she returned to an empty home. She knew, as soon as she stepped inside, that something was amiss. In muted shock she confirmed the obvious: her husband had left, taking with him all personal possessions; even the wedding picture in the living room had been removed. No explanations had been left behind. Ruíz was then 28 years of age, alone, and the mother of three small children.

Under these circumstances, employment became even more desirable, but the difficulty of reconciling home responsibilities with wage work persisted. Ruíz was well regarded at Shirley's, and her condition struck a sympathetic chord among the other factory women. In a casual conversation, her supervisor described how other women were leasing industrial sewing machines from the local Singer distributor and were doing piecework at home. By combining factory work and home assembly, she could earn more money without further neglecting the children. Mr. Driscoll, Shirley's owner and general manager, made regular use of homeworkers, most of whom were former employees. That had allowed him to retain a stable core of about twenty factory seamstresses and to depend on approximately ten homeworkers during peak seasons.

Between 1979, the year of her desertion, and 1985, when we met her, Ruíz had struggled hard, working most of the time and making some progress. Her combined earnings before taxes fluctuated between $950 and $1,150 a month. Almost half of her income went to rent for the two-bedroom apartment which she shared with the children. She was in debt and used to working at least twelve hours a day. On the other hand, she had bought a double-needle sewing machine and was thinking of leasing another one to share additional sewing with a neighbor. She had high hopes: "Maybe some day I'll have my own business; I'll be a liberated woman. . . . I won't have to take orders from a man. Maybe Miguel did me a favor when he left after all. . . ."

With understandable variations, Ruíz's life history is shared by many garment workers in southern California. Three aspects are salient in this experience. First, marriage and a stable family life are perceived as desirable objectives which are, nonetheless, fraught with ambivalent feelings and burdensome responsibilities.

Second, tensions surrounding the domestic sphere entail a contradiction between the intent to fulfill sexual roles defined according to a shared ideology and the absence of the economic base necessary for their implementation. The very definition of manhood includes the right to hold authority and power over wives and children, as well as the responsibility of providing adequately for them. Frustrations derived from the impossibility of implementing those goals are felt equally by men and women but expressed differently by each. Bent on restoring their power, men attempt to control women in abusive ways. Women often resist their husbands' arbitrary or unrealistic impositions. Both manifestations are imminently political phenomena.

Third, personal conflict regarding the proper behavior of men and women is related to the construction of alternative ideological universes and the redefinition of sexual roles. Women may seek personal emancipation, driven partly by economic need and partly by dissatisfaction with men's performance as providers. At the level of the household, economic and political conflict is experienced as the clash between personal inadequacies while broader structural factors remain obscure.

The absence of economic underpinnings for the implementation of patriarchal standards may bring about more equitable exchanges between men and women, as well as a feminist consciousness fostering individual well-being and personal autonomy. However, in the case at hand, such ideals remain elusive. Mexican garment workers, especially those who are heads of households, face great disadvantages in the labor market. They are targeted as a preferred labor force for jobs that offer the lowest wages paid to industrial workers in the United States; they also have among the lowest unionization rates in the country. Ironically, household atomization, partly caused by proletarianization and the ensuing breakdown of patriarchal norms, has not been followed by the elimination of similar patriarchal standards in the labor market.

Experiences like the ones related above can be found among Cuban and Central American women in Miami. However, a larger proportion have had a different trajectory. Elvira Gómez's life in the United States is a case in point. She was 34 years old when she arrived in Miami with her four children aged 3 to 12. The year was 1961.

Leaving Havana was the most painful thing that ever happened to us. We loved our country. We would have never left willingly. Cuba was not like Mexico: we didn't have immigrants in large numbers. But Castro betrayed us and we had to join the exodus. We became exiles. My husband left Cuba three months before I did and there were moments when I doubted I would ever see him again. Then, after we got together, we realized we would have to forge ahead without looking back.

We lost everything. Even my mother's china had to be left behind. We arrived in this country as they say, "covering our nakedness with our bare hands." My husband had had a good position in a bank. To think that he would have to take any old job in Miami was more than I could take; a man of his stature having to beg for a job in a hotel or in a factory? It wasn't right!

Gómez had worked briefly before her marriage as a secretary. As a middle-class wife and mother she was used to hiring at least one maid. Coming to the United States changed all that:

Something had to be done to keep the family together. So I looked around and finally found a job in a shirt factory in Hialeah. Manolo [her husband] joined a childhood friend and got a loan to start an export-import business. All the time they were building the firm, I was sewing. There were times when we wouldn't have been able to pay the bills without the money I brought in.

Gómez's experience was shared by thousands of women in Miami. Among the first waves of Cuban refugees there were many who worked tirelessly to raise the standards of living of their families to the same levels or higher than those they had been familiar with in Cuba. The consolidation of an ethnic enclave allowed many Cuban men to become entrepreneurs. While their wives found unskilled and semiskilled jobs, they became businessmen. Eventually, they purchased homes, put their children through school, and achieved comfort. At that point, many Cuban men pressed their wives to stop working outside the home; they had only allowed them to have a job, in the first place, out of economic necessity. In the words of a prominent manufacturer in the area:

You have to understand that Cuban workers were willing to do anything to survive. When they became prosperous, the women saw the advantage of staying at home and still earn additional income. Because they had the skill, owners couldn't take them for granted. Eventually, owners couldn't get operators anymore. The most skilled would tell a manager "my husband doesn't let me work out of the home." This was a worker's initiative based on the values of the culture. I would put ads in the paper and forty people would call and everyone would say "I only do homework." That's how we got this problem of the labor shortages. The industry was dying; we wouldn't have survived without the arrival of the Haitians and the Central Americans.

This discussion shows that decisions made at the level of the household can remove workers highly desired by employers from the marketplace, thus endangering certain types of production. In those cases, loyalty to familial values can mitigate against the interests of capitalist firms. Interviews with Cuban women involved in homework confirm the general accuracy of this interpretation. After leaving factory employment, many put their experience to good use by becoming subcontractors and employing neighbors or friends. They also transformed so-called Florida rooms (the covered porches in their houses) into sewing shops. It was in one of them that Elvira Gómez was first interviewed. In her case, working outside the home was justified only as a way to maintain the integrity of her family and as a means to support her husband's early incursions into the business world:

For long years I worked in the factory but when things got better financially, Manolo asked me to quit the job. He felt bad that I couldn't be at home all the time with the children. But it had to be done. There's no reason for women not to earn a living when it's necessary; they should have as many opportunities and responsibilities as men. But I also tell my daughters that the strength of a family rests on the intelligence and work of women. It is foolish to give up your place as a mother and a wife only to go take orders from men who aren't even part of your family. What's so liberated about that? It is better to see your husband succeed and to know you have supported one another.

As in our earlier example, several points are worth noting in the experience of Cuban garment workers. Perhaps the most obvious is the unambiguous acceptance of patriarchal mores as a legitimate guideline for men's and women's behavior. Exile did not eliminate these values; rather, it extended them in surprising ways. The high labor force participation rates of Cuban women in the United States have been mentioned before. However, it should be remembered at this time that prior to their migration only a small number of Cuban women had worked outside the home for any length of time. It was the need to maintain the integrity of their families and to achieve class-related ambitions that precipitated their entrance into the labor force of a foreign country.

In their descriptions of experience in exile, Cuban women often make clear that part of the motivation in their search for jobs was the preservation of known definitions of manhood and womanhood. Women worked in the name of dedication to their husbands and children and in order to preserve the status and authority of the former. Husbands gave them "permission" to work outside the home, only as a result of necessity and temporary economic strife. In the same vein, it was a ritual yielding to masculine privilege that led women to abandon factory employment. Conversely, men "felt bad" that their wives had to work for a wage and welcomed the opportunity to remove them from the marketplace when economic conditions improved.

As with Mexican women in southern California, Cuban women in Miami earned low wages in low and semiskilled jobs. They, too, worked in environments devoid of the benefits derived from unionization. Nevertheless, the outcome of their experience as well as their perceptions are markedly different. Many Cuban women interpret their subordination at home as part of a viable option ensuring economic and emotional benefits. As a result, they are bewildered by feminist goals of equality and fulfillment in the job market. Yet, the same women have the highest rates of participation in the U.S. labor force.

Conclusion

Our purpose in this chapter has been to investigate some dimensions of political action which influence the bargaining capacity of women within their households and in the larger wage economy. What are the lessons derived from this inquiry? Several issues for further consideration and research emerge from our comparison of Cuban and Mexican women's experiences in the garment industry.

First, data regarding Mexicans in southern California and Cubans in southern Florida point in two different directions: In the first case, proletarianization is related to a high number of female-headed households and households where the earnings provided by women are indispensable for maintaining standards of modest subsistence. In the second case, women's employment was a strategy for coping with the receiving environment and raising standards of living. These contrasting experiences involving the relationship between households and labor markets occurred despite shared values regarding the family among Mexicans and Cubans. While both groups share similar mores regarding the roles of men and women, their actual experiences have differed significantly.

Second, the unique and contradictory position that women have had over time forces us to shift the emphasis of political analysis beyond the public world into the household. It is within households that the pressures of gender, class, and ethnicity give rise to political options and

limitations. Negotiation, conflict, compromise, and resolution characterize the daily lives of women. To denude these phenomena of political
meaning can only be the effect of androcentric theories spun equally, at
times, by Marxists and non-Marxists. To include these minute but
significant events in the study of "the political" furthers our understanding of the participation of various groups of people in decision-
making processes, the sharing of power, and the distribution of
resources.

Third, our comparison of Mexican and Cuban experiences also shows
that the meaning of women's participation in the labor force remains
plagued by paradox. On the one hand, paid employment expands the
potential for greater personal autonomy and financial independence.
This should have a favorable impact upon women's capacity to negotiate
an equitable position within their homes and in the labor market. On the
other hand, women's search for paid employment is frequently the consequence of severe economic need; it expresses vulnerability rather than
strength within the home and in the marketplace. Under certain conditions, women's entry into the labor force also parallels the collapse of
reciprocal exchanges between men and women. Conversely, the "partnership for survival" illustrated by Elvira Gómez's perceptions of her
own life is not predicated on the existence of a just social world, but it is
made acceptable by an ideological universe entailing different benefits and obligations for the two sexes and shared equally by men and
women.

Fourth, our comparison underscores the impact of class on gender.
Definitions of manhood and womanhood are implicated in the very
process of class formation. At the same time, the norms of reciprocity
sanctioned by patriarchal ideologies can operate as a form of social adhe-
sive consolidating class membership. For poor men and women, the
issue is not so much the presence of the sexual division of labor or the
persistence of patriarchal ideologies but the difficulties of upholding
either.

Ultimately, our inquiry is about the factors—imperfect as they may
be—that empower or debilitate men and women and about the definition of a pact for collective survival. This is a central political question;
it is also a key feminist issue.

Notes

1. This chapter is based on the research project entitled "A Collaborative Study
   of Hispanic Women in Garment and Electronics Industries." Data collection

took place in the New York Metropolitan Area and in southern California between 1983 and 1986. Preliminary research took place in Miami-Dade County, Florida, during the winters of 1985 and 1986. Funds for research in southern California were provided by the Ford and Tinker foundations.

2. Relevant definitions and treatments of these terms are contained in the following writings: on gender—Kelly (1984); Benería and Roldán (1987); Scott (1986); on class—Aminzade (1981); Burawoy (1985); Przeworski (1980); Evans, Skocpol, and Rueschemeyer (1985); Wright (1985); on ethnicity—Bach (1986); Nelson and Tienda (1985); Portes and Bach (1985).

3. See, for example, Rowbotham (1980); and Fraser (1984).

4. See references in Jaggar (1983).

5. Hartmann (1976). For an elaboration and revision of the same framework, see Hartmann (1981).

6. Beechey (1979b); and Kessler-Harris (1975a).

7. The classic reading on this subject is still Zaretsky (1976).

8. Katznelson (1985).

9. Borjas and Tienda (1985).

10. See U.S. Bureau of the Census (1980); and Fernández-Kelly and García (1989).

11. Figures abstracted from the U.S. Bureau of the Census (1980) and the Census of Manufacturers.

12. Taylor (1980).

13. Taylor (1980).

14. Commission on California State Government, Organization and Economy (1985).

15. Portes and Bach (1985), p. 67.

16. Portes (1987).

17. Portes and Bach (1985), p. 135.

PART **III**

Electoral Politics

In 1920 the Nineteenth Amendment to the U.S. Constitution granted women the suffrage in all constituencies. The great women's social movement demobilized, and energies moved in two directions: (1) continued action through voluntary associations, some more formalized as pressure groups; and (2) electoral politics. Nancy F. Cott introduces these alternatives, which are expanded on by other authors in this part and in Part IV. Here distinctive and converging patterns of women's electoral participation are examined among black and white women; their opportunities to become members of party elites and the attitudes of those who do are analyzed; and the varying attitudes of women as voters and citizens are explored.

Cott argues for a continuity in women's political behavior in the period before *and* after 1920, focusing on their involvement in voluntary associations. Mass women's (or primarily women's) organizations such as the Parent-Teacher Association, patriotic societies, and religious groups and special interest organizations such as the Business and Professional Women's Clubs and the American Association of University Women flourished. Women's voluntarism became ever richer and articulated in more complex ways. There had been strong disagreements about tactics and strategy among suffragists before the Nineteenth Amendment. These continued. Some groups—the National Woman's Party was foremost—wanted to continue political struggle around single issues. Other organized women—for example, those in the League of Women Voters—opposed this. It was myopic to have expected a "woman's bloc" to emerge after suffrage was granted, given the class,

151

ethnic, race, regional, and ideological differences that separate women as well as men.

Women's electoral behavior and participation in the major parties in the decade following the passage of suffrage are examined by Kristi Andersen. She finds that a political socialization perspective which posits voting as a behavior to be learned offers only a first-order explanation. Women's registration as voters and election turnout increased regularly over the decade. To explain the patterns of variation observed, Andersen uses a core-periphery perspective. Although party politics was still a masculine sport at the end of the decade, attitudes opposing women's voting and involvement in partisan politics were fading among younger women.

The political participation of black women in the same decade is the focus of the chapter by Evelyn Brooks Higginbotham. She places these women in the context of black migration to the North and of black loyalty to the Republican party of Lincoln and emancipation. Black women were in politics to stay, but by the Hoover administration a move away from the Republican party was evident; that switch culminated in the 1930s, when black political activists joined the New Deal coalition.

M. Kent Jennings brings women's participation in party politics up to the 1980s. By 1984 the number of women delegates to the national nominating conventions had tripled for the Republicans and quadrupled for the Democrats from that in the 1948–1968 period. In 1984 women in both parties were still of lower status than men, and particularly less likely to be lawyers—a key advantage in being elected to state and national legislatures. Over time, Democratic women have cut the educational gender gap more than have Republicans. The voluntary organization membership profiles of male and female delegates have converged. Opinion differences between men and women delegates are greatest over the use of military force and women's issues. Women also feel that men are slow to open doors to women in politics.

David O. Sears and Leonie Huddy find remarkable gender similarity in the national electorate. Men and women hold similar political beliefs and policy preferences and equally support female candidates. Women are not a unified interest group. Like men, they are split by political ideology and party identification. These divisions in turn influence their evaluations of candidates and policy choices. The sharpest polarization Sears and Huddy find among women in the 1980s is the longstanding ideological cleavage over gender equality. Younger, well-educated, working, and high-income women support equality more than do other women. They argue that these differences among women are better explained by a symbolic politics model than by interest-based theories.

7

Across the Great Divide: Women in Politics Before and After 1920

Nancy F. Cott

The Nineteenth Amendment is the most obvious benchmark in the history of women in politics in the United States, but it is a problematic one for the viewer who intends to include more than electoral events in the category of politics. Concentrating on suffrage and the electoral arena means viewing women's politics through the conventional lens where male behavior sets the norm. Besides, there is real question whether women's political influence before and after the national achievement of woman suffrage can be compared if politics is restricted to the electoral arena. Against what kind of earlier evidence should one assess the facts that a tiny but increasing number of women gained elective and appointive local and state offices after 1920, that only a handful of women were elected as representatives to the Congress and none as U.S. senators or state governors (unless as widows of male officeholders), and that women obtained nominal parity in the national party structures only to gain no significant power? By what measure are these facts to be compared with the political gains or losses of the prior generation?[1]

1920 as a Dividing Line

The 1920 marker has been crucial to historians' treatment of women in politics and has undergirded claims that organized feminism declined in the 1920s. Despite cautions from observers at the time that "all feminists are suffragists, but not all suffragists are feminists," the suffrage victory

153

in 1920 is seen as the height from which feminism broke down; the earlier suffrage movement is assumed to be the matrix of women's politics and also a proxy for feminism.[2] If historians thus take the Nineteenth Amendment as an absolute dividing point, and merge feminism with suffragism, women's political actions to 1920 will coincide with feminist progress—but efforts of the following decades are suspended in limbo, without anchor or form-giver.[3]

The composite portrayal of women's politics in the 1920s supplied by historians emphasizes the following points: After the achievement of the vote, the large coalition movement among women disintegrated; now insiders rather than outsiders, women (ironically) lost influence within the political process. Suffragists' predictions of transformation in politics through women's contributions were not realized. No longer operating from strong women-only voluntary organizations nor avidly showing their strength as unified voices, women were not as aggressive as men in pursuing political advantage in a still highly male-dominated system. Historians have often evaluated women's progress in politics after 1920 with reference to the realization of a "woman bloc," in tacit parallel to the woman suffrage coalition (although the woman suffrage movement was not a voting entity but a great voluntarist effort formed around a single issue). This portrayal generally holds out the possibility of a woman bloc and links its failure to the destructive controversy over the Equal Rights Amendment, which was first proposed in 1923 by the minority National Woman's Party and then vigorously opposed by most other women's organizations.[4]

In this chapter I intend to complicate this portrayal, by showing that some of its elements are false and that it all looks different when the marker of 1920 is suppressed to some extent and the history is seen as continuous and related to the larger political milieu. Neglecting the political watershed of 1920 would be obtuse, and cavalier, since not only was the sex barrier to the ballot eliminated but also the movement for the vote ended. Too great a focus on the achievement of the Nineteenth Amendment, however, obscures the similarities in women's political behavior before and after it and the relation of that behavior to broader political and social context.

The sense of women and men, young and old, that they were living in a New Era after 1920 emerged not only from the news of women voting but from the experiences of recent world-historical disruptions—the Great War, the Bolshevik Revolution, the postwar strike wave and Red Scare in the United States, aborted revolutions in Europe, and widespread desolation, hunger, and epidemics. (As the poet Genevieve Taggard summarized drily, it had "something to do with a war and a revolution and five or six famines.'') Contemporaneous with the culmination of the woman suffrage campaign, other domestic political changes also took place. Historians' views of early twentieth century politics have become increasingly complicated, now more often ascribing internally contradictory aims and accomplishments to Progressive reform than unified intent. Claims that the ship of reform was dashed on the rocks of war have shifted toward findings of continuity (especially in organizational and associational structures and scale) between the 1910s and the 1920s. Although the ethos of the New Era in political outlook as well as social life is acknowledged to be distinct from the prewar years, that difference may be attributed to the fruition of scientific management and social engineering trends as much as to the rejection of Progressive idealism.[5]

Likewise, there were striking continuities in women's political choices and actions on both sides of 1920. Not only electoral politics followed women's gain of the ballot. Although it may be impossible to measure the comparative influence women as a group had in politics before and after the Nineteenth Amendment (and the lack of comparability should be openly acknowledged), it is possible to consider more carefully suffragists' promises and their results. Other elements in the usual portrayal need to be reassessed. Women's voting must be put in the context of men's voting—that is, in the context of popular political participation in the period. Perhaps most important, the organizational and political roles of women's voluntary associations—which, far from declining, multiplied in membership—must be considered within politics rather than outside politics. The problematic fiction of the woman's bloc looks different when these issues are taken into account.

The Suffrage Coalition a "Woman's Bloc"?

Although the campaign for suffrage is usually presented as a unity in contrast to the disunity of the 1920s, there is reason to see disunity among politically active women as typical of both the 1910s and 1920s. For instance, suffragists were opposed by female antisuffragists; white suffragists raised racial bars to blacks. In other matters great and small, from the conflicts between clubwomen and entertainers over the status and standards of dance halls to stand-offs between pacifists and preparedness advocates during the Great War, there were strategic, ideological, class-based, and race-based differences among groups of women that were acted out in the public arena before as well as after 1920. From 1869 on, within the suffrage movement itself there were successive deep divisions over strategy and method. Intense internal conflicts over leadership, finances, and tactics so racked the National American Woman Suffrage Association (NAWSA) in 1911 that long-time suffragist Reverend Olympia Brown called her colleagues' "shallow false talk of love excellence harmony &c &c . . . so false that it makes me vomit."[6] The bitter split between NAWSA and the Congressional Union–National Woman's Party leaderships beginning in 1913 was the latest but not the only such cleavage.

The way that suffragists built coalitions during the 1910s acknowledged that women had variant and perhaps clashing loyalties. Suffrage leaders purposely addressed defined groups (mothers, wage-earners, black women, white women, professionals) with specifically designed instrumental appeals, tacitly acknowledging that not all women shared the same definition of self-interest. Even nonvoting women took on partisan affiliations that mattered: In the final years of the suffrage campaign Maud Wood Park, head of congressional lobbying for NAWSA, was so aware of Republican and Democratic partisan loyalties clashing within her own congressional committee that she preferred to meet with its members individually. The women were so "inclined to be suspicious" of one another that full meetings of the committee were unproductive. Although distressed by the division, Park took it for granted that "party women could not be expected to free themselves from the prevailing currents of thought."[7]

Even when maintaining that women would exercise civic duties differently from men, suffragists rarely if ever portrayed a future voting "bloc" of women. (Because of the nature of their campaign, of course, they had experience marshaling not women's but men's votes.) It is striking that the one time that a small minority of suffragists *did* attempt to marshal women's votes into a voting bloc, they were condemned by the majority of their colleagues. In 1914 and 1916 the suffragist group the Congressional Union (CU), predecessor of the National Woman's Party, campaigned among enfranchised women of the western states to defeat all Democrats. They intended to "punish the party in power" in Washington for failure to adopt a constitutional amendment for woman suffrage. Their effort to make women's power at the polls count on a single issue inspired horrified rejection from mainstream suffragist leaders and little agreement from women voters. Alice Paul, architect of the CU's plan, had a definite conception of how a single-issue feminist bloc—not a generalized "woman bloc"—could operate in a two-party system to swing the balance: "To count in an election you do not have to be the biggest Party; you have to be simply an independent Party that will stand for one object and that cannot be diverted from that object."[8]

Very likely the CU strategy failed to evoke support from the bulk of suffragists not only because of its approach but because of its object—to unseat all Democrats, whether they as individuals supported woman suffrage or not. There was the thorn on the rose of any such proposal: a woman's bloc, to hold, had to make a single issue its clear priority, while candidates' positions on so-called women's issues would not stand alone but would combine with their positions on other questions that concerned women. NAWSA's judgment that the CU was misguided gave more evidence that women had differing priorities and tactics; perceiving that division, suffragists were unlikely to imagine women voting as one. When the National Woman's Party moved on to militant demonstrations, which NAWSA also deplored, Maud Wood Park found nothing more exasperating than having to answer congressmen's questions: " 'Why don't you women get together? You can't expect us to vote for you if you can't agree among yourselves.' " She pointed out as "mildly" as possible "that men, even within the same party, were not without their differences. But sauce for the gander was rarely accepted as sauce for the goose." Lest we assume that suffragists were too naive to recognize the coalition nature of their association, they remind us, as Harriot Stanton Blatch (daughter of Elizabeth Cady Stanton) reminded a colleague in 1918, "altho all sorts and conditions of women were united for suffrage . . . they are not at one in their attitude towards other questions in life."[9]

Suffragists spoke of issues—safeguarding children's health, eliminating political corruption, ending the liquor traffic, improving the economic leverage of women wage-earners—but rarely addressed exactly how or for whom women's votes would be collected, whether electing women to office was a high priority, or whether women's votes were adjuncts or substitutes for the established practice of lobbying and educational work by women's voluntary associations. As much as suffragists talked about women's inclinations, duties, and contributions, they rarely specified by what means, exactly, the injection of women's votes into the polity was to bring about change. Suffragists usually made very general or else modest claims and (interestingly) rarely touched on the subject of women in political office. True, there were some overarching retorts, such as Anna Howard Shaw's to an antisuffragist who objected that voting women would have little time for charity, "Thank God, there will not be so much need of charity and philanthropy!" There was rhetoric—equally vague—regarding women's inclination against war, such as the CU's claim that "a government responsible to all women, as well as all men, will be less likely to go to war, without real necessity." There were particular anticipations of women's efficacy, such as Florence Kelley's that "the enfranchisement of women is indispensable to the solution of the child labor problem." Typically, however, suffragists' proposals and predictions in the 1910s were locally relevant. It was claimed at the New York Woman Suffrage party's 1910 convention, for instance, that women's votes would help to alleviate the evils of inadequate inspection of milk, high prices, overcrowded classrooms, crime, prostitution, and child labor; the ballot would enable women to preside as associate justices in children's court and women's night court. During the 1915 New York campaign, Carrie Chapman Catt even warned suffragist speakers against promising "what women will do with the vote."[10]

The idea that women's votes would line up in one direction certainly existed in an implicit imprecise form, in the views of both suffragists *and* their opponents. As prospective voters, women were often expected to punish candidates who did not show deference to women's organizations' aims and to embrace those who supported Prohibition and social legislation. There was some evidence in the 1910s (mainly from Scandinavia) that women were "conservative" voters and some claims (from New York City) that women swelled the "radical" vote. When Washington, Oregon, and Arizona each adopted Prohibition shortly after adopting woman suffrage, women's votes were presumed to have turned the tide. Since the western states which enfranchised women early did not have extensive industries employing women and children, they gave little evidence whether women's ballots would decisively protect such vulnerable wage-earners. Shortly after New York women got the right to vote, however, four state legislators who had opposed minimum-wage legislation for women, child-labor laws, and other social legislation were unseated. Two of the four were replaced with assembly*women*. In Columbus, Ohio, in 1919, after women received municipal suffrage, their organizing and voter-registration work through voluntary associations succeeded in dumping the city boss who had been mayor for sixteen years, despite his organization's labeling them a "shrieking sisterhood." However, most big-city machine politicians had dropped objections to woman suffrage by the late 1910s after observing and reasoning that enfranchised women had *not* shown a habit of voting together to oppose existing political organizations. Claims about the impact of women's votes were so speculative and contradictory by 1919, in fact, that social scientists William Ogburn and Inez Goltra, after studying "how women vote," could conclude only that there might be some significant sex differences *or* that "the enfranchisement of women will have no other effect than approximately to double the number of votes previously cast." With more evidence, a 1923 study drew the similarly ambivalent conclusion that women neither "merely vote the same as men" nor vote "with marked independence."[11]

Voter Turnout During the 1920s

The unspoken notion that adding women to the electorate should transform politics did prompt some suffragists' disappointment in the 1920s, but they were not the only ones looking dourly at the scene. Both popular journalists and political scientists expressed a mood of skepticism, if not downright cynicism, about mass political participation. Social scientists stressed the irrational motivations driving individual political behavior, the inability of the mass public to make objective judgments in popular government, and the likelihood that politicians would manipulate these failings.[12] Observers' discouragement about democratic participation found corroboration in the deepening decline in voter participation, a trend continuous from 1896 and intensifying from the 1910s to the 1920s. Mean national turnout in the presidential election years 1920, 1924, and 1928 was just over half of the eligible electorate compared with an average of almost four fifths in the late nineteenth century. In the off-year elections between 1922 and 1930, little more than one third of the electorate voted, whereas nearly two thirds, on the average, had voted in the off-years between 1876 and 1896.[13]

The meaning of the decline in voter turnout is not absolutely clear, in great part because the meaning of Progressive reform—that is, whether its intents and/or effects were democratic or elitist—is not absolutely clear. In light of such reforms as direct election of senators, direct primaries, the initiative, referendum, and recall, it seems ironic, even tragic, that the Progressive era should have ushered in the decade of the lowest voter participation ever. But if Progressive reforms intended to keep the reins of the state in the hands of the expert or the economically powerful few—as some "reforms" more than others indicate—then the decline in voter turnout fulfilled rather than undid that aim. Voting reforms included the continuing disfranchisement of blacks and Populist or Republican whites in the South by means of poll taxes, literacy tests, and other bars to registration and balloting; more complicated and rigorous residency and registration requirements in northern states which limited immigrant voting; and, at the municipal level, replacement of district voting with at-large elections, which predestined minority interest-group candidates to fail.

While Progressive reformers embraced the salutary aim to eliminate corrupt influence-peddling and substitute neutral and informed standards, their emphasis on expert presence and management in the state also diverted control away from the populace to an elite of professional and business-managerial experts. The results could be seen institutionalized in the 1920s in various forms, from city-manager rule in municipalities, to federal and state commissions, to such quasi-governmental institutions as the National Bureau of Economic Research. "It is a misfortune for the woman's movement," mordantly commented Suzanne La Follette, a feminist and pacifist of antistatist inclination, in 1926, "that it has succeeded in securing political rights for women at the very period when political rights are worth less than they have been at any time since the eighteenth century." The most persuasive explanations of downsliding voter turnout from 1896 to the 1920s also have to do with the entrenchment of the Democratic party's hold on the South and the Republican party's domination of the North and West (and thus of the national government) to the extent that the interest of voters in partisan contest, and voter sense of efficacy, collapsed. The portrait of increasingly dispirited voters does not account for the vigor of third parties during the period, but it does account for the overall trend.[14]

Analyses in the 1920s pinned much of the blame for the contemporary drop in voter turnout on newly eligible women. Just before the presidential election in 1924, journalists and political scientists turned the spotlight on the "failure" of women to flock to the polls, although dependable data on voting behavior were very scarce.[15] Votes were not counted by sex except in the state of Illinois. In the 1920 national elections, slightly less than half of the eligible women in Illinois cast a ballot, while three quarters of the eligible men did. Early discussions based on that evidence generalized only downward, on the reasoning that Illinois women were more likely than most to vote because they had had the ballot since 1913. Women's voting participation actually varied greatly from place to place, group to group, and issue to issue. Fewer women than men voted, but the difference in their voting behavior was not as stark as initial extrapolations from the Illinois data established. Analysis via regression techniques has now made it clear that the 1920s' low turnout was due not only to women's behavior but also to male voters' sinking interest. Hull-House leader Jane Addams was on the mark when she responded to a magazine's question in 1924, "Is woman suffrage failing?" that the question ought to be "Is suffrage failing?"[16] (See Andersen and Higginbotham, this volume.) As Addams noted, the context in which to look at women's voting behavior in the 1920s is that of declining voter participation overall.

The Voluntarist Mode ✍

A few vigorous female voices, such as that of former National Woman's Party leader Anne Martin of Nevada, urged women to enter the electoral arena in force and move directly to claim "woman's share, woman's *half* in man-controlled government."[17] The much more general trend—and one deplored by Martin as merely "indirect influence"—was women's reliance on voluntary associations rather than the electoral arena for political efficacy. Since the early nineteenth century, women had influenced what took place in electoral and legislative halls from outside, not only by seeking suffrage but by inquiring about a range of health, safety, moral, and welfare issues. They had built a tradition of exercising political influence (one admittedly hard to measure), which continued vigorously once the vote was gained. Women's organizations' lobbying route should be seen as pioneering in the modern mode of exerting political force—that is, interest-group politics. This voluntarist mode, with its use of lobbying to effect political influence, and the kinds of interests pursued (that is, health, safety, moral, and welfare issues), prevailed in women's political participation both before and after 1920.[18] (See Lebsock, this volume.)

From recent histories one might gain the impression that women's voluntary organizations waned after 1920, but nothing is further from the truth. In her 1933 history of women, author and former National Woman's Party suffragist Inez Haynes Irwin observed that women were, if anything, *over*organized in voluntary associations during the 1920s and 1930s. She closed her book with a staggering list, from professional to civic to patriotic to social welfare to charitable to ethnic and religious women's organizations.[19] Although historians often cite as evidence of decimation in activism the contrast between the 2 million women in the NAWSA in the 1910s and the tiny proportion of that membership—probably 5 percent—who joined in the NAWSA's successor group, the National League of Women Voters (LWV), the two figures are not really comparable. The two organizations differed widely in form and intent: The first was a federation which pursued one specific goal, made few demands on its local members, imposed no homogeneity upon affiliates, and used all volunteer labor; the subsequent organization stated many aims (including civic reform, citizenship education, international peace, and women's rights), made strenuous demands on its local members, attempted standardized national procedure, and employed professional staff.

Quickly evolving into a "good government" rather than a feminist organization, its premise being to ready women for political life, the

LWV found itself, ironically, competing with women's partisan activity as much as preparing women for it. When all women became fair game for party organizations, Republican and Democratic women's divisions vied with the nonpartisan league for the time and loyalty of women interested in politics. Some leading NAWSA suffragists went directly into party organizations instead of into the LWV. Lillian Feickert, for example, a prominent New Jersey suffragist who was named vice-chairman of the Republican state committee in 1920, built the New Jersey Republican Women's Club on the grass-roots model of the New Jersey Woman Suffrage Association. Feickert claimed that three quarters of the suffragists joined; by the spring of 1922 the club claimed 60,000 members. Women's divisions in state and national party committees should be seen, as logically as the LVW, as successor organizations to the NAWSA.[20]

More generally, where one large or vital pre-1920 women's organization declined or ended, more than one other arose to take its space, if not its exact task. While the General Federation of Women's Clubs seemed to decline in vigor (although not clearly in membership), the National Congress of Parents and Teachers Associations (PTA) rose into a mass membership whose local units took up efforts similar to those of many unnamed women's clubs of the earlier generation, working to establish playgrounds, libraries, and health clinics, as well as lobbying at the national level on issues from film standards to international peace. More than quintupling during the 1920s, the membership of the PTA reached over 1.5 million by 1931. Its color bar (in effect) led to the founding in 1926 of a National Colored Parent-Teacher Association, which had at least the cooperation of the older group.[21]

The two national organizations that had labored most avidly on be-half of wage-earning women in the pre–World War I era did show drastic reductions in membership and resources in the 1920s. These were the National Consumers' League (NCL)—not strictly but for the most part a women's group—and the National Women's Trade Union League (NWTUL). Although both had set out auspicious programs in 1919, neither gained members nor momentum; their experience was more like that of labor unions than of women's associations. Both the WTUL's and the NCL's efforts had informed public consciousness to the extent that unions themselves and agencies of government took up the concerns raised by those voluntary associations. As pressure from women's voluntary organizations was instrumental in making local public health and school departments assume some responsibilities for sanitation and for children's safety, and in inducing states to institute social-welfare and protective labor legislation and the federal government to establish pure food and drug laws, likewise it was pressure from the WTUL and NCL (and other's women's groups) that led to establishing the Women's Bureau in the U.S. Department of Labor. The Women's Bureau's mandate was to investigate the conditions and protect the interests of wage-earning women; it also took on the WTUL's aim to educate the public, and, in alliance with the WTUL, staunchly defended sex-based protective legislation.[22]

The WTUL's intention to raise the trade-union consciousness of industrially employed women as well as sweeten their lives through association was seized by industrial clubs formed by the Young Women's Christian Association (YWCA). In 1926 the YWCA stopped requiring that members be Protestant Christians, and membership grew; by 1930 the organization boasted over 600,000 members, 55,000 volunteer advisers, and a dispersed professional staff of almost 3,500. The YWCA industrial clubs educated and helped to organize both black and white women workers in southern textile mills and brought them to testify before legislatures about industrial conditions. These clubs also served as recruitment grounds for summer schools for women workers. The summer schools themselves, founded during the 1920s by labor reformers and academics, formed a sequel to the WTUL cross-class efforts earlier in the century.[23]

The YWCA was also instrumental in bringing together white-collar women workers. The founding in 1919 of the National Federation of Business and Professional Women's Clubs (NFBPW) resulted from a conference of businesswomen called by the YWCA during World War I. Lena Madesin Phillips, a Kentucky-born lawyer who was drafted from her wartime YWCA position to become the first executive secretary of the NFPBW, warmed to the subject of encouraging business and professional women's teamwork, courage, risk-taking, and self-reliance. The slogan that the federation used to develop hundreds of local educational fundraising efforts during the 1920s, "at least a high school education for every business girl," indicated its orientation toward ordinary white-collar workers. Lawyers, teachers, and independent entrepreneurs also formed an important part of its membership. The clubs affiliated with the federation (required to have three quarters of their members actively employed) numbered 1,100 by 1931, including about 56,000 individuals. Scores of new associations of women professionals were also founded between 1915 and 1930, as were two more federations of such clubs, called Zonta International and Quota International.[24]

The alliance with professionals—social workers, social researchers, college and university professors—so noticeably important in efforts on behalf of women workers and in the YWCA in the 1920s was also apparent in the birth control movement. In 1919 Margaret Sanger, leader in the American Birth Control League, left behind her former socialist politics, along with her purposeful law-breaking and agitation in working-class communities and her emphasis on women's control of their own bodies. Sanger thenceforward emphasized eugenic reasoning about better babies. The American Birth Control League organized and educated the public and lobbied for the legalization of birth control on the premise of allowing "doctors only" to provide information and methods. Women who saw the virtues of that approach and volunteered their time for birth control in the 1920s were mainly middle-class matrons, more socially and politically conservative than the birth control advocates of the 1910s, and also more numerous. The American Birth Control League claimed over 37,000 members in 1926, almost 90 percent female. Fewer women followed the approach of civil libertarian Mary Ware Dennett, founder of the Voluntary Parenthood League, which stood on First Amendment rights and aimed to decriminalize birth control by removing it from federal obscenity statutes.[25]

While major women's organizations founded earlier, such as the Woman's Christian Temperance Union (WCTU) or the National Woman's Party, persisted, a host of organizations that women could and did join in the 1920s were new ones, founded during or after World War I. The American Association of University Women (AAUW), whose members had to be graduates of accredited collegiate institutions, evolved from the Association of Collegiate Alumnae into a truly national operation in 1921 under the new name and a decade later had 36,818 members in 551 branches. Black collegiate alumnae, excluded by the spirit if not the letter of the AAUW, founded their own national association in 1924, not only to promote mutual benefit, educational standards, and scholarship among their own race, but also to work toward "better conditions of contact" between white and black college women. In 1932 it had eight branches and almost 300 members.[26]

Group consciousness among minority-group women was a major source of new organizations. Both Jewish women and Catholic women founded numerous voluntary associations during the 1920s and 1930s.[27] Black women continued the National Association of Colored Women (NACW), the organizational hub which had been central to black suffragist efforts and had linked black clubwomen in communities across the nation. Its umbrella covered between 150,000 and 200,000 members in forty-one states in the mid 1920s. Many of its leaders also pursued their aims of racial uplift through male-dominated black organizations, especially the National Association for the Advancement of Colored People (NAACP), the Urban League, and the Commission on Interracial

Cooperation. (See Higginbotham, this volume.) All through the decade, black women campaigned vigorously against lynching and for the federal antilynching bill languishing in the southern-dominated U.S. Senate—their numbers far beyond Ida B. Wells Barnett's lone crusade in an earlier generation. Despite (or, perhaps, because of) the way that the NACW had brought women into political activism, its numbers declined by the end of the decade to about 50,000. Civil rights and welfare organizations of men *and* women were conducting the kinds of activities that the NACW had begun, and they had more benefit of white financial support. Lacking resources, in 1930 the NACW cut its departments from thirty-eight to two: the home and women in industry. But five years later Mary McLeod Bethune, a former president of the NACW and long-time laborer in the black struggle for freedom, led the way in establishing a new national clearinghouse, the National Council of Negro Women. She was emphatic that neither organizations dominated by black men nor those by white women had given black women sufficient voice.[28]

Other new organizations that women joined in the 1920s were patriotic, security-minded societies formed in the wake of World War I, including the American War Mothers and the American Legion Auxiliary, which grew from an initial 131,000 to over 400,000 members after ten years. The American Legion Auxiliary often worked in concert with the longer-established Daughters of the American Revolution (DAR), which more than doubled in size between 1910 and 1932, reaching 2,463 chapters and almost 170,000 members by the latter date. During the 1920s and 1930s these women's organizations—loudly anticommunist and enthusiastic in red-baiting—advocated military preparedness.[29] They positioned themselves against women's peace organizations, for international peace was *the* major item of concern among organized women in the 1920s.

In an unprecedented tide of public concern, a range of peace groups from the conservative and nationalistic American Peace Society, through Protestant church agencies, to the left-wing pacifist War Resisters League formed during and after the war. In the 1920s they proposed competing alternatives, including the League of Nations, the World Court, international arbitration conferences, disarmament, and non-cooperation with the military. Women could follow a number of avenues instigated and dominated by men; they appeared in all the peace societies, but clustered in their own organizations. Two groups were founded in 1919: the Women's International League for Peace and Freedom (WILPF), whose U.S. section included such luminaries of social reform as Jane Addams, Lillian Wald, and Alice Hamilton, and the much smaller, more extremely nonresistant Women's Peace Society. The founding of the Women's Peace Union of the Western Hemisphere and the Women's Committee for World Disarmament followed in 1921. In addition, the major women's organizations—the LWV, the AAUW, the WCTU, the NFBPW, and the PTA—all put international peace prominently on their agendas. In 1925 Carrie Chapman Catt, the former general of NAWSA, assembled from the memberships of the major women's organizations with peace departments the National Committee on the Cause and Cure of War (NCCCW). That collectivity met annually for many years and formed a basis for peace lobbying; it claimed a cumulative membership of over 5 million at the start and 8 million—or one out of five adult women in the United States—by the 1930s.[30]

The level of organization among American women after 1920 thus appears to compare very favorably with that before, even considering that voluntary memberships would have to increase by slightly more than a fifth to keep up with the growth in the adult female population. The number of women in organizations is compelling although memberships in the various organizations could and often did overlap, as had been no less true of the prewar generation. Repeated foundings and aggregate memberships make it clear that women were still joining women's organizations, as they had for generations. By their very constitution of specialized memberships (professional women, religious women, mothers, women of a particular political bent) and purposes (birth control, education, antilynching, peace, and so on), such organizations were as likely to sustain or even to rigidify the differentiations and diversities among women according to racial, ethnic, class, and political grounds, however, as to make women feel a common cause. The more purposive and specialized a women's organization, the more likely it was to be instrumentally allied with professional expertise and involved with the bureaucratic machinery of institutions, commissions, and conferences that developed rapidly in and outside government during the 1920s. It was also more likely to be working in concert with male-dominated organizations pursuing similar purposes. While these were women's organizations, they were not purporting to emanate from or to operate in a separate sphere, as had many of their forebears in the nineteenth century. Consequently, there was an omnipresent potential for the groups working on issues not peculiar to women—peace, for example—to self-destruct by routing their members toward male-dominated organizations that had more funds and thus seemed more effective (as happened with the NACW).

Carrying on the voluntarist legacy of prewar women's groups distinguished by their lack of the ballot, women's organizations in the 1920s and 1930s had the benefit of the new ethos that women were citizens who could and should participate in the public realm. These organizations benefited from the much increased rate of high school and college education among women and the lower birth rate, which together meant that there were many more women knowledgeable about social issues and not entirely occupied with childcare. At the same time, three quarters of all adult women were not gainfully employed. These factors created the pool of enfranchised women who peopled voluntary associations in the era between the two world wars, very probably the highest proportion of women engaged in volunteer associational activity in the whole history of American women.

Not all women's organizations entered politics, but most of the national organizations did. They adopted the mode of pressure politics— forwarding public education and lobbying for specific bills as they had during the suffrage campaign, rather than running their own candidates. Named the first president of the LWV, Maud Wood Park took the lead in 1920 in forming among ten women's organizations a Capitol Hill lobbying clearinghouse, the Women's Joint Congressional Committee (WJCC). The National League of Women Voters, the General Federation of Women's Clubs, the Woman's Christian Temperance Union, the National Congress of Parents and Teachers Associations, and the National Federation of Business and Professional Women's Clubs were all charter members. The WJCC promised to establish a lobbying committee on behalf of any item that at least five of its constituent members wished to forward; and it immediately started working on two different attempts, one for federal funds for maternity and infancy health protection (realized in 1921 in the Sheppard-Towner Act) and the other for removal of citizenship discrimination against American women who married aliens (partially realized in the Cable Act of 1922).

Describing the WJCC in 1924, by which time it included twenty-one organizations, Mary Anderson, director of the U.S. Women's Bureau, asserted with pride that "American women are organized, highly organized, and by the millions. They are organized to carry out programs of social and political action." She called the WJCC the "cooperative mouthpiece" of American women, conveying its members' opinions to Washington and bringing back to them news of legislators' doings. Women's organizations operated from motives and resources different from those of men's chambers of commerce, fraternal organizations, manufacturers' associations, and so on, in Anderson's view. Where men's pressure groups relied on economic power in politics and looked for commercial or financial advantage or professional gain, women's organizations were working without self-interest, for the public good, for social welfare, on largely volunteer talent, relying on their influence on public opinion and "upon their voting strength for their success."[31] Anderson's commentary highlighted how far certain women leaders persisted in assumptions formed before suffrage about women citizens' salutary disinterestedness. It also, unintentionally, explained why women's organizations (lobby as they might, and did) commanded only a weak position. Women could marshal only votes (in an era of widespread voter resignation) and public opinion. Men had the economic clout.

Voluntarist Diversity and Conflict

The considerable unity of method among women's organizations contrasted with the diversity—often acrimony—among their specific goals. (See Schlozman, this volume.) Although women formed groups of probably greater number and variety in the 1920s than they had ever before, it did not necessarily mean that they could work together nor could any particular group claim—without being countered—to speak politically for women. Differences among women's groups were at least as characteristic as their techniques of pressure politics. The controversy over the Equal Rights Amendment in the 1920s is well known: When the National Woman's Party had introduced into Congress in December 1923 an amendment to the U.S. Constitution reading "Men and women shall have equal rights throughout the United States and every place subject to its jurisdiction," it was immediately—and for decades after— opposed by the LWV and most other major women's organizations.[32] What is not so well recognized are the other equally important divisions among politically active women and the fact that these divisions were multiple and could cross-cut. Partisan loyalty has been wrongly slighted in historians' assessments of women's political behavior in the 1920s; partisan women not only conflicted across parties but also, importantly, with women who wanted to organize nonpartisan alliances.[33]

On the peace issue—where at first glance women seemed most wholeheartedly united—women's groups that urged disarmament were opposed by patriotic women's organizations that boosted military preparedness. To counter the antimilitarist impact that WILPF was making, the DAR and allied groups in 1924 formed a National Patriotic Council. When WILPF speakers testified in Congress in 1928 against the naval building program, for instance, members of the DAR and the Dames of the Loyal Legion were also present, and Mrs. Noble Newport Potts, president of the National Patriotic Council, outspokenly warned the House Naval Affairs Committee chairman about Dorothy Detzer, executive secretary of the WILPF, "That's a dangerous woman you've been talking to!" In that particular instance WILPF and other antimilitarists had the desired effect, and the 1928 cruiser bill did not pass. The House Committee, deluged by adverse mail, cut the authorization from seventy-one to sixteen vessels. Nonetheless, confidence that antimilitarism was "women's" stance was shattered. The impact that women activists made on one side or another of the pacifism/militarism question proved, ironically, the absence rather than the substance of gender solidarity. Right-wing women's confrontation and red-baiting of women pacifists and antimilitarists also led Carrie Chapman Catt, who intended to be moderate and mainstream, to leave out the WILPF and the Women's Peace Union when she organized the NCCCW. Regardless, ultra-patriotic women's organizations tarred Catt with the same brush that they used on the pacifists.[34]

On Prohibition—generally presumed in the 1910s to command women's support—the late 1920s revealed another crevasse. Pauline Morton Sabin recalled being motivated to found the Women's Organization for National Prohibition Reform (WONPR) when she heard Ella Boole, president of the WCTU, announce to the Congress, "I represent the women of America!" Sabin felt, "Well, lady, here's one woman you don't represent." A New Yorker born to wealth and elite social position, Sabin was president of the Women's National Republican Club, an active Republican fundraiser, and director of eastern women's activities for the Coolidge and Hoover presidential campaigns. Sabin first brought together women of her own class and acquaintance, but after she launched her organization formally in Chicago in 1929 with a national advisory council of 125 women from twenty-six states, it gathered much broader middle-class membership. Its numbers grew to 300,000 by mid 1931 and doubled that a year later, vastly exceeding the membership of the longer-established men's Association Against the Prohibition Amendment and surpassing the membership claimed by the WCTU. The WONPR actively challenged the stereotype that women supported Prohibition. For instance, it disputed the WCTU's public assurance that the 3 million women under the aegis of the General Federation of Women's Clubs (GFWC) endorsed the Eighteenth Amendment. After WONPR leaders dared the GFWC to poll its membership on Prohibition—emphasizing that WONPR members also belonged to GFWC clubs—the WCTU no longer made that assertion.[35]

The Fiction of the "Woman's Bloc"

"The woman 'bloc' does not tend to become more and more solidified but tends to become more and more disintegrated," journalist William Hard observed in 1923.[36] The quantity of evidence that women arrayed themselves on opposing political sides (even if they used gender-dependent justifications to do so) calls into question the very possibility of a woman bloc. Given the divisions among women and given the nature of the political system, a woman's voting bloc—or even the possibility of a lobbying bloc representing *all* women—must be considered an interpretive fiction rather than a realistic expectation, useful perhaps to some minds, but requiring a willing suspension of disbelief.

In the 1920s most politically active women, and the LWV as an organization, eschewed the notion of a woman's voting bloc in favor of women's diverse individuality. In her early leadership of the LWV, Catt made clear that it was not a woman's party intending to mobilize women's votes but a group dedicated to guiding women into the male-dominated political process and parties where change could be effected from the inside. Only a very few spokeswomen pointedly disagreed: Anne Martin, for instance, excoriated the decision to "train women for citizenship," saying that it handed women over to the Republican and Democratic parties "exactly where men political leaders wanted them, bound, gagged, divided, and delivered." The head of the Republican Women's Division believed, however, that voting women "do not want to differ from men on lines of sex distinction" and predicted that women would never vote for female candidates because of their sex alone but would choose the most qualified individuals. Grace Abbott, head of the Children's Bureau, said that women's voting record by 1925 showed that they were "trying hard to vote as citizens rather than as women, measuring a party or candidate in terms of their judgment on general community needs." Cornelia Bryce Pinchot, a leading Pennsylvania Republican, believed that women should enter politics to improve the position of their sex; nonetheless, as a candidate for Congress she found it counterproductive to isolate women as such in politics. She wanted to be listened to as an individual with views on many issues. Freda Kirchwey, influential left-leaning writer for the *Nation*, emphasized that "women are going to vote according to the dictates of class interest and personal interest as well as sex interest." To urge women otherwise, she contended, was to make them "forget they are human beings."[37]

Such remarks suggest that feminist impulses might scuttle the notion of a woman's bloc as reasonably as champion it. The fiction that women were unified in the political arena laid a foundation of feminist action, but also involved risks—most pointedly, the risks of denying women's diversity and individuality or prescribing a "woman's sphere" in politics. As much as suffragist rhetoric had stressed women's need to represent themselves and women's duty to become voters because their interests and expertise differed from men's, it had also stressed that women and men were equally citizens and individuals in relation to the state. A *New York Times* editorialist heard the suffragists' clarion to be that "women are people—human beings sharing certain fundamental human interests, aspirations, and duties with men." That very important strand of suffragist rationale was renewed in the 1910s along with rationales stressing women's differences from men; it justified and anticipated women's integration into men's political associations rather than the formation of a woman bloc.[38]

There were also strategically defensive reasons why most women active in politics did not pursue nor speak of their goals in terms of mobilizing a woman bloc. The notion of a woman bloc was portrayed as the deployment of destructive sex antagonism and was condemned in the harshest terms by mainstream male politicians as well as by right-wing ideologues. Once when the fledgling LWV did try to marshal a woman's voting bloc—in New York in 1920, trying to unseat Republican Senator James Wadsworth, an intransigent opponent of woman suffrage whose wife headed the National Association Opposed to Woman Suffrage—the organization was violently condemned by New York's Republican governor as "*a menace to our free institutions and to representative government.*" In the two-party system, Governor Nathan Miller said, "there is no proper place for a *league of women voters*, precisely as I should say there was no proper place for a *league of men voters.*" His attack differed only in degree rather than in kind from the blast of *The Woman Patriot*, a right-wing hyperpatriotic "news"-sheet published during the 1920s by former antisuffragists, which trumpeted that women's organizations on Capitol Hill formed an "interlocking lobby dictatorship" bent on "organizing women for class and sex war." The *New York Times*, too, censured the forming of a political organization by women, claiming that such formation presupposed that women were "a class, a group, something apart, . . . a class which apparently hates and distrusts men." In the *Times'* editorialist's view, such thinking not only signaled a "revival of sex-antagonism" but even amounted to a "socialist" theory of "a world divided into hostile classes."[39]

Although rarely proposed or envisioned by women leaders as desirable or likely, the notion of a woman bloc was denigrated, repressed, and ridiculed by defenders of "politics as usual" as fiercely as if it threatened them. Although the woman bloc could only have been an interpretive fiction, it was, curiously, a large enough looming specter for male politicians to slay it again and again. Those who have imagined that women entering politics in the 1920s should have or could have constituted a bloc of woman voters similar to the coalition formed on behalf of woman suffrage have underestimated how profoundly at cross-purposes to the existing party system such a proposition really was. Yet how else could women lobbyists, without economic resources to speak of (as Mary Anderson admitted), swing any weight? Women leaders in the political arena faced a classic double bind: damned outright for attempting to form a woman bloc, damned (in effect) by male politicians' indifference or scorn for failing to form one. There was the dilemma for women who intended to make it clear that politics was no longer a man's world.

Conclusion

An improved view across the great divide of 1920 clarifies the accomplishments of women in American politics and the limits to those accomplishments. It points up that the suffrage movement has its own history, overlapping the history of feminism and the history of women and politics before and after 1920 without being identical to either one of these subjects, as they are not identical with each other. A more continuous view highlights not only the immense organizational implications of women's lack of the ballot until the early twentieth century, but also the unique power of disenfranchisement to bring diverse women into coalition; it thus enables finer distinctions between the contribution of disenfranchisement to feminist mobilization and the ways that disenfranchisement has affected the history of women's behavior in male-defined politics. By taking fuller account of women's political efforts (including voluntary associations and lobbying as well as candidacies and voting), and by acknowledging that political efforts by various subsets of women may be mutually counterpoised (and yet still register as political activities of women), we might move the focus of inquiry after 1920 from the "woman bloc" to the possibility of a feminist bloc—the latter admittedly a grouping by politics and ideology rather than by sex.[40]

Notes

1. Of course twelve states had granted woman suffrage before 1917, and eighteen more did between 1917 and 1920, but the coverage was uneven—some

local, some presidential suffrage—and brief. See Scott and Scott (1975), pp. 166–168, for a convenient summary. On women and electoral politics after 1920, see Anderson (1929); Fisher (1947); Young (1950); Chafe (1972), pp. 25–47.

2. Winifred A. Cooley, "The Younger Suffragists," *Harper's Weekly*, September 27, 1913, p. 7. See also n. 4, below.

3. It is worth pondering if and how the history of women in politics and feminism would be rewritten if the Equal Rights Amendment had passed in 1982: Would the sixty years from 1923 (when it was first introduced into Congress) to 1982 be reconceptualized to reveal the ascending progress of equal rights, as the history of the "woman movement" from 1848 to 1920 has been conceptualized to reveal the ascending suffrage campaign?

4. See O'Neill (1969); Chafe (1972); Lemons (1973); and Alpern and Baum (1985). Gordon (1986), however, emphasizes former suffragists' continuing political activities.

5. Taggard (1925), p. 1. An excellent overview of the recent historical literature on the Progressive era is Rodgers (1982). Some works that influenced my thinking about the political context of the woman suffrage campaign are Filene (1970); McCormick (1981); Davis (1967b); Link (1959); Weinstein (1968); and Buenker (1973). The most influential reformulator of continuities between the 1910s and 1920s in terms of ongoing organizational and associational activities is Hawley (1979, 1981); see also Wilson (1975).

6. Olympia Brown to Catharine Waugh McCulloch, June 25, 1911; folder 236, Dillon Collection, Sarah Lawrence College. For the examples of conflict mentioned, see Terborg-Penn (1978), pp. 17–37; Gullett (1984), pp. 149–159; and Steinson (1982).

7. Park (1960), pp. 179–180. On the suffrage movement's coalition-building, see Flexner (1968); DuBois (1978); and Buechler (1986).

8. On the Congressional Union, see Flexner (1968), pp. 261–270, 275–277, 282–289; Bland (1972); Zimmerman (1964); Lunardini (1986); and for major accounts by participants, see Stevens (1920) and Irwin (1921). Paul's statement, from 1916, is quoted in Irwin (1921), p. 151.

9. Park (1960), p. 23; Harriot Stanton Blatch to Anne Martin, May 14, 1918, Anne Martin Collection, Bancroft Library. On the mixed nature of the suffrage coalition, see Buechler (1986) and Cott (1986).

10. Quotations from Shaw, Congressional Union, and Kelley in Kraditor (1971), p. 50; Schaffer (1962), p. 273; quotation from Catt's letter of October 9, 1915, to speakers, in Daniels (1979), p. 71.

11. Lemons (1973), pp. 92–93; Buenker (1970–1971); Ogburn and Goltra (1919); Rice and Willey (1924a).

12. See Purcell (1973), pp. 95–114, on political scientists; for a work of contemporary political cynicism by a journalist, see Kent (1928).

13. Burnham (1965), p. 10; see also Schattschneider (1960).

14. See Schattschneider (1960); Burnham (1965); Hays (1964); Weinstein (1968), especially pp. 92–116; Kousser (1974); Eakins (1972), pp. 163–179, 288–291. Compare the Cable Act's closing off marriage as a route to citizenship for immigrant women in Sapiro (1984). Quotation from La Follette (1926), p. 268.

    State-level woman suffrage campaigns in the 1910s moved progressively away from popular decision-making and toward more elite forums: Before 1915 all had sought popular referenda, but the later state campaigns sought woman suffrage through statutory actions of state legislatures, with rare exception; see McDonagh and Price (1985), p. 14.

15. Bourque and Grossholtz (1974) very effectively show that early 1920s analyses of female nonvoting—especially that of Merriam and Gosnell (1923)— were still being repeated in political science texts of the 1960s.

16. Jane Addams, quoted in "Is Woman Suffrage Failing?" *Woman Citizen*, April 19, 1924, pp. 14–16. Early analyses are Rice and Willey (1924a) and Keenleyside (1925); see also Merriam and Gosnell (1923). Recent treatments are Kleppner (1982) and Alpern and Baum (1985).

    Interestingly, scattered evidence now shows that black women, where they were not prevented by violence or by registrars (and that meant in a few cities), fulfilled both black suffragists' and white opponents' expectations by registering and voting in greater proportions in their communities than did white women—that is, in about the same proportions as black men. In Richmond, Virginia, in 1920, despite the fact that white women's applications were processed six times faster than blacks', black women registered to vote in equal numbers with black men while white women were outnumbered by white men three to one. Still, the absolute number of black women registered was too small to make an appreciable difference in black political power. Lebsock (1985), p. 9. In Baltimore, the black electorate increased from 16,800 to 37,400—that is, more than doubled—in 1921. Ida B. Wells Barnett credited the votes of black women organized by her Alpha Suffrage Club for the election in 1915 of Oscar de Priest as Chicago's first black alderman. Terborg-Penn (1983), pp. 265, 275.

17. Martin (1922), p. 14; see also Martin (1925); Kellor (1923); and compare Feickert's attitude in Gordon (1986).

18. Namely, Logan (1929), p. 32; Johnson (1972). Baker (1984) and Scott (1984b), pp. 259–294, have stressed the voluntarist political tradition among women in the nineteenth century, but its continuity after 1920 has received little attention, except very recently in the New Jersey study by Gordon (1986).

19. Irwin (1934), pp. 408–411, and Appendix. Compare O'Neill (1969), pp. 225–294; Freedman (1979).

20. The League of Women Voters (LWV) had branches in 45 states in 1931, with total membership probably under 100,000; see Breckinridge (1933), pp. 66–68; on the LWV program, see Lemons (1973), pp. 49–55; on Feickert, see Gordon (1986), p. 79. Charles Edward Russell (1924) noted that "at its last convention" the LWV "was assailed in unmeasured terms by ladies of a

strong partizan [sic] sympathy because it had not compelled all its members to be either Republicans or Democrats" (p. 730).

21. On the General Federation of Women's Clubs, see Wilson (1979), pp. 98, 100–101, 107, n. 26; O'Neill (1969), pp. 256–262; Breckinridge (1933), p. 39; on parent-teacher associations, see Breckinridge (1933), pp. 53–54, 79–80.

22. Chambers (1963), p. 7; Wolfe (1975); Dye (1980); Lemons (1973), pp. 25–30, 122–123; O'Neill (1969), pp. 231–249.

23. Breckinridge (1933), pp. 56–57; Kessler-Harris (1982), pp. 243–245; Wolfson (1929), pp. 130–131; Foner (1982), vol. 2, pp. 126–128; Frederickson (1977); (1985), pp. 169–171; Janiewski (1985), pp. 83, 151; Heller (1981, 1986).

24. Lemons (1973), pp. 58–59, n. 8; Breckinridge (1933), pp. 63–64. See also the Lena Madesin Phillips Collection, Arthur and Elizabeth Schlesinger Library, Radcliffe College.

25. One Connecticut volunteer wrote to another, for instance, commending a coworker for having "reached the best type of woman—those active in the Mother's Club and the League of Women Voters. They are women who are deeply interested in the subject of birth control and who will be extremely active and influential in the substantial conservative circles in Norwalk—of course, the more advanced, 'radical' set has always advocated birth control." [Mrs. Leonard D. Adkins] to Mrs. Day, July 21, 1928, in folder "Birth Control—Correspondence, A. G. Porritt, 1924–1932," box 2, Annie G. Porritt Collection, Sophia Smith Collection. See Kennedy (1970), pp. 100–101, 221–222; Gordon (1976), pp. 295–298; Jensen (1981a).

26. Breckinridge (1933), pp. 54–55, 79.

27. Both Hadassah and the National Council of Jewish Women had been founded by the generation before (and both claimed between 40,000 and 50,000 members by 1930) but in 1921, additionally, Junior Hadassah was formed, in 1923 the Conference Group of National Jewish Women's Organizations, in 1924 the Women's Branch of the Union of Orthodox Jewish Congregations of America, in 1925 the Women's Organization of the Pioneer Women of Palestine, and so on, through half a dozen more by 1935. The National Council of Catholic Women was formed in 1920, and a decade later there were 1,700 local societies of Catholic women, 50 Diocesan organizations, and at least 16 national societies (for example, the National Catholic Women's Union, the Catholic Daughters of America) affiliated with it. Breckinridge (1933), pp. 49–51, 58–59; Sochen (1981); Pratt (1978), p. 222.

28. Breckinridge (1933), pp. 77–79; Terborg-Penn (1983), pp. 269–270, 272–273; Giddings (1984), pp. 177, 183–185, 203–204. On southern white women's antilynching efforts, see Hall (1979).

29. Breckinridge (1933), pp. 43–49, 58.

30. De Benedetti (1978), esp. pp. 90–97; Chatfield (1971); Boeckel (1929), pp. 231–232; Jensen (1983); Breckinridge (1933), pp. 85–87.

31. [Mary Anderson], "Organized Women and Their Program," typescript, c. 1924, folder 84, Mary Anderson Collection, Schlesinger Library.

32. In 1943 the National Woman's Party changed the wording of the ERA to its current reading. On the controversy between women's organizations over the ERA, see O'Neill (1969), pp. 274–294; Chafe (1972), pp. 112–132; Lemons (1973), pp. 184–199; Rothman (1978), pp. 153–165; Kessler-Harris (1982), pp. 205–212; Becker (1981), pp. 121–151; Lunardini (1986); and Cott (1984, 1987).

33. When Florence Allen, for instance, was running for the Ohio Supreme Court in 1922, supported by a nonpartisan coalition of women, she was criticized by Mrs. George Gordon Battelle, chair of the women's state Republican Committee and frozen out by the visiting assistant U.S. attorney general, Mabel Walker Willibrandt (a Harding appointee), for diverting women's political activity away from loyal Republican channels. Allen (1965), pp. 66–67. Partisan/nonpartisan controversies bulked large in the first year or two of the LWV; see Lemons (1973), pp. 49–53, and Gordon (1986), pp. 34–39.

34. On the 1928 confrontation, see Foster-Hayes (1984), pp. 318–321; on conflicts among women's groups over peace issues, see Jensen (1983) and Cott (1987).

35. Sabin's politics disputed the shibboleth that women voted just like their husbands. Her husband, chairman of the board of the Guaranty Trust Company, was a politically active Democrat. Although the couple shared opposition to Prohibition, and Charles Sabin served on the executive committee of the Association Against the Prohibition Amendment (AAPA, founded early in the 1920s), the Women's Organization for National Prohibition Reform was an entirely independent organization which sought no help from the AAPA and rather quickly exceeded it in membership. Kyvig (1976); (1979), pp. 118–127; Carter (1977), pp. 96–99.

36. William Hard, quoted in "What the American Man Thinks," *Woman Citizen,* September 8, 1923; cited by O'Neill (1969), p. 264.

37. On Catt, see Lemons (1973), pp. 90–91; Martin (1925), p. 185; on Pinchot, see Furlow (1976); all other quotations are cited from Alpern and Baum (1985), pp. 60–62.

38. *New York Times,* November 30, 1918, p. 16. See Freedman (1979) and Cott (1986), pp. 50–54.

39. Lemons (1973), pp. 98–100; "Are Women a Menace?" *Nation,* February 9, 1921, p. 198; "The Interlocking Lobby Dictatorship," *Woman Patriot,* December 1, 1922; "Organizing Women for Class and Sex War," *Woman Patriot,* April 15, 1923; *New York Times,* November 30, 1918, p. 16; Cott (1987).

40. Compare the question of whether the subject of feminism is "women" or "gender justice" in Stacey (1983), esp. pp. 577–578.

8

Women and Citizenship in the 1920s

Kristi Andersen

> Disillusionment only can result from the claim that women when enfranchised will at once right wrongs, however deep-seated they may be in the body politic, and abolish corruption, though it is intrenched in an established, complicated system, and practised by astute and experienced men in the interest of their own personal profit; for such a claim is, in its nature, unreasonable, and doomed to disappointment.[1]

Unfortunately such warnings were not heeded, and the advent of universal suffrage for adult white women was surrounded with a mass of often contradictory expectations, fears, and predictions. Some of these expectations about how women would perform in their new role as voters were extensions of the suffragists' "expediency" arguments; others were based on claims of antisuffragists.[2] Many had, at their core, strong assumptions about basic differences between men and women with regard to their interests and their level of public-spiritedness. During the 1920s many articles, both scholarly and journalistic, attempted to argue that various of these hopes or fears had (or had not) been fulfilled.[3] However, this type of "evaluation" of the political behavior of women usually involved a quite arbitrary establishment of standards (what constitutes, for example, a "high" or "low" level of voting?), which were based on idealized and monolithic views of women. They often reached the conclusion that women's suffrage was "a failure" or "a disappointment."

In this chapter I place the assessment of women's electoral/political behavior in several contexts.[4] First, a useful, though not sufficient, perspective is to see postsuffrage American women not as a unique group but as one instance of a particular phenomenon which has been examined from various perspectives by political scientists. Additional instances would be other recently enfranchised groups such as nonproperty owners or blacks in the nineteenth century United States, or immigrants who do not become voting citizens until late in their lives.[5] Beyond this is the context of the arguments used by women themselves, during this period, to justify particular courses of political action. We can begin with the assumption that the Nineteenth Amendment added an important new dimension to women's citizenship, and in fact forced women as individuals and in groups to think about and define for themselves what it meant for them to "be good citizens." There were in the 1920s a number of different positions on what "women's citizenship" should or could be like, many of which focused on the role of parties in the American political system. One of the central issues facing women was how their newly expanded citizenship should be worked out in a system where parties played such a crucial role. Thus a third context, which needs to be analyzed, is that of the political parties themselves. The parties of the 1920s differed, as institutions, as coalitions, and as objects of citizens' loyalty, in several significant ways from the parties of today. The parties also varied a great deal from place to place, and this should be taken into account in developing a picture of women's political participation during this period.

Becoming Citizens

Although there were many hyperbolic predictions of sweeping changes, more judicious observers realized that the Nineteenth Amendment represented, rather than an automatic conferral of a different status, an *opportunity* to acquire a new role. Further, they recognized that for the vast majority of women, full integration into the political system[6] would be a relatively slow *learning* process. "The hope of a woman's vote, it would seem, lies in habit,"[7] said one observer in the middle of the decade.

The process by which newly enfranchised people (whether enfranchised as a group, like women, or because they come of age) are socialized into the values and behaviors appropriate in a particular political system—specifically the process by which they develop the habit of voting and a loyalty to a particular political party—has been examined at some length by political scientists.[8] In general, these researchers have accepted the argument that the *behavior* of voting, which includes both the information-gathering/choice process and the expression of a commitment to one or another party, serves to reinforce earlier learning, to deepen the commitment to the system, and to make it more likely that the individual will vote in the future. Formally, this model of the acquisition of partisanship (and the model can be extended to include the predisposition to vote) has been elaborated most clearly by Philip E. Converse, who predicts the aggregate level of partisanship of age cohorts by using factors such as the length of time they have been able to vote, their "inherited" partisanship, and the assumed resistance of older voters to the acquisition of new behaviors.[9] Converse's model is quite successful in making predictions for aggregates, rather than individuals. When the data are disaggregated, however, the model is much less successful: Within-group variation makes prediction more difficult.[10] Stein Rokkan provides examples of the kinds of variations which might affect the rates of participation of the newly enfranchised. Using Norwegian data, he demonstrates that "mobilization" or "integration into the political system" (that is, participation in elections and membership in parties) takes place first for new entrants who are at the "center" of society—those in more industrialized, urban, modern areas—and proceeds most slowly for those on the geographic and social peripheries.[11]

Certainly contemporary observers noted great variations in the extent to which women voted, particularly in the early 1920s. Further, many politicians, journalists, and scholars writing in the twenties commented on both the necessity of *habituating* women to political activity, particularly voting, and the variations in the rate at which this political learning progressed. Marguerite Wells, for example, writing in 1929, pointed out that women were *gradually* acquiring "voting habits" and that this was "precisely what is to be expected."[12] It also appears that the League of Women Voters heeded a learning-based argument: "An effort was particularly directed to the problem of arousing her interest and stimulating her participation before the habit of indifference should be deeply graven on her political character."[13] An interesting first-person account, which reveals the importance of voting as a habit and of the learned conviction that one *should* vote, appeared in *Scribner's* in May 1925.

> Each time I vote, I am more resolved never to do it again. It is all a question, every year, of the moral influence of my husband. . . . I bow to a conviction that I do not myself feel. The sense that it is a duty to vote is simply not in me . . . I am not mentally a citizen yet. Nor, for that matter, are most of the women who have been enfranchised only since 1920."[14]

When Carrie Chapman Catt, speaking to a celebratory gathering in New York in late 1920, said that "we are no longer petitioners, we are not wards of the nation," most suffragists could agree on the fact that women would now enjoy a new status. They were now, Catt said, "free and equal citizens."[15] The trouble was that there was no clear consensus on what exactly "being a citizen" meant for women. Antisuffragists had seen a woman as a special kind of citizen, who had the right to protection by a male-dominated society and whose obligations were to serve the community from her very special position as nurturer, cleanser, reformer.

Along with suffrage came a number of potential rights and obligations, but no clear agreement existed as to which of these was entailed by having the vote. For example, it quickly became clear that women were still in a special category with regard to the retention of their U.S. citizenship. The Cable Act of 1922, which allowed women to remain citizens if they married foreigners (though they were considered naturalized citizens!), needed strong efforts by the Women's Joint Congressional Committee to pass. Neither did the right to serve on juries follow directly from the right to vote, though many women assumed that it would or should. When pressed, in the 1920s and 1930s, many states ruled that the Nineteenth Amendment applied solely to voting; it did not confer other rights or obligations of citizenship.[16] In fact, some state constitutions were not amended to allow the election of women to legislative offices until the 1940s.[17]

Although there was little agreement on the implications of the right to vote for these other rights, it seemed clear that the fact that women could now vote in large numbers made it *more likely* that their rights to retain citizenship, serve on juries, and hold office would be conceded to them. One congressman said, after the passage of the Cable Act, that in his judgment "there was no particular force in the demand for this bill until the Nineteenth Amendment became a part of the organic law of the land."[18] Similarly, J. Stanley Lemons considers the record of states with regard to jury service as a measure of women's political "clout" in the 1920s: "Before 1922 when this power [of the women's vote] was unknown, 20 states gave jury service; but as the uncertainty began to evaporate, only one state granted it from 1922 to 1935."[19] Florence E. Allen, at the time an Ohio State Supreme Court justice, summarized the argument about the relationship between the right to vote and other rights: "Whether or not the ballot is exercised at all, whether or not it is exercised foolishly, there is a potential power in the franchise which makes its holder more influential than the one who does not have the vote. . . . [The voting right] carries with it other vital rights all along the line."[20]

Controversies About Women's Citizenship

What of the *obligations* of citizenship which devolved upon women with the advent of suffrage? Here the suffragists were divided among themselves, and their different views of how women *citizens* should act reflected the different arguments they had used in favor of suffrage, disparate views on essential male-female differences, and different ideas about the nature of the political system—particularly the role of parties in that system.

Women: Equal or Unique?

Logically, women who had accepted expediency-based arguments for women's suffrage tended also to accept the idea that women's participation should be directed toward the eradication of particular evils, such as sweatshops, high infant mortality rates, corrupt machines, and, sometimes, alcohol. This line of thinking was characteristic of the women Lemons calls "social feminists," whose political activities were issue-oriented and, at least in the early 1920s, often successful.[21]

The endorsement of expediency arguments was often based on belief in the unique interests and capabilities of women: the idea that they were perhaps better than men, and certainly more compassionate and moral. Women who took this position argued that women, as citizens, should set themselves apart from men—while of course they should vote, their "prime role would be to serve as a moral force, essentially outside the political structure, though not disassociated from it. Women would act as prodders to remind those within the system what course they must properly pursue."[22]

On the other hand, those who denied (or wished to deny) essential differences between men and women, at least in the aptitudes and abilities relevant to citizenship, felt that women citizens should now enter wholeheartedly into the male-dominated political world of parties and campaigns. This was sometimes argued in terms clearly reflecting a theory of citizen obligation. For example, Felice Gordon quotes a New Jersey League of Women Voters member in 1926, who argued that

perhaps we have failed to recognize fully that when we were enfranchised
. . . our own status and therefore our own obligations were definitely

changed. No longer outside the government . . . we were now inside and therefore obligated to assume the responsibility and to perform the full duties of citizenship through the regularly established governmental channels.[23]

These divisions can, at least crudely speaking, be collectively characterized as equalitarianism versus uniqueness; the former position tended to support the full participation of women in traditional partisan politics, while the latter de-emphasized (or sometimes shunned) party- or election-based politics in favor of a more moralistic and issue-based approach. Further complicating both contemporary debates and our analysis of them is another argument which reflects the Progressives' historical concern with the corruption of party politics. In essence, some women accepted the Progressive critique of parties, believing that parties produced self-interested politics by definition and, at least in the American context, corrupt politics as well. One of the most impassioned arguments of this type was that of Winifred Starr Dobyns, the first chair of the Republican Women's Committee of Illinois.

> Let us be frank. With some possible exceptions, the aim of the political organizations is not good government, patriotic service, public welfare. These are but phrases used for campaign purposes. Political organizations are, for the most part, designed to fill the pockets of politicians at public expense, to give jobs to thousands who find politics an easy way to make a living, to maintain men in office who can do favors for business. . . .[24]

Those who disagreed accepted some variations of the argument which Elizabeth Cady Stanton had made years before, when she argued that women, once they had the vote, *must* be involved with the parties "inasmuch as our demands are to be made and carried, like other political questions, by the aid of and affiliation with parties."[25] When Catt spoke to the February 1920 convention, which was the last meeting of the National American Woman Suffrage Association and the first of the National League of Women Voters, she reflected something of the era's negative view of parties, admitting that they needed reform, but urging women to enter the parties and change them from within.[26]

The major part of the proparty versus antiparty debate was carried out at the level of elites: Should well-educated, active women leaders try to work through parties or independently of parties? If they were to be involved in the parties, should they give, as the parties demanded, unconditional loyalty or should they withhold support until their demands were answered? Should women form separate women's organizations within the parties or party-support groups outside the official parties?[27] This debate had implications for mass politics as well, because the arguments made by both sides were accessible to women voters (for example, in the *Woman Citizen, Ladies' Home Journal,* and other publications) and because the position taken by elites in a particular locale could have had an important effect on the level and direction of the mobilization of female voters.

Women in Party Politics

Such debates about political parties are, of course, a familiar theme in American history. Americans have always been at least skeptical about political parties; George Washington spent much of his Farewell Address denouncing them. Currently, we are much more sanguine about political parties. Some version of the "responsible parties" model of politics is widely supported among social scientists and many members of the public—this is reflected in often-repeated concerns about the decline of the parties. We have, in other words, essentially accepted V. O. Key's claim that "we have contrived no other instrument quite so suitable for the translation of democratic theory into working reality."[28] But in some areas, notably California and the Midwest, in the late nineteenth and early twentieth centuries, the "party as enemy of democracy" argument was strong enough to allow Progressives and municipal reformers to establish nonpartisan elections and other antiparty measures. When we think of political parties today, we are likely to see them as unwieldy coalitions of groups and issues, on both the elite and mass levels. But "party" in the 1920s immediately conjured up the ideas of "machine" and "boss." It is important to keep this in mind when considering the postsuffrage arguments about how women should exercise their citizenship.

There are three themes in accounts of women's involvement in the political parties during the 1920s. One is the normative question of women's proper role, discussed in the previous section; this was the subject of much debate during the period. A second is the increasing participation of women at various levels of party politics during the 1920s. And the third revolves around the treatment of women by the parties and the male party leaders.

WOMEN IN PARTY ELITES   The Democratic National Committee (DNC) agreed in 1919 to have the national committeeman from each state appoint a committeewoman; in 1920 the convention was persuaded by Mrs. George Bass, chair of the Women's Bureau of the DNC, that both men and women should be elected. The Republican convention adopted similar procedures in 1924. Some states (eighteen by 1928) adopted similar policies of at least nominally equal representation within the party organizations.[29] Many women later complained that this did not guarantee them entry into the inner party councils and that, on the contrary, they did a great deal of work without gaining much power. But admission of the extent to which tokenism must have characterized the party organizations should not prevent us from realizing that by these rule changes thousands of women now had a stake, however small, in the parties' fortunes and some exposure, however minimal, to the realities of partisan politics. In 1928 Anne O'Hare McCormick, after interviewing male and female party leaders in a number of states, spoke of an "invasion" of women campaign workers: "Gone is the last safely masculine sport, save looking for new polar lands. . . ." "If anything," she continued, "women outnumber men at political meetings, and women speakers are becoming as numerous as men."[30]

Another measure of the slow but significant growth of women's involvement in party politics was their attendance at national party conventions. At the Republican conventions, for example, there had been a few (always fewer than 10) female delegates since 1892. In 1920, 27 women delegates attended; in 1924, 120; in 1928, 70; and in 1932, 87. Democratic conventions showed a similar pattern: from essentially none to 93 in 1920, 199 in 1924, 152 in 1928, and 208 in 1932.

While only 7 women were candidates for congressional seats in 1920, between 20 and 30 were party nominees in the election years between 1922 and 1930. The most extensive survey of women officeholders at state and local levels is in Sophonisba Breckinridge's 1933 study. She named 13 female secretaries of state, 4 clerks of state supreme courts, 3 state treasurers, and numerous appointees to advisory boards and commissions.[31] Information from secretaries of state allowed her to describe an upward trend in the number of women state legislators, as shown in Table 8.1:

Table 8.1 Women Serving in State Legislatures

	Number of Women	Number of States
1921	37	26
1923	98	35
1925	141	38
1927	127	36
1929	149	38
1931	146	39

By 1931 the only state never to have elected a female legislator was Louisiana.[32] Connecticut had elected 47 women to statewide offices by 1931.[33] Breckinridge presents four states' records of electing women to local government posts; these states had been surveyed intensively by the League of Woman Voters. (See Table 8.2.) The most frequently held offices were superintendent of schools and treasurer of towns, cities, and counties.[34]

Table 8.2 **Number of Women Elected to Local Offices**

	Connecticut	Michigan	Minnesota	Wisconsin
1925	29			
1926			127	58
1927	67	277	209	64
1929	178	590		158
1930			245	

Despite the clear increase in the number of women officeholders at subnational levels, as the decade wore on it was widely felt that women's interest in politics was on the decline[35] and that independent-minded and feminist women were less likely to be elected. Emily Newell Blair, for example, claimed that

> the kind of woman who could or would urge her state's member on a Resolutions Committee to vote for a measure which she thought was based on women's values, who could sway delegates at a convention, has all too often been succeeded by the wife of some office-holder whose aim in politics is to help him to success, or a woman who follows instructions from some men in order to advance herself to office.[36]

As Belle Moskowitz, the highly influential adviser to Al Smith, put it: "The major political parties are still man-made and man-controlled. Few of their leaders can work with women on a basis of equality."[37] Consequently, many women felt that they were not encouraged or allowed to gain independent power bases or even much real political experience. Some stated this belief even more strongly:

> There is no doubt that Mrs. Carrie Chapman Catt sounded the doom of feminism for many years to come when she urged the newly enfranchised American women . . . "to work for the party of your choice"—exactly where men political leaders wanted them, bound, gagged, divided, and delivered to the Republican and Democratic parties.[38]

So potential party activists were in a difficult position. While increasing numbers of women may have come to believe that to advance personal ambitions or to change public policy it was essential to work with and through the parties, this "choice" was (to them) unattractively constrained. First, it threw them into an unfamiliar and often unfriendly male world. Anne O'Hare McCormick's remark about "the last safely masculine sport" was not too far-fetched. A repeated observation about the effects of woman suffrage was that it made drinking, smoking, and bad language less characteristic of partisan politics and substituted more sex-neutral political arenas for the traditional bars, saloons, and barbershops.[39] But the smoke-filled room was not apocryphal in the 1920s, and its existence made it difficult for women to be directly involved in the work central to partisan politics.

Second, and more important, parties in the era of machines and bosses often demanded strict loyalty, with regard to issues and especially candidates, from their workers and active members—and, much more than today's parties, they had control of the sanctions to enforce such loyalty. This kind of unconditional support was objectionable to many of the activist women, even those who accepted the necessity of working within the parties. Gordon's study of New Jersey in the 1920s illustrates this tension. The New Jersey Republican Women's Club (NJRWC) criticized individual Republican legislators for particular stands or votes, and in particular advised members to vote against incumbent Senator William Edge because he was perceived as insufficiently committed to Prohibition. The NJRWC essentially broke with the party in 1923; the group and its leader, Lillian Feickert, were roundly condemned by party leaders.

> The Republican women . . . wanted to enter the political parties, but shuddered at the thought of playing the political game. First, compromise . . . was anathema to them. They sought the truth, knew the truth, and would not budge one inch from their chosen path. Those who opposed them were to be exposed in the public limelight, and defeated. This position led to indifference about . . . the primacy of party loyalty. "We women are for the Republican party right, but not right or wrong," Feickert often remarked.[40]

INDEPENDENCE OF PARTY? In Illinois, Republican women opposed a machine candidate in the primary; the machine candidate won. "By the code of party ethics," said Winifred Dobyns, "it was my duty as an officer of the party to swallow my disappointment and take up the cudgels for the successful candidate. How could I do so? I had said that I believed him to be totally unfit to hold office. Needless to say, I resigned."[41] And at the level of the presidential campaign, it was clear in 1928 that many of Hoover's supporters were not loyal Republicans. "When it became known that the New York delegates would probably be uninstructed on the first ballot, the New York State Republican Woman's Association threatened to vote for Smith if the Republicans failed to nominate Hoover."[42]

Certainly there was a sense at the time that this independence of party characterized not only the elite, activist women but the mass of women as well. An editorial in the *Woman's Journal* in August 1928 argued:

> The *Journal* does not believe there is a women's vote . . . [but] women haven't the long traditional party loyalty that men have. They may be enrolled Republicans or Democrats, but they vote as they please. Many of them have been keenly disappointed to find so few principles espoused by either party.

Goldstein found that women in Illinois were less likely to vote in primaries—another measure of their lower level of party loyalty. More generally, as the competitiveness of an election decreased, the rate at which women voted declined.[43]

The problem, from the point of view of women who wanted to have an impact on the political system, was that parties, by their nature, served the selfish interests of those who supported them; they were not serving the *public* interest. Various solutions were proposed. Margaretta Newell (Emily Newell Blair's sister) emphasized the need for women to discard many traditional "feminine" characteristics to be successful in party politics. Women, she wrote, are too diffident, trusting, modest, polite, and pacifistic to get anywhere in politics, which inevitably involves conflict. They need to "start fights," get publicity, gain followers by stressing issues, and take risks.[44]

Among those who found the problem more intractable, Winifred Dobyns, in her influential piece "The Lady and the Tiger," called for widespread and principled participation in primary elections by women (and men) "who are in the party but not of the 'organization' " and who are willing to mobilize public opinion and votes *against* their party if it puts up unqualified candidates. She stressed that this could not be done through the regular party organization: Catt's argument for "reforming from within" had been proved invalid.[45] Of course, there were those who disagreed, as exemplified by Elizabeth Green, the author of a 1925 article supporting party work called "I Resign from Female Politics."

Other female politicians, such as Anne Martin from Nevada and Alice Moyer-Wing from Missouri, felt that these kinds of principled individual actions were not enough: They proposed strong women's organizations within each party, not simply to work for men but to demand of the party organizations that women's interests be served. "Like all suppressed minorities in the political field, . . . women will get only as much as they organize for and demand effectually as a separate political force."[46] Similarly, Emily Newell Blair came to believe that a certain degree of political separatism was necessary to advance women's interests, if not the public interest. "We must pick out women in our own communities, in our states and in the nation. We must urge them to become candidates for public office. And then we must stand behind them and work for them as women."[47]

Voter Turnout

At the level of the ordinary woman citizen, these arguments may well have had little meaning, though the positions taken by local women's organizations and women leaders may have influenced turnout and general political involvement. Here the questions we are interested in have to do with the speed at which women became voters. Unfortunately the data that could be used to answer these questions definitively do not exist. Only Illinois kept men's and women's ballots separate, and only from 1913 to 1921.[48] Other states kept separate registration statistics for certain time periods, and some detailed work has been done which looks at registration in city wards and precincts.[49] In addition, there are contemporary accounts in the press, often based on estimates by party and campaign leaders, and a few early studies by social scientists.[50] Consequently, the present brief investigation of women's electoral participation in the 1920s is necessarily based on pulling together the scattered secondary sources that exist.

Even without adequate data, it is clear that expectations of an outpouring of female votes, enough to double the electorate, were not met. Instead, the number of votes cast in the 1920 election was only a 30 percent increase from 1916; in other words, the percentage of eligible voters who went to the polls declined over those four years. The coincidence of the record low voting turnouts of the twenties with the advent of women's suffrage has made it easy for political scientists and historians to assume that women's suffrage accounted for the decline in turnout. This hypothesis implies further (in the absence of data that allow separate analysis of male and female voting) that turnout among women was quite low; that many (if not most) women who received the vote did not make use of it. Paul Kleppner (1982) has used an ingenious array of data and statistical techniques to support Walter Dean Burnham's suggestion that "there is less than meets the eye in this famous woman-suffrage variable," a point to which I shall return later.[51]

I have argued above that the acceptance of arguments about basic differences between women and men made it difficult for women to work through the parties; it also fostered the assumption that women would vote as a monolithic unit—specifically, that they would vote "morally," for reform, against corrupt candidates and practices, and for "moralistic" laws such as prohibition. Certainly there were instances when the efforts of the League of Women Voters or other women's groups defeated "machine" candidates: Examples include the defeat of Theodore Bilbo in Mississippi in 1923 and the election of Gifford Pinchot as governor of Pennsylvania in 1921.[52] In general it appears to be the case that the "women's vote" was surrounded by uncertainty, and therefore feared by the politicians, in the early 1920s. When it became clear that turnout among women was not uniformly high and that women did not necessarily vote as a bloc, the "threat" of a "woman vote" and attention paid to it in the press declined.

As mentioned above, almost all studies that investigate male-female registration or turnout differentials find a great deal of variation by geographical/political unit. A study conducted by the Republican Women's State Executive Committee of New York of voting in the 1922 off-year elections found that "figures were strikingly varied." In one county the ratio of female to male voters was .95; in four others it ranged from .88 to .93. All these were rural and, with one exception, Republican. On the other hand, the county with the smallest ratio of women to men (.39) was also rural and Republican. In the boroughs of New York City ratios ranged from .57 to .69. "The statistics proved," it was concluded, "that the proportion of women who vote depends upon local conditions, rather than any general causes."[53] In a sample of Illinois counties the ratio of women to men voting for president in 1916 varied from a low of .44 to a high of .78.[54] Voter registration figures for Chicago wards in 1920 show that the male-female difference among wards (percentage of adults registered) ranged from 15 to 33 percentage points.[55] Earlier, Helen Sumner, in an exhaustive, survey-based study of women's political involvement in Colorado, found great variation also. As one example, the difference between men and women registrants in 1906 was only 2.3 percent in the city of Boulder, but 22.2 percent in the rural county of La Plata.[56]

Attitudinal Effects

If in some localities women were, from the start, voting at nearly the same rate as men, while in others a large male-female turnout gap persisted over the decade, possible sources of this variation need to be investigated. One factor which we might expect to inhibit women's voting, particularly in the years immediately following the ratification of the Nineteenth Amendment, is the persistence of antisuffrage attitudes. Some evidence exists that even leading antisuffragists voted and urged other women to vote. For example, in North Carolina, "though never a suffragist, Mrs. Bickett [the governor's wife] appealed to the women of the state to register and vote. May Hilliard Hinton, president of the North Carolina branch of the Rejection League [an antisuffrage organization], made a similar appeal."[57] In a *New York Times* article in 1928 a woman campaign worker was described as likely to be "a lady completely forgetful that she once crusaded to keep women safe in the home. There are no anti-suffragists now."[58] On the other hand, Charles Merriam and Harold Gosnell found in their study of Chicago that 13 percent of the women nonvoters they interviewed cited "disbelief in women's voting" or "objections of husband to women voting" as the primary cause of their failure to register or vote.

> One out of every nine female non-voters interviewed admitted that she had not adjusted herself as yet to the idea of women voting. The strength of this disbelief varied from a mild attitude of indifference toward women's civic responsibilities to a confirmed conviction that women should keep out of politics altogether. . . . [Some of] the disgusted anti-suffragists adopted somewhat of a superior attitude toward "the dirty game of politics that the men are wont to play."[59]

Thomas Jablonsky, in his study of antisuffragists, also claims that while some became "conscientious members of the voting public," others continued to believe that "politics were for men . . . despite their technical enfranchisement."[60] It was found in New York in the mid 1920s that "in every town" there were "some anti-suffrage women who refuse to take any part in politics."[61] All this suggests that variations in female registration and voting might be partially accounted for by persisting opposition to women's suffrage. Although there is no way of investigating this on an individual level, areas with particularly strong antisuffrage organizations, or records of voting against suffrage measures, or particularly traditional cultural norms with regard to women's roles could be expected to have lower turnout levels throughout the 1920s. In this context it is suggestive that Breckinridge's data show that in 1924 women constituted only 28 percent of the registered voters in Louisiana, while they were 42 percent in Pennsylvania and 44 percent in Rhode Island.[62]

Ethnicity and Class

This point about traditional values directs us to a consideration of another important source of variation in female political behavior: ethnic background. In Sumner's study those rural counties with large Mexican populations were those with the lowest levels of female involvement in politics. In all the areas she studied, the differences in voting rates between naturalized men and women were far greater than the overall male-female differential. Merriam and Gosnell found that the proportion of women giving opposition to female suffrage as a reason for not voting was highest among women of foreign parentage, particularly of German, Irish, and Italian extraction.

> The women voted in relatively larger numbers in those wards where rental values were the highest and where the proportion of foreign-born was the lowest. . . . An unduly large proportion of the non-voting adult citizens were women of foreign extraction living in the poorest residential sections of the city.[63]

Thus an intensive investigation of registration and voting patterns, particularly in the large northeastern cities, might well uncover variations in women's political behavior based on the cultural norms represented by ethnic divisions.

Traditional attitudes about women's role were also more prevalent among the working classes, as noted by Merriam and Gosnell. Sumner found that women turned out at a higher rate in the wealthier sections of Denver.[64] In Chicago Joel Goldstein found a positive association between social class and female turnout for presidential elections, though the relationship was reversed for mayoral elections. Breckinridge cited a League of Women Voters study of Minnesota which found that "the poorest voting record was held by women in domestic service."[65] It remains an open question whether traditional attitudes, and therefore lower voting rates, were particularly characteristic of rural areas in the twenties. Rokkan's center-periphery arguments and Herbert Tingsten's study of European voting patterns would lead us to expect such findings. Although the New York Republican Women's Committee study referred to above found some high female turnout in rural areas, it also found that in general turnout was lower in areas where conditions were harder and farms more isolated. In some places tradition dictated that men take a day off on election day, drive to the polling place and stay until dark talking politics. In this situation, noted Butler, women had no chance to vote even if they wanted to.[66]

The Impact of Organizations

Finally, there are numerous suggestions in contemporary accounts that the mobilization efforts of the parties and of women's organizations had a strong effect on the participation of women at the mass level. Merriam and Gosnell's study found that

> detailed studies of certain typical precincts brought to light the fact that women's political clubs have aroused an interest in voting among a very large proportion of adult female citizens of native parentage living in the best residential districts, and that the party organizations in working-class districts were very successful in bringing out a large proportion of the male vote, and, while less successful with the women voters, were improving in this respect.[67]

However, some women's groups in Chicago urged their members *not* to vote in primaries (particularly uncontested ones) as it would limit their political independence and freedom to have an impact on politics.[68] Butler found higher female turnout in 1924 in those New York counties where women had traditionally been active in civic organizations of all types and where these organizations were actively "encouraging their members to take part in the political life of the community."[69] Obviously these are merely hints, but research could usefully be done which attempted to link organizational activity and voting turnout.

Conclusion

All of these potential sources of variation in the way women behaved as they acquired their new role of potential voter serve to specify the general socialization model presented above. That is, depending on her previous political activity, the stance of local parties toward women, her husband's opinion, and her cultural and class background, we might predict that a given woman would be more or less likely to vote. In general, the socialization perspective would lead us to expect, over the period of 1920–1930, a gradual increase in women's voting turnout. Table 8.3 summarizes some diverse data which help describe this trend.

Table 8.3   Women as Percentage of Registered Voters

	Louisiana	Rhode Island	Vermont	Pennsylvania	Chicago
1920	18.2%	38.9%	24.2%		37.8%
1922	19.9	40.2			36.5
1924	28.4	44.1	44.2	41.8%	38.5
1926	29.1	42.8	44.8		36.4
1928	30.5	45.2	47.2		43.2
1930		45.4	46.9	44.4	41.7

Source: Breckinridge (1933), pp. 249, 250, 251, 252.

Tingsten's findings were similar. Longitudinal voting data beginning when women in various European countries received the franchise showed that, in general, the male-female differential gradually decreased over time. For example, in municipal elections in Norway, the difference in 1901 was 24 percentage points; this decreased to 12 points by 1934.[70]

For a variety of reasons, the presidential election of 1928 appears to be a turning point in this process. The League of Women Voters sponsored weekly radio broadcasts on politics; these were thought to have increased the interest of women in the campaign, particularly those in remote areas.[71] Certainly commentators at the time perceived the election to be of particular interest to women, and the papers were once more full of predictions about the likely impact of the women's vote. For example, a New York Times headline (July 9, 1928) read, "Woman Vote Plays Big Part This Year." There were several reasons for this perception; perhaps the most significant was the "moral" thrust of the campaign as it progressed, focusing on the issues of prohibition, immigration, and ethnic and religious tolerance which were thought to be close to women's hearts. Even though the previous eight years should have made it clear that women were not a monolithic voting bloc, this image was repeatedly resurrected during 1928, when it was routinely assumed that virtually all women would vote for Hoover.[72]

Less visible than the clubwomen for Hoover was another phenomenon: the entry into the active electorate of immigrant-stock women on the side of the Democrats. A few writers commented on this at the time. Eunice Fuller Barnard, in the New York Times Magazine, questioned the assumption that all women were dry and would vote for Hoover, suggesting that this myth had developed because a few women had been vocal leaders in the temperance movement. But she reminded readers that prominent Republican women favored repeal or modification and that some women prohibitionists (such as Nellie Tayloe Ross of Wyoming) favored Alfred E. Smith on the basis of other issues. Another writer spoke of Smith's strengths among women factory workers, social workers, and farmers.[73] Some polls—for example, those by the *Chicago Tribune* and an extensive Hearst newspaper poll—also found support for Smith among women.[74]

Postelection analyses indicated that there had indeed been a significant increase in the proportion of women voting. "Women were estimated to be 49 per cent of the possible electorate in 1928 . . . up from an estimated 35 per cent in 1924 and approximately 30 per cent in 1920."[75] According to Indiana Republican women, the women's 1928 vote in that state was 153,000 above that in 1924, while the men's vote remained unchanged.[76]

More specifically, it appears that many foreign-stock women who fell into Merriam and Gosnell's "habitual nonvoter" category began to vote in 1928. Naturalization rates for women were on the rise. In 1924 women accounted for only 9 percent of those applying for citizenship; in 1926 they were 17 percent, and by 1928 they were 22 percent.[77] This trend created a larger pool of potential female voters, and postelection analyses indicated that "women who had never before voted had turned out in remarkable numbers. This was notably true of women whose cultural patterns had most discouraged participation in the past—Irish and New Immigrant Catholics in the North, old stock Republicans in the South."[78] David Burner's research, based on unpublished Boston census reports, confirms a sharp rise in female registration in heavily Italian and Irish census tracts; he also cites newspaper accounts of heavy female voter turnout in New York City and in North Carolina.[79]

The importance of the 1928 election in mobilizing women on both sides of the partisan fence to vote, many for the first time, emphasizes the importance of placing the behavior of any newly enfranchised group in its political context. Deciding whether or not to vote is not a choice made in the abstract, but in the context of particular candidate choices, party images, and issue agendas. The 1920s represented the nadir of a long process of electoral demobilization that began with the election of 1896. As Burnham argues:

> This "system of 1896," as Schattschneider calls it, led to the destruction of party competition throughout much of the United States, and thus paved the way for the rise of the direct primary. It also gave immense impetus to the strains of antipartisan and antimajoritarian theory and practice. . . . By the decade of the 1920s this new regime and business control over

public policy in this country were consolidated. During that decade hardly more than one-third of the eligible adults were still core voters.[80]

Burnham stressed here and elsewhere that the decline in voter participation in the 1920s was a product not simply of the enfranchisement of women but of this larger process, including lessened party competition and the parties' attempts to avoid controversial issues.[81] Recently Kleppner has used turnout trends from years previous to women's suffrage to predict turnout levels in the 1920s; this allows him to measure the relative contribution of female suffrage and other factors to the low turnout rates of the 1920s. He concludes that "the lack of consistent results across states belies the sufficiency of a 'female suffrage' explanation." Instead, the explanation lies in the larger political system:

> [The] geographically extensive Republican hegemony could not fail to have had an impact on electoral turnout. . . . These were the political-environmental conditions that prevailed when most women were initially enfranchised. Politics generally lacked its earlier intensity and strong voter stimulus. . . . If for newly or recently enfranchised women the impact of weaker political stimuli was greater than for men, that was because their costs of participation were higher—they had to overcome standing and internalized norms that defined their sex roles as apolitical.[82]

As the decade progressed, and as the involvement of women in politics became less of a novelty, these costs decreased for some women; the perceived benefits of participation were, possibly, increased by the contentious 1928 election and, certainly, by the issues surrounding the Depression and the 1932 campaign. In 1928 journalists commented on the proliferation of women campaign workers, the ability of the radio to bring politics to the most isolated homes, and women's altered view of politics: "Their earlier inhibitions and fears are giving way, so that they are seeing politics as less of a grim duty and more of a game."[83] For good or ill, women became more used to the idea of women being involved as campaign workers, party officials, and, at times, candidates. In addition, contemporary observers in the mid 1920s were already noting generational differences among women: "Women who went through the fight for equal suffrage are inclined to be skeptical and more nonpartisan than men. . . . Women who inherited the vote without effort on their part are likely to be partisans; they were enfranchised into a party rather than into citizenship per se."[84] Merriam and Gosnell noted that attitudes against women's voting (in Kleppner's terms, overcoming them would be a cost of participation) were "still found to some extent among the older women, but they were beginning to die out in the new generation."[85]

Notes

I have benefited greatly from the comments and suggestions of the editors and the other authors, particularly those of Nancy Cott, Nancy Hewitt, Evelyn Brooks Higginbotham, and Susan Ware. I am grateful also to Sally Kohlstedt, Barbara Farah, and Virginia Sapiro for their comments.

1. Flexner (1909), pp. xviii–xix.
2. Kraditor (1965); Jablonsky (1978).
3. See also Freedman (1974).
4. I am concerned here primarily with women's voting and their participation in campaigns and in political parties and secondarily in women as candidates for elective office. I will not spend much time addressing the question of how women voted in the 1920s—for example, whether they constituted a "reform vote" or a "dry vote."
5. On the impact of nonproperty suffrage, see Vines and Glick (1967); on immigrants and voting, see Andersen (1979).
6. For present purposes, a good definition of "full integration" might include voting in roughly the same proportions as men and participating widely and confidently in electoral politics and other forms of political activity.
7. Gerould (1925), p. 452.
8. Among others, Converse (1969, 1976); Abramson (1974, 1976); Beck (1976); Glenn (1972); and Claggett (1980).
9. Converse (1969). What makes this type of analysis even more problematic for women, and why viewing women as simply one instance of the class of "newly enfranchised voters" is inadequate, is that women were not merely *un*practiced at voting or *un*socialized (as were, for example, nonpropertied males in some states in the early nineteenth century)—but had grown up, many of them, learning that women were *by nature unsuited* to politics, that by definition politics was a male concern.
10. Converse (1969), pp. 162–163.
11. Rokkan (1970).
12. Wells (1929), p. 207.
13. Breckinridge (1933), p. 247.
14. Gerould (1925).
15. Catt, cited in Adams (1967), p. 170.
16. Lemons (1973), pp. 68–73. See also Wheaton (1929).
17. Lemons (1973), p. 69.

18. *Congressional Record*, 87th Cong. 2d sess., LXII-9047. Cited in Lemons (1973), p. 66.
19. Lemons (1973), p. 73.
20. Allen (1930), p. 6.
21. Lemons (1973), p. 57. Jablonsky argues that many of the antisuffragists were also social feminists, but though they addressed the same problems, they believed that their solutions were "social," not "political," and that women's primary obligation was the molding of public opinion to support progressive laws. Jablonsky (1978), pp. 227–236.
22. Gordon (1986), p. 53.
23. Cited in Gordon (1982), p. 137.
24. Dobyns (1927).
25. Unpublished manuscript, "What Should Be Our Attitude Toward Parties?" excerpted in Stanton and Anthony (1981), p. 182.
26. Taylor (1966), pp. 229–230; Lemons (1973), pp. 50–51.
27. For an account of this debate in New Jersey, see Gordon (1982, 1986); Nichols (1983) has described similar arguments in Connecticut in the 1920s.
28. Key (1956), p. 11.
29. Blair (1929); Fisher and Whitehead (1944); Lemons (1973), pp. 86–87.
30. McCormick (1928), pp. 3, 22.
31. Breckinridge (1933), pp. 317–319.
32. Breckinridge (1933), pp. 322–324.
33. Nichols (1983), p. 48.
34. Breckinridge (1933), pp. 313–321.
35. As a possible indication of this decline, the *Woman's Journal* ceased publication in 1931.
36. Blair (1931).
37. Moskowitz (1930), p. 6.
38. Martin (1925), p. 185. See also Moyer-Wing (1928); Blair (1929).
39. For example, see Sumner (1909), p. 47.
40. Gordon (1986), p. 87.
41. Dobyns (1927), p. 44.
42. Morrison (1978), p. 24.
43. Goldstein (1973), pp. 110, 130.
44. Newell (1930), pp. 10–11.
45. Dobyns (1927), pp. 44–45.
46. Martin (1925), pp. 185–186.
47. Blair (1931), p. 544.
48. Goldstein (1973), pp. 23–25.
49. Burner (1967), pp. 68–70, 229–230; see also Lubbell (1951), p. 40.

50. Schlesinger and Eriksson (1924); Merriam and Gosnell (1924); Arneson (1925); Ogburn and Goltra (1919); Rice and Willey (1924a).

51. Burnham (1974), p. 1015.

52. Lemons (1973), pp. 91–103.

53. Butler (1924), pp. 529–530.

54. Data from *Illinois Blue Book* (1917–1919), pp. 582–584.

55. Figures from Goldstein (1973), p. 89.

56. Sumner (1909), pp. 25–29, 103.

57. Taylor (1961), p. 189.

58. McCormick (1928), p. 3.

59. Merriam and Gosnell (1924), pp. 109–110.

60. Jablonsky (1978), p. 139.

61. Butler (1924), p. 533.

62. Breckinridge (1933), pp. 250–251.

63. Merriam and Gosnell (1924), pp. 110–111; Sumner (1909), pp. 114–117.

64. Sumner (1909), p. 110.

65. Sumner (1909), p. 110; Goldstein (1973), pp. 110–120; Breckinridge (1933), p. 248.

66. Butler (1924), p. 532.

67. Merriam and Gosnell (1924), pp. 255–256.

68. *Chicago Tribune* (1914), p. 5.

69. Butler (1924), p. 531.

70. Tingsten (1937), chap. 1; also see Morrison (1978), p. 248.

71. Barnard (1928b); Morrison (1978), chap. 7.

72. See Taylor (1966), pp. 280–284.

73. Barnard (1928a); McCormick (1928).

74. Morrison (1978), pp. 249–263.

75. Morrison (1978), p. 248.

76. Taylor (1966), p. 286.

77. Butler (1929), p. 11.

78. Harbaugh (1963), vol. 3, p. 2118.

79. Burner (1967), pp. 229–230.

80. Burnham (1965), p. 23.

81. Burnham (1965); Burnham (1974).

82. Kleppner (1982), pp. 641, 643.

83. Barnard (1928a), p. 1.

84. McCormick (1928), p. 3.

85. Merriam and Gosnell (1924), p. 111.

9

In Politics to Stay: Black Women Leaders and Party Politics in the 1920s

Evelyn Brooks Higginbotham

Between 1900 and 1930 more than 1.5 million black men and women migrated from the South to the urban North. The massive trek, actually begun in the last decade of the nineteenth century, shifted into high gear during World War I when wartime demands from northern industry promised employment and most of all escape from the southern way of life—from its boll-weevil-ravaged sharecrop farming and from its segregation, disfranchisement, and lynching. In the decade between 1910 and 1920 the black population soared upward in such cities as Chicago (from 44,103 to 109,458), Detroit (from 5,741 to 40,878), Cleveland (from 8,448 to 34,451), New York (from 91,709 to 152,467), and Philadelphia (from 84,459 to 134,229).[1] Concentrated in the ghettos of urban centers, the migrants soon transformed their restricted residential opportunities into political opportunity.

With migration stepped up to even higher levels between 1920 and 1930, the growing significance of the black vote did not escape the attention of machine politicians. Blacks played an especially influential role in Chicago's machine politics. For instance, in the city's closely contested mayoral race in 1915, the black vote was critical to the victory of Republican William Hale Thompson. Moreover, growing black populations in the northern cities and border states precipitated the rise of black officeholders. In the first three decades of the twentieth century blacks increasingly sent their own to state legislatures, city councils, judgeships, and clerkships. In 1928 the political clout of Illinois blacks carried

Oscar DePriest, the first northern black congressman, to the House of Representatives.[2]

Invisible Politics

Black women played an active and valuable role in the electoral politics of the 1920s, but their role is, too often, overlooked as if an unimportant, even impotent factor in the profound political changes under way. Black political behavior during the early decades of the twentieth century has certainly been analyzed in a number of excellent studies. Unfortunately, the overwhelming majority treat black women as invisible participants, silent members of the black electorate. The literature, much of which was written between the 1930s and 1970s, fails to investigate, to any meaningful extent, either the black female vote or the role of black women leaders in getting out the vote.[3]

While the significance of the female vote has not received serious attention from the traditional literature on black politics, it also has been too easily dismissed by the recent scholarship in women's history. And though a growing body of research has appeared on the suffragist activities among black women leaders, very little is known about their political participation in the decade after the ratification of the Nineteenth Amendment.[4] Feminist scholarship has placed black women's club work firmly within the context of the organizational history of suffragism and has identified such individual leaders as Mary Church Terrell, Ida B. Wells Barnett, and Nannie Helen Burroughs as outspoken champions of women's suffrage in the first two deacades of the twentieth century, but this scholarship fails to recognize their continuing political activism after 1920. The passage of the Nineteenth Amendment, according to this research, appears to portend the end rather than the starting point of black women's involvement in electoral politics for the next decade. This assumption is based on the following realities.

On the eve of ratification, the handwriting on the wall boldly read, "The full meaning of the Nineteenth Amendment would be denied to black women." Historians of the woman's suffrage movement have exposed the racist and class biases of white women suffragists.[5] In a deliberate effort to win southern white support, they disassociated their cause from black voting rights issues. The white women's movement abandoned its earlier nineteenth century ties with the black freedom struggle in favor of an alliance with white supremacy. (See Lebsock, this volume.) The reversal reflected a fundamental shift not only in strategy, but also in the rationale upon which suffragism had rested. By the late nineteenth and early twentieth centuries, white suffragists argued from the position of expediency rather than justice. The National American Woman Suffrage Association, having adopted a states' rights policy toward its member organizations in 1903, paved the way for its southern wing to argue the expediency of woman's suffrage in nullifying the intent of the Fifteenth Amendment and buttressing the cause of white supremacy in general. An assent, if not a direct contributor to the disfranchisement and segregation of southern blacks of both sexes, the strategy assured the denial of black women's ballots. Carrie Chapman Catt, Alice Paul, Ida Husted Harper, and other luminaries of the women's movement added insult to injury by expressing their racist sensibilities in correspondence, segregated marches, and various public statements. The press reported the hard facts once ratification became reality. In state after state in the South, large numbers of black women turned out to register only to be turned back.[6]

Historian Rosalyn Terborg-Penn draws attention to the suffrage clubs of black women in the states that ratified the woman's vote prior to 1920, but she concludes that the postscript to the passage of the Nineteenth Amendment was one of frustration and disillusionment. By the mid 1920s discontented black feminists, Terborg-Penn posits, turned their eyes away from mainstream electoral politics to the renewed antilynching crusade, social service efforts, and separatist or Third World causes such as the International Council of Women of the Darker Races, Pan-Africanism, and the Marcus Garvey movement.[7] Although her assessment correctly emphasizes the hostile, racially charged environment that black women faced, it underestimates the continuing interest of black women leaders in the electoral process.

The work of Ida Wells Barnett, the great black feminist and antilynching crusader, illustrates the potential of black women leaders in mobilizing voters. Her autobiography tells of her activities with the Alpha Suffrage Club for black women soon after Illinois adopted woman's suffrage in 1913. She credited her club with the election of Oscar DePriest in 1915 as Chicago's first black alderman. The large black turnout also played the decisive role in the victory of William Hale Thompson.[8]

Migration and Woman Suffrage

When America returned to normalcy after World War I, the combined realities of Jim Crow and southern disfranchisement, of northern discrimination in housing and jobs, and of pervasive racism both customary and institutionalized created a set of social conditions as inimical to black progress as had existed in previous generations. Although their grievances were just as pronounced, black women, like their men, did not greet these objective conditions with the same degree of resignation and accommodation that had characterized the era of Booker T. Washington. Rather, their response was one of optimism, reflecting a reevaluation of their circumstances and a transformed subjective perception of their own power to bring about change. This subjective transformation was conditioned by new forces at work—namely, migration and the woman's vote. Both appeared to signal a break with the past.

Thousands upon thousands of migrants of voting age annually left states in the Deep South where voting restrictions had been most repressive. That these states simultaneously imposed the greatest economic and social restrictions upon blacks accounts for the eagerness of so many to uproot and search for greater economic and political freedom. Unskilled and semiskilled jobs in the northern cities offered wage rates considerably higher than the southern agricultural work in which most of the migrants previously had been engaged. Florette Henri's study of the Great Migration observes that "to farm workers in the South who made perhaps $.75 a day, to urban female domestics who might earn from $1.50 to $3.00 a week, the North during the war years beckoned with factory wages as high as $3.00 to $4.00 a day, and domestic pay of $2.50 a day." Despite the higher cost of living and the drastic reduction of factory employment for blacks after the war ended, the urban North's higher wages and greater economic opportunity relative to the South continued to lure hundreds of thousands of black migrants throughout the 1920s. For black southern migrants, the ballot box, no less than heightened employment opportunity and greater social mobility, served as a badge of freedom from the Jim Crow world they fled.[9]

When viewed as an indicator of voting behavior, employment suggests its positive role within the critical mix of urban opportunities that encouraged black women's political integration. Women constituted a sizable proportion of the northern black labor force. In 1920 the black married women's employment rate stood at five times that of white married women. In the largest northern cities in 1930 between 34 and 44 percent of black households had two or more members employed. Moreover, successive waves of migrants contributed to the growth of economic and social differentiation within the black urban community. The appearance of a black male and female elite composed of lawyers, educators, physicians, ministers, and entrepreneurs reflected a leadership ever mindful of black political interests and the importance of voter mobilization for the realization of those interests.[10]

Harold Gosnell indicates the political consciousness of black women in his classic *Negro Politicians* (1935), the earliest systematic study of urban black political behavior. More attentive to women than subsequent works by social scientists, Gosnell's several studies on Chicago politics were written in the 1920s and 1930s when the implications of woman's recently acquired right to vote were more consciously observed. Gosnell notes that black women "shared with their men folks an intense interest in politics." He reveals that in the 1923 local election relatively fewer black women than white used the antisuffragist argument as an excuse for not voting. While Gosnell does not dwell on the political mobilization of black women, he clearly acknowledges their importance in augmenting the black vote: "The huge increment in the absolute number of the estimated eligible colored voters between 1910 and 1920 was due largely to the adoption of woman suffrage in 1913 and to the flood of newcomers after 1914."[11] The conflation of woman's suffrage and black urban migration made possible greater political opportunity and leverage for blacks as a group. It also served to broaden black women's perceptions of their own influence and activism. Throughout the 1920s black women leaders, far from abandoning the electoral process, envisioned themselves in politics to stay.

The Black Press and Women's Political Consciousness

The black press served as an important vehicle for promoting the political concerns of black women. Varying in form from lengthy informative articles to mere blurbs, its news announced and promoted organizational activities and noteworthy persons and events rarely covered by the white press. Its pages featured the election or appointment of blacks to prominent and, just as often, quite obscure positions from across the nation. Papers such as the *Chicago Defender, New York Age, Pittsburgh Courier, Norfolk Journal and Guide,* and *Baltimore Afro-American* served not only their local markets, but a national one hungry for "race news." The *Chicago Defender,* which had the largest readership of all, is often cited for its influential role in the Great Migration out of the South during World War I. The importance of the black press did not go unrecognized by campaigning politicians. Robert L. Vann, editor of the *Pittsburgh Courier,* was appointed chairman of the publicity committee of the Colored Voters' Division of the Republican National Committee during the 1928 presidential race. Claude A. Barnett, of the Associated Negro Press, was secretary. In fact, the Hoover forces enlisted practically every black news editor on this committee.[12]

Black newspapers frequently reprinted or cited each others' stories along with those from such national magazines as the National Association for the Advancement of Colored People's *Crisis*, the National Urban League's *Opportunity*, and the National Association of Colored Women's *National Notes*. Through the Associated Negro Press important news releases were syndicated in the different papers. Hanes Walton draws attention to the historical role of the black press as a transmitter of political culture—as an agent of political socialization. Its role combated the negative black images presented in the white newspapers. The black press provided the counter orientation to forces affirming black inferiority. In its coverage of women's political activities during the 1920s, it also reinforced the idea of a prominent place for women within black political culture.[13]

The *Baltimore Afro-American*, a weekly during the twenties, concisely illustrates the way black women's political activities were portrayed. In the four issues appearing between September 17 and October 16, 1920, twenty-two articles covered one or another aspect of women's newly acquired right to vote. Three articles presented congratulatory responses by various black and white notables to the ratification of the Nineteenth Amendment. One noted the appointment of Lethia Fleming as head of the black woman's advisory committee to the National Republican party during the 1920 presidential campaign, while another covered Daneva Donnell's appointment as the only black on the first all-woman jury in an Indianapolis court. Five articles exposed the thwarted attempts of black women to register in the southern states. Nine reported political activities among women in Baltimore. Most of these activities took the form of meetings and rallies. One of the local stories featured the results of the first two days of registration in the city's predominantly black wards and concluded that "where the colored women are organized as in the 14th and 17th wards their registration nearly equals that of the men."[14]

The final three articles on black women and politics were represented in the column "A Primer for Women Voters," written by Augusta T. Chissell. Chissell, a member of the Colored Women's Suffrage Club of Maryland, designed the weekly column as a tool for political education. Readers were invited to write in questions, which she in turn answered.

> Question—There are some men who will be up for election in this state in November who have bitterly opposed woman suffrage. What do you think of supporting them?
> Answer—Women should weigh this question very carefully, not from the standpoint of resentment but from the standpoint of justice.[15]

Question—What is meant by party platform? And where may I go to be taught how to vote?

Answer—Party platform simply means what either candidate promises to do after he is elected. The Just Government League is conducting a polling booth at its headquarters. . . . You may go there and become acquainted with the whole order of things. You will also do well to attend the Thursday night meetings of the YWCA under the auspices of the Colored Women's Suffrage Club.[16]

Black women leaders used the press to voice their political concerns and programs throughout the 1920s.

Clubwomen and Politics

Even more important to the political activism of black women leaders was the organizational network already in place on the eve of the ratification of the Nineteenth Amendment. The National Association of Colored Women (NACW) had stood at the forefront of the suffragist cause among black women and became the logical springboard for future political work. By the 1920s the NACW came to represent the organizational hub of the women's club movement. It was the linchpin that united hundreds of women's clubs throughout the nation in shared goals and strategies of social service and racial uplift. Divided into districts, under which fell regional and state federations, the elaborate infrastructure established linkages and opened channels of communication between women's organizations in every black community in America. Through its national leaders and committees, plans were centralized and tasks divided. Through its biennial meetings and national magazine, *National Notes*, the NACW functioned as a clearinghouse, providing a communications network for the dissemination of information and the promotion of collective action.[17]

NACW members, largely of middle-class status, received wide coverage in the black press, and the leaders at the state and national levels were, more often than not, prominent in other progressive groups with respect to racial advancement, such as the National Association for the Advancement of Colored People (NAACP), the National Urban League, and the Commission on Interracial Cooperation. Some of these same leaders also occupied high places of influence within major religious organizations.[18] Tullia Hamilton's study of the first generation of NACW leaders reveals their privileged status vis-à-vis the great majority of black women. Most of the 108 leaders identified by Hamilton had been born in the South between 1860 and 1885, but had settled in the North a decade or two prior to the onslaught of migrants during the World War I period. Unlike the masses of uneducated and unskilled black women who were restricted to domestic service and other menial employment, NACW leaders enjoyed the benefits of education and greater employment opportunities. Approximately three quarters of them were married. Most of the clubwomen were career oriented; about two thirds were teachers and a small proportion were clerical workers and entrepreneurs.[19]

In 1926 the NACW boasted affiliated clubs in forty-one states. Its vast scope and influence prompted Mary McLeod Bethune, national president between 1924 and 1928, to remark: "Every organization is looking to the National Association of Colored Women for assistance in some line of advancement."[20] One organization that looked to the NACW for assistance was the Republican National Committee, which had enlisted outgoing president Hallie Q. Brown to direct its voters' drive among black women in 1924.[21] During the presidential race, the NACW's usual social service activities took a backseat to intense partisan politics. Its magazine, *National Notes*, encouraged political consciousness, shared ideas and strategies, and followed the progress of the campaign in the various states. The selection of Brown, NACW president between 1920 and 1924, reflected the Coolidge forces' recognition of her command over hundreds of thousands of black women.

As director of the Colored Women's Department of the Republican National Committee, Brown built her campaign network on the foundation of the existing regional, state, and local structures of her organization. She recruited her army of workers from the NACW's leadership—from women who had already proved their organizing abilities. Brown appointed Maria C. Lawton of Brooklyn to head the eastern division of the Republican campaign and Myrtle Foster Cook of Kansas to head the western division. At the time, Lawton held the presidency of the Empire State Federation, the association of clubwomen at the New York state level. Her mobilizing ability had been responsible for the tremendous growth in affiliated clubs since 1912. As organizer of the Empire State Federation in 1912 and president from 1916 to 1926, Lawton had expanded the number of clubs from a small concentration mostly in New York City and Buffalo to 103 in all parts of the state. Cook afforded the Republican party another strong mobilizing resource. As editor-manager of the *National Notes*, she transformed the nationally read magazine into a political organ for the Republican party.[22]

Black women's Republican clubs sprang up everywhere—led by clubwomen already in the vanguard of the civic and political affairs of their communities. The overall operation included precinct captains; ward chairmen; city, county, and district chairmen; together with state chairmen and national organizers and speakers. Each state chairman developed circulars and bulletins for her own territory and sent reports to the black press "with accurate and encouraging accounts of women's campaign activities." Their reports highlighted their cooperation in a cause that "has added to our lives a rich chapter of wider friendships with the mutual confidence born of close acquaintance and hard work." The campaign had a tremendous psychological effect on these workers, who described it as rewarding and personally enriching. Lawton referred to the campaign's emotionally fulfilling impact on black women workers. It became an "outlet for their pent up aspirations and ambitions to be counted as integral parts of the body politic."[23]

Reports from state chairmen and organizers revealed optimism in politics and a belief that their efforts were decisive to the electoral outcome. Although the Republican party had utilized black women leaders in the past, the election in 1924 involved their participation in more extensive, visible, and official ways. The state organizer from Rhode Island typified this attitude in her reflections on Coolidge's victory: "I am sure the work our colored women did during the last campaign helped materially to give the National ticket the large plurality it had in the Nation." Campaign reports indicate that there were hundreds of Coolidge-Dawes clubs and meetings in halls, churches, fraternal lodges, schools, homes, and on the streets. House-to-house canvassing appeared to be their most effective strategy, but bringing in speakers of national reputation also received a good response. Other interesting techniques were employed. The organizer for upstate New York outlined the following activities based on her tour of Elmira, Rochester, Auburn, Buffalo, and Niagara Falls:

> We found the forming of Coolidge-Dawes Clubs using pledge cards an excellent method for tabulating new voters and bringing in old voters who were in the class of stay-at-homes. Another method found very effective was Block Captains in every district. These, with their assistants, kept a list of new voters and registrants of old, in turn. These were given to the chairman of our Get-Out-The-Vote Committee. This committee of twenty women did Yeoman work on election day; no voter of their district was omitted.[24]

Organizers in West Virginia noted the role of special circular letters— one with an appeal to the ministry and another to women directly. West Virginia women also found the question box helpful in identifying issues of concern to voters. The report from Minnesota relied heavily on mass distributions—pamphlets entitled "Important Information for All Legal Voters," "Register Today" cards, and sample ballots. Iowa was the only state to cite telephone canvassing among its techniques. Kentucky reported its least successful technique—getting women to answer mail questionnaires.[25]

Florie Pugh of Oklahoma City held instructional meetings in the evenings and lectured on how to organize a precinct and district, the duty of a precinct committee woman, how to poll, how to get the voters registered, new voters, the necessity of voting by 10:00 A.M. on election day, and why black people should be Republicans. Lillian Browder, a precinct captain in Chicago, stressed the need to discuss gender politics in house-to-house canvassing. She found that women exhibited greater responsiveness and interest when told of legislation and political affairs vital to home life. Thus Browder talked to women about laws that touched upon their lives—for example, the Child Labor Law, the Pure Food Act, and the law regulating working hours for women, and she associated passage of this legislation with the Republican party.[26]

The presidential race of 1924 and Coolidge's ultimate victory reinforced a growing sense of political efficacy among black clubwomen. They interpreted their role as crucial to Republican victory, and they expected a continued relationship with the party and with political organizations among white women. Estele R. Davis, who served on the Speakers' Bureau during the Coolidge campaign, captured the perceived interconnection between their club movement and political participation:

> How little have we realized in our club work for the last twenty-five years that it was God's way of preparing us to assume this greater task of citizenship. I often wonder what would have happened without our organized club work which has not only trained us for service, but has created a nation-wide sisterhood through which we know the outstanding women of each state who are able to serve our race in the time of need.[27]

The National League of Republican Colored Women

Throughout the summer of 1924 women came to value the need for permanent organization at the state and national levels. In some states political clubs had operated since the adoption of women's suffrage, but in most the presidential campaign had spurred the desire for continued political work. Mamie Williams (Mrs. George S. Williams) and Mary

Booze, both NACW women and also the Republican national commit-teewomen from Georgia and Mississippi, respectively, urged the practi-cality of uniting black women's Republican clubs in a national organiza-tion.[28] On August 7, 1924, hours after the adjournment of the biennial meeting of the NACW, Williams and Booze reconvened a number of the clubwomen for the purpose of forming the National League of Republi-can Colored Women (NLRCW). Booze and Williams were named honor-ary presidents, while the official roster also included Nannie Burroughs of the District of Columbia, president; Sue M. Brown (Mrs. S. Joe Brown) of Iowa, vice-president; Daisy Lampkin of Pennsylvania, trea-surer and chairman of the executive committee; Mary Church Terrell of the District of Columbia, treasurer; and Mrs. Elizabeth Ross Hanes, parliamentarian. These women were well known for their visibility in political affairs and for their work with the NAACP and the Urban League.[29]

The NLRCW sought to become a permanent political force among black women, adopting the slogan "We are in politics to stay and we shall be a stay in politics." It distinguished its goals from that of the NACW and other groups that adopted partisan political activities on a temporary basis and specifically at election time.[30] While endorsing the Republican National Committee's appointment of Brown as director of colored women for the presidential campaign, the members of the NLRCW criticized the NACW for abandoning its nonpartisan image and expressed disapproval of its heavy coverage of the Republican campaign through the pages of the *National Notes*.

There are several explanations for this reaction on the part of women whose roles as leaders overlapped both organizations. First, the NLRCW ensured continuation of a partisan political emphasis by taking it out of the hands of an organization whose intentions and objectives had historically been to unite black women of all affiliations and persua-sions in the work of social service. The NACW's Citizenship and Legis-lative departments constituted integral parts of the organization's "lift-ing as we climb" philosophy, but they were designed to inspire civic duty and legislative study for race and sex advancement, not to advance specific political parties.[31] Second, rivalries existed between women. Some of the NLRCW women claimed that certain NACW leaders had used their position during the presidential campaign to further their own selfish personal ambitions.[32] On the other hand, individuals in the NLRCW might have perceived the new organization as a stepping-stone to a political appointment that had bypassed them in the last campaign.

The crossover of membership in the two organizations invariably blurred distinctions. Reports of campaign activities during the 1924 election were sent to Nannie Burroughs as well as to the NACW officials working with the Republican National Committee.[33] Members of the NLRCW often quoted the slogan of the NACW when confirming their attendance at an event sponsored by the former. In 1928 Daisy Lampkin wrote to Burroughs of Lethia Fleming, an outstanding Republican organizer in Ohio and leader in both the NLRCW and the NACW: "She seemed to confuse the two National organizations, but I made it clear to her that they are in no way connected." By 1926 the NACW, while continuing to urge women's political participation, had relinquished overt partisanship to the NLRCW.[34]

In 1924 Burroughs sent out a questionnaire to black women leaders throughout the country. The exact number mailed is unknown, and only twenty-three responses appear to exist—representing respondents from eleven states. While this number is too small to be representative of black women in general, the questions themselves reveal the major concerns of the NLRCW in the building of its program. Some of the questions read as follows:

—Did you hear of any vote selling among the women?
—What is being done to educate women as to the value of the ballot?
—Are Negro women taking an active part in local politics?
—Is it true that a number of women failed to register and vote because their husbands are opposed to woman suffrage?
—Did you hear that Whites who hire servants tried to influence their votes?
—What is the general attitude of the White women of your city toward Negro women since they have suffrage?
—Give the names of Congressmen from your State who have poor records on the Negro question.
—What should the Negro demand of the incoming administration?
—Who are the women in your city and State best qualified to organize political clubs to assist in the work?[35]

Meeting in Oakland in August 1926, the executive committee of the NLRCW presented its goals and intentions in the form of a resolution— copies of which were sent to Sallie Hert, a vice-chairman of the Republican National Committee and head of its Women's Division, and to the Associated Negro Press for distribution in all the black newspapers. The resolution requested formal and active affiliation with the Women's Division of the Republican National Committee and offered the services and counsel of its state leaders in the upcoming congressional election.[36]

The response by the Women's Division of the Republican National Committee could not have been more promising. Sallie Hert invited

Burroughs to represent the NLRCW at its first national conference of women leaders. Eighty-five women from thirty-three states met in Washington between January 12 and 14, 1927, to discuss their role in the Grand Old Party. The group included national committeewomen (Booze of Mississippi and Williams of Georgia being the only other blacks present), state vice-chairmen, and Republican women's clubs. The women discussed a variety of issues of direct interest to Burroughs: maintaining an ongoing functioning organization throughout the year, women's representation in the party organization, problems of organizing and fundraising, party integrity and loyalty, and overcoming differences among Republican women.[37]

Burroughs was among the seventy-five women to visit the White House and receive greetings from President and Mrs. Coolidge. She also heard talks by Secretary of War Dwight Davis and Secretary of Commerce Herbert Hoover. The high point for Burroughs was the opportunity to address the gathering. She began her remarks by stating: "I'm glad to be able to give a touch of color to this meeting. No political party in America is 100 percent American without this touch of color." She proceeded to inform her seemingly quite receptive audience of the work of her own organization.[38]

In May 1927 the NLRCW called its own three-day conference in Washington, D.C. Leaders from twenty-three states came together to discuss their concerns and to hear high-ranking officials in the GOP discuss issues and policies. Included among the array of speakers were Sallie Hert of the Women's Division, Virginia White Speel of the Republican Central Committee for the District of Columbia, Secretary of Labor James Davis, and Secretary of the Interior Hubert Work. Feelings of efficacy continued to run high among black women.[39]

The presidential election in 1928 witnessed NLRCW leaders in prominent campaign positions. Lampkin, chairman of its executive committee, was appointed by the Republican high command to direct the mobilization of black women voters in the East. Burroughs had deeply wanted the position, but her nonvoting status as a District of Columbia resident operated to her disadvantage. An eloquent orator, Burroughs was appointed to the National Speakers' Bureau and became one of the most highly sought-after speakers on the campaign trail.[40] Many NLRCW members journeyed to Washington for the inauguration of Hoover. They rejoiced in his victory. It seemed just as much their own.

By 1932 the honeymoon had ended between the black women and the Republican party. The Depression focused the attention of black leaders, male and female, on questions of economic survival. The Hoover administration had little to say to most Americans, least of all to blacks, on economic relief. Burroughs, like most blacks, continued to support Hoover in that year, but with increasing criticism of his policies toward the black poor. Nor had the party of Lincoln fared well in its civil rights record during Hoover's term. In the throes of unprecedented economic suffering, blacks came to challenge their traditional loyalty to the party responsible for their emancipation from slavery.[41]

Black leaders denounced the various racist actions of the Hoover administration. His efforts to "lily-white" the Republican party in the South, his segregation of the Gold Star Mothers, and his nomination of an avowed advocate of black disfranchisement to the Supreme Court incurred the wrath of black leaders throughout the nation.[42] However, for members of the NLRCW, the unhappy alliance between blacks and the administration was foreshadowed as early as Hoover's inauguration. In March 1929 the chairman of the Inaugural Charity Ball requested that Burroughs retrieve tickets "accidentally" sent to black women workers in the Hoover campaign. Burroughs acquiesced to Republican wishes for a segregated ball, but not without registering the protest of her coworkers: "It is not easy for me to get the others reconciled to embarrassments for which they are not responsible. One has said already, 'They use us in the crisis and humiliate us at will.' " In 1932 Sallie Hert's replacement by Lena Yost as head of the Republican Women's Division further alienated the black women. Yost lacked the sincerity and interest that had characterized Hert's relationship with the NLRCW. Burroughs's correspondence discloses increasing frustration with the party's solicitation of her support at election time, while at all other times treating her suggestions with "silent contempt."[43]

The League of Women Voters

Another organization that captured the interest of black clubwomen during the 1920s was the League of Women Voters (LWV). Lines of communication remained open between the NACW and black units of the LWV. While individual blacks held membership in some of the predominantly white state leagues, separate black leagues operated in Oakland, San Francisco, Los Angeles, Chicago, and St. Louis. Delegates from the Oakland, Chicago, and St. Louis groups were represented at the league's national conferences in the 1920s. They were also represented on the state boards of the California and Illinois leagues. Leaders of the black leagues were, at the same time, leaders of their state federated clubs—the constituent members of the NACW.

Hettie Tilghman, leader among black California women in the LWV, referred to the overlap in membership for the NACW and her state's two black leagues, the Alameda County League of Colored Women Voters and the San Francisco Colored League. She cited their political activities from the dual role of federated women and League of Women Voters. Delilah Beasley, active member of the NACW and the Alameda County League of Colored Women Voters, devoted press coverage to both in her column, "Activities among Negroes," which ran in the white daily, the *Oakland Tribune*. On November 25, 1925, she announced the interest of the Alameda County League of Colored Women Voters in the observance of World Court Day, scheduled for December 17. Her column also cited an article written by the president of the Alameda County League for the magazine of the NACW. The article, which had appeared a few weeks earlier in the *National Notes*, praised the California State League and National League of Women Voters for their efforts in securing the passage of specific legislation affecting women and children.[44]

On October 6, 1920, the St. Louis LWV organized a "Colored Committee" to bring before the larger body racial concerns related to education, health, child welfare, and citizenship. Nine years later, B.F. Bowles headed the committee, which functioned as an important liaison between the league and the large black female population in St. Louis. Under Bowles's leadership, the committee assumed a number of projects: gathering data on southern election laws and policies, offering lectures on pending legislation, holding citizenship schools, providing scholarships to black students, entertaining national league officers at gatherings in the black community, forming junior leagues among black girls, and contributing financially to the budget of the St. Louis league. In an editorial in the *St. Louis American*, Carrie Bowles, another black league member and member of the NACW, praised the St. Louis league for being "one of the very few leagues in the U.S. in which the colored members enjoy every privilege of the organization on terms of absolute equality." Writing in the national magazine of the NACW in 1928, Bowles again praised her city league for sending a black delegate to the eighth annual conference.[45]

Illinois black clubwomen also contributed to the work of the league. In 1926 the Illinois State League of Women Voters elected a black woman, Margaret Gainer, to membership on its board of directors. Gainer, also a member of the Illinois State Federation of Colored Women's Clubs, directed the latter's citizenship department, which included the program of the Illinois LWV. The Illinois State Federation constituted an extensive network of black clubwomen. It organized in 1899 and by 1926 comprised 92 clubs with 2,074 members divided into three districts: the Chicago and Northern, the Central, and the Southern.[46]

Several clubwomen in the Chicago area were league members. The Douglass League of Women Voters, the black unit of the league in the city, was headed by Irene Goins, a leader of the Illinois State Federation as well. On June 18, 1924, Florence Harrison of the national league met with the black members to discuss their plans for the development of citizenship schools. Attached to Harrison's report were the black women's plans for the national "Get-Out-the-Vote Campaign." In addition to incorporating the campaign into the citizenship program of the Illinois State Federation of Colored Women's Clubs, the Douglass League proposed:

> 1. Frequent meetings open and advertised, to be held in the Community Center . . . to which the League hopes to rally colored women from a large surrounding territory. At its meetings there will be from time to time (a) Ballot demonstrations (repeated); (b) Importance of registration (repeated); (c) Issues of the Campaign; (d) Candidates' meetings.
>
> 2. A system of home teaching for the colored women who cannot come to the Community Center . . . will be carried into the homes by members of the Douglass League.
>
> 3. "Excursion tickets" indicating a trip to the polls and asking "have you voted?" will be hung on tags on the doors in the neighborhood.[47]

News of league activities encouraged politically minded black women to seek membership in either separate or integrated units. However, they were usually discouraged. Delilah Beasley of Oakland exressed her frustration in establishing a black league in Los Angeles. Her efforts encountered prejudice throughout the state and especially in Los Angeles itself. Urging the formation of "full Colored Leagues" and auxiliaries to the white leagues, she stressed the need for black women to develop their own leadership, separate from whites so that "they do not antagonize the members of the White league by their presence." Yet Beasley did not demur from strongly recommending black representation on the general state board.[48]

On the other hand, Ohio black women opposed racial separatism in league work. Members of the Ohio Federation of Colored Women's Clubs had hoped to integrate various local leagues, after Sybil Burton, president of the state league, addressed their meeting and solicited their cooperation in mobilizing the vote. Ohio black women were ripe for participation. Burton admitted that the Ohio league found it unnecessary to execute educational classes for black women in the state because J. Estelle Barnett, a league member and black woman editor of the newspaper *In the Queen's Garden*, had used her paper to disseminate information on ballot marking and the necessity for voting.[49]

With no uniform guidelines, Burton preferred to leave the decision of accepting blacks to the individual leagues, whose racial policies varied by community. Oberlin accepted blacks freely and equally. Zanesville received black members, but made them unwelcome at their luncheons and other social gatherings. The Toledo league sought advice from the national league when black women desired membership. The general consensus of the Toledo league was against integration, but encouraged black women to form their own separate units. The Cincinnati league likewise contemplated the formation of an all-black unit. The reply from the national league tended to be discouraging in every way. While acknowledging that a few of the states had black leagues and a few others actually integrated individual black women into their ranks, Anne Williams Wheaton, press secretary, asserted: "Those who have expertise in this matter think it is far better not to encourage organizations of colored Leagues."[50] Rather than formal organization, the national league sought to address black issues through its Committee on Negro Problems—the name later being changed, at the request of black members, to the Committee on Interracial Problems. (See Jones, this volume.)

In 1921 the committee formed in response to a petition by southern black women whose suffrage rights were denied. Interracial in composition, the committee included representatives from states where "the colored vote is a material and accepted fact." Its purpose was to implement educational and citizenship training programs, not augment black league membership. Although plans were divised by its three successive chairmen, Julia Lathrop (1921), Minnie Fisher Cunningham (1921–1925), and Adele Clark (after 1925), the small committee left little in the way of accomplishment. A questionnaire was sent out to the states in 1927, but most did not reply, nor did the states that responded always do so thoughtfully and accurately. The ineffectiveness of the committee was evidenced in the infrequency of its meetings, all of which occurred informally at the national conventions and did not carry over into the interim period.[51] By the end of the decade the League of Women Voters had lost, largely by its own choice, the potential for being an important mobilizing force among black women.[52]

Conclusion

At the dawning of the 1930s, blacks found themselves on the brink of a political transition that would greatly accelerate in the next five years. The more dramatic collective action of blacks during the Depression and their strategic placement in the New Deal hierarchy have overshadowed the contribution of the previous decade to their political mobilization and increased political leverage. The ratification of the Nineteenth Amendment in 1920 lent significant impetus to black women's interest in the American political process, although the continuing legacy of racism conditioned the nature and extent of their participation. The racist policies of the National American Woman Suffrage Association continued in the 1920s with its successor organization, the League of Women Voters, to discourage black participation. Black women leaders, while organizing their own separate organizations, encountered racism from the very elected officials for whom they campaigned. Yet black women's discontent and frustration with white women's organizations, with the Republican party, and with a racist society in general during the 1920s did not translate into an abandonment of politics, but into the emergence of new leaders, alliances, and strategies.

In 1936, when the majority of black voters shifted to the Democratic party, the unswerving Republican allegiance of such leaders as Nannie Burroughs and Mary Church Terrell no longer won the applause of the black electorate. The Democratic party had shed its long-worn garb of white supremacy, its image as the party of the Solid South, segregation, and black disfranchisement. Under Franklin Roosevelt's New Deal, the Democrats came to be perceived as the party most receptive to black opportunity. Mary McLeod Bethune's visibility in the Roosevelt administration and Crystal Bird Fauset's membership on the Democratic National Committee expressed both the continuation of women's political activism and shifting opportunities for black women leaders. In 1932 Bethune sat on the Board of Counselors of the Women's Division of the Republican National Committee with such notable Republican stalwarts as Mrs. Theodore Roosevelt and Mrs. William Howard Taft. In 1936 she presided over Roosevelt's Black Cabinet.[53] Bethune's shifting allegiance symbolized the changed mood of the black electorate and, certainly not least of all, woman's prerogative to change her mind.

Notes

1. Henri (1975), pp. 50–59, 68–69; Kilson (1971), p. 175; Jones (1985), pp. 152–160.
2. Gosnell (1935), pp. 13–92, 180–190.
3. Lewinson (1932); Gosnell (1941); Drake and Cayton (1945); Wilson (1960); Kilson (1971); Katznelson (1976).
4. See, for example, Terborg-Penn (1983), pp. 261–278.
5. Kraditor (1971), pp. 138–171; Terborg-Penn (1978), pp. 17–27; Giddings (1984), pp. 129–130, 165–169, 177, 218–220.

6. "The Woman Voter Hits the Color Line," *Nation*, October 6, 1920.

7. Terborg-Penn (1983), pp. 261–278.

8. Barnett (1970), pp. 345–353.

9. Henri (1975), pp. 52–80; McAdam (1982), pp. 77–81; Gosnell (1935), pp. 16–19.

10. Henri (1975), pp. 54–55; Kilson (1971), pp. 170–182; Jones (1985), pp. 162–180, 190, 193–194.

11. Interview with Harold F. Gosnell, March 17, 1986, Bethesda, Maryland; also see Gosnell (1935), pp. 15, 19, 374; Gosnell (1968).

12. "Negro Republican Campaign Division," *Norfolk Journal and Guide*, August 11, 1928; also see press release "Republican National Committee, for Release Thursday, 2 August 1928," Nannie Helen Burroughs Papers, Library of Congress.

13. Walton (1985), p. 51.

14. See the *Baltimore Afro-American* for "Equal Rights League Sends Congratulations to Women"; "Colored Woman Sits on Jury"; "Committee of Women Named—Mrs. Lethia G. Fleming of Cleveland Is Approved Chairman," September 17, 1920; "Women Hit Color Line," October 8, 1920; "Vital Meeting—Come and Hear Why We Should Stand by Our Race Candidate," October 1, 1920; "Women Spring Big Surprise," September 24, 1920; "Women Make Good," October 16, 1920.

15. Augusta T. Chissell, "A Primer for Women Voters," *Baltimore Afro-American*, September 24, 1920.

16. Augusta T. Chissell, "A Primer for Women Voters," *Baltimore Afro-American*, October 1, 1920.

17. National Association of Colored Women, *National Notes*, April 1923, p. 18; Wesley (1984), pp. 55–100.

18. Giddings (1984), pp. 107–109, 135–136; Brooks (1988).

19. Hamilton (1978), p. 53.

20. Mary McLeod Bethune, "Biennial Report of the National Association of Colored Women, 1924–1926," *National Notes*, July and August 1926, pp. 3–4.

21. Hallie Q. Brown, "Republican Colored Women of America," *National Notes*, December 1924, p. 1.

22. "Report from the Western Division and the Eastern Division," *National Notes*, December 1924, pp. 2–3; Wesley (1984), pp. 91, 201–202.

23. "Report," *National Notes*, December 1924, pp. 2–3.

24. "Report," p. 4.

25. "Report," p. 4.

26. Gosnell notes a higher percentage of women precinct captains in the black wards. His roster showed as much as one fourth of the captains to be women in the black Third Ward in Chicago. See Gosnell (1968), pp. 61–63; "Campaign Experiences," *National Notes*, January 1925, pp. 13–14.

27. "Campaign Experiences," *National Notes*, January 1925, p. 13.

28. In the southern states black disfranchisement and Democratic hegemony combined to effectively nullify any hope of amassing votes for state and local office, but posts within the Republican party as well as federal patronage positions were still available to southern Republicans by virtue of the votes they delivered at the national conventions. The influence of black Republicans and their female officeholders such as Mary Booze of Mississippi and Mamie Williams of Georgia lay largely with the ability of the black Republican organization in each southern state to achieve recognition at the Republican National Convention. Termed "black and tans," these organizations distinguished themselves from the Republican organizations with overwhelmingly white membership—"lily-whites." The influence of the "black and tans" was keenly felt in the presidential nominations of McKinley in 1896, Taft in 1908 and 1912, and Hoover in 1928. See Lewinson (1932), pp. 170–176; Key (1949), pp. 286–289; and Walton (1975), pp. 133–135.

29. "Minutes of the Temporary Organization of the National League of Republican Colored Women, 7 August 1924," and "Minutes of the Subsequent Meeting of the NLRCW, 11 August 1924," Nannie Helen Burroughs Papers, Library of Congress.

30. "The National League of Republican Colored Women," *National Notes*, July 1928, p. 10.

31. Mary Church Terrell, "An Appeal to Colored Women to Vote and Do Their Duty in Politics," *National Notes*, November 1925, p. 1; Mary Church Terrell, "What Colored Women Can and Should Do at the Polls," *National Notes*, March 1926, p. 3.

32. Mazie Griffin to Burroughs, no date; Mamie Williams to Burroughs, January 5, 1925, Nannie Helen Burroughs Papers, Library of Congress; also see "Departments and Their Functions," *National Notes*, January 1925, p. 2.

33. See, for example: Frannie Givens, of the East-End Colored Women's Political Clubs, to Burroughs, October 20, 1924; Mary E. Gardiner, of the Women's Republican Club of Cambridge, to Burroughs, October 21, 1924; Susan B. Evans, state director of colored women's activities of the St. Paul Minnesota Republican State Central Committee, October 22, 1924; Elizabeth L. Gulley, of the Colored Division, Wayne County Coolidge-Groesbeck Club, Republican State Central Committee of Michigan, October 29, 1924; and Mrs. Charles W. French, Parliamentarian, Kansas State Federation of Colored Women, to Burroughs, October 30, 1924, Nannie Helen Burroughs Papers, Library of Congress.

34. However, the NACW's *National Notes* carried articles promoting the National League of Colored Women. See "Republican Call," *National Notes*, April 1927, p. 6; "The National League of Republican Colored Women," *National Notes*, July 1928, p. 10.

35. "Colored Women in Politics Questionnaire," Nannie Helen Burroughs Papers, Library of Congress.

36. "Meeting of the Executive Committee of the National League of Republican Colored Women, Oakland, Calif., 6 August 1926"; and Burroughs to Mrs. Alvin Hert, August 11, 1926, Nannie Helen Burroughs Papers, Library of Congress.

37. "Summarized Report of the Conference of the Republian National Committeewomen, State Vice Chairmen, and State Club Presidents, January 12, 13, 14, 1927," Nannie Helen Burroughs Papers, Library of Congress.

38. "Summarized Report."

39. "G.O.P. Women from Twenty-Three States in Session," *Afro-American* (Washington Edition), May 21, 1927.

40. Daisy Lampkin to Burroughs, July 2, July 17, October 8, 1928; Lampkin to Mrs. Paul FitzSimmons, October 8, 1928; Lampkin to Fellow Republican, July 17, 1928, Nannie Helen Borroughs Papers, Library of Congress.

41. Weiss (1983), pp. 3–33.

42. Gold Star Mothers were the mothers and widows of men buried in Europe who had died in active service during World War I. The U.S. government sponsored the women's passage to Europe in order to place wreaths on the graves. Black Gold Star mothers were sent over in separate and blatantly inferior ships. Weiss (1983), pp. 16–17.

43. Burroughs to Mrs. John Allen Dougherty, Chairman, Inaugural Charity Ball, March 2, 1929; Burroughs to Mrs. Sallie Hert, August 19, 1929, April 14, 1930; Susie M. Myers to Burroughs, May 3, 1932; Burroughs to Mrs. Ellis Yost, September 27, 1932, June 30, 1934; Burroughs to Mrs. Maude B. Coleman, September 8, 1936, Nannie Helen Burroughs Papers, Library of Congress.

44. Delilah L. Beasley, "Activities among Negroes," *Oakland Tribune*, November 22, 1925; Hettie Tilghman, "What the Study of Legislative Work Has Meant to Our Group," *National Notes*, November 1925, p. 3; "Miss Delilah L. Beasley," *National Notes*, March 1928, p. 8; Beasley, "California Women Preparing for Biennial Convention," *National Notes*, April 1926; Belle Sherwin to Sybil R. Burton, March 31, 1925, League of Women Voters Papers, Library of Congress.

45. Mrs. B. F. Bowles and Mrs. E. C. Grady, "The Colored Committee of the League of Women Voters of St. Louis, The First Nine Years"; Gladys Harrison to Ruth Siemer, October 14, 1929; Ruth Siemer to Miss Beatrice Marsh, June 30, 1930; and Beatrice Marsh to Adele Clark, July 2, 1930; also written sometime in the late 1920s but undated in Carrie Bowles, "Defends League of Women Voters," *St. Louis American*, no date; clipping and aforementioned letters in League of Women Voters Papers, Library of Congress; Carrie Bowles, "Women Voters' National League," *National Notes*, May 1928, p. 15.

46. "Mrs. Elizabeth Lindsay Davis . . . ," *National Notes*, April 1926, p. 1; "Illinois Federation of Colored Women's Clubs," *National Notes*, July 1926, p. 24.

47. "Excerpt from letter from Florence Harrison to Miss Sherwin dated 18 June

1924" and attached page, "Sent by Mrs. Rich to B.S. 1924," League of Women Voters Papers, Library of Congress.

48. Delilah L. Beasley to Mrs. Warren Wheaton, March 23, 1926; Mrs. Warren W. Wheaton to Delilah Beasley, March 25, 1926, League of Women Voters Papers, Library of Congress.

49. Sybil R. Burton to Belle Sherwin, March 27, 1925, League of Women Voters Papers, Library of Congress.

50. Agnes Hilton to Gladys Harrison, August 9, 1928; Anne Williams Wheaton to Agnes Hilton, August 17, 1928; League of Women Voters Papers, Library of Congress.

51. "Special Committee on Inter-Racial Problems, 17 April 1934"; "Report of the Special Committee on Interracial Problems to the Board of Directors, December 1927"; "National League of Women Voters—Report for the Committee on Negro Problems, April 1924–April 1925"; and "Committee on Negro Problems—Chairman Mrs. Minnie Fisher Cunningham, 11 July 1924"; League of Women Voters Papers, Library of Congress.

52. See, for example, a letter written by a black woman, Eva Nichols Wright, of Washington, D.C., to Belle Sherwin: "In reply to the question 'Are colored women of your city interested as members, in the League of Women Voters or the National Woman's Party? If not, why not?' The replies with two exceptions were negative. To the question 'To what extent do white women and colored women work together politically?' The same negative reply was received with three or four exceptions, and many expressed themselves as being discouraged." Eva Nichols Wright to Belle Sherwin, April 25, 1927, League of Women Voters Papers, Library of Congress.

53. Republican National Committee, Women's Division, *Organization News*, October 22, 1932, p. 2, in Nannie Helen Burroughs Papers, Library of Congress; Weiss (1983), pp. 137–148, 180–184.

10

Women in Party Politics

M. Kent Jennings

Introduction

Since the late 1960s the second women's movement and related processes have transformed the social and political landscape. The fuller incorporation of women into partisan politics, though perhaps a lesser manifestation, has been part of this alteration. One widely observed demonstration of this expansion occurred when the two major parties took a quantum leap by radically increasing the proportion of women delegates at the national nominating conventions. That there was great symbolic significance to that action is unquestionable. The substantive significance for the parties and for women is more problematic.

This chapter examines the topic of women's large-scale entry into party politics via the national nominating conventions. The conventions serve as convenient and meaningful vehicles for studying the incorporation of women into the institutions of the political parties. Although the demise of the political parties has been widely cited in the wake of personal campaign organizations, mass media blitzing, and shrinking party loyalty among voters, it is more accurate to say that the parties have changed rather than disappeared. In some ways—especially with respect to fund raising, resources at the national committee level, and state party organizational staffing—they have become stronger.[1]

While the national conventions are not the dramatic scenes of brokerage and power that they were at one time in American political history, they nevertheless command widespread attention in great part because of the nominating process that leads up to them. The delegates who attend these conventions continue to represent the mid to upper ranges of party leadership. Recent efforts to ensure that ranking public and party officials are guaranteed a certain number of delegate seats testify to the symbolic and practical importance attached to convention membership. Despite some intrinsic problems concerning just who or what it is that the delegates represent, they have been utilized to investigate various topics about the parties, including gender and politics. This chapter follows in that tradition.[2]

It is fortuitous for this study of women and politics seen through the prism of the national conventions that their presence in the parties increased so quickly. From an organizational or group point of view this was a radical departure, for the membership criteria appeared to change in a fundamental way. The announcement of this "new" class of membership raised a number of questions. Would the newcomers be welcomed? Would they threaten the old-timers? Would they have the requisite skills? Were they disadvantaged compared with the prior membership? Did they represent different interests and have different constituencies? Did they have different motives and drives? Did they have different agendas and different priorities? How much would they change the complexion of the parties? What would happen as the newcomers became regulars?

Several topics growing out of such questions will be pursued in this chapter. Thanks to the data base to be employed, most of these are treated in a longitudinal fashion. The analysis focuses on comparisons between men and women, primarily because men are the "oldtimers" and women are the "newcomers" in an organizational sense. Questions of differences, accommodation, and impact can be addressed through these comparisons. Six topics will be treated: (1) the wholesale incorporation of women into the party conventions, (2) the social roles and statuses which men and women bring to their party activities, (3) the voluntary organization profiles represented by men and women, (4) levels of officeholding and political ambition, (5) political preferences on issues of the day, and (6) beliefs about gender roles and the political parties.

The data to be used were obtained by the University of Michigan's Center for Political Studies from the Republican and Democratic delegates to the 1972, 1976, 1980, and 1984 national conventions. Questionnaires were sent to all delegates to these conventions. Across the four cohorts the average response rate for the Republicans was 53 percent and for the Democrats 44 percent.[3] Available comparisons between respondents and nonrespondents suggest only modest differences, thus indicating that the respondents, qua delegates, offer a reasonably representative look at the various party conventions. In interpreting the results it should be borne in mind that any convention is a reflection of stable and dynamic aspects of the parties and that the idiosyncrasies of particular aspirants for the nomination can bring elements into the convention which deviate considerably from preceding convention cohorts.

Breaking Through and Staying In

In many respects the story of women and the national conventions has two parts: The first accompanies the culmination of the women's suffrage movement in the early 1920s; the second, the rise of the second women's movement and the era of party reform beginning in the late 1960s. Starting with a handful of delegates and alternates around the turn of the century, the number of women did not increase until 1916, when they constituted about 1 percent of each party's gathering. On the eve of the passage of the suffrage amendment, both parties upped their representation of women in 1920 and increased that representation quite substantially—to over 10 percent—in the celebratory mood of 1924. By 1928 the celebration was over; the absolute number of women declined appreciably in both parties. In 1932 a rebound occurred, but over the next two decades the proportions fluctuated within a narrow band.[4] Women remained visible, but their failure to grow in numbers and importance reflected a society which itself was doing little to foster the notion of equal opportunity for women. (See Andersen, this volume.)

The political inequality of women was demonstrated in ways other than numerical inferiority. Throughout the pre–World War II period women were primarily represented among the ranks of convention alternates, a junior status in keeping with their assumed political involvement and ability. And women's roles at the convention, in terms of committee assignments and the like, showed an uneven and discouraging pattern of development.[5]

One salutary move associated with the emergence of women at the conventions was the decision of each party—the Democrats in 1920 and the Republicans in 1924—to have equal representation of men and women on their national committees.[6] These committees are nominally the chief rule-making bodies in the interim between elections. The practice of equal representation continues today and, indeed, the state committees and many local party committees are similarly composed. However, the more important point is that women, while present in nearly all twentieth century conventions, were only a small proportion of the convention totals and of the total to which they were entitled if the standard of statistical representation were to be used.

The first two decades after World War II witnessed a continuation of the prewar patterns. But the second part of the story about women and the national parties was about to emerge. Beginning in 1972 and continuing for the next four conventions, women far exceeded their earlier presence, as the following figures show:[7]

	Republicans	Democrats
1948–1968 average	15%	13%
1972	30	40
1976	31	34
1980	36	50
1984	44	50
1988	37	49

Several forces lay behind these dramatic increases, including the social and political upheavals attending the Vietnam War, the student protest movement, the civil rights struggle, and, of course, the second women's movement, which was just getting under way.

In the more immediate sense, however, the upsurge came from actions taken by the national parties, especially on the Democratic side. Following their tempestuous 1968 convention, the Democrats initiated a period of reform, the McGovern-Fraser Commission being the first and most influential proposing body. A key part of the reforms dealt with the composition of the nominating conventions. In particular the Democrats sought to ensure much heavier representation of highly visible demographic groups, including the young, nonwhites, and women.[8] Over the years the party has changed its rules a number of times as to how these quotas were to be achieved, at times making them essentially mandatory and at other times being less strict. But the goal of substantial if not perfect statistical representation of women has been a standard since 1972. For their part the Republicans, in keeping with their less centralized and strict control over convention composition, have adopted resolutions encouraging states to strive for proportionate representation of various demographic groups. In this regard they have clearly been most successful with respect to women.[9]

As the above figures show, the presence of women varies over time.

These variations reflect the rules in operation and the strategies of leading candidates and the national committees. The decrease of Democratic women in 1976, for example, was in reaction to the heavy criticism by traditional forces within the party to the debacle following the quotas-ridden 1972 convention. Perhaps the clearest example of strategic moves by a candidate is the 1984 Republican convention, in which the Reagan forces were apparently worried by several factors.[10] One was the general charge of being antifemale; a second was poll data showing that women supported the President far less than did men; and a third was the prospect that the Democratic convention, with a quota mandate for women, would appear to be much more egalitarian than the GOP meeting. Consequently, the campaign and convention managers worked assiduously to ensure that the Reagan-controlled state leaders included large segments of women as they made up their delegate slates. In fact, the result was the largest female contingent ever.

Beginning with the 1972 Democratic convention, the charge has often been made that women would not be appearing in the ranks of the party elites were it not for the presence of affirmative action motives. Indeed, the rationale of the Democratic reforms with respect to convention delegation composition assumed that affirmative action would be necessary to increase the presence of women at the conventions. But there are two views of the reason for the scarcity of women in previous conventions: One view is that qualified women were being systematically excluded from state delegations, that outright sexism accounted for their small numbers. A second, more benign view is that the pool of "eligible" women was much smaller than that of men. Hence when it came time to form the delegations, accurate representation of the pool of eligibles would result in a preponderance of male delegates. This was especially the case when the delegations were heavily loaded with major political figures and state party leaders, for the extant practices of institutional sexism and gender socialization had produced elites who were primarily male.

In any event, affirmative action was necessary to achieve a quick increase in female representation. Men as gatekeepers had to allow more eligible women in, or the pool of eligibles had to be defined in a different fashion. In keeping with a model of gradual and incremental change in large-scale organizations, we might expect that the use of affirmative action as a necessary lever would have decreased over time. We used the delegate study to estimate whether this was true. The delegates were asked: "Did the effort to see that your delegation was balanced by sex, race, and age play any role in your selection?" If there

Table 10.1   Belief That Affirmative Action Was Involved
in Being Selected As Delegate

	1972		1976		1980		1984	
	Men	Women	Men	Women	Men	Women	Men	Women
Democrats	31%	71%	19%	55%	29%	72%	24%	68%
Republicans	10%	37%	9%	26%	8%	24%	16%	41%

is a bias to these self-reports, it probably underestimates the balance criterion, for to admit it is to admit, in the eyes of some, that one could not qualify under the usual standards.

As expected, the Republicans were far less likely to cite the balance criterion (Table 10.1). Also, quite predictably, women were extraordinarily more likely than men to say that they were the beneficiaries of affirmative action. What was far less predictable, however, is the absence of a downward trend among women. One might have expected 1972 to be the high-water mark, with a subsequent gradual fall, especially within the Democratic party. That is patently not the case. In fact, among Republican women 1984 signals a high point, in large part because of the widely publicized attempt by Republican party officials to counterattack on the gender gap front. In that same year approximately two thirds of the Democratic women felt that their selection had been affected by the very fact that they were women.

On the one hand, it can be argued that women recognize that sexism is still so rampant that without such principles they would not be admitted. On the other hand, it can be argued that the pool of eligibles is still vastly different for men and women. In either case, men and women still accomplish organizational entry differently. In the following sections we shall see the degree to which that difference seems to be associated with social and political differences between men and women.

Comparing Gender and Party

Party is a major corollary or "determinant" of many of the attributes of interest to us; for that reason the results are given by gender within party. Nevertheless, it is also worthwhile to assess the degree to which gender contributes to elite differences once party is taken into account. The most straightforward way to do this (assuming interval-level data) is to construct multiple regression equations in which party and gender become the predictor variables and the attributes of interest become the dependent variables. However, the tabular results suggested that there were also some nonadditive, interaction effects between gender and party; that is, the combination of gender and party produced effects that were in addition to the summation of party and gender. In particular, the combination of being a Democrat and a woman appeared to exert special effects. Therefore, an interaction term was added to the equations.[11]

When applied to the question of whether affirmative action was involved in delegate selection, the use of the regression equations is enlightening. As adumbrated by the tabular results, both party and gender were strong predictors, which is to say that being either a Democrat or a woman increased very substantially the likelihood of feeling that affirmative action was at work in one's selection as a delegate. In fact for all but the 1980 delegates, gender was the strongest predictor once party was controlled (beta coefficients ranged from .30 to .36). Beyond these effects, however, there were also lesser but still significant interaction effects. Being a Democrat *and* a woman upped the likelihood of citing affirmative action more than would be expected based only on the (additive) results for party and gender. The unique position of Democratic women will also be encountered in other results to be presented.

Inequalities in Social Background

What people bring with them to the political arena in terms of social background and preparation is presumed to affect their standing and their effectiveness. Other things being equal, for example, individuals with more education will not only be accorded more prestige and recognition but will also possess derived traits (for example, high-level occupations) that will command recognition and may in fact have given them skills that are particularly valued in the political arena (for example, training in law). Even within this rarefied group of party elites, women continue to have less striking credentials than do men. What remains problematic is whether the gap has dwindled across the twelve years covered by our study and whether the trends extant in the larger society are being reflected at the elite level.

Initial comparisons were made in the three traditional domains of occupation, income, and education. We shall begin with employment and occupation, in part because they are the focal points of so much activity in the women's movement and in part because of their centrality for political status and influence. During the past two decades there has been a dramatic increase, especially among married women and mothers, in the rate of female employment in the general public.[12] Our party elites share fully in that development.

About one third of the Democratic women and over two fifths of the Republican women classified themselves as outside the labor force in 1972. That is almost exclusively a function of their self-labeling as housewives. Women in both parties recorded huge subsequent declines in that categorization, down to 6 percent among Democrats and 19 percent among Republicans. Some small portion of this shift may represent a newfound reluctance by women to call themselves housewives even if they are not in the labor force. But the great bulk of the movement undoubtedly comes from more women entering the job market. Whatever the reasons for these changes, it is generally conceded that, ceteris paribus, being employed carries more status in the world of politics and serves as a potential tool for political advancement. In the measure that this is so, women in each party gained much greater equality in the space of twelve years.

There is a very significant trait among the employed women. From one third to over one half of them were employed by governmental or educational agencies. Because the great majority of the educational employers are public institutions, we may safely refer to the combination of the two as public sector employment. Women are also far more likely than men to be in this sector, the ratios being roughly 2:1 among Republicans and 1.5:1 among Democrats across the years. By comparison, the proportion of the (nonagricultural) national work force employed in the public sector during this period was about 20 percent for women and 16 percent for men.[13] Thus the proportions, especially for women, are far higher among the delegates, and the differences between men and women are also much greater among the delegates. For women in particular, then, public employment is a key route to party power. All the more revealing is the fact that over one third of the GOP women, members of a party championing the private sector, were employed by public agencies.

Whether this differential ratio gives women an advantage is problematic. If the position is that of an elective or visible appointed official, the advantage is probably there. It is also true that simply being in public agencies heightens the likelihood of contact with a variety of political operatives and places one in a position to have access to desirable information. On the other hand, public employees are sometimes perceived negatively, as being bureaucrats, security conscious, and unambitious.[14] From this viewpoint, public employment would be a liability.

With time, women generally have come closer to men in the higher-status occupations. This is especially true within the Democratic party. By 1984 the proportion of women (50 percent) who were in professional or technical occupations nearly equaled the proportion of men (54 percent). The gap was still noticeable in the Republican party, but even there inroads had been made. However, the gap between men and women remained equally high in each party once the professional and technical jobs were distinguished from those requiring doctoral or equivalent training. Here the figures run about 25–35 percent for men and 3–10 percent for women. At the very apex of the occupational structure, then, men continue to hold an immense advantage. Ironically, in view of the GOP as the party of perceived higher status, more Republican than Democratic women were in clerical and office positions—in 1984 the figures were 6 percent for the Democrats and 13 percent for the Republicans.

Men and women party elites also differ rather markedly in what their work entails, according to results from the 1980 survey. Two domains which showed substantial gender differences in both parties concerned "supervising and coordinating the work of others" and "negotiating and bargaining with others." Among the 1980 delegates men were 11 to 24 percent more likely to be doing these activities "a lot." They held smaller margins (1 to 10 percent) with respect to "doing business with the government" and "dealing with the public." These differences are significant because the particulars of work can be converted into politically useful skills, traits, contacts, and interests. Therefore, employed men are better situated than employed women. In all probability the gaps between men and women would have been much larger in earlier years. Even in 1980, however, women were still disadvantaged by their workplace experiences.

Substantial gains have been recorded in the employment and occupational arenas, but the income of women delegates lags far behind that of men, as of course it does in the general public as well. The gap in personal income in the upper quartile remains fully as large among the 1984 delegates as it was among earlier cohorts. Although the gender gap in family income is much smaller, both the practical and symbolic significance of personal versus shared income is well known. Income is a key index of political power and status. Money is not only a resource that can be used directly; it also references the individual as successful, clever, and connected. If "money talks," then women party activists are still speaking in more muted tones.

A final characteristic to consider is that of education. Here again the parties differ. Democratic women have cut the gender difference in terms of training beyond the B.A. degree (63 percent for men and 51 percent for women), whereas it remains about the same in the GOP (56 and 25 percent). One very important distinction lies behind these figures. Although training in law is no longer the correlate of political success that it once was, it is nevertheless true that lawyers continue to constitute the largest occupational group in the most significant political bodies. Despite modest gains over the time period covered here, far fewer women than men have law degrees. Male proportions range from 20 to 27 percent compared with female proportions of from 1 to 6 percent.

If women and men differ with respect to occupational, educational, and income characteristics, the same is true with respect to other politically relevant statuses. Women in both parties are more likely than men to be unmarried, and the difference is especially noticeable among Democrats (39 percent for women and 26 percent for men in 1984). From 1976 onward at least one third of the Democratic women were not married at the time of the survey; moreover, the gap between them and Democratic men has grown over time. Age does not explain the gap in either party, for the age differences between the sexes are very slim.

It is not clear what is driving what here, whether less traditional women (in terms of marital status) are more attracted to party politics than similar men or whether the recruitment process is different. Nor is it clear whether not being married is a plus or minus in political party contexts. But the relative constancy of the gender differences in the GOP and the widening gap in the Democratic party suggest something fairly fundamental at work. One probable consequence of these differences is that the interests of "nontraditional" women are more likely to be represented in party councils.

A recurrent finding from research on women politicos is that the presence of young children often inhibits early entry into politics.[15] Among our delegates, the mean age of the youngest child was (with the exception of the 1972 Democrats) considerably higher among women than men, the gap ranging as high as 4.3 years among the 1984 Democrats. This suggests that women's entry into politics is delayed. However, because women typically become parents at younger ages than do men, this fact alone is not convincing.

The mean age of entry into politics, as recalled by the delegates, is more persuasive. In both parties women tended to be at least two years older than men when they first became politically involved. Although this may not seem like a large difference, the opportunity costs represented are substantial; extrapolated across a *political* lifetime, women have fewer political life chances. The lack of change between 1972 and 1984 in these comparisons indicates that contemporary developments in women's lives have not yet compensated for their later starting dates.

Indeed, the most arresting conclusion is how stable the sex differences in social attributes tended to be—leaving aside the very significant convergence in labor force participation and the lack of gender distinctions according to age and religious behavior. Men and women also continue to differ across a range of background factors even after taking party into account. Almost without exception these differences continue to operate to the disadvantage of women, even for these women who occupy the middling to upper strata of party and nomination politics.

Voluntary Organizations: Cut from Different Cloth

Almost by definition political party activists are joiners. They often acquire skills, experience, and visibility through their participation in voluntary groups. Involvement in such groups may provide an apprenticeship for a political career or serve as an adjunct to involvement with a party. Given that American political parties are holding corporations which encapsulate a wide range of interests, and that these often-conflicting interests must somehow be reconciled with each other, gender comparisons according to voluntary group activity are important for two reasons: (1) They indicate a possible basis of division within the parties according to gender, and (2) they point toward the differential recruitment of men and women into political elites.

Men and women delegates do not differ appreciably with respect to their *overall* rates of involvement in voluntary organizations. Using scores on two participation indexes,[16] we found that the absolute differences within party were minor. Republican men typically held a slight advantage over women, and by 1984 Democratic women held a slight edge over men. But similarity proved the rule.

Buried within this overall similarity is a high degree of gender specialization which is somewhat more acute within the Democratic party, but exists as well within the GOP. As the lower half of Tables 10.2 and 10.3 shows, men exceed women in the traditional male bastions of veterans' organizations, fraternal orders, labor unions, service clubs, and occupational groups. Women surpass men in such traditional female arenas as women's groups, abortion-related organizations, school-related organizations, and teachers' associations. Women also lead, though, in public interest groups and environmental organizations.

Table 10.2 **Membership in Voluntary Organizations Among Democratic Delegates**

Group	1972		1976		1980		1984	
	Men	Women	Men	Women	Men	Women	Men	Women
Environmental	NA	NA	22% <	42%[a]	21%	24%	31%	30%
Abortion-Related	NA	NA	12 <	32	12 <	30	14 <	40
Teachers'	NA	NA	17 <	22	18 <	28	15 <	25
School-Related	32 <	39	36 <	46	29 <	49	31 <	39
Public Interest[b]	50 <	58	32 <	60	35 <	53	37 <	55
Women's	3 <	35	11 <	41	14 <	58	14 >	60
Ethnic	NA	NA	30	31	28	28	32	30
Veterans'	NA	NA	28 >	07	25 >	6	21 >	4
Fraternal	NA	NA	40 >	15	35 >	16	32 >	12
Labor	25 >	11	29 >	19	31 >	21	28 >	23
Service	35 >	11	36 >	20	34 >	20	30 >	18
Occupational	58 >	34	59 >	43	52 >	35	53 >	43
Church[c]	53	51	54 >	43	55	52	48	47

[a]Percentage differences ≥ 5 are indicated by < and > signs.

[b]Called nonpartisan civic groups in 1972 and nonpartisan public interest groups in subsequent years.

[c]Entries represent frequent church attenders.

Contrary to popular opinion, women activists are not more involved in church life.[17] Nor are there appreciable gender differences with respect to ethnic groups, though here, as in several other instances, the party differences are large.

These results show that there is gender specialization and that it continues throughout the twelve-year period under observation. In this sense continuity prevails. There was a time when this specialization would have implied definite inequality, with men being enmeshed in organizations accorded more status and prestige, more centrally located in the sociopolitical world, and having more political clout. That assessment is less safe today, owing in part to how the political world has changed. Political issues more often associated with women's interests

**Table 10.3   Membership in Voluntary Organizations
Among Republican Delegates**

Group	1972		1976		1980		1984	
	Men	Women	Men	Women	Men	Women	Men	Women
Environ-mental	NA	NA	8%	11%	6%	8%	4%	6%
Abortion-Related	NA	NA	10 <	15[a]	15 <	22	19 <	27
Teachers'	NA	NA	3 <	8	3	6	5	6
School-Related	39 <	47	30 <	36	30 <	38	30 <	36
Public Inter-est[b]	37 <	50	13 <	24	13 <	25	13 <	21
Women's	3 <	11	2 <	36	3 <	36	4 <	42
Ethnic	NA	NA	8	4	7	5	9	6
Veterans'	NA	NA	37 >	8	39 >	10	37 >	8
Fraternal	NA	NA	44 >	24	41 >	23	40 >	20
Labor	8 >	3	4	2	4	2	4	3
Service	57 >	17	50 >	32	50 >	31	48 >	29
Occupa-tional	67 >	33	80 >	45	76 >	43	76 >	51
Church[c]	62	61	59 <	52	61 <	54	61	65

[a]Percentage differences ≥ 5 are indicated by < and > signs.
[b]Called nonpartisan civic groups in 1972 and nonpartisan public interest groups in subsequent years.
[c]Entries represent frequent church attenders.

have acquired greater importance on the political agenda. Abortion, divorce, childcare, equal opportunity in education and employment, comparable worth, and equal rights amendments have occupied the political limelight. Concomitantly, organizations with heavy complements of women have become more politically numerous and potent. (See Schlozman, this volume.) Organizations in which women predominate (at least among party elites), while perhaps not as mainstream as those dominated by men, are politically visible and influential.[18]

Two important changes occurred between 1972 and 1984. One was the increasing participation in what are labeled "women's" organizations, which is not surprising in light of the explosion of women's organizations during the 1970s, mostly on the left but also scattered throughout the political spectrum (especially if abortion-related groups are included).[19] Parties attract and are attracted by voluntary organizations that share their political sympathies. Parties need such groups for campaign and electoral support, and the groups need the parties in order to influence the nomination and electoral processes. What is less expected is that men became more involved in women's and abortion-related groups, surely a sign of topicality and the rising prominence of women's issues.

The second significant change that occurred was the movement of women into traditionally male-dominated groups. With varying degrees of success within the two parties women decreased their disadvantage in labor unions, service clubs, and occupational associations. Much of this gain can be traced to the upsurge of women in the work force. People in certain occupations are frequently obliged to join one or more job-related organizations. Community norms and a sense of civic duty often demand that members of some occupations also join a service club. Because these mainstream organizations remain critical actors in the political system and critical resource and training bases for individual political careers, women augment their own strength within the parties by their rising participation levels in such organizations.

Both party and gender contribute to the organizational profiles of these party activists. Moreover, the explanatory value of only these two traits is usually substantial, with most multiple correlation coefficients (R) ranging from .20 to .50. Three points are of special relevance. First, even with party controlled, gender is customarily a significant predictor of organizational activity. In 1980, for example, the delegates were asked about their level of involvement in thirteen different types of organizations. For all but three of these—church groups, ethnic/racial organizations, and environmental groups—gender was a significant predictor (beta coefficients ranged from .06 for labor unions to .43 for feminist organizations). Meanwhile, party proved to be a significant corollary for all but one type of organization (coefficients ranged from .05 to .30). In general, party tends to be more heavily associated with type of group involvement, but gender is quite "competitive." Second, gender has, indeed, become less associated with involvement in service clubs, occupation-based groups, and labor unions, all of which are key traditional bases for one or both parties. Finally, in contrast to the results for social background, there are no extra, interaction effects resulting from the combination of gender and party.

In addition to being indicators of political resources, membership in organizations may signify a political predisposition. To some extent people choose to join an organization according to their ideological orientation, but there is also little doubt that organizations mold and reinforce political orientations. In this sense it is clear that the complexion of the two parties would be quite different even without the marked increase of women participants. But women have brought their own blend of organizational ties to the parties, and the parties and their policies have changed as a result. Moreover, the issue and problem agendas at the conventions and the agendas of delegates qua party activists are perhaps even more affected by organizational interests.

Thus the different organizational profiles of men and women, coupled with the enhanced inclusion of women in the parties, seem likely to have had a substantial effect on the parties. Two vivid illustrations come from the Democratic party. In 1976 teachers' associations and unions helped secure the nomination of Jimmy Carter and helped shape the party platform. In 1984 the efforts of NOW and other women's groups were pivotal in securing the nomination of Geraldine Ferraro.[20] More generally, the sheer enlarged presence of women in the parties, with their special organizational profiles, has most likely had an anticipatory effect. Party leaders, knowing the group interests of women, are more likely to anticipate their demands and interests than would otherwise be the case.

Officeholding: Reducing the Gap

In the game of partisan politics, officeholding is the ultimate goal. Power and influence, respect and prestige, access and contacts accompany the attainment of public office. Parties live on the expectation and rewards of holding office. Individual careers are often shaped around the ambition for and attainment of office. In this section we first look briefly at the patterns of officeholding within the parties and then move on to the major subject of public officeholding.

As noted earlier, the parties began moving toward formal equality several decades ago in terms of party positions, by which we mean official party committee memberships and positions at the national, state, congressional, county, and municipal levels. Our surveys testify to the success of this effort.[21] Across all cohorts and within each party the differences between men and women in terms of the kinds of party offices they held were negligible—regardless of governmental level. If anything, women had a modest edge at the local level and, among Republicans, a similar edge at the state level. Over the twelve-year span the absolute proportion of party officials at the conventions varied, but the sex balance in officeholding remained throughout. Formal equality, however, does not necessarily bring power equality. In fact many politicos regard these party positions as only nominally important as power bases.

While parity in party officeholding is now standard, the same could hardly be said of public officeholding. The number of women officeholders, both elective and appointive, continues to mount, though the composition of Congress remains relatively untouched by these trends. The officeholding records of women delegates are not representative of all officeholders, though they should reflect national trends. They are probably least representative of nonpartisan offices, most of which are at the local level; and it is precisely at these local levels that women are making the most rapid gains in officeholding. For example, nearly one half of all school board members are now women, a stunning increase over the one tenth figure of the late 1960s.

Our results show the expected gains. In each successive cohort throughout the 1972–1984 period the proportion of women who were currently holding national, state, or local office rose. At the state level, for example, the gain was from 5 to 15 percent among Democratic women and 7 to 20 percent among Republican women. Had we been studying only women, we might well have rested with that happy conclusion. As it turns out, though, men exhibited the same *pattern* of growth in officeholding. It is not difficult to understand these parallel patterns. Especially within the Democratic party, there was a reaction to the composition of the 1972 convention, where officeholders were given short shrift, both numerically and strategically. By both formal and informal methods the Democrats in later convention years sought to bring in not only more party officials but also more public officials. In effect, this move benefited men more than women because the former occupy more high-status political positions.

A more positive light can be cast on these parallel gender patterns, positive from the perspective of gender equality. Women at least did not lose ground despite the parties' later emphasis on including officeholders at the conventions. Given women's lower initial rate of officeholding, this might have been an outcome. In addition, women did gain slightly more than men at the state and local levels. The most pronounced demonstration of this occurred in the Democratic party at the level of local officeholding, where women cut a deficit of 14 percent in 1972 to one of 4 percent in 1984. Finally, the heaviest gains for women came with the 1984 delegations. If this was a harbinger, then we should expect the officeholding gap to be further reduced in the future.

Modest Differences in Political Preferences

A key question accompanying the increased numbers of women in political circles is whether they would have political preferences at odds with those of men. The answer to that question is by no means straightforward because of the importance of such factors as critical mass points, elite socialization, and institutional lag in affecting the impact of newcomers on organizations. For present purposes we are simply interested in whether male and female party elites differ on policy issues and, by extension, whether the accelerated presence of women in the party elites has changed the parties' ideological complexions.

An extensive literature demonstrates that the most powerful discriminator of political preferences among political elites in the United States remains—despite some signs of slippage—that of political party itself.[22] That is no less true of party elites than it is of other political elites. Previous analysis of national (and state) convention delegates shows that the major analytic split for virtually all public policy issues occurs by party. Gender has tended to be of marginal significance except on issues that are of unique relevance to the interests of women or that seem to threaten the prevailing status and power relationships between men and women.[23]

Our study of delegates confirms this judgment, noticeably within the Republican party. A host of male-female comparisons on a variety of attitude objects reveals modest differences for the most part, though these differences virtually always showed women as being more liberal than men. These small to moderate contrasts tend to persist regardless of the delegates' level of involvement in presidential politics over an extended period of time. For example, an analysis of the 1972–1980 cohorts based on their (recalled) participation histories between 1972 and 1980 revealed gender differences in attitudes throughout, particularly among delegates who had lowered their participation levels during that period. Although we cannot expand upon the point here, the moderate GOP women were one of the most pronounced casualties of the Republican drift to the right during the 1970s.

The small policy differences between Republican men and women are exaggerated among Democratic delegates. Democratic women consistently take the more liberal position on most domestic and international issues; they evaluate liberal groups more positively and conservative groups more negatively; and they favor spending priorities that maximize the human and health services side of the public sector.[24] These differences are not large, with correlations (Pearson's r) between gender and issue position typically running from .10 to .30. Nevertheless, they definitely bespeak an element of liberal ideology that serves to alter the ideological cast of the Democratic conventions and, at a further remove, the composition of the party cadres and leaders.

Women and men have traditionally differed in their opinions about the use of military force, especially in the absence of officially declared or "just" wars.[25] This difference in orientation comes through in both parties, and it is one of the few in which Republican and Democratic women are about equally distant from their male colleagues—though the absolute scores are quite different. In 1972, with the Vietnam War winding down, women in each party were a little more likely than men to agree that the United States should cease all military and economic aid to South Vietnam, Laos, and Cambodia. The differences widened (assuming rough comparability in the questions) in 1984, when the delegates were asked whether they believed the United States should become more involved in the internal affairs of Central American countries. Women were more noninterventionist than were men, the corresponding tau-c correlations being .20 among Democrats and .21 among Republicans.

The sizable gap among the 1984 Republicans is intriguing considering the fact that those delegates were overwhelmingly pro-Reagan. Moreover, many of the women delegates had been handpicked to increase the proportion of women at the convention. A gender gap of this observed size within a conservatively dominated convention attests to fundamental differences between men and women in a very critical issue area. An accompanying point is that the "nonfeminist" issue that most divided Democratic men and women between 1976 and 1984 was whether defense spending should be increased or decreased (correlations ranged from .16 to .24).

As noted above, the most consistent differences between men and women within the parties have centered on so-called women's issues and activities. Again, this is particularly so within the Democratic party. On two central feminist issues—abortion and the Equal Rights Amendment—the two parties have taken increasingly polarized stands, and a moderate degree of conflict also exists within the parties. Among Democrats the women delegates were consistently more liberal than their male colleagues who, by conventional standards, were also very liberal (tau-c correlations ranged from .11 to .22 for the 1976–1984 period). Among Republicans the gender distance was not as great, but even with the growing conservatism women delegates remained the more liberal (correlations ranged from .01 to .14).

How much the federal government should do to help improve the social and economic position of women is an issue that divides the parties. Although Republican men and women do not differ appreciably on this score, within the Democratic party gender does make a difference. Democratic women are considerably more likely to feel that the government should play an active role (tau-c = .21 for the 1984 delegates). In a party long noted for its subscription to governmental action on the behalf of resource-poor groups, women emerge as being especially sensitive to the ameliorative needs of their gender.

To the extent that women's issues have been highly publicized and the focus of at least some convention decision-making in the form of the platform and nomination politics, it is apparent that the increased presence of women has affected these processes. Indeed, it might be argued that the anticipated and actual presence of large numbers of women at the conventions and in state and local party organizations affects the issue agenda and the strategies that the party and candidate organizations pursue. It is, of course, difficult to demonstrate in concrete fashion the operation of such "laws of anticipated reactions."

Nevertheless, as the multivariate analysis dramatically reveals, party is the key corollary of issue position. The vast interparty dissimilarities in ideology tend to swamp what modest differences are provided by gender. Democratic women stand out as being somewhat more liberal than would be expected simply on the basis of their being Democrats and female, but they are infinitely closer to Democratic men than to Republican women. Nor did the effect of gender change much between 1972 and 1984.[26] Intraparty variance continues to emanate more from broad ideological orientations and candidate support groups than from social traits such as gender. As we shall now see, however, gender forms a strong basis of intraparty conflict in one important attitudinal domain.

Conflict over Gender Roles and the Parties

The expansion of the nominating conventions to include large numbers of women has not yet reached the stage of the routine. Very substantial proportions of women delegates continue to believe that they are the beneficiaries of affirmative action. Incorporating a previously underrepresented and less resource-rich group into the parties could not be expected to proceed without hitches. Long-established norms and perceptions on the part of the established forces do not disappear with a change in rules nor do the trepidations and suspicions of the newcomers. Protestations to the contrary, men and women continue to view the "gender problem" in quite different fashion. A few examples illustrate this point.

A common complaint of women politicos and would-be politicos is that men, as the powerful gatekeepers, have been reluctant to open the gates to aspiring women politicians. Sometimes the accusation is one of outright sexism and at other times of poor political judgments. Men and women have dissimilar views about the prevalence of these restricting males in the political environment. One statement put to the delegates throughout our study period ran as follows: "Most men in the party organization try to keep women out of leadership roles." Responses could range from strongly agree to strongly disagree on the six-point scale.

Two strong messages emerge from the findings (Figure 10.1), where two sets of people viewing what is in principle an objectively verifiable behavior arrive at quite different conclusions based on their respective genders and their experiential histories. First, women are far more likely than men to agree that men do try to exclude women. Moreover, the gap is fully as large among Democrats in 1984 as it was in 1972 and is still substantial even among the 1984 Republicans.

The second point is that the trend is definitely in the direction of more positive perceptions. Men and women share in this trend, though for men the shift was sudden and came between the 1972 and 1976 cohorts. For women the change has been more gradual. Still, even by 1984 over two fifths of the Democratic women and one fourth of the Republican women could agree with the statement. In line with a model of gradualism, perceptions are changing, sexism is seen as less present, and women are not as mistrusting. Regardless of whether these shifts accurately reflect a change in the objective reality or are tainted by hearsay and misinformation, the degree of change augurs well for the incorporation of women into the elite strata of the parties.

Parties can change as a result of attitudinal shifts by individuals remaining within the parties or by new members entering and old members exiting. Significantly, the changes with respect to gender roles come as much from the processes of individual change as from population replacement. This can be demonstrated by comparing the responses obtained from the 1972 delegates in 1972 with the responses from these same individuals when they were resurveyed in 1981 and 1985. We found shifts of 20–25 percent among women and men in both parties. These attitude shifts brought the erstwhile 1972 cohorts into line with the attitudes of the 1984 convention delegates, almost none of whom were 1972 delegates. Owing to the historical effects associated with the

**Figure 10.1   Agreement That Men Try to Keep
Women Out of Leadership Roles**

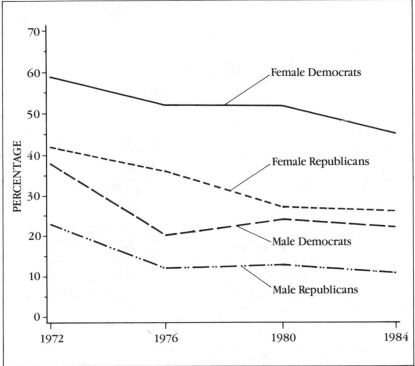

Note: Tau-c correlations between sex and the full range of responses among Democrats are, in chronological sequence, .27, .38, .36, and .35; corresponding correlations among Republicans are .22, .29, .17, and .26.

women's movement, old elites were moving toward convergence with the attitudes of the newer elites.

A more dramatic change occurred with respect to images of women's qualifications for a political life. One of the age-old charges laid against women is that they have less ability to remain dispassionate, to engage in restrained discourse, to make objective choices, and to act in a rational manner. Briefly put, the charge is that women are too emotional.

In 1972 and 1984 the delegates were asked to evaluate this statement in the strongly-agree to strongly-disagree format: "Most men are better suited emotionally for politics than are most women." A number of remarkable comparisons can be made according to party, gender, and

Figure 10.2 Agreement That Men Are Better Suited Emotionally for Politics

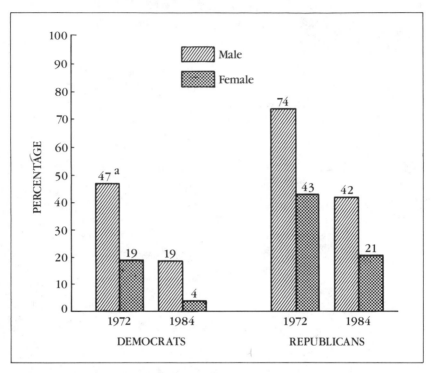

Note: Tau-c correlations between sex and the full range of responses among Democrats are .38 in 1972 and .29 in 1984; corresponding correlations among Republicans are .33 in 1972 and .32 in 1984.

time (Figure 10.2). Most impressively, agreement with the statement has dropped dramatically within each party and each sex. The 1972 figures would now be considered an embarrassment, especially among Republicans. But the decline is marked for the Democrats also, having almost reached a point of no possible further change among the Democratic women.

These universally steep declines again reflect a period or historical effect that, sparked by the women's movement, has worked to remove some old stereotypes about the "nature" of women and their ability to perform heretofore restricted jobs. Additional support for this position comes from examining the changes registered by the 1972 delegates who were resurveyed twelve years later. Men and women in both parties registered large drops (15–30 percent) in the proportions claiming that women were too emotional. As a result the 1972 party/sex cohorts, qua 1984 respondents, were virtually identical to their 1984 cohort counterparts. Even without organizational replenishment, the parties would have changed.

Despite these striking movements, the gap between men and women remains substantial within each party because men were initially so much more stereotypical in their attitudes. Each gender shifted, but at a roughly similar rate in absolute terms. We might view this pattern as an example of cultural lag on the part of males. In a fashion almost uncanny in its precision, the men in each party reached a point in 1984 that was virtually exactly where their female colleagues had been twelve years earlier! Admittedly, more men than women may always accept the proposition of women being too emotional. Nevertheless it is clear that men have been moving toward the beliefs held by women, rather than vice versa.

Another example of a cultural lag is seen in the parties. The 1984 figures for the GOP men and women echo almost exactly those of the 1972 Democratic men and women, respectively. Given the demythologizing of gender differences, it seems highly unlikely that the Democrats will retreat from their stance. What is much more likely is that the Republicans will continue to move in the direction of the Democrats because of supporting demographic, social, and structural trends. Moreover, it must be recalled that the 1984 Republican conclave was very Reaganesque in composition, and even under those conditions the twelve-year shift was marked. A convention with more representation from the party's moderate wing would undoubtedly have shown a more pronounced rejection of the "emotional woman" image.

One spectacular affirmation of women's coming of political age was Geraldine Ferraro's nomination as the Democratic party's vice presidential candidate. Although her presence apparently had little effect on the outcome of the election,[27] her nomination was hugely important in a symbolic sense. Seeking high political office was no longer a gender role restricted to men (though minor parties had put women on the ticket in the past). Despite, or perhaps because of, the historical precedent being set by the Ferraro candidacy, there was considerable controversy over her presence on the ticket and what it meant for the party and for women in general.

Our 1984 respondents reacted to two statements about Ferraro, one having to do with the extent of her impact on support for the Democratic ticket and the other with how much she strengthened the future prospects of women seeking national office. Predictably, the two parties differed sharply, the 1984 Republicans judging that she hurt the ticket (61 percent versus 26 percent for the Democrats) and that her presence would provide only modest help for future women aspirants (35 percent versus 83 percent). Republican women were almost as negative as Republican men in their views.

In addition to these large interparty differences, there were pronounced contrasts between Democratic men and women. Whereas 36 percent of the men said that Ferraro helped the ticket a lot or somewhat, the figure was 55 percent among women. Although the discrepancy was not as great with respect to Ferraro's impact on women political aspirants, men again took a less positive view (31 percent compared with 46 percent of the women). It is important to note that judgments rather than attitudes are being compared here. These Democratic elites interpreted the same phenomenon differently according to the perceptual filter supplied by gender.

In sum, gender is a consistent demarcator of attitudes toward women's roles in politics in general and within the political parties in particular. This conclusion is reinforced by the results of the multiple regressions, in which party and gender were used as predictors of gender role attitudes. In virtually all instances both party and gender were substantial predictors, with the lion's share of the standardized regression coefficients ranging from .15 to .40. Party tends to be slightly more powerful than gender, but gender is clearly a major determinant, especially in contrast to its nonexistent-to-minor influence with respect to public policy preferences (see preceding section).

Furthermore, the contribution of gender has altered very little over time despite changes in the absolute positions taken by men and women. Illustratively, the beta coefficients for the "women are too emotional" item were .27 for party and .31 for gender among the 1972 delegates; the figures for the 1984 delegates were reversed to .27 for gender and .31 for party. The influence of gender even increased in one instance. The coefficients for the "men exclude women" item were .31 for party and .21 for gender among the 1972 delegates; the corresponding figures among the 1984 delegates were .27 and .27.[28] In some other cases the impact of gender has waned slightly. While the expansion of female representation in the parties may not have widened conflicting views between men and women, it has certainly affected the proportions holding them. Without women, high-level party gatherings would be much less "feminist" in their attitudinal complexion.

Conclusion

Political parties tend to change slowly. Two of the more abrupt changes in the organizational histories of the two major parties occurred when they opened up the national conventions to women, first in the 1920s and half a century later in the 1970s. Partly because the first opening was associated with the single, concrete accomplishment of female suffrage, a period of exceedingly slow change followed the initial rush of enthusiasm and accomplishments. Women's roles in the political parties (and in public office) leveled off at a modest rate. Not so after the second big expansion of women in the party conventions, which was tied to more general reforms and changes in the parties. This expansion also accompanied the onrushing feminist movement—with its multiple goals—and was fed by structural changes such as delayed age of marriage, lower birth rates, and much greater female participation in the work force.

It is very unlikely that the place of women in the parties will retreat, unless women find that other organizational outlets are more suitable. If nothing else, the symbolic importance of virtual parity guarantees women a significant role in future party conventions. Indeed, the very fact that a large percentage of women still feel that affirmative action is involved in their selection as delegates testifies to the importance the parties attach to equitable if not equal representation of the sexes.

As our evidence demonstrates, the parties have been altered as a result of the sizable presence of women. The configuration of voluntary group interests represented is clearly different, as is the attitudinal profile concerning gender roles and politics. Similarly, the substantial gender contrasts in terms of social and political backgrounds mean that the party conclaves are different than they were in the old, preform days. Because of the overwhelming importance of candidate support groups and ideological factions within each party, it is hard to argue that the enlarged presence of women has made a dramatic difference in the public policy preferences of these party meetings and, at a larger remove, the parties more generally. What seems much more likely is that the enlargement has affected, partly by the rule of anticipated reactions, the agendas of the conventions, the framing of certain problems and issues, strategic considerations involved in the nomination process, and the voting patterns on platforms and resolutions. Whether the parties are stronger or weaker as a result of the much greater inclusion of women depends upon the criteria being invoked. Clearly, they are stronger in the sense of statistical representation of the populace and in the sense of bringing varied interests to the parties. They are arguably less strong in the sense of comprising experienced politicos with ampler social, economic, and political resources.

What should not be overlooked in an assessment of the impact on the parties are the changes that are occurring among women within the parties, at least as represented by our subjects. Perhaps most significantly there has been an increase in the proportion of women who hold (and have ambitions to hold) public office. This increase has not been dramatic, but it seems to be of a piece with other developments wherein women are gradually acquiring social, economic, and political positions formerly reserved primarily for men. Women's gains in employment and in some forms of higher-level occupations also signify a rise in indicators long associated with power and influence in American politics. So, too, does their growing participation in women's organizations and their movement into some organizations formerly dominated by men.

At the same time, it is important to note that the increasing involvement of women in the parties has not worked to lessen their sense of gender role consciousness. They have not been assuaged in that they are still more likely than men to see obstacles for women in politics. Thus there remains a lively tension between achievement and progress on the one hand and perceived inequalities and deprivation on the other. This tension, fostered and sustained by broad-ranging structural changes and the institutionalization of the women's movement, promises to maintain the parties as a focal point for observing the interplay between gender and politics.

Notes

Support for the research on which this chapter is based came from the Russell Sage Foundation. I would like to acknowledge the skillful assistance of Debra Dodson and Laura Stoker.
  1. See, for example, Price (1984), pp. 32–46; and Cotter, Gibson, Bibby, and Huckshorn (1984).
  2. See Jennings and Thomas (1968); Jennings and Farah (1981); Costantini and Craik (1972); Kirkpatrick (1976); and Jackson III (1975).
  3. Data were collected in 1972 for the 1972 cohort, in early 1981 for the 1976 and 1980 cohorts, and in early 1985 for the 1984 cohort. In view of the lag between convention service and survey date, the results for the 1976 cohort should be interpreted cautiously at some points. The Ns for the four convention cohorts are as follows, beginning with the 1972 cohort: Republican males = 550, 632, 750, 546; Republican females = 313, 329, 351, 509; Democratic males = 977, 646, 764, 711; Democratic females = 742, 404, 852, 874.

Embedded within the design is a three-wave panel of the 1972 delegates and a two-wave panel of the 1976 and 1980 delegates. A description of the study up through the 1981 data collection is contained in Miller and Jennings (1986). Initial funding for the research came from the Twentieth Century Fund and subsequent funding from the Russell Sage Foundation.

4. See Breckinridge (1933), chap. 17, for the period up to 1932; and Fisher and Whitehead (1944) for the period up to 1944.

5. Breckinridge (1933) and Fisher and Whitehead (1944).

6. David, Goldman, and Bain (1960), p. 327.

7. Reported figures on the sex composition of the conventions vary slightly from one account to another. The pre-1988 figures used here are taken from a tabulation reported by Lynn (1984). The 1988 figures are from party sources.

8. A detailed accounting with respect to women and the key role of the newly formed National Women's Political Caucus in the 1971 deliberations is presented in Shafer (1983), chap. 17.

9. See Price (1984), chap. 6, and Huckshorn and Bibby (1983), for descriptions of the various reform efforts in each party devoted to the question of delegate composition.

10. See Mueller (1987).

11. The effects of gender, party, and the interaction between them were estimated using ordinary least squares regression analysis, with "effects-coding" of the two dummy variables (gender and party). In reporting such results throughout this chapter, standardized coefficients (betas) will be used and only those coefficients significant at the .01 level or lower will be cited.

12. The proportion of all women who were in the labor force rose from 37 percent in 1965 to 46 percent in 1975 and 54 percent in 1985. U.S. Bureau of the Census, *Statistical Abstract of the United States, 1986b* (1986), p. 398.

13. U.S. Department of Labor (1979), pp. 1, 818; and U.S. Department of Labor (1984), pp. 3, 324.

14. See, for example, Kilpatrick, Cummings, and Jennings (1964), chap. 10.

15. See Lee (1976).

16. One index counted the absolute number of claimed memberships across a long list of organizational types. A second index took into account the reported level of activity in the organization.

17. For a summary of differences at the mass public level, see Wuthnow and Lehrman, this volume.

18. For reports on national and subnational activity see, inter alia, Costain (1982); Gelb and Palley (1979); Freeman (1984); and Schlozman, this volume.

19. See Knoke, this volume, for an analysis of the incentive structures and participation patterns differentiating women's organizations from other types.

20. See, for example, Frankovic (1987).

21. Respondents were queried about their contemporary and past officeholding with respect to over fifteen types of positions.

22. For example, Price (1984); and Epstein (1983).

23. For example, Kirkpatrick (1976); McClosky, Hoffman, and O'Hara (1960); Soule and McGrath (1977); Jennings and Thomas (1968); Kelly and Burgess (1986); Hauss and Maisel (1986); and Brudney and McDonald (1986).

24. Compare similar results at the mass public level in Shapiro and Mahajan (1986).

25. Smith (1984).

26. Furthermore, it does not appear that the situation was much different before 1972. An analysis of the 1972 female delegates according to whether or not they had been delegates to previous (nonreform era) conventions revealed scant differences, thereby suggesting that the women brought in by virtue of the reform movement were not very different—*in terms of public policy preferences*—from the small band of women who attended previous conventions.

27. See Frankovic (1985); and Hagner, Knight, and Lewis (1986).

28. Interaction effects are weak for this set of relationships, though to the extent that they are present they indicate that Democratic women are disproportionately liberal.

11

On the Origins of Political Disunity Among Women

David O. Sears / Leonie Huddy

The women's movement has long tried to mobilize American women as a self-conscious, solidary political force. The strength of these efforts has waxed and waned over the years, perhaps peaking in the early 1920s and again in the 1970s. There have been some big and dramatic successes, such as the passage of the Nineteenth Amendment guaranteeing women's suffrage; some less successful but nonetheless impressive efforts, such as the near miss of the Equal Rights Amendment (ERA); and various indications of steady long-term progress, such as an increasing number of female candidates and elected officials.

Many activists have striven to mobilize women into a cohesive political group, in the model of a labor union or a solidary ethnic group. Successful group mobilization would be marked, presumably, by such indicators as bloc voting, preferential voting for female candidates, unified support for government policies benefiting women, and support for political candidates based on the degree of their support for women's issues.

It is commonly assumed that groups are most readily mobilized politically around common interests. Women would seem, on the face of it, to share interests as much as do members of many other groups that evidence political solidarity and wield political clout. Women figure prominently as society's caregivers, taking the major responsibility for bearing and caring for children, and so are particularly affected by legislation linked to reproductive rights, childcare, and childraising. Middle-aged and older women take on the responsibilities of caring for aged parents, an ill spouse, or other relatives, and thus are similarly affected by government health care policies. In the workplace, women are paid less than men, in part because traditionally female occupations are financially devalued and in part because childraising responsibilities result in discontinuous work experiences that are less conducive to career advancement. Furthermore, they face the burdens of widespread stereotyping and discrimination in the workplace that prevent entry into more highly paid, traditionally male professions and positions of greater responsibility.

Despite these seemingly common interests, women have not been effectively mobilized politically. We would argue that the problem is not that women have low levels of political participation, but that they are not a unified political bloc. The major focus of the chapter is an analysis of the reasons for this disunity, particularly a contrast between a tangible-interest explanation and a major alternative that focuses on symbolic predispositions.

Ineffective Mobilization

In the past, one obvious barrier to the political mobilization of women was their generally low level of political involvement relative to men, as reflected in lower political interest, willingness to express opinions, level of ideological thinking, sense of efficacy, and turnout. (See Andersen, this volume.) These differences have largely disappeared, however. Women express opinions on political issues much more frequently than they did in the past. They now feel as politically efficacious as men and register and vote in equal numbers. The major remaining difference is that women are still less involved in conventional campaign activities; they pay less attention to campaign media coverage and give less money to campaigns than men do. But the resurgence of the women's movement in the late 1960s led to a substantial increase in women's active political participation. This partial eradication of political apathy and political exclusion among women in the 1970s and 1980s thus should have removed a powerful barrier to their political solidarity.[1]

Nevertheless, women still are not likely to act as a solidary political group if they are not politically unified. Group unity is generally marked by both homogeneity of opinion within the ingroup and marked difference of opinion between ingroup and outgroup on issues relevant to the group. For example, blacks have tended both to support overwhelmingly (in the 80–90 percent range) federal antidiscrimination intervention in such areas as jobs and public accommodations and to take markedly more problack positions than do whites (about half of whom support such intervention).[2]

By these criteria women do not now form a unified political group. This can be seen by reviewing a number of political dimensions relevant to gender on which the public as a whole tends to split rather evenly. In most of these cases there is no consistent "gender gap," and both gender groups are split quite thoroughly.

First, women might be expected to show greater support for the entry of women into public office. In fact, in 1984 the gender difference in evaluations of Geraldine Ferraro were trivial, and almost as many women were negative as were positive about her, as will be seen. Similarly, a study of five tight statewide elections pitting female against male candidates in 1982 showed no marked tendency for voters to favor candidates of their own gender, and women were as divided about female candidates as men were about males. Finally, in the 1930s women were substantially more likely than men to say that they would support a fully qualified woman for President, though they were deeply divided then. The gender difference no longer holds; both women and men tend to support such candidacies. In the present era, then, women seem not to support female candidates more than men do, and indeed usually show the usual partisan divisions about them.[3]

Second, from a standard interest group mobilization perspective, the largest differences in political attitudes between women and men should be on issues directly affecting women's own tangible interests, such as employment opportunities, reproductive rights, and access to affordable childcare. In the 1930s and 1940s women were substantially more supportive than men of liberalized roles for women, particularly their suitability for paid work and political office. However, gender differences on such women's issues diminished through the 1960s, so that contemporary research typically turns up almost none. Indeed, both genders tend to be deeply and equally divided on most of them. One prime example is that women and men did not differ in support for the Equal Rights Amendment, the issue most explicitly promoting women's collective interests, during the late 1970s and early 1980s when it received the most publicity and its fate was largely determined. And, as is well known, each gender was quite divided on its merits, partly accounting for its defeat. Data on other such examples will be presented below. In brief, much research has shown both that women and men do not differ and that women are quite divided on such key questions as whether "the woman's place" is properly in the home, whether women should be drafted, how much discrimination there is against women, and how much support there is for women's organizations or legalized abortion.[4]

Third, women as a group might have a distinctive set of policy preferences on issues that are not so directly concerned with the group's main interests. From the early days of political behavior research into the 1960s, there were few gender differences in party identification, partisan voting, the economic issues central to the New Deal, or the anticommunist and racial issues that achieved political prominence in the decades following World War II. The few exceptions were that women were consistently more conservative morally than men and more strongly opposed to war and the military. As a result most observers felt that gender was not of great import on the most consequential political issues.[5]

Beginning in the 1970s, however, women began to report more Democratic votes and party identification than men did. In the 1980s Ronald Reagan polarized the genders more than other recent Presidents had, resulting in gender polarization on party identification. Today the "gender gap" extends as well to issues of force and violence, "risk-aversion" on toxic waste and nuclear power, and "compassion" policies concerning unemployment, social security, education, and health. Finally, women continue more than men to support traditional morality on alcohol and drug abuse, pornography, sex and birth control, and prayer in the schools.[6]

Fourth, women might give more weight than men to women's issues when arriving at partisan choices. Ronald Reagan and his Republican party took rather unsympathetic stances on women's issues, and leaders of the women's movement were outspokenly opposed to his administration. But the evidence suggests that women were no more inclined than men to cast their votes on the basis of candidates' positions on women's issues. Jane Mansbridge found that support for the ERA had an equal effect in 1980 on women's and men's Reagan-Carter vote choices, and a small one at that. Kathleen Frankovic reported that support for such women's issues as ERA and abortion had about the same small influence on women's job approval ratings of Reagan as it did on men's ratings in the 1980–1982 era. And Ethel Klein and Carol Mueller reported similar findings from 1972 and 1976 surveys. The one exception is that Klein found substantial gender differences in the impact of women's issues on the presidential vote in 1980. But the weight of the evidence seems to be against strong gender differences in this respect. Rather, women's greater opposition to Reagan is more likely to have been caused by their greater opposition to his advocacy of the use of force—that is, his war, defense, Soviet, and nuclear power policies.[7]

So women do not seem to act politically as if they were unified on the basis of shared interests. On most issues and candidacies that are seemingly relevant to gender, women do not differ materially from men, and both genders show considerable disunity. Neither is particularly distinctive as a social group. The central problem for us then becomes one of explaining women's political disunity.

Two Models of Women's Political Disunity

The central purpose of this chapter is to present and test two different models of the origins of women's political disunity. The first is an interest-based model. This, broadly speaking, proposes that women respond politically on the basis of their own current personal experience and realistic interests. Their basic political allegiances should reflect such interests, as should their views of the appropriate roles for each gender and their policy and candidate preferences. The alternative we propose, a symbolic politics model, suggests instead that ordinary citizens' political thinking is dominated by longstanding predispositions, normally acquired much earlier in life without consideration of one's real interests, which are activated by relevant symbols in the current political arena.[8]

Interest-Based Model

Many utilitarian philosophers, behaviorists, and contemporary economists would contend that egoistic hedonism is the dominant determinant of human behavior. Applied to politics, such interest-based theories would view ordinary citizens' political preferences as emerging from their own tangible outcomes—from the pleasures and pains of ordinary life and/or the costs and benefits of past political events or future alternatives. A considerable amount of research has tested the effects of such interests on ordinary citizens' political thinking. In general it has defined self-interest in terms of the short- or medium-term impacts that political issues and candidacies have on the material well-being of the individual (and his or her immediate family). This definition excludes nonmaterial interests (such as spiritual well-being, social status, or moral righteousness) and long-term or "enlightened" self-interest, because they tend to make the concept of self-interest tautological and tend to pose intractable problems of falsifiability.[9]

Short-term material interests may vary in three ways: The costs and benefits might be retrospective, current, or prospective; individuals may or may not be aware of their own motives; or the relevant outcomes may affect the self as opposed to the wider social group with which the individual feels community. Only the last distinction is consequential for our analysis. Self-interest theories typically emphasize outcomes that materially affect the individual. Group interest theories, on the other hand, emphasize the actual or perceived economic interdependence among group members, whether or not such collective interests are central to the fate of the group member in question.[10]

If interest-based theories are to be useful in understanding women's political diversity, the logical starting place is with interests that divide them, because of women's differing personal experiences at work, at home, or both. We will concentrate on four general areas.

First, young children generally have a greater impact on the lives of women than of men, since women are usually the primary caretakers. Their care may present the most serious problems for particular subsets of mothers, such as working mothers, who cannot do full-time childcare themselves, and single mothers, especially those with low income, who may be financially pressed. Such mothers should have greater vested interests in a wide variety of government programs that help with childcare and education or those that target subsets of mothers, such as Aid to Families with Dependent Children (AFDC).

Second, economic disadvantage might serve as another source of political cleavage. Women in general are economically disadvantaged relative to men, owing to lower employment rates, lower income when employed, the greater incidence of elderly women, and so on. These economic interests should impact most on the most economically disadvantaged women. Poorer women should then show the greatest gender solidarity, since political unity might help remedy economic problems such as lack of access to employment, inadequate or inequitable levels of pay, postdivorce financial declines, loss of earning capacity in old age through death of a husband, and the like. Even among working women, there may be further distinctions that are politically important, such as between single women who derive their entire income from their employment and their married counterparts who benefit from a second income, or between women earning a lot and those earning a little.

Third, some women's participation in the paid labor force might divide women politically. Most specific legislation concerning job discrimination and affirmative action, and court decisions mandating redress of pay inequities, affect working women more directly than homemakers, the retired, or full-time students. Therefore working women should have a greater stake in government policies affecting women's employment. Moreover, those currently in, or aspiring to join, higher-status male-dominated occupations in business and the professions are in sectors most likely to require affirmative action or equitable pay scales, and so may benefit the most in simple monetary terms from such government policies. Professional women may also have the most difficulty adjusting their work lives to accommodate childrearing. These considerations would suggest that the most advantaged working women would have most to gain through the greater political unity of women.[11] This hypothesis conflicts with the economic-disadvantage hypothesis in certain respects, a point to which we will return.

Fourth, some women might have a particular sense of group interest about these matters that would transcend their own self-interest. A feeling of solidarity with women, mixed with a sense that women have been treated poorly, might generate preferences for policies and candidates that would most benefit women. It could in principle do so whether or not the individual woman in question would especially benefit herself. Presumably not all women share this same feeling of solidarity, so it, too, may contribute to political disunity.

Most studies in other political realms have shown that, generally speaking, only the most direct indicators of self-interest have much influence in politics, and indeed even they often do not.[12] Among women in particular, existing evidence is mixed. On the negative side, economically disadvantaged women have not supported the ERA or affirmative action programs any more than have affluent women. On the positive side, low income contributed to opposition to Reagan more among women than among men in 1984. There is also some evidence that working women support women's issues more, and the legitimacy of male power domination less, than do nonworking women, which could result from their personal experience with discrimination or knowledge of such incidents involving other women. Still, this early evidence is mixed and fragmentary, suggesting the need for further research on the contribution of women's divided interests to their political disunity.[13]

Symbolic Politics Model

A symbolic politics approach assigns a central political role to the basic political attitudes learned earlier in socialization and evoked by effectively loaded political symbols in adulthood. A mother with teenage children is incensed by the practices of a local abortion clinic and pickets it, not because abortion affects her directly but because it violates her lifelong values and religious beliefs. Such "symbolic predispositions" are presumably often acquired in early-life socialization, prior to entry into the work force and full exposure to the other interests and experiences of full adulthood, though acquisition may extend well into young adulthood.

According to this view, a social group would be politically unified only if its members shared such political predispositions. Thus some of the political unity that does exist among women, as reflected in the "gender gap," could be explained by their common socialization and consequent shared predispositions. For example, females might generally be socialized to more compassionate and caring views of their interpersonal obligations than males. Or females may be taught different political attitudes than males as part of their direct political socialization, such as more sympathy for the poor, elderly, and children, and more antipathy toward war and violence. Either way, the symbolic politics view ascribes adult attitudes to the residues of earlier learning.

By this reasoning, disunity among women should result from divisions on such symbolic predispositions. Indeed, much of it has been shown to originate in cleavages on such potent symbolic predispositions as general egalitarian values, political ideology, party identification, morality, and religiosity.[14]

Gender Beliefs

So far, we have addressed women's disunity principally in terms of attitudes toward political issues and candidates. But women are quite sharply divided in their beliefs about appropriate gender roles, feminism, and the women's movement, as seen earlier. What are the sources of this disunity? In principle, the simple theoretical contrast between interests and symbolic politics should be relevant to them as well.

Beliefs about women's roles focus on whether women should share roughly the same roles as men in jobs, schools, family life, and other aspects of ordinary life or whether the two genders should play quite different roles. These beliefs are applied daily in the ways women live their personal lives, so they may well be profoundly affected by adult personal experiences. In particular, women's experiences in the workplace and having a family of their own ought to test and modify those beliefs. And it is widely believed that *feminism* and support for the women's movement grow directly out of women's experiences with stereotyping, prejudice, and discrimination, and their real economic and social difficulties, in the manner described above. So it is plausible that these gender beliefs are products of women's real interests.

On the other hand, both feminism and beliefs about gender roles may fit a symbolic politics model better than they do an interest-based model.

Feminism is a highly political ideology, originating as the core of an intensely political movement. Any attitude that is more a creature of the political arena than of daily life is less likely to be greatly influenced by personal experiences, as indicated by the considerable research cited earlier showing that political attitudes usually are not strongly influenced by self-interest. Attitudes toward feminism might then more plausibly be expected to be acquired as part of the political socialization process, like other basic attitudes centrally concerned with the political arena. But in this case, the relevant political socialization may occur only infrequently in the preadult period. Although feminism has a considerable history in American political thought, as a number of other chapters in this volume indicate, it was relatively dormant between the 1920s and the late 1960s. By the time feminism again became widely visible, most adult Americans now living were already well into adulthood. So if they acquired attitudes toward feminism through the symbolic politics process, it is more likely to have been by linking it to other fully formed symbolic predispositions in adulthood.

Beliefs about women's roles may also be a product of the symbolic politics process, but have a slightly different dynamic. They are usually socialized in childhood, as much psychological research has shown. Little girls and boys quickly learn the conventional differences in anatomy, dress, appropriate behavior, and tastes and interests. Individual differences within each gender in such sex-typed beliefs and behaviors also emerge at this time. It is doubtful that this early learning has much to do with any very explicitly political socialization, any more than does early learning about food and sleeping habits, relationships with siblings, and other standard childhood matters. But among young adults, beliefs about gender roles, like feminism, have become politicized to some extent in recent years. During the 1960s, consciousness-raising groups, and slogans such as "the personal is political," were among the attempts to politicize gender role beliefs. It seems likely that they did become somewhat politicized—though less than feminism itself—and to that extent, they too should prove to have been influenced by the individual's other symbolic predispositions.[15]

An Empirical Test

There has been, to date, no systematic comparison of the interest-based and symbolic politics perspectives in accounting for women's political disunity. In the remainder of the chapter we make this comparison empirically. The goal is to uncover the key causes of cleavage among women and to determine why they have not become more politically united, given that to some extent they do have common interests and are more actively engaged by politics than they were in the past.

The key propositions of the interest-based theory are that (1) women form different political attitudes than men because their self-interests and group interests are different; and these interests contribute to political disunity among women by affecting (2) their basic political predispositions (such as party identification and political ideology) and (3) their attitudes toward gender roles and the women's movement; and (4) both interests, and the gender beliefs that arise from them, affect women's attitudes toward women's issues and relevant political candidates.

The symbolic politics theory would predict, instead, that (1) women's interests bear little connection to their basic symbolic predispositions, since their socialization circumstances should have antedated awareness of those interests; (2) symbolic predispositions, rather than real interests, dominate the formation of attitudes toward women's issues, support for gender-relevant candidates, and gender beliefs; and (3) gender beliefs can be traced back to earlier socialization experiences. The analysis that follows tests these conflicting propositions.

Sample and Dependent Variables

Our data come from the 1984 National Election Studies (NES) survey, a large (N = 2,257) and representative sample of American adults who were interviewed both before and after the 1984 presidential election.[16] Six dependent variables were used. Two were policy positions: (1) *government aid to women*, a single item on support for greater government spending to improve the social and economic position of women; and (2) *opposition to abortion*, a scale based on two items on legalized abortion and evaluation of antiabortionists. Two were candidate evaluations: (3) *opposition to Reagan*, an additive scale composed of (standardized) feeling thermometer and job approval ratings of Reagan; and (4) *support for Ferraro*, the first woman nominated as a major-party candidate for Vice President, measured with a 100-point feeling thermometer item. And two were beliefs about gender: (5) *support for gender equality*, a three-item additive scale (alpha = .70) based on the standard NES sex role item which pits an equal role for women and men in business and government against women's role in the home; disagreement that men are better than women at running things; and disagreement that men are better equipped emotionally for politics than women; and (6) *support for feminism*, a two-item additive scale based on perceived closeness to feminists and a feeling thermometer item on the women's liberation movement.

Self-Interest and Group Interest

Our earlier discussion of women's interests juxtaposed with the data available in the 1984 NES survey lead us to test the effects of four types of self-interest and group interest. Our analyses test both their simple main effects and, where appropriate, interactions between two or more variables. All four types of interest should produce more support for gender equality and for feminism, and for the other dependent variables as follows:

(1) *Child-oriented responsibilities:* Mothers of preadult children, or mothers who are single or working outside the home, or mothers who are single and working, or single with relatively low personal income, ought to support government aid to women and be anti-Reagan and pro-Ferraro, since their campaigns differed markedly on women's issues. The links of child-oriented responsibilities to support for abortion rights are less clear: Those with a family already (and especially those with special financial and childcare problems) might seem to have a stake in controlling the family's further expansion, but unmarried working women could jeopardize their employment with unwanted children.[17]

(2) *Economic disadvantage:* Women with low personal income or declining personal finances, women who are single and/or nonworking, and those who combine low income with being single or nonworking or both should be most in need of government aid, their economic viability should be most jeopardized by unwanted children or cuts in government funding for abortions, and they should be most opposed to the budget-cutting Reagan and supportive of Ferraro.[18]

(3) *High-income workers:* Working women, those with high personal income, and/or those with improving personal finances should be most likely to have workplace roles in traditionally male-dominated areas. They should be most likely to encounter job discrimination and to benefit from government programs such as affirmative action and pay equity. Therefore they should be most supportive of government aid to women and be anti-Reagan and pro-Ferraro. Such women also have much to lose professionally by unwanted children, who could produce serious interruptions in their careers, and thus should be motivated to support abortion rights.

(4) *Economic group interest:* Two variables indexed a sense of group

interest (that is, perceived interdependence with women as a group)—perceived declining finances for women as a group and perceived economic closeness to women as a whole.

Symbolic Predispositions

The four symbolic predispositions used were the standard NES (1) *party identification* and (2) *political ideology* questions; (3) *sociopolitical egalitarian values*, a six-item scale on equal opportunity, equal rights, giving everyone an equal chance, and problems created by giving some people more of a chance in life than others; and (4) a *religiosity* scale, with items on frequency of church/synagogue attendance, perceived importance of religion, degree of guidance provided by religion in day-to-day living, and born-again religious experience. In each case the liberal position is keyed as high.

Symbolic Politics

As in previous studies, women and men did not differ significantly from each other on women's issues. Gender differences on all six dependent variables were trivial in absolute terms and none was statistically significant, even in this large sample. Moreover, women (like men) were deeply divided on each of these variables. Our main analyses, then, are aimed at explaining this disunity among women.[19]

To start with, interest-based theories would suggest that women's symbolic predispositions originate in their real interests. If this were the case, interests would indeed have great power. Moreover, we could not then legitimately compare interests and symbolic predispositions as simultaneous predictors of our dependent variables. Fortunately, the two sets of variables turn out to be only weakly associated. Among women, most (21 of 28) of the correlations between the four predispositions and the seven interest variables were in the expected direction, but they were quite small. The median was +.06, and the mean was +.04 (with the expected direction coded as positive). Only four involving self-interest exceeded +.10; the largest was +.24, between personal finances and party identification, no doubt reflecting the emphasis President Reagan had placed upon improvement in voters' personal finances during the 1984 campaign (the correlation for men was +.34). It seems unlikely, then, that these symbolic predispositions were much influenced by women's self-interest or group interest.

We turn, then, to our major analyses, testing the effects of interests and symbolic predispositions on the dependent variables. Table 11.1 shows the bivariate correlations and Tables 11.2–11.4 show the regression analyses on women's issues, candidate evaluations, and gender beliefs, respectively. In these latter cases, we first conducted regressions with symbolic predispositions or interests separately, and the variance explained by each is shown at the bottom of the tables. The regression coefficients for analyses incorporating all variables are presented in the main body of each table. Not displayed in the tables, but referred to in the text, are a series of two-way and three-way analyses of variance that test various possible interactions between interest variables. Rather than proceeding through the data in lockstep fashion, we will present the main themes, referring to the tables as appropriate.

The Dominance of Symbolic Predispositions

In general, the symbolic predispositions have considerably more predictive value than does self-interest or group interest. This can be seen in three ways. First, for women the median correlation of the dependent variables with symbolic predispositions is almost three times as large (.24) as it is with interests (.09). For men the correlations are very similar: .23 and .08, respectively (see Table 11.1). Second, the great majority of the regression coefficients for symbolic predispositions are statistically significant (79 percent for women and 75 percent for men; see the main bodies of Tables 11.2–11.4), while only about one third of the interest terms are significant (40 percent for women and 31 percent for men). Third, the symbolic predispositions as a set explain considerably more of the variance in each of the dependent variables than do the interest variables (see the bottom of Tables 11.2–11.4). Sometimes the difference is quite large; the symbolic predispositions explain over five times as much variance in attitudes toward feminism or Geraldine Ferraro as does self-interest, and three times as much in attitudes toward abortion or Ronald Reagan. Even when the difference is smaller, as with government aid to women and gender equality, symbolic predispositions dominate.

By all three criteria, women do not differ much from men in the power of either symbolic predispositions or interests. On certain issues—most notably abortion, gender equality, and feminism—women's symbolic predispositions have greater power than men's. Women's interests have more power than men's in two cases, government aid to women and gender equality, and we will return to explore them in more

Table 11.1 Bivariate Correlations

	Government Spending for Women		Abortion Rights		Reagan Opposition		Ferraro Support		Gender Equality		Feminism	
	Women	Men	Women	Men	Women	Men	Women	Men	Women	Men	Women	Men
Symbolic Predispositions												
Equality	.34	.38	.19	.04	.40	.40	.36	.37	.32	.24	.40	.34
Religiosity (low)	.00	−.03	.42	.37	.08	.09	.05	−.05	.23	.16	.17	−.01
Ideology (high)	.24	.21	.23	.16	.37	.37	.29	.27	.17	.11	.29	.23
Party identification	.20	.23	.10	.08	.59	.57	.46	.46	.13	.04	.22	.27
Self-Interest												
Children under age 18	.15	.02	−.05	−.16	.03	−.12	.02	−.04	.12	.03	.03	−.04
Single	.13	.00	.03	.14	.12	.10	.02	.06	−.04	.00	.03	.05
Low personal income	.04	.16	−.22	−.08	.06	.22	−.02	.10	−.26	−.16	−.08	.14
Declining personal finances	.13	.13	−.03	.00	.29	.34	.17	.18	−.09	−.07	.00	.13
Not working	−.03	.09	−.15	−.05	.05	.11	−.03	.02	−.27	−.13	−.09	.08
Group Interest												
Declining women's finances	.20	.16	.10	.08	.24	.28	.14	.11	.01	.05	.12	.12
Economic closeness to women	.11	.06	.09	.03	.04	.05	.03	.05	.09	.05	.10	.10

Table 11.2 Origins of Support for Women's Issues

	Government Spending for Women		Abortion Rights	
	Women	Men	Women	Men
	1	2	3	4
Symbolic Predispositions				
Equality	.62(.07)**	.64(.07)**	.37(.11)**	−.09(.11)
Religiosity (low)	−.04(.02)*	−.03(.02)	.38(.03)**	.33(.03)**
Ideology (liberal)	.10(.03)**	.08(.03)**	.14(.04)**	.11(.05)*
Party identification (Democratic)	.04(.02)	.05(.03)	.05(.04)	.09(.04)*
Self-Interest				
Children under age 18	.45(.10)**	.08(.12)	−.30(.15)*	−.69(.19)**
Single	.35(.10)**	−.16(.12)	−.15(.15)	.40(.19)*
Declining personal finances	.06(.03)*	.02(.03)	−.05(.04)	.00(.06)
Low personal income	.01(.01)	.03(.01)**	−.08(.02)**	−.05(.02)**
Not working	−.04(.11)	.06(.13)	−.20(.16)	−.19(.20)
Group Interest				
Declining women's finances	.16(.04)**	.09(.04)*	.15(.06)**	.11(.06)
Economic closeness	.55(.27)*	.90(.74)	.40(.40)	1.72(1.18)
R^2 Contributed by				
Predispositions only	14.7	16.9	21.0	15.3
Interests only	9.7	6.1	7.0	5.9
Age and education only	1.5	0.6	5.8	3.9
Predispositions and interests	19.5	19.1	24.7	19.2

Source: 1984 National Election Studies pre-post surveys.

Note: The entries are unstandardized regression coefficients, with standard errors in parentheses.

*p < .05
**p < .001

detail. But the similarities of the two genders stand out a good bit more than the differences. All these findings would seem to support a symbolic politics notion more than an interest theory.

Aside from the general dominance of the symbolic predispositions, some are stronger than others. Egalitarian values have the strongest effects, significant on each dependent variable, while party identifica-

Table 11.3 Origins of Candidate Support

	Reagan Opposition		Ferraro Support	
	Women 1	Men 2	Women 3	Men 4
Symbolic Predispositions				
Equality	.82(.10)**	.70(.10)**	8.30(1.05)**	7.88(1.02)**
Religiosity (low)	.04(.03)	.09(.03)**	−.04(.29)	−.63(.29)*
Ideology (liberal)	.20(.04)**	.18(.04)**	1.48(.41)**	1.12(.42)**
Party identification (Democratic)	.57(.03)**	.51(.04)**	4.26(.35)**	4.00(.40)**
Self-Interest				
Children under age 18	.03(.13)	−.38(.16)*	−.61(1.47)	−1.18(1.68)
Single	.21(.13)	.00(.16)	−2.61(1.46)	1.08(1.75)
Declining personal finances	.23(.04)**	.29(.05)**	1.08(.44)*	.96(.51)
Low personal income	.00(.01)	.04(.01)**	−.26(.16)	.01(.14)
Not working	.31(.14)*	−.28(.18)	.05(1.58)	−3.68(1.86)**
Group Interest				
Declining women's finances	.21(.05)**	.28(.06)**	.83(.56)	.00(.59)
Economic closeness	−.17(.35)	.67(1.01)	−1.39(3.86)	7.41(10.77)
R^2 Contributed by				
Predispositions only	43.4	41.3	28.1	27.9
Interests only	13.1	19.7	4.5	4.8
Age and education only	0.9	1.9	0.3	0.3
Predispositions and interests	47.6	47.6	29.1	28.6

Source: 1984 National Election Studies pre-post surveys.

Note: The entries are unstandardized regression coefficients, with standard errors in parentheses.

*p < .05
**p < .001

tion and ideology produce smaller but still significant effects in almost every case. Differences in their roles across the dependent variables are generally as would be expected. Egalitarian values are especially important in determining support for gender equality and, to a lesser extent, support for special government aid to women. Intense religiosity has its strongest effects on opposition to legalized abortion, presumably from Protestants and Catholics alike. The major conventional partisan attitudes, party identification and ideology, play their strongest roles in evaluations of candidates Reagan and Ferraro. But this evidence of a textured response aside, the most striking outcome is the consistent power of the symbolic predispositions and the rather inconsistent, and weaker, effects of interests.

Pure Symbolic Issues

Three of our dependent variables turn out to be almost pure symbolic issues, in the sense that they yield virtually no interest effects at all. Feminism, as the primary political manifestation of the women's movement, fits the symbolic politics model quite well. Indeed, Table 11.4 (columns 5 and 6) indicates strong effects of the symbolic predispositions on the feminism scale for both women and men; they account for 20.4 percent and 15.7 percent of the variance, respectively, and almost all terms are strongly significant. The results are similar for women and men. Moreover, none of the interest variables is significant for women by any of our criteria: the mean correlation is $+.06$ and the maximum is $+.12$; and none of the regression coefficients is significant.

Reagan and Ferraro were evaluated almost exclusively in terms of symbolic predispositions, as shown in Table 11.3. The only consistent effects of interest variables were that Reagan drew greater opposition, and Ferraro greater support, from women who felt that their own and/or women's finances in general had deteriorated. But the same held true for men, so these effects are more likely to be due to the centrality of Reagan's management of the general economy as a campaign issue in 1984 than to women's distinctive interests.

Interests

While, writ large, the dominance of symbolic predispositions seems to be the clearest conclusion of the research, there is merit in a more fine-grained pursuit of the role of interests. Our strategy for this more detailed canvass will be to evaluate each interest hypothesis in terms of four considerations: Is the main effect of the interest variable significant among women, considering (1) the bivariate correlation and (2) the regression coefficient, and (3) are any of the predicted interactions of interest variables significant among women, using an analysis of variance? If one or more of these three yields a significant effect among women, then, (4) is the effect significantly stronger among women than men? The interest theories presumably require a positive answer to this

Table 11.4 Origins of Gender Beliefs

	Gender Equality				Feminism	
	Women 1	Men 2	Women 3	Men 4	Women 5	Men 6
Symbolic Predispositions						
Equality	.94(.09)**	.68(.09)**	.78(.09)**	.62(.09)**	1.089(.103)**	.768(.100)**
Religiosity (low)	.15(.03)**	.10(.03)**	.12(.02)**	.09(.03)**	.083(.028)**	−.028(.028)
Ideology (liberal)	.04(.04)	.06(.04)	.05(.03)	.02(.04)	.186(.040)**	.127(.041)**
Party identification (Democratic)	.08(.03)*	.00(.04)	.09(.03)**	.03(.04)	.110(.034)**	.131(.040)**
Self-Interest						
Children under age 18	.41(.13)**	−.04(.15)	−.16(.14)	−.23(.16)	−.088(.144)	−.120(.165)
Single	−.42(.13)**	.02(.16)	−.23(.12)	−.20(.16)	−.174(.143)	−.048(.171)
Declining personal finances	−.10(.04)*	−.06(.05)	−.03(.04)	−.02(.05)	−.065(.043)	.042(.050)
Low personal income	−.10(.01)**	−.06(.01)**	−.06(.01)**	−.03(.01)*	−.027(.015)	.027(.014)
Not working	−.67(.14)**	−.36(.17)*	−.11(.14)	−.05(.19)	−.074(1.54)	−.007(.183)

Group Interest

	(1)	(2)	(3)	(4)	(5)	(6)
Declining women's finances	−.02(.05)	.03(.05)	.01(.05)	.03(.05)	.104(.055)	.061(.057)
Economic closeness	.45(.35)	1.59(.97)	.14(.33)	1.37(.96)	.740(.377)	2.77(1.06)**
Age	—	—	−.03(.00)**	−.01(.01)*	—	—
Education	—	—	.29(.03)**	.16(.03)**	—	—
R^2 Contributed by						
Predispositions only	14.5	8.1	14.5	8.1	20.4	15.7
Interests only	12.3	3.9	12.3	3.9	3.5	4.9
Age and education only	—	—	23.2	7.7	—	—
All variables	24.1	12.3	33.8	15.6	21.7	17.2

Source: 1984 National Election Studies pre-post surveys.

Note: The entries are unstandardized regression coefficients, with standard errors in parentheses.

*p < .05
**p < .001

last criterion. We find two cases in which interest effects meet these criteria.

Interest-Based Support for Government Aid to Women

Prima facie, women's interests should perhaps be the most directly energized by the general question of governmental spending to improve the social and economic position of women. And indeed among women, five of the seven interest variables produce significant bivariate correlations (Table 11.1) and regression coefficients (Table 11.2). In contrast, only two of the regression terms are significant for men. In toto, interests account for somewhat more variance for women than for men: 9.7 percent versus 6.1 percent. This pattern of results encourages us to pursue the more specific interest hypotheses posed earlier.

First, women with preadult children do support government aid to women most. The bivariate correlation is significant for women (r = .15) but not for men (r = .02). The same holds for the regression coefficients, and the difference is quite substantial (Table 11.2). However, none of the four interactions of motherhood with other presumed dimensions of its burdens (being single, working, both single and working, or single and low-income) proved significant for women. So these data yield some limited support for the child-responsibility hypothesis.

Second, economically disadvantaged women also especially favored government aid for women. Both being single and having a declining personal financial situation significantly increased support for such government aid among women, and more than for men in the regression analyses (Table 11.2). However, the two other indices of economic disadvantage—low personal income and not working—had no effect among women, and several interactions of these disadvantage variables yielded no evidence for the hypothesis: Low-income women who were single, not working, or both showed no special support for government aid to women. In short, two of the seven tests of the economic disadvantage hypothesis were positive, reflecting some limited support for it, as well.

Finally, the group-interest hypothesis focuses on perceptions of women's shared economic fate. Perceiving that women's finances were generally declining did promote women's support for government aid, and more than it did among men (see Table 11.2). So did feelings of economic closeness to women (though these proved to be so rare that they could not be said to yield much sense of group interest; only 3.5 percent of the women and 0.5 percent of the men felt economically close to women). On balance there is some suggestion of a group-interested response among women to the policy question of government spending on women.

In short, we do find some evidence that women responded to the question of special government aid to women in a self- and group-interested manner. The strongest supporters of government aid to women were women who had special burdens of childrearing, who were economically disadvantaged, and/or who had a sense of shared economic disadvantage with other women.

On the other hand, the strength of these effects should not be exaggerated. None of the eight hypothesized interaction effects was significant; even the main effects were not large in absolute terms (the average bivariate correlation for the interest effects was .10 among women); and the simple main effects among women were in the final analysis not much larger than those among men (the comparable average was .09 for men).

High-Income Workers

Both legalized abortion and beliefs in gender equality seem also to draw self-interested support from women, but, consistent with our high-income-worker hypothesis, from affluent working women rather than the disadvantaged poor. The correlations in Table 11.1 show that high-income and working women especially support legalized abortion, while the same does not hold for men. The regression equations summarized in Table 11.2 indicate that at least the former effect holds up with other variables controlled. Moreover, childless women and men alike are the strongest supporters of legalized abortion, as shown in Table 11.2. It is specifically the *lack* of childrearing burdens that contributes to women's support for legalized abortion, as revealed in two significant interaction effects: Childless working women and childless, single, high-income women show the greatest support for it (and greater than do comparable men). The strongest supporters of legalized abortion, then, were high-income working women, especially those with no children.

Similarly, higher-income and working women were the strongest supporters of equal gender roles; the correlations were .26 and .27 for women (as opposed to .16 and .13 for men), and the regression coefficients were significant for women, and higher than for men, as shown in Table 11.4. Among women, the interest variables cumulatively contributed 12.3 percent to variance explained, as opposed to 3.9 percent for men. And married women, who for the most part have access to a second income, supported gender equality more than did single women; again, there was no comparable effect among men (see Table 11.4). These data seem to yield further support for the higher-income working women hypothesis: Among women, the core supporters of gender equality are affluent working women, not the most child-burdened or economically deprived nor those with a sense of solidarity with deprived women.

Two other similar interactions also appeared. High-income working women were most opposed to Reagan and most supportive of Ferraro, as were single mothers; neither was true for men. These interactions should probably be interpreted cautiously, since they were the only two that reached significance of the eight interactions predicted for each dependent variable.

There is an important problem in interpreting these findings, however. Previous research has also clearly shown that better-educated and younger women show the greatest support for gender equality and women's issues.[20] Yet age and education are also correlated both with working and higher income and with the symbolic predispositions that best predict attitudes toward abortion and gender equality. Both the mass movement of women into the workplace and their ability to increase their income significantly have occurred disproportionately in the younger generation and among the college-educated. At the same time, egalitarianism and political liberalism have also been greatest among the young and well-educated women.

It is possible, then, that the greater support for legalized abortion and gender equality among high-income working women is not due to their personal experiences in the working world, as the self-interest interpretation would have it, but is simply an artifact of a symbolic politics process. The distinctive socialization of the younger generation, occurring in part in institutions of higher education, may be responsible for both their pro-equality symbolic predispositions and their ambitions for high-income working roles.

To test this, we regressed attitudes toward legalized abortion and gender equality on age and education. Considered alone, the latter prove to have powerful effects, especially for women, accounting for 5.8 and 23.2 percent of their variance, respectively. But even more dramatic is the fact that in both cases adding age and education to the regression equations eliminates the effects of working and sharply diminishes those of higher income (though the latter is still significantly greater for women than men). The symbolic predisposition terms prove to be largely unaffected, so this does not seem to reflect a symbolic politics process. But it does show that there is considerable overlap between the self-interest effects, on the one hand, and those of age and education, on the other. More precise measures of self-interest would be required to distinguish its effects from the direct effects of youth and higher education.

Failures of Other Interest Hypotheses

Aside from these few exceptions, the interest hypotheses did not for the most part yield a great deal. The child-oriented responsibilities, economic disadvantage, and group-interest hypotheses generated only isolated significant effects on the dependent variables other than government aid to women. Our five child-oriented predictions yielded only three positive effects out of twenty-five comparisons, which seems most likely simply to reflect chance. Our seven economic-disadvantage predictions yielded virtually no significant effects aside from the government aid question. And the group-interest items yielded little that was unique to women: The bivariate correlations were very similar for women and men (Table 11.1), and but four of the twelve regression coefficients were significant for women (Tables 11.2–11.4).

Gender Beliefs

Gender beliefs play a crucial role in both interest and symbolic politics theories. On the one hand, they should help form women's attitudes toward gender-relevant political issues. On the other, they should themselves be based on interests or symbolic predispositions and, if the latter, in earlier socialization experiences.

In fact, gender beliefs do prove to have some impact on the other four dependent variables. The average correlations across the four dependent variables were, for women, .24 for gender equality and .32 for feminism; for men, .22 and .26. The increments in variance explained by adding these two gender belief variables to the regressions shown in Tables 11.2 and 11.3 were, for women and men, respectively, 3.6 and 6.9 percent for aid to women, 2.8 and 3.4 percent for abortion rights, 0.4 and 0.7 percent for opposition to Reagan, and 7.4 and 4.8 percent for support for Ferraro.

We have already seen that attitudes toward feminism are largely explained by symbolic predispositions, while beliefs about gender equality are explained partly by them and partly by the adult personal experiences suggested by interest theories. This divergence of the two forms of gender belief persists when we consider the symbolic politics hypothesis that their origins lie in early socialization (or resocialization) experiences.

We obviously cannot measure precisely the exact socialization experiences that our respondents had with respect to gender roles. But we can do so indirectly. We have seen that egalitarian beliefs about gender are most common in upper-middle-class, urban social environments. Therefore, individuals reared in those environments are most likely to have been exposed to egalitarian gender socialization. Accordingly, we indexed the presumed gender egalitarianism of the individual's preadult socialization environment with father's occupation, mother's employment status, and urban-rural origins.[21]

These three socialization indicators were indeed significantly linked to beliefs about gender equality for women. In a multiple regression equation, they accounted for considerably more variance in women's support for gender equality than in men's (9.1 and 3.9 percent, respectively). In contrast, they have almost no predictive value at all in accounting for support for feminism, explaining only 2.8 percent of the variance among women and 1.9 percent among men.

This leaves us with two further questions. First, why does socialization explain beliefs in gender equality for women, but not very well for men? And beliefs in gender equality are better explained by more proximal interests and symbolic predispositions for women than men, as well. The variance accounted for by both interests and symbolic predispositions in beliefs about gender equality was 24.1 percent for women and 12.3 percent for men. The reason for both phenomena would seem to be that the manifest content of beliefs about gender equality is primarily concerned with women, not men. The specific items used to measure them focus on *women's* roles specifically. The gender equality items ask whether *women* should be in the home or in the workplace, political office, and so forth, and whether or not *women* are adequate in public roles. By this argument the reverse would be true for questions about male roles.

The second question is why socialization fails to explain attitudes toward feminism even among women. Feminism, as the political arm of the concern for gender equality, ought to have become a highly symbolic attitude object during the past two decades: It was frequently in the news; it was surrounded by hot emotion; its meaning was consensual and well understood; and so it was likely to have attracted stable and strong affects in the general public.[22] As a result, attitudes toward the women's movement should fit the symbolic politics formulation even more closely than do beliefs in gender equality.

Yet we should note, too, that there is clear evidence that attitudes toward feminism have not been acquired by our adult respondents as part of their preadult socialization. Rather, they appear to have been acquired through a process of embedding feminism in the other symbolic predispositions with which they entered adulthood. Indeed, women's attitudes toward feminism are more firmly and exclusively rooted in other symbolic predispositions than is gender equality for women or feminism for men. Presumably this is because feminism is likely not to have been a core aspect of most current adults' preadult political socialization, as an attitude object that only relatively recently reemerged publicly. Still, feminism, unlike gender equality, is largely a political matter, and therefore a product of specifically political predispositions.

In short, there are interesting differences between the two forms of gender beliefs. Beliefs about gender roles seem partly to have been socialized in early childhood, prior to contact with the political world. They may also stem (though the evidence is susceptible to alternative interpretations) from women's private, nonpolitical, adult experiences, with managing a family and in the workplace. And they seem to have become politicized to some degree, and so to be linked to basic symbolic predispositions. In contrast, support for feminism tends to be derived primarily from the political values people hold in their adult lives, men as well as women. In that sense feminism is a classic "symbolic" political issue, except that it appears to be derived from other political values rather than itself being a product of early-life socialization.

Conclusions

Have women become a cohesive political bloc? Relative to men, women have supported Reagan less, opposed the use of force more, and support so-called compassion issues more. While such differences are persistent over time and across studies, their magnitude has been relatively slight. Moreover, there is no such gender gap on issues of particular relevance to women, such as government-supported childcare programs, affirmative action hiring and promotion policies, and the ERA. Nor are there gender differences in support for female candidates, even Geraldine Ferraro, the first woman on a major-party presidential ticket. Women would seem more to be politically fragmented than to form a cohesive, mobilized, political force.

The reason for this fragmentation is that women are split over such basic sociocultural values as equality, political ideology, political party preferences, and religiosity. These divisions go back in large part, if not completely, to political socialization in earlier life and are equally prevalent, and politically consequential, among men. These predispositions in turn are the foundation for candidate evaluations and support for women's issues. They also indirectly influence candidate and policy choices through their influence on beliefs about gender equality and feminism.

There was considerably less evidence that women's political disunity is due to interest-based cleavages among women. In two cases, however, there did seem to be meaningful evidence of a distinctively self-interested response on the part of women. The greatest support for special government aid to women did emerge from women burdened by young children, from those who were most economically disadvantaged, and from those feeling a sense of common group interest with disadvantaged women. While these hypotheses were not uniformly supported across our several empirical tests, and women did not differ dramatically from men, the data did reveal some role for self-interest and group interest.

The other main support for the self-interest hypothesis concerned high-income working women. The greatest support for abortion rights and for gender equality was among working women with relatively high levels of personal income. Similarly, high-income working women most opposed Reagan and supported Ferraro, quite unlike men. These distinctive attitudes of high-income working women are perhaps the clearest support for the self-interest idea, though as indicated above they are open to other interpretations.

Elsewhere, support for the interest hypotheses was much weaker, and interest-related differences were dwarfed by differences based on predispositions, as in much earlier research. Women, like men, tend to respond to them primarily in symbolic terms. Having said that, perhaps some caveats are in order. As mentioned earlier, we follow a considerable body of other research in working with a relatively narrow definition of self-interest. The purpose of this narrowing is to align the concept with everyday usage ("selfish, pocketbook politics" and the like) and to specify it in testable and falsifiable form. This decision has certain costs, however, including the exclusion of possibly important sources of motivation such as long-term or "enlightened" self-interest.

A second caveat is that our tests of self-interest are in some respects rather crude. The dependent variables we use are rather global, which may hinder the operation of self-interest. In a study of the California tax revolt, Sears and Citrin found that recipients of public services preferentially supported funding those service areas targeted quite specifically to their own needs.[23] If political self-interest requires the matching of a quite specific personal need with an equally specifically targeted public policy, a more sensitive test of women's interests might predict their attitudes about childcare, pay equity, affirmative action, and so on. Presumably the tax dollars such programs would require would be a selfish disincentive for some women, especially those with high income who do not personally benefit from them, and that should be taken into consideration as well.

Our indices of interests are also rather global. For example, not all high-income working women are equally personally vulnerable to the need for a legal abortion; younger, sexually active women would surely be more self-interested in abortion policy than would postmenopausal and/or nonsexually active women. Comparable men also have some self-interest in the issue, although presumably less than women. Further research could well narrow the tests of self-interest in both respects and test its effects more precisely.

With respect to these symbolic predispositions, we have assumed that they are truly longstanding and causally prior to the other variables in our model. Some researchers have recently argued that such predispositions as party identification are not static, but may be modified in response to such events as the individual's perceptions of current government performance. This is a long debate that cannot be addressed here in detail. Our view is that the present approach allows our interpretations if three assumptions are granted: (1) that these predispositions are among the most stable attitudes in the general public in our era; (2) that they are highly stable in absolute terms; and (3) that the symbolic politics theory requires only that they be stable over a substantial period of the lifespan, not necessarily from preadult life. The current literature supports these assumptions, we believe.[24]

One unresolved question concerns the great polarization among women over questions of gender equality. Working, high-income, younger, well-educated women tend to support the notion of gender equality, while nonworking, low-income, older, less well educated women oppose it. The same trends exist among men, but they are not nearly as polarizing. What lies behind these divisions? Is it that older, less well educated women are more socially, politically, and religiously conservative? Or is it because younger, better-educated women work in male-dominated occupations and so have more to gain from women's equality? We are simply unable to resolve this question with our data.

Finally, it seems likely that new issues will surface as women's policy agendas broaden. An obvious example is that as young women continue to enter the work force at very high rates, the need for widespread, accessible childcare will deepen. Beliefs about the priorities to be given to women's roles as mothers and workers would seem likely to be central to their attitudes about an expanded government role in supplementing the family's role in childcare and in allowing both parents to work. Thus, our finding that American women are quite divided over gender beliefs suggests that they will continue to be divided over women's issues as well, even when such issues are in the political limelight. Although this disunity may reduce women's collective influence over public policy, it probably does have the advantage of helping to maintain attention to the many issues that bear on women's well-being.

Notes

Thanks are due to the editors of this volume, to an anonymous reviewer, and to Cary Funk, Tom Jessor, and Rick Kosterman for their helpful comments on earlier drafts of this manuscript. The chapter was completed while the first author was a Guggenheim Fellow and a Fellow at the Center for Advanced Study in the Behavioral Sciences. We are grateful for the financial support provided to the latter by National Science Foundation grant #BNS87-00864.

1. Baxter and Lansing (1983); Klein (1984); Mansbridge (1986).
2. Schuman, Steeh, and Bobo (1985).
3. Zipp and Plutzer (1985). In 1936, 40 percent of the women and 27 percent of the men said that they would vote for a qualified woman for president (Erskine 1971). The gender gap on this item had reversed by 1963 (53 and 61 percent, respectively, supported a woman; see "Women and Men" 1982). By 1978 about 80 percent of each gender did so (Fleming, 1986).
4. For example, women were almost evenly divided in 1972 on the existence of discrimination and support for legalized abortion (55 and 48 percent, respectively), and moderately supportive of the ERA in 1981 (67 percent favorable; the comparable figures for men were 54, 54, and 68 percent); see "Women and Men" (1982). A useful summary of the earlier data may be found in Erskine (1971). Fleming (1986) reviews some of the later findings. Also see Daniels, Darcy, and Westphal (1982); Mansbridge (1985); Shapiro and Mahajan (1986); Klein (1984); Tedrow and Mahoney (1979).
5. Berelson, Lazarsfeld, and McPhee (1954); Campbell, Converse, Miller, and Stokes (1960); Sears (1969); Lane (1959); Hero (1966); Verba, Brody, Parker, Nie, Polsby, Ekman, and Black (1967).
6. For a thorough review, see Smith (1984); also see Frankovic (1982); "Women and Men" (1982); Shapiro and Mahajan (1986).
7. Klein (1984); Mansbridge (1985); Frankovic (1982); Mueller (1986); also see Sears, Huddy, and Schaffer (1986) for similar findings. It should be noted that these studies have not looked closely at differences in impact across various women's issues. As Mansbridge has pointed out, Reagan's supposed opposition to the ERA was less a factor in the women's vote than was his inhospitality to nontraditional work roles for women. This issue needs further exploration.
8. Sears, Lau, Tyler, and Allen (1980); Sears, Huddy, and Schaffer (1986).
9. Sears and Funk (1990).

10. Sears and Kinder (1985).
11. Freeman (1975).
12. Sears and Funk (1990); Green (1988); Citrin and Green (1988).
13. Sears, Jessor, and Gahart (1984); Shaffer (1985); Poole and Zeigler (1981, 1985); Gurin (1985); Crosby (1982); Del Boca and Ashmore (1984).
14. Sears, Huddy, and Schaffer (1986); Del Boca and Ashmore (1984); Fleming (1986); Marmon and Palley (1986); Tedin et al. (1977).
15. There could be subtler patterns, as well. Klein (1984) and others have suggested that women's gender beliefs are based in interests and real adult experiences, whereas men's are based more in abstract political socialization and symbolic predispositions. For a further test of that idea, see Sears, Huddy, and Schaffer (1986).
16. The data were made available by the Inter-University Consortium for Political and Social Research. Neither the original collectors of the data nor the consortium bear any responsibility for the analyses or interpretations presented here.
17. In fact, Hewlett (1986) goes so far as to argue that political emphasis on abortion has occurred at the expense of family and childcare issues, effectively alienating mothers.
18. Personal income, rather than household income, is emphasized because government policies are likely to have a more direct effect on women's personal income. There is a clear dissociation between personal and household income among women that is not present among men. Men in the NES sample, for example, report average personal incomes of $14,000–15,000 and average household incomes of $17,000–20,000. Women, on the other hand, earn on average $9,000–10,000 but live in households with average incomes of $14,000–15,000.
19. These items provide good illustrations of women's disunity; for example, their mean evaluation of Ferraro was 58.9, and of women's liberation, 59.0, on 100-point scales; and on whether women were as emotionally suited to politics as men, 3.1 on a 5-point scale. Both genders had more consensus on general principles of gender equality; for example, women averaged 5.7 on the 7-point scale concerning women's roles extending beyond the home and 4.0 on a 5-point scale concerning whether women were equally good at running things.
20. Klein (1984); Poole and Zeigler (1985).
21. For the relevant data, and a more extensive justfication for this procedure, see Miller and Sears (1986).
22. See Sears (1983) for an analysis of what makes some attitude objects highly symbolic.
23. Sears and Citrin (1985).
24. Evidence of such adulthood modification may be found in Fiorina (1981). On the remaining points, see Converse and Markus (1979); Jennings and Niemi (1981); Sears (1983); Jennings and Markus (1984).

Continuities and Discontinuities in Women's Political Voluntarism

Women's (or primarily women's) social movements such as temperance and suffrage pioneered interest group politics. Despite their greater participation in electoral politics and integration in party politics, women's activity in interest group politics has continued to be substantial. Part IV includes a historical look at the characteristics of members of the League of Women Voters and its role in training women in politics, a study of women in contemporary religion, an analysis of the ERA ratification campaign in Illinois, and two studies of women in pressure politics today.

A 1950s survey of members of the League of Women Voters offers Susan Ware a window on women's political activity in that period and after. The League was primarily a middle-class organization that offered women a chance to engage in nonpartisan politics on many levels. Ware compares the picture she finds with that drawn in *The Feminine Mystique* by Betty Friedan. Membership in the League was the starting point for some women who later entered electoral politics or social movements such as civil rights or women's liberation.

The relationship between religious groups as voluntary organizations and women's politics is examined by Robert Wuthnow and William Lehrman. They point out that in the United States religious organizations have a legal status similar to other voluntary associations. Comparing today's split in the Christian churches between liberals and conservatives with the late nineteenth century split between fundamentalists and modernists, Wuthnow and Lehrman find that present divisions

279

involve members, not just leaders, and have occurred within, not simply between, denominations. Overall, religion has facilitated women's political participation, but in support of varying goals. Most recently, it has been conservative Republicans who have capitalized on the churches as a resource for political mobilization.

Jane J. Mansbridge examines the operation of feminist pressure group activity at the state level. She compares two women's organizations (NOW and ERA Illinois) that campaigned for ratification of the Equal Rights Amendment, and attributes to their different political bases and alliances the uneasy relations between the two organizations working for a common goal. The organizations attracted different groups of women, and consequently offered different incentives for participation. The result was two different sets of tactics often characterized by lack of smooth collaboration, sometimes by clashes.

Two complementary chapters focus on women in national-level pressure group politics. Kay Lehman Schlozman compares *organizations* representing women, and their resources and activity in Washington, with predominantly male organizations. Although women now serve as Washington representatives in 22 percent of all organizations, they are much more highly concentrated in women's organizations. Such organizations, even when they are not feminist by self-description, most often include women's issues on their agenda. The chief disadvantage of women's organizations is lack of resources; in response, they work together more often than do other organizations. David Knoke compares *members* of women's pressure organizations with members of professional and recreational pressure groups. He explores reasons for joining, incentives, the decision-making process, participation, and commitment. He finds that members of women's associations are distinctive in their high level of activism, a characteristic he attributes to their organizations' democratic decision-making structures.

12

American Women in the 1950s: Nonpartisan Politics and Women's Politicization

Susan Ware

The 1950s continues to fascinate and, in many ways, to elude historians studying American women. The postwar years are full of contradictions: the heightened emphasis on domesticity which Betty Friedan termed "the feminine mystique" and a steady, indeed dramatic, increase in women's wage force participation; in the 1950s the seeming political apathy and the nonparticipation of women; and in the 1960s and 1970s the explosion of social turmoil, especially the revival of feminism. Yet some historians are beginning to question this one-dimensional view of the 1950s. Unlocking the mysteries of the 1950s has the potential of not only encouraging a more diverse portrait of American womanhood in that decade, but also providing the key to understanding the role of continuity in shaping the lives of twentieth century American women.

We begin our search for the elusive 1950s by considering the League of Women Voters (LWV). As political scientist Louise M. Young asserted in 1952, "The history of the League is the autobiography of the enfranchised female sex in the United States."[1] Although never a mass organization, the League produced a corps of committed volunteers whose contributions to the functioning of government, especially on the local level, were vital to the democratic process in the United States. Its style of intensive study, training for citizenship, and grass-roots political action show one direction that women took in public life. In communities across the nation, local Leagues stimulated and legitimated women's political aspirations, providing channels for the cultivation of women's talents at a time when traditional organs of political expression, such as the Democratic and Republican parties, were uninterested in training women for leadership.

This chapter addresses several questions about the League of Women Voters in order to locate its historical significance. To what extent did the LWV provide women in the 1950s with an opportunity for political action? What kinds of women joined the League in the communities? How does the League's history compare with Friedan's concept of "the feminine mystique"? And more broadly, did the League's facilitation of women's politicization and potential empowerment serve as a bridge to the activism of the 1960s?

The League of Women Voters' philosophy was based on a belief in the responsibility of individual citizens to be active and informed participants in the democratic process; voter information and citizenship training are still readily associated with it. The League chose a distinctive route to achieve political influence: It was rigorously nonpartisan. While individual members were expected to enroll as registered voters and even participate in partisan politics while associated with the League, none of its officials could hold a political position. Nonpartisan, however, did not necessarily mean nonpolitical. The League consistently took strong stands on major governmental questions and lobbied aggressively for causes it believed in; it prided itself on its commitment to internal democracy at the grass-roots level, believing that the real vitality of the organization came from local initiative. It acted only after a rigorous period of study in which its membership reached a consensus about the proper course of action.[2]

The LWV remains largely unstudied for a variety of reasons. Generally, there is a lack of attention given to women's organizations in the fields of history and political science, a situation which only recently began to change as women's studies challenged traditional disciplines. Another factor is the unwarranted assumption that because the League is not a self-interested political group, it is outside the mainstream of political activity and therefore uninteresting. Also, since everyone seems to know what the League does, there is little incentive to subject the organization to intensive scrutiny.[3]

A final barrier has to do with the League's institutional structure. Until the 1940s the National League of Women Voters (as it was known) functioned under a structure inherited from the National American Woman Suffrage Association, whereby the organization was basically a federation of state leagues. After a major reorganization put into effect at the 1944 national convention, the League became an association of members, in which each member joined the League of Women Voters of the United States (its new name) and worked through her local League.

State Leagues had the responsibility of dealing with state issues and chartering local Leagues. Local members, however, predominantly worked through their local organizations on state and national issues. A further structural change occurred in 1948 with the introduction of the unit system, small discussion groups of fifteen to thirty members. Such a structure maximized the importance of local Leagues.[4]

Profile of League Members in the 1950s

To concentrate on the national leadership of the League of Women Voters—its conventions and programs, the recruitment patterns of leaders, its sophisticated lobbying tactics, and its links with other women's organizations—may be important and fascinating, but it misses the essence of what it was like for the average "Leaguer." We can capture some of the unwritten history of the local Leagues by examining a study done by the Survey Research Center of the Institute for Social Research at the University of Michigan between 1956 and 1958. The results, presented in five volumes of interpretation and data,[5] illuminate the relationship of the individual member to her League as well as the patterns that facilitated effective League functioning at the local level. Of special interest is the broad demographic profile of the typical League member, which confirms the view that the LWV was a group of well-educated, well-off community women.

Here are some of the highlights of this composite portrait of the League's 128,000 members in 1956:[6]

Age: The median age for members was 45.3 years. Presidents of local Leagues were below the median (43 years), while board members were even younger (40 years). The age of membership varied regionally, with the West boasting the youngest members (41.4 years) and the South the oldest (47.2 years). Furthermore, the oldest members tended to be found in metropolitan and county Leagues, while not surprisingly the youngest were found in suburban Leagues.[7]

Marital status: Eighty-two percent of League members were married. Metropolitan Leagues had the lowest proportion of married women (70 percent), and suburban Leagues had the highest (87 percent). The proportion of presidents and board members who were married was even higher (92 percent), suggesting that marriage facilitated, rather than hampered, leadership in the League. Those who were not married were about equally divided between women who had never married and women who were widowed. There were very few divorced women in the League in the 1950s.[8]

Education: Half the League members had completed college. The percentage was even higher for presidents (65 percent) and board members (56 percent), which suggests that education was an important factor in leadership selection. Thirteen percent of League members had a postgraduate degree, while only 3 percent had not finished high school. Yet this was not a uniformly super-educated group. The largest category of members had some college, but had not graduated.[9]

Employment: Somewhat less than one third (28 percent) of League members were employed either full or part time, a percentage similar to women's general employment statistics for the decade. Employment was highest in metropolitan areas (39 percent) and small cities (34 percent) and lowest in suburbia (21 percent). That one out of five suburban League members held jobs shows how prevalent employment was becoming even among the white middle-class women who were the bulk of League members. The rest of the survey, however, had very little to say about such women or the kinds of jobs they held. It did note that only 18 percent of presidents and 19 percent of board members were employed.[10]

Income: The median family income of League members was $9,385, more than twice the 1955 national median family income of $4,421.[11] Presidents had the highest median income ($10,467); since presidents were the least likely among League members to have outside employment, it seemed that husbands' incomes expedited assumption of leadership duties. The North Central and West regions were below the median income, as were small city and county Leagues. The wealthiest Leagues were located in metropolitan and suburban areas.[12]

Other data complete the profile of the League member and what the League meant to her. Leaguers were real "organization women." Only 15 percent belonged to fewer than two other organizations; more than one third belonged to five or more.[13] The median length of membership for women in the League was 4.1 years, although this probably was higher since membership figures did not reflect whether women had belonged to other Leagues in other communities.[14] More than half had joined within five years, although a tenth had been with the League for fifteen years or longer.[15] Most typically (40 percent), women learned about the League through friends.[16]

League members saw the main purpose of their organization as the political education of the public, with specific attention given to women's political participation. Only 4 percent considered its purpose as supporting legislation.[17] Forty-nine percent of the League members surveyed cited the local program as the most meaningful activity for them. The reasons are fairly obvious: The problems were closer to home, and it was possible to effect changes. However, there was also broad support for the national program, especially its voter service. The area of League structure that held the least relevance for the local Leaguer was the state program, which was cited by a mere 7 percent as "most interesting."[18]

The survey discovered that members derived a high level of satisfaction from their participation in the League. An active 37-year-old member, wife of an engineer and mother of three school-age children, who gave ten hours a week to her metropolitan League, observed: "The League keeps me on my toes, educationally and politically. It gives me an outlet to work constructively, without social obligations which I would find binding on my time. It seems to meet just often enough to keep me interested and not too often so I can't get my work done here [at home]. I've made some wonderful friendships, learned a lot, and enjoy it. . . ."[19]

Members spent different amounts of time on League activities. One third spent less than an hour per week; the average participation was one to two hours per week (although one out of twenty gave a day a week). In general, women's activity levels were linked to four factors: time available, husband's attitude, interest in the League's program, and ability to work with other women. The factor of husband's support was "perhaps the most important situational determinant of whether she will be active."[20] Husbands would be called on for occasional babysitting when their wives went off to meetings. In addition, if their wives did not work, they would have to pay the cost of luncheons and other expenses incurred by League participation. Husbands themselves involved in organizations were more likely to be tolerant of their wives' activities.

The main reason for limited activity in League functions was, not surprisingly, "not enough time." The 55 percent who cited lack of time as their reason usually attributed it to family responsibilities, home affairs, or children, but the figure also included 16 percent who gave work as their reason. (This is one of the infrequent references to women's employment patterns in this study.) In general, the "not enough time" response covered a wide range of factors, leading the researchers to conclude that if a woman was really interested in the League, she could find the time.[21] For example, 30 percent of the women without young children were active as compared with 20 percent of those with children under age 5. These figures can be read two ways. A small child reduced activity by about one third. This means that even with preschool children, women's activity was two thirds as high as women without them.[22] Researchers also found that the number of children under age 12 did not have an adverse impact on the effectiveness of board members. In fact, childrearing responsibilities often enhanced a woman's effectiveness in the League.[23]

The League in Its Community

One interesting aspect of the Michigan survey was its attempt to sample community attitudes toward the LWV, or at least the attitudes of a cross-section of 509 women aged 25 to 64 in the urban three fifths of the United States where the League was found.[24] Approximately half of those women had heard of the League; recognition was highest (78.0 percent) among the wives of professional and managerial workers and lowest among the semiskilled and unskilled industrial workers (35.4 percent). The prevailing view of the League was "as a group which takes the initiative in interaction with other groups in the community, within a broadly 'political' sphere of activity, and which has a definite but by no means exclusive interest in women."[25] On the whole, the image of the League member was a positive one, with many interviewees (especially, again, those of the business class) seeing members as "interested in politics, government and world affairs, intelligent and well-informed, hard-working and devoted."[26]

The section on community attitudes underscores the general message conveyed by the survey: The League was predominantly an organization that appealed to and was made up of white, educated, middle-class women. This is further confirmed by a section devoted to how cross-sectional League membership was. The survey compared data from personal interviews with the previously mentioned sample of 509 community women with material collected from a representative sample of 227 League members. One of the most obvious differences concerned where the women in the two samples lived. During the personal interviews, the researchers (all women) recorded a judgment about whether their subject lived in a good, average, or below-average neighborhood. Three quarters of League members lived in good neighborhoods compared with one quarter of all women in the community. There were practically no League members from below-average neighborhoods, whereas 29 percent of all women lived in these areas.[27]

The disparities were just as great in the areas of education and income. Of the League members, 78 percent had some college education, including 28 percent with a B.A. and 18 percent with some graduate work. The comparable figure for all women interviewed was 14 percent. Although many community women had some high school, only 5 percent of League members had *not* graduated from high school. In terms of income (a variable that clearly was related to the neighborhood in which the subjects lived), 54 percent of League members had family incomes greater than $10,000, a level of economic security achieved by the families of only 9 percent of all women in the sample. Only 6 percent of League members had family incomes below $5,000, leading the researchers to conclude that "few wives of men in clerical, sales, factory work, or personal service work are found in the League."[28]

These figures bring home with striking clarity the class composition of the LWV. It was drawn almost entirely from wives of professional and managerial workers, who lived in the best neighborhoods of their communities, had exceptionally high levels of education, and had incomes well in excess of the national average. These were a privileged lot, belying the survey's description of the League as "a large and diverse group, encompassing women with a variety of personal, social, and economic characteristics."[29] It could more accurately have been called the League of Affluent Women Voters.

Was it realistic for the League to think of becoming more representative? A desire to attract more members was one of the few specific suggestions that League members (especially active ones) volunteered in their interviews.[30] But they did not necessarily want a cross-section of the community. Instead, they had in mind targeting and initiating into membership women who were generally like themselves.

The profiles of the potential members gleaned from the general community sample hint at the changes that might have been implemented to achieve a slightly broader membership base. Take "Mrs. A.," a 35-year-old mother of five with number six on the way. She was the wife of a mechanic, active in community affairs such as the Den Mothers and the church; her husband participated in union activities and Catholic groups. She was very interested in politics and had once considered running for a minor office on the Democratic ticket. Right now she was too busy with her family, but the interviewer thought she might be interested in the League later. "Mrs. A." might, however, be held back by the fact that she knew no League members (the major source of recruitment); that she lived in a home that was not up to standards of the average League member (the interviewer described the home

as terribly run down, with furniture that "could well be used for kin-
dling wood"); and, tactfully, that "she may have some problem with
money."[31]

"Mrs. C." presented problems on a different level: She was black.
Her husband was a painter, and they lived with their children in an
average neighborhood, where she was active in church and school organizations. She occasionally supplemented family income by selling
Seventh Day Adventist books, and she found time to take courses at a
local junior college. Here, the surveyor discreetly looked forward to the
potential adjustments Mrs. C.'s membership would cause: "Mrs. C. is,
in some aspects of background and belief, different from the typical
League member. There is the possibility that integration of Mrs. C. into
a local League might require an adaptability on the part of both the local
League and Mrs. C. beyond that ordinarily required." Although the
League of Women Voters did have integrated Leagues in the 1950s, it
was unusual for black women to join the organization.[32]

The problems inherent in increasing the diversity of the League again
highlight the narrow class basis of its members. Since the LWV was one
of the largest and most influential women's political organizations before the 1960s, this finding reinforces the fact that very few "women's"
organizations really reached much of a cross-section of women. In this
case, the League had its greatest resonance for members of the white
middle class who were more educated and wealthy than the average
woman. Even attempting to include some blue-collar wives who paralleled the typical League profile called for fairly drastic departures in
League style, especially on a social level, changes which were neither
desired nor implemented. On the positive side, the homogeneity of the
League's membership probably increased its effectiveness, certainly in
its members' ability to work well together.

The Historical Context of the League Survey: The 1950s

So far this portrait of the League of Women Voters has been fairly
ahistorical, rich in demography but devoid of real issues or people.
Except for occasional references to suburban Leagues and income clues,
this could be the picture of almost any decade. But this survey was not
conducted in a historical vacuum: It was taken in the midst of the period
of the "feminine mystique." These historical connections are worth
pursuing.

The idea that women's place was in the home was hardly a new idea
in American life, but the message was promoted with special stridency

in the immediate aftermath of World War II. A constellation of factors came together to reinforce women's domestic roles in new, and powerful, ways: the maturation of a consumer economy, an expanding middle class, the growth of suburbia, the baby boom, and the new intellectual currents in psychology and social sciences. These factors were obviously interrelated: On the one hand, the increased birth rate made it easier to think of women primarily as mothers; on the other hand, the growth of suburbia provided a specific locale for the child-centered family culture of the 1950s.[33]

The late 1940s and 1950s were rife with an explicit antifeminism that made this period especially inhospitable for those women who aspired to life beyond the confines of their suburban dream houses. This antifeminism was typified by such books as Philip Wylie's *A Generation of Vipers* (1942) and Marynia Farnham and Ferdinand Lundberg's *Modern Woman: The Lost Sex* (1947), which used Freudian psychology to argue that feminists were neurotic because they had turned their backs on their biological roles. The thrust of the new school of functionalism, although pretending toward objectivity, was also profoundly conservative. When analyzing social behavior and institutions in terms of their consequences (or functions) for larger social systems, too often "the function is" was translated into "the function should be." Nowhere was maintenance of the status quo more apparent with this analysis than in gender roles: Society functioned best when women were homemakers and men were breadwinners. Evidence that women took these messages to heart was reflected in their declining college and graduate school enrollment rates throughout the 1950s.[34]

Friedan captured the stories of this lost generation of women in *The Feminine Mystique* (1963). In this highly successful feminist tract drawn from popular culture and advertising, Friedan caustically challenged the prevailing culture of the 1950s which told women that "the highest value and only commitment for women is the fulfillment of their own femininity."[35] In a pointed indictment of the trap of suburban domesticity, Friedan identified "the problem that has no name": "As she made the beds, shopped for groceries, matched slipcover material, ate peanut butter sandwiches with her children, chauffeured Cub Scouts and Brownies, lay beside her husband at night—she was afraid to ask even of herself the silent question—'Is this all?' "[36]

Friedan's book struck a resonant chord among American women in the early 1960s, especially the educated, upper-middle-class white women in suburbia who were its primary subjects.[37] For our purposes, the superficial resemblance between the women that Friedan wrote about and the Michigan survey's profile of the typical 1950s League of

Women Voters member is intriguing. Friedan claimed that she had first uncovered "the problem that has no name" while analyzing the responses of two hundred of her Smith College classmates to open-ended questionnaires on the occasion of their fifteenth reunion. For the most part, these women had enjoyed an elite education, lived predominantly in suburbia, and were married to professional or business men. In 1957, at the time of their fifteenth reunion, they were in their late 30s. The League women shared a similar general demographic profile: high access to education, marriage to white-collar or professional workers, and concentration in the most desirable neighborhoods of suburbia or small towns. In age, the average Leaguer was only a few years older than Friedan's Smith classmates.

The League, Its Members, and the Feminine Mystique

Did the League members of the 1950s suffer from a terminal case of the feminine mystique? Not at all. Rarely in the volumes of survey material or its supporting correspondence was there any manifestation of frustration, boredom, or conflict between activity outside the home and women's domestic roles. There was no hint of defensiveness about being a modern, activist woman volunteer of the 1950s. In fact, the survey presented strong evidence that the members were quite fulfilled by combining familial roles with participation in local and community affairs.

Why do the women surveyed in the League seem so happy and productive, while Friedan's educated, white middle-class housewives seem so miserable and unfulfilled? In part, the answer has to do with the focus of each study: Both found what they were looking for. The LWV-Michigan project was concerned with issues of membership, leadership, and effectiveness; it was not structured to elicit responses about frustration or boredom, nor did it provide a vehicle for venting feelings of personal discontent.[38] At the same time, Friedan, as scholars and contemporaries at the time have consistently pointed out, overdrew her pictures of the 1950s: Not only was the feminine mystique not a phenomenon unique to the postwar world, but many women managed to lead active and interesting lives even at its height.[39]

If Friedan had stuck with her original interpretation of the Smith questionnaires, the gap would have been even narrower. In a 1961 article published in the *Smith Alumnae Quarterly*, Friedan presented a far more upbeat and positive assessment of her contemporaries than she would just two years later in *The Feminine Mystique*. The main complaint of these Smith-educated suburban wives and mothers was not that they led boring, empty lives, but that their lives were too fragmented because of their varied activities. Although only one tenth were working full time, three quarters had satisfying interests outside their homes and families. They participated in a dizzying range of volunteer activities, including starting cooperative nursery schools, serving on school boards, working against desegregation, founding mental health clinics, and organizing choral groups or theaters-in-the-round. Almost one third were active in local party politics. While three fifths admitted that they did not find homemaking totally fulfilling, they made a point of claiming that they were "not frustrated" as suburban housewives. And almost two thirds already had concrete plans for work or study when their children were grown: "The Republican precinct committeewoman intends to study law; the mother of four who fought for better schools will teach remedial reading; the League of Women Voters leader plans to run for the legislature."[40]

The popularity of *The Feminine Mystique* has in many ways biased the questions asked of women's lives in the 1950s. The typical middle-class woman was neither totally frustrated nor completely fulfilled; she was neither pathologically lonely nor radiantly happy. She could be a little of both, which is why Friedan's book touched so many women.

The complicated lives led by suburban women in the 1950s in part explain the appeal of the League of Women Voters. From 1950 to 1958 League membership increased by 44 percent; historian Eugenia Kaledin has argued that the League "had the most impact on the political lives of middle-class women" of any organization at the time.[41] The League provided an important outlet for the family- and community-oriented woman to participate in activities beyond her home. It was a visible and established force in communities across the country. It was there, it was respectable, and it was available; women knew where to turn. Groups such as the LWV and the PTA created public roles for women denied access to the usual sources of power. And they made these roles available on the local level, where women could most easily make political contributions without necessitating drastic changes in their familial arrangements. The League had been serving that function since women won the vote, but its legitimization and facilitation of women's political activity was probably especially important during the antifeminist backlash of the 1940s and 1950s.

The League was also important because it served as a vehicle for political training and socialization for women in the 1950s and beyond. Such apprenticeships prepared women not only for entry into conventional electoral politics but also for participation in change-oriented protest movements such as civil rights and feminism. The results of such training were not always immediately apparent in the 1950s, however. The typical member was in her 30s or early 40s and still tied to family responsibilities, but she was preparing herself, consciously or unconsciously, for the future. Lucia Bequaert, who pinpointed the wide range of practical skills and advocacy techniques that women developed in organizations like the League, concluded, "While one cannot measure the effect on society of changed individual attitudes, there is no doubt such personal changes remain just below the surface, fermenting and transforming, until a later opportunity for realization presents itself."[42] The political ferment of the 1960s provided just that opportunity.

League Members and Electoral Politics

In the 1960s and 1970s League women excelled in electoral politics, especially on the state and local level. Participation in the League of Women Voters was one path by which women entered state legislatures. Women came to politics through voluntarism and community activity more than through such traditional male routes as business and law. For example, Jeane Kirkpatrick's study of 46 women serving in state legislatures in 1972 found that about 40 percent were active in the League.[43] Irene Diamond's profile of women legislators in 1971–1972 found that 22 percent participated in League activities.[44] Ruth Mandel's study of the new women candidates captured the League's pervasive influence perfectly: "Very frequently, and all over the country, one hears political women echoing the remark, 'I got my training in the League of Women Voters.' "[45]

Very often, the transition to electoral political activity was a direct outgrowth of the years of experience women had gained in the League. A commentator in the 1920s had called the LWV "a sort of water wings for women to use before they swim out a real distance from shore,"[46] and this ability to provide its members with a well-rounded political education was still true decades later. One former president of a local League recalled in 1972:

> After many years in the League, it seemed a natural thing to move into political affairs. I never had any problems talking on an issue or selling anybody on an issue, but the whole concept of selling myself was something that I had never really done. I had always had doubts about my own abilities and through the years in the League I was convinced of my capabilities. Serving as president, speaking a lot in public, increased my self-confidence enormously.[47]

Another woman was a "ready recruit" for elected office:

> I spent twenty years in the League of Women Voters and I was working on
> a major state project. I had served on my local finance board for two terms.
> I knew the community activities—of the nonpolitical type. Then I was
> asked to run by some close friends who were very active in the Democratic
> Party, and then I decided to run.[48]

When these interviews took place in the early 1970s, the average woman legislator was in her late 40s. The years of League activism they mention, however, place them squarely back in the 1950s, precisely the period covered in the Michigan survey.[49]

Other scattered evidence suggests that League members were using their political talents, if not immediately in the mid 1950s, then soon after. In 1964 one out of every 38 League members in Illinois was participating in government at the policy level in either the state legislature, boards of education, or commissions in such areas as the status of women or fair employment practices.[50] The Georgia League was credited with the elimination of Georgia's poll tax, and the Michigan League gathered 209,000 out of the 320,000 signatures on a petition for a state constitutional convention in 1963. Overall, the League was especially active on legislative redistricting, a salient political issue after the 1962 Supreme Court decision in *Baker* v. *Carr* which mandated "one person, one vote."[51]

Harder to quantify, but just as likely, is the participation of former and current League members in the social protest movements that rocked America in the 1960s and 1970s. League members were some of the first involved in the desegregation battle, especially in the South. Women whose study groups had spent the 1950s learning about water resources or product safety were certainly predisposed to join the burgeoning environmental and consumer movements of the 1960s; and League groups which studied such issues as public housing and the differences between district and at-large elections soon found themselves deeply involved not only in city politics but in civil rights. And for the issue most directly concerned with women—the revival of feminism—the League not only provided recruits but eventually, by 1972, support for major elements of the feminist agenda, such as the Equal Rights Amendment.[52]

Uncovering the activism of the League of Women Voters members, both that which is documented in the Michigan survey for the 1950s and that which is visible in the extrapolation of women's expanding political roles in the 1960s and 1970s, changes the accepted view of women in the postwar period. First, it provides more evidence that the one-sided picture which Friedan painted of neurotic, unhappy housewives does not convey either the complexity of many middle-class women's lives or the contributions such women made to their communities and public life. Second, it suggests previously overlooked continuities in women's postwar political behavior. It is too simplistic to contrast the doldrums of the 1950s with the explosions of the 1960s and 1970s. The examples of politically active women who channeled their energies through the LWV suggest that women's community-level activism remained vibrant in the 1950s and that such activism was destined to have both short-term and long-term effects. Without denying the harsh antifeminist climate of the 1940s and 1950s, or claiming that activity in the immediate postwar period reached anywhere near the levels it would during the social upheavals of the 1960s and beyond, many women still managed to make contributions on their own terms. At a time when there were so few institutional encouragements to women who had aspirations beyond the home, this activism represented a major accomplishment.

Postscript

After the University of Michigan presented its research findings to the League of Women Voters, the League distributed copies to its national board members and all presidents of state Leagues, but did not send the five volumes of findings to the general membership because they considered the reports too technical for wide readership. The LWV and the Survey Research Center did, however, collaborate on the development of a self-survey manual so that local Leagues could collect and analyze data about themselves. Only four of these self-surveys were completed. Local Leagues found these projects consumed too much "womanpower," and when outside funding dried up, they were abandoned.[53]

In general, the leadership of the League was quite pleased with the results of the Michigan project. Even if, in the words of the national organization secretary, the survey had "produced few truths unknown to the experienced Leaguer,"[54] it had uncovered a strong reservoir of support for the basic principles and operation of the League. Percy Maxim Lee, the organization's president from 1950 to 1958, interpreted the survey results as "abundant evidence that the basic concept, structure and procedures of the League are highly effective."[55] The national board agreed with that positive assessment.

Although the Survey Research Center hoped to continue studying the structure of the League, the League of Women Voters chose not to continue its association with the University of Michigan. The results of the initial project had validated and legitimated what the League was doing, especially on the local level. Now the League was eager to turn its attention outward—rather than inward—once again. In a turnaround from the traditional interpretation of the League of Women Voters as an organization devoted to all study and no action, it proved to be much more interested in doing a community survey than a self-survey. Its political agenda diverged from the research agenda of the Institute for Social Research. In the words of one experienced Leaguer, they concluded that they would be better off not measuring the size of the mountain they had to move, but using their time and energy to move the mountain.[56]

Such a reaction could come only from an organization that was supremely confident of its membership and its goals, indeed of its basic structural soundness. Unlike the women Friedan popularized in *The Feminine Mystique*, the League of Women Voters was not suffering from a crisis in women's identity.

Notes

1. Young (1950), p. 67. Louise Young is completing a manuscript of the history of the League of Women Voters for the Greenwood Press.
2. For an excellent elaboration of these goals, see Wells (1938).
3. One book that does in fact pay attention to the LWV is the study of the issue of reciprocal trade in the 1950s by Bauer, Pool, and Dexter (1963). Symptomatic of their treatment, the authors call the chapter "The Ladies of the League."
4. League of Women Voters of the United States (1960), pp. 36–37.
5. Material on the survey is found in boxes 1373 and 1445 of the League of Women Voters Papers, Library of Congress (hereafter LWV Papers).

    Report I, "The League Member Talks About the League" (October 1956), summarizes material from interviews with a sample of League members about their activities and attitudes about the League.

    Report II, "Community Attitudes Toward the League" (February 1957), is based on interviews with a sample of women living in urban areas who were not League members.

    Report III, "Some Problems of League Membership: Cross-Sectional Membership, and Member Activity" (August 1957), deals with widening the base of League membership and increasing the level of League activity.

    Report IV, "Organizational Phase, Part I: Factors in League Functioning" (August 1957), discusses similarities and differences among League members in different regions of the country and in different types of Leagues, as well as between leaders and members. It includes an appendix on demographic characteristics of League membership.

Report V, "Organizational Phase, Part II: Factors in League Effectiveness" (April 1958), examines how effectiveness in local Leagues is affected by leadership behavior, decision-making processes, size, and member participation.

This chapter concentrates on the individual League members rather than on how the organization functioned as a unit. For discussions of the LWV based on models of effectiveness within organizations, see Likert (1958); Likert (1960); and Tannebaum (1960).

6. Mary Ann Guyol, the League's public relations director in the 1950s, tried unsuccessfully to publicize the survey in the national press. She speculated that "one reason a writer might not want to tackle the assignment is that there is so little for the writer to do. All the research—usually done by the writer—is handed to him on a silver platter; there are two things he can do with it: knock holes in it or go along with it. If he does the latter it is likely to result in a puff-piece which most writers don't want to do" (Guyol memo, September 30, 1957; LWV Papers). One course of action for this chapter would have been to review and rerun the original data tapes (Guyol's "knock holes in it" strategy). Instead, I have chosen to use the demographic data more interpretively as a historical source—in her phrase, "go along with it."

7. Report IV (1957), pp. 107–108.

8. Report IV (1957), p. 115.

9. Report IV (1957), pp. 108–109.

10. Report IV (1957), pp. 114–115. In 1955, 31 percent of American women were employed. Banner (1974), p. 255.

11. U.S. Bureau of the Census (1970), p. 296.

12. Report IV (1957), pp. 118–120. These findings were drawn from mail questionnaires sent to a sample of 2,905 women in 104 local Leagues, of which 2,150 were returned. Many of these demographic areas were also covered in the personal interviews administered to an independently drawn sample of 227 League members. With the exception of family income (which the researchers thought was underestimated in the returned questionnaires), the differences between the two samples were insignificant. The team took this congruence in results as validation of their survey techniques. See Report IV (1957), pp. 120–122.

13. Report I (1956), pp. 2, 10.

14. Report IV (1957), pp. 112–113.

15. Report I (1956), p. 6.

16. Report II (1957), p. 32. This recruitment pattern differed significantly from other organizations studied by the Survey Research Center, where only 15 percent reported learning about an organization from friends. On the other

hand, relatives were a much less important source for recruitment in the League than for other organizations surveyed.

17. Report I (1956), p. 57.

18. Report I (1956), p. 36.

19. Report III (1957), p. 29.

20. Report III (1957), p. 43. Studies of women political candidates have also found that husbands' support was an important factor in women's decisions to seek elective office.

21. Report III (1957), p. 24.

22. Report III (1957), p. 25. In another part of the survey, researchers found that the number of children under age 12 who lived at home with a member was .98—lower than might be expected at the height of the baby boom, but no doubt linked to the median age of mid-40s when many children would have been over age 12. Not surprisingly, the number of children under age 12 per member was highest in suburbia (1.2) and lowest in metropolitan areas (.47). See Report IV (1957), p. 117.

23. Likert (1958), p. 9.

24. Unfortunately, despite the title of "Community Attitudes Toward the League," the researchers did not sample the attitudes of men in the community.

25. Report II (1957), p. 4. See also pp. 1 and 8.

26. Report II (1957), p. 16.

27. Report III (1957), pp. 2–3.

28. Report III (1957), pp. 4–7.

29. Report IV (1957), p. 106.

30. Report I (1956), pp. 41–47. The other issue that they mentioned was an increase in the level of partisanship allowed—64 percent wanted greater permissiveness for partisan political activity for board members. See Report IV (1957).

31. Report II (1957), pp. 11–13.

32. Report II (1957), pp. 14–15.

33. General background on women in the 1950s can be found in Kaledin (1984). Other useful sources include Chafe (1972); Rupp (1982); and Woloch (1984).

34. Rupp (1982), pp. 35–36, 40–42; Solomon (1985), pp. 186–198.

35. Friedan (1963), p. 37.

36. Friedan (1963), p. 11.

37. Friedan (1976), pp. 38–51.

38. The only place in the Michigan survey at all likely to elicit any frustration was described in Report III (1957), pp. 39–41. A sample of League members was asked reactions to a series of pictures, including the following: "In the foreground of this picture is a woman standing behind a fence, looking out

into the distance. Behind her is a modern looking home outside of which play two small children. There is a car in the foreground. The fence extends all around the house. Our aim was to learn from the stories respondents told, whether they felt the woman was 'fenced-in'—restricted—by the fence. An example of a 'fenced-in' response is: 'Looks like she's restless and would like to go to the city but she can't because she has to stay with the children.' An example of a response which is not a 'fenced-in' response is: 'She's sort of standing against the fence and dreaming, maybe waiting for her husband to come home.' Using those criteria, almost half of the relatively inactive members saw the fence as restrictive, whereas only one in three of the moderately active members, and one in four of the active members, expressed concern about being tied down." Yet it is difficult to place too much weight on this finding, since both the sample responses seem capable of being interpreted as "fenced in."

39. See Kaledin (1984). For a critique from another angle, see Komarovsky (1962), which found no evidence of status frustration among blue-collar wives.

40. Friedan (1961), pp. 68–70.

41. Kaledin (1984), pp. 33–34. For a general overview of League activities in the 1950s, see League of Women Voters of the United States (1960), pp. 37–44.

42. Bequaert (1976), p. 217.

43. Kirkpatrick (1974), p. 44.

44. Diamond (1977), p. 177.

45. Mandel (1981), p. 137.

46. Gruberg (1968), p. 91. The quotation is from Ernestine Evans, *Century Magazine*, August 1923, p. 514.

47. Kirkpatrick (1974), pp. 64–65.

48. Kirkpatrick (1974), p. 77.

49. Continuing to use a generational approach, League alumnae already prominent in national public life by the 1950s represented women whose League activism had been in the 1930s and 1940s. The list of women politicians who got their start in the League includes Senator Maurine Neuberger of Oregon; Eugenia Anderson, Truman's ambassador to Denmark; Representative Edith Green of Oregon; Olive Remington Goldman of the United Nations Commission on the Status of Women; Ella Grasso of the Connecticut General Assembly, and later secretary of state and governor; Representative Chase Going Woodhouse of Connecticut; and Oveta Culp Hobby, Eisenhower's secretary of health, education, and welfare. For further information, see Kaledin (1984); Kirkpatrick (1974); Diamond (1977); Sapiro (1983); and Gruberg (1968).

50. Gruberg (1968), p. 92. Over 80 percent of these Illinois activists had served on their local boards, suggesting that the women who were most consistent in continuing with further political activities were those who had sought and

been chosen for leadership positions in the local and state Leagues. Whether this high level of activism also prevailed for a more ordinary (nonboard) member remains unclear, although unlikely. It does seem that there were many League members who had no aspirations beyond a bit of community involvement. For them, the League served a useful, if limited, purpose in providing a vehicle where with as little as several hours a week, a woman could feel that she was making a contribution to her community and her own self-development.

51. Gruberg (1968), p. 90.

52. Kaledin (1984), p. 92. For the changing activism of the League over the course of its history, see Ware (1985).

53. For more extensive material on the self-surveys, see the LWV Papers. The reaction of the Hinsdale, Illinois, League, which spent two years on the project, is typical: "Had we known the time and effort that would be involved, we doubt if we would have done it." See Mrs. Paul Cleveland to Mrs. Otis Ingebritsen, December 11, 1961; LWV Papers.

54. Mrs. Paul Cleveland and Mrs. Ralph Newton, September 23, 1960; LWV Papers.

55. Quoted in foreword to Likert (1958).

56. Mrs. Paul Cleveland to Mrs. Ralph Newton, September 23, 1960; LWV Papers.

13

Religion: Inhibitor or Facilitator of Political Involvement Among Women?

Robert Wuthnow / William Lehrman

Across a large wooden desk in an office adorned with theology books, two women faced the pastor of a medium-sized nondenominational church. One was a college professor; the other, a professional musician. Both held advanced degrees from elite universities. As members of the pastor's church, they had spent long months planning an annual retreat for women of the congregation. At issue was whether the Eucharist could be celebrated at the retreat, a task previously performed only by the pastor himself. The pastor, wishing to cooperate and above all avoid conflict within his parish, worried about the members' reactions. When he asked if he could take the matter before his all-male Board of Elders, the women agreed, but not before tense words left the pastor flushed and embarrassed.

Although neither woman considered herself a "feminist" (in fact, both rather disliked the concept), they were well schooled in theological and secular arguments about women's roles. Both felt scandalized by this conversation and, in retrospect, would see it as a turning point. They began to think more liberally about such issues as women's ordination as members of the clergy, abortion, and the Equal Rights Amendment. Within two years, both had left the church for more supportive religious environments. While neither became a political militant, each gradually came to participate more intensively in the political struggles she deemed important.

The path to political involvement sometimes follows a circuitous route. For some, it winds through ivied halls and consciousness-raising groups; for others, church basements and religious retreats. Although the experience of these two women may be unique, their story addresses the complex relations between religion and political involvement among American women. How salient a role does religion play in the lives of American women? What relation does religion bear on feminist orientations? Does religion promote a particular kind of political view? Is it an inhibitor or facilitator of women's political involvement?

In setting up a strict wall of separation between church and state, the founders of the United States ensured that a different pattern would emerge in the relations between religion and politics than had been common in Europe. No political party would come to be identified with a particular religious organization, nor could parties advocate a special brand of religious commitment. If religious groups were to participate in the political arena, they would be equal to other voluntary associations, joining people in bonds of common interest but not seizing governmental control. It was the strength of these voluntary associations, especially churches, that most impressed Tocqueville when he visited the new nation some half century after its War of Independence.

The wall of separation established by the framers of the Constitution also contributed immensely to the continuing strength of American religion: In removing the state as a source of fiscal assistance and political legitimation, religious organizations were forced to compete actively with one another for voluntary support. And as the nation's economic well-being expanded, churches received generous support. During the critical half century prior to World War I, when religious participation declined dramatically in most of Europe, more than 150,000 new churches were founded in the United States at a total cost of approximately $1.3 billion, resulting in a church membership growth (as a proportion of the population) from a mere 18 percent in 1870 to an impressive 43 percent by 1916. Over the next half century, while religious organizations were suffering badly throughout much of Europe as a result of war, economic hardship, and political parties that aimed at curbing the influence of state religion, the strength of religion in the United States continued to increase. By the 1980s the United States boasted twice as many churches per capita as France, West Germany, or the United Kingdom. On a per capita basis, Bibles were being purchased in the United States at a rate twice that in the United Kingdom, five times that in West Germany, and eleven times that in France. And on the average in a given week, 40 percent of the American public attended religious services compared with 27 percent in West Germany, 25 percent in France, and only 15 percent in Great Britain.[1]

With resources of this magnitude religion has remained a vital force in American politics, despite formal sanctions against the mingling of church and state. One need only recall the civil rights movement or the antiwar protests of the late 1960s or read about the political aspirations of television preachers such as Jerry Falwell and Pat Robertson or the lobbying efforts of religious groups on behalf of nuclear disarmament to recognize the enormous importance of religious commitment in American politics.

Gender Differences in Religious Commitment

It is important to account for religion in any consideration of American women's political involvement since gender differences continue to characterize patterns of religious commitment. By nearly every indicator, women in the United States manifest greater attachment to religious beliefs and practices than do men. According to recent national surveys, only half as many women (6 percent) as men (11 percent) claim to be without any religious faith.[2] By a margin of 46 to 35 percent, women are more likely than men to report having attended religious services within the past seven days. Two thirds, compared with fewer than two fifths among men, say they read the Bible (at least once a month). And by a margin of 57 to 37 percent, women are more likely than men to report having given a lot of thought to developing their faith. Indeed, significant percentage point spreads differentiate women from men on almost every kind of religiosity measure: Women are 18 points more likely than men to say that their religious commitment has been a positive experience; 17 points more likely to say that their relation to God is a very important source of self-worth; 16 points more likely to say that they would read religious literature when faced with personal problems; 15 points more likely to report that they try to seek God's will through prayer; and 14 points more likely to indicate that religion on the whole is very important in their lives.[3]

That women demonstrate greater commitment, on the average, to religion than men can be interpreted as part of the traditional role women have played until very recently: mother, housekeeper, guardian of traditional values, participant in voluntary associations, and, as women, marginally connected to the labor force and to sources of social status such as education and professional occupations. Religion's role in secular society has run in many of the same channels: an extension of the family, a promoter of traditional values, an institution relegated to the private sphere, associated with localistic values, and peopled frequently by the culturally disadvantaged. Many have argued that for these reasons women have found religion to their liking. If one needs to get away from the children for awhile or needs solace from the comforts of otherworldly promises, houses of worship are the place to go.[4]

Less commonly recognized is the fact that gender differences in religious commitment seem remarkably immune to the changing roles that women have begun to play. For instance, higher levels of education and greater rates of participation in the labor force among women should presumably wipe out some of the gender differences in religious commitment. When women and men with college educations are compared, however, the differences persist. Even when *younger*, college-educated women are compared with younger, college-educated men, no reduction is evident. Nor do the differences dissipate much when younger, college-educated, full-time participants in the labor force are compared with their male counterparts.[5]

Evidence from earlier studies of religious commitment also suggests that gender differences in religiosity have not diminished substantially with time. For example, a question asked in a 1944 survey about belief in life after death produced a 6-point gap between men and women; the same question asked again in 1960 generated a 10-point difference; and in 1981, an 11-point difference.[6] On church membership rates, some evidence does suggest that gender differences may be smaller now than they were in the past. But the reason cannot be traced to declining membership rates among women. Instead, membership has actually grown among both men and women. The growth, however, has been faster among men than among women, resulting in some convergence between the two: A 1926 religious census showed that 63 percent of adult females and 48 percent of adult males were church members, a 15-point gap; in 1985 the proportions were 73 and 63 percent, respectively, only a 10-point gap.[7]

On the whole, then, it appears that gender differences in religious commitment may be more deeply rooted than has often been believed. In the long run, the changes in American gender roles that have taken place in recent decades may lead to greater similarities in religious commitment levels among women and men. For the time being, however, religion remains an activity that can scarcely be ignored in considering women's involvement in American politics. Religion remains a vital aspect of the public and private lives of the vast majority of American women: Nearly three quarters consider themselves church members, one half attend religious services at least once every week, more than two thirds attend at least once a month, four tenths claim they pray *more than once a day*, seven tenths say their relation to God is very important to their self-worth, and three quarters consider their religious faith the most important influence on their life. It is also worth noting that these kinds of differences cannot be restricted simply to the rank and file. Among political leaders women tend to be disproportionately involved in religious activities. For example, a 1983 study of women holding political offices showed that women were members of religious organizations three times more often than were male officeholders.[8]

Feminism and Religion

Even if American women continue to register high levels of religious commitment overall, sharp levels of difference can be observed between women with feminist orientations and women with more traditional gender orientations. The feminist movement, particularly since the 1970s, has drawn a more favorable response from those women whose religious commitment is relatively weak: young, better educated, professional women, with more secular orientations toward life. A study conducted in California in 1973, for example, showed that only 38 percent of those women whose convictions were grounded in traditional beliefs about God said they favored equal rights for women compared with 64 percent whose convictions stemmed from a combination of secular ideas from the social sciences, literature, and humanistic psychology.[9] For church members, the feminist movement seemed too much a part of the counterculture, too closely associated with sexual experimentation, too much in sympathy with abortion and permissive moral standards. One church-goer told an interviewer, "I would associate [feminism] with across-the-board liberality, a weak view of [Biblical] inerrancy, a lenient view of abortion and capital punishment." Another, commenting on feminists who wanted to introduce nonsexist language into religious services, remarked, "They're open to homosexuality and they lean toward favoring pro-choice over pro-life on abortion."[10] To feminist leaders, these kinds of responses only reinforced suspicions that churches were enemies rather than potential allies. As one leader lamented, "The churches have contributed an enormous amount of money, time and organizing toward the goal of crushing us, especially on the issues of abortion and the ERA."[11]

As the movement progressed, feminism gradually acquired some support within many religious organizations. Study groups were formed to explore ways of integrating inclusive language into standard formats for religious services. Most of the major denominations gradually followed up on decisions permitting women to be ordained as members of the clergy. As a result, women gradually entered the ranks of religious hierarchies, assumed positions in local congregations as well as in seminaries and denominational bureaucracies, and played an increasingly instrumental role in challenging traditional gender concepts in theological literature and in ecclesiastical practice. Even when results were less than satisfactory, efforts to bring about change within religious hierarchies often led to the creation of religious feminist networks which later provided a platform for more general political involvement. In the 1970s, within the Catholic church, for example, an increasing number of religious women became "radicalized" by the broader social unrest of the period and began to link with the larger feminist movement, supporting the ordination of women and opposing the church's official stance on contraception and abortion. Some of these movements became directly involved in demonstrations, protests, lobbying, and other political activities.[12] In addition to working for change within the church, religious women began voicing opinions on a wide range of political issues, including prison reform, homosexuality, racial and ethnic equality, and U.S. policies in Latin America. Much of the work of these movements was also directed at reforming the theological presuppositions from which positions on political issues were derived. By the end of the 1970s, therefore, a considerable degree of innovation had been generated.

Nevertheless, the slow implementation rate of many religious organizations, together with broader social differences in the type of clientele most readily attracted to the churches, led to wide disparities between the religious involvements of feminists and nonfeminists. A study of Catholic women, for example, showed that only 26 percent of those with feminist orientations and with at least some college education attended church regularly compared with 49 percent of those with nonfeminist orientations and with comparable levels of education. By a margin of 20 percent to 40 percent, the feminists were also less likely to express confidence in the church's leadership.[13] Other evidence shows similar differences among most Protestant denominations, although some significant exceptions do appear. Baptist women with feminist orientations are 16 points less likely to attend church regularly than are Baptist women with nonfeminist orientations. Among Lutheran women the difference is 15 points. And among women in small, fundamentalist sects, it rises to 21 points. The exceptions are the two predominantly liberal denominations—Presbyterian and Episcopalian—and Jews; these groups contain a majority of women with feminist orientations, unlike the other denominations. Among Presbyterians and Jews, feminists are no less likely to attend church regularly than are nonfeminists. And among Episcopalians, feminists are 11 points *more likely* to attend regularly than are nonfeminists.[14]

The exceptions indicate that feminism and religion need *not* be incompatible. The Episcopal church, for example, not only has *reacted* to the changing interests of women, but also has played an *active* role in sponsoring gender consciousness-raising groups for both sexes, providing counseling and other services for women making the identity transitions, and teaching about the sexism in traditional theological language and liturgy. The broader tendency in American religion, nevertheless, appears to run against feminist involvement in religious organizations. Early socialization, in some cases, orients potential feminists away from churches, if only because they grow up in households where religious observance is low. Studies suggest that the experience of attaining higher education leads students who become involved in causes such as feminism away from conventional religion.[15] As the opening story about the two women illustrates, we see that in some cases church women who become more involved in feminism may become less actively engaged in religion, switch to denominations in which they feel more at home, or defect from religion entirely.[16] Whatever the sequence, the result is that religious organizations (with the few exceptions mentioned) tend to be populated with women who lean away from feminist orientations, and these are the same women who tend to be the most active members in the organizations. At the grass-roots level, therefore, churches may be better able to mobilize sentiment against than for feminism. This possibility, of course, has obvious portent for the character of women's involvement in politics.

The Split Between Liberals and Conservatives

Within American religion, the division between liberals and conservatives is similar to the one separating feminists and nonfeminists, but it combines theological, moral, social, and political orientations as well. Although it has deep roots in American history, its present manifestation can be traced largely to developments occurring since the mid 1960s. We have discussed these developments elsewhere in greater detail, but a brief overview will suffice to suggest their relevance to the current role of religious organizations in women's politics.[17]

The present split between religious liberals and religious conservatives is heir to, and the most recent reincarnation of, the division that developed nearly a century ago between modernists and fundamentalists, a division that pitted Biblical literalists, who emphasized individual salvation, against a theological view influenced by historical criticism of the Bible and oriented as much toward a "social gospel" as toward personal piety. Religious conservatives, at present, trace their roots to the fundamentalism of this period, while religious liberals stand more in the tradition of the modernists. Beyond certain theological continuities and some rhetorical use of the earlier labels, however, the present division is largely discontinuous with the earlier controversy.

Compared with the present division, the earlier dispute between fundamentalism and modernism was quite limited. It was fought mainly by theologians and often turned on subtle theological arguments to which the general church-going public had little response or knowledge. At the time it occurred, the population remained overwhelmingly conservative in its religious views and largely avoided identifying with the labels used by either the fundamentalists or modernists. The source of the dispute was centered largely on two northern Protestant denominations—the Northern Baptists and the Presbyterian Church U.S.A.—and was hardly an issue outside these denominations. The South was too solidly conservative to feel the frenzy of dispute dividing these two northern denominations. Catholics had solved their own "modernist" dispute much earlier and remained separated from their Protestant cousins by deep tensions. Even within major denominations, such as the Methodist church and the Episcopal church, theological and ecclesiastical "distinctives" rendered any broader coalition of fundamentalists or modernists virtually unworkable. Most important, the fundamentalist-modernist controversy failed almost entirely to enlist support for any broader political causes. Indeed, the famous Scopes Trial was about the only aspect that drew national attention. And this episode, by most accounts, marked the beginning of the end for the fundamentalist movement. By the end of the 1930s, the disputes had subsided—the Great Depression with its financial exigency made it impossible for the fundamentalists to continue their annual national conventions, which had provided them with publicity and a means of coordination. Also, by the middle 1930s, the most adamant fundamentalists had split away from their parent churches and formed small sectarian denominations.[18]

During the 1940s and 1950s, contention continued between fundamentalists and modernists, but other issues began to overshadow these earlier conflicts: battles between Protestants and Catholics, strategies for inspiring church growth, evangelistic campaigns, and a general closing of ranks, first against the Axis in World War II and then against communism during the Cold War. With fairly widespread theological consensus, emphasis on evangelism, and indifference to social issues, religious organizations in the 1950s were able to enjoy a remarkable, if brief, period of peaceful coexistence.

The beginnings of the present conflict between American religious liberals and conservatives can be traced primarily to the broader social turmoil of the 1960s. The civil rights movement, and then the protest movement against U.S. involvement in Vietnam, shattered many assumptions that had prevailed among religious leaders about the proper way of addressing the public sphere. Rather than attempting to shape individual consciences, religious leaders began taking a more active role in social and political protest activities. "Clergy activism," as it was called, was controversial from the beginning. Within most of the large denominations, special interest groups began to mobilize, some with the purpose of promoting greater activism and others aimed at resisting it. By the end of the 1960s, fractures between conservatives and liberals had begun to show in many of these denominations. Conservatives favored more traditional theological views, wanting churches to concentrate on personal evangelism and deeply disliking the new activism on social concerns. Liberals tended to support clerical activism and favored the broader positions on social issues that their denominations' hierarchies were taking. A number of mergers and proposed mergers among major denominations also fanned the flames of controversy. Some dissidents broke away to form their own denominations; others mobilized national organizations to pitch battles within their denominations.

By the end of the 1960s, a major presence on the theological right was mobilized. Calling themselves "evangelicals," the leaders of this movement had quietly founded a number of national organizations in the 1940s and 1950s and had seen these organizations become increasingly successful as a result of proselytization, natural increase, and recruitment among dissatisfied members of more established religious organizations. Groups such as the National Association of Evangelicals, Campus Crusade for Christ, and Youth for Christ, as well as the Billy Graham crusades, major training grounds such as Wheaton College (Illinois) and Fuller Seminary, and rapidly growing evangelical denominations formed the nucleus of this movement. Consciously repudiating ties with earlier fundamentalists or with ultraconservatives, the leaders of the evangelical movement focused primarily on evangelism, preached a relatively moderate back-to-basics theological curriculum, and devoted great effort to building up their own institutional base. As yet, they remained largely free of political engagements.

During the early 1970s, two highly consequential developments became evident among evangelicals. The first was a distinct turn to the *left* among younger evangelical leaders as a result of their feelings about the Vietnam War, some exposure to the rethinking of moral issues provoked by the student counterculture, and their overall participation in the rapid expansion in higher education. These younger leaders added diversity to the evangelical movement but largely failed to attract any mass following. The second development consisted of several unrelated occurrences which gradually stripped the older evangelical elite of its position as the movement's mouthpiece. Leaders who had actively supported American involvement in Vietnam, had supported Nixon (before and during Watergate), and were prolife (before and after the 1973 Supreme Court ruling) felt confused and, in the case of Watergate, embarrassed. The result, in retrospect, appears to have been a temporary leadership gap among evangelicals—a gap that was very soon filled by another, more conservative, more politically active set of leaders.

The new leadership that emerged among American evangelicals in the middle 1970s consisted primarily of preachers in command of large television viewing audiences: Jerry Falwell, Jimmy Swaggart, Pat Robertson, Jim Bakker, Rex Humbard, and a few others. They had virtually no ties to the older evangelical leaders and, in fact, differed from them in several dramatic ways. The new leaders came largely from the South, were trained mostly in fundamentalist "Bible colleges" rather than universities or liberal arts colleges, had close ties to the most rapidly growing conservative denominations (especially Independent Baptists and Assemblies of God), and commanded vast financial resources through their television ministries. They were also much more outspoken on issues such as abortion, communism, and sexual morality and saw great danger in the Equal Rights Amendment (ERA) and, more generally, in feminism.

By the late 1970s, by way of the national media, the new evangelical leaders had captured prominence as the voice of religious conservatism and, indeed, had created a sizable constituency among evangelicals at the grass-roots level. According to one poll, close to three quarters of all evangelicals identified themselves as right-of-center theologically and more than nine tenths took conservative positions on issues such as abortion, homosexuality, and pornography.[19] Only one fourth favored the activities of controversial New Right groups such as the Moral Majority, and even fewer claimed membership in such organizations; nevertheless, they backed the same kinds of issues and increasingly felt that church leaders should be speaking out about them.[20] Members of established denominations continued to be divided on many of these issues. Liberals found strength in the larger numbers of denomination members who had gained college educations and who sympathized with the positions that their denominational bureaucracies were taking on issues such as abortion, nuclear disarmament, and the ERA. Conservatives, in the same denominations, increasingly found themselves more in sympathy with the New Right leaders' positions.

At present there is a deep division between religious liberals and religious conservatives. According to one national survey, the public is split almost evenly between those who identify themselves as "religious conservatives" and those who identify themselves as "religious liberals." Two of three people believe the division between these two groups constitutes a major cultural problem. The same study also documented exceptionally high levels of negative stereotyping of each side by the other and found that relatively small proportions on either side report having pleasant contacts with the other. Liberals tended to view conservatives as rigid, narrow-minded, moralistic, and unloving fanatics; conservatives saw liberals as morally loose, biblically illiterate, and unloving pawns of church bureaucrats who probably did not understand what Christianity was about. And these divisions cut directly through most of the established denominations: Catholic conservatives, Baptist conservatives, and Methodist conservatives had much more in common with one another than they did with liberals in their own denominations.[21]

Unlike the earlier fundamentalist-modernist cleavage, the present split appears to have much broader roots in the general population: It divides virtually every major Protestant denomination as well as Catholics and Jews. Religious views also have a closer relationship to views on political and social issues than they had in earlier times. This last point is especially relevant to the present discussion of political involvement.

Prior to the early 1970s, religious orientations and political orientations showed little correspondence with one another. This relationship was in fact probed repeatedly in empirical studies because most social scientific theories of religion suggested that a distinctly conservative religious orientation should also be associated with conservative political views. A review of these studies published in 1973, however, demonstrated that these expectations were largely unsupported. Studies using any number of different measures of religious commitment, including conservative belief and participation in conservative denominations, showed that there were about as many negative relationships or nonrelationships with political conservatism as there were positive relationships.[22]

More recent studies, especially those conducted since the late 1970s, show much stronger relationships between religious orientations and political orientations. There are exceptions: Religious conservatives and liberals often agree on specific policy issues having to do with taxation, housing, research and technology, or foreign affairs. But on other issues religious conservatives and liberals are divided. In the national survey mentioned earlier, for example, the two sides disagreed on abortion and school prayer, perhaps for obvious reasons, and on government spending for welfare programs.[23]

Although all implications of the current split between religious liberals and conservatives have not yet been explored, several possible implications for the character of women's political involvement deserve consideration. One implication is that religious orientations, given religion's salience for most women, are likely to influence the *direction* in which women's political energies are invested. If they become involved at all, religiously conservative women seem increasingly likely to become involved in conservative political causes, while religiously liberal women are likely to engage in liberal political causes. A second implication is that political involvement in general may be encouraged by the present polarities in American religion. In other contexts, people who are polarized on political issues (that is, who take extreme positions) tend to be more politically active than people who take middle-of-the-road positions. Likewise, since religious views are now highly polarized for many people, and these views relate closely to political issues, this may mean that political involvement will increase. Finally, religious liberals and conservatives need to be understood in the context of each side's propensities, which have shown considerable variation from one period to another, to engage in political activities.

Until the early 1970s, research on the relation between religious orientation and political involvement generally showed that religious liberals were more likely to be politically involved than religious conservatives. Researchers saw an inherent tendency toward political withdrawal in fundamentalist theology. The most plausible interpretation, however, was that, at the time, religious conservatives were very much in the minority in most denominational settings; they were faced with denominational hierarchies that were becoming increasingly embroiled in liberal causes such as civil rights and antiwar protests; and, disagreeing with these broader forms of clergy activism, they made moral capital of their situation by arguing that religious people should avoid political involvement.[24]

Since the mid 1970s, however, the patterns found in these earlier studies have been reversed. Almost all of the studies conducted between 1978 and 1981, whether national or regional, showed that religious conservatives were actually more likely than religious liberals to be politically involved. Religious conservatives encouraged their clergy to speak out on political issues, wanted their churches to become more politically involved, were more likely to believe that good religious people had political responsibilities, and were more likely to be registered to vote and to vote than religious liberals. This pattern was all the more noteworthy because religious conservatives included large numbers of people—the elderly, rural dwellers, and southerners—whose political involvement has characteristically been below average. Religious conservatives apparently had found their political voice. Their clergy and their religious periodicals encouraged them to become more involved in political campaigns; television preachers tried to arouse their indignation about issues such as abortion and pornography, and movements such as Moral Majority coordinated efforts to raise money, lobby, and enlist new voters.[25]

As the tensions between religious liberals and religious conservatives have deepened, both sides appear to be more interested in mobilizing their constituencies for political purposes. Now we examine how these and the other religious developments that we have considered fit together as factors in the political mobilization of American women.

Religion and Political Participation

There are two competing theories on the relations between religion and political participation. The older of the two derives from Tocqueville and focuses on the mobilizing potential of participation in voluntary associations. In Tocqueville's view, religion was a positive force in American politics because it could mobilize people in secondary groups for political purposes. From this perspective, religion was a means of forging ties among people with common interests, of exposing them to collective issues, and of training them for leadership and interpersonal relations. Unlike their counterparts in Europe, Americans might not engage directly in politics as a religious group, but would presumably cultivate relationships and obtain information for facilitating their participation. The alternative view stems more from Marxist theory and regards religion, in Marx's famous phrase, as "the opium of the people" which inhibits political involvement. Simply put, people are generally faced with limited time and energy and, therefore, must choose between becoming involved in religion or in politics. If they turn toward religion, the argument goes, they will focus on otherworldly rewards and personal piety to the exclusion of trying to make a difference in this world through participation in the harsh realities of politics. In various ways, this view has been implicit in much of the secular feminist literature. According to some formulations, religion is similar to traditional familial gender roles which need overthrowing so that women can gain an effective political voice.

Previous research lends some support to both of these theories. Some studies have found positive relations between involvement in church activities and political participation, controlling for a variety of other factors.[26] In contrast, other research has shown that people whose meaning systems were oriented toward religion were less likely than people with other meaning systems to favor political reforms or to be involved in political activism.[27] The two sets of findings are not necessarily contradictory, however. The Tocquevillian argument focuses mainly on the effects of religious *involvement;* the Marxist argument, on conservative religious *ideology.* Both may be relevant to different kinds of political participation. Neither view, though, has been examined with specific reference to women's political participation.

To examine the relations between religious involvement and political participation among women, data were analyzed from the National Election Surveys conducted by the Center for Political Studies at the University of Michigan during the presidential elections of 1976, 1980, and 1984.[28] Political participation was measured by a standard set of items asking about attendance at political meetings, talking about politics, working in the campaign, and making political contributions.[29] The results showed that women who attended religious services frequently were significantly more likely than women who attended them infrequently to score high on political participation in 1980 and 1984 but not in 1976.[30] Thus, the results gave partial support to the Tocquevillian idea that religious involvement can help to mobilize political participation.

The data were also examined to determine whether religious involvement is more conducive to political participation for certain women. In 1976 few differences in political participation were evident for any of the subgroups. During the 1980 election, the Reagan campaign and conservatives more generally seemed to capitalize on churches as a resource for political mobilization. Women who showed the strongest positive relations between church attendance and political participation included opponents of the ERA, those who felt the government should provide fewer welfare services, those who felt government had gotten too powerful, and registered Republicans. Those who voted for Carter showed a negative relation between church attendance and political participation. In contrast, those who voted for Reagan showed a positive relation.[31]

The 1984 election continued the pattern established in the 1980 election. Reagan supporters and Republicans were the most likely to show positive relations between church attendance and political participation. Like those of his predecessor, Mondale's supporters were *less* likely to participate in politics if they went to church regularly than if they did not. Conservatism also appeared to reinforce the relation between church attendance and political participation. For example, those who favored increases in defense spending and who thought a woman's place was in the home were more likely to be politically involved if they were religiously involved, whereas their liberal counterparts did not show these patterns.[32]

Overall, then, the dominant tendency at least in the 1980 and 1984 elections has been one in which religion mobilized political conservatives more than political liberals. That this was the case may not be surprising, given the much publicized rise of the "religious right" during this period. Several points about these findings should be emphasized, however. First, the *failure* of Democratic candidates to utilize the churches for political mobilization appears to be as significant as the Reagan supporters' success in exploiting this resource. Second, these findings contradict those of some other studies, as well as the conventional wisdom advanced in the popular press, which suggested that the religious right was inconsequential in recent elections. The reason for this contradiction is that those studies focused only on the role of religious preference in relation to candidate preference and failed to address the relation between religious involvement and political participation. Third, the Reagan administration seems to have shifted successfully the base of its mobilizing potential among women churchgoers from an early populist, antigovernment constituency in the late 1970s to a prodefense constituency in the mid 1980s. Finally, antifeminists appear to be more adept at linking religious involvement with political participation than profeminists.

These conclusions are limited, of course, to what can be inferred from broad statistical tendencies in the population at large. There is, in fact, evidence that social movements on a smaller scale have successfully linked women, religion, and political participation among constituencies with *liberal* agenda as well as among those with conservative viewpoints. Indeed, the issue of mobilization within focused movements, whether liberal or conservative, is quite different from that of broad political participation at the grass-roots level. Relatively little information is available for many of these movements, but some of the more general contours of their organization and activity can be outlined.

On the conservative side, several antifeminist movements have developed with clear political objectives and close ties to religious groups. The most visible of them is Concerned Women for America, founded in 1979. Described by its leaders as "a positive alternative to the militant feminism that threatens American society," its stated objectives include exposing antifamily movements, fighting the erosion of traditional moral standards, organizing a grass-roots movement, and lobbying in state and federal legislative bodies. Specific issues on which Concerned Women has lobbied include abortion, pornography, parental rights, national defense, free choice in education, and the free enterprise system. In addition to explicit concern for religious values and frequent references in publications to God and Christ, the movement is closely allied with both the religious and the political right. President and founder Beverly LaHaye is married to Moral Majority board member and American Coalition for Traditional Values president Jim LaHaye. Other members of the advisory council of Concerned Women include the wives of Jerry Falwell, Senator Jesse Helms, and television evangelists Jimmy Swaggart, James Kennedy, and Jack Wyrtzen.

In addition to movements like Concerned Women that are organized by and specifically for women, other conservative movements with large numbers of women have been especially concerned with gender issues and have combined religious and political appeals in their efforts at mobilization. In studying the prolife movement in California, for example, Kristin Luker found that the leaders were overwhelmingly women with strong religious convictions and close ties to conservative religious organizations.[33] At the national level, conservative activists such as Phyllis Schlafly and Connie Marshner have been closely involved in the development of Moral Majority, Christian Voice, Religious Roundtable, and other New Right organizations, all of which have taken strong stands against the Equal Rights Amendment and have styled themselves as "profamily" supporters.

More generally, the role of religious television appears to have been especially important in mobilizing support among women for conservative political causes. Not only are women more likely to watch religious television programs than are men, they are also more likely to watch these programs for longer periods of time each week, to send money, to have positive opinions on them even if they do not watch, and to support many of the political issues favored by the television preachers.[34] The role of religious television in providing a common identity and an outlet for political inclinations is especially important for women whose lives are otherwise "privatized" because of small children, nonparticipation in the labor market, or old age. The significance of this role is amplified because local churches often do not favor direct political participation or they contain too much political diversity to encourage organized political involvement. A survey of women in evangelical Protestant churches in New Jersey, for example, showed that Moral Majority supporters were relatively scattered and in most churches did not constitute a substantial critical mass.[35] Under these circumstances, the capacity of religious television, combined with direct mailing and telephone hookups, to link individuals directly with a national political movement becomes all the more important.

On the liberal side, women's organizations have enjoyed a long and venerable history as part of most denominations' formal structure and for many years have included certain kinds of political issues among their agendas. One of the oldest of these organizations is the International Association of Liberal Religious Women, founded in 1910. Its objectives include not only the promotion of liberal religious ideas and ecumenical cooperation among religious women, but also the promotion of peace and, more recently, equal rights for women in all countries. Another is Church Women United, founded in 1941 as an ecumenical movement including both Protestants and Roman Catholics, currently represented in every state by more than 2,000 local organizations. It has taken an increasingly active role in national and international politics. Recent actions taken by the movement's executive council include support of the sanctuary movement for refugees from Latin America, support of New Zealand's declaration of its waters as a nuclear-free zone, opposition to the U.S. government's decision to mine Nicaraguan harbors, adoption of a resolution deploring apartheid in South Africa, sponsorship of civil disobedience at the South African embassy in Washington, and lobbying against the MX missile and against federal funding of Contra operations in Nicaragua.

Many of the liberal Protestant denominations, as well as groups within the Roman Catholic church and within the Jewish religion, have witnessed a rise in political consciousness and political mobilization among women as part of the movement toward greater inclusion of women in clergy and other leadership roles. In part, this development is the result of women clergy and seminary students becoming politicized to gain inclusion. Finding ideological support for their cause in the broader feminist movement, many of these leaders have gone on to challenge other manifestations of gender bias within their churches and to support broader initiatives for legislative and political reform.

At present, a relatively wide variety of women's movements, in operation under specifically religious auspices, number liberal political issues among their objectives. These movements fall primarily into three categories: movements having bureaucratic sponsorship from organized denominations or other religious bodies, movements organized separately from any established religious bodies but subscribing to established Judeo-Christian beliefs, and movements organized around other religious beliefs and usually expressing self-conscious opposition to the Judeo-Christian tradition. An example of the first is the United Churches of Christ Coordinating Center for Women in Church and Society. Sponsored by the hierarchy of the United Churches of Christ, its activities consist chiefly of publishing a quarterly newsletter which contains articles and announcements on political issues ranging from toxic waste disposal to economic justice for the elderly; cooperating with other national organizations in lobbying on political issues; maintaining a support network among clergy women; sponsoring various conferences and publicizing literature; and promoting religious and political involvement among women at the grass-roots level through chapters in local churches. Similar organizations exist among women in the Church of Christ, Methodist church, Episcopal church, Presbyterian church, and Roman Catholic church. Illustrative of the second kind of movement (lacking sponsorship of an established religious body) is the Coalition on Women and Religion. Organized in 1973 in Seattle, it represents women of all faiths and is dedicated primarily to furthering the spirituality of women. Its activities have included endorsing local and national legislation on issues such as the ERA, abortion, and displaced homemakers bill; supporting ordination of women clergy; preparing study materials on religious and cultural attitudes toward women; sponsoring workshops and panels; making television appearances; and sponsoring a credit union for women and a shelter for abused women and children. The third category includes a wide variety of post-Christian, occult, witchcraft, mystical, Buddhist, meditative, and therapeutic movements. Mostly small and, because of opposition from anticult groups, relatively apolitical and quiet, some of these groups have nevertheless been active in promoting political consciousness among women and have occasionally become involved in political activities.

Judging from the survey results mentioned earlier, women's movements combining liberal political and religious goals have not been as successful in mobilizing participation in electoral activities as have conservative movements. Yet, in some ways, this failure may be attributable to the broader reforms sought by many of the liberal movements. Rather than focusing primarily on specific candidates or referenda, these movements have been concerned with fundamental reorientations of language and self-identity as well as political attitudes. Much of the published literature that has emerged from the religious wing of the feminist movement has been concerned with recasting basic religious symbols and practices in more inclusive language. Trial liturgical experiences, curriculum materials for the instruction of children, role modeling through the inclusion of women in clergy and other leadership positions, and consciousness-raising groups and personal counseling have all been part of the broader programs of these movements and organizations. Basic to all these activities is the assumption that the political cannot be separated from life and that life involves conceptions of self and reality which transcend, and yet permeate, the political.

Conclusion

Familiar theoretical notions which conceive of religion and politics as entirely separate spheres, or which view them as competing loyalties, have been belied by the events of recent years. In the United States, as in the Middle East, Northern Ireland, the Philippines, and Latin America, religion and politics continue to intermingle in complex and important ways. The extent of this intermingling is as consequential for women's politics as it is for politics in general. To the degree that women's political involvement is also shaped by special circumstances, however, this involvement is a product of the changing configurations of American religion and of the role of women in religious organizations.

In a broad overview of this kind, it has been possible to suggest only some of the religious conditions that seem most relevant to the consideration of women's political involvement. Among these are the fact that women have been, and continue to be, relatively more involved in religious activities than men have been; that women with feminist orientations tend to be relatively less involved in religious organizations, thereby leaving these organizations in the hands of women and men with antifeminist orientations; and that American religion has become deeply polarized between liberals and conservatives, the two sides being especially divided over issues such as abortion, pornography, ordination of women, and women's roles in the family. In considering these various conditions, we have found that their political implications do not always run in the same direction. Simple projections are, for this reason, impossible to make. Nevertheless, most of the tendencies that have been described point in the direction of religion facilitating, rather than inhibiting, political involvement among women.

The evidence, focusing directly on the relations between religious involvement and political involvement among women, also points toward religion as facilitator rather than as inhibitor. The vast institutional infrastructure of American religion has been a significant resource for launching women's movements, both on the left and on the right. At the individual level, women who are more involved in religious organizations have also been more involved in political activities, at least in the last two presidential elections. In addition, evidence indicates that conservative women are more likely to manifest a positive relationship between religious involvement and political involvement than are liberal women. It remains to suggest some of the reasons for this difference.

One possibility, as already suggested, is that the relative absence of feminists (and probably of politically liberal women more generally) in the churches has left conservatives with a stronger voice in religious organizations. A second possibility is that the religious right, in general, has become more politically aroused, perhaps because of issues such as abortion and school prayer. The greater political involvement of conservative religious women, therefore, may simply be a reflection of this larger development. Finally, it is important to note that the political and religious styles of liberals and conservatives are in some respects quite different. Conservatives tend to be more actively involved in their local churches, and these churches are more likely to be organized into small denominations with relatively high degrees of local autonomy. When conservatives become politically involved, therefore, it is likely to be either at the local, grass-roots level or through the activities of the "televangelists." Religious liberals, in contrast, tend to be less actively involved in their local churches, are more likely to belong to large denominations with well-organized national bureaucracies, and have a long tradition of organizing special-purpose groups. Their style of political involvement, therefore, often takes the form of drafting official policy pronouncements, endorsing political platforms, or lobbying through national organizations. Which method is more effective remains an open question. But clearly, the application of religious pressure to the political arena has serious consequences, both for religious organizations themselves and for the social standing of American women.

Notes

1. The figures reported in this paragraph are discussed more extensively, along with other European comparisons, in Wuthnow (1988).
2. For this and subsequent figures, see Gallup (1982). Figures not reported in this volume are from the authors' analysis of other Gallup surveys of nationally representative samples conducted between 1980 and 1984.
3. These differences between men and women are also evident in most European countries, despite the fact that overall levels of religious commitment are much lower. Our analysis of data collected in 1983 by the *Eurobarometer* survey, for example, showed that the proportion of those who said they were "religious" was 7 points higher for women than for men in France, 6 points higher in Belgium, 4 points higher in the Netherlands, 15 points

higher in Germany, 10 points higher in Italy, 8 points higher in Luxembourg, 10 points higher in Denmark, 25 points higher in Ireland, 14 points higher in the United Kingdom, and 11 points higher in Greece. Differences of 12 percentage points on the average separated men and women on reporting that God was "very important" in their lives.

4. For an early empirical study concerned with the "comforting" qualities of religion for women, see Glock et al. (1967).

5. We analyzed data from the General Social Survey Cumulative File, 1972–1984, which contains information from approximately 10,000 men and women in national surveys conducted during the years indicated. For the entire sample, women were 12 percentage points more likely than men to say they attended religious services almost every week or more often. The differences ranged from 8 points for members of Protestant sects to 13 points for Baptists and Methodists. Controlling for level of education, the differences were 15 points among Protestants with at least some college training, 10 points among Protestants with no college training, 8 points among Catholics with some college training, and 14 points among Catholics with no college training. Among men and women under age 40, there was a 12-point spread for those with some college training, a 9-point spread for those with no college training. And among full-time participants in the labor force, the difference among men and women with some college training was 7 points; and among men and women with no college training, 9 points.

6. Erskine (1965); Gallup (1982).

7. Douglass and Brunner (1935); Gallup (1985). Douglass and Brunner attributed the lower rates of religious membership among men to the demands of farming. By implication, the partial convergence of rates among men and women may be a function of urbanization. Other characteristics of urbanization, such as shift-work in industry, however, would seem to militate against this explanation.

8. Center for the American Woman in Politics (1983).

9. Wuthnow (1976), p. 261.

10. Becker (1986).

11. Spretnak (1982), p. 396.

12. Several of the groups that gained national prominence were the National Assembly of Religious Women, the National Coalition of American Nuns, the Institute of Women Today, and the Womanchurch Movement.

13. Greeley and Durkin (1984).

14. These results are based on an analysis of data from the General Social Survey Cumulative File, 1972–1984.

15. For example, see Wuthnow (1978).

16. Some evidence suggests that "assortative switching" according to educational levels does occur across denominational lines; for example, those with higher levels of education switch to denominations with already higher than

average educational attainment, such as the Presbyterian and Episcopal churches; see Wuthnow (1988).

17. See Wuthnow (1988).

18. This history is discussed in greater detail in Wuthnow (1988). Some disagreement exists among historians concerning the social correlates of the fundamentalist-modernist controversy; for example, Kleppner (1970) presents data from the Midwest for the late nineteenth century that suggest a relation between religious and political orientations. A more authoritative discussion of the 1920s and 1930s is available in Szasz (1982).

19. Gallup (1982).

20. Wuthnow (1983).

21. Wuthnow (1987).

22. Wuthnow (1973).

23. Other evidence from national polls shows that the public tends to identify itself politically in much the same terms as it identifies itself religiously. For example, three quarters of those who identified themselves clearly on the religious "right" said they were right of center politically, while two thirds of those on the religious "left" placed themselves left of center in political philosophy. See Gallup (1982). Most of these studies have not examined the views of women and men separately, but there seems to be no reason to expect that the results would be different for women than for the public at large. Indeed, the political differences between religious conservatives and religious liberals might even be more pronounced among women, given the extent to which issues of special interest to women, such as the Equal Rights Amendment and abortion, have been debated by religious organizations.

24. This literature is reviewed in Wuthnow (1983). For a longer-range view of evangelicals' involvement in politics, especially during the nineteenth century, see Hammond (1979).

25. Wuthnow (1983).

26. For example, see Olsen (1972).

27. See Wuthnow (1976).

28. Women who said they attended church or synagogue "almost every week" or more often were compared with women who said they attended "once a month" or less.

29. Respondents were assigned a value of "high" if they scored two or more on the scale.

30. The percentages who scored high on political participation among high church attenders and low church attenders, respectively, were 17 and 12 percent in 1984, 16 and 12 percent in 1980, and 16 and 14 percent in 1976: only the 1980 and 1984 results were statistically significant at the .05 level of probability.

31. The percentages who scored high on political participation among high church attenders and low church attenders, respectively, were 19 and 9

percent among women who disapproved of the ERA, 30 and 17 percent among women who were registered as Republicans, 24 and 14 percent among women who felt the government had gotten too powerful, and 21 and 13 percent among women who felt that the government should provide fewer welfare services. All of these relations were significant at or beyond the .05 level. The differences were not significant among women in the contrasting subgroup on each of these items (for example, those who approved of the ERA, Democrats, and so on). The differences among Carter voters were 9 and 17 percent, respectively; among Reagan voters, 26 and 22 percent. These differences were only marginally significant (at the .15 level).

32. Specific percentages scoring high on political participation in 1984 for women who attended church regularly and women who did not, respectively, were: 23 and 16 percent among Republicans, 20 and 15 percent among Reagan voters, 17 and 21 percent among Mondale voters, 19 and 12 percent among persons who wished to increase defense spending, and 16 and 8 percent among persons who felt that women's place was in the home. These differences were significant at or beyond the .05 level; differences among contrasting subgroups were not significant.

33. Luker (1984), pp. 196–197.

34. These conclusions summarize findings from the authors' analysis of national survey data collected in 1984 as part of the Annenberg/Gallup study of religion and television.

35. Survey of women in twenty-three evangelical churches conducted in 1985 by Bruno & Ridgway Associates.

14

Organizing for the ERA: Cracks in the Façade of Unity

Jane J. Mansbridge

In both the suffrage movement and the movement to ratify the Equal Rights Amendment (ERA) to the U.S. Constitution, American feminists acted with extraordinary external unity. From 1910 to 1920 in the mobilization for the suffrage movement, and in the late 1970s in the mobilization for the ERA, feminists of widely differing intellectual priorities, personal styles, and collective needs pooled their energies for a short, intense period in order to produce the near national consensus required to pass a constitutional amendment. Since then, feminist mythology has exaggerated the internal unity of these periods, holding them up as examples of the heights from which the women's movement has fallen and to which it ought to aspire again. It is the task of this chapter, in conjunction with Cott's chapter on the suffrage, to puncture that myth of internal unity.

Both suffrage and the ERA shared one characteristic—the possibility of presenting the feminist goal as simply fulfilling the promise of liberal democracy. Suffrage extended to women the voting rights of citizenship. The ERA, in principle, extended the remaining rights. In neither case did these amendments to the Constitution, in fact, portend important substantive social or economic reforms, although speculation on the amendments' possible indirect effects played a major role in both outcomes. Portrayed as no more than extensions of classic liberal rights, both innovations had a chance to garner the public and legislative support, including a two thirds vote in each house of Congress and a majority in three quarters of the states, required to amend the Constitution.

The potential portrayal of both amendments as relatively contentless extensions of rights also enabled women activists with widely differing longer-run priorities to piece together a powerful temporary alliance.

Historians sometimes describe the suffrage movement as "falling apart" once victory was achieved, implying that better organization or deeper feminist commitment could have kept it together. In fact, as Cott's chapter demonstrates, there were deep and genuine divisions over strategy and method in the suffrage movement from 1869 on.[1] Members of the coalition dampened their disagreements while the battle lasted—both to help the cause of suffrage and because they had little time or energy left to develop potentially different and profound positions on issues other than suffrage itself. Nor was it obvious, after suffrage had been won, what the next step should have been. Feminists in the National Woman's Party, for example, wanted to introduce an Equal Rights Amendment that would abolish protective labor legislation, while feminists with backgrounds in socialism or social reform wanted *more* social legislation aimed at poor and working women. After the suffrage victory, both were free to develop their sometimes conflicting understandings of, and solutions to, the problems of women in their era.

Unlike suffrage, the ERA was defeated. This defeat, like the earlier victory, released an eruption of divergent thinking on issues such as maternity leave, joint custody, no-fault divorce, abortion, sexuality, and pornography. Indeed, even during the ERA ratification campaign from 1972 to 1982, differing intellectual priorities among feminists were not hard to identify. This period saw the coining of the now-standard distinctions between "liberal feminists," "socialist feminists," and "radical feminists."[2] But along with differing intellectual priorities, the external unity of the movement masked a variety of personal needs among ERA activists.

Social movements, generally speaking, are distinguished from sects and other groups working for change by the breadth of their appeal. That breadth ensures considerable internal diversity. Activists in the movement may all agree on one end, but will usually want that end for different reasons and will benefit from different means. Accordingly, any attempt to mobilize a large constituency may founder on differences in the activists' motivations, interests in the way the work is done, and personal styles. The struggle for the ERA, as the most recent of the two examples of a national feminist coalition in the United States, illustrates how mass coalitions must be built not only from different kinds of activists but from widely differing kinds of organizations. This chapter argues that the organizations will differ in large part because their dependence on free labor forces each organization to specialize in the kinds of incentives it offers its members. The different incentives in turn lead the organizations to adopt different tactics in the struggle.

The chapter does not attempt to explain the ERA's defeat. The ERA was defeated by a combination of factors—backlash from Supreme Court decisions in the 1960s and 1970s (in particular *Roe* v. *Wade*), the deceleration in progressive reforms during the 1970s, the political mobilization of fundamentalist Christians, the rise to prominence of conservatives opposed to the ERA in the Republican party, the extraordinary gender imbalance in the legislatures of the nonratifying states, and the decisions by feminists to interpret the ERA as a potentially radical document.[3] Differences in the styles, experiences, and tactics of the organizations supporting the ERA explain only a small part of its defeat. They do, however, exemplify the fragility of any social movement's unity.

Volunteering and Free Riding

In the early 1960s Mancur Olson identified an organizational "Catch 22" in public goods.[4] A "public good," in the terminology of economists, is a good that, once brought into being, can be enjoyed by everyone, not just those who paid for it. For this reason, Olson pointed out, self-interested individuals will not pay a price for a public good. Bluntly put, if an individual gets only what she pays for, no more and no less, anyone who wants and can afford the good will have to pay. But when everyone can get the good, having paid or not, it makes individual sense not to pay. Thus, from this "economically rational" viewpoint, volunteering time, money, or energy for a public good like ERA ratification appears as an unnecessary cost. Since those who have not worked will benefit as much as those who have, the "rational" strategy is to do nothing and "free ride" on the efforts of others.

Organizations have traditionally handled the "free rider"problem by (1) coercing or punishing the slackers in some way, (2) rewarding those who work with benefits that go to the workers only ("individual" rewards or benefits),[5] and (3) persuading potential workers that the cause is good and worthy of free giving. Between 1972 and 1982 virtually every ERA activist worked primarily for the third reason. This kind of motivation meant that sometimes activists preferred to be right rather than to win and made ERA decisions accordingly.[6] Motivations, however, are rarely pure. Potential ERA activists were also enticed into volunteering time and money because they got some individual rewards from their activity. The differences in these individual rewards helped produce important tactical variations among the organizations. Assuming that all the activists worked primarily for reasons of principle, not for individual reward, this analysis will explain the diverse tactics that pro-ERA organizations adopted in their ratification campaigns by looking at the range of individual rewards that those organizations could offer their members.

Differing Incentives

In the United States' pluralist democracy, the mass organizations that most influence public policy have large and stable memberships based on the continuing individual benefits they can offer their members. Women's organizations in general, and the ERA organizations in particular, were comparatively weaker: None could offer members much in the way of individual benefits. For instance, the National Organization for Women (NOW) could offer new friendships, mutual support, companionship, and solidarity to some members—like young women, the newly divorced, the newly conscious feminist, or the recent migrant to a new city. It could also offer one-time participation in a consciousness-raising group. But members did not need to maintain their formal organizational affiliation to keep getting these benefits. Because NOW had few ongoing individual benefits to offer, its membership drives had to rely on emotional identification and moral exhortation. Whenever women, rightly or wrongly, felt somewhat more threatened, or whenever the president of NOW happened to write a particularly moving letter of appeal, membership in the organization would rise. But as the critical moment faded into history, membership would drop. The organization could offer no individual rewards to make its members feel the rationality of paying their dues consistently year after year. It had to rely instead on nationwide moral appeals, which in turn generated the tactics of mass demonstration and advertising in the national media.

ERAmerica, and such affiliates as ERA Illinois, had a seemingly more stable base as a religious, professional, civic, and labor coalition. The statewide coalition of ERA Illinois, for example, had a board of about fifty members, of whom about forty represented organizational participants in the coalition (the Federation of Business and Professional Women and the League of Women Voters, for example, were active partners in the coalition; NOW was sometimes a partner; the United Auto Workers were an inactive partner). However, ERAmerica and its affiliates faced the typical problems of broadly based coalitions. Each constituent organization had priorities different from those of the coalition; few provided consistent financial support; and only a couple tried to enlist individual members in the coalition's work of passing the ERA. As a consequence, a few ERA Illinois board members, those who had caught the political bug and enjoyed politics for its own sake, did most of the work. As we will see later, ERA Illinois's reliance on its members' love of politics generated tactics that some legislators denounced as "meddling."

The Federation of Business and Professional Women (BPW) had at its disposal the important individual benefit of professional contacts with other women in business, government, and the professions. However, the very emphasis on professional networking and self-help that drew women to BPW also worked against the organization's involvement in state politics—where ERA had to pass—because politics of this sort means conflict, and conflict does not facilitate business contacts. The League of Women Voters (LWV) provided relatively isolated homemakers with a chance to maintain adult social contacts, continue their education, and do some good. Again, however, the LWV's specializing in projects that everyone agreed were good (its policy being determined by consensus) attracted members who preferred studying "good government" issues to clashing with opposing interests in partisan state politics. Both BPW and the LWV found it hard to enter into the political struggles in state legislatures. Instead, these organizations' reliance on nonconflictual membership incentives generated tactics stressing public education.

In addition to the formal organizations, other social groups had particular reasons for joining in the ratification campaign, and these reasons, in turn, affected their tactical choices. Lesbians, for example, supported the ERA primarily for the same reasons of principle as other feminists, but they had as well a commitment to feminism deriving from their deeper rejection of male oppression and values. They also had the individual incentive of meeting other lesbians. Their reasons for joining to some extent affected their tactics. Having "come out" at great personal cost, declared lesbians often wanted to carry at ERA demonstrations banners that identified them as lesbians. They were defending the legitimacy of their way of life. After lesbian—and socialist—banners had triggered considerable anti-ERA propaganda, NOW decided to prohibit both, producing among many members of the lesbian community a deep disaffection from the ERA cause.

Feminist lawyers involved in the ERA campaign also had the same reasons of principle as other feminists for supporting the ERA. In addition, however, almost all had joined the ERA movement as part of their continuing commitment to radical or liberal legal reform. These lawyers were divided both organizationally (as paid consultants to ERA organizations, unpaid volunteers, and academics writing in law journals) and philosophically (on many issues, including the importance of the ERA, the benefits of eliminating legal gender distinctions, and the legitimacy of the very language of rights). But in practice on some matters the different philosophies formed a single perspective, and the structural roles often blurred. The small feminist lawyer community in Washington discussed ERA issues among themselves both formally and informally and played several of the roles described above. Consequently, even the paid staff lawyers thought that they were serving a broader liberal or radical "public" interest, or at least a "feminist" interest, as opposed to simply furthering goals that the ERA organizations had set. This commitment affected their tactics. For example, the lawyers could have suggested to the ERA organizations that, on the precedent of the First Amendment, the ERA would not apply as strongly to the military as to civilians (women draftees probably would not be sent into combat on the same basis as men). This interpretation would have countered one of the ERA opponents' most effective arguments. Yet no one, not even a staff lawyer for one of the more conservative ERA organizations, called attention to this interpretation. In this community of feminist lawyers, the possibility of such an argument was ruled out for reasons that had relatively little to do with the ERA per se.[7]

Mutual Reinforcement

Social movements are characteristically highly decentralized.[8] Decentralization has the advantages of flexibility, adaptability, innovation, and membership commitment. But the decentralist advantage of not requiring national agreement on, say, the means to a given goal, which encourages local innovation, entails a corresponding disadvantage: The participating organizations do not need to hammer out a single policy on those means. When individuals and organizations can act without consultation, their insularity lets them avoid hard questions and discordant information.

Subgroups in a decentralized organization also reinforce their members' perceptions or misperceptions of reality. ERA activists in the states, for example, often began to see the ERA as an end in itself. Each argument with an angry opponent, each attempt to convince an uncertain neighbor, each phone call to a talk show or letter to the editor, each visit to an irritated legislator made a little scar on the soul, healed only (if at all) by friends recounting similar experiences, extending sympathy, and affirming the mutual goal. As the small, but emotionally poignant, costs cumulated,[9] the ERA became much more than a practical instrument for improving the lives of American women, much more even than a symbol that would inspire women. For some activists the ERA became a public symbol of their own lives' meaning. While the appeal to principles usually leads recruits to care more about being right than winning, this intense personal involvement sometimes led local activists to care more about winning than about being right. Getting something called "the ERA" through the legislature and capturing those last two or three votes became a goal in its own right, worth almost any sacrifice, including perhaps some of the character of the ERA itself.

Meanwhile, other activists, living in an entirely different world, were reinforcing the collective perceptions of their fellows. Communicating between these worlds caused problems different from the classic problems of individual autonomy versus collective good. These were problems of the autonomy of small groups where members felt more responsible to one another than to a movement that spanned the continent.

A Close Look at Illinois: Two Memberships, Two Tactics

In order to attract and keep their activists, ERA Illinois and NOW (the two ERA organizations in Illinois that I examined) chose different ways of mobilizing public opinion and changing legislative votes. NOW, a national organization that had come to rely heavily on direct mail contributions, tried to generate national media coverage through mass rallies, demonstrations, and television ads. ERA Illinois, the statewide ERA umbrella organization, while affiliated with a national coordinating organization, had no existence outside Illinois and depended on the energies of local women who had a longstanding interest in state politics. Accordingly, ERA Illinois leaned toward tactics that involved its members in the activities they liked most—district-based local organizing and building personal relationships with state leaders from the two political parties. Both strategies had weaknesses and strengths. But in Illinois, as in the other states, members practicing one activity tended to see the others at best as self-serving or deluded, and at worst as undermining the cause.

In 1982 NOW organized a mass demonstration in Springfield, the state capital. Thousands of women wearing white marched the wide streets toward the capitol dome and chanted, "What do we want?" "ERA!" "When do we want it?" "Now!" Yet far from rejoicing at this demonstration of support, the members of ERA Illinois, who talked every day to the legislators, agonized over the way the demonstrations were provoking legislative anger, even among legislators sympathetic to the cause. For these were the legislative sessions' harried last days, and the demonstrators demanded so much time that the legislators could not get their business done.

For their part, NOW leaders felt extreme frustration when the ERA Illinois president (a Republican) and vice-president (a Democrat), sporting ERA buttons, attended a fundraising dinner for Governor Thompson at which President Reagan and the most powerful ERA opponents in the Illinois house were the principal speakers. NOW members picketed outside the dinner (as they had picketed everywhere throughout the state where Reagan came to support Republican reelection candidates) to draw attention to the President's opposition to the ERA and to his many national policies that hurt the poor, who are primarily women. They had no qualms about picketing this fundraising dinner, because Governor Thompson, a liberal Republican who nominally supported the ERA, had chosen the second speaker at the dinner, a conservative Republican and arch opponent of the ERA, as his running mate for lieutenant governor. How could the ERA Illinois president and vice-president justify attending a $250-a-plate fundraising dinner for Governor Thompson where these two key opponents of the ERA were honored speakers?

Members of ERA Illinois, however, believed that picketing this dinner hurt the ERA because although it would generate national publicity against Reagan, it would further alienate the Republican state leadership, whose help was essential in getting the ERA passed. In addition, they argued that their free tickets to the fundraising dinner served as an entrée for distributing pro-ERA literature around the tables. Making the ERA a straight Republican/Democratic issue would surely kill it, they thought, since the Republicans were the majority party in the house. As one put it:

> [NOW's leaders have] worked only with the Democrats and have simply almost ignored the Republicans, who are the majority party, and the leadership of the Republican Party, which has every prerogative to use the gavel in dozens of different ways to frustrate their efforts. . . . They must have ceased to believe that to keep communications open was the better part of wisdom. It seems to me an unworkable policy.

The two tactics developed naturally from the two groups' different membership needs. Each group attracted people with different political sympathies, ages, and ways of life. ERA Illinois, a nonpartisan body, had for several years had a Republican president. When the president of ERA Illinois ran for the state senate in 1982, she pledged to work for "public assistance only for those truly in need" and for "a balanced state budget." The next president of ERA Illinois, a schoolteacher, commented at a meeting, "If the parents would teach their kids responsibility, respectability and religion . . . at home, we'd have no problem with them at school!" NOW, on the other hand, had an almost exclusively Democratic membership. Indeed, as one Illinois NOW leader put it, "Most of our members would identify themselves as socialist, without knowing what it meant." NOW, working with Democratic politicians, developed ERA strategies that tended to benefit the Democrats, while ERA Illinois, working with Republicans, created ERA strategies more sensitive to that party's needs.

In part, the differences had to do with style. NOW members often thought that ERA Illinois was composed of ladies who sat with their hands in their laps expecting the Republican leadership to change because the ladies were so nice. The members of ERA Illinois were mostly over age 40, older than most active members of NOW. ERA Illinois was also more sedate: In the first ERA Illinois meeting that I attended, none of the women wore jeans, one wore a pantsuit, and exactly half wore skirts—compared with my first NOW meeting where half the women wore jeans and half wore slacks. More than half the women at ERA Illinois wore some kind of makeup compared with only one of the women at the NOW meeting. The ERA Illinois women saw themselves as representing the grass roots. They laughed together, as they traded recipes during a potluck lunch, at the contrast between their homey activity and the images they imagined state legislators had of the average ERA activist. Notwithstanding their conservative presidents, their age, and their more local backgrounds, these women were genuine feminists. ERA Illinois meetings usually began with someone passing around a news item about women or the ERA that had made her mad or a joke that spoke to women's plight. They welcomed a member's newborn to "his first feminist meeting," and in my later interviews every woman I talked with identified herself as a feminist. One ERA Illinois leader responded with irritation to the charge of "niceness" by saying:

> I don't think niceness makes anybody change. But there is only one way to keep a rapport going with the people who are in a position to make or break a piece of legislation, and that is to keep communicating, to be sensitive to that person, to keep relaying what you know, what you hear, to other people in the party who have your best interest in mind, your issue in mind. And look for the moment when you might use some devi-

ous tactics to get what you need done. I don't think there is anything productive about making an enemy out of leadership unless you see a moment when some kind of an extreme action is going is accomplish what you need accomplished.

And this is what the NOW people are so annoyed about, is that they see us continuing to talk to Republicans and to Republican leadership, and they see us as traitors.

But the NOW activists, eyeing the activities of some of the members of ERA Illinois, concluded that ERA Illinois members were only trying to advance their careers in the Republican party.

The two groups differed not only in age and style but also in political background. The typical NOW member was not born in Illinois and did not necessarily expect to spend her life there. In my local NOW chapter many members were recent migrants to the state, at least half were under age 40, several were lesbians, and many were unmarried. They recognized their ignorance of state politics, and in my first meeting one woman suggested that the chapter set up a "legislative task force" to teach members more about the state legislature. One NOW leader, summarizing her constituency, said, "We have a lot of people who know about reproductive rights, affirmative action, and all the feminist issues—but they don't know a thing about street lights." While these NOW members might eventually settle in Illinois and become local political leaders, at the time of the ERA campaign they were mostly "cosmopolitans" who had joined the organization primarily to share their feminism in an atmosphere of mutual support.

Because this generalized feminist ideology made NOW a multi-issue organization, many state legislators tied the ERA to other feminist causes, especially legal abortion. The NOW leadership was aware of this dilemma. In the major ratification push of 1980 in Illinois, NOW's national office set up its ERA ratification office several blocks from the Chicago main NOW office, specifically to ensure that literature, posters, and other reminders of NOW's multi-issue approach would not be present. New direct-mail members often joined NOW solely because of the ERA, while active chapter members were still concerned with the range of feminist issues and often resented the fact that NOW's national office was devoting time and money to the ERA rather than using it to preserve abortion rights or promote other feminist causes. Occasionally, when responding to questions about the ERA's effect on abortion, these members defended a woman's right to abortion instead of taking the official NOW position that there was no connection between the two issues. ERA Illinois, on the other hand, was proud to have engaged in its coalition a number of Roman Catholic organizations, which opposed abortion as a matter of principle. The leaders of ERA Illinois saw both NOW's support for abortions and the generally distracting effect of other issues as detrimental to the ERA.

NOW's active members had a larger goal in mind than simply ratifying the ERA. For many new members, working for the ERA was a radicalizing experience. It opened their eyes to the underlying attitudes of many legislators, friends, family, colleagues, and bosses. For many, the ERA provided their first political activity. In a NOW bus going to Springfield in 1980, I interviewed one woman who had driven from Colorado to Illinois, using her entire yearly vacation from her secretarial job to work for the ERA. Having encountered the women's movement when the first issue of *Ms.* was shared around her office, she had become a direct-mail member of NOW, and for years had been politically active only by sending postcards to legislators when the *NOW Times* sent out a call. But when the ERA began to falter, she had sent money and then volunteered her time and now her one vacation. Another woman, from a town of 25,000 in New Mexico, had joined the town's NOW chapter after listening to a feminist interview at the radio station where she worked. Her group had raised money to send her to work for the ERA in Illinois because she was the only one of them not working from "8 to 5." An older black woman told me that she had watched on television the ERA demonstration organized by NOW in Chicago and had wanted to join them, but this was the first moment in which she had the time to participate. Like almost everyone on the bus, she had never been to Springfield before.

Viewing ERA work as the first step to committed feminism, both NOW's leaders and most of its active members considered the ERA only one battle in an ongoing, much longer war. They valued each demonstration, each phone call soliciting support, and each television ad not just for its effect in passing the ERA itself, but for its value in sensitizing all women to feminist political issues. Moreover, NOW functioned as a national, not just a local, organization and relied more on direct-mail membership than on constituent chapters. Once NOW became visibly involved in the national ERA struggle, its direct-mail membership began to increase dramatically.[10] This meant that the organization naturally leaned toward activities that had a national impact, like television ads and massive demonstrations (which received national media coverage), rather than toward local organizing in districts with wavering legislators, particularly when these districts did not even have a NOW chapter.

While NOW depended on people who had joined for a range of

feminist reasons, ERA Illinois largely relied on a few women who in their unions, churches, or League of Women Voters chapters had followed state politics the way a fan follows baseball. At the first ERA Illinois meeting I attended, the president spent more than two hours giving an update on each of the state legislators, with a style so informal in its references that at least half the time I did not understand which legislator was being discussed. She updated members on the legislators' personal and political status, including who had said what to whom at what restaurant, who was getting divorced, who had a hard race ahead in the next election, who was being maneuvered out of power by a group of local committeemen, and how all this affected the probable lineup of ERA votes in the upcoming legislative session. No one who had not immersed herself in the details of Illinois politics could have followed this discussion.

During a break at another ERA Illinois meeting, I turned to a nurse from south Chicago who had been almost as quiet as I, assuming that she, too, was confused. Hoping to strike up a tentative alliance among the unsophisticated, I asked where she lived. "District 27," she replied, leaving me as ignorant as I was before. Had I asked the same question at a NOW chapter meeting, it is inconceivable that anyone would have described where she lived by naming her legislative district. Indeed, several would not even have known the numbers of their legislative districts, much less have expected other people to know where a district identified by a number was located. For the ten to fifteen people who were extremely active in ERA Illinois, this kind of response was second nature. As one board member put it, they were "political animals."

Organizationally weak, ERA Illinois kept its larger membership by offering a nonradical way of supporting the ERA and by bringing together through a coalition all the state supporters of the ERA—from unions to businesses. The most active members were attracted because the work gave them the chance to live and breathe intrigue, high drama, and history-in-the-making while also doing good. Such a strategy produced tactics that some legislative ERA sponsors considered counterproductive and a naive interference in legislative planning. ERA Illinois members often wanted to be "in" on the action even though the legislators managing the amendment sometimes did not want them in. Moreover, this strategy did not generate many active members. The prerequisite of mastering so much information drove away the politically unsophisticated. Thus, despite the enthusiasm of its most active members, ERA Illinois was not equipped to organize at the district level. There were simply not enough "political animals" around.

Tactics and Members

We need not assume that NOW and ERA Illinois consciously chose their tactics in the ERA struggle in order to attract and keep their membership. Both natural selection and self-selection were at work. Natural selection ensures that if a voluntary association does not find viable ways of attracting and holding members, it goes out of business. The organizations that cannot adapt die off. Those that survive have, by definition though often by accident, characteristics suited to their particular ecological niche. Self-selection also operates in evolution. People join organizations to find people like themselves, and if they do not, they quit the organization instead of trying to change it. The active membership of NOW used national media campaigns and nationally televised demonstrations not only because these events brought in new members, but because they gave the old members the vital feeling of belonging to a larger, world-historical feminist cause. People who did not find such activities exciting were not very likely to join NOW. And people who joined because they found such drama appealing, even if it was not "cost effective" in terms of ERA ratification, usually wanted more. "As for the value of our demonstrations," one local NOW leader told me, "they were morale boosters for us." The active membership in ERA Illinois, by contrast, was attracted to one-on-one or small group meetings with individual legislators and to electoral campaigning. People who did not share this interest simply fell away. Biases in self-selection made it hard for either organization to survey, "rationally," all alternative tactics for ratifying the ERA and to choose among them solely on the basis of their legislative payoff.

Unity, Suffrage, and the ERA

According to some calculations, the ERA lost in the states by seven votes.[11] Such a narrow defeat makes it possible to claim that any one of many factors "caused" the defeat. But it is hard to attribute much of the defeat to coalitional disunity. Different tactics can be useful in mobilizing different constituencies, and even, on occasion, in appealing to different legislators. Different tactics also make it possible for a conservative group to "side with" the legislators, urging them to act before the more radical group gets out of hand. The alternation of sweet reason and threat, sometimes called a "Mutt and Jeff" or "good cop/bad cop" act, can be extremely effective.

Moreover, in the course of the ERA ratification campaign, activists in all the proponent groups learned a great deal. They had never been naive—in the sense of not being willing to "play the game"—but now they were experienced in partisan politics, both in the legislature and at the district level. By 1982, when voters had elected a number of women to state legislatures, a core of legislative leaders had begun to emerge with longstanding ties to different feminist organizations and an ability to work with these organizations to develop effective political strategy. Also by 1982 feminist groups had come to see the necessity of full-time paid political lobbyists, who could work with sympathetic legislators, identify weaknesses in the opposition, and help the activist organizations coordinate their strategies. But 1982 was also the year the ERA died, and with it the symbol and the conviction of being close to victory that had galvanized hundreds of thousands of women into activism. Just as the ten-year campaign for the ERA was beginning to build feminists in the unratified states into a politically sophisticated force, the money, the time, and the skills slowed to a trickle. The crisis over, most women turned to other things. And the feminist organizations, which were never able to give their members important individual benefits, began to lose membership and thus political power.

The women's movement fragmented with the death of the ERA because the need for strategic coalitions aimed at a specific issue and appealing to many kinds of women had vanished. The "once in a lifetime" cause was no longer available to generate extraordinary membership and monetary support. The history of the suffrage movement reveals a similar pattern of different tactics, different bases for membership, and, after the struggle was over, different philosophical strands. While we do not have adequate historical data from either of these periods to compare the unity or disunity of the coalitions, quite probably factors other than the ability of suffrage organizations to mute divisions explained its success, just as other factors explained most of the ERA defeat.

The greatest success of both the suffrage and the ERA movements may have been the gains produced in feminist and antifeminist consciousness by the process of thinking about and organizing for the two amendments. The ERA, for example, brought the ideas of the feminist movement directly into the smallest towns of the South and the Midwest. If this is the case, it is at least arguable that the subtle process of consciousness-raising must take place through many diverse organizations, so that women with different individual styles and needs can find organizations that respond to those needs.

Structural divisions will remain a central problem in any mass mobilization: the organizations and political strategies involved in mobilization will almost always demand a great deal of time from volunteers. Given the nature of individual incentives for volunteering, it can sometimes be counterproductive to urge expanding the base of a particular membership, as Ware (this volume) reports happening in the League of Women Voters. Individuals join organizations not only to support a cause but to be with people like themselves. Social benefit is often one of the few individual rewards an organization can offer. If the pleasures of membership homogeneity provide such an important base for individual rewards, heterogeneity can threaten an organization's very viability. Individuals often move in their lives from one mode of gratification to another, and even on one issue and at one time can be attracted to different organizations to fill different personal needs. Organizations often have to specialize in order to produce a particular ambiance for their members. To the degree that internal homogeneity increases organizational viability in voluntary organizations, the most effective larger organizational model will be coalitional and federalist. The most important outstanding research task, moreover, will be uncovering the conditions under which coalitions among groups with various individual incentives are most easily built.

Notes

The research on which this chapter is based was funded in part by faculty grants from Northwestern University, by the Center for Urban Affairs and Policy Research at Northwestern University, and by a Rockefeller Foundation Humanities Fellowship. I would particularly like to thank the Institute for Advanced Study in Princeton and the National Endowment for the Humanities for providing the collegial environment and time that made this chapter possible.

1. Cott, this volume, and Cott (1986). DuBois (1986) insightfully explores the differences in strategy, produced in part by differences in class, racial sensitivity, and partisan affiliation, that divided the American suffrage movement from 1848 to 1869.
2. For example, Jaggar (1983).
3. See Mansbridge (1986). Wuthnow and Lehrman, this volume, reinforce my argument that the effect of fundamentalist political mobilization was enhanced by the failure of ERA proponents to use the liberal churches as effectively as the opposition used its churches.
4. See Olson (1971 [1965]) and Hardin (1982).
5. The usual term is "selective" incentive. See Knoke, this volume, for a fuller discussion of incentives.

6. This is the larger theme in Mansbridge (1986). Much of this chapter has been adapted from chapters 10 and 12 of that book. Quotations in this chapter derive from taped interviews conducted in 1981–1982 with activists in the ERA ratification campaign in Illinois. The work is also based on participant observation in Illinois from 1980 to 1982 as an independent member of the board of directors of ERA Illinois, with the announced aim of collecting data for a book that would examine how organizational incentives affect tactics.

   For the strong effect of "normative" incentives in organizations connected to the women's movement, see Knoke, this volume, especially Table 16.2.

7. See Mansbridge (1986), chaps. 7 and 8.

8. Gerlach and Hine (1970).

9. Having paid a price, emotionally or otherwise, people often upgrade in their minds the worth of the good they have paid for. Festinger (1957).

10. Boles (1982) points out that due to NOW's 1977–1979 "shift in focus to a national campaign instead of one centered on the legislatures in unratified states," NOW's annual budget soared from $700,000 in 1977 to $8,500,000 in 1982, and its membership from 55,000 to 210,000.

11. Steiner (1985), p. 100.

15

Representing Women in Washington: Sisterhood and Pressure Politics

Kay Lehman Schlozman

Pressure politics is a sphere of political activity characterized by reliance on the most traditional kind of old-boy political network, the unabashed pursuit of narrow self-interest, and, often, considerable skepticism about activity undertaken in the name of the public good.[1] Although women have only recently joined the ranks of professional lobbyists in large numbers, they have a long history of involvement in pressure politics. Their efforts on behalf of suffrage for women and social reforms brought them into the halls of government in Washington and the state capitals as advocates for causes in which they believed, if not as wheeler-dealers for hire. And if the methods of grass-roots lobbying that now figure so importantly in the arsenal of techniques of influence of virtually every organization on the Washington scene were not actually invented by the early suffragists, these brave women surely pioneered in their use and refinement.

Over the past two decades, a great deal has been written about the politically salient gender differences among individual citizens. However, we are only beginning to probe women's involvement in private organizational activity in contemporary Washington politics. This relative inattention to women's participation in the pressure sphere and the organizations that represent their political interests probably reflects not only the well-documented tendency among political scientists to overlook and undervalue the political contributions of women but also their tendency in recent years to de-emphasize the study of organized interests in Washington. Political scientists of the 1950s and early 1960s placed competition between organized private interests at the heart of the distinctively pluralistic character of American politics.[2] The group theorists' perspective was later subjected to serious criticism by analysts who argued that organized interest activity had neither the determinative role in governing nor the benign effect on public life that had once been attributed to it.[3] In the aftermath of these intellectual debates, however, students of politics turned their attention elsewhere.

Recent developments have stimulated renewed concern with pressure politics among academic observers.[4] Over the past two decades there has been an explosion in the volume of organized interest activity in Washington: Not only are organizations doing more to influence policy outcomes, but many more are on the scene—both those that are new and those that were at one time apolitical but have now been mobilized politically. Among the newcomers to Washington are many organizations that represent women in national politics—visible ones pursuing an array of policy objectives, such as the National Organization for Women (NOW) and the Women's Equity Action League, as well as less conspicuous and more specialized ones, such as the Center for Women Policy Studies and the National Conference of Puerto Rican Women. Recent studies of women's activity in national politics have taken note of the significance of these new women's organizations and the support given by traditional women's organizations such as the National Federation of Business and Professional Women's Clubs and the American Association of University Women in policy controversies over women's issues.[5] However, there has been no systematic, comprehensive survey of the organizations that represent women in Washington. This chapter seeks to fill that gap by training many of the same questions used to probe the role of gender in various arenas of American politics—the attitudes, priorities, and characteristic political styles of women and the impediments to their equal participation in political life—on the organizations that represent women in national politics.

Pressure Politics in American Politics

Of the forms of citizen activity, pressure politics has traditionally assumed a characteristic shape and played a particularly weighty role in the United States. In contrast to their counterparts in the democracies of Europe, American interest groups have long been distinguished by their voluntary character and autonomy from government, as well as by the vigor of their activity and the richness and variety of the interests they represent.[6] The fundamental contours of organized interest activity were laid down during the nineteenth century. Lobbyists like Samuel Ward—who served ham boiled in champagne at his nightly banquets and paid off legislators' gambling debts—perfected the techniques of direct contact with policymakers. Similarly, methods of grass-roots lobbying were developed long before the arrival of the electronic technologies that now facilitate citizen mobilization: Unaided by computers, the Anti-Saloon League had a mailing list of over half a million sympathizers in the early 1900s.[7]

Although substantial numbers of women have entered the ranks of government-affairs professionals only recently, they have long been active in this realm. As Cott's chapter in this volume demonstrates, women have historically lobbied for causes to which they were committed, most notably votes for women as well as such social reforms as temperance and child labor laws. In addition, a small number of women's organizations such as the League of Women Voters and the Women's International League for Peace and Freedom are long-term Washington activists.

The stunning expansion in the volume of Washington pressure activity in recent years is related to a variety of factors: among them, the increasing scope of federal government involvement; procedural changes (especially in Congress) which have created new opportunities for influence by private organizations; the social ferment of the 1960s and the concomitant citizen mobilization around such issues as civil rights, consumer protection, and environmental preservation; and the countermobilization by business interests threatened by these developments.[8] Such trends, of course, have increasingly brought women into politics. An important component of the citizen protest of the 1960s was the revival of the women's movement; the movement has begotten new organizations, many of them active in Washington, dedicated to promoting women's interests.

The link between protest activity rooted in social movements and organizational formation is a longstanding one in American politics. Although there is a venerable tradition of middle-class protest in American politics, direct action tactics have traditionally been the weapon of the weak and excluded. Effective and sustained protests can provide a vehicle for those who lack the resources for more conventional forms of political activity to draw attention to their concerns, build support for the cause, and pressure policymakers to take action.[9] However, as Mansbridge's chapter in this volume points out, such tactics may not always be the most instrumental choice. Sometimes protests backfire: At the same time that they may help to win converts to the cause and generate sympathy within the public and the media, they may alienate the policymakers who make the ultimate decisions. Hence, in deciding to sponsor protest activity, organizational leaders often calculate explicitly whether the risk to policy objectives is justified by the payoff in terms of internal organizational enhancement. Indeed, one argument holds that NOW's shift in strategy in 1977 from a focus on lobbying the state legislatures to a protest-centered and media-oriented national campaign for ERA ratification sacrificed political effectiveness to the dictates of organizational maintenance.[10]

Furthermore, the residue of protest activity is frequently a symbolic policy response that defuses the immediate pressure but may not address the real grievances that animated the citizen action.[11] To realize and consolidate substantive political benefits usually requires the kind of coordinated effort and sustained vigilance and follow-through that are difficult to achieve in a decentralized political movement relying on volunteer leadership and a rank and file whose enthusiasm may wane when symbolic victories have been attained.

The nearly universal response to the problem besetting social movements—the need to routinize enthusiasm—has been organization. The organizational legacy of social movements can assume a variety of forms. In the multiparty systems of Europe, particularly in a nation like the Netherlands, a social movement may leave a new political party in its wake. American history is also littered with minor parties like the Prohibition and Right-to-Life parties, some of which have had a significant, indirect effect on politics. However, the institutional and cultural biases in favor of a two-party system in the United States imply that such parties are very unlikely actually to share in governing power. Another outcome, illustrated by the incorporation of contemporary Swedish feminists into the Social Democratic party or late-nineteenth century American agrarian radicals into the Democratic party, is the absorption of a social movement by one of the existing political parties.[12] This, however, is a somewhat unusual development. In the United States a citizens' movement seeking to supplement mass action with more readily sustained forms of political participation ordinarily moves into interest group politics. It seems that pressure politics in the United States is relatively permeable to new organizations and that it is somewhat easier here than elsewhere to make the transition from protest to organized interest politics.[13] In following this trajectory, the contemporary American women's movement has taken a course that is unique among its counterparts in other Western democracies. Although there is variation in the degree to which contemporary women's movements in Europe have pursued strategies of protest, electoral impact, or policy influence, in no case have they institutionalized their presence in organized interest politics.[14]

Attention to the defeat of the Equal Rights Amendment (ERA), an important but substantively symbolic measure, may have obscured the degree to which the organizations bequeathed by the women's movement have had an influence on policy.[15] For example, it is possible that if established women's organizations, accustomed to monitoring developments in the capital, had not insisted that the Equal Employment Opportunity Commission deal with the accumulating complaints of sex discrimination, the Civil Rights Act of 1964 might never have been implemented on behalf of women.[16] Similarly, if there had been no women's organizations on the scene in Washington to keep an eye on the details as regulations were being written in the executive branch, the legislative gains of the Equal Credit Opportunity Act of 1974 might have been undercut.[17] On issues ranging from pension rights to equal opportunity in vocational education to the assignment of women in the armed forces, the continuing scrutiny and activity of women's organizations have had an impact on policy.

In spite of such accomplishments, there is considerable disagreement about the strategic wisdom of the movement of women's organizations into mainstream pressure politics. In particular, there has been a conflict within NOW over the relative efficacy of strategies of protest or insider influence.[18] On a more fundamental level, a radical feminist might question whether such narrow policy successes even matter so long as women continue to be oppressed by a patriarchal, capitalist order. Indeed, according to this perspective, such trivial victories might be counterproductive, the feminist equivalent to embourgeoisement. Might not women's new ability to compete for Rhodes scholarships or secure auto loans from a bank—the fruits of efforts by women's organizations—undermine the development of the ideological fervor essential to mass-based political action?

While there is little precedent within the American tradition for radical mass action and many examples of social movements that have been absorbed into mainstream politics, opting for an ongoing organizational presence in Washington need not preclude forays into direct action or electoral politics, however. The range of techniques of influence available to an organization that has established an institutionalized presence in Washington is very broad. Protest, electoral, and pressure politics are not mutually exclusive alternatives.

The Study

This chapter seeks to elucidate the role of women in pressure politics by focusing on the organizations that represent women in Washington. In order to obtain a systematic understanding of these organizations and their place in the larger context of national politics, data from a survey of Washington representatives in organizations of women having offices in the capital are used to investigate the nature and activities of these organizations.[19] These data complement those of Knoke (this volume) about the members of women's organizations. We consider the kinds of organizations that represent women in Washington and the nature of their ideologies and policy concerns; the extent of their collective presence and the degree to which that presence can be considered feminist; the level of their resources; the degree to which women in government relations have a distinctive political style; the extent to which they face discrimination by policymakers; the techniques these organizations use to influence political outcomes; and the degree to which the community of organizations of women is divided or united politically.[20]

An organization was included in the sample if it fulfilled one of two criteria: It makes a self-conscious claim to represent women, or a majority of its rank-and-file members are women. The 1984 *Washington Representatives* directory[21] was used to locate 89 such organizations with their own offices in the capital. (For a more complete description of the sample and a discussion of some of the problems involved in locating these organizations, see Appendix 15.1.) Interviews lasting roughly an hour and a half each and consisting of open- and closed-ended questions were conducted during the late summer and fall of 1985 in 76 of these organizations with the person whose job title, as listed in the directory, indicated that he or she would have the most comprehensive understanding of the organization's involvement in politics. Seventy of the respondents were women; six were men.

Although their participation in Washington pressure politics guarantees that all these organizations are in the political mainstream, they are a diverse set. They include women's rights organizations such as the Center for Women Policy Studies and the Older Women's League; associations of women professionals such as the National Association for Women Deans, Administrators and Counselors; and groups of women of a particular ethnic or religious derivation such as the Organization of Pan Asian American Women. In addition, they include organizations that are not specifically women's organizations but which have a high proportion of female members: unions and professional associations in fields such as nursing and occupational therapy having a disproportionate share of women. As shown in Table 15.1, these organizations can be grouped into four categories: women's rights organizations; "caucuses," or organizations of women from particular occupations or religious or ethnic backgrounds; occupational groups; and a heterogeneous residual

Table 15.1   Examples of Washington-Based Women's Organizations

Kind of Organization	Number
Women's Rights	18
National Women's Law Center National Women's Political Caucus Older Women's League Project on Equal Education Rights	
Caucus	19
Association for Women in Science Mexican-American Women's National Association National Council of Catholic Women Women in Communications	
Occupational	21
Amalgamated Clothing and Textile Workers Union American Library Association Association of Flight Attendants Home Economics Education Association	
Other	18
American Association of University Women Future Homemakers of America National Abortion Rights Action League Women's International League for Peace and Freedom	

group that includes one New Right organization whose expressed purpose is to represent women's interests.[22]

Because the questions in the survey of organizations representing women replicated many in an earlier survey (conducted between October 1981 and April 1982) of 175 Washington-based organizations of various types, it is also possible to make comparisons between women's organizations and other kinds of organizations such as corporations and trade associations. Thus, it is possible to examine the extent to which the politically relevant characteristics and activities of organizations of women are typical of all organizations active in Washington; characteristic only of those—such as civil rights, social-welfare, and citizens' groups—that operate at a disadvantage in Washington politics; or unique to organizations representing women.

In making such inferences, however, it is important to recall certain differences between the earlier sample and the survey of organizations representing women. First, the earlier sample had been designed deliberately so that organizations having large, active, and affluent offices in Washington would have a higher probability of being selected than organizations fielding smaller, less active, and less well financed operations.[23] Therefore, one would expect the organizations in the earlier study to be more active and to have fewer resource problems. In addition, the organizations of women differ substantially from those in the earlier sample with respect to the overall distribution of kinds of organizations. Most important, while there are several organizations of women business professionals among the women's organizations, there are no business organizations—corporations or trade and other business associations. Fifty-six percent of the organizations in the earlier sample fell into this category.[24]

How Much of a Presence?

Eighty-nine organizations representing women in Washington sounds like a lot. Yet, it is well known that, across branches and levels of government and across historical eras in the United States, women are underrepresented among political elites. Is this not true of organized interest politics as well? One way to answer the question is to focus on women as Washington representatives. Clearly, increasing numbers of women are entering a field once dominated almost exclusively by men and are becoming government affairs experts for Washington-based organizations. When Lester Milbrath interviewed a random sample of 114 Washington lobbyists in the late 1950s, only 7 percent of his respondents were women.[25] As shown in Table 15.2, two and a half decades later 36 percent of a sample of 489 organizations having offices in Washington, chosen at random from the 1985 *Washington Representatives* directory, list women among their government affairs professionals; of the 1,089 individuals listed, 22 percent are women.[26] Although social-welfare organizations and, not surprisingly, women's organizations are especially likely to include women on their professional staffs, these women Washington representatives are distributed among all types of organizations. Turning the figures around, it is interesting to note that 49 percent of the female and 61 percent of the male Washington representatives represent business organizations—corporations or trade and other business associations.

When it is a matter of representation by organizations rather than individuals, however, it becomes very difficult to measure under- and

Table 15.2 Women as Washington Representatives

	Percentage of Organizations Listing Women as Washington Representatives (N = 489)	Percentage of All Washington Representatives Listed Who Are Women (N = 1,089)
All Organizations	36%	22%
Corporations	36	20
Trade and other business associations	31	17
Professional associations	32	23
Unions	31	11
Citizens' groups	42	23
Social-welfare groups	50	47
Civil rights groups	33	26
Women's organizations	100	100
Governments	42	31
Other	29	21

Source: Figures derived from a random sample of organizations drawn from Arthur C. Close, ed., *Washington Representatives—1985* (Washington, D.C.: Columbia Books, 1985).

overrepresentation in the way that we can, say, for electoral turnout. Because the Washington pressure community includes groups organized around an array of dimensions—from occupation, race, age, and gender to hobbies—and because individual organizations vary substantially in both the number of members they enroll and the level of resources they command, harmonizing the principle of political equality for individuals with collective representation is difficult.[27] Although an exact count is impossible, a reasonable estimate is that women's organizations account for only 1 to 2 percent of all organizations with representation in Washington. (Two of the 175 organizations included in the earlier study are women's organizations; an additional four are unions having a majority of women among their members.) In short, whatever the difficulties in specifying what an unbiased pressure system would look like, it is safe to conclude that women, as well as broad publics and the disadvantaged, are underrepresented in the Washington pressure community.

A Feminist Presence?

To what degree do these organizations bring a feminist, not simply a female, presence to Washington pressure politics? Table 15.3—which presents information about the membership, staffing, organizational self-identification, organizational agendas, and ideologies of these organizations of women—provides some insight into this question. These organizations certainly constitute a female presence in the capital. The membership in these organizations is overwhelmingly female—a finding that is hardly surprising since that is one criterion by which they were chosen. However, across the various kinds of organizations, the proportion of women among members is matched by a nearly equal or even higher proportion of women among the professional staff.[28]

Whether these organizations also constitute a feminist presence is a much more difficult question. Given the controversial nature of the term "feminist," it seems appropriate to consider the question from various perspectives rather than to select a single definition. As shown in Table 15.3, there is considerable variation across the different kinds of organizations when it comes to organizational identity. In an open-ended question, respondents were asked to give a shorthand label that would place their organization in a recognizable category. Naturally, this item elicited a wide variety of answers. Taken together, only a third of the respondents mentioned anything about being a women's or women's rights organization, and just over a fifth of the respondents gave this answer exclusively. The pattern of responses is interesting: While none of the respondents from the occupational groups and very few of those from the caucuses said anything about being a women's organization, the overwhelming majority of the respondents from the women's rights groups did so.

A similar, if less pronounced, pattern emerged when respondents were asked, in an open-ended item, to name the three most important policy issues confronting their organizations. Given the diversity among the organizations, the range of issues is to be expected. What is note-worthy, however, is that two thirds of all the respondents included a women's issue on the list of three.[29] As shown in Table 15.3, once again there are differences across the various kinds of organizations. Not sur-prisingly, the overwhelming majority of the respondents from women's rights organizations (83 percent) mentioned women's issues exclusively. However, only among the occupational groups did a majority (62 per-cent) mention no women's issues at all.

As a follow-up, respondents were asked to indicate the level of their organizations' activity on nine specific issues affecting women, ranging from the ERA to the problems of minority women to the rights of wives, ex-wives, and widows.[30] Interestingly, the relationship between organi-zational policy agenda and level of activity on behalf of these nine wom-en's issues is very weak. (The zero-order gamma is .12. Controlling for organizational position on feminist goals, the first-order partial gamma is .10.) Organizations with an agenda dominated by women's issues are only slightly more likely than organizations with no such priorities at all to indicate a high level of activity across the board. In addition, the pattern across different kinds of organizations is less distinct. There seems to be a certain degree of organizational specialization: The wom-en's rights groups are especially likely to be active on behalf of women who are poor; the caucuses, on behalf of equal educational opportunity; the occupational groups, on behalf of childcare. The women's rights groups—which are otherwise the most feminist—are not the most ac-tive across the board. While they are overwhelmingly likely to have an exclusively feminist organizational agenda, many of them concentrate on a few issues. Thus, the women's rights groups did not score espe-cially high on a scale (ranging from 0 to 27) measuring total activity on all nine issues. In fact, the occupational groups, which tend to be larger and better staffed, had the highest average score on this scale. Their en-hanced resources may permit them to diversify their political efforts in a way that the smaller organizations cannot.

With respect to organizational ideology, it is not so much the differ-ences as the similarities across various kinds of organizations that are striking. Respondents were posed a deliberately vaguely worded item that asked them to characterize their organizations' position "when it

Table 15.3 Organizations Representing Women in Washington——How Feminist?

	Women's Rights Groups (N = 18)	Caucuses (N = 19)	Occupational Groups (N = 21)	Other (N = 18)	All (N = 76)
A. Membership (average percentage women)	91%	97%	76%	90%	88%
B. Professional Staff (average percentage women)	97%	99 + %	74%	94%	90%
C. Organizational Self-Identification					
Women's organization	67%	0%	0%	24%	22%
Women's organization and other	11	17	0	18	11
Other identification	22	83	100	59	68
	100%	100%	100%	101%	101%
D. Organizational Agendas Three Most Important Policy Issues					
Women's issues only	83%	28%	10%	25%	36%
Mixed agenda	17	67	29	31	36
No women's issues	0	6	62	44	29
	100%	101%	101%	100%	101%

Activity on Women's Issues (percentage "very active")

ERA	29%	58%	57%	39%	47%
Equal workplace rights	44	53	52	44	49
Comparable worth	28	37	33	39	34
Problems of poor women	65	26	48	17	39
Problems of minority women	41	47	62	17	43
Equal educational opportunity	31	53	35	56	44
Rights of wives, ex-wives, and widows	53	21	10	33	28
Childcare	12	16	57	33	31
Abortion	27	26	10	28	22
Scale of activity on all issues (average score)	9.4	9.2	10.0	9.4	9.5

E. Ideology
Position on feminist goals

Strongly support	94%	53%	70%	47%	67%
Somewhat support	0	41	25	47	27
Basically neutral	6	6	5	0	4
Somewhat opposed	0	0	0	0	0
Strongly opposed	0	0	0	7	1
	100%	100%	100%	101%	99%

Note: Percentages may not total to 100 because of rounding.

comes to feminist goals"—without offering any definition for the term. The respondents from women's rights organizations, not surprisingly, expressed virtually unanimous support. However, the level of support emanating from respondents from other kinds of organizations is noteworthy. Only one respondent (from the New Right organization mentioned earlier) indicated organizational opposition. Otherwise, three respondents expressed organizational neutrality. The remainder voiced some level of organizational support, usually strong.

Clearly, there is no simple relationship among organizational policy agenda, activity on a broad range of women's issues, and support for feminist goals. Yet, understanding the ways that particular organizations sort themselves into various patterns helps to clarify the extent to which these organizations, taken together, constitute a feminist presence in Washington. For example, ten of the organizations can be considered all-around activists: That is, they are supportive of feminist goals, their top priorities are dominated exclusively by women's issues, and they are active on a range of these issues. The all-around activists are organizations of various types: several women's rights groups with a broad involvement in women's issues—for example, the National Women's Political Caucus and the Women's Legal Defense Fund; two caucuses, one occupational and one religious; a union of workers in the secondary labor market, the Service Employees International Union; and the Coalition of Labor Union Women. Six of the organizations could be labeled issue specialists. Like the all-around activists, they are committed to feminist goals and women's issues dominate their policy agendas. However, they are relatively inactive when it comes to the broad range of women's issues and focus on a few specific issues: four are women's rights groups—for example, the Coalition for Women's Appointments, which concentrates solely on getting more women appointed to governmental positions; the other two are reproductive rights groups.

The six organizations that can be considered fellow travelers exhibit almost the opposite pattern. While they are ideologically supportive of feminist goals and involved politically on a range of women's issues, they do not list any such issues among their highest priorities. Most of the fellow travelers are unions—for example, the International Ladies' Garment Workers' Union (ILGWU), whose primary concerns are focused on its own industries. Not surprisingly, the ILGWU, which organizes diminishing numbers of workers in an industry besieged by imports, does not place any women's issues among its three most important policy concerns. Nevertheless, under the direction of political veteran Evelyn Dubrow, the ILGWU's Washington office manages a remarkably high level of involvement on issues explicitly affecting women.

A diverse group of six organizations—containing organizations as different from one another as the Association of Teacher Educators and Women Strike for Peace—can be considered passive supporters. While they support feminist goals, they place no women's issues on their agendas and exhibit low levels of activity on the range of such issues. Finally, there are four organizations that do not support feminist goals. Of the three that expressed ideological neutrality, one—Ex-Partners of Servicemen, which focuses solely on the issue of the pension and benefit rights of former military spouses—has an agenda dominated by women's issues but is not active across the board; the other two are occupational caucuses like the National Association of Women Highway Safety Leaders that indicate no involvement with women's issues either as policy priorities or as secondary objects of political activity. The final organization, the only one indicating outright opposition to feminist goals, is the New Right organization, which has a mixed policy agenda and is very active on a variety of women's issues—of course, on the opposite side from all of the other organizations under consideration.[31]

Having reviewed both the various patterns of involvement on issues affecting women as well as the aggregate responses to the survey items, we can now pose the question, "How feminist a presence do these seventy-six organizations constitute?" To a certain extent, the only possible rejoinder to such a question is "Relative to what?" Compared with local branches of NOW, these organizations taken together are not overwhelmingly feminist. However, it is important to recall that organized pressure politics is both the most professionalized and the most mainstream sphere of citizen involvement. Considering these characteristics, the nature of the Reagan administration, and the decade that it has reflected and shaped, the level of feminist commitment and activism seems surprising. Only one organization opposes feminist goals; three more are neutral. An additional six are supportive of feminist goals, but do not back up their support either by placing issues affecting women among their highest policy goals or by being active on behalf of such issues. The remainder, however, not only support feminist goals but go beyond tacit support in terms of either agenda or overall activity. For a diverse set of organizations operating in a realm of insider politics, this is indeed a more feminist presence than might have been expected. In short, it seems that these organizations constitute a substantial, though not a radical, feminist presence in Washington.

Experience in Washington Politics

The period since 1960, particularly since 1970, has witnessed a phenomenal increase in the number of organized interests. Fully 40 percent of all organizations with offices in Washington as of 1981, and 48 percent of the organizations representing women, have been founded since 1960; 25 percent of all organizations, and 38 percent of the organizations of women, since 1970.[32] Thus, women's organizations are somewhat, though not substantially, younger than average. This growth, however, has not been uniform across all kinds of organizations. A mere 6 percent of the corporations—as opposed to 50 percent of the civil rights, social-welfare, and citizens' groups[33]—have been born since 1970. With respect to organizational birth rates, there are even wider disparities among the women's organizations. Only 10 percent of the occupational groups with predominantly female memberships have been founded since 1970. In contrast, the women's rights organizations include a very high percentage of newcomers (82 percent since 1970) even when compared with organizations that might be expected to resemble them most closely—civil rights, social-welfare, and citizens' groups. To summarize, the explosive growth in the number of organizations since 1960, and especially since 1970, has operated unevenly across various kinds of organizations; however, it has left many new organizations of women—in particular, women's rights groups—in its wake.

Although many of these organizations are relatively new to the Washington scene, they are run by staff whose experience compares favorably with that of other Washington-based organizations.[34] Overall, respondents in both surveys have an average of eleven years of experience in government relations. Interestingly, the respondents from the women's rights organizations, by far the most recent organizational arrivals, have slightly more than average experience. The respondents from women's organizations show a small, but not substantial, disadvantage with respect to another measure of experience—having worked for the federal government. It is well known that organizations of all kinds take advantage of the expertise gained from working for the federal government by hiring through what is commonly referred to as the "revolving door." Fifty-eight percent of the respondents in the earlier study, and 46 percent of the respondents in the women's organizations survey, reported having worked for the federal government.[35]

Operating at a Disadvantage in Pressure Politics

For several reasons women's organizations operate at a disadvantage in Washington pressure politics. The first has to do with political resources. There are a variety of resources, ranging from an active and committed membership to a reputation for credibility and trustworthiness to extensive contacts, that are useful in pressure politics. However, its convertibility into other resources gives money a primacy among those resources. Indeed, it can be argued that organized interest politics contrasts with other forms of citizen politics—most notably electoral and social-movement politics—in the degree to which it is hospitable to the conversion of market resources into political ones.[36] At several points in both surveys, respondents expressed a desire for greater resources. Respondents were shown a list of eight political resources and asked, if they could enhance their organization's stock of two of the eight, which they would choose. Also, the replies to two open-ended questions—each of which elicited a wide variety of answers—included expressions of need for greater financial resources. The first question asked respondents to consider a recent policy controversy in which the organization had sustained a defeat and to explain why the defeat had occurred. A number of respondents in both surveys cited lack of resources as the reason. The second question asked respondents to discuss the greatest sources of frustration in being a Washington representative. Again, a number of respondents mentioned lack of resources.

Substantial differences across various organizational categories arise in the perceived need for more resources. (See Table 15.4.) Respondents from business organizations, especially corporations, only rarely expressed a need for greater financial resources. In contrast, those from women's rights groups and from citizens', civil rights, and social-welfare groups indicated a need for greater financial resources much more frequently. Clearly, women's organizations are not alone in their perception that lack of resources is a handicap to policy effectiveness. Still, this fact should not obscure either the meaning or the potential political implications of the aggregated figures in Table 15.4: When compared with respondents from a sample of *all* kinds of organizations active in Washington politics, representatives from organizations of women are substantially more likely to express a need for greater financial resources.

In another way women's organizations operate at a disadvantage in Washington politics. Reagan's Washington was not a particularly congenial environment for organizations representing women. It has sometimes been thought that administrations come and go while the Washington pressure community marches on undisturbed, its relationships with policymakers in Congress and the agencies remaining unaffected. Recent research demonstrates the inaccuracy of this view. Various administrations—of differing partisan or ideological coloration—are not equally hospitable to all kinds of organized interests.[37]

Respondents in both surveys were asked a series of questions about

Table 15.4 Perceived Resource Needs

	Would Like to Enhance Budgetary Resources	Insufficient Resources Cited as Source of Ineffectiveness in Recent Policy Controversy	Insufficient Resources Cited as Biggest Source of Frustration
All Organizations			
Washington representatives study (N = 175)	34%	19%	14%
Women's organizations survey (N = 76)	63	27	38
Citizens', Civil Rights, and Social-Welfare Groups			
Washington representatives study (N = 33)	61	57	42
Women's rights groups (N = 18)	72	53	53
Women's Caucuses (N = 19)	56	35	39
Occupational Groups			
Washington representatives study (N = 32)	43	23	4
Women's groups (N = 21)	43	11	29
Business Organizations			
Corporations (N = 52)	9	2	5
Trade and other business associations (N = 45)	38	13	9

whether the 1980 election, and the consequent change to Republican control of the Senate and White House, had made any difference to their organizations. The replies, which fall into a reasonably predictable pattern, indicate that the implications for pressure politics of the arrival of the Reagan administration had already become apparent by the fall of 1981. Once again, the responses of the representatives of various kinds of women's organizations resemble those given by respondents from parallel organizations. Ninety-three percent of the respondents from occupational groups in the earlier survey, and 90 percent of those from their counterparts in the women's organizations study, indicated that life had become harder in terms of either substantive policy outcomes or political access. Similarly, 82 percent of those from citizens', civil rights, or social-welfare groups interviewed in the earlier survey, 78 percent of the respondents from women's rights groups, and 79 percent of those from the caucuses mentioned that things were more difficult since the change of administrations. In contrast, only 17 percent of the respondents from trade or other business associations and 9 percent of those from corporations discussed such difficulties when interviewed in 1981–1982. Thus, in this way as well, organizations of women operate at a disadvantage in contemporary Washington, a disadvantage they share with other organizations. However, once again, it is important not to ignore the overall effect in focusing on the extent to which this circumstance is not unique to women's organizations. Overall, 39 percent of the respondents in the Washington Representatives Study indicated that Republican control of the White House and Senate had had a negative impact on their fortunes. Respondents from women's organizations, 78 percent of whom gave such replies, were twice as likely to see such negative consequences.

In one respect representatives of women's organizations operate at a special disadvantage that is not shared equally with their counterparts in similar organizations: Most of those who represent organizations of women in Washington are themselves women, and women in government relations seem to be the objects of discrimination. Respondents in the women's organizations survey were asked a series of questions about the treatment of women Washington representatives by policymakers.[38] As shown in Table 15.5, at some point during this series of items over two thirds of the women respondents—spread more or less evenly across the various kinds of organizations representing women—indicated that women operate at a disadvantage as Washington representatives. Several comments were made. The most frequent was that women are not taken seriously. Respondents also mentioned that women are excluded from the old-boy networks that are critical to suc-

Table 15.5 Perceived Discrimination Against Women Washington Representatives
(Women's Organizations Survey: women respondents only)

	All Organizations	Women's Rights Groups	Caucuses	Occupational Groups	Other
Operate at a Disadvantage (not taken seriously by male policymakers, excluded from old-boy networks, etc.)	67%	72%	68%	62%	65%
Impact of Gender on Ability to Operate Effectively					
An asset since I represent women	30%	53%	12%	13%	41%
An asset	20	0	29	33	18
No difference	23	24	18	20	29
A liability	27	24	41	33	12
	100%	101%	100%	99%	100%

cess in Washington pressure politics, that men are threatened by women as Washington representatives, and so on.[39] Since these comments constitute subjective perceptions rather than objective observations, a skeptic might argue that they are not evidence of gender discrimination. One way to check is to consider the responses of the few men who were interviewed.[40] The six men in the sample were much less likely than the women from similar kinds of organizations to describe their organizations as feminist in either ideology or agenda. Interestingly, however, five of them commented on the disadvantage suffered by women in government relations. While we should not overinterpret the importance of only six cases, this seems to suggest that the women respondents are not simply imagining a handicap imposed by their gender.

In spite of the widespread perception that women suffer discrimination in government, less than a third of the female respondents consider their own gender a liability—and half said they consider it an asset—to their ability to operate effectively as Washington representatives. How can these figures be reconciled with the comments about discrimination against women in government relations? Table 15.5 shows that, upon probing, over half of the women (and all of those from women's rights organizations) who said being a woman was an asset linked that statement to the fact that they represent large numbers of women; they noted that being a woman helps under such circumstances because it lends credibility to policy advocacy and facilitates cooperation with other organizations representing women. When these respondents are excluded, a plurality of the remainder—spread somewhat unevenly across the various kinds of organizations of women—indicated that they consider their gender to be a liability. Once again, it is interesting to note that of the five men who answered this question, four indicated that they considered *their* gender to be an asset; the other said that it made no difference.

Coping with Disadvantage

We have seen that organizations representing women confront special problems in Washington politics. Some of these—the scarcity of resources and the hostility of Reagan's Washington—are shared with citizens', civil rights, and social-welfare groups. The burden of discrimination against women in government relations, however, is borne disproportionately by representatives of women's organizations.

How do representatives of women's organizations cope with this circumstance of relative disadvantage? One way may be by working harder. In an attempt to learn whether women have a distinctive style in pressure politics, respondents were asked whether there are any significant differences in the ways that men and women approach being a Washington representative. A majority (62 percent) perceived some difference, but there was no consensus as to the nature of such a difference. Respondents made various points: Of those who saw a difference (13 percent of all who answered the question), 19 percent remarked that women in government affairs are more sensitive and humane than their male counterparts; even smaller proportions said that women are more concerned with issues (10 percent), less comfortable with power (7 percent), or less likely to take bribes (4 percent). Nearly half (45 percent) of those who saw a difference (30 percent of all who answered the question) made some comment to the effect that women are forced by the old-boy network to be more careful, to work harder, and to have their facts in order. Taking these comments together, there does not appear to be a single characterization of a feminine style in government affairs— unless perhaps it is that women are more likely to play by the rules.

When it comes to strategies of influence, as opposed to style, there is even less evidence of a distinctive approach. In brief, political operatives in organizations representing women in Washington cope with the disadvantages they face by acting like the boys and joining forces with women. In terms of political strategies, organizations of women cannot be distinguished by what they do, how much they do, or where they do it. Respondents in both surveys were shown a list of 27 different techniques of policy influence and asked to specify which ones their organizations used. The list included traditional forms of articulating positions, such as testifying at hearings, as well as nontraditional forms, such as staging protests. In addition, the list incorporated techniques mobilizing differing kinds of political resources—money, information, constituency size and cohesion, and the appeal of organizational cause. Finally, it embraced methods appropriate to various institutional arenas—legislative, executive, and judicial.

The results of this inquiry indicate that all organizations—including organizations representing women—do a lot. Women's organizations use many techniques, averaging 18 of the 27 techniques of influence (only slightly less than the average of 19 for the organizations in the Washington Representatives Study). These figures are particularly impressive in light of the fact that the earlier sample was deliberately designed to increase the probability of selecting large and active organizations.

Women's organizations are also typical in the nature of their activity.

As shown in Table 15.6, women's organizations tend overall to engage in the same kinds of techniques of influence as other organizations. (The correlation coefficient for the percentage of organizations in each sample using each of the techniques of influence is .88. The Spearman rank-order coefficient is .87.) There are, however, some exceptions to the overall pattern of similarity. For example, there are several insider activities, involving participation when policy is made, at the top of the scale. While all organizations use these techniques extensively, respondents from women's organizations were somewhat less likely than those in the earlier study to report that their organizations testify at hearings, present research results or technical information, shape the implementation of policies, or help to plan legislative strategy or to draft legislation. This seems to imply that women's organizations are excluded from the everyday interactions with policymakers that provide opportunities for influence. However, the meaning of this finding becomes somewhat clearer when the figures are broken down for particular kinds of organizations. (Complete data on which the generalizations in this paragraph and the following three paragraphs are based can be found in Appendix Table 15.A.) Among organizations of women, the occupational and women's rights groups use these techniques at the same rates as all other kinds of organizations. However, the caucuses—either because they have differential access to, or differential desire to participate in, policymaking processes—are quite a bit less likely to employ such methods of influence.

The divergence between organizations of women and other organizations is greater when it comes to filing suit, and the pattern is somewhat different. Once again, the caucuses are distinctive: Respondents from only 21 percent of the caucuses indicated that their organizations file suit. However, the women's rights groups, perhaps because they have a somewhat mixed record of success in the courts, are also less likely to file suit. Fifty percent of the respondents from women's rights groups, compared with 72 percent of those from civil rights, social-welfare, and citizens' groups, indicated that their organizations go to court.

The pattern for contributing to electoral campaigns, somewhat different again, reflects the differences between the samples in the distribution of various kinds of organizations. Disparities among organizations with respect to available resources and restrictions on nonprofit organizations having 501(c)(3) tax status imply that different kinds of organizations are differentially likely to use this technique. Business and occupational groups—in particular, corporations and unions—are especially likely to make campaign contributions. Since 56 percent of the organizations in the earlier study are corporations and trade or other business

Table 15.6 Percentage of Organizations Using Techniques of Exercising Influence

Technique	Washington Representatives Study	Women's Organizations Survey	Difference
1. Testifying at hearings	99%	84%	−15%*
2. Contacting officials directly to present your point of view	98	91	− 7
3. Engaging in informal contacts with officials	95	93	− 2
4. Presenting research results or technical information	92	79	−13 *
5. Sending letters to members of your organization to inform them about your activities	92	93	+ 1
6. Entering into coalitions with other organizations	90	91	+ 1
7. Attempting to shape the implementation of policies	89	75	−14 *
8. Talking with people from the press and media	86	92	+ 6
9. Consulting with government officials to plan legislative strategy	85	74	−11
10. Helping to draft legislation	85	68	−17 *
11. Inspiring letter-writing or telegram campaigns	84	82	− 2
12. Shaping the government's agenda by raising new issues	84	83	− 1

13. Mounting grass-roots lobbying efforts	80	79	− 1
14. Having influential constituents contact their legislators' offices	80	79	− 1
15. Helping to draft regulations, rules, or guidelines	78	63	−15 *
16. Serving on advisory commissions	76	84	+ 6
17. Alerting members of Congress to effects of a bill on their district	75	66	− 9
18. Filing suit	72	45	−27 *
19. Making financial contributions to campaigns	58	29	−29 *
20. Doing favors for officials who need assistance	56	46	−10
21. Attempting to influence appointments to public office	53	59	+ 6
22. Publicizing candidates' voting records	44	45	+ 1
23. Engaging in direct-mail fund raising for your organization	44	60	+16
24. Running ads in the media about your position on issues	31	33	+ 2
25. Contributing work or personnel to electoral campaigns	24	29	+ 5
26. Making public endorsements of candidates for office	22	30	+ 8
27. Engaging in protests or demonstrations	20	41	+21 *

*Significant at .01 level, two-tailed t-test.

Appendix Table 15.A   Percentage of Organizations Using Each of Techniques of Exercising Influence

Technique	Citizens', Civil Rights, and Social-Welfare Groups	Women's Rights Groups	Caucuses	Occupational Groups Washington Representatives	Occupational Groups Women's	Corporations	Trade and Other Business Associations
1. Testifying at hearings	100%	94%	74%	100%	90%	98%	100%
2. Contacting officials directly	97	94	79	97	95	100	98
3. Informal contacts	94	94	95	94	95	98	96
4. Presenting research results	94	89	58	94	90	94	91
5. Sending letters to members	90	83	95	94	95	85	96
6. Entering into coalitions	94	89	90	97	95	96	84
7. Shaping implementation	94	88	63	84	86	90	89
8. Talking with press and media	97	100	84	97	90	67	89
9. Planning legislative strategy	84	72	58	81	86	90	84
10. Helping to draft legislation	71	78	47	88	90	86	89
11. Inspiring letter-writing	84	78	84	91	90	83	82
12. Shaping the government's agenda	100	83	79	84	86	79	78
13. Mounting grass-roots lobbying	75	72	79	91	90	81	76

14.	Having constituents contact	66	72	68	88	86	77	84
15.	Drafting regulations	81	72	37	75	90	85	73
16.	Serving on advisory commissions	69	88	74	91	95	74	73
17.	Alerting members of Congress to effects	66	61	53	72	90	92	69
18.	Filing suit	72	50	21	84	71	72	73
19.	Contributing to campaigns	22	22	0	72	62	86	53
20.	Doing favors for officials	48	56	28	64	55	62	52
21.	Influencing appointments	50	44	53	75	81	48	47
22.	Publicizing voting records	72	11	32	62	76	28	36
23.	Direct-mail fund raising	69	82	42	53	57	19	40
24.	Running ads in the media	34	18	10	38	48	31	27
25.	Contributing work or personnel to campaign	25	17	0	50	57	14	22
26.	Endorsing candidates	25	17	5	62	57	8	9
27.	Engaging in protests	31	33	47	59	52	0	4
	Average number of 27 techniques of influence used	19	17	15	21	22	18	18

associations, the overall figure for the earlier study is enhanced. Among the organizations of women, the women's rights and occupational groups contribute to campaigns at rates comparable to those of their counterparts in the earlier study.

Almost the obverse pattern obtains for the use of protests and demonstrations. Again, there are substantial differences among various kinds of organizations, with the business organizations distinctive in that they eschew protest almost without exception. Thus, in this case the overall figure for the earlier sample is depressed by the predominance of business organizations. There are, however, interesting discrepancies across the various kinds of women's organizations in the willingness to use protest as a tactic. Considering both the greater feminist commitment among the women's rights groups and the well-publicized battles within NOW over the relative merits of protests and more traditional modes of seeking influence, it might be expected that the women's rights groups would be especially likely to take to the streets. On the contrary, respondents from the women's rights organizations were less likely than those from either the occupational groups or the caucuses to report using protest tactics. (In fact, all of the respondents from unions indicated that their organizations protest.) This finding was confirmed by the responses to another item. Respondents were asked to describe their organizations' use of protests and demonstrations: Six of the seventy-four respondents who replied indicated that their organizations take the initiative in sponsoring demonstrations, of which five were from unions and only one from a women's rights group.

In spite of the discrepancies that emerge from Table 15.6, the similarity between women's organizations and other kinds of organizations is the dominant pattern. In addition, women's organizations focus their energies on the same institutional targets as other organizations. (See Appendix Table 15.B for complete data.) Respondents were asked to evaluate the importance of Congress, the White House, executive agencies, and the courts as targets of organizational activity. For all kinds of organizations, Congress is the most important focus of effort; the courts the least. (Not surprisingly, respondents from women's rights organizations were most likely to report that the courts are a very important target of activity.) For the executive branch the pattern is somewhat different. Respondents from business organizations were particularly likely to consider the executive branch a very important focus of activity—a pattern that presumably reflects both the special relevance of the substance of the regulatory process for business and the Reagan administration's hospitality to business organizations.

Appendix Table 15.B   Institutional Targets of Organization Activity

Recognizing that the focus of your activity may change from issue to issue or even over the life span of a single issue, in general, how important is [each institution] as a focus of your organization's activity: very important, somewhat important, or not very important?

	Congress	White House	Executive Agencies	Courts
All Organizations				
Washington representatives study	89%	55%	65%	22%
Women's organizations	86	35	39	19
Citizens', Civil Rights, and Social-Welfare Groups				
Washington representatives study	91	42	42	33
Women's rights groups	83	47	35	41
Women's Caucuses	74	26	42	11
Occupational Groups				
Washington representatives study	87	42	64	21
Women's groups	95	24	43	10
Business Organizations				
Corporations	94	67	68	18
Trade and other business associations	86	60	79	17

Note: Percentages are those responding "very important."

Working Together

Several chapters in this volume discuss disagreements among women—within the mass public, within the women's movement, and between the women's movement and women opposed to the ERA and abortion. Such conflicts are also common within the organizations included in this survey. Fully 72 percent of the respondents, spread more or less evenly across the various kinds of organizations, indicated either that over the past few years there had been issues that had generated conflict or differences of opinion among the rank-and-file members or within the leadership of the organization or that there are groups or factions within the organization that tend to be in conflict with each other over and over again. The bases for such conflict are diverse indeed—including, for example, disputes over political tactics (15 percent) and over internal organizational issues (11 percent). The most common source of disagreement, however, is political issues, with 56 percent of the respondents mentioning some policy issue as the source of dissension. Such disagreements seem to be especially common within the caucuses (67 percent) and considerably less frequent within the women's rights organizations (38 percent). In addition, a number of the respondents from occupational groups (38 percent) mentioned conflict over some issue peculiar to the occupation that the members of the organization share.

Disagreement over women's issues in particular is relatively common. Thirty-two percent of the respondents mentioned internal conflict over a women's issue—most commonly, abortion (17 percent). However, in disputes over such issues the source of contention is often not what position the organization should take, but whether the organization should take a position at all. For example, in the organizations where the respondent reported difference of opinion over the ERA (15 percent), the question was more likely to be whether to depart from the usual agenda of concerns by becoming active on behalf of the ERA than whether to weigh in on the side of the pro- or anti-ERA forces.

In contrast to these indications of dissension within organizations there is compelling evidence of extensive cooperation among organizations of women.[41] Like all organizations, one way women's organizations attempt to maximize their policy influence is by joining forces with other organizations, a strategy that is consistent with an ideology that stresses cooperation over competition. As we saw in Table 15.6, 90 percent of the respondents in the Washington Representatives Study and 91 percent of the respondents in the women's organizations survey indicated that their organizations enter into coalitions with other organizations. Whether because they are committed ideologically to cooperation, because they are smaller and less well-heeled financially, or because they have not achieved as high a level of insider status, this is a particularly important activity to organizations of women. When asked to choose the three activities on the list of 27 that consume the greatest share of organizational time and resources, 38 percent of the respondents from women's organizations—as opposed to 20 percent of the respondents in the earlier study—indicated that joining coalitions consumes time and resources. As a matter of fact, no other technique was cited more frequently by the respondents from women's organizations. (In the earlier survey, joining coalitions ranked sixth in terms of the number of respondents, indicating that it is a time- and resource-consuming activity.)

In order to understand this cooperative behavior, let us consider the replies to questions in both surveys asking respondents to name any organizations they consider to be their allies—or their antagonists—on most issues. (Data on which this discussion is based can be found in Appendix Table 15.C.)[42] In general, all organizations tend to find their allies from within their own community: corporations tend to cite business organizations as allies, and unions to cite labor organizations. This is true of women's organizations as well. Seventy-five percent of the respondents in the survey of women's organizations named other women's organizations as consistent allies. (Of these, 4 percent also indicated that they have opponents among women's organizations.) Fully 94 percent of the respondents from women's rights groups specified allies but no antagonists from among other women's organizations. New Right organizations were the most frequently mentioned foes. Forty-two percent of the respondents, including 67 percent of those from women's rights organizations, named New Right organizations as antagonists; in fact, 29 percent of the respondents and 44 percent of those from women's rights organizations specifically designated the one New Right group in the sample as an opponent.

Table 15.7, which gives results for several items about coalition building scattered throughout the interview, amplifies these findings. Part A contains the figures for the proportion of respondents from different kinds of organizations representing women who spontaneously named other women's organizations in answer to the open-ended inquiry about the organization's consistent allies. At another point in the interview respondents were asked whether, in building coalitions, the organization was likely to make special efforts to join forces with other organizations representing women or whether the organization would be equally likely to work with any organization sharing its point of view (part B). Finally, respondents were shown a list of all of the organizations in the sample and asked to specify how often their organization cooperated in joint efforts with each one. Part D gives, for each organization category, the average number of organizations on the list with which respondents indicated they frequently or sometimes engage in joint efforts.

Several themes emerge from Table 15.7. First, it is clear that these organizations do not confine their coalitional activities to organizations representing women. On the contrary, 56 percent of all respondents indicated that they would work with any organization sharing a com-

Appendix Table 15.C Patterns of Competition and Cooperation Among Organized Interests

	Business Organizations	Labor Organizations	Citizens', Civil Rights, and Social-Welfare Groups	Women's Organizations	New Right Organizations
Women's Organizations Indicating They Have:					
Allies only	3%	22%	36%	71%	1%
Both allies and antagonists	0	0	0	4	1
Antagonists only	22	4	1	3	42
Neither allies nor antagonists	75	74	63	22	55
	100%	100%	100%	100%	99%
Citizens', Civil Rights, and Social-Welfare Groups Indicating They Have:					
Allies only	0%	15%	67%		
Both allies and antagonists	6	6	3		
Antagonists only	58	3	9		
Neither allies nor antagonists	36	76	21		
	100%	100%	100%		
Women's Rights Groups Indicating They Have:					
Allies only	0%	22%	33%	94%	0%
Both allies and antagonists	0	0	0	0	0
Antagonists only	22	0	0	0	67
Neither allies nor antagonists	78	78	67	6	33
	100%	100%	100%	100%	100%

Unions Indicating They Have:

Allies only	0%	79%	45%		
Both allies and antagonists	16	5	0		
Antagonists only	53	0	0		
Neither allies nor antagonists	32	16	55		
	101%	100%	100%		

Women's Unions Indicating They Have:

Allies only	0%	100%	90%	60%	0%
Both allies and antagonists	0	0	0	0	0
Antagonists only	80	0	0	0	60
Neither allies nor antagonists	20	0	10	40	40
	100%	100%	100%	100%	100%

Corporations Indicating They Have:

Allies only	66%	2%	0%		
Both allies and antagonists	23	11	6		
Antagonists only	0	19	48		
Neither allies nor antagonists	11	68	46		
	100%	100%	100%		

Trade and Other Business Associations Indicating They Have:

Allies only	63%	12%	0%		
Both allies and antagonists	23	2	0		
Antagonists only	9	23	36		
Neither allies nor antagonists	5	63	64		
	100%	100%	100%		

Note: Percentages may not add to 100 because of rounding.

Table 15.7 Coalition Building Among Women's Organizations

Question	All Women's Organizations	Women's Rights Groups	Caucuses	Occupational Groups	Other
A. Are there any organizations you consider to be your allies on most issues? Any organizations you consider to be your opponents on most issues?					
Names consistent allies and no opponents among women's organizations	71%	94%	79%	52%	61%
B. In building coalitions with other organizations on a policy issue, is your organization likely to make special efforts to join forces with other organizations representing women, or is your organization equally likely to work with any organization that shares its point of view?					
Women's organizations	21%	31%	33%	10%	12%
Some of each	24	38	6	24	29
Any organization sharing point of view	56	31	61	67	59
	101%	100%	100%	101%	100%

C. Combined results of A and B

Women's organizations	21%	31%	33%	10%	12%
Some of each	24	38	6	24	29
Any organization—allies among women's organizations	31	25	44	29	24
Any organization—no such allies	25	6	17	38	35
	101%	100%	100%	101%	100%

D. How often do you cooperate in joint efforts with each organization [on this list]: frequently, sometimes, almost never?

Average number of women's organizations cooperated with "frequently" or "sometimes"	30	42	28	23	29

Note: Percentages may not add to 100 because of rounding.

mon viewpoint, and 80 percent indicated that they would do so at least some of the time. (Fully two thirds of the respondents in each organization category gave such replies.) Still, these data indicate that while they do not cooperate exclusively, they do cooperate extensively with other women's organizations. Within this general tendency to join forces with other organizations representing women, there are substantial differences among the various kinds of organizations. On all these measures the respondents from women's rights groups were the most likely—and those from the occupational groups the least likely—to indicate that they ally with other women's organizations. The figures in part D were further broken down to show the frequency of joint activity with various kinds of organizations of women. This analysis indicated the centrality of the women's rights groups to coalitional efforts: Women's rights groups seem not to confine their joint efforts to other women's rights groups; rather, they seem willing to work with all kinds of organizations representing women. Respondents from women's rights groups were more likely to mention caucuses as frequent or sometime partners than were respondents from the caucuses; similarly, respondents from women's rights groups were more likely to mention occupational groups as partners than were the respondents from the occupational groups.

With the exception of the hostility between many of the organizations in the survey and the one New Right group (as well as the prolife position taken by the National Council of Catholic Women, an organization that is otherwise active on many women's issues), there is evidence of extensive cooperation and very little antagonism among the organizations in the study. However, this is not evidence that organizations of women march in a phalanx on all issues affecting women. Rather, the pattern is one of partial mobilization, issue-specific alliances in which some of the organizations are active while the majority sit on the sidelines. And, as Mansbridge's chapter in this volume demonstrates, such joint ventures may unite somewhat uneasily organizations having common goals but very different styles.[43]

Conclusion

It is commonplace to inquire whether the contemporary women's movement is dead. This chapter makes clear that although the second wave women's movement has been transformed and institutionalized, it is not yet time to write its epitaph. One legacy of the movement politics of the 1960s and 1970s is a vigorous presence in Washington pressure politics, a diverse group of nearly 90 organizations representing women in the capital. Considering that this is an arena of mainstream political activity in a city dominated by a hostile administration, these organizations could be considered a feminist presence in Washington—in spite of variations on measures of feminism from organization to organization and across different kinds of organizations. For several reasons—their slender financial resources, the antagonism of the Reagan administration to the causes that many of them champion, and the discrimination women face in government relations—these organizations of women operate at a disadvantage. The first two of these burdens are shared with organizations such as citizens', civil rights, and social-welfare groups; the last, of course, is borne disproportionately by organizations representing women.

By and large, organizations of women use the same techniques and train their efforts on the same institutional targets as other organizations active in Washington. Like other organizations, they attempt to multiply the effect of their activities by forming alliances with like-minded organizations; and like other organizations, they find such mutually interested partners within their own community. In short, one way that organizations of women seek influence in Washington is by allying with other organizations of women.

The strategy of acting like the boys while joining forces with women is not unique to Washington pressure politics. Women legislators seem to adopt a similar strategy—as do women who are attempting to make their way in academic departments, law firms, and many other institutions long dominated by men. A question much discussed both among feminists and in the media is whether, as more and more opportunities become available to women in what were once exclusively male preserves, women must simply act like men or whether they can enjoy the fruits of these opportunities without sacrificing a distinctive style. The experiences of advocates for women in Washington pressure politics suggest that wherever they are a small minority lacking critical resources (money, tenure, partnership, seniority, whatever matters for the institution in question) and operating in an arena with a long history and deeply established folkways, women are in no position to write, or rewrite, the rules. If they wish to participate in pressure politics—and not to participate would have undeniable consequences for the way in which the federal government treats women—those who represent women in Washington have little choice but to follow rules they did not set. In fact, the way policymakers treat women in government affairs may dictate that these women have less autonomy than their male counterparts in defining a distinctive style. As mentioned earlier, a number of the respondents in the survey indicated that they felt constrained by their gender to work harder in order to be taken seriously. Under the circumstances, to follow rules constructed by men while supporting other women on behalf of issues affecting women may be the most instrumental response.

Appendix 15.1

The 89 organizations in the original sample were located as follows. Using the 1984 *Washington Representatives* directory, a list was compiled composed of all organizations having "women" in their names. A small number of organizations obviously composed of women (for example, Future Homemakers of America) and organizations described in the directory as women's organizations (for example, Project on Equal Education Rights) were added. Among these organizations was one New Right organization that makes a self-conscious claim to represent women—although it clearly does so in a manner very different from the other organizations in the sample. Other New Right organizations—for example, the Conservative Caucus—were excluded because they make no such claim, even though the substance of their positions on issues like the ERA or affirmative action might accord completely with the positions taken by the one New Right group.

To locate the occupational organizations, census data were used to compile a list of occupations dominated by women. Then, the *Washington Representatives* directory was used to locate all the organizations that might represent such occupations in Washington. These organizations were telephoned to ascertain the proportion of women within the membership of the organization. The twenty-five occupational groups with a majority of women were included; the small number without were not.

On the basis of the dual criteria of self-conscious representation of women or a majority of women among members, it was decided to include pro-choice groups but to exclude pro-life groups. Unlike pro-life groups, reproductive rights groups do claim to be champions of the rights of women. Furthermore, 63 percent of their members are women. With respect to the criterion of gender composition of membership, telephone calls to the pro-life organizations listed in the *Washington Representatives* directory elicited the response that the organizations did not have even approximate information about the proportion of women among their members. Hence, there was no way to ascertain whether pro-life groups are organizations composed primarily of women.

Respondents in 76 of the original 89 organizations were eventually interviewed. Seven refused to be interviewed—a refusal rate of 7.9 percent, which compares favorably with the refusal rate of 12.5 percent in the 1981 Washington Representatives Study. Of the remaining six organizations, four had either closed their Washington offices or gone out of business entirely, and two could not be reached after repeated attempts.

Notes

The research on which this chapter is based was supported by a grant from the Russell Sage Foundation.

I am grateful to Rosalie Whelan, who supervised the interviewing, and Eleanor Byrne, who assisted with data processing. I would also like to thank the editors and other authors of this volume as well as Anne Costain and Joyce Gelb for their helpful comments on earlier drafts.

1. For example, in their discussion of the various organizations that lobbied actively on trade issues during the 1950s, Bauer, Pool, and Dexter (1963) entitle the chapter devoted to the one organization that was not narrowly self-interested "The Ladies of the League."

2. See Bentley (1908); Truman (1952); Latham (1952); and Dahl (1956).

3. See, for example, Schattschneider (1960); Olson (1971 [1965]); McConnell (1966); and Lowi (1969).

4. Among the recent studies are Moe (1980); Hayes (1981); Wilson (1981); Chubb (1983); Walker (1983); Berry (1984); Smith (1984); McFarland (1984); Salisbury (1984); and Laumann and Knoke (1987).

5. Freeman (1975) and Costain (1980, 1981) discuss the emergence of organizations representing women in Washington. Furthermore, Costain (1978); Boles (1979); Tinker (1983), esp. Fraser and Kolker essays; Gelb and Palley (1987), esp. chap. 3; and Mansbridge (1986) discuss the organizations representing women in the context of analyzing the politics of particular policy issues. In addition, Palley (1987) places special emphasis upon organizations representing women in her discussion of women and politics in the 1980s.

6. For a discussion of the peculiar character of associational life in American democracy, see Handlin and Handlin (1961), chap. 5. Neocorporatist analysts of European democracies tend to dispute that organized interests are of greater importance in American politics. See, for example, Schmitter and Lehmbruch (1979) and Lehmbruch and Schmitter, eds. (1982). For a discussion of this perspective, see Schlozman and Tierney (1986), pp. 392–394.

7. On Samuel Ward, see Schriftgiesser (1951), p. 14. On the Anti-Saloon

League, see Odegard (1928), p. 76. Herring (1929) also contains a historical account of lobbying as traditionally practiced. For a discussion of the historical precedents for much of what is considered new in contemporary pressure activity, see Schlozman and Tierney (1983), pp. 363–366.

8. For a discussion of the recent explosion in organizational activity in Washington, see Schlozman and Tierney (1983).

9. This theme is explored in Lipsky (1970), chaps. 1, 6, and 7.

10. Boles (1982).

11. Edelman (1964), chap. 2. A common pattern in American politics is that legislative victory is eroded by lackadaisical implementation by the executive branch or hostile interpretation by the courts.

12. On the case of feminists in Sweden, see Kelman (1984).

13. For an elaboration of the perspective presented here, see Schlozman and Tierney (1986), pp. 399–405.

14. On this theme, see Dahlerup (1987) and Katzenstein (1987), as well as the other essays in these edited volumes.

15. Palley (1987), p. 152, makes an especially strong assertion to this effect in her statement that "interest groups in the women's movement have profoundly influenced the policy process."

16. Freeman (1975), pp. 177–190.

17. Gelb and Palley (1987), chap. 4.

18. One of the principal positions taken by victorious candidate Eleanor Smeal in the hard-fought 1985 election for the presidency of NOW was the need to concentrate on tactics of confrontation. See Lemley (1985). Although they do not discuss feminist politics per se, Piven and Cloward (1977) make a strong case that participation in mainstream organized interest politics is not helpful to movements for social change.

19. The term "Washington representative"—one that has considerable currency these days, presumably because it suggests a broader range of professionally related activities and greater professional distinction than "lobbyist"—is potentially confusing. It denotes not a member of the House or any elected official, but rather any one of the government affairs experts who staff or are retained by organized private interests in the capital.

20. It should be noted that this research design neglects many aspects of women's involvement in pressure politics. First of all, extensive pressure activity is found in the state capitals—where, for example, the battle over the Equal Rights Amendment was fought. In addition, the women who represent organizations of women having offices in Washington constitute only a small proportion of the women government affairs professionals in national politics. Many more, of whom there are growing numbers advocating causes ranging from clean air to manufacturers of candy bars, work in the Washington offices of other kinds of organizations—corporations, trade associations, consumer groups, and the like—or in the law, public relations,

and political consulting firms that serve the government relations needs of organizations that do not maintain offices in the capital.

21. Close, ed. (1984). Because respondents were promised that neither their names nor the names of their organizations would be mentioned without their permission, it is impossible to give a complete list of the organizations in the survey. All organizations mentioned did grant such permission.

22. In making coding decisions, an attempt was made to place ambiguous cases into the residual category and, thus, to keep the other categories as pure as possible. One particularly difficult decision was how to treat reproductive rights organizations. Although it is possible to think of them as women's rights organizations, it seemed safer to place them in the "other" category. To test this decision, however, all the data were run again coding the reproductive rights organizations as women's rights groups. There was little consistent or appreciable effect. With the exception of a single variable (the percentage of women among members) the values on all variables for reproductive rights groups lie somewhere between those for women's rights groups and those for organizations in the "other" category. The overall results as reported in the text, however, remain unchanged no matter how the reproductive rights groups are coded.

23. For a description of the technique used to generate the earlier sample, see Schlozman and Tierney (1986), pp. 411–413.

24. A final potential source of noncomparability may, in fact, be more tractable. Four years separate the two studies, during which time Washington changed. Washington in the Reagan era was clearly less hospitable to organizations representing women than it had been under previous administrations. However, as discussed below, data from the earlier study indicate that the implications of the 1980 election for pressure politics in Washington had already become obvious by the fall of 1981. Hence, it seems that the time period separating the two surveys may be less of an impediment to making systematic comparisons than might originally have been thought.

25. See Milbrath (1959), p. 372.

26. As originally drawn, the sample included 500 organizations. However, it was impossible to discern the sex of twenty of the individuals listed representing eleven of the organizations.

27. These issues are probed in Schattschneider (1960), chap. 2; Dahl (1982), pp. 82–85; Schlozman and Tierney (1986), chap. 4. See Schlozman and Tierney (pp. 73–74) for a discussion of the extent to which men are represented in the pressure system, either by organizations specifically established to represent their interests or by their dominant role in the unions and business and professional associations that form the preponderance of the organizations active in Washington.

28. The figures in Table 15.3 (for professional staff) refer to the gender composition of these organizations' Washington offices only. Thus, they omit branch offices or organizational headquarters outside Washington, if any.

The careful reader might note that in Table 15.2 all of the Washington representatives listed as representing women's organizations are female, while an average of only 90 percent of the professional staff of the 76 organizations in this study are women. Two factors account for the apparent discrepancy. First, the *Washington Representatives* directory does not pretend to be an inclusive listing of all professional staff. Rather, the directory lists staff concentrating on government relations and may exclude those whose central concern is, for example, fund raising or membership education. In addition, in any comprehensive categorization of Washington-based organizations, the occupational groups in our sample—which average 74 percent female on their Washington staffs—would be considered unions or professional associations. As indicated above, they have been included here because a majority of their members are women.

29. Because it ultimately must involve addressing the thorny issue of how we define what is in the best interests of an individual or group, the question of what women's interests are—and, therefore, what is a women's issue—is an extremely complex one. (For an abstract discussion of the nature of political interests and a review of the relevant literature, see Schlozman and Tierney 1986, chap. 2.) In practice, however, it was not difficult to distinguish between two kinds of organizational policy goals. When the policy sought would affect a collectivity defined by a characteristic (for example, occupation) other than gender, then the issue was not classified as a women's issue—even if the group in question is predominantly female. For example, the respondent from the Amalgamated Clothing and Textile Workers Union cited job safety regulation and restrictions on imports as important policy issues; the respondent from the Home Economics Education Association mentioned federal funding for vocational, consumer, and homemaker education. In neither case are the presumed beneficiaries women per se, but in both cases the group is disproportionately female. Still, these were not coded as women's issues. In contrast, when the category of beneficiaries was women—or some subgroup of women such as ex-wives or minority women—then the issue was considered a women's issue.

30. This list raises the same knotty theoretical question of what constitutes a "women's issue" referred to above. In actual practice, however, the list—which was constructed after extensive consultation—gave respondents no difficulty.

31. The remaining organizations all show some kind of mixed pattern—support for feminist goals and at least one women's issue among the top three policy priorities or a moderate level of activity on a range of women's issues.

32. The figures for the organizations of women have been adjusted slightly to make them comparable to those for the catalog of organizations having offices in Washington as of 1981.

33. Unfortunately, the small number of such organizations in the earlier Washington Representatives Study renders impossible analysis of these categories separately.

34. Gelb and Palley (1987), p. 3, make a similar point about the professionalism of feminist advocates in Washington.

35. These figures mask at least one anomaly: that 85 percent of the respondents from trade and other business associations have worked for the federal government. Otherwise, the figures vary within a much narrower range, from a low of 38 percent for the occupational groups in the women's organizations survey to a high of 56 percent for the women's rights groups. If trade and other business associations are omitted from the calculations, 49 percent of the respondents in the Washington Representatives Study reported that they had worked for the federal government.

36. For an elaboration of the argument summarized here, see Schlozman and Tierney (1986), chap. 15.

37. See Peterson and Walker (1985); and Schlozman and Tierney (1986), pp. 202–206.

38. Unfortunately, these items were not included in the earlier survey. It would have been useful to get the reactions both of a larger number of men and of women representing a greater range of organizations. Thirty-two of the 175 respondents in the earlier survey were women.

39. The replies to an analogous set of questions about the behavior of *women* in government lend additional perspective to these findings. Respondents were also asked whether, in their dealings with Washington representatives, female policymakers in the government treat women differently from men (and, if so, how). A majority of the female respondents, 53 percent, indicated that women in government were more supportive of women in government relations; 35 percent said that it made no difference or that it depended upon the circumstances or the particular policymaker; only 12 percent said that they were less supportive of women Washington representatives.

40. Four of the male respondents represent small professional associations, a fifth represents a large union of white-collar workers, and the sixth represents a reproductive rights group.

41. The observations of those who have studied the policy controversies surrounding women's issues lend strong support to the conclusions in this section about the importance of coalitional efforts among organizations of women. See, in particular, Gelb and Palley (1987); Palley (1987); and the case studies of policy controversies in Tinker (1983).

42. An aggregate category includes both general references to that category as well as mentions of specific organizations falling under that rubric. For example, the "business" category includes general references to "corporations," "trade associations," or "business," as well as references to particular organizations such as the American Petroleum Institute or the Business Roundtable. For a further explanation of these coding categories and amplification of the results, see Schlozman and Tierney (1986), pp. 283–284.
    For the purposes of this analysis, unions and professional associations

having a majority of women among their members were categorized as unions and professional associations, respectively, rather than as women's organizations. In addition, the one New Right group in the survey was not classified as a women's organization.

43. Although the number of male respondents is small—and, therefore, any conclusions must be extremely tentative—there is evidence that the coalitional activity of organizations representing women is not merely alliance building among the mutually interested, but sisterhood. The six men in the sample were much less likely than women from the same kinds of organizations to report either that their organizations are sympathetic to feminist goals or active on women's issues or that their organizations tend to form alliances with other organizations representing women. Indeed, when the occupational groups represented by men are removed from the analysis, the occupational groups are no longer distinctive with respect to the various measures of feminism in Tables 15.3 and 15.7. In short, although there are only a handful of men in the sample on which to base such a conclusion, it seems to matter whether an organization is represented by a man or a woman: Organizations of women represented by men are on several measures—ideology, agenda, and propensity to join forces with other organizations of women—demonstrably less feminist.

16

The Mobilization of Members in Women's Associations

David Knoke

Women's associations constitute a small proportion, perhaps 75 to 90 groups, of the 13,000 national associations.[1] The associations studied in this chapter are formal organizations, with predominantly female memberships, that take explicit stands favoring improved women's status and opportunities in the larger society. They seek social and legal changes on issues including employment practices and pay equity, job training, health and reproductive rights, family law, racial and educational discrimination, and general governmental policies. Although some women's associations—such as the League of Women Voters and the American Association of University Women—have been active for many decades, many—such as the National Organization for Women (NOW) and the Women's Equity Action League (WEAL)—are outgrowths of the social ferment of the 1960s and 1970s movements for equity and change.[2]

As newcomers to the expanded pressure group system,[3] the women's organizations face many of the membership mobilization, resource acquisition, and collective decision-making problems that older associations solved. Using data from a survey of U.S. national association members, this chapter examines members' reasons for joining and mobilization processes for collective action. Members of women's organizations are compared with members of professional and recreational associations. The six women's associations whose members were surveyed are politically liberal or reformist, perhaps broadly feminist, but radical in neither rhetoric nor tactics. My focus on individual members complements Schlozman's chapter, which considers how women's organizations operate within the Washington interest group scene.

Political Mobilization

American associations provide significant contexts for the political participation of their members.[4] Survey and case studies[5] of specific organizations[6] consistently show that organizational involvement is intimately tied to participation in larger political arenas, apparently because of an association's internal political activities. In a 1967 national sample of adult Americans, Sidney Verba and Norman Nie found that 62 percent of these respondents belonged to at least one organization (and 39 percent to two or more), 40 percent were active members, and 31 percent belonged to a group in which political discussions took place.[7] In a value-added process, the combination of active membership and exposure to political stimuli—even within such manifestly nonpolitical groups as hobby clubs—greatly boosted participation in conventional political activities (voting, campaigning for candidates, working on community problems). The relationships seemed to be robust, independent of socioeconomic status and personal propensities toward activism.[8]

An association's capacity to stimulate political activity appears to operate through several processes that bridge internal organization structures and external environment.[9] With increased interpersonal contacts that extend beyond kin and workplace networks to a diversity of people including political activists, organizations raise the salience of public affairs and political issues and newcomers become aware of the efficacy of political action as a solution to group problems. The organization is a micro-democracy in which face-to-face resolution of controversies reinforces participatory values and norms.[10] Because of the small scale and voluntary nature of many associations—especially those with local branches and chapters—many members gain valuable experience and confidence in leadership tasks. Thus, an association can serve as a springboard to subsequent engagement in adversary party politics. Finally, when the association's goals require frequent interaction with government authorities, its mobilization efforts will draw many individuals into a variety of political activities, ranging from letter-writing to visiting public officials to demonstrating.[11]

The analyses reported below begin with earlier investigations showing that organizations are important to their members' participation in the larger political system. Much less is known about how organizations mobilize their members for collective action. Relatively little empirical attention has focused on the importance of incentives and decision-making procedures for mobilizing member participation. American pressure group politics comes from a strong voluntary action tradition rooted in eighteenth and nineteenth century individualism.[12] But in the modern political context, with the rise of large-scale powerful institutional actors,[13] the political vitality and effectiveness of mass membership associations depend more than ever upon the ability to attract members and to secure their continuing involvement. The next section discusses a political economy model that is useful for framing research questions about collective action in organizations: Why do people join these associations? How important are different types of incentives? What is the internal distribution of power and influence over organizational decision-making? And how do these various factors affect members' participation and commitment to their organizations? Data from the association survey provide some answers to these questions.

The Political Economy Model

The research reported in this chapter was guided by a theoretical framework, elaborated in greater detail elsewhere.[14] This political economy model of associations emphasizes two intertwined activity systems—the incentive system and the internal polity—which involve two questions: How does the organization acquire sufficient resources for collective use, and how does it reach decisions on the allocation of these resources? Individuals must decide whether and how many personal resources (financial and participatory) to commit to an organization. An association must collectively decide how to use its pooled resources to further its internal and external goals. At two analytic levels (the individual and the organizational), these dual decisions are the source of this political economy model.

INCENTIVE SYSTEM   For decades, scholars have debated about people's motives for joining and contributing to collective action organizations. The controversy centers around whether organizations must offer valuable private inducements or whether they can expect their members to commit their time and energy for selfless, altruistic reasons. Incentives are sets of benefits offered to organization members in exchange for contributions to the group.[15] Some theories argue that people respond primarily to selective incentives—rewards that are not shared with outsiders. For example, members join and pay dues to an association only if they receive benefits such as journal subscriptions, group insurance, social parties, and assistance with job searches that are not offered to nonmembers.[16] Other theories argue that people can be motivated to join and contribute to groups whose main incentives are the production of public goods—benefits also available to persons who are not members of the organization.[17] For example, noncontributors to a women's rights association cannot be excluded from enjoying access to legal abortions or from the benefits of an Equal Rights Amendment enacted through the association's political efforts.[18]

Some previous research suggests that organization members may be mobilized by both types of incentives.[19] A person may enjoy the selective goods offered by an association and also be attracted to the nonselective benefits of public goods produced through the organization's collective efforts. Further, some people may find that the very effort of helping to create a public good is satisfying in itself, which is a selective incentive aspect of public goods production. Obviously, not all members are equally predisposed to respond to each type of incentive. Within some organizations and among some individual members, public goods incentives may carry greater weight than selective inducements. In other associations, direct service benefits or social activities may be more appealing to members than such public goods as influencing women's rights legislation. While some authors, such as Mansbridge (in this volume), believe that political organizations must specialize in their incentive offerings, associations need not restrict their inducements to a single kind of incentive.

INTERNAL POLITY   Using incentives to gain control over members' resource contributions is only half the function of an association's political economy. The internal polity must also make collective decisions about how these organizational resources should be spent for different objectives, such as legislative lobbying or more direct services to the membership. The extent to which leaders' and ordinary members' interests are taken into account varies among organizations. In some groups, a small leadership clique completely dominates all major decisions (American unions, such as the Teamsters, are notorious oligarchies), while other organizations maintain elaborate procedures to foster extensive membership inputs at every stage of the decision-making process (the League of Women Voters is known for its participatory democracy). An association's distribution of influence affects a member's willingness to become involved in activities that are essential to achieving the organization's goals.[20] Students of organizational democracy suggest that if decision-making power is more widespread, rather than relegated to a few, then members are more likely to become strongly committed to the collective decisions and hence to be more enthusiastic and supportive of the association's efforts.[21]

Scattered evidence suggests that internal political structures shape both member mobilization and resource contribution utilization.[22] Associations that encourage members' involvement in collective decisions usually reap the gains of a heavily involved and highly committed membership. But organizations that prevent or constrict members' involvement in internal politics, encourage apathy and detachment, at best, or generate hostility and withdrawal of contributions, at worst.

Research Questions

We compare incentive systems and internal polities of women's associations with those of professional societies and recreational groups. The women's organizations closely resemble politically oriented social movement organizations, while other associations are routinized service-oriented organizations with less salient social change objectives. Consequently, the women's associations' incentive systems should be more diverse and the governance structures more democratic, as they attempt to stimulate their mass memberships' involvement in organizational affairs. The professional and recreational groups depend more on leadership activities, hence they require less diverse inducements and less participatory governance structures. The following research questions guided our comparisons of these groups:

1. What is the range and diversity of selective and public goods incentives that attract members to join and become involved in their associations? Do women's association members tend to have interests in a more heterogeneous mixture of incentives?

2. What are the distributions of decision-making characteristics of associations? Do the women's groups exhibit more decentralized and democratic politics?

3. What is the relative importance among selective incentives and public goods incentives for inducing member involvement in their associations? Are women's group members more likely than members of other types of associations to participate because of public goods incentives?

4. What impact do the decision-making structures have on members' participation and commitment? Are women's organization members more likely than members of the other groups to be involved because their groups' political structures are democratic?

The answers require multivariate comparisons of the members of women's associations with those of other types of collective action organizations.

Data and Measures

The data come from the National Association Study (NAS), a project to investigate the political economies of American associations. A list of all U.S. national women's associations was compiled from the most recent editions of *Washington Representatives* and the *Encyclopedia of Associations*. These 86 organizations were ranked by the reported membership size. A sample of eight associations was selected, proportional to membership size. Leaders of these eight associations were asked permission to mail self-administered questionnaires to a sample of their membership. Two organizations—NOW and WEAL—both declined participation without stating the reasons for their decisions. We have no evidence that the members of these two organizations are similar to or differ from those of the cooperating groups. Confidentiality was promised to the six participating organizations and their members, so that names and specific details cannot be revealed here. However, sketches are offered below to suggest the general attributes of these groups.

Associations A, B, and C have more than 100,000 members each, are structured into state and local chapters, and hold regular meetings. These periodic opportunities for face-to-face contact permit members to engage in networking for social and professional contacts. Each organization maintains national headquarters in Washington, D.C., with a dozen or more staff members engaged in member service and lobbying activities. All three groups offer their members a diversity of services, ranging from research and data dissemination to group travel plans. In addition, they sponsor legislative action efforts. Their members are mainly middle class. Associations A and C have specific occupational and educational requirements for membership.

Associations D, E, and F are much smaller, with D and F having only a few thousand members each and all three having small staffs. Only F is headquartered in Washington. D draws its members mainly from one large urban area. E serves an occupational clientele with interests in advancing to managerial positions through leadership training. Associations D and F are not occupation-specific, but attract persons with interests in altering the economic and legal conditions of women in the workplace. Given their small resource bases, these groups provide fewer direct services to their members, although periodic workshops and training programs are offered. All six associations use legislative lobbying activities or litigation to pursue their political and legal objectives.

In 1986 eight-page questionnaires were mailed to 3,900 members of the six associations, selecting every *k*th member on the current mailing list after a random start. Larger samples (800 to 1,000) were drawn from the larger organizations than from the smaller ones (400 to 500). After a second mailing to nonrespondents, a total of 2,208 usable questionnaires was obtained, which, after deletion of improperly listed addresses, represents a 58 percent response rate.[23] The questionnaires consisted mainly of closed-ended (forced-choice) items that required respondents to check off specific categories reflecting frequency of behaviors or attitudinal orientations. Central to the present analysis are three types of measures:

1. Six reasons why members originally joined their organizations, and a checklist of the importance of 28 incentives.
2. Perceptions of decision-making influence by various groups within the organization and respondents' interest and activity in six recent issues that were identified by national organization leaders.
3. Participation in association activities, contributions of time and money, and overall commitment to the organization.

Unfortunately, space limitations prohibit detailed descriptions of specific scale items and their methods of construction.

Throughout the analysis, the women's association members are compared with 6,538 members of 29 other U.S. national associations in the National Association Study (NAS).[24] These groups fall into four categories: 12 professional societies with political goals, 4 recreational organizations with political goals, 8 professional societies, and 5 recreational groups without political objectives. This classification was based on telephone interviews in which organizational informants indicated whether "influencing public policy decisions of the government" was a major goal or moderate goal versus a minor goal or not a goal of the association (only 4 of the 29 informants chose the lowest category). As the women's organizations all have substantial commitments to public policy influence, their most appropriate comparison is with the two professional and recreational categories that also have substantial political objectives.

Incentives

Association members' interests in organizational incentives were measured by two sets of survey questions: The first set asked about the

Table 16.1   Reasons for Decision to Join Organization

	Type of Association				
Reasons for Joining	Women's (N = 2,208)	Political Professional (N = 2,348)	Political Recreational (N = 1,242)	Nonpolitical Professional (N = 1,531)	Nonpolitical Recreational (N = 1,417)
Lobbying or political activities	72%	46%	42%	26%	30%
Social or recreational activities	63	31	53	37	60
Direct services offered to members	59	72	51	66	76
Job-related	47	92	11	86	39
Expected to join by other people	27	42	18	39	24
Membership was a gift	3	2	6	2	3

importance of reasons for joining; the second asked about the importance to the respondent of current activities. The specific items in each set were chosen, on the basis of theory and previous research, to span a wide variety of inducements, including both selective goods and public goods incentives. The public goods incentives referred to such organizational actions as legislative lobbying, emphasis on general principles or goals, and public education programs. Selective incentives included social opportunities for members, the provision of information, material goods, and occupational or career benefits. The memberships of different types of associations exhibited distinct patterns of interest in these various incentives.

Respondents were asked how important each of six reasons was in their original decisions to join their associations. Respondents could check as many as applied, indicating "major reason," "minor reason," or "unimportant reason." As Table 16.1 shows, for all respondents only about 3 percent received their memberships as a gift, but the other five choices showed substantial variation. "Direct services offered to members by the organization" was the most frequently given reason (67 percent of all respondents, and a majority of each type of organization). Great differences occurred among the associations across the other reasons. Professional society members were more likely to cite job-related and others' expectations as reasons. Social-recreational activities were mentioned most frequently by the women's association members (63 percent), followed by majorities of both types of recreational groups. For a large majority in the women's associations (72 percent), lobbying or political activities was a major or minor reason for joining. But for other associations, especially both nonpolitical categories, the percentage was much smaller.

Substantial differences among organizations persisted when members checked a list of 28 organizational incentives that were "important . . . organizational activities to you personally as a member." Respondents could choose answers on a 4-point scale ranging from "not important" to "extremely important."[25] As Table 16.2 shows, the configurations varied markedly over the five types of associations.[26] The women's association members attached greater importance to normative incentives and lobbying incentives than did the members of other types of organizations. Members of women's associations and members of the nonpolitical recreational groups considered social-recreational activities equally important. (Among the nonscaled incentives, "opportunity for community service" was endorsed by two thirds of the women, a substantially higher percentage than that of the other association members.) The women's groups ranked lowest on material incentives and in the middle on informational and occupational inducements.

Finally, to examine the incidence of multiple incentives, Table 16.3 shows the percentage distributions across combinations of four types of incentives.[27] A majority of members in the women's associations (51 percent) and in the political professional associations (52 percent) expressed high interests in three or more types of incentives. Indeed, the two distributions are nearly identical, although the professionals were somewhat more likely to score below average on all four types of incentives. Large majorities in the other three types of organizations emphasize two or fewer types of incentives. Nonpolitical group members were especially likely to consider none of the incentives as important.

Decision-Making

To examine the internal polities of associations, three types of indicators of organizational decision-making were available:

1. Perceived decision-making decentralization, based on members' responses to six items (5-point Likert-type scales ranging from "strongly disagree" to "strongly agree").[28]

Table 16.2   Importance of Organizational Incentives to Members

Type of Incentive		Type of Association			
	Women's	Political Professional	Political Recreational	Nonpolitical Professional	Nonpolitical Recreational
Normative Incentives					
Emphasizing main principles, goals	67%	50%	62%	43%	45%
Information/ public relations programs	66	47	48	32	35
Educating general public about organization	63	71	60	43	53
Holding local chapter meetings	59	38	35	22	35
Enhancing public status of organization	39	62	27	34	44
Stressing general prestige of organization	38	33	36	25	28
Mean on 4-point scale	2.62	2.50	2.32	2.06	2.24
Lobbying Incentives					
Lobbying governments on legislation	70%	53%	45%	29%	29%
Changing values, beliefs of public	66	62	49	41	42
Changing the lives of nonmembers	26	12	8	18	4
Endorsing political candidates	23	15	17	10	7
Mean on 4-point scale	2.47	2.10	1.94	1.81	1.70

Table 16.2   (Continued)

		Type of Association			
Type of Incentive	Women's	Political Professional	Political Recreational	Nonpolitical Professional	Nonpolitical Recreational
Informational Incentives					
Publishing newsletters, magazines	55%	79%	56%	73%	79%
Providing information/data services	53	60	42	50	53
Sponsoring research activities	51	51	37	42	42
Holding a national convention	32	45	23	58	28
Mean on 4-point scale	2.41	2.70	2.20	2.63	2.55
Occupational Incentives					
Improving members' incomes, conditions	39%	41%	15%	26%	13%
Professional, business contact opportunity	36	55	10	42	26
Helping members with job searches	31	50	12	49	17
Mean on 4-point scale	2.07	2.45	1.43	2.18	1.64
Social-Recreational Incentives					
Opportunities to form friendships	45%	24%	36%	39%	45%
Raising money for charitable organizations	26	11	24	8	13
Enhancing members' cultural lives	25	19	24	13	21

Table 16.2   (Continued)

Type of Incentive	Women's	Political Professional	Political Recreational	Nonpolitical Professional	Nonpolitical Recreational
			Type of Association		
Social or recreational activities	24	9	29	17	41
Mean on 4-point scale	1.99	1.64	1.94	1.69	1.99
Material Incentives					
Offering group insurance plans	9%	13%	16%	7%	15%
Certification, licensing programs	8	37	16	12	30
Group purchasing, marketing opportunities	7	14	16	15	26
Mean on 4-point scale	1.34	1.74	1.55	1.46	1.78
Nonscale Items					
Opportunity for community service	66%	37%	43%	24%	28%
Seminars, conferences, workshops	65	71	34	57	56
Representing members in negotiations	27	26	17	11	16
Awards, recognition ceremonies	14	24	18	29	27

Note: Percentages are those responding "very important" and "extremely important."

2. Perceived differences in influence between the organizational president (or chair) and the membership ("influence slope"; see Tannenbaum, 1968) and the imputed influence sum of the two organizational roles ("total influence").[29]

3. Average levels of expressed interest in issues facing the organization, and average levels of activity on those issues, for as many as

Table 16.3   Incidence of Multiple Incentives

Type of Incentive	Women's (N = 2,208)	Political Professional (N = 2,348)	Political Recreational (N = 1,242)	Nonpolitical Professional (N = 1,531)	Nonpolitical Recreational (N = 1,417)
All Four Types	27%	25%	15%	13%	17%
Lobbying with Two Others	20	20	13	15	7
Normative, Social, and Utilitarian	4	7	4	9	12
Two Types	25	20	27	20	24
One Type	19	14	24	18	20
No Incentives	6	14	17	25	20
Total	101*	100	100	100	100

*Does not total to 100 because of rounding.

six issues provided to the project by organizational leaders.[30] For the women's organizations, about half the listed items involved matters internal to the organization (such as raising dues) and half concerned external political objectives (such as equal rights, job training, and pay equity).

Table 16.4 reports the mean membership responses to these five scales. In every instance, the women's organization members have the highest values: They see their organizations as more decentralized, with smaller influence differences between the president and the general member, and the members report more interest and activity in issues than members of the four other kinds of organizations. The nonpolitical recreational clubs tend to exhibit the opposite configuration of political characteristics.[31] However, the differences between types are much smaller than the variations among members within similar types of organizations.

The average levels of decision-making, influence, and issue participation can be analyzed as characteristics of the 35 organizations, not just as individual members' attributes. Figure 16.1 shows the joint pattern of the issue activity index and the total influence measure. Each point on the scatterplot represents a particular association's average values on the two variables. The tendency for these points to fall along a line that slopes toward the upper right of the figure implies that associations whose members are very active on organizational issues are also likely to perceive high levels of influence shared by both leaders and members.

Table 16.4 Mean Responses to Organizational Decision-Making

Decision-Making Indicator	Type of Association					
	Women's (N = 2,208)	Political Professional (N = 2,348)	Political Recreational (N = 1,242)	Nonpolitical Professional (N = 1,531)	Nonpolitical Recreational (N = 1,417)	Eta^2 (N = 8,746)
Perceived Decentralization	3.35	3.07	3.09	3.05	3.02	.045
Influence Difference	0.77	1.25	1.15	1.33	1.89	.032
Total Influence	7.08	6.72	6.73	6.63	6.73	.020
Issue Interest	3.19	2.83	2.98	2.60	2.50	.135
Issue Activity	1.99	1.30	1.43	1.43	1.29	.162

(For the 35 associations, the linear correlation between activity index and total influence is +.65, a large enough number to imply more than chance.)[32] Figure 16.1 also shows that women's associations are unique: The four associations with the highest scores on both variables are women's groups, with Association E (one of the smaller organizations but with an extremely active membership) the highest. These empirical relations suggest that associations that distribute power to both leaders and members have substantial membership involvement in collective decision-making, and women's organizations are especially adept at creating these conditions.

Participation and Commitment

To test how internal politics translates into participation and commitment, a variety of members' participation measures were collected. A factor analysis revealed that these items clustered into two subsets: activities taking place within the organization's boundaries and participation requiring external contacts.[33] Table 16.5 shows the percentages of respondents in each type of organization who said they performed a particular activity during the past year "regularly" or "sometimes" (as opposed to "rarely" or "never"). Two summary 4-point scales were created by averaging across all items in each factor. The women's association members displayed substantially higher participation levels than did members of the other organizations. More than half had held an office compared with fewer than one sixth of other association members. Women are more likely to have worked on special projects, contacted other members, provided transportation, solicited donations, and represented the organization to other groups. These activities are undoubtedly facilitated by the existence of local chapters for five of the six women's groups (all except Association F). Of the 29 other organizations, only 16 are organized at the state or local level, thus making such personal interactions more difficult.

On external participation activities the women's groups are distinctive, with a third to a quarter having recently contacted government officials, worked in a political candidate's campaign, or signed a petition on behalf of the organization. One in ten members picketed or demonstrated compared with negligible proportions in the other four groups. Women's groups did not contribute significantly more time or money than other organizations. The recreational political members gave the most money, primarily because of a few large donors (5 percent said that they gave $3,000 or more during the past year). Both recreational polit-

Figure 16.1   Scatterplot of Organization Means on Issue Activity Index and Total Influence for 35 Associations

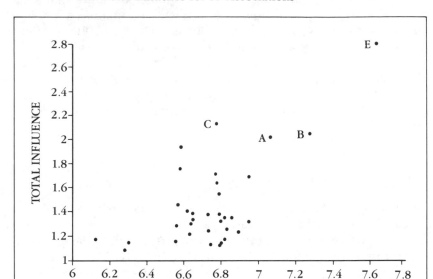

ical and women's association members worked more than four hours for their groups each month, almost double the time commitment of professional society members.

The final set of analyses compares the participation and commitment between the two categories, the women's groups and all others (more detailed analyses of the latter appear in Knoke, 1988). Multiple regression equations were estimated for each of these two samples, using three dependent variables: internal participation, external participation, and organizational commitment.[34] In each equation, the independent variables were the incentive and decision-making measures discussed above, an indicator of local chapters or branches, and personal attributes of members.[35] The columns in Table 16.6 display the estimated regression coefficients for a particular equation. Adjacent pairs of columns compare the results of the same equation estimated for women's and other associations' members.[36]

For the two internal participation equations, all four types of incentives exert roughly similar effects: Members who are motivated by normative and by social incentives are more likely to participate or be committed, while those members attracted by utilitarian or lobbying incentives are less involved. However, the magnitudes of the latter two incentive types are much smaller than the former two, as shown by the absolute magnitudes of the standardized regression coefficients. Indeed, in both equations the normative incentive scale is clearly the single most important predictor of internal participation. Turning to the four decision-making variables, several contrasts between the two equations are noteworthy. Having an interest in organizational issues produces a much smaller participation effect among the women's associations. Perceived decentralization has no significant effect for the women, but reduces others' participation levels. When total influence and the influence difference between president and members are high, women are more likely to participate in organizational affairs, but the influence difference effect is negative for other members. Finally, as might be expected, the existence of subunits (local chapters) is conducive to higher participation in both types of groups.

The two external participation equations (third and fourth columns of Table 16.6) reveal that normative incentives and lobbying incentives are both significant motives to participate. For women's associations, the issue interest coefficient is almost twice as large as the one for the other groups, possibly because their groups are more likely to emphasize issues external to the association. Another major contrast is the effect of local chapters: Having them helps to mobilize members of the other groups, but it *reduces* external participation among the women's groups. However, since only Association F had no local chapters, the extent to which this relationship generalizes is not clear.

Members who find utilitarian benefits important are less likely to be highly committed to their groups (fifth and sixth columns of Table 16.6). Several decision-making measures are also important. Members who are highly interested in the issues, who believe that decisions are decentralized, and who perceive shared influence are more likely to be strongly committed. Having local chapters reduces commitment for women's association members, although once again the unique situation with Association F may be responsible for this conclusion.

Table 16.5 Participation and Contributions

		Type of Association			
Participatory Action	Women's (N = 2,208)	Political Professional (N = 2,348)	Political Recreational (N = 1,242)	Nonpolitical Professional (N = 1,531)	Nonpolitical Recreational (N = 1,417)
Internal Participation					
Phoned or contacted other members	54%	32%	32%	40%	32%
Ever held office in organization	53	14	18	14	11
Voted in organizational elections	51	52	27	40	30
Worked on special projects	51	17	29	16	17
Tried to recruit new members	49	46	38	23	32
Attended conferences or workshops	39	32	19	36	19
Provided transportation to members	31	8	20	9	12
Represented organization to other groups	29	15	19	12	16
Solicited donations for the organization	25	5	17	3	5
Gave or loaned equipment and supplies	20	11	20	11	17
Mean Internal Participation Scale	2.07	1.61	1.62	1.58	1.54

400

External Participation

Contacted government officials	32%	12%	14%	3%	3%
Worked for a political candidate	26*	4	5	2	2
Signed a petition for the organization	25	7	8	2	4
Wrote letters to papers, magazines	16	5	7	5	5
Picketed or demonstrated	10	—	—	—	—
Mean External Participation Scale	1.65	1.17	1.19	1.08	1.09
Mean Contributions					
Amount of Money Given Annually	$60.36	$77.45	$166.07	$78.35	$50.35
Monthly Hours Devoted to Organization	4.4	2.1	4.3	2.3	3.7

*Excludes members of Association B.

401

Table 16.6 Standardized Regression Coefficients (b*) Predicting Member Participation and Commitment by Incentives and Decision-Making Measures, for Women's and Other Associations

Independent Variable	Internal Participation		External Participation		Organizational Commitment	
	Women's Associations (N = 2,208)	Other Associations (N = 6,538)	Women's Associations (N = 2,208)	Other Associations (N = 6,538)	Women's Associations (N = 2,208)	Other Associations (N = 6,538)
Incentives						
Normative	.42***	.32***	.19***	.07**	.33***	.35***
Social	.21***	.15***	.06*	-.07	.04	.05**
Utilitarian	-.13***	-.07***	-.06*	.03	-.10***	-.05**
Lobbying	-.07**	-.09***	.14***	.21***	.03	-.04*
Decision-Making						
Issue interest	.06**	.19***	.17***	.09***	.21***	.18***
Decentralization	.03	-.09***	.07**	-.04*	.21***	.14***
Influence difference	.06**	-.04*	.06*	-.06***	.06**	.01
Total influence	.09***	.07***	.04	.03	.13***	.06***
Subunits	.14***	.11***	-.11***	.11***	-.11***	-.03
Multiple R^2_{adj}	.353***	.224***	.169**	.119**	.352***	.235***

Note: Each equation also includes members' age, income, and education; and for other associations, gender and type of organization (dummy coding).
*p < .05
**p < .01
***p < .001

Discussion

We have learned that the members of the women's associations are distinctly different from the members of other organizations. As indicated by the political economy analyses (reasons for joining, combinations of diverse incentives, perhaps of collective decision-making, involvement in organizational issues, levels of participation, and commitment to the group), the women's associations have exceptionally activist populations with strong roots in their organizations' cultures. Through more diverse inducements and organizational processes, their members are mobilized at high levels of participation. Also, their members' personal resources, used for the collectivity, have been more effectively tapped. These findings mark the women's organizations as unique among American associations for their high levels of activism.

Only when comparing the process by which these political-economic attachments translate into participatory acts do the women resemble the members of professional societies and recreational associations. That is, with modest exceptions, the net magnitudes of incentives and decision-making variables on both internal and external participation and on commitment are very similar. Especially important in predicting involvement are interest in normative incentives, high interest in organizational issues, perceptions of decentralized decision-making and of high influence, and (for external participation) strong interest in lobbying incentives. The similarity in multiple regression equation estimates between the two types of organizations should not obscure the fact that women's association members generally have higher values on the independent political-economic factors, thus leading to higher average levels of participation and commitment compared with other group members.

Notably missing in these equations were major effects from such selective goods as the utilitarian incentives. Only the social-recreational incentives measure produced a small positive effect, confined to the internal participation equation. In our study the rational choice theories, which assert the importance of selective inducements for eliciting contributions from the members of public goods–oriented collectivities, receive scant support. The women's associations, closely resembling social movement organizations, uniformly emphasize public goods objectives among their major goals. Normative incentives—stressing the organization's main principles and goals, enhancing its public stature and prestige, and informing the larger community about the organization—proved to be robust predictors of member participation and commitment for all types of organizations. And, again, the women's associations ranked exceptionally high on these indicators. The notion that collective action organizations can foster intense involvement by offering their members private goods inducements that are unrelated to the group's manifest purposes is clearly erroneous. Indeed, the negative effects of utilitarian incentives imply that such offerings only attract peripheral persons whose participation and commitment do not extend beyond cashing in on these immediate benefits. However, to the extent that friendships and sociable interactions are private goods enjoyable only through membership, this type of inducement produces modest organizational benefits, at least in promoting internal participation.

The results of these analyses also underscore the importance of democratic organizational decision-making structures for building commitment to the collectivity. Those organizations with centralized decisions, low total power, large power gaps between leaders and the rank and file, and member apathy about organizational issues are the least effective in stimulating member involvement. A contrasting configuration characterizes "participatory" social organizations able to motivate intense loyalty and resource contributions among their mass memberships. The women's associations, more so than others, have discovered how to structure and maintain open-access political economies that are conducive to high-energy involvements.

The present analysis investigated relationships within associations at a given time. Missing is an understanding of the temporal processes through which member mobilization occurs. For example, the existence of local chapters apparently provides an important context for face-to-face interaction that helps bind members to their national organizations. No evidence is yet available about the historical formation of such local social structures: Do they emerge through indigenous community dynamics? Are they imposed from above by a hierarchical national body? And what difference does it make for the ultimate creation of participatory organizations? Does the close relation of women's associations to the recent women's social movement generate special conditions of collective action that are absent from more conventional professional and recreational associations? Some answers to questions that require a historical perspective on women's associations are better addressed in other chapters of this volume.

Notes

Research supported by grants from the Russell Sage Foundation and the National Science Foundation (SES82-16927 and SES85-08051). Data were collected by the Center for Survey Research at Indiana University, Kathryn Cirksena, field director, and by the Minnesota Center for Social Research, Rosanna Armson, field director.

1. Based on recent editions of *Washington Representatives* and the *Encyclopedia of Associations*. See later sections for details of the sampling procedures.

2. Freeman (1979).

3. Berry (1977, 1984); Salisbury (1984); Schlozman and Tierney (1986).

4. A recent survey (Knoke 1986, p. 14) discovered that nearly half of all associations agree that "influencing public policy decisions of the government" is one of their major or moderate goals. Labor unions were the most likely to act as interest groups (85 percent), followed by trade associations (58 percent), professional societies (53 percent), and social and recreational organizations (22 percent).

5. Verba and Nie (1972); Olsen (1982).

6. Wilson (1973); Mansbridge (1980).

7. Verba and Nie (1972), p. 176.

8. Verba and Nie (1972), p. 199.

9. Olsen (1982), p. 32.

10. But see Mansbridge (1980) for cautions concerning the unity or diversity of interests within the collectivity.

11. Political mobilization is most effective when the organization can create an intense psychological bond by which the member "is willing to let the group serve as a source of identification and direction for his or her own beliefs and behaviors" (Wilson and Orum 1976, p. 194; Knoke, 1981). For example, Knoke found that social-influence association members contacted government officials on behalf of their organizations most frequently when their attachments to the group (measured by communication frequency) were strong and the organizations explicitly mobilized their memberships for collective action (Knoke, 1982). The empirical evidence for the politicizing function of associations comes from a handful of general population surveys in which only a few questions were asked about organizational involvement. In-depth examinations of small-scale democracies typically rely upon case studies or narrowly defined types of associations: labor unions (Dickerson, 1982), fraternal organizations (Schmidt, 1973), churches (Wood, 1981), historical social movement organizations (Gamson, 1975), and social influence associations (Knoke and Wood, 1981).

12. Tocqueville (1947).

13. Salisbury (1984); Schlozman and Tierney (1986).

14. Knoke and Wright-Isak (1982); Knoke and Prensky (1984); Knoke and Adams (1987); Knoke (1986, 1987).

15. More formally, incentive systems are patterned resource transactions between members and their organization. The key feature of an incentive

system is an exchange of organizationally controlled values (material and symbolic) for an individual's financial and participatory resources that are needed by an association to pursue its collective goals.

16. Knoke and Wright-Isak (1982) developed a "predisposition/opportunity" explanation of the relationship between individual motives and organizational incentives. (See Clark and Wilson, 1961 and Fireman and Gamson, 1979 for similar incentive schemes, using somewhat different labels.) They argued that members' interests in organizational incentives fall into three broad categories: utilitarian, affective, and normative. The first two consist of material and interpersonal rewards that are available only to group members. The third consists of purposive values (such as fairness, equity, altruism, and other moral injunctions that relate to fundamental association purposes) that may also benefit nonmembers, yet nevertheless powerfully motivate members to become involved in a collective action organization.

17. A public good is available to anyone who fits its eligibility qualifications, regardless of his or her contributions to the organization that produces the good.

18. According to Mancur Olson's classic *The Logic of Collective Action* (1965), organizations will attract insufficient member contributions if they offer only public goods as inducements. Rational calculations lead people to maximize their benefits by taking a "free ride" on others' efforts. Olson argued that to overcome this problem, organizations must offer selective inducements, either coercion or positive incentives that reward members with private goods, whose consumption is restricted to only those members making contributions to the organization (p. 51).

19. For example, Moe's analysis of members of five large economic associations found that their extensive packages of economic services "are widely used and valued by members, and they typically have greater inducement value than politics . . . [but] it is still true that a good many members join for political reasons—and, in fact, except in the Printers, most of the respondents in each group indicate that politics plays a pivotal role in their decision to maintain membership" (1980, pp. 217–218).

20. Scott et al. (1981); Jennergren (1981).

21. Michels' famous "iron law" argued for the inevitability of oligarchic control even in nominally democratic organizations (1949). Meister similarly proposed a phase- or life-stage model of gradual transformation from egalitarian democracy to administrative domination (1984, p. 146). Mansbridge pointed out that small social organizations with common interests, equal respect among members, and face-to-face decision processes are strongly constrained to practice consensual or "unitary" democracy rather than the "adversarial" mode that characterizes larger social organizations where conflicts of interest are more prevalent (1980).

22. Gamson's investigation of historical social movement organizations indi-

cated that centralized organizations were more successful in containing tendencies toward paralyzing internal factional splits, while bureaucratized organizations were more successful in attaining external goals (1975, pp. 89–109). Freeman (1979), analyzing the social organization of women's liberation, argued that the younger, decentralized organizations were compelled to devote large portions of their resources to group maintenance needs, while older, more formalized organizations could devote greater efforts to external goal attainment. In a contextual analysis of members from thirty-two social influence associations, Knoke (1981) found that members' commitment and attachment to their organizations increased significantly with both frequency of communication and participation in decision-making.

23. The range was from 67 percent for Association B to 48 percent for Association E.

24. The first phase of the NAS began in 1984, when telephone interviews were conducted with the leaders of 459 associations, sampled at random within five major types of organizations (trade associations, professional societies, labor unions, recreational associations, and others) to represent the estimated 13,000 national associations. The second phase began in 1985 when eight-page questionnaires were mailed to samples of members from 20 professional societies and 9 recreational associations, selected proportional to membership size from the list of associations participating in the first phase. Eight-page questionnaires were mailed to members of these 29 associations, selecting every kth member on the current mailing list after a random start. Overall, 6,538 usable questionnaires were returned, with an average response rate of 64 percent.

25. The respondents were instructed, "If an activity is not performed at present by [the organization], just leave it unanswered and go on to the next item." Although most respondents appeared to follow these instructions, the fact that small numbers checked various incentives known not to be offered as important implies that some persons might have been indicating their desires for such incentives rather than their actual use. However, as no way exists to separate preferences from consumption, all respondents' self-reports are taken at face value.

26. The 28 incentive items are grouped in Table 16.2 according to the results of a principal components factor analysis with oblique rotation. High loadings on six factors were attained by 24 items, with four items not loading highly on any factor. The six factors accounted for 58 percent of the variance. The summary scale scores for each factor, reported in Table 16.2, were constructed by averaging equally weighted item responses across 4-point item scales from "not important" (1) to "extremely important" (4).

27. The six incentive scales were each dichotomized as close as possible to their overall sample medians. The information, occupational, and material scales were treated as a single "utilitarian" index. Respondents were classified as

interested in a particular type of incentive if they attached above-average importance to that scale.

28. These items appeared among 18 statements in a section titled "Decision-Making in the Organization." A principal components factor analysis with oblique rotation yielded high loadings for six items on the first factor, which accounted for 24.0 percent of the variance. These items are:

> Leaders' decisions more often reflect their personal interests than the wishes of the members.
>
> Power over major policy issues is concentrated in the hands of a few people.
>
> The leaders of (organization name) sometimes make decisions that have little support from the rank-and-file members.
>
> If people disagree about policy decisions, there are formal ways for them to voice their opposition.
>
> Major policy decisions are made only after wide consultations at all levels of the organization.
>
> The (organization name) leaders can be trusted to make the best decisions possible.

The coding on the last three items was reversed, to be consistent with the direction of the first three. A high average score across all six items indicates disagreement with the statements, hence a perception that power over organizational policy decisions is widespread and not concentrated in the leaders' hands.

29. Respondents rated six different roles according to "how much influence do you think that each of the following persons or groups have in determining the policies and actions of [organization name]?" Each position could be rated on a 5-point scale from "none" to "very great deal." The president–general membership comparison was used because all 35 organizations had such positions, while some lacked executive directors, committees, and other elected officials.

30. These issues were presented as short statements of the substantive contents. Members were asked to check for each issue the "level of interest or concern that you had or have about each issue category" on a 4-point scale from "no interest" to "major interest." They then were asked to indicate "how active you are or were in the [organization name] on that category," again using a 4-point response scale from "not active" to "highly active." Every organization provided at least two issues for the questionnaire. The women's groups were much more involved in issues, with 5 groups listing six issues and 1 group listing five issues. Among the other organizations, only 17 listed six issues, 8 listed five issues, 3 listed four issues, and 2 listed only two issues. To take into account these differences, members' issue interest and issue activity levels were computed by averaging responses across items.

31. The last column in Table 16.4 gives the correlation ratio (eta-square), which shows the proportion of total variation in each decision-making variable that lies between the five types of associations. Except for the two issue indicators, these ratios are relatively small (although all are statistically significant, given the large sample sizes). Thus, while the women's group members are clearly distinct from the others, considerable within-category variation remains to be accounted for by other factors.

32. Correlation coefficients ranging from +1.00 to −1.00, with zero indicating no relationship and an absolute value of 1 indicating perfect predictability of one variable from the other. Other high correlations among the decision-making variables occurred among the 35 associations: +.68 between decentralization and total influence, −.76 between decentralization and influence difference, and +.59 between total influence and issue interest. These covariations all suggest that decision-making characteristics tend to be consistent across organizations.

33. The principal components analysis with oblique rotation showed that the internal participation items loaded on the first factor with 34.8 percent of the variance, while the external participation items accounted for 10.9 percent. The two factors were moderately correlated at r = +.38.

34. This measure is the response to the question, "Personally, how committed do you feel to the [organization name]?" on a 5-point scale from "not committed at all" to "very strongly committed." The women's organizations' mean was 3.09; the mean for all others was 2.74. All statistics are based on unweighted cases.

35. The equations also included members' personal attributes—age, gender, income, education—and dummy variables for types of organizations. As these effects are not theoretically important, their coefficients are omitted from Table 16.6 to conserve space. Because the measures are scaled in arbitrary units, only the standardized regression coefficients are presented. These estimates show the effect that a one-standard-deviation difference in an independent variable has upon the dependent variable, after holding constant the additive effects of all other variables in the equation. For example, in the internal participation equation of the women's association members, the .42 coefficient for normative incentives means that a one-standard-deviation difference in the importance of normative incentives produces an average .42 standard deviation higher level of internal participation. The adjusted R^2 for an equation shows the proportion of the individual variation in dependent variable that can be explained by the additive effects of all the variables in the equation.

36. For those readers not familiar with regression analysis, the standardized coefficient (b*) of an independent variable reveals both the direction (negative or implied positive sign) and the strength (magnitude of the number) of that variable's effect upon the dependent variable, holding constant (controlling for) the effects of all the other independent variables. For example,

in the first column of Table 16.6, the .42 coefficient for Normative Incentives means that a woman whose interest in normative incentives was exactly one standard deviation (a measure of dispersion or spread) higher than another woman's would be .42 standard deviation higher on the internal participation scale. Because all the variables are measured in standard deviation units, comparisons between coefficients within the same equation are meaningful. Thus, the .42 Normative Incentive effect is twice as strong as the .21 Social Incentive effect, and more than three times the − .13 Utilitarian Incentive effect (the negative sign means that women's association members with higher interest in utilitarian incentives are *less* likely to participate in internal activities). None of the four decision-making variables affects internal participation by as much as one-tenth standard deviation. The multiple R^2_{adj} at the bottom of each equation is the coefficient of determination, adjusted for degrees of freedom. It indicates how much of the variation in the dependent variable is accounted for (explained by, in a statistical sense) by the additive linear effects of all the independent variables in the equation. For the women's internal participation equation, the .353 value means that slightly more than one third of this variation is explained by the independent measures (thus, about two thirds is not accounted for).

The Politicization
of Gender

Part V examines some of the ways in which masculinity and femininity have been socially constructed or reconstructed in the twentieth century through political processes, including legislation and policymaking, litigation, and pressure group activities. The focus moves from women primarily as actors to women and gender as objects of action.

Barbara J. Nelson examines the gendered nature of welfare legislation. She suggests that gender-specific systems of welfare arose from the parallel development of Mothers' Aid (and later Aid to Dependent Children), legislated for women in the home who had lost their primary wage earner, and of Workmen's Compensation, legislated for employed men who had lost their wages due to work-related disability.

In a case study of Farmer Labor women in Minnesota, Elizabeth Faue offers a picture of their efforts to establish gender parity in the New Deal politics of welfare. These women acted in the belief that women's rights and responsibilities were linked to their marital status. Nevertheless, they were temporarily successful in integrating the power structure of local politics and in promoting sex equality in relief and employment policies. Over the decade of the 1930s there was a decline, however, in gender-based politics and its replacement by a more conventional politics, increasingly conservative on gender issues.

The changing legal climate of women's rights in the 1970s and 1980s is examined by Jo Freeman. She argues that the courts have resolved the debate about equality versus protection in favor of equality. The court cases she analyzes lead Freeman to conclude that an "intermediate

411

scrutiny" of sex as a suspect classification has emerged in the federal law. There has been a revolutionary change in opportunities for women, but there is need for further change in institutionalized sex role differences and the concept of adult dependency.

Another overview of legal change in an arena which strongly affected women is Herbert Jacob's chapter on divorce reform. Despite its apparent link to women's issues, divorce reform occurred with little involvement of feminists. He sees three reasons for this: Women had not penetrated decision-making agencies; feminist organizations were concentrating their efforts on the national rather than the state level; feminist priorities lay elsewhere. Only when some of the long-term consequences of no-fault divorce (in the form legislated by some states, at least) became evident did feminists become more active on the issue.

Division among women, in this case among feminists, is also discussed by Alida Brill. She probes the roots and characteristics of the contemporary split among feminists over pornography. WAP—Women Against Pornography—an organization that campaigns through advertising and direct street-corner appeals to passersby, calls for legislative control of pornography. FACT—Feminists Against Censorship Task Force—upholds a contrasting civil libertarian position and also supports women's (and men's) access to fantasy through pornography. Brill analyzes the passionate rhetoric of advocates on both sides and uncovers some of the dilemmas and contradictions that feminists face over this issue.

Yet another division among women—that among female conservative activists—is examined by Rebecca Klatch. The two groups are the social conservatives, whose world view is moral, hierarchical, and defensive of conventional female roles and the status that derives from them; and the laissez-faire conservatives, whose world view conceives liberty as fundamental and opposes government intervention in private life. Although the laissez-faire world view supports some positions that are shared with feminists, it diverges on issues of gender roles and the role of the state in combating discrimination. Hence, even though the two groups of women in the New Right are uneasy partners and may eventually split, a coalition of laissez-faire conservatives and feminists over abortion rights is unlikely.

17

The Gender, Race, and Class Origins of Early Welfare Policy and the Welfare State: A Comparison of Workmen's Compensation and Mothers' Aid

Barbara J. Nelson

In the last decade there has been an outpouring of research on state formation[1] and more recently on the connection between state formation generally and the creation of the welfare state in industrial democracies. The recent work on welfare state formation has been led by Theda Skocpol, Ann Shola Orloff, John Ikenberry, and Kenneth Finegold, among others.[2] One major conclusion reached through their research is that, in large part, the relatively late emergence of the welfare state in the United States (during the New Deal) is due to an earlier distrust of corrupt parties as the administrators of benefit programs and the lack of an alternative, neutral bureaucracy to undertake this task. In the state formation research, the sex, race, and class of the potential clients of new social programs do not figure importantly in the discussion of the emergence of a socially undifferentiated welfare state.

At the same time that the research on state formation was under way, feminist interpretations of power and politics, including feminist critiques of the welfare state, also developed. Feminist scholars examining the welfare state—including Mary McIntosh, Lisa Peattie, Martin Rein, Virginia Sapiro, Jennifer Schirmer, Elizabeth Wilson, Eli Zaretsky, and myself, among others—are much less unified in approach and topic.[3] For the most part, this work covers current welfare programs from various theoretical perspectives; and if a summary of a divergent literature is possible, it suggests that the welfare state has incorporated long-lasting political tensions by reproducing and reinforcing profound social inequities between groups while also improving the material conditions of

413

beneficiaries. By and large, this work is not focused on the origins of welfare policies and the welfare state. The existing historical work does not typically compare programs designed for men with those designed for women.

There has been little convergence between the state formation research and the feminist critiques of the welfare state. Indeed, it is striking that while the questions asked by both groups of scholars may occasionally run parallel to each other, the sources used in analysis rarely overlap. When the concerns that motivate these researchers are examined together, an important and provocative set of questions emerges. Is the state gendered and if so how? How can theories of state formation and theories of the welfare state illuminate one another? Arising from feminist theories of difference, how do gender, race, and class intersect in the creation of the U.S. welfare state?[4] What is the role of comparative case studies of welfare programs in contributing both to an understanding of events and to a more richly elaborated social theory?

The sum of these questions, and others like them, is more an agenda for interdisciplinary research than the subject of a single essay. The more focused aim of this work is to initiate a critical reconceptualization of the origins of the U.S. welfare state. Specifically, I shall present the beginnings of a historically grounded argument for viewing U.S. welfare policy and ultimately the welfare state as fundamentally divided into two channels, one originally designed for white industrial workers and the other designed for impoverished white working-class widows with young children.[5] The origins of this two-channel welfare state can be seen through the parallel development of Workmen's Compensation and Mothers' Aid between 1900 and 1920. Workmen's Compensation, which initiated the white male worker's channel, resulted from the politics of regularizing industrial production and was strongly linked to the ideology of welfare capitalism and the administrative practices of scientific management. Mothers' Aid, which initiated the white female caretaking channel, resulted from the politics of women's political incorporation and was linked to the Poor Law tradition and the administrative practices of the Charity Organization Society movement.

This chapter is organized in two parts. The first section summarizes the state formation approach to a socially undifferentiated welfare state and presents a feminist critique that argues that the origin of a two-channel welfare state is a product of the Progressive period's labor-power relations between the sexes, races, and classes. The second section compares the content and structure of Workmen's Compensation and Mothers' Aid to show the legacy these programs left as the welfare state developed. This comparison illuminates the longstanding welfare state tensions between productive, domestic, and reproductive labor, tensions that separate individual male workers from family-centered female nurturers.[6]

State Formation, Feminism, and the U.S. Welfare State

In a series of wide-ranging and important articles, Theda Skocpol, John Ikenberry, and Ann Shola Orloff have transformed scholarly thinking on the origins of the U.S. welfare state.[7] The authors agree with the widely held view that the Great Depression ushered in the welfare state, acknowledging, however, that early welfare policies existed beforehand. The authors sought new answers to the longstanding question, "Why was the United States so much later than western European countries in establishing its welfare state?" These scholars report that social policies, especially national schemes of social insurance, developed comparatively early in some western European countries because, in the first instance, political parties needed to recruit newly enfranchised members of the electorate and because, in the second instance, policies could be developed and administered through existing politically neutral national bureaucracies, themselves a remnant of the autocratic past. Applying these criteria to the U.S. case, the authors reject as inaccurate or incomplete any explanations for the late development of the U.S. welfare state based on the strength and persistence of liberal values, differential rates of industrialization, or differential power of the working class.

Skocpol, Ikenberry, and Orloff demonstrate that the United States did not meet the political and administrative requirements for creating a welfare state until the mid 1930s. The reasons, they assert, rest in part on the comparatively early franchise of white men, which was largely completed by 1840. The early creation of what social scientists routinely, though erroneously, call a "mass electorate" helped to create patronage-based rather than programmatic parties. (Programmatic parties developed in part to woo the waves of voters that periodically washed into the European electorate as the franchise was sequentially liberalized for men.) The authors further argue that Americans distrusted the corruption of public officials that accompanied patronage-based parties. The citizenry was unwilling to countenance the distribution of public benefits by public officials. A federal system of powerful states and a concomitantly weak national government with a relatively small permanent bureaucracy in Washington and underdeveloped national administrative capacities completed the list of political liabilities that inhibited the systematic development and adoption of welfare policies and the creation of the welfare state.

Administrative underdevelopment and the corruption of political parties in the United States kept the one large "welfare" program of the nineteenth century—Civil War Pensions—from becoming the entering wedge for social insurance in the twentieth century. The Civil War Pension system was a large enterprise. In 1912 it had 860,000 beneficiaries (covering *two thirds* of the nonsouthern white native-born men over age 65) and cost $153 million.[8] These pensions were, however, a product of the patronage-based parties. They were not intended to be an instrument of social amelioration (though they certainly acted as one); they did not rest on a belief in collective responsibility for commonly experienced economic dislocation; their administrative irregularities were widely known and deplored; and they offered the model of a pension fully funded from the general revenue at a time when joint employee-employer insurance systems, some with additional public revenue contributions, were the typical policy in western Europe.[9]

The crisis of the Great Depression forced the beginning of welfare state building through the vehicle of the Social Security Act. Uniform, nationally administered programs for all major types of problems and constituencies were suggested during the development of the Social Security Act. As finally passed, however, the law reflected the political considerations of a federal system of government and the weight of existing state-level welfare programs. Only old age retirement benefits were nationalized and made uniform. Unemployment compensation and a revised Mothers' Aid program remained administered and at least partially funded at the state level.[10]

The state capacities approach does not emphasize any aspects of the politics or composition of clientele. This is not due to assuming that all members of the working class were equally the beneficiaries of welfare programs. The authors acknowledge that early welfare programs assisted the most integrated members of the industrial working class in the United States: northern white men, struggling to become or remain unionized and employed in mining, heavy manufacturing, and transportation; and, to a much lesser extent, their widows.[11] But as always the interest is in state formation. Elsewhere Skocpol specifies that the economic class interests of both the working class and capitalists shaped and were shaped by the particularly American forms of state development. Wide geographical distances and a federal system made it difficult for both workers and owners to establish national movements and institutions designed to benefit from centralized action and planning.[12] But even Skocpol's limited discussion of class is not extended to other groups. Perhaps this is because the main thrust of the new state-building literature compares state formation among and between nations, and its authors have not focused their comparative methodology on the consequences of gender and race on questions of welfare state formation within one country.

A feminist commentary on the political and administrative approach to the origins of the welfare state must surely begin with a series of "What if?" questions. What if the United States had really had mass-based political parties? What if women had achieved the franchise in 1878 when the "Anthony Amendment" was first introduced in Congress by California Senator A. A. Sargent?[13] Or, more interestingly, what if women had won the vote in, say, 1890 when the National American Woman Suffrage Association was formed, *and* the 1890s had not brought about the systematic disenfranchisement of southern blacks? Would these new groups of voters have been integrated into patronage-based political parties? Would they have posed a programmatic challenge for the parties? Would that challenge have altered the climate for social reform? And would any change in party program have been sufficient to overcome the underdeveloped administrative capacities of government, capacities so necessary to the establishment of welfare programs? None of these scenarios was likely, but taken together they alert us to the gender and race components of the process of political incorporation driving welfare state formation.

On a more concrete level, feminist critiques of the welfare state are widely divergent in their approaches and often quite theoretical in their presentation. Liberal, radical, socialist, and Marxist feminists each bring a specific perspective.[14] As suggested earlier, their major concern has been how the welfare state simultaneously reinforces profound social inequities between groups, especially but not only the sexes, while also partially ameliorating the financial distress of beneficiaries. At the center of these approaches are questions about the relationships between productive, domestic, and reproductive labor; about the relationships of labor broadly defined to political and economic power; and about the state's role in reproducing or altering labor-power relationships.

Understanding the origins of the U.S. welfare state requires an examination of labor-power relations at the time of the first benefit programs. At every level—material, ideological, and political—labor-power relations were partially defined by structural differences between women and men, blacks and whites, and wage workers and other producers and owners. Materially, women and men did not participate in the same kinds of labor. In the first two decades of the 1900s men constituted roughly 80 percent of the paid labor force. By 1920 nearly 45 percent of the male labor force was engaged in wage labor in mining, manufacturing, or transportation.[15] Women workers were found more frequently in service and domestic occupations. Unlike male workers, women workers were overwhelmingly single, although a larger proportion of married black women worked for wages. By and large, after marriage both black and white women's work was concentrated in often-arduous reproductive and domestic labor, although some working-class or poor women also worked for wages in their homes by doing piecework or taking in boarders.

Gender, race, and class differences can also be seen in the political activities of the Progressive period. The two powerful, locally based parties of the nineteenth century waned in an era when men's political and economic interests were no longer mostly community based. White male voter turnout declined markedly. In the South, black men were actively denied the franchise. At the same time, as historian Paula Baker writes, "men increasingly replaced or supplemented electoral participation with the sorts of single issue, interest group tactics women had long employed."[16] Unions played an odd role in these changing politics. Craft unions, as represented by Samuel Gompers and the American Federation of Labor, favored workplace gains for workers and distrusted governmental interventions in labor relations, in part because those interventions had mostly been detrimental to labor's interests. Gompers also resisted unionizing women, favoring protective legislation that both eliminated female competition for male jobs and kept male wage structures intact.

Simultaneously, the beginning of the twentieth century witnessed the increasing power of several mass movements promoting (mostly white) women's empowerment. Founded before women won the vote, indeed often actively working for women's suffrage, the organizations representing these mass movements focused on women's empowerment both in the family and in public life. These efforts drew upon and supported such powerful women's institutions as the Woman's Christian Temperance Union, the National American Woman Suffrage Association, the National Woman's Party, parts of the settlement movement (notably Hull House), women's colleges, and women's social and religious organizations of all kinds. White women depended significantly on these mostly separate women's institutions to create the organizational, material, and psychological basis for political activism.[17] Black women, denied access to many institutions established by white women, more frequently used a combination of all women's and mixed sex groups (especially churches) as a springboard for political action. The range of actions undertaken by white and black women's groups both defended and undercut gender relations premised on separate spheres.[18]

The ideology of separate spheres provided the cultural interpretation for labor and political experiences divided by gender.[19] (I would argue that the ideology of separate spheres also supported a general world view valorizing social relations based on inequitable racial and class differences.) The ideology of separate spheres argued that women and men had separate but complementary interests, skills, and abilities and gave many women a vehicle for political action through images of moral guardianship analogous to motherhood and for civic housekeeping analogous to domestic responsibilities. In content, the ideology of separate spheres glorified the white, middle-class, Protestant ideal of motherhood, an ideal that insisted that paid work and motherhood did not intersect. This view carried with it not only a recognition of the double burden placed on wage-earning mothers, but also the clear possibility of vastly restricting women's lives to the domestic sphere.

The gender, race, and class differences in labor experiences and politics suggest that the different social groups were differentially able to express their interests in how the risks of industrial capitalism should be socialized. Blacks were the least powerful economically and politically and were largely absent from the politics and benefits of early welfare programs. Most lived in the South and were bound to a tenant agricultural system or an industrial sector paying very low wages.[20] Black men were increasingly disenfranchised in practice, and black women, like all women, had not yet won the vote. White women were excluded from electoral politics, from the organizational power of unions, and from the economic power of the market, but they, and a minority of black women, did have the organizational base of women's voluntary groups that were capable of articulating a "woman's" perspective on political questions. Mothers' Aid, a limited governmental program available primarily to white women and based on reproductive rather than paid labor, resulted from their actions. White male industrial workers had somewhat better economic resources, and of course they also had the vote, but they expressed no great trust in political solutions to labor's demands. Workmen's Compensation, an industrial initiative supported by labor and ratified by politics, resulted from the position and efforts of white industrial workers.

Workmen's Compensation and Mothers' Aid

The discussion of labor-power relations in the Progressive period shows that the first welfare programs in the United States arose from very different work and political circumstances. A comparative history of Workmen's Compensation and Mothers' Aid demonstrates that these two programs, representing two clusters of labor-power relations, initiated a two-channel welfare state. Workmen's Compensation defined the first channel, which was male, judicial, public, and routinized in origin. Mothers' Aid defined the second channel, which was female, administrative, private, and nonroutinized in origin.

At the turn of the century, much of American industry ran on a model of unchecked, ruthless competition. In heavy industry, competition and dangerous production processes exacted an enormous toll. In a yearlong study of heavy industry in Allegheny County (Pittsburgh), Pennsylvania, undertaken in 1907–1908, Crystal Eastman found that there were 195 industrial deaths among 70,000 steel workers, 125 industrial deaths among 50,000 railroaders, and 71 industrial deaths among 20,000 miners. In addition to the fatalities, a three-month study of hospital records revealed that 509 workers required hospitalization for nonfatal work-related injuries.[21] The drive for Workmen's Compensation arose from public outrage over figures like these, especially when they were compared with much lower figures in western Europe.

Businessmen as much as workers had a need to regularize and limit the social and economic costs of industrial accidents. As the death and injury toll increased, the costs of acquiring employers' liability insurance rose dramatically. Nationally, U.S. businesses paid $200,000 in premiums in 1887, a figure that rose to $35 million in 1912.[22] The increasing cost of insurance in part reflected the expansion of manufacturing and the rise in the number of workers. But increasing costs were also a function of increasing liability caused by the fact that manufacturers were losing their common law protections against responsibility for industrial accidents.

In the nineteenth century, employers were protected from tort liability in industrial accidents by three common law defenses: the fellow servant doctrine, the assumption of risk, and contributory negligence. The fellow servant doctrine asserted that a fellow employee was responsible for the negligence of other workers and had a duty to inform himself or herself of the possible bad work habits of colleagues and endeavor to correct these dangerous habits. The assumption of risk doctrine allowed employers' notice of dangerous conditions to absolve them of their liabilities on the grounds that workers had been alerted to the risks they faced and had thus willingly assumed them. Likewise, the courts disallowed any claims where workers had contributed in any way to the situation that caused the accident. Unions lobbied vigorously against these defenses, especially the fellow servant doctrine, and began to have some successes in state legislatures, especially in the railroad industry, the favorite whipping boy in many agriculturally dominated state legislatures.[23]

With their legal defenses diminishing, some businesses were willing to look for a way to predict, regularize, and limit their liabilities. The original vehicle for designing this policy was the American Association for Labor Legislation, a protocorporatist group of reform-minded capitalists from large businesses, labor leaders, social reformers, and a few politicians. Later, the National Civic Federation (NCF), a similarly constituted group which had more consistent support from union leaders, worked on this issue. Samuel Gompers, who had participated in the NCF, had initially been skeptical of Workmen's Compensation and only came to support it after he realized that there was a national consensus for it.[24] Moreover, labor was not united in wanting to give up the right to sue employers, an option that had been retained in the English Workmen's Compensation law. Many local unions favored that approach, which did not get much attention from reform politicians.[25] Many reformers thought the best law would have eliminated tort liability through a state-managed, if not state-financed, insurance program that replaced a high percentage of wages over a reasonably long period of time. Not surprisingly, the laws that were passed often used private insurance, replaced a low percentage of wages for a short duration, and, importantly, employed a formulaic approach to long-term disability.

For less serious accidents, Workmen's Compensation functioned like a poorly paid sick leave. After a waiting period, a successful claimant received some small percentage of his or her wages. Long-term disability was handled differently, being reimbursed according to a dismemberment schedule, yielding a flat sum for, say, the loss of an arm or a leg. These schedules were attacked as a "product of guesswork and 'crude bargaining.' "[26] They did have the virtue of greatly routinizing the decision rules for assigning benefits. Routinized decision rules allow for the same funding decision to be made easily by different officials.

The routinization of decision rules about eligibility deserves more attention. Comparing the administrative origins, ideologies, and practices of early welfare policies helps us better understand the two-channel welfare state. The administrative style of Workmen's Compensation blends judicial forms with procedures borrowed from the scientific management school of business management, which was adopted by many large corporations in the Progressive period. It is important to remember that Workmen's Compensation was designed to replace a tort liability system. By accepting Workmen's Compensation, beneficiaries gave up their right to sue employers for damages. Once a method to negotiate constitutional issues was devised in 1912, non-southern states adopted Workmen's Compensation with great rapidity.[27] By 1920 forty-two states and three territories passed Workmen's Compensation laws. The administration of each state's program was greatly facilitated by the publication in 1914 and revision in 1920 of Samuel A. Harper's *The Law of Workmen's Compensation,* a digest presenting Illinois's pioneering law, a case commentary on its provisions, and, importantly, a *model set of forms,* forty-six in all (!), covering almost every aspect of the Workmen's Compensation process.[28]

Three qualities of this group of forms are especially important because they alert us to themes in administrative design. First, the forms are legal in layout and origin and reflect the fact that the Illinois Industrial Commission, which had jurisdiction and oversight of Workmen's Compensation cases, had a quasi-judicial character. This judicial quality leads to the second characteristic of the forms as a whole: They are intended to be public documents in the way that most other legal documents presenting judicial decisions are intended to be open to public scrutiny. This does not mean that the records of the commission were not treated with care, merely that there is a clear physical and cultural presumption of publicness, itself a norm associated with the political place and power of men.

The third quality of these forms is the extent to which they demonstrate that Workmen's Compensation rests on a set of established, routinized decision rules. The tables for computing wage replacement and the extent of disability, which are part of Harper's book but which would not necessarily have been available to claimants, can be seen implicitly in forms that refer to weekly wages, medical expenses, and extent of injuries.[29] Even time is rationalized by the decision rules and through the forms. Successful claimants knew how long they would receive payments and at what level, a clear break from the temporal and fiscal uncertainties of relief under the Poor Laws or through charity organization activities.

The administrators of Workmen's Compensation used these forms in a bureaucracy whose structure and practices were in part modeled on the scientific management school of corporate administration. Beginning at the turn of the century, large corporations, cushioned from price competition, began to experiment with corporate welfare. The administrative model they used came from the scientific management movement, which organized personnel relations on the principle of " 'cold blooded science' rather than sentimentalism."[30] The drive for the new organizational form was fueled by the national integration of technology-dependent industries, increased dependence on continuous production processes, and geographically widespread production and distribution, all of which required higher levels of uniform administration.[31] The businessmen and lawyers who promoted Workmen's Compensation and staffed organizations like the Illinois Industrial Commission looked to the law and scientific management when they needed to create new bureaucracies in an age of underdeveloped governmental capacities.

Workmen's Compensation set a course that other social insurance programs followed, indeed improved upon. In fact, the hallmark of social insurance eligibility became straightforward decision criteria in the service of highly routinized decision-making and dispassionate, if not exactly scientific, management. This was and is the administrative style linked with work-based benefits. For many years the vast majority of direct beneficiaries of these programs were white men. Contemporary research clearly shows that routinized decision rules, and concomitantly simpler application procedures, contribute markedly to client satisfaction with insurance programs and reinforce the social legitimacy of the clients as being deserving of their benefits.[32] Hence, in Workmen's Compensation we see the confluence of the major elements of the first channel in the welfare state: socially legitimate, standardized decision criteria supporting insurance programs whose eligibility is based on wage work employing white men. The legalism of Workmen's Compensation did not carry over to the social insurance programs of the New Deal, but the public, male quality did.

Industrial accidents, not to mention industrially related disease, took their toll on families. The death or disability of a breadwinner was an economic as well as a personal catastrophe. If a mother was left without the income of a male breadwinner, her family suffered tremendously. If she needed to support her family aided only by her children's income, she was at a wage disadvantage compared with a man working the same number of hours. If she worked in a manufacturing job, her wages would average only two thirds of her male counterpart's.[33] Manufacturing work was difficult to find and it took single mothers away from their homes, creating a crisis of unsupervised children at home.[34] Thus many women chose to do piecework at home or to take in boarders. Both types of work yielded lower income than most jobs performed outside the home, and taking in boarders could put both the women and their children in danger of possible sexual exploitation.[35]

Charity arrangements at the turn of the century often exacerbated these problems, although these arrangements varied substantially from place to place. In some cities and counties government maintained a strong role in supporting the elderly or children in their own homes, an approach to dependency that was rooted in local ethnic politics and economic arrangements.[36] Beginning in 1877, however, a number of large eastern cities did away with public outdoor relief, that is, goods or services provided publicly to the poor in their own homes. The new local policies more or less exclusively favored institutional care in almshouses or orphanages, institutions that originally developed with surprising rapidity and endurance in the antebellum period. Institutional care was augmented by a system of private charities making *small*, short-term gifts to noninstitutionalized people. In many cities this relief work came to be monitored by Charity Organization Societies whose tasks were to register, track, and refer poor people in need. These societies also popularized the role of "friendly visitors" who examined the cause of each family's want. Personal visits and administrative control, rather than relief, "formed the basis of . . . [a] 'science' of . . . therapeutics that was supposed to relieve philanthropy of sentimentality and indiscriminate almsgiving."[37] Hence the administrative style of the Charity Organization Society movement is called "Scientific Charity." Neither institutionalization nor piecemeal private relief coordinated by social workers offered solutions to the dilemma of work and child supervision confronting single mothers, however.

Although institutionalization was a popular policy in some communities in the nineteenth century, the public became increasingly unwilling to mix children with other paupers and demanded the creation of separate orphanages.[38] By the Progressive era, the label orphanages was misleading, since, as Ann Vandepol writes, "these asylums quickly developed into the major social mechanism for sustaining children of low-income parents faced with unemployment, financial collapse, or death of a male breadwinner. At many asylums half-orphans (children with one parent alive) outnumbered full orphans by a wide margin. In California by 1900 there were 5,399 half-orphans and only 959 full orphans housed in institutions throughout the state."[39] Some charity workers and reformers much preferred foster care to placing the children of indigent families in asylums or orphanages. Homelike settings were believed to be better at molding character than was institutional care. Similarly, education rather than child labor was viewed as better for children and, in the long run, for family finances. Settlement-house Progressives such as Florence Kelley and Jane Addams favored keeping a child in his or her own home, and in school, if possible.

"School pensions" were the first policies designed to respond to keeping children of widows in school without forcing families to forgo the children's earnings.[40] The grants were available only on a very limited basis in a few jurisdictions. Moreover, school pensions did not fully address the tensions between earning a living and supervising one's children that single mothers felt. What were single mothers with young children to do? Theirs was an extreme dilemma of dependency—on male income, on children's income, and on their obligations to care for children and be housekeepers.

The movement for the more universal, in-home support of the children of impoverished widows received a national platform at the 1909 White House Conference on Children, whose report stated that "children of parents of worthy character . . . who are without the support of normal breadwinners, should as a rule be kept with their parents, such aid being given as may be necessary to maintain suitable homes for the rearing of children."[41] Although a preference for supervision over wage-earning was expressed in the conference, the Resolutions Committee stopped short of supporting public outdoor relief for mothers with dependent children. Even Homer Folks was not yet convinced of the propriety of public aid to single mothers with children at this time.[42] Folks's position demonstrates the power of the Charity Organization Society movement's opposition to public outdoor relief, which they felt encouraged laziness and dependency. Charity Organization Society spokespeople Mary E. Richmond and Edward T. Devine further condemned Mothers' Aid in that it was neither a pension given for past service nor a universal support for all mothers, as a proper policy might have been.[43] So, too, the Charity Organization Society opponents of Mothers' Aid could not help but have known that this program would signal the loss of their hegemony over defining the forms of relief.

The Charity Organization Society movement lost its battle against Mothers' Aid. Mothers' Aid had wide popular support among the General Federation of Women's Clubs and the National Congress of Mothers and Parent-Teacher Associations. Mark H. Leff describes their membership as "principally middle-aged, middle-class, poorly educated married women. These women sensed a waning influence in an emerging industrial system that created a new social hierarchy." These groups worked with the National Consumers' League, some suffrage groups, and the Woman's Christian Temperance Union to pass state laws. They were successful as an effort of women organized for women, working with the aid of sympathetic male politicians.[44] Most of this organizing predates national suffrage, although activity in states that gave women suffrage before the Nineteenth Amendment was especially strong. The movement for Mothers' Aid can certainly be seen as part of women's drive for political incorporation, both in the content of the policy and in the effort to win political citizenship.

Unlike Workmen's Compensation, which had a large contingent of working-class leaders, Mothers' Aid was a movement often but not exclusively led by middle-class women in sympathy with working-class and poor women. Middle-class support ranged from the college-educated women of the settlement movement who saw themselves as part of a workers' movement to the homemaking women of the organizations described above. The *Delineator*, a magazine reaching 5 million, took on Mothers' Aid as one of its causes.[45] Leff reports that in Chicago immigrant newspapers with working-class readership supported Mothers' Aid. The American Federation of Labor did endorse a Mothers' Aid resolution in 1911, although Mothers' Aid was never a priority for organized labor.[46]

The first statewide "Mothers' Aid Law" passed in Illinois in 1911. In point of fact, it was a loosely written law funding needy parents, and it was revised and substantially tightened in 1913. Like many early laws the revised legislation limited eligibility de facto to widowed mothers with children under the school-leaving age, who could prove both citizenship and three years' residence in the county in which they applied.[47] By 1919 thirty-nine states had passed similar laws. As time passed, many states offered benefits to women who were deserted or whose husbands were disabled or incarcerated. The rapid diffusion of Mothers' Aid occurred largely because in twenty-nine states the laws permitted rather than required local governments to give these grants. Similarly, very few states contributed to local payments. Local option and local funding made for highly variable coverage. Local control also meant that local norms dictated client selection. A study undertaken in 1931 by the U.S. Children's Bureau reported that beneficiaries were overwhelmingly white: Only 3 percent of clients were black, and another 1 percent were other women of color.[48] For women of both races, Mothers' Aid reached only a tiny proportion of those eligible by the admittedly stringent criteria of the day, and benefits were well below the levels of "health and decency" promulgated by the U.S. Children's Bureau.[49] The limited, indeed punitive, aspects of the female channel of the welfare state were in place from its origins.

In many places the initial implementation of Mothers' Aid fell to the Charity Organization Societies or their members, even though these organizations often opposed such laws.[50] The first task confronting administrators was to remove children from child-minding institutions, returning them to their mothers. This action saved the localities the difference between the costs of their institutional care and their home-based care, and met the implicit demand of all new welfare policies to save money. Both Workmen's Compensation and Mothers' Aid were promoted as good investments which saved money for taxpayers and society in general.[51]

Not only did opponents often participate in the initial implementation of Mothers' Aid, but they also influenced its organization in lasting ways. Scientific Charity's particular view of casework, which was intrusive while attempting to be uplifting, and which allowed for enormous discretion on the part of caseworkers owing to the imprecision of and difficulty in applying eligibility standards, became the administrative hallmark of income-tested benefits for mothers financed by the general revenue. As in the case of Workmen's Compensation, the public sector—in this instance usually the newly created Juvenile Court rather than the Industrial Commission—was administratively inexperienced and underdeveloped.[52] Public officials again looked outside government for administrative models, this time adopting the practices traditionally used by the Charity Organization Societies rather than legalistic forms or the practice of scientific management. In 1914 A. E. Sheffield described the intake, decision-making, and monitoring procedures of the Massachusetts Mothers' Aid law this way:

> The mother makes application of the overseer of the poor in her place of residence. He investigates her need, fitness, and resources, filling out a blank form which the board has prepared for the purpose, and ending with his recommendation. This information and advice he sends to the state board [of charities]. The supervisor then assigns one of the five women visitors to make a second independent investigation, and reviews the recommendation of the overseer in the light of the two findings. The result of her study of the case, whether approval, disapproval or suggestions on treatment, she embodies in a letter to the overseer in question. In the course of her work she is in constant conference with the superintendent of the adult poor division, a man who has the advantage of many years acquaintance with the individual overseers. The chairman of the committee goes over cases that present some deviation from the usual types, while the committee itself considers special cases and all general questions of policy.[53]

This entitlement process differs notably from the intake procedures used in Workmen's Compensation. In Workmen's Compensation an employee merely had to give notice of the injury to his or her employer. A standard form existed for this report, but any written notice containing the required information would suffice.[54] (See Figure 17.1.) The employer then sent a claim to the quasi-judicial commission governing the program. The employee also had to undergo a physical examination by a doctor of the employer's choosing if the employer requested such an examination. The doctor, an external agent appealing to external, "scientific" norms, determined the extent and duration of disability. The doctor filled out a simple form which was also sent to the commission.[55] Although the medical decision rules and their application became more complex over the years, the initial intake process in Workmen's Compensation was quite straightforward compared with that in Mothers' Aid.[56]

Figure 17.1

WORKMEN'S COMPENSATION

NO. 40

ILLINOIS INDUSTRIAL COMMISSION

NOTICE TO EMPLOYER OF ACCIDENTAL INJURY AND CLAIM FOR
COMPENSATION THEREFOR

To ....:
   (Write name of employer here.)
      ....:
      (Write address of employer here.)
   You will take notice that the undersigned was on the .... day of
.............., A. D. 19. . , injured by an accident arising out of and in the
course of his employment, while employed by you at ...., Illinois.
   Name of employee ....
   Post office address ....
   Relationship to claimant ....
      (State whether notice given by injured person or by dependent.)
   Claim for compensation is for ....
   Cause of the accident ....
....
   Nature of the injury is as follows ....
....
                  (Signed:) ....

NOTE.—This notice must be filled out by the injured workman or someone in
his behalf, or in case of his death, by a dependent or dependents, or someone in
their behalf. It should be served upon the employer as soon as practicable after
the accident, and not later, in any event, than thirty days thereafter. See §24 of
Act.

Source: Harper (1920), p. 636.
Note: This is the least legalistic Workmen's Compensation form, perhaps because it was
considered an internal communication to the employer, who used a separate, more typical
form to report to the Illinois Industrial Commission.

A key difference in the administration of the two programs is that
Mothers' Aid was given in return for an ongoing service rather than in
response to a realized risk. For instance, the administrators of Workmen's Compensation cared if alcohol contributed to accidents (such
claims were denied), but they did not care about, or, more important,
could not control, a beneficiary who spent all of his or her benefits on
drink. The behavior of Mothers' Aid beneficiaries, on the other hand,
was closely monitored. Thus it was the *capacity to care* that was sup-

ported in Mothers' Aid; or said another way, the program recognized not only women's economic dependency on men and children for adequate family income but the dependency of children (and adult men and elderly relatives) on women's domestic and reproductive labor, which had both emotional and material components. This was not, however, a mutually equal dependency.[57]

Moreover, by preferring caring to earning, Mothers' Aid reinforced low-wage work for beneficiaries because the work paying low wages, like in-home clothing assembly or domestic work outside the home, was most likely to meet the requirement that employment not affect supervision. In the early days of Mothers' Aid, the rhetoric of a sharp division between paid work and supervision did not match the reality of beneficiaries' experiences. For example, a 1923 study of the implementation of Mothers' Aid in nine locations showed that 52 percent of mothers receiving aid also worked for wages, certainly not the image of full-time domesticity underpinning the popular political debate.[58] Mothers' Aid reinforced and subsidized low wages for some poor, single mothers lacking a man's income.

The Mothers' Aid application and case investigation forms demonstrate the program's commitment to establishing a woman's capacity to care. As a group, they represent the continuous, administrative, private, and nonroutinized character of the program. Figures 17.2 and 17.3 reproduce the Illinois (Cook County) Mothers' Aid application and case investigation forms in use in 1919. These forms are typical, even moderate, examples of their genre, chosen to make a comparison with Illinois's model Workmen's Compensation forms, as published in 1920. The Mothers' Aid forms were clearly designed to be part of an ongoing, internal (that is, private, bureaucratic) process. The distant, final, public, and judicial qualities of the set of Workmen's Compensation forms are missing.[59] The U.S. Children's Bureau distributed both examples of Mothers' Aid laws and administrative forms to a well-developed network of activists, educators, and politicians. Thus the administrative practices and forms developed in localities, all of which arose from the ideological and practical necessities of a program requiring long-term monitoring, were widely available.[60]

The eligibility decision rules in Mothers' Aid were not the formulaic past-wages-and-percent-of-disability tables used in Workmen's Compensation. Mothers' Aid administrators did try for clear policies, but the specification of those policies was difficult because they encompassed a large number of variables, many of which were qualitative and defined against the family norms of white middle-class Protestants. An example of such a variable is the requirement that mothers be "morally fit," a

Figure 17.2

LAWS RELATING TO MOTHERS' PENSIONS.

[Forms used in Juvenile Court of Cook County (Chicago).]

APPLICATION CARD.

Surname .... | Man's first .... | Woman's first .... | Date of application ....

Alias .... | Other names needed for identification ...... | Social state ....

Cross references ....

Date.	Res. No.	Street.	Rooms.	Floor.	F. or R.	Rent.	How long.	Sanitary condition.	Landlord or agent. Address.	Dist.

First names.	Date of birth.	Birth-place.	Occupation or school with grade.	Wages.	Left sch. at age of.	Amt. of ins.	Prem.	Cause of death.	Date of death.	Mental or physical defects and illiteracy.	Docket number.
Man. 1 .... **Woman's maiden name.**											
2. .... **Children.**											
3. .... **Others in family.**				Kin-ship.	To.	Contributes to family.					
12.				....	....						
13.					...	....					

Union.	Lodge.	Benefit society.	Other sources of income.	Amt.	Pawns.	Install-ments.	Debts to.	Amt.	For.
		Weekly benefit.							

Race.	Length of time in—			Marriage.			Previous marriage.	Property.
	County.	State.	U.S.	Date.	Place.	By whom.		
Man								Do you own any? ....
Woman ...								What, if any, did your husband leave? ....

Relatives.	Address.	Kinship.	To.	References.	Address.	Connection.	Of.
				Church or Sunday school. Original religion. Man .... Woman .... Children			

State of Illinois, County of Cook, ss:

——— ——— being first duly sworn, on oath doth depose and say that the written statements under the various printed headings on the opposite side of this application card were voluntarily made by this affiant and written thereon by direction of this affiant and that the statements thereon, both written and printed, are true in substance and in fact.

Subscribed and sworn to before me this ——— day of ——— A.D. 19—.

——— ———.

——— ———, *Notary Public.*

Source: U.S. Department of Labor, Children's Bureau (1919), p. 75.

Figure 17.3

LAWS RELATING TO MOTHERS' PENSIONS.

REPORT OF INVESTIGATOR.

Previous addresses.	Rent.	When.	How long.	Previous addresses.	Rent.	When.	How long.

Employer.	Address.	Of No.	Wages.	R., I., or S.	Date. From—	Date. To—	Position.	Department.	Foreman.

Agencies and persons interested.	Address.	Capacity.	Date.	Disabilities.	Of No.	Date.
....	....	....	....	Accident Chronic physical disability .	....	......
....	....	....	....	Epilepsy .... Insanity .... Subnormal mind	....	......
....	....	....	....	Industrial accident .... Occupational disease	....	......

Institutional care of.	Of No.	Date.	Tuberculosis		
....	....	....	Venereal disease .... Maternity	....	......
....	....	....	Imprisonment .... Death	....	......

Source: U.S. Department of Labor, Children's Bureau (1919), p. 76.

term which included sexual behavior, use of alcohol and tobacco, presence of boarders, and housekeeping skills. Moreover, administrators and chroniclers of the program experienced a tension over wanting to portray the management of the programs as both scientific and flexible enough to be compassionate. Flexibility and nonroutinized decision rules went hand in hand with repeated scrutiny. Beneficiaries of Mothers' Aid never really knew for certain how long they could maintain their eligibility. Uncertainty over the duration of benefits became a longstanding characteristic of the motherhood channel of welfare policy and the welfare state.

The Aid to Dependent Children system, which nationalized the scope of the Mothers' Aid programs and partially subsidized them, subsumed the administrative style given to Mothers' Aid by the Charity Organization Society interpreters of the Poor Law tradition. This administrative style was characterized by moralistic, diffuse decision criteria, high levels of bureaucratic discretion, and many levels of managerial cross-checking. While it was designed to be efficient and accountable, it was also cumbersome and repeatedly intrusive.

The motherhood channel of the welfare state initiated by Mothers' Aid differs from the one cut by Workmen's Compensation in most aspects except race. Through the type of "work" they recognized and the politics of local control, both programs often excluded blacks. This practice was reinforced in the Social Security Act when leaders of the National Association for the Advancement of Colored People were unable to convince senators that domestic workers and farm laborers, fully 60 percent of the black labor force in 1930, should be included in categories of employment covered by the old age insurance program.

The U.S. welfare state has been fundamentally shaped by the legacy of Workmen's Compensation and Mothers' Aid, perhaps quite out of proportion to the original scope of the programs and the good they accomplished. The welfare state has two channels, carved out of a set of a specific gender, race, and class relationships during a period of political volatility and demands for political incorporation by women; supported by an ideology and practice of separate spheres; and institutionalized through different types of administrative practices. The first channel, based on the paid labor of white men, took its form from the existing administrative capacities of the law and welfare capitalism. The second channel, based on reproductive and domestic labor of white women, took its form from the Charity Organization Societies' social work techniques. The programs on which these channels are based predate the centralized creation of a U.S. welfare state during the New Deal.

These origins should be considered as strongly directing but not binding the events that followed. The gender, race, and class relations of work and politics and the administrative capacities of American government have changed in the last seventy years, and the force of those changes can be seen by canals that connect the motherhood and paid-work channels of the welfare state. The dramatic rise in the number of working mothers of all races employed in jobs covered by Social Security indicates all the complexities inherent in a two-channel welfare state predicated on the separation of wage-earners and childbearers. Social theory and social policy need to be reexamined in this light.

I would like to thank Nancy Johnson, Julie Luner, and Sarah McGrath Johnson for research assistance and Linda Baumann, Ellen Carlson, and Louise Straus for administrative support. Staff of the Minnesota Historical Society Research Center were very helpful in locating Workmen's Compensation and Mothers' Aid records. Clarke Chambers, Sara Evans, Linda Gordon, Barbara Laslett, Ray Marshall, Theda Skocpol, Louise Tilly, and the anonymous reviewers for this volume offered helpful comments.

Notes

1. Held et al. (1983); Krasner (1984); Nordlinger (1981); Skowronek (1982); Tilly (1975).
2. Skocpol (1985); Orloff and Skocpol (1984); Skocpol and Ikenberry (1983); Skocpol and Finegold (1982); and Skocpol (1980).
3. McIntosh (1978); Nelson (1984); Nelson (1985); Peattie and Rein (1983); Sapiro (1986); Schirmer (1982); Wilson (1977); and Zaretsky (1982).
4. Giddings (1984); Eisenstein and Jardine (1980).
5. A word is in order on the racial and ethnic comparisons used in this research. Aggregate census data and program reports for the period I am examining do not, as a rule, include material on people of Asian, Hispanic, or American Indian background. The text compares only the experiences of U.S. blacks and whites.
6. Using the convention employed by the majority of writers, this chapter defines welfare policy as those programs at least partially funded and managed by government in response to the loss of income due to old age, disability, unsupported motherhood, fluctuations in the business cycle, and the phases of capitalist development. A fuller definition would also include educational policy (Katz 1983), private benefits (Nelson 1985), and labor policy (Offe 1984).
7. See note 2 above.
8. Rubinow (1913), pp. 405–407.
9. Rubinow (1913), pp. 351, 354, 362.
10. Skocpol and Ikenberry (1983), pp. 129–130.
11. In this, Orloff and Skocpol (1984) and Skocpol and Ikenberry (1983) stand apart from a longstanding interest in welfare state research. Shalev (1983) reviews two generations of research on the (re)distributional consequences of welfare programs.
12. Skocpol (1985), pp. 25–27.
13. Flexner (1968 [1959]), pp. 173–175.
14. See note 2 above and Eisenstein (1981); Gelb and Palley (1987); and Glassman (1970).

15. U.S. Department of Commerce (1923), table 51, p. 54. The categories "Manufacturing and Mechanical Industries," "Extraction of Minerals," and "Transportation" contain some artisans (for example, goldsmiths) and some managers, but as large categories they overwhelmingly comprise industrial and commercial wage-earners.

16. Baker (1984), p. 639.

17. Sklar (1985).

18. Gilkes (1985); Jones, this volume.

19. Rosenberg (1982), pp. 1–28.

20. Jones (1985), pp. 134–135; Quadagno (1984). Southern planters did not have to work specifically to exclude blacks from Mothers' Aid or Workmen's Compensation. Local option in benefits and local control of hiring effectively limited these programs to whites.

21. Lubove (1968), p. 46.

22. Lubove (1968), p. 51.

23. Weinstein (1968), pp. 41–43; Skocpol and Ikenberry (1983), pp. 106–115; Friedman and Ladinsky (1978); Asher (1983).

24. Weinstein (1968), p. 48; Dresher (1970), p. 14.

25. Lubove (1968), pp. 55–57.

26. Lubove (1968), p. 59.

27. Tishler (1971); Lubove (1968).

28. Harper (1920), pp. 591–643. The U.S. Department of Labor (1917) also promoted Workmen's Compensation and its legalistic administrative style.

29. See especially form no. 10, "Application for Adjustment of Claim"; Harper (1920), pp. 601–603.

30. Berkowitz and McQuaid (1978), pp. 120–127.

31. Berkowitz and McQuaid (1980); Chandler (1977), pp. 287–314.

32. Nelson (1979, 1981).

33. Aldrich and Albeda (1980).

34. Gordon (1985). "Single mothers" is a contemporary term, and not one that these women would have used for themselves. They would have described themselves as widowed or deserted or, less frequently, divorced.

35. Gordon (1985).

36. Gratton (1986), pp. 154–173; Katz (1983).

37. Trattner (1974), p. 85.

38. Fewer institutions of all kinds were available for black children. See, for example, Kremer and Gibbens (1983).

39. Vandepol (1982), p. 224.

40. Halbert (1915).

41. *Proceedings of the Conference on the Care of Dependent Children* (1909), pp. 9–10.

42. Wedel (1975), pp. 283–284.

43. Lubove (1968), p. 102; Almy (1915), p. 155.
44. Leff (1973), pp. 408–409.
45. Wedel (1975), p. 299.
46. Leff (1973), p. 407.
47. Abbott and Breckinridge (1921), p. 12.
48. U.S. Department of Labor, Children's Bureau (1933), pp. 13–14.
49. Goodwin (1986).
50. Wedel (1975), p. 330; Edmonds and Hexter (1915), p. 5.
51. Wedel (1975); Katz (1983).
52. For a discussion of the role of the courts (though not specifically the juvenile courts) in state formation, see Skowronek (1982).
53. Sheffield (1915), p. 73.
54. Harper (1920), pp. 450–458.
55. Harper's 1920 compendium of forms does not include one to be used as a model for doctors to report their findings. Such forms did exist prior to 1920, at least in Minnesota, where the archives of Workmen's Compensation claims include a Physician's Certificate asking seven questions and allowing no more than three lines for each answer.
56. Nagi (1969).
57. Sapiro (1986).
58. Nesbitt (1923), pp. 11–13.
59. There were Mothers' Aid forms that were not only legalistic looking but actual legal documents, such as the petition to the Juvenile Court for Mothers' Aid funds. These documents ratified and transmitted decisions made elsewhere.
60. Thompson (1919).

18

Women, Family, and Politics: Farmer-Labor Women and Social Policy in the Great Depression

Elizabeth Faue

What kind of men are these who can play politics with human suffering?[1]

Marian Le Sueur, a political activist and a member of the Farmer-Labor Women's Federation (FLWF), raised this question in the context of the political debate on relief during the Great Depression, voicing the demands of many women that welfare boards protect men, women, and their families from the consequences of economic crisis. Le Sueur, along with other women of the Farmer-Labor Association (FLA), recast employment and relief as family issues, maintaining a strong connection between work and welfare as rights and the continued preservation of the child-centered family. This chapter explores some of the issues surrounding the historic position of the Minnesota Farmer-Labor party and its women members. It considers the extent to which these women shaped politics during the Depression years and under what conditions they became active in the family politics of relief and unemployment. It also explores the failure of their efforts. This historical account of women in progressive politics in one state offers us a close look at the process of women's integration into party politics at the state and local levels and helps us understand the national politics of relief and the family in the Great Depression.

The Farmer-Labor women became active by placing social concerns on Minnesota's political agenda, specifically in the area of family politics—relief, economic assistance, and the peripheral issues of health, working conditions, and childcare. In Minneapolis, the state's largest

city, women of the Hennepin County Farmer-Labor Women's Club
(FLWC) played a central role when they established an oversight committee for the relief department, protested against relief cutbacks, and
lobbied local and state officials for new, more egalitarian policies.

The success of these Minnesota women was due to several factors.
Their actions drew upon a Progressive legacy that affirmed the power
and duty of the state to ameliorate social conditions, promote equality,
and protect the family. Further, because they incorporated family ideology, Farmer-Labor women could claim moral authority in the political
arena, reinforced by the socially recognized importance of women's concerns for home and family. As Susie Stageberg, a Farmer-Labor colum-
nist, once stated, women were "not essentially politicians", but they
could be "tremendously effective propagandists when political issues
touch vital points of [their] lives."[2] In "The Contribution of Women to
the Farmer-Labor Party," Stageberg documented the involvement of
women: ". . . when in 1930, loans were called that could not be met, and
homes began to rock at their very foundations, the women so affected
fairly crashed the gates of the Farmer-Labor Party. Nearly 500 women's
clubs were organized."[3] These women acted on the belief that women
not only were but should be political activists during a crisis that
threatened their homes and families.

While the Farmer-Labor program for economic assistance and social
insurance placed it to the left of the political spectrum in the United
States, its use of family rhetoric in shaping and defending its policies did
not differ significantly from that of mainstream American political parties. Farmer-Labor policy capitalized on the historical role of the state in
privileging the family system of male wage-earning and female parenting roles. Under conditions of prolonged economic crisis, intraparty
factionalism, and declining political fortunes, the politics of the Farmer-
Labor party became increasingly conservative on family and welfare
issues in the late 1930s. In many respects, family ideology became the
only common ground for a splintering Farmer-Labor coalition.

The adherence of Minnesota's progressive party to "traditional" family politics illuminates the changing relationship of women, family, and
welfare in the United States as a whole. New Deal solutions to the Great
Depression nationalized the economy and the welfare state. As a result,
the federal government formalized the inequality of women and their
secondary status in the labor force. Nationally, as in Minnesota, family
welfare and women's equality were subordinated to the economic recovery program.

The content of family politics during the Depression includes the
evolution of relief programs in the 1930s, the orientation of these pro-

grams with regard to family and nonfamily women, and the connections between family and work policies. This chapter is divided into four sections. The first lays out the background history of the FLA and the existing state apparatus for welfare and labor legislation. The second examines the activism of Farmer-Labor women in the politics of relief, focusing on the Hennepin County FLWC; and the third discusses relief and employment legislation at the state level. The fourth section explores divisions among women in the Farmer-Labor movement and the extent to which they explain the increasingly conservative politics of the family in the 1930s.

The Farmer-Labor Party in Minnesota

Prior to the 1930s, the Minnesota state legislature had passed programs which later provided the foundation for relief and social insurance during the New Deal. In 1913 the legislature created a mothers' pension system to provide subsistence-level relief to families where the mother was widowed or her spouse was in a state institution or was under a warrant for nonsupport of children. The state FLWF and the Minnesota League of Women Voters sponsored further measures in the state legislature to appropriate state funds to support local pensions; however, the programs remained dependent on local options. During the 1920s, when no state monies were appropriated, only Minneapolis and St. Paul used mothers' pensions widely as a relief allowance. Resistance to taxes necessary to support the new system prevented many counties from providing support for dependent children.[4]

From 1915 to 1930 the state legislature also passed social programs that became the skeleton of services to come. While none of these directly gave communities assistance in emergency relief, they provided basic coverage in old age assistance and workmen's compensation oversight. Also, in the years before the Great Depression, the Working People's Non-Partisan League and later the Farmer-Labor party promoted the adoption of public works programs and unemployment insurance.[5]

The inadequacy of state programs for relief was demonstrated by the lack of response to the agricultural and industrial crisis of the 1920s and 1930s. While every Farmer-Labor platform called for the passage of farm assistance and unemployment relief, the state government remained under the control of conservative legislators and was influenced by business associations. Direct relief for farm and urban families came from local welfare boards that were unable to meet the crisis. State unemployment levels rose from 8.2 percent in 1930 to 23.4 percent in less than three years.[6] In 1932 over 12 percent of the population was on the city relief rolls in Minneapolis. The Family Welfare Association, a major source of private relief in Minneapolis, had to transfer the majority of its cases to the city Board of Public Welfare.[7] The escalating crisis left local communities, even those with as large a tax base as Minneapolis, dependent on bond issues to meet the costs of emergency assistance.[8]

During the Depression, relief eligibility, distribution of relief funds, and decisions to participate in federal relief programs were made within the local arena. In Minneapolis this process became politicized because unemployment and relief issues entered into the realm of conflict between local labor unions and the employers' association. The city council and the board of public relief disputed both the acceptance and distribution of federal and state monies. In major strikes during the decade, a local alliance of businessmen pressured the Minneapolis Board of Public Welfare to deny relief to striking workers.[9]

The economic crisis in Minnesota's agriculture and cities provided the basis for new organizing and political initiatives by the Farmer-Labor party. Under the leadership of Floyd B. Olson, the Farmer-Laborites were able to capture the state administration in 1930. Winning the governor's office, however, did not translate into adoption of the Farmer-Labor program. While the Farmer-Labor party retained control of the governorship for the next eight years, it was unable to budge Republican control of the state legislature. Even in 1936, with Farmer-Labor electoral support at its greatest, the state senate remained in Republican hands, which deadlocked the legislature on the passage of relief bills. Monies for existing programs were often held hostage by the hostile state senate, while legislation that complied with federal programs for relief funds was used as a bargaining tool to restrict other Farmer-Labor initiatives.[10]

The chief accomplishments of the Farmer-Labor party in these years were the abolition of labor injunctions, passage of a moratorium on farm mortgages, institution of significant tax reform, and development of a constituency among the unemployed.[11] Relief appropriations, however, had to pass the state legislature. Only federal pressure forced state parties into writing legislation that made state programs compatible with social security and emergency relief.[12] The F-L party's broader proposals for wide-ranging health measures, unemployment insurance, and governmental regulation never went beyond the committee level in the Republican-dominated senate. In addition, battles over party patronage, accusations of corruption, the new power of the federal government, and ideological conflicts disrupted the control that the Farmer-Labor party exercised in state government and caused major disaffection among the party's voters.[13]

The Minnesota state legislature responded to the economic crisis with emergency relief measures during Governor Olson's first term of office (1931–1933), but it was not until the federal government began channeling funds through the Federal Emergency Relief Agency that local and state relief efforts expanded to meet the problem. The emergency relief funds and later work relief programs through the Civil Works Administration and the Works Progress Administration (WPA) divided responsibility for unemployed wage-earners and "unemployables" between federal and local authorities.[14] The two systems of local and federal aid mirrored divisions between steady wage-earners and widows that earlier characterized state programs. As the federal government's role in relief and social insurance grew, so, too, did the discrepancy between men's and women's rights in the welfare state. The right of wage-earners to a steady job underwrote men's position in the primary labor force; women's right to assistance as mothers provided them with family income but also helped to structure their position in the labor force as secondary and disadvantaged.[15]

Women in the Farmer-Labor Coalition

Women's substantial representation as members, activists, and public officials in the Farmer-Labor party gave them a voice in shaping social policy.[16] While their role in the Non-Partisan League, a precursor of the FLA, seemed at times an auxiliary one, women were visible not only at picnics and fundraisers but as league organizers, educators, and candidates.[17] In Minnesota one of the four women elected to the state legislature in 1922 (the first year women were eligible for legislative office) was a league member and labor organizer, Myrtle Cain. Other women ran as candidates for office; several served on state school and library boards, and two were elected to the state legislature in the late 1920s and early 1930s. Women were even more visible, however, as appointed officials (and as recipients of party patronage) under the Farmer-Labor governorships of Olson and Benson.[18]

It was in the Depression decade that women Farmer-Laborites shifted the focus of their organization away from exclusively social functions toward a role in the political sphere. As the Farmer-Labor political organization grew stronger in Minneapolis and St. Paul, the FLWF became an avenue for party office and political activism. In 1932 Farmer-Labor women in Minneapolis formed their own club separate from the Farmer-Labor ward clubs. Organizers and officers from the three main cities in the state—Minneapolis, St. Paul, and Duluth—soon dominated the Women's Federation.[19] With the predominance of urban women in the organization, there was increasing emphasis on party concerns, political education, and social-welfare policies.

In the 1936 election the Women's Federation played its most important role in organizing women voters in support of incumbent governor Olson and the Farmer-Labor ticket. The Farmer-Labor Women's Cavalcade, which featured principal speaker Marian Le Sueur[20] and organizer Hulda Lundquist, toured state women's clubs with a sound truck, musical recordings, and political literature through the fall campaign. Women developed new educational materials, ran a campaign booth at the state fair, and raised funds.[21] Their reward for these efforts was that one third of the delegates on the state central committee of the FLA were women, marking the largest representation of women in the history of any political party. Farmer-Labor women demanded and received appointments to specific posts in the state government.[22]

Ideologically, the FLA membership divided between ostensibly mainstream Farmer-Laborites who perceived their constituency as farmers and craft unionists (and who were avowedly anticommunist) and "popular front" Farmer-Labor supporters who chose to join in an informal coalition with and give support to members of the Communist party or were members themselves.[23] The visibility and power of popular front party members in the Benson administration antagonized the anticommunist factions in the FLA.[24] Parallel developments in the Farmer-Labor Women's Federation splintered the organization into the state federation (which was not directly affiliated with the FLA) and the local FLWCs (many of which were affiliated with the state FLA through county and ward clubs). The state Women's Federation was dominated by conservative (and often older) women who had joined it from the Non-Partisan League, while the local clubs were in many instances controlled by popular front supporters, especially in Minneapolis (the Hennepin County FLWC), in Duluth, and on the Iron Range in northern Minnesota.[25]

Farmer-Labor Women and the Politics of Relief

The factionalism that surfaced in the Farmer-Labor Women's Federation was reflected in the contradictory and inconsistent family policy of the FLP during the Great Depression. The Hennepin County FLWC (which Minneapolis women dominated) played a vital part in shaping the politics of relief as it developed in response to the Depression. Women from this group became involved in the struggles over relief eligibility in the city and were a primary force on the Board of Public Welfare. One member, Selma Seestrom, was instrumental in fighting for supplementary aid for relief workers.[26] The Hennepin County group also played a role in developing and promoting public support for state relief measures.

Support of the welfare board by the county FLA and its women's club helped to balance the opposition to relief by the local employers' association. The Minneapolis city council divided along party lines as Farmer-Labor and Republican council members fought over relief policy. Even after the election of a Farmer-Labor mayor in 1935, the Board of Public Welfare remained a political battleground. The city's relief funding was dependent on bond issues, so Republican council members were able to use the bonds as a lever to force Farmer-Labor delegates off the welfare board. Employer organizations and conservatives on the city council also used the threat of a tax strike as a weapon against Farmer-Labor initiatives.[27]

The Hennepin County FLWC acted both independently and in alliance with other labor and relief groups to investigate abuses in the welfare system and to force the welfare board to respond to local needs. In 1935 the Hennepin County group placed one of its members, Myrtle Cain, on a committee to investigate practices of the Minneapolis Board of Public Welfare. After it had investigated over 1,500 cases, the committee concluded that the city relief system should eliminate its casework approach to relief. Further, the investigating committee found that welfare workers refused to disburse rent payments unless relief clients asked for them at the office, that there were wide discrepancies in budgets, and that relief investigators had heavy caseloads. The number of cases for social workers alone had increased from 30 to 175 in the years between 1930 and 1935.[28] To keep informed on welfare board activities, the Hennepin County FLWC established an oversight committee called the labor committee for relief and headed by FLWC members Myrtle Cain, Marian Le Sueur, Hilda Humphner, Myrtle Hillerman, and Eva Baltuff.[29]

The Citizens' Alliance of Minneapolis, the local employers' association, exerted continual pressure on the relief department to restrict relief and to reduce allotments. In the spring of 1936, for example, the alliance lobbied to end welfare payments to workers who had been on strike against the Strutwear Knitting Company for eight months. At that time, the Minneapolis welfare board rewrote regulations to restrict the number of single men and women eligible for assignment to the WPA. Backed by the Minnesota State Industrial Commission, the welfare board denied allowances to hundreds of women already on relief. The women were forced to accept domestic jobs that paid $1 to $3 per week as maids or servants in private homes. While workers picketed the local WPA office demanding "that no relief client, man, woman, single, married or homeless be required to accept work unless at union wages" and while the restaurant and hotel workers' union, Miscellaneous Workers local 665, fought the move by asking for an $8 weekly minimum wage for women domestics, the Hennepin County FLWC defined the root problem as women's unemployment.[30]

A Hennepin County FLWC committee, including welfare board member Selma Seestrom and federation members Jessaline Scott (wife of an alderman and a former union activist), Marian Le Sueur, and Myrtle Harris (a labor organizer), found that the welfare board "ha[d] made an organized effort to force single girls who are on relief to accept jobs as domestics in homes at starvation wages, resulting in forcing these girls to accept employment at substandard wages and possibly forcing them into prostitution. . . ."[31] While the women's committee was "heartily in favor of seeing that these girls are employed," they condemned the practice of forcing women to work at low wages. Further, the committee found that most single women on relief were not qualified for domestic service but had clerical and business backgrounds.[32]

In 1937 the caseload for the Minneapolis relief department reached a peak at nearly 18,000 cases.[33] Since the city council had made issuance of new relief bonds contingent on severe cutbacks in relief eligibility, the department was in financial crisis. The cuts included the removal of all single men under age 45 and all single women under age 35 for four months; a reduction in the clothing allowance; the requirement that all resident adult children or relatives contribute to family income; and the exclusion of all workers who either owned a car or could obtain credit.[34] Local agencies in both Minneapolis and St. Paul began to reinvestigate relief clients; and the Ramsey County Welfare Board secretary in St. Paul announced that the county would close dental clinics for relief clients, reduce allotments, and force clients to dispose of all personal property except homesteads.[35]

The Hennepin County FLWC protested the new relief rules that would force "widows and their children . . . to dispose of small personal property," eliminate aid to men and women who owned homes, and take all single men off relief.[36] In particular, the FLWC was disturbed by reports of landlords refusing to rent to relief clients with children, and they demanded an investigation of housing conditions.[37]

Supported by the Minneapolis Central Labor Union, the Farmer-Labor women publicly lobbied against the new relief proposals. When a court order forced the city Board of Public Relief to accept the claims of single men but retained its restriction on single women, the Farmer-Labor women responded:

> We are amazed at this brazen attempt to force the single women of Minneapolis into resorting to the worst forms of existence. Such an action by the welfare board is but an invitation to increase the white slave traffic, and is so utterly callous and such a vicious attack against the single women of this city that every decent person must rise to protest it.[38]

The Minneapolis Labor Committee for Relief (headed by the FLWC officers and including delegates from the Minneapolis Central Labor Union, organizations of the unemployed, and representatives from the Farmer-Labor party) was instrumental in pressuring the council both publicly and through state channels to change its policies. Following a third warning by the Farmer-Labor state relief administrator to cut off state aid, the Minneapolis Board of Public Relief finally rescinded regulations denying single men and women aid.[39]

Gender and the Welfare State

A broad definition of relief eligibility for unemployed men and women was a high priority for FLWC throughout the decade; but by 1939 factionalism and electoral defeat had eroded the effectiveness of the women's organization even in local government. When in 1938 Congress passed the Emergency Relief Appropriation Act (the Woodrum Act), a measure which effectively cut WPA programs in half, labor unions and unemployed organizations took the lead in protesting the changes.[40] While many Farmer-Labor women participated as union members, the FLWC did not play a prominent role in press accounts. One consequence was that while relief issues continued to have gendered implications, women no longer had an autonomous organization to voice their concerns. In part, the decline of the club was directly related to the decline in power of the Farmer-Labor party. Also, the arena of struggle had shifted.

The Emergency Relief Appropriation Act of 1939 implemented the cuts in relief spending through a revision of eligibility requirements for WPA employment. First paper aliens, old age pensioners, and workers who could receive Aid to Dependent Children (ADC) or unemployment insurance were barred from WPA work.[41] The overall program cut several millions of dollars in direct relief appropriations to state and local governments. Finally, the bill increased the burden on local governments to provide compensatory relief and heightened competition over federal work relief jobs.

Among the first affected in Minneapolis were 900 women who were dismissed from work relief jobs because of their eligibility for ADC. While many of the women were not eligible for the program, they lost their jobs before they could arrange intake interviews. The WPA's evaluation and firing rules created personal hardships for these women. The waiting period before a woman and her dependents could receive ADC benefits jeopardized any surplus saved; and if denied eligibility, women had little choice but to accept any available employment.[42] Reapplication for WPA employment took several weeks. Even for women who were granted benefits, ADC paid less than the $60 a month security wage women were earning on WPA. Because of the pressures to drop the number of workers on relief rolls, all working mothers were vulnerable. Union leaders intervened on behalf of those dismissed, but only twenty or so were immediately reinstated. The vast majority had little option but to apply for relief. WPA officials also refused to reinstate any women who could become eligible if they swore out a warrant citing abandonment or failure to support.[43]

The state ADC system was overloaded because of the recently completed investigation of women transferred from the local mothers' allowance system. The new federal system had only twelve case workers in Minneapolis, and the department could handle only sixty new cases each month. At this rate, some of the women laid off from WPA would have received their interviews nearly three years after being laid off, by which time many would have been ineligible.[44]

On the issue of women and eligibility for work relief, the Farmer-Labor Women's Federation was virtually silent. Their organization foundered on ideological rifts, and their state party lost control of local government in Minneapolis. While the minutes of the FLWC and the local Hennepin County Farmer-Labor paper revealed concern over the restructuring of the WPA and the consequences of relief cuts, local Farmer-Labor women did not lead this struggle. They gave moral support to a strike of WPA workers in July, 1939, but were not visible either in the strike or in the trial that followed.[45]

As historians Susan Ware and Lois Scharf have argued, the gender-neutral language of the New Deal masked a family agenda.[46] High levels of unemployment made the effect of government assistance programs on women and their families a central issue in the family politics of the 1930s. The isolation of women and their economic dependency made the question of their eligibility for relief a controversial topic, particularly when federal policy and local governments concerned with welfare costs promoted the dismissal of women from the WPA rolls. That Minnesota, and especially its principal city, Minneapolis, rejected easy solutions to the problem was due in part to the pressure of groups at both the state and local levels for higher levels of relief and broad categories of eligibility. This concern, however, worked in tandem with moralistic approaches to the welfare system which intervened in the private lives of welfare families over child custody and promoted work relief because it kept people off "the dole."

Under the New Deal, social programs assumed that women had a single relationship to the relief system as members of family units. This assumption often made programs providing for single women vulnerable to cutbacks in light of their "marginal" need. Female-headed households faced different forms of discrimination. As potential recipients of mothers' pensions (or later ADC), their access to employment and/or better-paying work relief was severely limited. Finally, their fitness as mothers became a focal point for criticism of the relief system.[47]

This was in contrast to the treatment of men as relief recipients. While New Deal federal programs placed a high premium on finding work for unemployed men through various relief administrations, there was little consideration of the needs of women workers in the design of such programs as the Civil Works Administration, the Emergency Relief Administration, and the WPA. Officials and legislators concerned with families left destitute by the Depression assumed that family men should be the principal recipients of such aid.[48] Yet federal programs under the New Deal did not distinguish between men on the basis of family status, and local programs which attempted to make this distinction failed. Women, whether single or married, did not have the same access to wage work and were presumed not to need or require access to public employment.

Employment Legislation

Issues surrounding regulation and implementation of relief on the local and state levels must be seen in the context of the developing social and employment policies worked out under the New Deal. The Farmer-Labor program in Minnesota promoted a more egalitarian approach to social insurance. In both federal and state level proposals, Farmer-Laborites urged the adoption of unemployment insurance for all workers, regardless of work history, sector of employment, or marital status.

The proposal included a program of national health insurance and maternity benefits for women workers. Introduced into the U.S. Congress by Farmer-Labor Congressman Ernest Lundeen, unemployment insurance also became a central part of the Farmer-Labor platform in 1932, 1934, and 1936. In its refusal to categorize workers by work history or current employment status, the Lundeen-Dunn bill was the broadest proposal for social insurance considered in the 1930s. The inclusion of maternity and health benefits was a serious attempt at ameliorating the effects of childbearing on women's access to federal resources.[49]

Another provision of the Lundeen-Dunn bill was to establish a social security administration, which would be controlled at the federal level and encompass all forms of economic assistance from unemployment and old age pensions to ADC grants.[50] This administration would have provided a means of bridging the division in the welfare state between wage-earner and dependent benefits while shifting the emphasis away from the moral aspects of economic assistance programs like ADC.[51] The New Deal social security program included generous grants to states in support of ADC, but continued local control made eligibility difficult to attain, set benefits below the subsistence level, and reinforced existing social divisions in entitlement programs.

The issue of women's right to wage work transcended the welfare arena in the 1930s. The issue of married women's access to work was settled by the federal government through clauses in the Economy Act of 1932.[52] Local and state governments wrestled with the problem of women and work throughout the 1930s; in Minnesota both labor and political groups were engaged in debate over the access of women, particularly married women, to work and to party patronage. Women in the Minnesota state government had weathered early attempts to bar them from employment under the Olson administration with support from the Farmer-Labor party. But in the aftermath of the Roosevelt recession of 1937 and with the continued high levels of unemployment, bills were introduced in the state legislature to bar married women from state employment. Only through an intensive lobbying effort in cooperation with the Business and Professional Women's Clubs, the League of Women Voters, and the state Bureau of Women and Children were civil service and state employment bills purged of their discriminatory restraints.[53]

The Farmer-Labor Women's Federation exerted pressure on the party through resolutions and political work to retain women's access to patronage jobs. In a resolution written in 1938, the Hennepin County FLWC complained that many married women were being discriminated against in state employment. Given the commitment of the Farmer-Labor party to "justice for all, regardless of sex," women resolved that

> regardless of whether or not a woman is married she is entitled to work.
> . . . If a married woman has merited an appointment or position by virtue
> of her activity in the farmer labor movement, her married state should not
> bar her from seeking such employment . . . no married woman already
> employed should be discharged on the ground of her being married.[54]

Resolutions were followed by specific demands. In Hennepin County, the FLWC discovered that the Minneapolis Board of Public Welfare had begun to discriminate against married women in hiring after a group of women employees asked for leaves of absence during pregnancy. At a gathering of over fifty women, the Farmer-Labor women argued that "such attempts to discriminate against minority groups represent the first step in a long chain of steps tending to isolate and defeat minority groups with the final view of embracing a decreased standard of living on the American people."[55] While the protest was aimed at stopping discrimination against married women in particular, it was framed within the language of equality for minority groups, signifying a reluctance to base their claims on gender.

During legislative sessions in 1937 and 1939, Farmer-Labor and women's advocates sponsored legislative measures which indirectly affected the conditions of and access to work for women. In 1938 the legislature passed a minimum wage law for women, hoping to revitalize legislation passed in 1923 but rendered ineffective by a Supreme Court decision in 1925.[56] This legislation was considered vital to the improvement of women's economic condition in the state, but the opposition of employers in the garment and apparel industries, laundries, and the hotel and restaurant trade prevented the easy passage or implementation of the programs.

The Minimum Wage Advisory Board established a minimum wage for women in 1938 ranging from $11 to $15 per week. Wage adjustments for the first six months alone totaled over $15,000. Court cases plagued the efforts of the board to enforce either general wage levels or wages by industry.[57] The formal agreement of major industrial groups and unions to set wage scales in 1939 did not lessen the opposition of small businesses, and the wage law continued to be controversial. As late as 1943 a business challenged the law not only on constitutional grounds but with the argument that minimum wage laws pertained only to single, self-supporting women. In *Tepel* v. *Sima*, the defendant argued unsuccessfully that married women were not covered by the law.[58]

Similarly, the Farmer-Labor party supported measures to regulate the hours of women's work. In 1933 the Farmer-Labor House led the way to a 54-hour law restricting women's labor.[59] Further efforts in 1937 to limit the hours of work to the 8-hour day/44-hour week failed in repeated attempts in the state legislature. Opposition forces included not only the Republican majority but the state Business and Professional Women's Clubs.[60] Eventual passage of the bills did little to alter the wage and working conditions of women, as the legislation did little to ameliorate unemployment for these workers.

The passage of these bills coincided with efforts in the legislature to restrict the number of women eligible for work relief and to bar or restrict married women workers. In a time of unemployment, the regulation of women's work fostered discrimination on the behalf of private and public employers, and the passage of national unemployment and labor standards laws which supposedly covered all steadily employed wage-earners did little to change this. Inequality of women in the labor market was further underwritten by their lack of eligibility for social insurance. As Judith Baer has argued, protective labor legislation in the late 1930s and 1940s was one of the principal means of justifying discrimination against women.[61]

Politics, Gender, and Generation

Divisions in political orientation in Minnesota Farmer-Labor politics had a significant impact on state social policy during the Great Depression. They also had another dimension, which reflected generational differences in political orientation and understanding of the state's role. The older generation of women (and men) in the FLA had common origins in Progressive reform. As a group, the older Farmer-Laborites gained experience in the temperance, suffrage, and pacifist movements and the socialist politics of the Non-Partisan League. They embraced a vision of the state as an impartial instrument which could serve to ameliorate school and economic conditions.

The Progressive social program that dominated early Farmer-Labor politics in Minnesota, therefore, evolved from three central propositions: first, that reproduction, sexuality, and gender were inextricably intertwined; second, that social and political behavior was fundamentally based on biological sex; and, finally, that motherhood and wage-earning were separate and gendered vocations that lay the foundations for the public claims of women and men.[62] As a consequence, Farmer-Labor women believed that social policy should be gendered.

More to the point, the rhetoric and strategy of the older generation of women Farmer-Laborites expressed an innate distrust of the violent and competitive nature of men collectively and relied upon state and families to control and channel men's aggression. In their minds, the violence of poverty and of war was related to the nature of masculine governance. Susie Stageberg, the Farmer-Labor activist, wrote:

> It is heartbreaking to think how slowly we emerge from the jungle morass of physical violence. Men seem so definitely inclined to that type of prowess that we often wonder if one of the most effective cures of war will not have to be the placing of the so-called "weaker sex," the mothers of the world, in places of national authority and international diplomacy.[63]

An angry sense of betrayal and the belief in gender differences gave women the necessary political authority upon which to base their demands for autonomy and equality in the Farmer-Labor movement. The escalating war in Europe and the economic crisis at home caused women like Stageberg to conclude that "men [had] disqualified themselves as protectors of the human family."[64] It was a belief which transcended rural/urban divisions among women in the Farmer-Labor Women's Federation and was rooted instead in generational experience.

Younger Farmer-Labor women had a different view. They aligned themselves with the politics of equality rather than the politics of protection. They understood that the achievement of suffrage made them equals with men, rather than moral superiors; and they chose integrationist rhetoric and strategy. They wanted to participate in the mainstream of the Farmer-Labor movement. While the women were for the most part urban in origin, this was not the only attribute they shared. The youngest generation of Farmer-Labor women was more likely than the older generation to have labor union membership and organizing experience and to have had experience as wage-workers. Prominent within their ranks were many present and former teachers who belonged to the American Federation of Teachers and women active in clerical unions in the Minneapolis–St. Paul area.[65]

In addition, the shift in political orientation reflected larger changes in the American political system. If older generation Farmer-Laborites had learned their politics from the Socialist party, the young women identified for the most part with the popular front. While the older generation embraced gender-linked pacifism (many were members of the Women's International League for Peace and Freedom), young women identified with antifascist politics. Young Farmer-Laborites took an antiwar and anti-interventionist stance for most of the decade but later supported American entrance into the war.

More important, young women of the Farmer-Labor party chose strategies that reflected a different perception of women's role in the public sphere. Women in the Progressive period had petitioned, lobbied, and educated; women Farmer-Laborites of the 1930s demonstrated, protested, and demanded. They lacked the perception of the older generation that the public claims of women must be based on their role as mother and consumer. While women of the FLWC had sought to promote their ends by organizing the Women's League Against the High Cost of Living in the early 1930s, the younger generation for the most part chose to avoid identifying their politics as "women's." Instead, they framed their politics and demands in a rhetoric of equality.

A number of Farmer-Labor women activists did not fit into these generalizations. Analysis of the differences between generations of women, however, provides some important insights into both factionalism and contradiction in Farmer-Labor family policy. Estelle Freedman has argued that the departure from older, woman-centered reform politics to the integration of women in the party structure had grave implications for the fate of feminism in the twentieth century. Women, she believed, were more successful when they pursued a politics of separatism.[66] The inroads of Farmer-Labor women into the party politics and state government in Minnesota would seem to contradict this view.

Women's early Farmer-Labor activism on relief issues was geared toward investigatory committees, petitions to the mayor, and lobbying for social legislation, all of which had strong parallels in the Progressive period. By 1935 the politics of relief—especially as it was practiced in Minnesota's largest city, Minneapolis—used public protest to force higher relief appropriations and to enjoin the city welfare board from implementing restrictive relief rules.

The focus of Hennepin County Farmer-Labor women on the demands and needs of single women, however, suggests that women of both generations shared an understanding of the rights and responsibilities of women based on their marital status. Shifting their priorities away from widows and children, younger women became much more concerned with "the worker and his family," a trend which revealed a theoretical and political blindness to gender issues. The claims of gender equality were more loudly heard among the younger generation, but their perception of women's vulnerability had not changed: Women's dependence on the wages of a primary male worker (or the state equivalent) still reflected their assumed status and role in society.

Conclusion

The efforts of the Farmer-Labor women to promote relief programs and improve the conditions of women's health and labor in the 1930s demonstrated their fundamental commitment to economic and social change in the context of a family-centered society. While there were deep divisions among them, Farmer-Labor women shared a concern for the welfare of families and the protection of women and children. In an era when men's and women's claims for employment and on state resources conflicted, Farmer-Labor women saw no contradiction. They envisioned a society able to provide for the welfare of all citizens.

During the 1930s Farmer-Labor women shaped relief policies and forced the implementation of egalitarian regulations on local welfare boards. In Minneapolis they forced the welfare board to rescind regulations restricting the eligibility of single and married women and penalizing nonfamily women with work requirements. On the state level, women in the Farmer-Labor party and the Women's Federation supported broad-based programs for social insurance, sought a minimum wage for women workers, and fought legislation to restrict the employment of married women. Divisions among women in the movement, however, undercut their effectiveness as advocates for women and led to the decline of the Farmer-Labor Women's Federation.

The prolonged depression of the 1930s and the differing demands of urban and rural women put a strain on the politics of family in the Farmer-Labor party. Indeed, as the decade of the 1930s came to a close, conflict over policy and ideology caused a deep rift within the FLP and in the Women's Federation itself. Deeply involved in the struggle of workers and the unemployed, some women resorted to solutions that seemed to cut across the fabric of family values that had been the base of Minnesota's Farmer-Laborism. Older women, resentful of popular front control of the party, actively supported the expulsion of its supporters from the Women's Federation and from the party itself. Even as the coming of World War II brought calls for state and national unity, these debates in the Farmer-Labor party could not be healed. Ironically, the politics of family, protectionism, and relief became increasingly divisive as a new concern for women's equality brought about changes in the welfare state.

Minnesota's Farmer-Labor party sharply posed the problems of family and welfare in the 1930s by challenging the state and federal government to guarantee the right of individuals to subsistence. Even on the left, however, these issues proved divisive as Progressive policies of protection gave way to the new politics of entitlement. In a real sense, the Farmer-Labor party reached the limits of redistributive politics in the economy. In the nation, as in Minnesota, consensus about the role of the state in promoting the general welfare disintegrated when it threatened basic assumptions about gender and the family. The divergence of opinion between the party and the electorate became so great that it halted further growth in the party and began to erode the gains of the early 1930s.

The history of Farmer-Labor women illuminates the role of women activists in the changing American political culture. Generational differences in gender consciousness, in understanding the state's role, and in political tactics marked a turning point in women's political history. While women lost an autonomous base of power when they dissolved the Farmer-Labor Women's Federation, there were compensations. Like their counterparts in federal New Deal agencies, women in both the popular front and mainstream factions of the Farmer-Labor party were successful in integrating the power structure of politics.[67] Although they did not acquire electoral power, women Farmer-Laborites directly shaped and implemented policy as government bureaucrats in ways only dreamt of by the women activists of previous eras. Although the decade of the 1930s witnessed a decline of a separate women's politics, it promoted women's activism in general politics. If feminism as an organizing principle of politics was dormant in that generation, the Farmer-Labor women's high levels of participation and their politics of equality demonstrate that feminism as political practice never entirely disappeared.

I want to thank Sara Evans, Barbara Nelson, Edward Tebbenhoff, Susan Ware, Louise Tilly and Pat Gurin, and Ann Watson of the Russell Sage Foundation for their comments and suggestions.

Notes

1. *Farmer Labor Leader*, "Woodshed for Some Solons Says Woman Speaker," April 15, 1933.
2. Stageberg (1940).
3. Stageberg (1940).
4. Koch (1967), pp. 327–338, 418–423; Minnesota State Council of Social Work (1935).
5. Asher (1973); Mayer (1951), pp. 17–36.
6. Douglas (1936), p. 41.

7. U.S. Federal Emergency Relief Administration (1934); Segner (1937).

8. Koch (1968).

9. Koch (1968).

10. Mayer (1951); Gieske (1979); Valelly (1984).

11. Valelly (1984).

12. Patterson (1969), pp. 56–73.

13. Haynes (1984); Valelly (1984).

14. Patterson (1969), pp. 74–101.

15. Nelson, this volume.

16. Throughout this chapter, generalizations about women in the Farmer-Labor party assume white ethnicity. Minnesota, the state, and its principal urban areas of Minneapolis, St. Paul, and Duluth, had a small minority population of no more than 2 percent, the majority of whom were black. This does not mean, however, that there was no black support for the Farmer-Labor platform. See *Minnesota Leader*, April 11, 1936, for an instance of black women organizing in the Rondo neighborhood of St. Paul.

17. Starr (1983).

18. For example, Violet Johnson became tax commissioner; Laura Naplin, a former state senator, became inspector of hotels and restaurants; Marian Le Sueur served first on a board for utilities and natural resources and later on a temporary basis on the state board of education; Mercedes Nelson served as a permanent education board commissioner; Florence Huber served on the minimum wage advisory committee. On women in the Non-Partisan League, see Starr (1983); women legislators are covered in Fraser and Holbert (1977).

19. Farmer-Labor Women's Clubs of Minnesota (1932); Farmer-Labor Women's Federation (1936a).

20. Marian Le Sueur was a prominent woman socialist and organizer. She organized for the Non-Partisan League, was involved in workers' education, and held a number of different posts in the Farmer-Labor government. She was also the mother of author Meridel Le Sueur. Le Sueur (1955).

21. Farmer-Labor Women's Federation (1936a, 1936b); *Minnesota Leader*, September 5, 12, 26; October 3, 17, 1936.

22. *Minnesota Leader*, March 28, May 23, 1936.

23. Haynes (1984), pp. vii, 9–70. The "popular front" did not employ the term at the time. As Haynes notes, they used the identifiers "left-wing," "the Benson faction," and "progressives" while their opponents called them "communist sympathizers," "radicals," or "Stalinists."

24. Gieske (1979), pp. 251–281; Haynes (1984), pp. 9–70.

25. *Minnesota Leader*, January 21, 1939; *Our Time*, December, 1939, p. 6.

26. Koch (1968).

27. Koch (1967), pp. 254–295.

28. Koch (1967), p. 255.
29. *Minnesota Leader*, December 21, 1935; January 11, 1936.
30. *United Action*, February 14, June 5, June 26, 1936.
31. *Minnesota Leader*, April 11, 1936.
32. *Minnesota Leader*, April 11, 1936.
33. Segner (1937); Koch (1967), pp. 255–256.
34. Koch (1967), pp. 278–280.
35. *Minnesota Leader*, July 24, 1937.
36. *Minnesota Leader*, August 7, 1937.
37. *Minneapolis Tribune*, September 7, 1937; *Minnesota Leader*, September 11, 18, 1937.
38. *Minneapolis Journal*, September 15, 1937.
39. *Minnesota Leader*, September 18, October 30, 1937.
40. Faue (1987).
41. *Minneapolis Labor Review*, December 9, 30, 1938; January 20, 27, 1939; *Northwest Organizer*, December 7, 1938; February 9, 1939.
42. *Northwest Organizer*, January 28, 1937.
43. *Northwest Organizer*, February 2, 9, 1939.
44. *Northwest Organizer*, February 2, 9, 1939.
45. Hennepin County Farmer-Labor Women's Club, Minutebook (1939–1940), Minnesota Historical Society.
46. Scharf (1980); Ware (1982).
47. Faue (1987).
48. Schwartz (1984).
49. Olson (1934); Van Kleeck (1934); Douglas (1936), pp. 74–83. For Farmer Labor women's support of the bill, see Stageberg (1938); Farmer-Labor Women's Federation (1938).
50. Douglas (1936), pp. 69–83; Van Kleeck (1934).
51. Lubove (1968), pp. 91–112.
52. Scharf (1980); Scime (1983).
53. Florence Burton, Superintendent, Division of Women and Children, Minnesota Industrial Commission, to Mary Anderson, Director, Women's Bureau, January 29, 1937; RG 86, Records of the Women's Bureau, Box 1290, Correspondence, Minnesota Industrial Commission, National Archives and Record Service (hereafter NARS).
54. Handwritten resolution by the Farmer-Labor Women's Club Committee on Women's Organization, dated 1938; in the Madge Hawkins Papers, Alpha, "Farmer-Labor Women's Club" folder, Minnesota Historical Society.
55. *Minnesota Leader*, April 9, 1938.
56. The case was *Adkins* v. *Children's Hospital*, 761 U.S. 525. Dietrickson (1926);

Minnesota Minimum Wage Commission (1922). On the national scene, see Chafe (1972), pp. 79–82; Baer (1978), pp. 92–99.

57. *Minnesota Leader*, April 30, June 11, 1938; *Justice*, July 15, 1938; Advisory Board, to Mr. J. D. Williams, Chairman, Industrial Commission of Minnesota, February 14, 1938, Box 1488; Florence Burton, Superintendent, Division of Women and Children, Minnesota Industrial Commission, to Mary Anderson, March 10, 1939, Box 1476; Summary, from *Federal Supplement*, vol. 24, 370, folder "Western Union Telegraph Co. v. Industrial Commission of Minnesota," Box 1476; RG 86, Division of Legislation and Standards, Material Related to Court Decisions, Minnesota, NARS.

58. Appellant's brief, no. 203, Municipal Court, Ramsey County, Caroline S. Tepel, appellant, 33166, v. William Sima, d.b.a., Sima Bakery, December 31, 1942; RG 86, Division of Legislation and Standards, Material Related to Court Decisions, Minnesota, Box 1476, NARS.

59. *Farmer Labor Leader*, August 15, September 3, 1933.

60. Florence Burton to Mary Anderson, January 29, 1937; RG 86, Box 1290, Correspondence, Minnesota Industrial Commission, NARS.

61. Baer (1978), pp. 66–67; Keyssar (1986).

62. Gordon (1976); Nelson, this volume.

63. Stageberg (1938).

64. Stageberg (1938).

65. There are no complete membership lists for the Farmer-Labor Women's Federation, and these generalizations are based on data collected on the leadership of the organization using the *Minnesota Leader*, city directories, and manuscript sources. There are also some brief sketches in the Women's Annual for 1936. Farmer-Labor Women's Federation (1936a).

66. Freedman (1979); Shaffer (1980); Farmer-Labor Women's Federation (1936a).

67. For the continuation of progressive women's politics in the New Deal, see Ware (1981).

19

From Protection to Equal Opportunity: The Revolution in Women's Legal Status

Jo Freeman

Between 1963 and 1976 Congress and the courts made revolutionary changes in women's status in law and public policy. Congress led the way by passing the 1963 Equal Pay Law, which for the first time committed the federal government to improving women's economic position. It followed this up with the prohibition of sex discrimination in employment as part of the milestone 1964 Civil Rights Act. In the early 1970s Congress sent the Equal Rights Amendment to the states and added to the books numerous laws whose primary thrust was to prohibit discrimination in a wide variety of federal programs and to encourage equal opportunity for women.

Parallel to this development, the Supreme Court fundamentally altered its interpretation of women's position in society. Until 1971 the judicial approach to women was that their rights, responsibilities, opportunities, and obligations were essentially determined by their position in the family. Women were viewed first and foremost as wives and mothers. Their individual rights were subservient to their class position. From this perspective virtually all laws that classified by sex were constitutional; their purpose was to protect a dependent group. Today most such laws have been found unconstitutional. Furthermore, the remaining laws and practices that treat the sexes differently are subject to more scrutiny than they were in the past, and the Court is particularly disapproving of rationalizations that encourage dependence.

Equality versus Protection

The woman suffrage movement was not a united movement. It had two distinct branches with different strategies and goals which were not abandoned even after suffrage was attained. The moderate, and larger, branch, dominated by the National American Woman Suffrage Association (NAWSA), is given most of the credit for the Nineteenth Amendment. Under the leadership of Carrie Chapman Catt, NAWSA mobilized the ratification campaign through its state chapters. Even before final ratification Catt successfully urged her followers to disband the feminist organization and form a nonpartisan, nonsectarian League of Women Voters (LWV) to encourage women to work within the parties and support a broad range of social reforms.

Under the banner of the National Woman's Party (NWP), the militant feminists had used civil disobedience, colorful demonstrations, and incessant lobbying to get the Nineteenth Amendment out of Congress. Once it was ratified, they decided to focus their attention on the eradication of legal discrimination against women. This strategy was suitable to the NWP's particular strengths as well as its feminist ideology. The vehicle through which the NWP sought to attain legal equality was the Equal Rights Amendment (ERA), written by its guiding light, Alice Paul. First introduced into Congress in 1923, it was strongly opposed by the LWV, the newly created Women's Bureau of the Department of Labor, the National Women's Trade Union League (WTUL), the National Consumers' League (NCL), and most other women's organizations. Their opposition was based on the one fact about the ERA on which everyone could agree, that it would abolish protective labor legislation for women.[1]

Protective labor legislation was a generic label for a host of state laws applicable only to women, which restricted the number of hours women could work and the amount of weight they could lift, occasionally required special benefits such as rest periods, and sometimes prohibited night work or work in certain occupations. This legislation was passed at the turn of the century in an attempt to curb sweatshop conditions. Its proponents had originally intended these laws to apply to both sexes, but the Supreme Court declared them a violation of the right to contract.[2] However, the Court upheld an Oregon law that restricted the employment of women in factories, laundries, or other "mechanical establishments" to ten hours a day, on the grounds that women's

> physical structure and a proper discharge of her maternal functions—
> having in view not merely her own health but the well-being of the race—

justify legislation to protect her. . . . The limitations which this statute places upon her contractual powers . . . are not imposed solely for her benefit, but also largely for the benefit of all. . . . The reason rests in the inherent difference between the two sexes, and in the different functions in life which they perform.[3]

Reasoning based on inherent differences between the sexes both physically and socially was not unprecedented. Ever since the Court decided the first sex discrimination case in 1873 it had maintained that "the paramount destiny and mission of women are to fulfill the noble and benign offices of wife and mother." What made *Muller* so important was its assertion that "this difference justifies a difference in legislation." *Muller* made legal sex discrimination the law of the land.[4]

The NWP originally intended the ERA to serve as a means of eradicating laws which limited women, not those that protected them. The ERA was aimed primarily at the plethora of laws which restricted women's property rights, disadvantaged them under state family laws, or barred them from holding office or serving on juries. However, the overwhelming conclusion of legal authorities was that the amendment would nullify or throw open to question all legislation aimed at women. After an attempt at compromise wording the NWP admitted that the ERA would eliminate protective laws, but asserted that it would be to women's advantage because such laws only limited women's opportunities.[5]

The conflict between those who favored the ERA and those who favored protective labor legislation reflected a fundamental difference of perspective over the meaning of equality. The NWP favored absolute equality of opportunity. Laws based on the assumption that women were weaker than men portrayed them as " 'semi-invalids,' stricken with the incurable 'disease' of womanhood." Feminists felt that women would never achieve economic freedom if assumed to be perpetually shackled by the "malady" of "maternity." The very phrase "protective legislation" implied that women were second-class citizens. Reformers, on the other hand, accepted fundamental differences in physiology and family role as incontrovertible. True equality required different treatment. While reformers believed that women had a right to work, they assumed that women's real contribution to society lay in the separate sphere of the family and that the burdens placed on those who had to work required special consideration. The protection of legislation was necessary to put women on an equal plane with men.[6]

For the next few decades, each side devoted itself to undermining the position of the other. The Women's Bureau took the lead, organizing what historian Cynthia Harrison has called the "Women's Bureau Coalition" of organizations opposed to the ERA. It conducted studies to show that protective labor laws did not handicap women and testified to this before legislative committees. Its director, Mary Anderson, was "convinced that in some cases the Woman's Party was used as a front by the employers' association that wanted to kill legislation for women."[7] The NWP argued that "whatever the effects on women of sex legislation aimed to protect them, it has been a real protection to men by slowing down the competition of women for their jobs." Although all labor unions, including those whose members were mostly women, supported protective labor legislation, the labor movement's lack of interest in organizing women and occasional opposition by its leaders to laws applying to both sexes gave credence to the NWP's views.[8]

Lacking the prestige of a government agency or the large membership of the opposition women's organizations, the NWP relied on protest and publicity to promote the ERA and oppose protective legislation. NWP members were wealthy enough to attend conferences on women all over the world where they expressed their views and persistent enough to persuade the House and Senate judiciary committees to hold hearings on the ERA every few years. They were particularly vociferous at Women's Bureau convocations, if necessary disrupting them to discuss the ERA. As a result of a confrontation at a 1926 Women in Industry conference, the Women's Bureau conducted a major study on the effects of protective labor legislation, predictably concluding that protective laws for women helped rather than hindered them.[9]

During the Depression feminists who believed that every woman had a right to work and reformers who wanted to protect women for the good of their families joined in common cause against federal and state policies designed to remove married women from the labor force. Public sentiment had long disapproved of women continuing to work after marriage. As unemployment grew, the traditional argument that working wives were undermining the family and neglecting the home was bolstered by the claim that they were taking jobs away from unemployed men who needed them to support their families. Many state and local governments ordered the dismissal of wives from public jobs, and thousands of them (particularly teachers) lost their positions.[10] In 1932 the federal government joined this movement when Congress passed Section 213 of the National Economy Act, which prohibited husbands and wives from working in the federal civil service at the same time. Because the act was attached to a desperately needed appropriations bill, it was passed by Congress over the joint opposition of all politically active women and signed by President Hoover, who nonetheless censured Section 213.[11]

For the next five years the NWP and the Women's Bureau Coalition fought an uphill battle until Congress repealed Section 213 in July 1937. Even though they lobbied, wrote letters, compiled studies, and publicized personal horror stories, their efforts were drowned out by the thousands of letters sent to periodicals and newspapers opposing the employment of married women. When mass polling began in the mid 1930s, it showed that 80 percent of all respondents opposed wives working if their husbands could support them. The opponents of Section 213 also lacked the support of the Roosevelt administration, though Eleanor Roosevelt called it a "very bad and foolish thing."[12]

President Franklin Delano Roosevelt began his presidency with a mandate to alleviate the suffering caused by the Depression. During the first hundred days of his administration Congress passed a large package of economic reform and social welfare legislation. These laws were challenged in the courts, and by 1935 the Supreme Court was pronouncing many of them unconstitutional on the grounds that they exceeded the government's authority. The same Court continued to strike down state labor legislation that it felt violated an individual's right to contract. In response to the Depression and the resulting disintegration of the wage structure, many states had enacted new minimum wage and other regulatory laws with somewhat different language in hopes that they would pass muster.[13]

Although based on precedents of almost fifty years, these decisions were usually made by a slim 5-to-4 majority. It was not until 1937, after Roosevelt had been overwhelmingly reelected and precipitated a major constitutional crisis by proposing to increase the size of the Court to fifteen, that the balance of power shifted in favor of greater governmental authority.[14] The "switch in time that saved nine" was by a single Justice, Owen J. Roberts. In *West Coast Hotel* v. *Parrish* the Court ruled 5 to 4 that Washington state could set minimum wages for women because the state "had the right to consider that its minimum wage requirements would be an important aid in carrying out its policy of protection."[15] Only a few months before, Roberts had voted differently, and the Court had invalidated a similar New York law because it found no essential difference between it and one declared unconstitutional in 1923.[16]

This decision was followed by several others in which Justice Roberts's crucial vote favored expanded government powers and permanently reversed the Court's direction. In June 1937 one conservative Justice resigned to be replaced by Hugo Black, and in July Roosevelt's "court-packing" plan was dropped. In 1938 Congress passed the Fair Labor Standards Act (FLSA), which established minimum wages, regulated workers' hours, and limited child labor. Since it applied to both men and women producing goods for interstate commerce, it was immediately challenged, but was upheld by the Court in *U.S.* v. *Darby* in 1941. Although the decision was primarily concerned with other issues, the Court noted that the fixing of minimum wages and maximum hours for either sex was no longer open to question.[17]

These two decisions—*West Coast Hotel* and *Darby*—were a watershed. The former specifically demoted liberty of contract from its pedestal of fundamental rights, and the latter implicitly extended this demotion to men as well as women. But in doing so the Court cemented even further the exception for women carved out by *Muller*. Long after the Progressive era ended, the goal of reformers to use state power to protect all workers from the vicissitudes of the free market was finally achieved. The legality of sex-specific laws remained as a residue.[18]

Transition

During the 1930s and early 1940s the coalition of women's organizations that opposed the ERA slowly disintegrated as the social reform movement which fed them died out. Some of the key organizations of the reformers, such as the WTUL, completely disappeared. Others, such as the LWV, turned their energies to other problems. The type of well-educated, socially concerned woman who had formed the active membership of reform organizations during the first third of the twentieth century went to work for New Deal agencies in the second. But by the late 1930s the network they had created in the federal government began to shrink. Most of Roosevelt's appointments of women had been to independent agencies newly created to deal with the Depression. Some of these agencies were declared unconstitutional by the Supreme Court, and others were later abolished or saw their budgets slashed in the interests of economy.[19] At the same time, support for the ERA expanded beyond the NWP to include the National Federation of Business and Professional Women's Clubs (NFBPW); social clubs such as the Soroptimists; and organizations of women lawyers, dentists, osteopaths, real estate agents, accountants, and physicians. Many NWP activists were founders or members of these groups.[20]

Although some industrial working women supported the ERA as a result of losing their jobs because of protective labor legislation, over time the division became increasingly one of class or, more specifically, occupation. Women in or associated with women working in industry, particularly unionized industries, opposed the ERA because they supported protective legislation. Business and professional women supported the ERA because they saw protective labor legislation as a barrier to their effectively competing against men in their professions. Indeed it was the attempt of protectionists to bring women in mercantile establishments under the protective umbrella which pushed NFBPW from neutrality to support for the ERA. From the businesswomen's perspective, clerical and retail sales jobs were not industrial ones and these workers were potential executives and managers who should not be protected from promotions and the responsibilities that went with them.[21]

Despite the Depression, these developments subtly shifted the balance of opinion in favor of the ERA. After 1936 congressional subcom mittees reported the ERA favorably virtually every year. When the FLSA was passed and affirmed by the Supreme Court in *U.S.* v. *Darby*, the momentum behind the ERA increased considerably. Although the Court decisions did not sway the true believers, such as Mary Anderson of the Women's Bureau and leaders of the NCL and the LVW, it rendered their position much less persuasive. Their argument was undermined still further when World War II brought large numbers of women into the labor force who were not visibly harmed by the suspension of protective labor laws in the war industries. And the inclusion of support for the ERA in the 1940 Republican platform gave it legitimacy. In 1942 the full Judiciary Committees of both houses in Congress voted favorably for the ERA.[22]

Although aided by circumstances, this increase in momentum was not accidental. During the twenties and thirties Alice Paul had lived abroad and devoted most of her time and attention to international activities for equal rights. The war in Europe forced her return in 1941 to the United States where she resumed active leadership of the NWP, reorganizing and revitalizing it. Recognizing the similarity of the wartime attitude toward democratic ideals and slogans about equality with that of the suffrage era, she began a massive publicity campaign. Successes included endorsements of the ERA by noted public figures such as Nobel novelist Pearl Buck, artist Georgia O'Keeffe, and actresses Helen Hayes and Katharine Hepburn; newspapers, such as the *New York Herald Tribune* and the *Christian Science Monitor;* and major women's organizations such as the General Federation of Women's Clubs.[23] In 1944 both political parties endorsed the ERA in their platforms.

In response, opponents formed the National Committee to Defeat the Un-Equal Rights Amendment (NCDURA) late in 1944. The composition of this new anti-ERA coalition reflected the political changes of the previous two decades. The original Women's Bureau Coalition had been a coalition of *women's* organizations, most of which had been formed during the Progressive movement. The NCDURA reflected the rise to power of organizations involved in the New Deal coalition. Its twenty-seven affiliated groups were mostly labor unions, joined with those remaining organizations of the original coalition that had kept the anti-ERA faith through the years (NCL, YWCA, LWV). It also included some additional women's organizations, such as the National Council of Catholic Women, and new organizations, such as the National Council of Negro Women.[24]

The NCDURA's first move was to propose an alternative to the ERA in the form of an Equal Pay Act (EPA). The idea that women should receive equal pay for equal work was not a new one—and equal pay laws existed in a few states—but there had been no organized effort to pass federal legislation. Opponents of the ERA had long argued that the proper legislative route was "specific bills for specific ills," not blanket prohibitions. The EPA was aimed at an acknowledged "ill" that had become even more apparent during the war when women moved into previously male jobs. While the NCDURA saw the proposal as meritorious in its own right, it hoped that this "positive alternative" would preempt the ERA. This presented a dilemma to the NWP. Caught between its fear that the EPA would deflect interest from the ERA and a concern not to be seen as against all bills on women, it was publicly neutral and privately opposed. The NWP was particularly concerned that the proposed bill would be enforced by its archenemy, the Women's Bureau, and that since the language only prohibited paying women less than men, not vice versa, the EPA was just another form of sex-specific protective labor legislation. The NWP argued that equal pay would undermine women's job opportunities by removing the economic incentive for employers to prefer them to men.[25]

As an anti-ERA measure the EPA was not successful, and the Senate voted on the ERA for the first time on July 19, 1946. However, the vote was unexpected and the supporters unprepared. The tally of 38 to 35 was well below the two thirds required for a constitutional amendment.[26] Nonetheless, expectations of favorable action in the next Congress were high because "there has been a subtle change in the public attitude toward [the ERA.]"

> . . . the recent war brought about a shift in the strategic positions of the opposing factions . . . [because] these things happened: In the interests of high production, most "protective" industrial laws were waived by State legislatures and labor boards. Women in industry worked side by side with men around the clock. WACS, WAVES, SPARS and women Marines took over strenuous jobs, some of them on front-line assignments. Nurses

worked at advanced battle field stations. WASPS flew cumbersome bombers and "hot" fighter planes under the Ferry Command, establishing an excellent record.[27]

To reverse the flow of support, the NCDURA proposed the "Status Bill." Introduced on February 17, 1947, the bill declared the policy of the United States to be that "in law and its administration no distinctions on the basis of sex shall be made except such as are reasonably based on differences in physical structure, biological or social function." Instead of enforcement provisions, it proposed the creation of a Commission on the Legal Status of Women to study sex discrimination. Along with this "more positive" approach the NCDURA decided that it needed a more positive name and became the National Committee on the Status of Women (NCSW), headed by Mary Anderson, former head of the Women's Bureau.[28]

In January 1950 the ERA was debated on the Senate floor once again. When the Status Bill was overwhelmingly rejected by 65 to 18, ERA opponents made their next move. At the end of the debate, Senator Carl Hayden (D. Ariz.), at the suggestion of the Women's Bureau, proposed an amendment which read: "The provisions of this article shall not be construed to impair any rights, benefits, or exemptions now or hereafter conferred by law upon persons of the female sex." ERA proponents were caught by surprise, and many senators, whose support for the ERA had been on the record but never very strong, took advantage of the opportunity to vote for both amendments. The Hayden rider passed 51 to 31 and the ERA, thus vitiated, passed 63 to 19. This strategy was repeated when the ERA once again came to the Senate floor in July 1953. This time the rider passed by 58 to 25 and the ERA by 73 to 11.[29]

When Eisenhower was inaugurated in 1953 ERA proponents thought that its time had finally come. Eisenhower favored the ERA, albeit weakly, as did the new appointee to head the Women's Bureau, Alice Leopold. Although Leopold withdrew the bureau's longstanding opposition, the new Secretary of Labor, a Democrat and official of the Plumbers Union, continued the department's policy of official opposition, albeit muted. In effect the administration withdrew from the arena, leaving the battle to Congress, where key committees were headed by ERA opponents.[30]

The gap left by the defection of the Women's Bureau was filled by organized labor. In 1957 Esther Peterson became the legislative representative of the industrial union department of the AFL-CIO and orchestrated an anti-ERA lobbying campaign. Her main weapon was the Hayden rider, which was supported even by members of Congress listed as sponsors of the ERA. The ERA's main sponsor in the House, Representative Katherine St. George (R. N.Y.), tried to find substitute language that would not undermine the amendment, but since the rider was really just a ploy to kill the ERA, no compromise could be found. The ERA seemed blocked at every turn.[31]

Between 1946 and 1953 the NWP was embroiled in internal disputes and suffered a serious decline in membership. After many decades of keeping the faith, many NWP stalwarts had died or retired and its active members were few. Its journal, *Equal Rights,* ceased publication in 1954. Although by then many other organizations supported the ERA, the NWP maintained exclusive rights to leadership of the struggle. The NFBPW, which opened an office to work on the amendment in 1947, often found its efforts thwarted by the NWP, which "reacted to any suggestion that they give up control of the campaign with hostility." It could still get the ERA introduced into every new Congress, but it could not get it out.[32]

Turning Point

The ERA hit its nadir in 1960 and also began its resurgence. The key person in both these developments was Esther Peterson. As an adviser to presidential candidate John F. Kennedy, she convinced the Democratic party to drop the ERA from its 1960 platform in favor of a vague expression against barriers to employment based on sex and "equality of rights under law, including equal pay." After Kennedy was elected she asked, and received, appointment as director of the Women's Bureau and was also made an assistant secretary of labor. Few other women received such important appointments, a lack of action for which Kennedy was roundly criticized.[33]

Peterson had two major items on her agenda to improve the status of women: passage of the EPA and derailment of the ERA. To accomplish the first she organized a concerted lobbying campaign which drew upon the expertise and contacts Peterson had developed as a lobbyist for the AFL-CIO. Although the final bill was narrower than Peterson and EPA advocates had wanted, and covered only 61 percent of the female labor force, when passed in 1963, after numerous hearings and intensive lobbying, it committed the federal government to its first active efforts to improve the economic position of women.

One of Peterson's first recommendations to the new President was the creation of a national commission on women, one of the components of the 1947 Status Bill once proposed by ERA opponents. To avoid the NWP lobbyists, the President's Commission on the Status of Women was created by Executive Order 10980 on December 14, 1961. Members were selected to represent mainstream opinion on women and to come up with suggestions that would be acceptable to the administration. Marguerite Rawalt, a former NFBPW president, was the sole ERA supporter. Eleanor Roosevelt was asked to chair the President's Commission, and when she died almost a year later, she was not replaced.

> Peterson . . . and her colleagues used the presidential commission on women to stop the E.R.A. dead in its legislative tracks. Peterson reasoned that Congress would not be likely to act on the E.R.A. while the matter was under consideration by a presidential panel. In addition, she presumed that eventually the Commission would offer substitute recommendations which would continue to stymie the Amendment's progress. Peterson regarded the Commission's most important function to be the creation of an alternative program of "constructive" action to improve women's status, a possibility which before had always been blocked by the E.R.A dispute.[34]

The commission did offer a middle ground. After much debate and many alternative proposals on wording, the final report declared: "Equality of rights under the law for all persons, male or female, is so basic to democracy . . . that it must be reflected in the fundamental law of the land. . . ." The commission acknowledged unreasonable distinctions based on sex in state laws and practices which discriminated against women. It considered three different ways to achieve "greater recognition of the rights of women": (1) test litigation challenging laws under the Fourteenth and Fifth Amendments to the Constitution, (2) the ERA, and (3) state legislative action. The commission expressed a preference for the first and third routes, but did not explicitly oppose the ERA. In deference to Marguerite Rawalt, it declared that the ERA "need not *now* be sought." The report called instead for "judicial clarification . . . in order that remaining ambiguities with respect to the constitutional protection of women's rights be eliminated."[35]

Although the President's Commission gave Congress an excuse to abstain from further consideration of the ERA, it also was a key element in its resurgence. Governors in all but one state were prompted to create their own state commissions on the status of women. These prepared extensive reports documenting discrimination against women in their states. It was at the third annual conference of the state commissions in June 1966 that the National Organization for Women (NOW) was formed. In 1967 NOW formulated an eight-point Bill of Rights which included the ERA. It also supported a woman's right to choose abortion, which prompted board member Elizabeth Boyer to leave NOW and form a separate organization, the Women's Equity Action League (WEAL), which concentrated on eliminating employment and education discrimination, particularly through litigation and lobbying.[36]

It was several years before the ERA became a NOW priority. Initially, NOW was more concerned with changing the guidelines on sex discrimination promulgated by the Equal Employment Opportunity Commission (EEOC), which had been created by Title VII of the 1964 Civil Rights Act. The addition of "sex" to the section of the act prohibiting discrimination in employment on the basis of race, color, creed, and national origin was more opportunistic than planned. It was not brought up in committee and no hearings were held. Instead it was a floor amendment in the House made by a male ERA supporter from Virginia which received several hours of humorous debate before it passed 168 to 133. The NWP had wanted to amend all the relevant sections of the Civil Rights Act, but it could find support only for the employment section, and this was shaky. Alice Paul considered such maneuvers as "sideshows" to the ERA campaign, engaged in only because the organization did not want to see any group given rights not also given equally to women. Throughout the 1950s the NWP lobbied for the inclusion of sex discrimination in Executive Orders prohibiting race discrimination by government contractors and had tried to add "sex" to other civil rights bills. Despite opposition from the Women's Bureau, the "sex" amendment was passed in the House, primarily by a coalition of Republicans and southern Democrats. It was not removed in the Senate because the Johnson administration wanted to minimize the differences which would have to be ironed out in the House-Senate Conference and because the President had made several public statements in January 1964 on the importance of bringing more women into government.[37]

The EEOC chose to follow what it felt was the true intent of Congress rather than the actual wording of the law and ignored the sex provision. The first executive director of the EEOC publicly stated that the provision was a "fluke" that was "conceived out of wedlock."[38] Initial guidelines prohibited segregation of want ads by race but permitted them by sex. The EEOC also supported state protective labor legislation, forcing opponents to go to court. Several of these cases were handled by lawyers on behalf of NOW, including *Weeks v. Southern Bell Telephone*, the first major decision by an appeals court. The Fifth Circuit's ringing denunciation of "protection" in March 1969 was cited in virtually all subsequent cases.

Southern Bell . . . would have us "assume" on the basis of a "stereotyped characterization" that few or no women can safely lift thirty pounds, while all men are treated as if they can. . . .

. . . Title VII rejects just this type of romantic paternalism as unduly Victorian and instead vests the individual woman with the power to decide whether or not to take on unromantic tasks. . . . The promise of Title VII is that women are now to be on an equal footing.[39]

This ruling that state protective laws were preempted by Title VII and therefore invalid was consistently followed by other courts, thus paving the way for reconsideration of the Equal Rights Amendment.[40]

Since the traditional opponents of the ERA had based their opposition on the need to maintain protective labor legislation, they were neutralized by its invalidation. Several unions were impressed by the numerous legal complaints filed by blue-collar women about the restriction of their job opportunities by protective labor legislation. The United Auto Workers endorsed the ERA in 1970 and was soon followed by others. The AFL-CIO, however, did not change its position until late 1973. The Women's Bureau switched in 1969 when the Nixon administration appointed as its director Elizabeth Duncan Koontz, a black former president of the National Education Association (NEA) from North Carolina who, like the NEA, was an ERA supporter.[41]

In 1970 the emerging women's liberation movement became a major public phenomenon with massive press publicity. This generated an enormous momentum for the ERA and eventually for additional legislation to eliminate sex discrimination. The first governmental body to endorse the ERA was the Citizens' Advisory Council on the Status of Women, a successor to the President's Commission. It did so on February 7, 1970. The second was the President's Task Force on Women's Rights and Responsibilities, which had been created the previous year by Nixon to appease feminists. It prepared a report with detailed policy proposals to improve the status of women, including presidential endorsement of the ERA, which was held up for six months because it was "too strong." Much of the legislation to be introduced into Congress in the next ten years was first spelled out in the task force report, *A Matter of Simple Justice*.[42]

In May 1970, in response to disruptions by NOW members of February hearings on the eighteen-year-old vote, hearings were held in the Senate Judiciary Subcommittee on Constitutional Amendments, chaired by ERA sponsor Birch Bayh (D. Ind.). In June the new secretary of labor endorsed the ERA at the Women's Bureau's fiftieth anniversary conference, where the task force report was also released. During that conference Representative Martha Griffiths (D. Mich.) announced that she was sponsoring a discharge petition to release the ERA from the House Judiciary Committee whose Chair Emmanuel Celler (D. N.Y.) had locked it up for almost twenty years. The House voted on the ERA for the first time in August 1970; it passed by 350 to 15. The Senate voted to add two amendments: one to exempt women from the military draft and another to permit prayer in public schools. Therefore the ERA was dropped for that session. When it was reintroduced into the next Congress, the House Judiciary Subcommittee held new hearings and Celler tried once again to block the ERA in committee with a crippling amendment. Nonetheless, it reached the floor again on October 12, 1971, where it passed 354 to 24. In the Senate the following March, Sam Ervin (D. N.C.) proposed eight separate substitutes that all met with resounding defeat. The final vote for passage was 84 to 8.[43]

Passage of the ERA came at a unique point in its history. It had been debated for years by mutual antagonists who would not compromise an inch. Meanwhile, social and legal changes had undermined the basis of the opponents' position. Between 1970 and 1972 opposition was greatly attenuated. The ERA became a symbolic issue on which everyone could agree. Yet even as this agreement was reached, a new opposition was developing. Ironically, it was from the right, which had usually supported the ERA during its lengthy stay in Congress. This opposition grew and eventually consumed more moderate forces, even as the ERA gained support from ancient foes to the left.

Legislation

Although the ERA was not ratified, the two-year battle had some very beneficial side effects. It impressed Congress with the serious constituent interest in women's rights and facilitated liaisons between feminist organizations and congressional staff. With this impetus the same Congress that sent the ERA to the states passed a bumper crop of women's rights legislation—considerably more than all relevant legislation previously passed in the history of this country. These laws (1) expanded the coverage of Title VII and the enforcement powers of the EEOC; (2) prohibited sex discrimination in all federally aided education programs (Title IX); (3) added sex discrimination to the jurisdiction of the U.S. Commission on Civil Rights; (4) prohibited sex discrimination in state programs funded by federal revenue sharing; (5) provided free daycare for children of poor families and a sliding fee scale for higher-income families (vetoed by President Nixon); (6) provided for a childcare tax deduction for some parents; (7) added prohibitions against sex discrimination to a plethora of federally funded programs including health training, Appalachian redevelopment, and water pollution.

Subsequent Congresses have not passed as many major laws, but they have been active. New laws include the Equal Credit Opportunity Act; the Women's Educational Equity Act, which provides grants to design programs and activities to eliminate stereotyping and achieve educational equity; creation of the National Center for the Control and Prevention of Rape; an amendment to the Foreign Assistance Act requiring that particular attention be given to programs, projects, and activities which tend to integrate women into the national economies of foreign countries; prohibitions of discrimination in the sale, rental, or financing of housing; an amendment to Title VII to include pregnancy in employment disability insurance coverage; admission of women to the military academies; and the addition of still more antidiscrimination provisions to federally funded programs. The states have also been active arenas in the last fifteen years, prohibiting sex discrimination in employment, housing, and credit; and in some states prohibiting discrimination in insurance, education, and public accommodations. Many states have followed the lead of the federal government in conducting studies to identify gender-based distinctions in their laws and recommend changes. Most of these studies were in response to efforts to adopt a state ERA or ratify the federal amendment.[44]

Sex and the Supreme Court

The proposal of the President's Commission that women seek "judicial clarification" under the Fifth and Fourteenth Amendments was not a new idea. It had been tried during the nineteenth century without success. After *Muller* declared that sex was a reasonable basis of classification, further efforts were futile. Although the rationale of *Muller* had rested on public concern with maternal health, it was cited as a precedent in support of excluding women from juries, different treatment of the sexes in occupational licensing, and excluding women from state-supported colleges.[45] To understand why *Muller* was so important one has to understand the structure of legal analysis that has developed around the Fourteenth Amendment. The simple language of Section I imposed restrictions on state action that had previously been imposed only on the federal government:

> No state shall make or enforce any law which shall abridge the privileges or immunities of citizens of the United States; nor shall any State deprive

any person of life, liberty, or property, without due process of law; nor deny to any person within its jurisdiction the equal protection of the laws.

The Supreme Court ruled in 1872 that the "privileges and immunities" clause did not convey to citizens any rights that they had not previously had, and it thus shut off that avenue of legal development.[46] The "due process" clause was for many decades used to undermine state economic regulations such as protective labor laws applying to both sexes. This left the "equal protection" clause. Initially, the Court ruled that race and only race was in the minds of the legislators when the Fourteenth Amendment was passed, but its coverage was soon expanded to include national origin and alienage. However, what is prohibited is not *all* official discrimination, but only *invidious* discrimination. If a *compelling state interest* is served by discrimination—such as the need to integrate school districts—distinct laws or state practices based on race or nationality are permitted. The essence of this approach is that certain classifications made by the state are "suspect" and thus subject to "strict scrutiny" by the courts. Unless there is a "compelling state interest" they will be struck down as unconstitutional. Classifications that are not suspect are not subject to the same searching inquiry by the courts. The state need only show that there is a "rational basis" for their existence, and the court will then defer to the legislature.

In practice, classifications that are subject to strict scrutiny are almost always invalidated as unconstitutional. Classifications that need only a rational basis have almost always survived challenges to their constitutionality. The courts have shown great deference to state legislatures and have gone out of their way to construct rationalizations for legal distinctions that to the untrained eye seem to be extremely flimsy.[47] The consequence has been a "two-tier" system in which the type of analysis applied to a classification, rather than the reason for the classification, determines the outcome of its constitutionality. The "strict scrutiny" test is usually fatal, while the "rational basis" test is usually meaningless. Thus, in order to eliminate a legal classification, the courts must be convinced that strict scrutiny is necessary.

In 1961, only two years before the President's Commission urged courts to examine the validity under the Fifth and Fourteenth Amendments of the "laws and official practices discriminating against women, to the end that the principle of equality become firmly established in constitutional doctrine,"[48] the Supreme Court had upheld sex discrimination as valid. Reviewing the conviction of a Florida woman by an all-male jury for murdering her husband, the Court upheld a law exempting women from jury service unless they registered a desire to serve with the clerk of the circuit court. Even though this virtually ensured that there would be no women in the jury pool, the Court justified it as acceptable because of women's "special responsibilities" as the "center of home and family life."[49]

Ten years after *Hoyt*, the Supreme Court began to take a different view. The turning point came in 1971 when the Court unanimously held unconstitutional an Idaho statute giving preference to males in the appointment of administrators of estates. In *Reed* v. *Reed* the Court found the "administrative convenience" explanation for the preference for males to have no rational basis.[50] Although unexpected, this development was not unforeseeable. During the previous few years the Court had been adding a bit of bite to the rational basis test by looking more closely at state rationalizations for *some* classifications that did not trigger strict scrutiny. During the previous two years the emerging women's movement had become publicly prominent, and the ERA had been battling its way through Congress.

One sign of this "sea change" in public attitude was given by the American Civil Liberties Union (ACLU), a traditional opponent of the ERA. In 1968 its national board had rejected a proposed policy statement about women's legal rights which would challenge sex-specific legislation. Two years later, Suzanne Post and Faith Seidenberg, NOW's vice president for legal affairs, organized a women's caucus at the ACLU's 1970 national biennial meeting. It persuaded the board to pass a resolution supporting the ERA and litigation to foster women's rights. Shortly thereafter a staff member spotted *Reed* in a legal publication while it was still in the Idaho courts. The ACLU became co-counsel and asked Ruth Bader Ginsburg, a professor at Rutgers Law School, to write a major portion of the brief presented to the Supreme Court. The change was not solely due to pressure from within. In the preceding few years the ACLU's affiliates had been bombarded with requests by women to take on sex discrimination cases. Ginsburg's students had likewise brought cases in state courts to her attention. After *Reed* the ACLU obtained a major grant from the Ford Foundation for a Women's Rights Project. Ginsburg argued several key cases before the Supreme Court, and the ACLU wrote amicus briefs in others, but there was never any strategy to bring cases in a particular order to achieve a particular result.[51]

The next key case was brought before the Court in 1973 after Air Force Lieutenant Sharon Frontiero challenged a statute that provided dependent allowances for males in the uniformed services without proof of actual economic dependence, but permitted such allowances for females only if they could show that they paid one half of their husbands' living costs. Eight members of the Court found the statute unconstitutional but they split on the reasons. Four applied strict scrutiny, thus granting sex the long-sought status of a "suspect class." Three applied the traditional rational basis test, but found the statute unconstitutional on the authority of *Reed*. One Justice concurred without giving an opinion. Justice Rehnquist was the sole dissenter. If only one more justice had joined the plurality opinion, "legal equality," or at least as much as any other group had, would have been achieved.[52]

In cases after *Reed* and *Frontiero* the Court applied a "strict rational basis" standard with greater and greater scrutiny, until in 1976 a new standard, subsequently referred to as "intermediate scrutiny," was articulated. On the surface, *Craig* v. *Boren* did not appear to be a momentous case and was not sponsored by any of the feminist litigation groups. It concerned an Oklahoma law that prohibited selling "3.2" beer to men under age 21 but allowed sales to women over age 18. The state's rationale for this law was that more than ten times as many males as females between the ages of 18 and 21 were arrested for drunk driving. The Court found the law unconstitutional, holding that "classifications by gender must serve important governmental objectives and must be substantially related to achievement of those objectives." The Court was not satisfied that "sex represents a legitimate, accurate proxy for the regulation of drinking and driving."[53]

After *Craig* the Court no longer wrote plurality opinions in which some justices supported use of strict scrutiny in gender cases and others concurred or dissented on a different basis. Instead, the "heightened scrutiny" of the new intermediate standard was applied consistently, though not unanimously, usually to strike down laws that made distinctions by sex. Yet even before *Craig*, the language of decisions after *Reed* reflected a very different approach by the Court to women's status. No longer was family status the determinant of women's legal status. Instead, the very articulation by a state of the desirability of women's economic dependence or women's unique responsibility for family obligations led the Court to view it as irrational. Two cases decided in the spring of 1975 illustrate this profound transformation from the assumptions of *Hoyt* and earlier cases that a woman's family role created a valid basis for classification by sex.

Weinberger v. *Wiesenfeld* challenged a provision of the Social Security Act that provided benefits for the surviving widow and minor children of a working man covered by the act, but only for the minor children of a covered woman. The unanimous opinion of the Court pointed out that

> since the Constitution forbids . . . gender-based differentiation premised
> upon assumptions as to dependency . . . [it] also forbids the gender-based

differentiation that results in the efforts of female workers required to pay social security taxes producing less protection for their families than is produced by the efforts of men.[54]

A month later the Court went further in *Stanton* v. *Stanton*, a Utah case in which a divorced father ceased paying child support to his daughter when she reached age 18, but continued it for his son on the ground that in Utah girls were no longer minors after age 18, but boys were until age 21. It found:

> No longer is the female destined solely for the home and the rearing of the family, and only the male for the marketplace and the world of ideas. . . . If the female is not to be supported so long as the male, she hardly can be expected to attend school as long as he does, and bringing her education to an end earlier coincides with the role-typing society has long imposed.[55]

The Supreme Court has continued to strike down state statutes which reinforced role-typing and economic dependency, or which rested on "archaic and overbroad generalizations." In doing so it has invalidated statutes that provided for social security benefits payable to widows but not to widowers,[56] for alimony for wives but not for husbands,[57] permitted an unwed mother but not the father to block adoption of illegitimate children,[58] paid welfare benefits to families with unemployed fathers but not unemployed mothers,[59] and paid workers' compensation death benefits to widows, but to widowers only if they could prove economic dependency.[60]

However, the record of the women's rights litigants is not unblemished, as the Court has not ruled against *all* sex distinctions. Both before and after *Craig* the Court has looked favorably on statutes that it felt operated "to compensate women for past economic discrimination." *Califano* v. *Webster* upheld a social security provision that, prior to 1972, permitted women to eliminate more of their low-earning years from the calculation of their retirement benefits than men could eliminate, because it "works directly to remedy some part of the effect of past discrimination."[61] *Kahn* v. *Shevin* upheld a Florida statute giving widows, but not widowers, a $500 property tax exemption. The Court ruled that the state law was "reasonably designed to further state policy of cushioning the financial impact of spousal loss upon the sex for which that loss imposes a disproportionately heavy burden."[62]

The other rationale that the Court has employed to uphold some sex distinctions is that men and women are not "similarly situated." *Schlesinger* v. *Ballard* upheld federal statutes that allowed more time for female naval officers than for male officers to attain promotion before mandatory discharge on the ground that they served the goal of providing women equitable career advancement opportunities. The Court found that because women were restricted from combat and most sea duty, it would take longer for them to compile favorable service records than it took men. Therefore, "the different treatment of men and women naval officers . . . reflects, not archaic and overbroad generalizations, but, instead, the demonstrable fact that [they] are *not* similarly situated with respect to opportunities for professional service."[63] This explanation was also relied on to uphold a California statute that made statutory rape a crime that only males could commit against females. The state supreme court had already subjected the classification to "strict scrutiny" and found that the statute served a "compelling state interest" in preventing teenage pregnancies. Applying the lesser standard of "important governmental objectives," the U.S. Supreme Court came to the same conclusion, but only by ignoring the dissent's objection that a sex-specific statute was not "substantially related to a stated goal as long as a gender-neutral one could achieve the same result."[64]

These cases led in turn to *Rostker* v. *Goldberg*, which contested the requirement that males but not females register for a potential draft. Giving great weight to the legislative history, the Court noted that Congress's thorough consideration of the issue had clearly established that its decision to exempt women was not the "accidental by-product of a traditional way of thinking about females." It concluded that the "purpose of registration . . . was to prepare for a draft of *combat* troops" and that "women as a group . . . unlike men as a group, are not eligible for combat." Because men and women were not "similarly situated" with regard to military service, it was not unconstitutional to distinguish between them. "The Constitution requires that Congress treat similarly situated persons similarly, not that it engage in gestures of superficial equality."[65]

Although the Court has not adopted the same standard for sex cases as it has for race, religion, and national origin, for both categories there are some exceptions to the mandate for equality, usually ones involving rectification for past inequalities. However, cases permitting different treatment of the sexes on the grounds that they are not "similarly situated" could, under a different Court, lead the way to a modern version of *Muller*. On the surface it might seem desirable for the Court to require equality where men and women are similarly situated and to make exceptions apparently in women's favor where they are not, but there are very few circumstances in which men and women are similarly situated. *Muller* was also perceived to be in women's favor from the perspective of reformers of the time. Yet later courts, and legislatures, relied on it to restrict women's opportunities.

These deviations from the pure feminist approach should not detract from recognition of the revolution in judicial thinking on women that has occurred since 1961. Sex is not yet a suspect class, but legal sex discrimination is no longer sanctioned as a necessary protection for a dependent class. What is even more remarkable is that the revolution took place in such a short period of time for judicial doctrine. True, the 1937 Court changed directions in only a few months, but the decisions both before and after the change were by a vote of 5 to 4 and the country was in the midst of a major crisis. Most of the decisions on women's rights made since 1971 have been by comfortable pluralities. The extent of the revolution is perhaps best seen in two challenges to national service organizations that have traditionally excluded women from membership—the Jaycees and the Rotary Clubs. Not only did the Court rule that any "slight infringement on Rotary members' rights of expressive association . . . is justified because it serves the State's compelling interest in eliminating discrimination against women," but even Chief Justice Rehnquist joined in the unanimous ruling.[66]

The Next Revolution

While the finishing touches are being applied to the legal revolution of the 1970s, the stage is being set for the next act. As revolutionary as were the changes in public policy toward women, there is still a fundamental assumption that the principal economic unit is the two-parent family, only *one* of whom is the primary wage-earner, with the other being cast in a supporting role. It is this assumption that feminist theory and feminist policy proposals need to challenge. Feminist proposals must recognize that all adults should have responsibility for the support of themselves and their children, regardless of their individual living situation, and that all are entitled to policies that will facilitate carrying out this responsibility regardless of sex, marital status, or parental status. Acceptance of this idea would require an entire reconception of what is women's role in the labor force, what is a family, and what are our social obligations to it. It would also involve the recognition that one cannot have primary responsibility both to a career and to a family and that rather than divide such responsibilities by sex as they are now, modifications should be made in both so that women and men can participate equally in both.

The revolution in consciousness wrought by the women's liberation movement has resulted in acceptance of the idea of "equal opportunity." This view asserts that women who are like men should be treated equally with men. Although drastically different from earlier views, it accepts as standard the traditional male lifestyle, and that standard in turn assumes that one's primary responsibility should and can be one's job, because one has a spouse (or spouse surrogate) whose primary responsibility is the maintenance of house and family obligations. Women whose personal lifestyle and resources permit them to fit these assumptions, could, in the absence of sex discrimination, succeed equally with men.

But most women cannot do this because our traditional conception of the family, and women's role within the family, makes this impossible. Despite the fact that only 20 percent of all adults live in units composed of children plus two adults, only one of whom is income producing, our entire social and economic organization assumes this as the norm and maintains that it is socially desirable for one class of adults to be economically dependent on another. Consequently, couples who equalize family responsibilities, or singles who have them all, pay a price for deviancy. Women who spend the greater part of their lives as dependent spouses only to find their "career" ended by death or divorce pay a price for conformity. The fact that a majority of the population are paying these prices is compelling some reforms, but a total reorganization is necessary.

This reorganization must be one which abolishes institutionalized sex role differences and the concept of adult dependency. It needs to recognize the individual as the principal economic unit, regardless of what combinations individuals do or do not choose to live in, and to provide the necessary services for individuals to support themselves and help support their children. In pursuit of these goals, programs and policies need to make participation by everyone in the labor force to the full extent of their abilities both a right and an obligation. They should also encourage and facilitate the equal assumption of family responsibilities without regard to sex, as well as develop ways to reduce conflict between the conduct of one's professional and private lives. While transition policies are necessary to mitigate the consequences of adult dependency, the goal should be abolition of the sexual division of labor. These policies should not be ones which permanently transfer dependency from "breadwinners" (male earners) to society in general, nor should they be ones which encourage dependency for a major portion of one's life by extolling its benefits and minimizing its costs. Instead, transitional policies should be ones which educate women to the reality that they are ultimately responsible for their own economic well-being and are entitled to the opportunities to achieve it.

Needless to say, the consequences of revising our policies to focus on the individual rather than the family as the basic economic unit, to deliberately eradicate the sexual division of labor in both the family and the work force, to establish equal participation in the labor force as a right as well as an obligation, and to institutionalize the support services necessary to achieve the above would not merely be felt by women. Such policy changes would reverberate throughout our entire economic and social structure. Thus, one should not anticipate their achievement in the near future. But one will not be able to anticipate their achievement at all until the ideas are raised and the need for change understood. To do this the movement needs to return to its origins and begin the process of questioning and consciousness-raising all over again.

Notes

1. Lemons (1973), chap. 7; Chafe (1972), chap. 5.
2. Baker (1964), pp. 91–96; *Lochner* v. *New York,* 198 U.S. 45, 53 (1905).
3. *Muller* v. *Oregon,* 208 U.S. 412, 422 (1908).
4. *Bradwell* v. *Illinois,* 83 U.S. (16 Wall.) 130, 142 (1973). *Muller* at 412–413.
5. Lemons (1973), p. 187.
6. Becker (1981), pp. 49, 51; Chafe (1972), pp. 125–129.
7. Harrison (1988), p. 8; Anderson (1951), p. 171.
8. Quotation from Alma Lutz in Chafe (1972), pp. 124–125.
9. Anderson (1951), pp. 165–170; Becker (1981), p. 212; Chafe (1972), p. 119; Lemons (1973), pp. 192–195; *Equal Rights,* January 30, 1926, pp. 402–403; U.S. Department of Labor, Women's Bureau (1928). See Baker (1964), pp. 401–404, for a summary.
10. Becker (1981), pp. 138–139; Scharf (1980), chaps. 4 and 5.
11. Scharf (1980), pp. 46–47. The one compromise was the substitution of spouse for woman, even though everyone knew it was the wife who would lose the job.
12. Gallup (1972), p. 136; Scharf (1980), p. 50; Becker (1981), p. 203; Ware (1981), p. 79.
13. Baker (1964), p. 405.
14. Tribe (1978), p. 449.
15. *West Coast Hotel* v. *Parrish,* 300 U.S. 379, 399 (1937).
16. *Morehead* v. *Tipaldo,* 198 U.S. 587 (1936).
17. *U.S.* v. *Darby,* 312 U.S. 100 (1941).
18. See Goldstein (1979), p. 44, on the strategy of obtaining social welfare legislation by the technique of women-and-children first; see Baer (1978) for a fine review of the cases, history, and politics of this era.

19. Ware (1981), pp. 117–124.
20. Lemons (1973), p. 204; Becker (1981), pp. 197–199, 226–227.
21. Lemons (1973), pp. 24, 196, 199–200.
22. *Congressional Digest*, April 1943, p. 106.
23. Becker (1981), p. 182; Paul (1972–1973), pp. 440–442; Pardo (1979).
24. Harrison (1988), pp. 19–23.
25. Harrison (1988), pp. 40–44. See Berger (1971), p. 331, for the view of an NWP National Council member.
26. *Congressional Record*, July 9, 1946, p. 9405; Pardo (1979), pp. 127–133.
27. *Congressional Digest*, December 1946, p. 290.
28. Harrison (1988), pp. 26–30, 94; Rawalt (1983), p. 53. The NWP derisively referred to it as the Biological Status Bill; Pardo (1979), p. 147.
29. *Congressional Record*, January 25, 1950, pp. 872–873; *Congressional Quarterly Almanac* (1950), p. 539; *Congressional Record*, July 16, 1953, pp. 8954–955; *Congressional Quarterly Almanac* (1953), p. 386; Harrison (1988), pp. 31–32.
30. Harrison (1988), pp. 33–35.
31. Harrison (1988), pp. 38, 85; Harrison (1982), p. 124.
32. Rupp and Taylor (1987), pp. 74–75; Hole and Levine (1971), p. 80.
33. Harrison (1988), pp. 86, 88, 116.
34. Harrison (1982), p. 378.
35. President's Commission on the Status of Women (1963), pp. 44–45.
36. Freeman (1975), chaps. 2 and 3.
37. *Congressional Record*, February 8, 1964, pp. 2577–584; Pardo (1979), pp. 161–162; Paul (1972–1973), p. 615; Zelman (1982), pp. 45–47, 61, 67, 70; Brauer (1983), pp. 37–56. Edith Green (D. Ore.) was the sole woman to vote against the "sex" amendment.
38. Herman Edelsberg, at the New York University 18th Conference of Labor, quoted in *Labor Relations Reporter*, August 25, 1966, pp. 253–255.
39. *Weeks* v. *Southern Bell Telephone and Telegraph*, 408 F.2d 228, 235–236 (5th Cir. 1969).
40. Freeman (1975), pp. 76–77, 212.
41. Freeman (1975), pp. 209, 212.
42. Freeman (1975), pp. 148–150, 207, 212.
43. Freeman (1975), pp. 213–220.
44. U.S. Department of Labor, *1983 Handbook on Women Workers* (1983), chap. 7.
45. *Commonwealth* v. *Welosky*, 276 Mass. 398, 414, 177 N.E. 656, 664 (1931), certiorari denied, 284 U.S. 684 (1932); *Quong Wing* v. *Kirkendall*, 223 U.S. 59, 63 (1912); *State* v. *Hunter*, 208 Ore. 282, 288, 300 P.2d 455, 458 (1956); *Allred* v. *Heaton*, 336 S.W.2d 251 (Tex. Civ. App.), certiorari denied, 364 U.S. 517 (1960); *Heaton* v. *Bristol*, 317 S.W.2d 86 (Tex. Civ. App.), certiorari denied, 230 (1958).

46. *Slaughter House Cases*, 83 U.S. (16 Wall.) 36 (1872).
47. Tribe (1978), pp. 994–1002. "Strict scrutiny" is also employed where fundamental rights, such as voting, travel, procreation, criminal appeals, or those protected by the First Amendment, are involved.
48. *American Women* (1985), p. 45.
49. *Hoyt* v. *Florida*, 368 U.S. 57, 62 (1961).
50. *Reed* v. *Reed*, 368 U.S. 57 (1971).
51. Phone interview with Ruth Bader Ginsburg, now a judge on the D.C. Circuit Court of Appeals, April 16, 1984; phone interview with Faith Seidenberg, Syracuse attorney, June 5, 1987; letter of June 26, 1987, from Suzanne Post to author.
52. *Frontiero* v. *Richardson*, 411 U.S. 677, 692 (1973).
53. *Craig* v. *Boren*, 429 U.S. 190, 197, 204 (1976).
54. *Weinberger* v. *Wiesenfeld*, 420 U.S. 636, 645, 652 (1975).
55. *Stanton* v. *Stanton*, 421 U.S. 7, 14–15 (1975).
56. *Califano* v. *Goldfarb*, 430 U.S. 199 (1977).
57. *Orr* v. *Orr*, 440 U.S. 268 (1979).
58. *Caban* v. *Mohammed*, 441 U.S. 380 (1979).
59. *Califano* v. *Westcott*, 443 U.S. 76 (1979).
60. *Wengler* v. *Druggists Mutual Insurance Company*, 446 U.S. 142 (1980).
61. *Califano* v. *Webster*, 430 U.S. 313, 318 (1977).
62. *Kahn* v. *Shevin*, 416 U.S. 351, 355 (1974).
63. *Schlesinger* v. *Ballard*, 419 U.S. 498, 508 (1975).
64. *Michael M.* v. *Superior Court of Sonoma County*, 450 U.S. 464, 472 (1981).
65. *Rostker* v. *Goldberg*, 453 U.S. 57, 74, 76, 79 (1981).
66. *Rotary International* v. *Rotary Club of Duarte*, 481 U.S. 537 (1987); *Roberts* v. *U.S. Jaycees*, 468 U.S. 609, 623 (1984).

20

Women and Divorce Reform

Herbert Jacob

It is a striking coincidence that divorce laws changed radically during a period of intense activity by feminists, beginning as the new feminist movement was becoming organized in the late 1960s and reaching a peak during the 1970s, a decade that could be called "the woman's decade." Then, during the early 1980s as the movement's political force seemed spent, divorce law reform came to an end.

Although these were years of extraordinary feminist activity if judged by the flourishing of feminist organizations, by the publication of feminist magazines and specialized journals, and by the efforts to obtain ratification of the Equal Rights Amendment, there were few connections between feminist activity and divorce reform. The twentieth century feminist movement exerted little influence on the shaping of mid twentieth century divorce law, even though many people had long considered home, family, and children women's issues and some nineteenth century feminists such as Elizabeth Cady Stanton had been outspoken leaders in the liberalization of divorce laws.[1] This chapter explores why, in most states, women and feminists failed to mobilize around the revision of the nation's divorce laws and what can be learned about the political role of women and feminists from this experience.

Divorce Law Revision in the 1970s and 1980s

The policy arena I examine, involving a complex set of legal changes, requires an explanation because few outside the club of family law scholarship have followed its development. Four major changes were sought and largely adopted: (1) the introduction of no-fault divorce, (2) alterations in the rules governing child custody, (3) modifications in child support payment, and (4) revisions in alimony and in the division of property after divorce. The new laws had the potential for fundamentally altering the status of many women and families in the United States.

After 1965 every state addressed these four issues; and none escaped policy alteration in at least one area. However, changes came in separate waves of legislative and of judicial action.

The first revision, which affected property division after divorce, began quietly in the 1930s but became briefly controversial in the 1980s. The early changes were so obscure that much of the legal community erroneously continued to believe that at divorce title to property still governed property division.[2] In reality, by the mid 1980s many states had adopted the quasi–community property concept of marital property and mandated equitable distribution between husband and wife at divorce. This occurred without any self-conscious reform movement.

The first explicit reform campaign targeted the grounds for divorce. In 1966 New York was the first state to broaden its traditional divorce grounds, but it did not expressly adopt the no-fault standard. In 1969 California embraced no-fault openly and was followed quickly by many other states. Within four years, thirty-six states had adopted no-fault as at least one way of obtaining a divorce; by 1985 the last state (South Dakota) had adopted no-fault divorce.[3] Many states, however, never explicitly adopted no-fault provisions but permitted divorce after a period of separation (for example, New York) or on grounds of incompatibility (for example, Oklahoma). Such procedures came to be considered the equivalent of no-fault divorce in legal circles.

In the 1970s child support became a target of legislation, but, unlike other areas of divorce law, it spilled over to the national arena because of the connection existing between child support and the federal program providing Aid to Families with Dependent Children (AFDC). The initial federal thrust in this field came in 1950 with an amendment to the Social Security Act known as NOLEO (Notice to Law Enforcement Officials), which was intended to facilitate the welfare agencies' collection of delinquent support payments from fathers. Congressional interest broadened with the establishment in 1974 of a parent locator service for finding fathers who were delinquent in their child support payments and whose children were relying on AFDC[4] and with other ways of fostering more efficient means of collecting child support payments. In 1984 Congress mandated withholding funds from delinquent fathers' paychecks and income tax refunds to force payment of child support; in 1988 the measure was extended to all fathers, not only to delinquent fathers or fathers of children on welfare.[5]

Child custody law followed a different path and included a different set of issues: jurisdictional questions concerning parents living in different states,[6] which affected only a small minority of divorced families; and, more important, the erosion of the "tender years" doctrine which favored maternal custody for young children.[7] The most dramatic change, however, occurred in the early 1980s when joint custody was adopted as an optional or mandatory arrangement for children of divorced parents. Between 1980 and 1985 twenty-seven states endorsed some form of joint custody, joining the five states already possessing such authority.[8]

Another dimension of the process of change of divorce laws was that the reform activities occurred in a variety of political arenas. The most visible site was the legislature as it considered altering statutes governing divorce and ancillary matters. These activities involved both Congress and state legislatures, although state legislatures made most of the decisions. Auxiliary study commissions formed to investigate the need for reform and to devise legislative solutions also existed in many states. In addition, the National Conference of Commissioners on Uniform State Laws (NCCUSL), a quasi-governmental body, promulgated model state laws which could serve as launching grounds for individual state legislative efforts. Finally, courts sometimes played a prominent role in revising state divorce laws. The most conspicuous case occurred in 1979 when the U.S. Supreme Court decided that alimony statutes that discriminated according to sex were unconstitutional because they violated the equal protection clause of the Fourteenth Amendment;[9] that decision led many states to reconsider their alimony and property division laws in order to make them neutral with respect to gender.

We are thus examining a large matrix of activity: twenty-six years (1963–1988); a variety of policy provisions (grounds for divorce, child support payments, criteria for custody, and presumptions about family property); and the interplay of advisory, legislative, and judicial bodies in decision-making. Yet, though divorce law is complex, it is not as complicated as many policy processes. Divorce law revision never became a campaign issue in elections. Moreover, polls rarely tested public opinion; between 1945 and 1966, for instance, a Gallup poll asked about divorce laws only three times, and none of these polls questioned the public about attitudes toward no-fault.[10] With one exception, public bureaucracies did not concern themselves with divorce law because it did not involve their interests. The exception was welfare agencies with welfare clients who were divorced mothers driven into poverty by the lack of child support. These agencies collected child support from delinquent fathers. The Department of Health, Education, and Welfare consequently supported national legislation to assist state agencies in collecting such support for welfare clients.[11]

The Role of Women and Feminist Groups in Changing Divorce Law

The faint presence of women and feminist organizations and their variable influence on family law revision has at least three plausible explanations:

1. Women had not effectively penetrated decision-making agencies and, therefore, had no avenue for representing feminist views.
2. Feminist organizations were inadequate to the task, both because they organized too late and because they focused on national rather than state issues.
3. Feminist organizations concentrated on other, higher priority issues.

Women in Decision-Making Arenas

Representation of an interest requires a significant number of spokespeople who are ready to articulate a collective interest and who are situated to take advantage of organizational opportunities. In a legislature, for instance, members must identify with a cause, and then they are more likely to espouse this cause effectively if they also hold some legislative leadership positions.

Men have sometimes represented feminist interests, most notably before women had the vote or held legislative, judicial, or executive positions. However, since the suffrage, women have increasingly relied on women to represent feminist concerns. This has required that a significant number of women identify with the feminist cause, but not every woman in public office espouses feminist concerns. Thus, of interest to us are (1) the number of women who held a decision-making post and might have supported feminist interests and, where possible, (2) the numerical strength of those women who publicly identified with feminist causes.

The representation of women in public office has varied widely both by place and by date. In the judiciary, where divorce law was routinely litigated and interpreted, there were very few women; by 1977 only 110 state judges of a total of 5,940 were women.[12] On the other hand, the number of women legislators has increased steadily. In 1963–1964, as divorce revision began, 351 women served in state legislatures;[13] twenty years later 992 women had seats.[14]

As women became more prominent in legislatures, their participation increased in the passage of divorce laws. Initially, no women played a significant role, as exemplified by the 1966 New York revision where the legislative committee was chaired by a man with the assistance of a professor of family law at New York University, who was also a man. Women testified as mental health professionals or as individuals with marital problems, but no women's organizations appeared.[15] At that time, there were only four women serving in the assembly, none of whom played a visible role in the new law's consideration, and no woman served in the New York Senate.[16]

Two years later, women played a considerably larger role in the effort of the NCCUSL to formulate a uniform marriage and divorce act. A handful of women held strategic positions and some of them used their platform to promote feminist ideas.

Originally, the NCCUSL effort was entirely a male initiative, the result of agitation by two male attorneys from New Jersey. When the NCCUSL formed its drafting committee, no women were selected to serve. The committee first hired Robert Levy of the University of Minnesota to be its reporter, or the equivalent of executive director, with the responsibility to provide drafts to the committee. Only after several months when Levy recruited Herma Hill Kay, a law professor from the University of California, did a woman join the committee in an influential position.[17] In addition, law dean Soia Mentschikoff, one of the handful of women who belonged to the NCCUSL, played a key role at one meeting.[18] However, neither Kay nor Mentschikoff apparently viewed their role as representing women; they were highly regarded professionals acting as experts in promoting preferred policy positions without regard to the policy implications for women. I was unable to find any indication that Kay had feminist concerns in mind in the correspondence and memoranda in Levy's files or in interviews with Levy or Kay. Mentschikoff was remembered by Levy as playing a crucial role in one committee meeting where it decided to recommend limiting judicial discretion in granting a no-fault divorce. This issue, however, was not perceived as a feminist concern. Two other women who were members of the committee's advisory board brought their feminist views to the fore: Alice Rossi urged upon Levy equal division of marital property and time-limited alimony,[19] and Jessie Bernard proposed that a mother's childcare be counted as equivalent to a financial contribution to the family's well-being.[20] Overall, however, feminist voices were not frequently raised during committee drafting sessions or at the conference debates when the NCCUSL formulated the Uniform Marriage and Divorce Act.[21]

While the NCCUSL debated the Uniform Marriage and Divorce Act, California and Iowa were considering their pathbreaking laws that would permit divorce *only* through a no-fault procedure. Kay strongly influenced the California effort at the prelegislative stage. She presented the nucleus of the subsequent no-fault proposal at legislative hearings in 1964 and was perhaps the most influential member of the Governor's Commission on the Family that drafted the no-fault law in 1966. The legislative effort, however, was spearheaded by male members; no woman legislator played a prominent role in the committee deliberations or the floor debate.

Iowa considered and adopted a no-fault statute at almost the same time as California. Originally, the Iowa study committee had no women members, and its minutes do not reflect any substantial contribution by the two women who eventually joined.[22] Likewise, contemporary news reports indicate that the handful of female Iowa legislators did not play a key role in the law's adoption, even though they were somewhat more numerous than their California counterparts.[23]

Not only did few women play a substantial role in the formulation of early no-fault proposals, but no evidence exists of feminist prodding. The surviving legislative record, in addition to my interviews,[24] failed to show testimony by feminist groups at legislative hearings on no-fault during the early years. Individual women (and men) told of their divorces at such hearings, but there was no group representation of women. In Iowa the study committee did not even hold public hearings. Thus, at its beginning, legislative deliberations of no-fault were not penetrated by feminist thinking. Clearly, no-fault was not the product of women, in large part because women were not present or did not speak up as the new laws were being enacted.

The presence of women in state legislatures steadily increased during the 1970s, and as divorce law issues entered the legislative arena, they had an opportunity to be heard. When welfare administrators sought to reduce welfare costs by seeking federal legislation that would force payment of delinquent child support, some congresswomen played instrumental roles. By 1984 the issue had become an integral part of the women's caucus agenda, and Congresswoman Pat Schroeder (Colorado) was a key figure in the law's passage.[25]

At the state level, both grass-roots and official participation by women was strongest during debates, in New York and Wisconsin, about legal provisions for dividing property at divorce. The Woman's Bar Association of New York and a New York County Bar Association committee chaired by Julia Perles played decisive roles in formulating New York's marital property act. The National Organization for Women (NOW) drafted its own bill requiring equal division of property and obtained sponsorship from an ardent member and supporter, Senator Linda Winoker. The debate centered on the choice between NOW's bill and the bill written by women in the bar associations, which required equitable division. It was not, however, just a dispute between women. One of the women legislators in New York referred to one of the early debates on property law reform as "a battle of the sexes."[26] However, male legislators from both parties, such as Democrat Albert Blumenthal and Republican Gordon Burrows, played key roles in persuading the legislature to adopt the equitable division bill rather than continue with the existing law, which distributed property according to who held title.

The contrast between Wisconsin and Illinois, which adopted divorce bills in 1977, is a sharp one. In Wisconsin, according to Fineman's account,[27] feminist women exerted considerable influence: Wisconsin feminist groups both helped formulate the legislation and pushed it through the legislature. They were in a somewhat more advantageous position than women in California and Iowa in 1969–1970; there were 10 women legislators of 99 in the Wisconsin assembly and 2 of 33 in the senate. Also, women in the Wisconsin legislature had held committee leadership posts for many sessions, and more than half of the women in the legislature were dedicated feminists.[28] On the other hand, in Illinois feminists were never mentioned in my interviews as exercising influence over the formulation of the legislation. In fact, women held the same proportion of seats in each legislature (10 percent in the assembly and 6 percent in the senate), but far fewer of the Illinois legislators were committed feminists and fewer held leadership positions. According to the public record and interviews, the revision of the law governing property division in Illinois passed with scarcely any participation by the women members of the Illinois legislature or lobbying by feminist organizations.[29]

Finally, at the end of the 1970s and the beginning of the 1980s, more than half the states adopted new rules on child custody at divorce. This legislation promoted joint, rather than sole, custody, undermining the presumption that mothers should have sole custody and giving fathers a considerably greater chance to obtain a share of legal or physical custody of their children. In some states, women legislators played a substantial role in these decisions; they sponsored the statute in eight of the twenty-six states on which we possess such data. This should not be interpreted as a feminist initiative, however, because many of the women who sponsored these bills did not consider themselves to be representatives of the feminist cause. Instead, women legislators played a prominent role in custody legislation because many male legislators perceived this to be a "woman's" issue.[30]

Thus, the degree to which women influenced divorce legislation seems relative to their legislative strength. If custody bills had been presented in the 1960s, they, too, would have been sponsored by men since so few women were serving in state legislatures. By the late 1970s the contingent of women in legislatures was large enough for them to figure prominently in what were commonly dubbed "women's" bills. However, the presence of women alone did not assure feminist input into the legislation. Where women served and feminists were among them, a feminist viewpoint was sometimes articulated, even though it usually did not prevail. Since much of the legislation passed before feminists became numerous in state legislatures, many of the divorce revisions were spearheaded by men, and the feminist influence remained nominal.

The Organizational Capacity of Feminist Groups

The weak presence of feminist groups in deliberations about divorce law revision reflects more than the paucity of women in decision-making positions. It also demonstrates a consequence of organizational frailty among feminist groups. The first wave of divorce reform occurred just as feminist groups were forming; and later reforms came when these groups had not yet acquired a continuing capacity to work effectively at the state level.

The contemporary feminist movement dates from about 1961 when President John F. Kennedy established the President's Commission on the Status of Women, a move which was followed in the next two years by the establishment of parallel organizations in 14 states.[31] In June 1964 the first national conference of these state commissions convened with representatives from 24 state commissions; by the following year 44 state commissions sent representatives. At the third national conference in 1966 a handful of activists, disappointed by the conservative thrust of the meetings, formed the National Organization for Women.[32]

Two years later, as a consequence of further policy disagreements, the Women's Equity Action League (WEAL) and Human Rights for Women, an organization dedicated to legal action, split off from NOW.

NOW, however, remained the dominant organization of the feminist movement, although it suffered from severe organizational problems throughout those early years.[33] At the same time that NOW and WEAL were forming, numerous local groups of activist women sprang up which were, as Freeman describes, even less well organized than NOW and less capable of systematic legislative activity at the state level.[34]

In the late 1970s as the Equal Rights Amendment (ERA) became the primary feminist concern, these groups sought a more active role in state capitals. With the fight to ratify the ERA, NOW and other groups established state organizations directed at enlisting legislatures to the feminist cause. However, most states, where ratification of the ERA was achieved with little struggle, did not acquire strong statewide organization through their efforts. In other states, such as Illinois, the struggle continued for years and drained resources from other potential women's projects.[35]

On balance, however, feminist groups remained more oriented toward influencing the federal government in Washington than toward swaying state agencies in state capitals.[36] This was particularly the case for NOW, which was a national organization focused on Washington rather than a federation of state groups interested in local legislation. It concentrated on Congress, on obtaining favorable administrative action from such federal agencies as the Equal Employment Opportunity Commission (EEOC), and in litigating before the Supreme Court.

Even though the feminist movement made a strong impression on the United States during the 1970s through the mass media and events like the August 1970 women's strike, women's organizations did not penetrate all the sectors of the policy process. To claim a voice in divorce law change, feminists needed continuous representation in state capitals, a requirement which the fledgling movement could not meet.

The Low Priority of Divorce Law Revision

Social movements and interest groups do not select their policy objectives indiscriminately. They target policies which threaten fundamental values of their adherents or which provide exceptional opportunities to advance the well-being of their supporters.[37] Divorce law revision did not attract the feminist movement because it neither threatened basic values nor promised widespread benefits.

The new feminism of the 1970s organized around labor market issues more than around family policies—in part a reflection of the roots of the movement in the activities of the National Commission on the Status of Women and its state counterparts, and in part their dependence on assistance from the Women's Bureau, a Department of Labor agency. The Women's Bureau was instrumental in organizing the early conferences on the status of women and in spurring their organization at the state level.[38] The report of the 1963 conference included a chapter entitled "Women Under the Law," which encompassed concerns about divorce law and its impact on women; however, this chapter followed other chapters on education and counseling, on home and community, on women in employment, and on labor standards.[39] The "Women Under the Law" chapter highlighted the need for constitutional recognition of equal rights for women, for recognition of international conventions on human rights, and for elimination of gender discrimination in jury service. Only after these matters were discussed did the chapter take up divorce law or "personal and property rights." The paragraphs that focused on rights of women during marriage also mentioned the need for more widespread recognition of marriage as a partnership in which each partner gains an interest in the property acquired during the marriage, and that property interests should extend through the termination of the marriage by either death or divorce.[40] But instead of calling for action, the conference only urged legal research on such matters as alimony, support, and property settlements and did not mention no-fault or child custody. In many respects, the report was a pioneering document, even in its discussion of family law. However, family law concerns clearly were not at the top of the agenda.

A summary of the committees established by state commissions, published in 1964, indicates that of the thirty-two states represented, none had a committee on family or domestic relations law issues, although some had committees that handled broader issues such as "women under law," "legal rights," "legal treatment," and "legal status."[41]

After the 1964 Civil Rights Act included in Title VII a prohibition against sex discrimination, nascent feminist groups directed much effort toward obtaining its enforcement. The EEOC, charged with enforcing these provisions, was initially hostile to them. Consequently, feminists expended much effort in changing the EEOC's views, an effort which served to reinforce the earlier concern with labor market issues.[42]

In 1968, while California, Iowa, and the NCCUSL were considering divorce law reform, the Citizens' Advisory Council on the Status of Women issued a report on family law and policy. This report considered the entire range of issues and made some modest recommendations. It neither endorsed nor opposed no-fault divorce, although it supported permitting divorce after a voluntary separation of one year. Its recommendations on property division cautiously endorsed equitable division of marital property (without using those terms). It advocated deciding child custody on the basis of "the best interests" of the child with neither parent given automatic preference, but there was no discussion of joint custody.[43] The task force, including only one of the leaders of the nascent women's movement (Marguerite Rawalt), evidently did not have a substantial impact on the state commissions. For instance, at the fourth national conference of the Commissions on the Status of Women just a few months after the report's issuance, it was the subject of discussion on the last morning of a three-day meeting in the context of all the other recommendations made by the Citizens' Advisory Council.[44]

Feminists were not uninterested in family law. Freeman reports that at the 1973 NOW convention, the workshop on family, marriage, and divorce attracted the largest attendance of any meeting.[45] In the NOW archives at the Schlesinger Library, there are statements on divorce law by NOW leaders, such as the speech by Elizabeth Spaulding in August 1974 before the Connecticut NOW conference urging that provisions to improve the economic circumstances of divorced women be included in divorce legislation.[46] However, statements about divorce legislation do not appear to have been central to NOW's agenda. In NOW's earliest years, when California was adopting no-fault, Ruth Ehrlich, NOW national politics chairman for the West, summarized NOW's California political activities at the 1970 NOW convention but did not utter one word about no-fault divorce legislation.[47] Later, the low position of family issues was reflected in an appropriation of only $4,393.80 for 1977 for NOW's task force on marriage, divorce, and the family.[48]

NOW focused on such issues as the elimination of job discrimination, the liberalization of state abortion laws before *Roe* v. *Wade*, and the ERA.[49] Once the ERA was proposed to the states, it captured the prime position on the agenda and monopolized the resources and attention of feminist groups. The ERA was particularly draining for state groups because the amendment required ratification by state legislatures. Feminist groups tended to lobby for the ERA rather than for the revision of domestic relations law. Family law issues were also neglected in the realm of litigation, where most activity by such groups as Equal Rights Advocates and the Women's Law Fund centered on employment discrimination and reproductive freedom.[50] There was one notable exception when the Women's Rights Project of the American Civil Liberties Union intervened in a case attacking the provisions of a Georgia alimony statute which permitted alimony only to wives. Ruth Bader Ginsburg submitted the feminist arguments for gender neutrality in divorce laws in an amicus brief. The ensuing 1979 decision in *Orr* v. *Orr* required gender neutrality in alimony laws and caused many states to review the entire array of laws making insidious distinctions between men and women.

Thus, activists in the women's liberation movement usually focused on issues that struck at seemingly more fundamental issues than divorce law reform. Winning equality in the market place, gaining control over their own bodies by abortion law reform, and achieving constitutional recognition of equal rights had priority over divorce law revision.

At the same time, proponents of divorce law reform presented their proposals in ways unlikely to attract attention from feminists or other potentially interested groups. The reforms were cloaked as narrow technical alterations rather than as the fundamental changes they were. Their sponsors did not address feminist issues; instead they regarded their work as procedural reform.

The proponents of no-fault supported it on the ground that it addressed the problems of fraud and perjury in divorce proceedings. Many perceived no-fault as simply legitimizing the existing practice of granting divorce with no real inquiry into the causes of a marriage's breakdown. They also argued more broadly that no-fault reduced acrimony in divorce by replacing an adversarial procedure with a more conciliatory one. This strategy does not reflect a conscious effort to exclude feminists; these proponents of no-fault simply did not consider feminism as relevant. As lawyers, they presented their proposals in procedural terms and in this way inadvertently avoided the feminists' concerns.

Later proposals that affected child support payments, property division, and custody arrangements were presented somewhat differently. Many legislative revisions of property laws resulted from the Supreme Court's 1979 decision declaring sex-based alimony statutes a violation of the Fourteenth Amendment's equal protection clause. The changes, therefore, often came about as a legislative attempt to update state laws. Improvements in child support administration were originally proposed to reduce state and federal welfare budgets and initially were applied solely to welfare recipients, a group that did not enjoy strong support from the feminist movement (which was more oriented toward the middle class than the working class). Such provisions did not apply to all delinquent payers, regardless of their welfare status, until 1984.

Property law revisions had more apparent relevance to the feminist agenda since they directly affected the division of wealth between men and women and the economic welfare of divorced women. However, highly legalistic terminology obscured the matter and made it appear too complicated to tackle as a popular issue. For example, the Louisiana revision of 1980 altered the "legal regime" of "the community of acquests and gains."[51] The South Carolina provision reads:

> In every judgment of divorce from the bonds of matrimony the court shall make such orders touching the maintenance, alimony, and suit money of either party or any allowance to be made to him or her and, if any, the security to be given as from the circumstances of the parties and the nature of the case may be just.[52]

In addition, marital property provisions were embedded in a maze of statutory provisions: some dealt with alimony (a part of the family code); others, with property rights *during* a marriage (a part of the civil code); and still others, with property rights upon the death of a spouse (a part of the probate code).

In addition, child custody also did not attract attention as a central issue of feminist organizations, reflecting, I think, a fundamental ambivalence about children among some feminists. On the one hand, children are often a hindrance to women seeking a career,[53] given the inadequacy of childcare facilities and the antipathy of many employers toward female employees' taking time off for mothering duties. For divorced women, children impose a heavy financial burden which is usually not fully compensated for by child support payments from the absent father.[54] On the other hand, most women are deeply attached to their children and are ready to make enormous sacrifices for their sake. Thus some women welcomed the removal of the automatic presumption that children should go to mothers at divorce, while others saw it as a severe deprivation. A further complication arose in the observation that removing the presumption in favor of maternal custody might diminish a mother's bargaining strength at divorce and reduce a father's child support obligation.[55] Although some feminists voiced their opinions on this issue, it did not immediately mobilize organizations to take a strong stand.

Consequently, divorce law revision did not appeal to feminists as a central concern for various reasons. My evidence indicates that in the early stages of divorce law reform, feminist groups acted as if divorce law revision would not provide significant opportunities for the immediate enhancement of women.[56] Also, they felt that no-fault proposals did not pose a visible threat to the status of women; on the contrary, the proposed changes appeared to be enlightened. In later years, when property and child custody provisions were changed, the feminist movement was preoccupied with other concerns. Like the concerned feminists in the nineteenth century who found their divorce law reform interests usurped by a mobilization around suffrage, the feminists in the twentieth century experienced a similar condition with the emergence of the ERA and labor market issues.[57]

Thus, feminist groups put in only occasional appearances in the debates over divorce laws. They were more frequently active in discussions over bills with explicit economic consequences such as property division laws, but even then they were not always present. The ERA, abortion laws, and proposals affecting the economic well-being of women ranked higher on their agenda. Given their limited resources, feminist groups mostly chose to remain silent on divorce law revision.

In the mid 1980s feminist organizations began to change their perception of the adopted divorce reforms.[58] No-fault provisions attracted considerable criticism because they allegedly disadvantaged divorcing women.[59] California women sought to end the perceived injustices incurred under equal distribution of property, while New York women searched for alternatives to the norm of equitable distribution. Joint custody also attracted opposition because it allegedly decreased the bargaining power of women and harmed children. Thus feminist organizations, armed with studies such as Lenore Weitzman's,[60] the analyses stemming from panel studies,[61] and continuing reports from the census on the economic suffering of households headed by women, may have learned that divorce laws did indeed affect central values. The debate begun in the 1980s, however, found feminists at a disadvantage because the statutes that they were attacking had just been "reformed."

Comparisons to Other Groups

Divorce law revision did not occur in a complete interest group vacuum. Four groups provide particularly instructive comparisons with women and feminists in considering the recent history of divorce law: bar associations, men's rights groups, the Catholic church, and the new radical right. Space permits only brief descriptions of their activities but will suffice to highlight the problems encountered by feminist organizations.

LAWYERS   The bar played an important role in all of the revisions I have discussed. In many instances, individual lawyers, or some segment of the organized bar, initiated the divorce reform proposals; in most cases, legislatures asked for the opinion of the bar. This is not surprising because lawyers have an acknowledged expertise in domestic relations law and a financial stake in its operation. During California's debates over no-fault, for instance, it was not unnoticed that the change would reduce the flow of divorce to nearby Nevada.[62] In 1980 the New York bar's economic interests also were evident in the fundamental revision of property division, which spurred an enormous amount of litigation that made divorce expensive for many clients and remunerative for many attorneys.[63]

On the other hand, the bar did not operate entirely from a position of strength. The divorce bar commands little respect in the legal profession; it is only a notch above collection attorneys and perhaps on a par with criminal and personal injury practice. In other words, the family law sections of state bar associations were not influential powerhouses. It is instructive that no state adopted without change the Uniform Marriage and Divorce Act recommended by the prestigious National Conference of Commissioners on Uniform State Laws; most states eschewed its grand structure while selecting only a handful of its provisions.

Nevertheless, economic interest and expertise as well as assured access to legislatures motivated lawyers to become involved in divorce law changes. Many lawyers served in legislatures and often monopolized positions on the judiciary committees that considered divorce legislation. The absence of feminist opposition only reinforced the influence of attorneys.

MEN'S GROUPS   Men's rights groups played a much more limited role. They were active from the beginning, appearing before legislative committees (for instance, as early as 1964 in California).[64] In California they supported no-fault because they wished to remove divorce entirely from the courts and because a strong element in their rhetoric was antilawyer. There is no evidence that their testimony was taken seriously by the committees. However, in the 1980s men's groups—which were not necessarily the same as those active in the 1960s—were exceptionally successful in pressing for joint custody. These groups in some ways resembled the young turk faction of the feminist movement that Freeman describes. They seemed to have no national structure and could not claim a large membership. But because they focused on the narrow issue of joint custody, they succeeded. Their argument had much intuitive appeal: If it was good for children to have two parents during a marriage, it would also be good for them to have the benefit of both parents after a divorce. Their adherents appeared to be motivated by a mixture of concerns. On the one hand, some men appeared genuinely outraged that existing law favored maternal custody as a matter of presumption and made it exceedingly difficult for fathers to obtain custody without a bloody fight; on the other, some were probably motivated by financial considerations because with joint custody they were likely to be assessed lower child support payments.

Access for men's rights groups was easier than access for feminists: Men constituted the overwhelming majority of every legislature. A large proportion were fathers, some of whom were divorced. Together with the intuitive appeal of the issue, these facts permitted men's rights groups to succeed in their efforts to promote joint custody. Again, the absence of feminist opposition was probably important to their success. Indeed, in many instances they convinced a woman legislator to sponsor the legislation.

THE CATHOLIC CHURCH   The church provides a very different case because its concern was largely defensive. Unlike lawyers or men's rights groups, the church sought to protect its interest in stable marriages. It opposed all divorce as a matter of doctrine and therefore was troubled by proposals that would make divorce more obtainable. In states with large Catholic populations, the church was able to translate its concern into political influence, and these states were among the last to adopt no-fault. In New York, for instance, the church, long opposed to the liberalization of divorce laws, succeeded until 1966 in making divorce all but impossible because it was available only upon a showing of adultery. Only with the crumbling of Catholic influence, which occurred as Cardinal Spellman aged and as the result of the liberalization that accompanied Vatican II, were New Yorkers able to revise their divorce laws. But, New York never explicitly embraced no-fault. No-fault also came late to Wisconsin (1977), Pennsylvania (1980), and Illinois (1983), each of which had large Catholic populations. Church opposition played a conspicuous role in each instance.

Like men's rights groups, the church focused its concern narrowly. It took no position on child support, child custody, or property division because those changes did not touch on the church doctrine of the sanctity of marriage.

In some cases, the church, like feminists, did not have automatic access to legislatures. However, in states with large Catholic populations there were always a substantial number of Catholic legislators. In addition, the church—with its interest in other matters such as abortion and parochial education—often had lobbyists in the state capital, and it could use its network of parishes to publicize its positions. The church was in a position to make its voice heard even though it did not usually prevail.

THE RADICAL RIGHT   Because of its stance for traditional family structures, the new radical right had a large stake in divorce revision. The rhetoric of the radical right leads one to expect vigorous opposition to the changes that took place in family law because, in almost every instance, those changes reflected nontraditional norms of family life. Yet, the radical right was even more conspicuously absent in these debates than feminists.[65] Legislative transcripts did show opposition to these changes on the grounds that they would undermine family life, but the organizational muscle of the radical right—its lobbyists and mail campaigns—were totally absent. This may have occurred because the radical right faced problems similar to those of feminists. It organized late, arising largely in the mid 1970s as a response to the abortion issue after *Roe* v. *Wade*. In addition, just as the ERA drained the energy of feminists, abortion sapped the resources of the radical right.

Conclusion

The political presence of women and feminists during the revision of divorce policy in the United States after 1960 must be judged in its historical and social context. If one could devise an absolute scale of political influence, women and feminists would undoubtedly register a very low rating. They rarely molded policy and, usually, failed to register concerns or articulate preferences. But such an absolute scale is misleading; it does not take into account what was possible, what other causes engaged feminists, or what other groups were doing.

The weak presence of women and feminists in the divorce law reform arena clearly is associated with the low ranking of divorce policy among feminist issues. Until the later 1970s many feminist organizations acted as if they were unaware of divorce policy developments; they lacked the organizational resources needed to monitor legislative proposals in all capitals. In addition, proponents of change in divorce law framed many of their bills so that potential opponents, like feminists, would not become alarmed. The proposals were introduced with rhetoric about reducing fraud and ameliorating familial conflict (no-fault), cutting welfare costs (child support), complying with Supreme Court decisions (marital property), and motivating fathers to remain in contact with their children (joint custody). Thus, divorce revision rarely tapped the central concerns of organized feminists. Few women would have considered the changes peripheral, but perhaps equally few thought they were central.

In addition, relatively few women and still fewer avowed feminists held decision-making positions in legislatures and courts. Therefore, they could not mold divorce policy, a fact that often forced advocates of a feminist position to argue from the outside rather than operate as insiders.

The contrast with the experience of lawyers, men's rights groups, and the Catholic church is striking. In each case, some central and well-perceived interest motivated a focused and largely successful activity. Each of these groups was better endowed with political resources than were the feminists: They had easy access, possessed expertise, or received respect. In the case of the church and bar associations, they also had well-established state lobbying organizations that knew how to track legislative proposals.

The similarity to the experience of the radical right is equally instructive. Like feminists, the radical right was not mobilized on divorce revision; it organized too late to engage in the debate over no-fault; and it expended almost all of its energies on other overriding issues (for feminists, the issues were the ERA, abortion reform, and labor market discrimination; for the radical right, opposition to abortion and the ERA).

A different kind of influence, however, cannot be ignored: In the 1970s the feminist rhetoric surfaced in many debates about divorce law even without specific appearances by feminists or feminist groups. Marriage was increasingly described as a partnership of equals; the need to make family law gender-neutral was scarcely debated after the Orr decision; acceptance of the marital property concept hardly raised an eyebrow. The feminist movement had indeed raised the consciousness of many policymakers to women's needs. Had divorce revision been on the agenda of the states in the 1950s, it is likely that the character of the reforms would have been different. Thus, in a subtle way, feminists exercised influence even when they did not visibly participate in the law-making process. Although specific provisions reflecting feminist goals for divorce law remained beyond their reach because there were too few women in office to make a difference and because the issues did not engage the core agenda of women and feminists, their rhetoric won many diffuse or symbolic victories.

The research on which this chapter is based was funded in part by Grants #SES-83-19321 and SES-85-16112 from the National Science Foundation and the Hawkins Chair in Political Science at the University of Wisconsin. I am also grateful to Hugh Bohlender, Georgia Duerst-Lahti, Jo Perry, and Laura Wolliver for assistance with the research on which this chapter is based, and to Jo Freeman, Karen O'Connor, and the editors of this volume for their comments on earlier drafts. None of the above is responsible for the views expressed herein.

Notes

1. Lutz (1974), pp. 112–113, 261–266; Griffith (1984), pp. 101–102, 159–160.
2. Cheadle (1981), pp. 1269–313.
3. This summary is derived from reading the annotated statutes of each state and, where necessary, their session laws.
4. Cassetty (1978), pp. 1–21.
5. *New York Times*, September 27, 1988.
6. See the pattern of adoption of the Uniform Reciprocal Enforcement of Support Act of 1950, 1958, and 1968 and the Uniform Child Custody Jurisdiction Act of 1968. Council of State Governments (1986), pp. 327–328.
7. Luepnitz (1982).
8. Folberg (1984), pp. 266–305; slightly different figures are given by Weitzman (1985), pp. 430–435, who based her count on an earlier compilation.
9. *Orr v. Orr*, 440 U.S. 268 (1979).
10. Gallup (1971). The General Social Survey also periodically asked whether divorce laws should be easier or more difficult but also did not inquire about attitudes toward specific legal changes.
11. Cassetty (1978), pp. 1–21.
12. Center for the American Woman in Politics (1978), p. xix. See also Cook (1984), pp. 191–218.
13. Werner (1968), p. 42.
14. U.S. Bureau of the Census, *Statistical Abstract of the United States, 1985* (1985), p. 251.
15. *Transcript of Public Hearings of the New York Joint Legislative Committee on Matrimonial and Family Law*, October 20, 1965; October 27, 1965; November 30, 1965; and December 1–2, 1965.
16. *New York Red Book* (1966).
17. Robert J. Levy Papers, letter from Levy to Maurice Merrill, March 21, 1968.
18. Interview with Levy, November 8–9, 1984.
19. Letter to Levy from Rossi, January 8, 1969.
20. Levy Papers, 1970 file.
21. The debates may be found in the *Handbook of the National Conference of Commissioners on Uniform State Laws and Proceedings of the Annual Conference Meeting* (1970).
22. Iowa State Archives, materials relating to Divorce Laws Study Committee.
23. The *Des Moines Register* and *Des Moines Tribune* were examined for the days after major legislative action took place. The data on the gender of legislators come from an examination of the rosters of the legislatures as published in the Iowa and California blue books.
24. In California: Herma Hill Kay, Richard Dinkelspiel (the co-chair on the Governor's Commission which formulated the no-fault law), Aiden Gough (ex-

ecutive director of the commission), Donald Grunsky, and James Hayes (the senate and assembly sponsors of the bill), and Kathryn Gehrels (one of the original developers of the no-fault idea in California). In Iowa: Loren Sloan, Robert Frederick, and Elizabeth Shaw (all members of the Iowa Study Committee).

25. *Congressional Quarterly Almanac, 1984* (1985), p. 463.
26. Interview with Karen Burstein, March 30, 1985.
27. Fineman (1983), pp. 789–886.
28. These observations, and those on Illinois, are based on an examination of the legislative biographies in the official manuals published by each state for the 1977 legislative session. A legislator is counted as a "committed feminist" here if she listed a feminist organization among her affiliations.
29. This is based on reading the transcripts of the debates in the Illinois house and senate in 1977 for April 7, May 19, May 20, and June 23, and interviews with Assemblyman Alan Greiman (July 10, 1984), Marshall Auerbach (August 14, 1984), Senator William Marovitz (October 26, 1984), and Senator Eugenia Chapman (April 26, 1986).
30. The source is questionnaires sent to state legislative leaders. The states in which women sponsored joint custody legislation are Florida, Idaho, Illinois, Louisiana, Michigan, New Mexico, Ohio, and Oklahoma.
31. East (1983), p. 10.
32. This account draws heavily upon Freeman (1975). See also Hole and Levine (1971).
33. Freeman (1975), pp. 71–102.
34. Freeman (1975).
35. See Mansbridge, this volume.
36. See the account of legal changes at the federal level in Freeman, this volume.
37. Berry (1984).
38. Duerst-Lahti (1985).
39. *American Women* (1965).
40. *American Women* (1965), p. 10.
41. Citizens' Advisory Council on the Status of Women (1964).
42. Freeman (1975), pp. 186–190.
43. Citizens' Advisory Council on the Status of Women (1968).
44. Commission on the Status of Women (1968).
45. Freeman (1975), pp. 99–100.
46. NOW Archive, Schlesinger Library, box 15, folder on marriage, divorce, and the family.
47. NOW Archive, Schlesinger Library, box 15, folder on marriage, divorce, and the family.
48. NOW Archive, Schlesinger Library, P10/Task Forces, Marriage, Divorce, and the Family, 1976–1977.

49. Freeman (1975).
50. O'Connor (1980), pp. 93–139.
51. Louisiana Civil Code Annotated, art. 2327, 1980.
52. Code of Laws of South Carolina, Title 20-3-130, 1985.
53. Gerson (1985).
54. Weitzman (1985), pp. 262–322.
55. Schulman and Pitt (1982), pp. 538–577; and Weitzman (1985), p. 361.
56. See, for instance, *Do It Now*, March 1970; *Women's Rights Law Reporter*, Spring 1972, p. 17; and *Do It Now*, December 1974.
57. Leach (1980), pp. 144–145, 310; Lutz (1974); Griffith (1984).
58. *New York Times*, August 17, 1986, sect. 4, p. 8.
59. Weitzman (1985).
60. Weitzman (1985).
61. Duncan and Morgan (1980); Corcoran, Duncan, Gurin, and Gurin (1985).
62. *Los Angeles Times*, July 24, 1969, pt. 1, p. 3; and California Assembly (1965), p. 137.
63. *New York Times*, January 13, 1983, pt. 3, p. 1.
64. California Assembly (1964).
65. Conover and Gray (1983).

21

Freedom, Fantasy, Foes, and Feminism: The Debate Around Pornography

Alida Brill

From the antiquated "filthy pictures" to the sophisticated horrors of modern pornographic films or the technological ease of sex videos for home use, pornography has long been with us as both notion and reality. The decision about what should, or can, be included in the free exchange of ideas is never a simple one, but in the case of pornography the definitional task itself becomes a venture into a fun-house hall of mirrors. Depending on the angle taken or the mirror used, the logic of control or freedom takes on a different image and shape. The attempt to control or eliminate pornography raises an eternally perplexing question in a democratic society: At what cost freedom? At what loss control? It is unlikely that any definition could successfully end the now centuries-old argument about the lewd versus the erotic, the sensual versus the offensive, the obscene and worthless versus the validly "socially redeeming."

Even with the *Miller* standard,[1] the problem of naming or placing the "correct" labels on the "proper" categories is difficult. Its virtual impossibility is well expressed in the oft-quoted words of Justice Potter Stewart: "I can't define it, but I know when I see it."[2] What should be done about the public and published portrayals of sexual behavior is not a new political struggle, nor a new frontier for legal philosophy. What is unusual at the present time is the cast of characters participating in the current drama-debate about the role pornography can play in a society founded on freedom and espousing a concern for the equality of its citizens. Ronald Dworkin defines the problem:

It is an old problem for liberal theory, how far people should have the right to do the wrong thing. . . . If we assume that . . . the people who publish and consume pornography do the wrong thing, or at least display the wrong sort of character, should they nevertheless have the legal right to do so?[3]

The current issues go beyond the challenge of finally, reliably identifying what is or is not obscene, pornographic, or otherwise repugnant. Instead, they confront another question: To what extent should (or can) a society tolerate a freedom which, by its exercise, many argue, humiliates, degrades, or harms half the population?

Not surprisingly, this battle about the control of pornography has captured a significant amount of feminist attention. The pornography debate has moved away from the consideration of constitutional protections and censorship to encompass major women's issues and to present a challenge to feminism. In this instance, the value of free expression collides with feminist goals and ideology, and feminist ideology, in turn, conflicts with presumed constitutional provisions and guarantees. In these developments, some women are participating in political strategies which, if successful, would force censorship. Most ironically, these strategies, and the beliefs from which they grow, locate feminists and members of the New Right on the same side for the first time. Censorship as a tool is not an unknown feature of conservative politics; it is, however, a seemingly less appropriate tactic for the advocates of women's rights. Other feminists, because of their suspicion and mistrust of any legal remedy that would prescribe restriction, find themselves in the unhappy situation of being accused of championing the cause of pornographers.

Contemporary feminists opposed pornography early in the development of the women's movement. The well-publicized "Take Back the Night" demonstrations, followed by a volume of the same name edited by Laura Lederer, predate the current drama by about ten years. Some feminist leaders have devoted large amounts of time and writing to the harmful effects of pornography.[4] The elimination or reduction of pornography has been a part of the radical feminist agenda for some time. It is fair to say that the existence of pornography is not a new feminist concern; certainly for a serious and vocal group, pornography has long been a focus for anger and for reform. Previously, however, feminist protests and other political strategies[5] surrounding pornography did not threaten to split the movement or significantly alienate allies. Organizations such as Women Against Violence Against Women and Women Against Pornography (WAP) had their roots in the antirape and antibattery efforts of the 1970s.

In 1985, however, a significant departure in strategy occurred. Andrea Dworkin, a noted feminist writer and strong opponent of pornography, and Catharine MacKinnon, a law professor, proposed a novel ordinance that they hoped would sidestep the traditional obscenity versus freedom arguments by taking the issue out of the domain of the First Amendment. Defining pornography as an infringement on women's civil rights and basing cases on the proof of actual harm, the Dworkin-MacKinnon strategy attempted to have an ordinance enacted in a number of cities. They succeeded, temporarily, in Indianapolis.[6] It is this ordinance and its approach that have so divided the feminist community.

An organization known as FACT (Feminists Against Censorship Taskforce) was formed and opposed the Indianapolis ordinance. "FACT feminists" question the presumed link between pornographic images and violent behavior against women, thus undercutting or challenging what has always been a main contention of "WAP feminists."[7] FACT feminists challenge the uncomfortable alliance with the New Right and its fundamentalist colleagues, fearing that such dubious liaisons (whether admitted or not) will eventually thwart feminist goals and destroy any chance for true equality.

One of the arguments advanced by feminists opposed to pornography is that pornography is an evil parallel to racism. Just as the definition of pornography eludes us, so does its placement in a human and cultural context. Pornography is more vexing and problematic even than racism. Although some psychologically troubled people might perceive antiblack or anti-Jewish materials as sexually arousing, the primary purpose of racist propaganda does not have sex at its foundation. Not unlike pornography, the ideology of racism does include power over others who are perceived as inferior or weak; racism, however, does not also include the pleasure and the confusion of what is sexually arousing. Racist materials call into question the conflicting values of free expression and legitimate protections, as does pornography, but pornography cannot be completely separated from that most fundamental thing which makes us human. Unlike other animals, only human beings are capable of intense sexual drives whether or not reproduction is possible.

Pornography is a by-product not only of our cultural history but of our human condition and cannot be confined to the sexless air of judicial interpretations about constitutional legality. At its most repulsive outer limits, or at its more benignly erotic edge, pornography is a topic we still find troubling to discuss openly. The racist analogy does not apply because pornography is not simply terrifying and dangerous, but can often be allied with the sexually magical. Whether about men and men, women and women, or men and women, the current pornography debate requires us to confront the reality of sexual complexity in order to unscramble its role in current feminist thought and political activity.

Every actor in this drama has a different script, each reflecting a legitimate reading of various American traditions. The pornography debate is a story which, one might say, contains something for everyone. Sex and violence, power and money, heroes and martyrs, angels and devils, class warfare and the U.S. Supreme Court. It is a play in four acts: freedom, fantasy, foes, and feminism, and each act is replete with facts and fallacies.

Freedom

The . . . argument which expresses concern that curbs on pornography are the first step toward political censorship . . . [has] an underlying assumption that the maximization of freedom is a worthy social goal. [A] source of protection for pornography would be a general right to do what we please as long as the rights of others are respected. Since the production and distribution of pornography violates the rights of women—to respect and to freedom from defamation—among others—this protection is not available.[8]

We are characteristically pre-occupied with freedom. . . . It isn't that we look to provide for freedom in this place or that as that we seek to create a society that has freedom as its setting and environment.[9]

Women need the freedom and the socially recognized space to appropriate for themselves the robustness in what traditionally has been male language. Laws such as the one under challenge here would constrict that freedom.[10]

Freedom is the primary concept that permeates all discussions about pornography; and while much of the debate is consumed by the loftier principles of the First Amendment and its possible infringement, there are other freedom issues beyond those involving speech and expression. That is, there are different kinds of freedoms at stake, such as those involving the privacy of sexual behaviors, as well as the notion of sexual freedom itself.

In reviewing the positions of the various actors—FACT, the American Civil Liberties Union (ACLU), WAP—what becomes clear is that they are arguing about vastly different kinds of freedoms. One could say that they are not in the same conversation. Essentially, the WAPs believe that to defend the indefensible, pornography, is to harm the already vulnerable and weak of society. If the views that must be protected by the guarantees of freedom of expression are the ones that preach a hatred of women and a justification for women's pain and inequality, the WAPs would argue that the First Amendment is no friend to women and as such does not deserve female reverence. While much of the WAP literature and the attempts to sidestep the traditional First Amendment considerations recognize constitutional reality, WAP feminists are in essence talking about the centrality of another kind of freedom—freedom from harm, pain, humiliation, and degradation.

An interesting question is why some feminists have fixated on pornography and its violent images of women as proof of the continuing exploitation of women and why others have fixated on the importance of safeguarding freedom as necessary ultimately for all women's safety, even at the expense and sensitivity of women in particular instances.

The diverging feminist positions might best be characterized by the difference between the concepts of *freedom from* and *freedom to*. For the WAPs, the desire to have *freedom from* a harmful world motivates the regulation of pornography; and in the ACLU/FACT view, the *freedom to* engage in pornographic modeling, distribution, and consumption is a highly regarded right. In the civil libertarian portion of the debate, pornography issues also involve the guarantees of privacy—the freedom to buy pornographic materials and to use them in the privacy of your home. Pornography is a part of the "new" privacy claims that are a far cry from the rather passive rights Brandeis described as the "right to be let alone." People now want to do something in their privacy, and one of the things they want to do is to partake of pornography.

Perhaps in their advocacy for an unrestricted First Amendment and an active use of the rights of privacy, the FACT and ACLU forces have closed their eyes to the most virulent forms of pornography. By virtue of the importance placed on the First Amendment, they must deal primarily with the image alone and its right to exist as a form of speech or expression rather than with the implications of how the image came to exist.

When confronted with the question of repugnant violence as in the questionable "snuff" films in which women are apparently savagely murdered on screen, including one in which this was done to a pregnant woman, the civil libertarians argue that if the law was indeed broken in order to make the films, then criminal statutes cover criminal offenses such as kidnapping, battery, and murder. Feminists opposed to these violent depictions consider the constitutional protection of such films as ludicrous at best since if the acts had been committed, they would have been illegal and punishable by law.

However, not all pornography depicts such abhorrent behaviors and not all pornographic stars are prisoners of sex-crazed moviemakers. Most people know the story of Linda Marchiano (the Linda Lovelace of *Deep Throat*) who has testified to her abuse and rape during the making of the film. Even if the Marchiano story was exactly as she portrays it, not all women who star in pornographic films can be assumed to be captives. It is impossible therefore to avoid the question of the freedom of women to participate in the economy of the pornography industry. As John Dixon has stated:

> We can advise adults against the consequences of overeating, smoking, mountain climbing, prostitution and acting in pornographic films but we should not prevent their choosing these activities. . . . We cannot reasonably prevent persons from acting in pornographic films on the grounds that such labor is exploitative or degrading.[11]

By following another line of reasoning, derived from an understanding that the entire structure of our culture has been one that renders women powerless over both their personal and public lives, the questions might be: Can there be any question of personal, sexual freedom if women have no power? This argument would assert that any woman who engages in a pornographic act, at home for her pornography-consuming husband, or in front of the cameras for pay, is doing so under culturally induced duress and force. If one does not have a free life, one cannot actually exercise any real degree of freedom over any part of one's life. The argument continues that if the pornography industry is run by men for the pleasure of men and the profit of men, there cannot be freedom for women in such a system unless equality is established in all aspects of the pornographic industry from production to consumption, a proposition that is both counterintuitive and unlikely.

No matter how appalled individual FACT or civil libertarian feminists may be by the existence of pornography's worst examples, they must regard the First Amendment as sacred. Their arguments center exclusively around the protections of freedom offered by the Constitution. They see the liberties we enjoy as interdependent and fragile. Any legislated censorship of pornography passed for the benefit of women could one day harm blacks, homosexuals, and ultimately come back around to harm the very women who sought this shield. If liberties are fragile and interconnected, a compromise could lead to a collapse of the entire structure of freedom—like a constitutional house of cards. In the civil libertarian play, the chief actors must be freedom and access—for it is only in complete and unrestricted openness that truth can have its day.[12]

What pornography should be called in order to discredit and destroy it has been a topic of concern to feminists for some time. In her essay "Pornography, Oppression and Freedom: A Closer Look," in *Take Back the Night*, Helen Longino argues that pornography degrades women, and a society's tolerance of pornography validates the notion that women are not equals, hence not qualified to participate in its political life.[13]

The notion of seeking remedy from the harm of pornography is not new. The harm foundation had already been laid when MacKinnon and Dworkin drafted their proposed ordinance. What is novel about the ordinance is that it takes pornography out of the criminal domain and places it squarely within the civil rights/discrimination framework. The similarity between the MacKinnon ordinance and other feminist critiques of pornography is the link between pornography's very existence and a denial of equal rights to women in a variety of spheres. In passing the ordinance, the Indianapolis City Council agreed with the premise of the ordinance and found that pornography

> is central in creating and maintaining sex as a basis for discrimination. Pornography is a systematic practice of exploitation and subordination based on sex which differentially harms women. The bigotry and contempt it promotes, with the acts of aggression it fosters, harm women's opportunities for equality of rights in employment, education, access to and use of public accommodations and acquisition of real property; promote rape, battery, child abuse, kidnapping and prostitution and inhibit just enforcement of laws against such acts; and contribute significantly to restricting women in particular from full exercise of citizenship and participation in public life, including in neighborhoods.[14]

The main concern of the WAP feminists is the deprivation of full enfranchisement caused by pornography. It is the link between the political participation of women and pornography as well as the placing of these diminished citizenship rights of women into the sphere of sexuality that makes the MacKinnon approach particularly interesting.

> Pornography is a practice of discrimination on the basis of sex, on one level because of its role in creating and maintaining sex as a basis for discrimination. It harms many women one at a time and helps keep all women in an inferior status by defining our subordination as our sexuality and equating that with our gender.[15]

What does the MacKinnon-Dworkin ordinance say? It defines pornography as one or more of the following:

> Women are presented as sexual objects who enjoy pain or humiliation; or
>
> women are presented as sexual objects who experience sexual pleasure in being raped; or
>
> women are presented as sexual objects tied up or cut up or mutilated or bruised or physically hurt, or as dismembered or truncated or fragmented or severed into body parts; or
>
> women are presented being penetrated by objects or animals; or
>
> women are presented in scenarios of degradation, injury, abasement, torture, shown as filthy or inferior, bleeding, bruised, or hurt in a context that makes these conditions sexual; or
>
> women are presented as sexual objects for domination, conquest, violation, exploitation, possession or use or through postures or positions of servility or submission or display.[16]

Different from criminal proceedings under the existing obscenity laws (as provided by the Court's reasoning in *Miller* and before that in *Roth*), this ordinance provides for civil actions, based on the allegation of discrimination. Thus, the ordinance has at its foundations a complaint procedure involving the Office of Equal Opportunity, through hearings at the equal opportunity boards, and ultimately relief at the court level.

This strategy is one based almost exclusively on evidence of harm or injury. But the ordinance and the legal theory MacKinnon uses as the ordinance's foundation also provide a particular kind of feminist critique of the liberal state:

> In the philosophical terms of classical liberalism, an equality-freedom dilemma is produced: Freedom to make or consume pornography weighs against the equality of the sexes. Some people's freedom hurts other people's equality. There is something to this, but my formulation . . . comes out a little differently. If one asks whose freedom pornography represents, a tension emerges that is not a dilemma among abstractions so much as it is a conflict between groups. Substantive interests are at stake on *both* sides of the abstract issues and women are allowed to matter in neither. If women's freedom is as incompatible with pornography's construction of our freedom as our equality is incompatible with pornography's construction of our equality, we get neither freedom nor equality under the liberal calculus. Equality for women is incompatible with a definition of men's freedom that is at our expense. What can freedom for women mean, so

long as we remain unequal? Why should men's freedom to use us in this way be purchased with our second-class civil status?[17]

Pornography is MacKinnon's patriarchy or, had she been of another era, the "demon-rum" of this century. Unlike her temperance sisters, however, MacKinnon stops short of pronouncing the end of evil with the end of pornography. She also avoids the thorny issue of the subordination and inequality of women in places in the world where there is no pornography.

By placing pornography within the domain of discrimination and under the larger consideration of equality, MacKinnon seeks to move away from the censorship considerations present in other attempts to control pornography. Although, if successful, her ordinance would clearly have to rely on censorship as the tool of enforcement, by casting the argument in this manner, she places the spotlight on something other than the First Amendment. If one adopts the MacKinnon strategy, and to do so one must first be able to accept the foundations of her argument, then the courts are the obvious choice as the ultimate arbiters of what is or is not pornographic. MacKinnon would have us believe that the decision to be made is not the more simplistic one about suppression of materials, but rather a more general one about civil rights, in which seeking legal remedy is appropriate. What is difficult to comprehend is the MacKinnon leap from pornography to the wholesale denial of women's civil rights and a full enjoyment of citizenship claims, a leap reminiscent of the sweeping statements made by the temperance feminists that harm is caused by alcohol and drunken men.

In her study of women's involvement in the temperance movement, Ruth Bordin discusses the symbolic power of temperance for nineteenth century women. The following quotation, discussing the motivations of the political actions of women in the last century, could easily describe today's attraction to the antipornography campaign. As men's use of alcohol underscored women's vulnerability in the nineteenth century, so pornography is seen as underlining female weakness in the 1980s.

> Women's attraction to temperance in the last quarter of the 19th century can be explained in terms of symbolism. Nothing was as destructive to a powerless woman's existence as a drunken husband. He could destroy both her and her family.
>
> The wife and mother has no legal remedies. She has no political remedies. She is forced to suffer from this lack of control.
>
> In the Crusade first and later in the WCTU women were taking control.[18]

Many of the same issues apply to the pornography struggle. Women are perceived to be harmed both actually and psychologically by the behavior of men; male behavior becomes the symbol of women's powerlessness. In the nineteenth century the powerlessness was a consequence of unfair property, divorce, and inheritance laws as well as the reality that most women did not work outside the home and had little recourse for supporting themselves even if they could get rid of a drunken husband. Today's pornography struggle is set against the modern backdrop of the fight for equality and recognition, from the home to the workplace. In the temperance and the pornography instances, men's behavior is the symbolic and dramatic announcement of women's condition. The overindulgent, unchecked, and animalistic behavior of men is perceived as the cause of women's pain and sorrow. Whether it is the immoderate use of alcoholic beverage or the "ungentlemanly" sexual behaviors of both the pornographer and the consumer of pornography—it is the male appetite, seemingly wild and insatiable, that is the villain.

MacKinnon draws on the logic of the *Ferber* case for an injunction to remove pornographic materials from sale, or at least from public view. In *Ferber* the Court upheld an anti-child-pornography statute prohibiting persons from "knowingly promoting sexual performances by children under the age of 16 by distributing material which depicts such performances." It is a landmark case not just because of the First Amendment limitations it imposes but also because of the Court's tacit admission that, prior to the appearance of a visual image, sexual acts may have occurred. Perhaps it is this that causes MacKinnon to draw on *Ferber* as a resource for the control of adult pornography.[19]

There is, however, a great complication involved in deriving any feminist argument, particularly a legal one, from a precedent based on the protection of children. Although MacKinnon insists that "women are not children," she goes on to add "but coerced women are effectively deprived of power for the expressive products of their coercion."[20]

In short, she is not convincing; her reliance on the *Ferber* logic equates women with children, or at the least assigns them to the same category of legal protection. The use of the *Ferber* decision in building the case for the control of pornography illustrates one of the paradoxes present in the pornography battle: It is virtually impossible to make a plea for control, whether couched in sophisticated legal reasoning or not, that does not in some way return to a more traditional understanding of the need to protect women from harm. This is particularly ironic because many of the leading WAP activists are the more "radical" feminists, or were once so considered. Although the word "radical" is always a problematic label, the point here is simply that the persons associated with the movement against pornography are not those one would expect to see supporting a traditional view of women's natures or lives.

Much scholarly attention has been given to civil libertarian concerns about the control of pornography, from both a legal and a feminist perspective. The one document that best exemplifies this side of the argument is the brief filed in the Seventh Circuit Court of Appeals by FACT and authored by Nan Hunter and Sylvia Law. This brief was prepared for the lawsuit against the MacKinnon-Dworkin ordinance. It is particularly useful for the discussion here since it is FACT's direct response to the ordinance and to the MacKinnon reasoning.[21]

The Hunter-Law brief confronts the MacKinnon-Dworkin ordinance on the freedom and the equality dimensions. Hunter and Law do not confine themselves to the rather straightforward considerations of the First Amendment and suppression of expression through censorship. Although the brief begins in much the way one might predict for a civil libertarian position, the authors quickly proceed to much more complex terrain in their discussion of the difficulties of achieving and maintaining sexual freedom for women.

> The violent and brutal images which Appellants use as examples cannot obscure the fact that the ordinance authorizes suppression of material that is sexually explicit, but in no way violent. . . . The material that could be suppressed . . . is virtually limitless.[22]

Hunter and Law provide an interesting shading to the traditional First Amendment concerns when they suggest that the ordinance could be employed to suppress not simply violent depictions of women, and not only pornography. If one accepts the cultural underpinnings of the strategy proposed by MacKinnon and Dworkin, they continue, why would feminists want to stop at regulating pornography?

> While the sweep of the ordinance is breathtaking it does not address . . . the far more pervasive commercial images depicting women as primarily concerned with the whiteness of their wash, the softness of their toilet tissue and whether the lines of their panties show when wearing tight pants. Commercial images, available to the most impressionable young children during prime time, depict women as people interested in inconsequential matters who are incapable of taking significant serious roles in societal decision making.[23]

The above aptly illustrates the "separate conversations" metaphor. Given the premise that censorship is a general harm, then the suppression of even commercial advertising infringes upon the guarantees of free speech, and by implication projects a "chilling effect" on all forms of speech. If, however, one's primary goal is the removal of harm and unfairness to women, perhaps the "limitless" potential of the ordinance is a hopeful, not an ominous, sign.[24]

The FACT brief is striking in how little it deals with the history of women's inequality or the origins of male dominance, which in turn is played out in pornography. Law and Hunter talk instead about how women have been injured by the erosion of freedom under the guise of the protection of women. They carefully trace the history of a variety of legislative acts and laws that have long been viewed as antiquated and harmful to women. They argue that the ordinance cuts into deeply personal freedoms of women and not only the more public ones of free expression.

In their view all forms of control lead to unwanted suppression, and any attempt to remove the harm caused women by pornography diverts feminist goals and treats women as unequal, childlike, and vulnerable. Their brief traces previous laws which regulated sexual behaviors and contends that such laws imposed a double standard of legal codes and cultural norms. Hunter and Law, then, place the ordinance in the land of the double sexual standard. Throughout the brief an important point is that the ordinance denies women the freedom to be sexual and the right to choose what is enjoyable and reject what is not. Hunter and Law argue that the ordinance "resurrects the notion that sexually explicit materials are subordinating and degrading to women."[25] They build a case against the ordinance on this foundation, relying on the history of such restrictions as those on birth control information (not remedied until the *Griswold* decision in 1965),[26] the Mann Act, statutory rape laws, and the like. Their arguments are perhaps best summarized by the following passage:

> Society's attempts to "protect" women's chastity through criminal and civil laws have resulted in restrictions on women's freedom to engage in sexual activity, to discuss it publicly and to protect themselves from the risk of pregnancy. These disabling restrictions reinforced the gender roles which have oppressed women for centuries. The Indianapolis ordinance resonates with the traditional concept that sex itself degrades women, and its enforcement would reinvigorate those discriminatory moral standards which have limited women's equality in the past.[27]

For FACT feminists all liberties are linked together. The various elements present in the pornography struggle are all secondary to the essential argument about the place of freedom in society. For these feminists the historical fragility of liberty, the recency of sexual freedom for women, and the still emerging case law on women's equality, coupled with the unavoidable reliance on the mechanism of control, outweigh other concerns about the possible effects of pornography on individual women's lives. Instead, they say, build the structure of freedom large enough and strong enough and everyone can live there. If women need protection, it is in freedom's house.

Fantasy

> You ask Mr. X what he finds essential in a girl. He replies without hesitation: purity, innocence. . . . Meanwhile, in the depths of his serene gaze, a ghost is raping a virgin. But wait. He didn't see a thing, and if you pointed it out to him, he'd object and be right to do so. For fantasy is, in a sense, innocent.[28]

> We desperately want to be bound, battered, tortured, humiliated, and killed. Or to be fair to the soft core, merely taken and used. This is erotic to the male point of view. . . . Fantasy expresses ideology, is not exempt from it.[29]

> It is true that many women have masochistic fantasies and can be sexually aroused by pornography. . . . This does not make it harmless. It does not mean it is healthy.[30]

> . . . it is comforting to recall that it is *certainly* not the case that the thoughts and expressions of persons are related to what they actually *do* in any simple and direct way. To be a human being in any culture we have knowledge of means that one has learned to *use* fantasy and to distinguish it from reality.[31]

Fantasies abound in pornography and in the discussions surrounding it. Is pornography simply the visual enactment of generalized male fantasy? Is it fantasy that causes pornography, or pornography that leads to fantasy, which leads to evil and violence? What is the shape and texture of female fantasy? And what is the vision of a world without pornography?

Presumably pornography could not exist if there were no sexual fantasies in people's souls. Despite all the arguments about pornography, no one seems to dispute the existence of sexual fantasy. WAP feminists say that male fantasy, imbedded as it is in a hostile culture, inevitably involves desires that are harmful or degrading to women and that male sexual fantasy itself is a problem.

For these feminists the depictions of women in the pages of *Playboy* or other softer versions of pornography are unacceptable. These portrayals deliver the message that a woman, submissively posed, is inviting the sexual advances of a man. By their standards, this cannot be a freely given invitation but instead represents intrusion, or worse. Other feminists, however, feel that women can find sexual arousal through traditional forms of pornography and that to deny women that access not only curtails a kind of freedom, but in essence censors fantasy, which might otherwise lead to more profound sexual experiences for women: "By defining sexually explicit images of women as subordinating and degrading to them, the ordinance reinforces the stereotypical view that good women do not seek and enjoy sex."[32]

The fantasy of a woman's sexual life has moved through time from the notion of what she should want to what she can want and back to the notion of what she should want. At an earlier time, women, associated with motherhood and purity, were considered above sexual desire. Those wanting sexual experiences other than within the most proscribed marital domains were labeled whores. Just as prevalent in popular culture has been the notion that women do want sexual encounters, in fact, that women crave sex, and that men, through romance, aggression, or rape, will show women just how much they want to be sexually engaged. In a feminist fantasy vision, perhaps the sexual desires of women must include, or indeed be premised upon, complete equality in desire and behavior. Yet, we are still living daily lives in a world far from equal and still without a new model of sexuality for women.

The old dichotomy of the woman as madonna or whore may not be articulated directly in the pornography controversy, but underlines it. Even with sexual liberation and a relaxation of cultural norms about sexual behavior, women, at least heterosexual women, still have not constructed a fantasy life that could be identified as uniquely their own. While FACT feminists argue that censorship also harms the sexual development of women, it is clear that to date the sexual freedom women have experienced is not outside the confines of the cultural definitions of male and female sexuality. In forms of the mass media not considered pornographic, the message conveyed is about how to be alluring to a man, how to make a man want you, and so forth. *Ms.* devoted an entire issue in October 1985 to men, including articles about how to flirt with a man. Sexuality is not dead, but articles in *Ms.* or in the pages of *Cosmopolitan* do indicate that there has not been much change in the portrayals of the basic concept of sexuality between men and women. It is still largely the game of search and submission—with men making the choices and defining the rules of the game.

What then will happen to sexual fantasy for women? Do women have an opportunity to develop or create a form of feminist sexual response? Understandably, the WAPs are concerned with the removal of pornography, not the creation of a new version of fantasy for women. In their refusal to address what might be an acceptable eroticism, however, they invite the criticism levied by Hunter and Law. Their lack of consideration of the reality of desire and what may bring pleasure to women returns to the ground of the "good girl/bad girl" of the past.

In her essay "Who Is Sylvia? On the Loss of Sexual Paradigms," Elizabeth Janeway confronts the lack of a female-defined sexual identity. Who we might be in a world where women's sexual roles have not been so culturally proscribed is a conjecture relevant here. There is not a robust pornography industry catering to women's "needs," because the age-old game is still with us and simply does not lend itself to the production of such depictions. In Janeway's discussion of "Mary and Eve" she suggests ways that feminists might take charge of the male-created myth of Eve the Temptress and turn it into a liberating fantasy. The work of Carole Vance and others who are exploring new forms of sexual expression for women is responsive to Janeway's plea for a new model.

> Certainly Eve represents freedom, an explicit denial of the shackling lessons of chastity which forced us to reject the reality of our own feelings. Eve is undomesticated; the doll figures of the media are just attempts to draw a tamed version. She invites us to enjoy our own pleasure. Freedom, delight, wildness, a dionysian testing of edge experience—all this is alluring to those who were not permitted them in the past. . . . More important to women's own inner reality is the fact that Eve is not our own creation. We find license for pleasure within this paradigm, but that cannot disguise the clear evidence that *our* pleasure is not primarily there. In the Eve image of female sexuality there is no true sense of internal experience, no vision of a female self choosing, enjoying, directing and controlling her own pleasure.[33]

The FACT feminists fear that passage of a pornography ordinance or the enforcement of obscenity laws will destroy the fragile beginnings of open female sexual fantasy. While abhorrent pornography would disappear if the WAPs have their way, the FACT forces argue that so would the opportunities for women to begin to define for themselves a female sexual fantasy.

A number of FACT members and signers of the amicus brief are lesbian groups and coalitions; it is easy to see how lesbian images, fantasy, and identity could be adversely affected. The lesbians involved in the anticensorship campaign believe that such restrictions begin to set the stage for repression of all sexually explicit materials, including lesbian erotica. Even more important is their belief that such widespread control of materials could open the door to the repression of behavior defined by some as "deviant."

The cultural implications of fantasy and pornography deserve an entire article and have been the focus of much scholarly thought. Within the confines of this chapter, it is possible to mention only some of the dominant themes present in the literature about the intertwining of culture and fantasy.

What is sexual fantasy? It is that moment of imagination, embellished memory, received image, or depiction that we find exciting or arousing. But to whom and when, and in what manner does this occur? Some feminists assert that male sexual fantasy has dictated the boundaries of feminine beauty as well as female sexuality. Thus, the air-brushed, unreal beauty of a *Playboy* centerfold defines the reality of male fantasy of what a beautiful woman is—even what a woman is *supposed* to look like. That male fantasy dictates the standards for beauty and that this leads to a kind of cultural sexism is unquestionable. The message of *Playboy* is that fantasy (at the least) is only possible with young, very trim, and flawless women; hence it perpetuates the sexist myths of what a woman really is—or must strive to be. Should it then, by extension, mean that magazines like *Playboy*[34] be made illegal, and if so, have we then made a certain kind of male sexual fantasy itself illegal?

Joanna Russ's *Magic Mommas, Trembling Sisters and Puritans and Perverts* offers a particularly useful feminist criticism of the above:

> As for the men's magazines, surely heterosexual men's desires to look at women's bodies is in itself perfectly acceptable. What's not acceptable is that the images sold to men are plastic and unreal, and that such sale takes place as part of a deeply sex-hating and woman-hating society. But the attack on pornography seems to be going in the wrong direction. Sexual fantasies, to judge from women's, don't make much sense if taken at face value.[35]

Pornography and culture is the chicken and egg game. Which came first? Which reinforces the other? Susan Griffin, in one of the most lucid statements on the cultural aspects of pornography, writes that ". . . the pornographic mind is the mind of our culture. In pornography we find the fantasy life of the mind."[36] What sets Griffin apart from MacKinnon is her broader cultural critique of pornography's history:

> . . . in pornography a "woman" is not a *woman*, she is a symbol. She is denied a self that is human. As we look more deeply into a culture which has fashioned itself after the pornographic mind, we will find that sadism and masochism have not been derived from the biological behavior of men and women as some theorists have supposed, but rather that the ideas of masculine behavior and of female behavior have been shaped by culture to embody sadomasochism.[37]

Further questions present themselves. Is pornography born from culture, or has culture evolved to include pornography? Will the elimination of the worst of pornography change the culture or begin to alter it? Herein lies the fundamental, and probably insurmountable, difference in the two feminist positions. The WAPs see the end of pornography as at least a window on a new world—the remaking of a culture. The FACTs see the control and censorship involving repression, which, if unchecked from the outset, would lead to the destruction of guarantees of particular importance to women. The leitmotif of the debate then is this: The WAPs would protect women from a variety of asserted evil consequences; the FACTs would protect mechanisms relevant to society in general, so that women, in particular, might continue to enjoy freedom.

The hardest question however remains: Is pornography no more than depiction of desire and fantasy, however vile? Or is it aggression or forced submission against women? Griffin concludes:

> All death in pornography is really only the death of the heart. Over and over again, that part of our being which can feel both in body and mind is ritually murdered. We make a mistake, therefore, when we believe that pornography is simply fantasy, simply a record of sadistic events. For pornography exceeds the boundaries of both fantasy and record and becomes itself an act. Pornography *is* sadism.[38]

If pornography is not behavior, then it becomes the offensiveness itself which must become the rationale for its removal—a punishment for the portrayal of private notions played out in the public arena. Unless, of course, we return to the question of whether pornography can be linked to the hateful acts that happen. Here is the strongest part of the WAP argument: Pornography causes violence against women. This causal statement is so complex and fraught with measurement problems that verification is impossible.[39] Yet this is where the strongest claim for censorship must ultimately rest. It is a sexual version of the famous "shout fire" in a crowded theater. Is there a fire or not?

Foes

> Women do not believe that men believe what pornography says about women. But they do. From the worse to the best of them, they do.[40]

> Men are not attack dogs, but morally responsible human beings. The ordinance reinforces a destructive sexist stereotype of men as irresponsible

beasts with "natural physiological responses" which can be triggered by sexually explicit images of women. . . .[41]

To the extent that women ignore the connections between our vulnerability to attack by the men in our lives . . . and pornography as an institutionally supported expression of the deepest misogyny, our efforts to put a stop to violence against women are bound to fail.[42]

The antipornography movement has attracted women from many sectors of women's liberation. But this unity has a high price, for it requires that we oversimplify, that we hypothesize a monolithic enemy, a timeless, universal male sexual brutality.[43]

At the heart of the struggle lies the question: Who is the foe? The real enemy? Many WAP feminists argue that the entire system is the culprit, which makes apparent the logic of the MacKinnon approach to system transformation through legal remedy. Beneath all WAP strategies or actions, however, is an assumption, or a conviction, that men are the enemy: dangerous and to be reckoned with. And, since institutions, indeed culture itself, are male creations, or at the least highly male identified and dominated, the belief that men *and* the system are the dual foes is not a contradictory vision.

The rhetoric of the WAP movement is a rhetoric of militancy; the terms are placed in the context of a war to be won. Many actors in the WAP drama once professed a separatist feminist vision.[44] Much of the WAP rhetoric is reminiscent of this earlier view, and their proclamations sound a familiar refrain: Men are evil; they cause pain; they must be vanquished. Or, at minimum, they must be controlled and stopped from causing harm.

This notion of man as foe again raises one of the most difficult issues for this century's feminism—the question of sexuality, in particular the thorny question of sameness and difference. Are men and women natural foes, inevitably at odds with one another, because they are so inherently, so genetically, different from one another? Or is it our uniqueness as human beings, differentiated from animals, and not our gender distinctions that govern us? Following the latter assumption, some resolution (fraught though it may be with sexual complications) of the pornography issue is possible because we are more the same than we are different. While FACT feminists acknowledge that women are hurt by pornography, they do not see the world in the same way that the WAPs do and criticize the seemingly one-sided vision of the WAPs: ". . . the ordinance is wholly blind to the possibility that men could be hurt and degraded by images presenting them as violent or sadistic."[45]

When Dworkin writes of men, she writes unmistakably of the enemy. One of WAP's most articulate and visible leaders, Dworkin denies any compromise or solution to the pornography question short of complete restraint. She cuts into the Law and Hunter argument, claiming that the individual behavior of men is not really the crucial question. For her, whether or not men "are attack dogs" is irrelevant. All men engaged in sexual intercourse, at any time or in any setting, are, by definition, behaving in a hostile and hurtful manner. Dworkin would not concede that if men controlled themselves and stopped producing and consuming pornography, they would become acceptable. The need to stop pornography goes much further, and the rationale cuts much deeper, for man is the enemy, a most vile creature whose only salvation might lie in teaching himself not to have erections. In Dworkin's terms, all sexual intercourse is the physical outcome of male hatred for women.[46]

Although Dworkin represents the most radical end point of WAP ideology and rhetoric, it would not be wise to dismiss her message. Stripped of its more inflammatory words, Dworkin expresses the core of WAP belief: Men can never redeem themselves from their "other" or enemy status; the very reality of their gender precludes redemption. Since their natural sexual response to women is both painful and cruel, men, in the most literal WAP vision, can be neither trusted nor reasoned with. Whether expressed in conventional male-female sexual encounters, or in pornographic consumption or production, the only possible outcome of male sexuality is abuse of women.

For the WAP feminists who have remained consistent in their views over the last decade and a half of the women's movement, this is not a new depiction of men or a new definition of women's situation in society. One is reminded of the split from the radical left which was caused primarily by the feminist realization of the New Left male's view of women and led ultimately to a call to arms for many feminists. Women rallied around the cry, "I do not take my enemy to my bedroom." It is important to note that the vision, for those feminists who have kept faith with it, is essentially unmodified. In this light it may be helpful to the discussion of men as foes to read again a small piece of rhetoric from an early and important manifesto—the SCUM (Society for Cutting Up Men) Manifesto:

> SCUM will couple-bust—barge into mixed (male-female) couples, wherever they are and bust them up. . . . The few remaining men can exist out their puny days or can go off to the nearest friendly suicide center where they will be painlessly gassed to death.[47]

As feminists entered an intense debate which led, ultimately, to the formation of two distinct branches of the movement, the radicals produced more manifestos directed at shocking women into action; publication of *Notes from the First Year* laid the groundwork for a more seriously separatist trend; and the women involved in "Cell 16" debated the relevance of men for any part of life. Celibacy, separatist strategies (of both a benign and a more violent nature), and sabbaticals from marriage were all suggested as ways to preserve female energy and to keep undiminished the power of the radical movement.[48] The antecedents of the pornography struggle began in those days. How to treat, characterize, or "dispose" of the other gender became an increasingly divisive and complex issue; it is the remnant of this profound disagreement between feminists that is so evident in the tensions around pornography.

Another dilemma emerges in this immediate drama that addresses the very definition of a foe. What of the nonfeminists who have supported the MacKinnon ordinance as well—namely, New Right and fundamentalist groups? John Stolenberg, a founder of Men Against Pornography, an organization allied with WAP, has said that "we are reaching women on the New Right."[49] FACT feminists insist that the only issue on which there could be agreement among these groups is pornography and what to do about it; indeed, they argue that the motivations for control are very different, and any alliance with these groups can be detrimental to women.

Although the alliance with the New Right is largely unacknowledged by WAP, it is a very real phenomenon. The ordinance, which began as a feminist initiative in Minneapolis and Indianapolis, ended up in Suffolk County, New York, and in Maine as initiatives sponsored by the New Right and a reorganized or reconstituted version of the Decency League. Feminist presence was barely visible in later versions of the ordinance. New Right antipornography efforts make the image of a fun-house hall of mirrors especially vivid. Little is as ironic as the members of the ultra-right and representatives of WAP engaged in warm and friendly conversation following the filming of a television panel show in the spring of 1986, while FACT representatives were insulted or ignored by their feminist WAP sisters.

Empirical research seems to indicate that these nonfeminist groups are foes, not friends. New Right opponents of pornography also reject other aspects of freedom or equality for women, including the right to abortion, the passage of the ERA, and questions of sexual preference and other lifestyle options.[50] For conservatives opposed to pornography, as demonstrated by the Meese Commission, conventional morality and a belief in the purity and sanctity of womanhood lead to an ideology valorizing a traditional lifestyle for women. Their desire to reform society, and turn back the clock to a time when a different code was honored, has special irony because they believe that they are responding to a higher order. This ideology, which proscribes universal values that must be enforced, could lead, of course, to the banning of all sorts of books and literature.

Conservative and fundamentalist support of censorship is not surprising; what is surprising is how little the WAPs seem to mind. Thus, the pornography battle poses interesting questions about the meaning of liberal and conservative ideologies. In this configuration, pornography is the hated target and the tactics to eliminate it are the same for WAPs and for conservatives. WAPs may in fact see censorship as a very specific weapon against one particular enemy, but others see it as a more general approach to a larger "problem" of moral decay.

For FACT feminists the foes are the ideological strangers. It is the crusade against repression and censorship that unites them, not the opposition to men, or to pornography, or even to the inequities of life in a sexist world. Here the WAP point about the disloyalty of defending those who bring harm to women is well taken. For there is no reason to believe that one's ACLU brothers care more about the rights of women than they care about the rights of Nazis to march; for various profound reasons they cannot. One might assume that the ACLU defends the rights of pornographers and the rights of Nazis (while in some sense "holding their noses"), but at heart, for civil libertarians, all groups must have equal standing. What unites a civil libertarian view and gives it cohesiveness is a commitment to an enduring ideology of individual rights. The civil libertarian agenda that the FACTs have subscribed to, then, is not differentiated for women; the FACTs see neither irony nor conflict in taking refuge in a shelter where the overall ideology of individual rights means that some roommates are incompatible with others.

Feminism

Whereas liberal feminism sought to include women in the mainstream, radical feminism embodies a rejection of the mainstream itself.[51]

I think this doubleness of experience may explain the bitterness of the fight against pornography . . . and the phenomenon of the sides being so very horrified by each other because they are perpetually talking past each other. When A attacks violence and B hears her attacking sexual freedom,

B will defend sexual freedom and A will hear B defending violence. You see how it goes round and round, louder each time. . . .[52]

The separate conversations metaphor of this battle has been illustrated throughout this chapter. The FACT feminists believe that the structure of the WAP fight endangers the health of feminism. Russ, for example, writes that "as Virginia Woolf says, a battle that wastes time and energy is as ill-advised as one that wastes lives."[53]

Betty Friedan, who perhaps best exemplifies liberal, reform, egalitarian feminism, has said that the true obscenity of our society is the obscenity of poverty.[54] Like others allied with FACT, she believes that the questions of racism and the continued sorrow of the lives of poor women should be the primary concerns of feminism. WAPs see an even greater sorrow in the reality of incest, rape, and battery; for them, pornography is a direct cause of this violence. They are much less concerned with empowerment through other means—equal pay, reversing the feminization of poverty, and so on. Two anticensorship activists underline this clash of values and motives:

> . . . in general, today's antipornography campaigns achieve their energy by mobilizing a complex amalgam of female rage, fear and humiliation in strategic directions that are not in the long term best interests of our movement. A politics of outrage—which can be valuable and effective— can also seriously fail women in our efforts to change the basic dynamics of the sex-gender system.[55]

> If the approach to pornography had served to highlight the causes of women's oppression through a critique of women's sexual exploitation, its galvanizing effect would have been very different. . . . There has been, among the antipornography feminists a series of subtle shifts in ideas about the forms and causes of women's oppression. From an appreciation of the multidimensional reality of masculine dominance, vocal feminists have been increasingly narrowing their focus to one dimension: the sexist and sexually explicit representation of women: pornography. Women's attention has been diverted from the causes to the depictions of the oppression.[56]

The temperance analogy is again relevant, for like temperance's attempt to remove liquor but leave unchanged the property and marriage laws, pornography legislation seeks to remove a representation, but not the underlying causes, of women's pain. It is the one-issue dimension of WAP that the FACT feminists claim is the dangerous strategy; that one cause has become the central focus of some of the most active and articulate feminists clearly would frighten those who see a broad women's program as essential. It is, however, the obsessive and singular nature of the WAP movement that characterizes it as a social movement.

It is unlikely that the battle around pornography will destroy the feminist movement or split it apart irreparably, as has been argued. There is, in this drama, a collision of values, and therefore the impossibility of absolute victory for either side. It may, however, produce a more humane and just society in the end. There is little hope that this break can be healed; it is at the core of what splits radical and moderate reformers.

Where and how to draw the line? That is the question with which this chapter began, and with which it ends. If in the ideal WAP vision *Playboy* must be removed from newsstands, then the FACTs must argue that nothing can be eliminated, and if the WAPs hear that nothing can be eliminated, they in turn must cling to the position that each and every piece of pornography must be stamped out. It is the route of ordinance, the resort to legal remedy that presents such an interesting paradox for these radical women.

What may ultimately prove most destructive to the WAP feminist approach is the interest of the New Right in this strategy. With the involvement of fundamentalists and the New Right, the stage is set for a modern Comstockian version of a value system which would dictate sex education as well as censorship. Why are the WAPs so reluctant to acknowledge these dangers, and so unwilling to compromise on a less far-reaching ordinance? One cannot ignore the conservative trend in American life, the popularity of antipornography and antiabortion crusades. Whether defined as a *moral* issue or a *feminist* issue, it is not accidental that antipornography campaigns happen when there is a prevalence of conservative opinion.

Perhaps the WAPs will win; this is less difficult to imagine than it once was, in light of the Bush presidency and the inevitable changes on the Supreme Court. What is more important to note here, however, is that the fight to eliminate pornography is being carried out on a traditional battleground, a symbolism that cannot be overlooked. The question of morality is replayed for women over and over again. Earlier women without protection in divorce, without the right to inherit from their own fathers, and with no adequate devices for the prevention of pregnancy saw sexual purity as a way to a better life and survival itself. Despite the modern players, this drama is an old one; the traditional battleground for reform has become a radical encampment. But the eternal question continues to plague women's political life: How to reconcile one's "womanness" with one's "citizenship," in the dual realm to which women are forever consigned.

I am grateful for the insights offered by the members of the Women and Politics Seminar, and am especially indebted to Jane Isay and Harriet Pilpel, Esq., for their editorial wisdom.

Notes

1. The Court held that, in addition to being without redeeming social importance, the work must also lack "serious literary, artistic, political and scientific value."
2. *Jacobellis* v. *Ohio*, 378 U.S. 184, 197 (1964).
3. Dworkin (1985), p. 35.
4. Robin Morgan is an example of a leading feminist who wrote very early on the role of pornography in causing pain and harm to women.
5. Such as pickets against *Playboy*, tours of the "red-light districts or combat zones" of cities, and other consciousness-raising devices designed to force women and men to face up to the realities of pornography, live sex shows, and the like.
6. On February 24, 1986, the Supreme Court struck down the proposed statute, by summary affirmation—a decision without opinion—after lawsuits had been filed by a united group of First Amendment advocates and booksellers. It should be noted that the Court was actually affirming the lower court's free speech findings against the ordinance.
7. For the ease of discussion and analysis the terms "WAP feminists" and "FACT feminists" will be used as descriptions of those sharing the views of these organizations, and not only to describe the actual members of the organizations. That is to say, these terms will be employed as a shorthand way of referring to those essentially opposed to pornography and to those fearing the repercussions of control. It is not to suggest that all people possessing these attitudes are actively involved or affiliated with a specific organization. Many other groups, splinters and branches of the original FACT and WAP groups, also exist, as well as women who are passionately attached or committed to one side or the other who are not, however, officially affiliated with a group. As the purpose of this chapter is to highlight the overarching philosophical dilemmas in women's political participation and not to present a structural analysis of feminist organizations, the reader is asked to indulge the author with these concise referents when they are used.
8. Longino (1980), pp. 52–53.
9. Dixon (1984), p. 6.
10. Hunter and Law (1985), p. 31.
11. Dixon (1984), p. 7.
12. It should be noted that the American Civil Liberties Union is opposed to all obscenity statutes and believes that both the *Roth* and *Miller* standards as set

forth in those cases should be repealed (American Civil Liberties Union, 1985).

The ACLU opposes any restraint on the right to create, publish or distribute materials to adults or the rights of adults to choose the materials they read or view, on the basis of obscenity, pornography or indecency. . . . The ACLU has long maintained that all definitions of obscenity from the Supreme Court's 1957 definition (*Roth* v. *United States*) . . . to *Miller* v. *California* . . . is erroneous because this type of judgement is inevitably subjective and personal. Courts and juries continue to differ over what constitutes obscenity, often including in that category materials that have won world-wide acclaim.

—American Civil Liberties Union
Ordinances for Governance

13. Longino (1980), p. 53.
14. MacKinnon (1985), p. 20.
15. MacKinnon (1985), p. 27.
16. MacKinnon (1985), p. 33.
17. MacKinnon (1985), p. 8.
18. Bordin (1981), p. 162.
19. In this case the Court held that the *Miller* standard need not be applied in cases of child pornography and "[that] child pornography [is] a category of material outside the protection of the First Amendment." It emphasized that the "prevention of sexual exploitation and abuse of children constitutes a government objective of surpassing importance." Being cautious not to overextend the ruling, the Court noted that this holding was limited to live performances by children—mere descriptions retain their constitutional protection.
20. MacKinnon (1985), p. 37.
21. Amici Curiae Brief of Feminist Anti-Censorship Task Force et al. (1985).
22. Hunter and Law (1985), pp. 1–2.
23. MacKinnon-Dworkin Ordinance, p. 3.
24. For example, the recent decision by the 7-11 chain of stores to remove *Playboy* and such magazines was hailed as a victory by many feminists, despite its conservative origins—coming at the same time as the Meese Commission report on pornography.
25. Hunter and Law (1985), p. 4.
26. *Griswold* v. *Connecticut*, 381 U.S. 479 (1965).
27. Hunter and Law (1985), pp. 7–8. "The Mann Act was premised on the notion that women require . . . special protection from sexual activity."
28. Robbe-Grillet (1985), pp. 44–45.
29. MacKinnon (1985), p. 41.

30. Russell (1980), p. 218.

31. Dixon (1984), p. 9.

32. Hunter and Law (1985), p. 43.

33. Janeway (1980), p. 585.

34. I am referring here to those forms of pornography in which violence is superseded by the notions of sensuality and desire—the so-called soft porn.

35. Russ (1985), p. 114.

36. Griffin (1981), p. 3.

37. Griffin (1981), p. 49.

38. Griffin (1981), p. 56.

39. It is interesting to note that WAP spokespeople say in interviews and in the literature they distribute how many women are battered or raped per minute; this is always said within the context of eliminating pornography. It is taken as a given by WAPs that pornography and rape or battering go hand in hand, if in fact they are not viewed as one and the same event. A series of empirical studies consider the causal possibilities of pornography and violence. See Bart, Freeman, and Kimball (1985); Malamuth and Check (1985); Linz, Penrod, and Donnerstein (1986); and Shepher and Reisman (1985).

40. Dworkin (1979).

41. Hunter and Law (1985), p. 39.

42. *Sourcebook for the 12th Annual Conference on Women and the Law* (1981), p. 211.

43. Snitow (1985), p. 113.

44. Although it should be noted that many women involved in the FACT movement were also radical feminists who once identified with a more separatist view of liberation.

45. Hunter and Law (1985), p. 40.

46. See Dworkin (1987).

47. "SCUM Manifesto." In Morgan (1970), p. 105.

48. For an excellent discussion and analysis of the difference in radical and liberal feminism, see Echols (1986).

49. Stated during the Channel 13 television program "Symposium on Pornography," Spring, 1986.

50. McClosky and Brill (1983).

51. Echols (1986).

52. Russ (1985), pp. 107–108.

53. Russ (1985), p. 113.

54. Friedan (1986).

55. Snitow (1985), p. 108.

56. Burstyn (1985), p. 25.

22

The Two Worlds
of Women of the New Right

Rebecca Klatch

The 1980s witnessed a resurgence of conservative activism commonly termed the "New Right." Although no consensus exists on the exact boundaries of the New Right, generally the phrase is used to delineate a network of people and organizations that came into prominence in the mid-1970s, including conservative politicians such as Jesse Helms, Orrin Hatch, and Jack Kemp; conservative think tanks such as the Heritage Foundation; general purpose organizations such as the Conservative Caucus, the National Conservative Political Action Committee, and the Committee for the Survival of a Free Congress; as well as the religious sector, including prime-time preachers, the Moral Majority, and groups working against such issues as abortion, gay rights, and pornography. In fact, the New Right is not a cohesive movement whose members share a single set of beliefs and values. Rather, there is a fundamental division within the New Right based on different—and even opposing—views of human nature, men's and women's roles, the function of government, and the ideal society.

This schism within the New Right is historically based and continuous with the Old Right of the 1950s. Seymour Lipset and Earl Raab's classic study of the American Right from 1790 to 1970 finds a continuous marriage of interest between two groups: those based in the less educated, lower economic strata, highly religious, and drawn to the *social issues* of right-wing movements; and those rooted in the highly educated, higher income strata, less religious, and committed above all to *economic conservatism*.[1] Thus, despite claims that what is new about the

New Right is its attention to the social issues,[2] in fact social conservatism is *not* a distinguishing characteristic of the New Right. The issues may have shifted from temperance and Darwinism to the ERA and school prayer, but noneconomic issues have typically played a part in right-wing movements.

If social conservatism is not a distinguishing mark of the New Right, what *is* unique about the New Right is the visible presence of women throughout the conservative movement.[3] Although virtually all past research looked exclusively at male activists, recent research, particularly by feminist scholars, examines female involvement on the right. While these studies are a welcome and necessary addition to the lack of knowledge about women, virtually all of the research concentrates exclusively on female participation in antifeminist activities.[4] Typically, conclusions are reached about "right-wing women" based on involvement in anti-ERA or antiabortion organizations. Yet this is a limited portrayal of women of the right. By focusing only on women involved in the social issues, we get an incomplete picture of female activism. Just as the New Right is not one cohesive movement, neither are right-wing women a monolithic group.

My own study, based on two years of field research, analyzes a diverse group of female activists and finds a fundamental division in world view among women of the right. I present these two distinct ideologies as ideal types, labeling them the social conservative and laissez-faire conservative world views. Analysis of this schism is based on three sources of data. (1) I conducted in-depth interviews, ranging in length from one-and-a-half to four hours, with thirty female activists. All activists are self-identified and labeled by others as conservative. The women included in the sample either were referred to me by others after I explicitly stated that I wanted to talk to women of the New Right or were affiliated with organizations identified as part of the general movement called the New Right. The one group consciously excluded was women whose primary or sole affiliation was with the right-to-life movement.[5] The entire sample supported the 1980 election of Ronald Reagan, with nearly all criticism falling to the right of Reagan's policies. Many of the women interviewed supported the 1964 presidential campaign of Barry Goldwater as well. Thus, the organizations and political beliefs represented in this study range from the conservative branch of the Republican party to the more "extreme" ideology of such groups as the Libertarian party and the Moral Majority.[6]

Comparing the background of the women in the sample reveals the varying social bases of each type. Although all activists interviewed are white, social conservative women tend to be somewhat older than laissez-faire conservative women, with the average ages being 45 years and 38 years, respectively. While the sample as a whole is disproportionately Catholic due to the location of the majority of the interviews in Massachusetts, the social conservative group is virtually all Catholic and Fundamentalist Christian, while the laissez-faire conservative camp is divided between Catholics and more ecumenical Protestants, with a minority of Jewish constituents. Further, while the sample overall is highly educated, with nearly all women having completed a college education, laissez-faire conservative activists hold more postgraduate degrees than do social conservative activists. Overall, there are slightly more married than single women. Of those married, more fall into the social conservative group, and all but two of the married women have children. The laissez-faire group includes two divorced women who are living with men, as well as another woman living with her fiancé, a lifestyle not found among any of the social conservative activists. While the clear majority (90 percent) of the sample are employed outside the home, all women who are full-time homemakers are located within the social conservative group. Half of the overall sample hold jobs directly tied to their political beliefs—employment in conservative organizations, as Reagan administrators, and so on. The laissez-faire group, however, includes more women who have training and/or who hold professional positions distinct from their political work—engineer, college professor, and so on. Although no conclusive statements can be made from the small sample in this study about all conservative activists, these findings parallel the demographic differences among the two constituencies of the Old Right.[7]

(2) I took extensive field notes during participant observation at conservative conferences and organizational meetings.[8] (3) I examined the printed literature of organizations affiliated with those interviewed as well as literature obtained at conferences and meetings.[9]

Obviously, one must be cautious in generalizing from the small sample in this study about the population as a whole. While the interviews with local activists took place in Massachusetts, a state that is disproportionately liberal and Irish Catholic, the field data from conferences and the textual analyses do draw upon a national pool of activists. Moreover, because the basic division in political beliefs at the heart of this analysis is consistent with the findings regarding the dual social base and ideological tensions historically present in the American right, there is reason to believe that the findings here are true for the New Right as a whole. In fact, other analysts of the New Right have sketched out ideological strains that parallel the division found here regarding social and laissez-faire conservatism.[10] Nonetheless, any conclusive statements about the overall distribution of right-wing beliefs require a national study based on survey analysis.

After briefly examining the main differences in belief among women of the right, the remainder of this chapter focuses on the varying perceptions of gender roles, gender discrimination, and feminism. Because confidentiality was assured, all excerpts from the interview data included in this chapter remain anonymous.[11]

Social Conservatism and Laissez-Faire Conservatism

Every ideology has a central lens through which the world is viewed. Vision is refracted through this lens, coloring all perception. Social conservatives view the world through the lens of religion, meaning specifically Christianity or the Judeo-Christian ethic. In looking at America, social conservatives see a country founded upon religious beliefs and deeply rooted in a religious tradition. The family stands at the center of this world, representing the building block of society. The family's role as moral authority is essential; the family instills children with moral values and restrains the pursuit of self-interest.

Implicit in this image of the family is the social conservative conception of human nature. Humans are creatures of unlimited appetites and instincts. Left on their own, the world would be a chaos of seething passions, overrun by narrow self-interest. Only the moral authority of the family or religion tames human passions, transforming self-interest into the larger good. The ideal society, then, is one in which individuals are integrated into a moral community, bound together by faith, by common moral values, and by obeying the dictates of the family and religion.

While this is the ideal, the social conservative vision of contemporary America sees a morally decaying country in which the basic unit of society is crumbling. Moral problems not only are the root of America's ills, but take precedence over all other issues. Social conservative activists see themselves as having a special mission: to restore America to health; to renew religious faith, morality, and decency; and to return America to the path of righteousness of the Founding Fathers.

While religion is the central lens of social conservatism, laissez-faire conservatives view the world through the lens of liberty, particularly the economic liberty of the free market and the political liberty based on the minimal state. Laissez-faire belief is rooted in the classical liberalism associated with Adam Smith, John Locke, and John Stuart Mill.[12] Hence, the concept of liberty is inextricably bound to the concept of the individual. As the primary element of society, the individual is seen as an autonomous, rational, self-interested actor. Rather than viewing humans as creatures of unlimited passions, laissez-faire conservatives view humans as beings endowed with free will, initiative, and self-reliance. The larger good is not ensured through the maintenance of moral authority and the restriction of self-interest. Rather, the laissez-faire ideal poses a society in which natural harmony exists through the very pursuit of self-interest. The aim of the good society is to elevate the potential of humans by bringing their creative and productive nature to fruition.

America is awarded a special role in history as the cradle of liberty. Yet, like social conservatives, laissez-faire conservatives deplore the current direction and spirit of America. It is the erosion of liberty, however, rather than moral decay, which is of utmost concern. America's departure from the ideal of the limited state and the unfettered market threatens the individual's economic and political liberty. Thus, laissez-faire conservatives unanimously name economic problems as the top priority of the nation; economic issues and, secondarily, defense issues take precedence over all other concerns.

In sum, social conservative activists use their influence to return the United States to its moral foundation. Laissez-faire conservative activists are trying to restore the nation's economic foundation. To social conservatives, renewal of spiritual faith, religious devotion, and righteous living will create a stable and ordered America. To laissez-faire conservatives, protection of the free market and a strengthening of individual initiative, self-reliance, hard work, and pride will assure the productivity and security of the country.

Perceptions of Gender and Feminism

The perception of the proper roles of men and women in society distinguishes the two constituencies of the New Right. Social conservative women believe in a strict division of gender roles as decreed by the Scriptures. Gender is envisioned as a hierarchical ordering with God and Christ at the top, followed by men, and then women.

While male and female roles are each respected as essential and complementary components of God's plan, men are the spiritual leaders and decision-makers in the family. One woman, active in the promotion of school prayer, articulated her notion of the masculine ideal:

> God made man and He made woman to complement each other. I like it that way. . . . Since I've been born again, I've come to realize what a real

man is. A *real man* is like Jesus. . . . Look at the men who founded this country. They were all real men—George Washington, Thomas Jefferson, John Adams—they were real heroes. They all believed in God.

It is women's role to support men in their positions of higher authority. A woman's role is not simply to help her husband, but essentially is defined in terms of altruism and self-sacrifice. This belief in women's natural orientation to others is reflected in the voice of a pro-family activist in Massachusetts who told me:

Being a mother has enhanced my life *so much.* Before I had children I was always worried about how my hair looked or my clothes, but now I no longer worry about that as much. I'm no longer self-centered. It feels so good because now I put six people ahead of me. I am giving something important to my children and to future generations.

The social conservative world is rooted in a firm conception of the proper roles of men and women which, divinely ordained, are essential to the survival of the family and to the maintenance of a moral, ordered, and stable society. Men and women have clearly defined, separate functions. Because gender roles are delineated in such unambiguous terms, any blurring of roles is viewed as a threat. A Family Forum member expressed her fear of this threat in the following story:

Tonight we took the kids out to Papa Gino's for dinner. While we were sitting there, these three girls came in dressed up in baseball outfits. They looked just like boys. From the back you couldn't tell the difference. They had it all down—even drumming on the table. And the way they walked, everything! They were about fourteen. Here's my twelve-year-old son sitting there and what is he to think? What effect does that have on my son to see this sameness? He won't be able to tell the difference between the sexes seeing things like that.

In order to reaffirm the essential line dividing the sexes, Jerry Falwell sermonizes about the super-masculinity of Jesus. Denouncing the portrayal of Christ as having long hair and wearing flowing robes, Falwell asserts: "Christ wasn't effeminate. . . . The man who lived on this earth was a man with muscles . . . Christ was a he-man!"[13]
While social conservatives envision a man's world as distinct from a woman's world, no such distinctions are visible in the laissez-faire view of gender. There is a notable absence of commentary on gender roles. There is particularly no mention of the need for male authority and female submission or of women's natural orientation toward others. In

fact, these very beliefs contradict the fundamental values of the laissez-faire conservative world view. Listen, for example, to the words of one woman, active in public education, speaking about her view of gender:

> I believe women used to be considered property; that was terrible. I *do* believe in differences between the sexes. For example, I can't do all the things men do in terms of strength; but difference does not mean inferiority. I think women are strong, competent, able. Women have to get over their roles as shy, pretty, helpless and always nice. Men who are successful and competent get really scared and threatened when they discover a strong woman. I've had people treat me that way.

In short, the social conservative vision of a hierarchical ordering of authority of men over women is antithetical to the laissez-faire conservative ethos. Faith in individual self-reliance and free will, and belief in the liberty and autonomy of every individual, extends to women as well as to men. One woman interviewed, who heads an antitax organization, reacted to my description of this study by saying:

> Why study *women* in politics? After all, women are no different than men. When you come down to it, some men are aggressive, some women are aggressive; some men are shy, some women are shy. It's only because people *expect* particular reactions or traits in men and women that it is so. We are really only people.

Further, in contrast to the social conservative activist who praised the selflessness of the mother role, this tax reform activist responded to *her* days as a homemaker by saying:

> Ontological guilt—do you know what that is? The feeling that you're not doing enough, that if only you could get something more from your life— that is what I felt as a homemaker. Now I have really found myself. I never feel as if I haven't done enough. Every moment is consumed in my work which is a fulfillment of my beliefs.

The gap between the two worlds' perceptions of gender is also apparent in a comment made by one Washington leader, active in defense and Republican women's organizations. Reacting to the ideas of social conservative leader George Gilder, she said:

> It would be almost like saying I don't belong in the workplace to believe that stuff, wouldn't it? There's sort of an over-emphasis on family, that every woman's got to have children to be fulfilled kind of thing and you've

got to give your twenty years to the kitchen or whatever. I mean, hell, how can you spend twenty years in the kitchen today? Everybody's got a Cuisinart. It takes fifteen minutes to prepare a gourmet meal today.

These varying perceptions of gender result in opposing views of gender discrimination. Because social conservatives adhere to a hierarchical ordering, they believe that positional differences between women and men do *not* imply inequality. For example, pro-family leader Connie Marshner denies that discrimination is the cause of women earning fifty-nine cents to every dollar earned by men. Rather, it is because women *choose* to work part time or temporarily that they are paid less than men. She argues that "[feminists] would not entertain the idea that women may not want to work as hard or that in school they may not want to take as challenging courses."[14] Similarly, Phyllis Schlafly claims: "The fact that there may be only eighteen women out of 535 members of Congress does not prove discrimination at all. . . . The small number of women in Congress proves only that most women do not want to do the things that must be done to win elections."[15]

Social conservative women argue that being female actually is beneficial. As one national organizer told me: "It's a great advantage being female. I get away with things I could never do if I were a man! I get in to see corporate leaders, I get through to people on the phone. There's never been a time where I felt I couldn't do something because I'm female."

Laissez-faire activists, on the other hand, are inclined to recognize and deplore the unequal treatment of women. Discrimination is denounced as interfering with the individual's ability to climb to the height of her talents. Both men and women must remain unconstrained by external interference, free to follow the dictates of their own initiative. Recognition of prejudice against women in politics is evident in a story told by an activist in Massachusetts:

> Once I was on this panel debating the mayor and he argued against my comments about waste in government by saying, "When was the last time you cleaned out your refrigerator? Did you throw anything out of that?" And then, "Why aren't you home with your children?" I got the audience on my side because I said, "Gee, it's embarrassing. I can't remember when the last time was that I cleaned my refrigerator. Actually, I think my husband did it." I hate that kind of attitude.

Another laissez-faire activist complained about the tendency to pay men for their political efforts while expecting women to volunteer their time.

Laissez-faire conservative women are also more likely to acknowledge discrimination against women in the work world. An engineer active in the Libertarian party reports:

> I worked for a corporation. I came up for promotion. It was between me and this man. They gave it to him. I asked my boss, "Was I qualified to get the promotion?" and he said, "We gave it to him because he has a family." I said, "I didn't ask you if he had a family, I said was I qualified." I quit two weeks later. I figure any place that doesn't value me and my work doesn't deserve me. . . . Sure, there's discrimination. But I'm not going to get upset over a person's attitude about women or blacks. I can go somewhere else. Also, you can boycott a place so that other people know about it.

Although laissez-faire women share recognition of discrimination with feminists, they react to such bias purely in voluntaristic terms. Women who are discriminated against should, on their own initiative, leave the job and enter the free market to choose another one. Another laissez-faire activist who reported discrimination in hiring responded by reading books on the psychology of organizations, trying to understand "how things are run and what I'm up against in order to make my way." Individualistic solutions, rather than collective actions, are the way to fight unequal treatment.

The two worlds' varying perceptions of gender also imply different views of feminism. To social conservatives feminism represents one of the primary forces of moral decay responsible for America's decline; by challenging traditional gender roles, feminism threatens the family and religious dictates. Among laissez-faire conservatives, on the other hand, there is a noticeable absence of commentary on feminism. Feminism does not represent one of the primary foes of freedom. In fact, laissez-faire women adhere to part of the feminist vision.

Social conservatives charge feminists with renouncing the family as a source of repression and enslavement, a tool used by men to entrap and oppress women.[16] The International Women's Year Conference held in Houston in 1977 concretized the perception of feminism as an anti-family force. Sponsored by the United Nations, the conference brought together women from all over the country to consider "women's issues." Social conservatives were shocked by the delegates' support for the ERA, gay rights, federal funding of abortion, government-sponsored childcare, and contraception for minors without parental consent, all seen as a threat to the traditional family. In opposition to such measures, a network of activists and organizations came together calling themselves "the pro-family movement."

Inextricably bound to the association of feminism as anti-family is the perception of feminism as an extension of the new narcissism, a symbol of the Me Decade. Pro-family leader Onalee McGraw explains, "The feminist movement issued an appeal that rapidly spread through our culture urging women to liberate themselves from the chains of family life and affirm their own self-fulfillment as the primary good."[17] Feminism threatens to replace the higher moral authority of the family with women's self-interest. When individuality and freedom of self are paramount, the ultimate result is what Marshner labels "macho feminism."

> Macho feminism despises anything which seeks to interfere with the desires of Number One. A relationship which proves burdensome? Drop it! A husband whose needs cannot be conveniently met? Forget him! Children who may wake up in the middle of the night? No way! To this breed of thought, family interferes with the self-fulfillment, and given the choice between family and self, the self is going to come out on top. . . . Feminists praise self-centeredness and call it liberation.[18]

The underlying fear of social conservative women is of a total masculinization of the world. If everyone pursues his or her own interest, no one will be left to look out for the larger good, to be the nurturer and caretaker.

Further, feminism also denigrates the very status of the homemaker. Feminism explicitly belittles homemakers by labeling their work as drudgery, as ungratifying, and as glorified babysitting. The feminist call for women to go beyond the housewife role, to step into the male world of paid labor, denies the importance and the satisfaction derived by those content with their homemaker status. As one local anti-ERA activist explains:

> The women's liberation movement looks down on the housewife. She should be the most respected person as she is bringing up future generations. But women's liberation puts her down and says, "All she does is stay home all day and wash dirty diapers." ERA won't do anything for these women.

The conflict between feminists and homemakers becomes a tug-of-war between two lifestyles. There is no peaceful coexistence between women following traditional ways and those women seeking new paths and new careers. Rather than accepting and valuing each lifestyle, social conservatives view feminism as promoting new roles for women at the expense of the old, thereby disregarding the worth of women's work in the home. Social conservatives are appalled, for example, by feminist assessments of the monetary value of housework, believing such efforts reduce a relationship based on love to purely quantitative value.

While feminists—not men—are blamed for attacking the status of homemakers and for degrading the traditional female role, beneath this blame is an underlying distrust of men, particularly evident in discussions of the ERA. In social conservative eyes the ERA would have eliminated the homemaker's most valuable property right: the right to be provided for by her husband. The existing remedies a wife has if her husband neglects his responsibilities, such as purchasing goods on her husband's credit and letting the store handle collection of payment, would be destroyed. Worst of all is the fear that a man who stops loving his wife will be freed of all responsibility to support his spouse. Phyllis Schlafly warns:

> Consider a wife in her 50's whose husband decides he wants to divorce her and trade her in on a younger model. This situation has become all too common, especially with no-fault divorce in many states. If ERA is ratified, and thereby wipes out the state laws that require a husband to support his wife . . . the most tragic effect would fall on the woman who has been a good wife and homemaker for decades, and who can now be turned out to pasture with impunity because a new, militant breed of liberationist has come along.[19]

The underlying assumption is that men are creatures of uncontrollable passions and lust, who have little sense of loyalty or commitment. Only moral *and legal* authority can restrain the savagery of male nature. Opposition to the ERA, then, speaks to the fear that homemakers will be left most vulnerable if legal binds on men are lifted. Feminists are responsible for removing the safety valves that currently protect women. With men free to "do their own thing" the homemaker will be left with nothing to hold on to. As Mrs. Billy Graham put it, the women's liberation movement is "turning into men's lib because we are freeing them from their responsibilities. I think we are being taken for a ride."[20]

Ironically, this same fear of women's precarious position is voiced by feminists in recognizing that all women are just one man removed from welfare. Yet while social conservative women try to ensure women's rights and entitlements within marriage, thereby binding men to a stable family unit, feminists seek security through ensuring women's economic independence from men.

Just as there is little commentary on gender roles in laissez-faire ideology, so, too, there is a noticeable absence of response to feminism.

Where social conservatives see feminism as threatening to blur the sacred differences between women and men, disrupting the natural hierarchy of authority, laissez-faire conservatives see no such separate spheres, view both men and women as individuals, and reject the notion of a "natural hierarchy of authority." Where social conservatives reject feminism as encouraging women to be self-interested, laissez-faire conservatives uphold individualism as an ideal, embracing the extension of self-interest to all. Where social conservatives view the emphasis on women's self-fulfillment as narcissistic, laissez-faire conservatives applaud each individual's attempt to rise to his or her talents, believing that it adds to the wealth of the nation.

Although laissez-faire conservatives also opposed the ERA, they did so for entirely different reasons. The ERA was viewed as a misguided way to eliminate gender discrimination because it implied the growth of big government. It symbolized the expansion of bureaucratic control, the federalization of one more area of life, resulting in encroachment on individual liberty. One female activist put it this way: "There are two parts to the ERA. The first part regarding equality I agree with, but I don't think we need that. That's already established by the Constitution. . . . But the second part I don't agree with. The second part gives the government the right to enforce equality." Typically, laissez-faire conservatives responded to the ERA by calling for individual efforts to fight discrimination or by proposing changes on a state or local level.

This fundamental opposition to big government is also evidenced in the stance laissez-faire conservatives take toward other "women's" or "family" issues, further separating the two worlds of the right. While opposition to daycare, abortion, and homosexuality is at the very core of social conservatism, all seen as evidence of the moral decay of American society, laissez-faire conservatives *support* these very issues. To them, abortion or homosexuality are private, individual matters; government legislation of such issues intrudes on individual liberty. As one activist explains: "Personally I'm against abortion. But I think it's not for the government to decide. I think it's an individual woman's choice whether to have an abortion or not." Another activist put it this way: "I believe life begins at conception, but I don't see how you can legislate that. I much prefer the way it is now . . . women are not butchered. But do I want government to pay for abortions? Well, no, because that's not morally justifiable." Typically, this laissez-faire activist is pro-choice but against government-sponsored abortion. The government has no right to deny a woman's choice, but should not fund her abortion either. Many laissez-faire activists also support day care as long as it remains in private hands. In one Reagan administrator's words: "I think we need to expand day care. . . . If a woman has to work an eight hour day to make money, she needs day care. I just don't believe the government should pay for it. I think it should be in private hands."

Laissez-faire conservatives support women's equality, women's choice regarding abortion, and day care, but believe these matters are best left to individual decision-making. They deplore the use of government as a means to assure anyone's rights. Thus, while laissez-faire conservative women are closer to feminists in their view of gender roles and discrimination, it is the very means to achieve women's equality which separates laissez-faire conservatives from most feminists. While most feminists call for federal support in addressing women's needs, laissez-faire conservatives oppose any further reliance on big government. While many feminists look toward collective solutions to remedy inequality, laissez-faire conservatives look toward individual solutions as a way to end discrimination. While feminism itself does not pose a threat to the laissez-faire conservative world, affirmative action and other such measures *do* threaten to encroach upon the economic and political liberties of the individual. In short, liberty must not be sacrificed in the quest for equality.

The Paradox of Right-Wing Women's Activism: Women In and For Themselves

The question inevitably arises concerning the seeming paradox of the social conservative woman. Given her adherence to traditional gender roles in which men are breadwinners and protectors, and women are helpmates and caretakers, how does the social conservative woman understand her own position as a political activist? Does her activism contradict her beliefs?

Social conservative women do not see a tension between their political involvement and the traditional female role. In fact, these "new" political roles are defined within the bounds of traditional gender ideology. Female activism is conceptualized as the power behind the throne, women altruistically working for the benefit of a larger cause. Schlafly, for example, includes an assertive political role in her ideal of womanhood, what she terms "the Positive Woman": "The Positive Woman accepts her responsibility to spin the fabric of civilization, to mend its tears, and to reinforce its seams. . . . God has a mission for every Positive Woman. It is up to her to find out what it is and to meet the challenge."[21]

Marshner has another name for this expanded female role: "the new traditional woman." In explaining the new traditional woman, Marshner distinguishes between conventions and traditional values. Conventions are mutable, changing with the times. Thus, certain changes in gender roles must be seen as a mere shift in conventions. For example, the fact that more women today feel that boys should be as responsible as girls for doing the laundry does not challenge traditional values; this merely indicates a change in convention because doing laundry is a morally neutral act. On the other hand, traditional values are external; traditional values are moral norms which must be followed without exception. Fidelity is a moral norm; thus, adultery is always wrong. Similarly, a man being the head of the household is a traditional value. It is not immoral for a woman to earn more money than her husband does. But it *is* immoral to reject his authority. The man must remain the leader in the family.[22]

Thus, neither Marshner nor Schlafly sees any contradiction in the activism of the social conservative woman. It is, in fact, woman's role as moral gatekeeper which allows her to adopt these new positions, bringing moral purity to a world filled with sin.

There is no apparent paradox to laissez-faire women's activism. Because they do not see women as bound to traditional roles, there is no seeming contradiction between their beliefs and their own role as public leaders. In fact, Jeane Kirkpatrick speaks of the need for more women to be in positions of power in order to act as role models breaking through traditional roles.[23] Laissez-faire conservative women do *not* conceive of themselves as the caretakers of society, altruistically at work for the benefit of all. Instead, they see themselves as no different from men, self-interested actors working for a political cause.

The paradox of right-wing women is *not* that social conservative women are vocal and active as they call for traditional roles. Despite the prevalent assumption that antifeminist women are "a brainwashed flock,"[24] "lackeys" of men,[25] the paradox is that those women who are furthest from feminists in their beliefs actually *do* act in their own interests *as women*, while laissez-faire women, who actually share a portion of the feminist vision, do *not* act in their collective gender interest. Far from suffering from false consciousness, social conservative women are well aware of their interests and act to defend their status as women. Rather, the conflict between social conservative women and feminists derives from their radically different interpretations of male and female. Because social conservative women define femininity in terms of traditional roles of male breadwinner/female caretaker, they seek to extend and secure female rights *within* the context of marriage and the family.

To borrow a phrase from Marx, social conservative women act as women *for* themselves, while laissez-faire conservative women remain women *in* themselves.[26] Gender identity is central to the political involvement of social conservative women; recognizing their commonality with other traditional women, they seek to protect women's place as a group. Laissez-faire women's activism is *not* motivated out of concern regarding gender; they do *not* act in the collective interest of women and therefore remain women in themselves. For laissez-faire conservatives it is individuals, and not men and women *as* men and women, who are threatened by the foes of freedom. Thus, laissez-faire women act as members of the marketplace, not as members of their gender group, in their effort to return America to strength and freedom.

Clearly, there is a relationship between a woman's social location and her values and beliefs. It is not coincidental that a woman with a devout religious upbringing who is a full-time homemaker is likely to see the family at the center of the world and to adhere to a traditional ideology regarding gender. Nor is it a coincidence that a single professional woman in her mid 30s who is devoted to her career does *not* see the family as central and holds nontraditional attitudes about men's and women's roles. As Kristin Luker puts it, commenting on women on either side of the abortion debate, "We might say that for pro-life women the traditional division of life into separate male roles and female roles still works, but for pro-choice women it does not."[27] As applied to women of the New Right, traditional gender roles "work" for social conservative women not simply because of faith, but because they themselves are more likely to be in life situations which correspond to traditional roles. Laissez-faire women, on the other hand, who are more likely to be single, divorced, or living with men outside of marriage and who have higher levels of education and hold more professional positions than do social conservative women, are in life situations and have social resources outside of the traditional female sphere.

The Future of Women of the New Right

We have seen how the motivation behind the activism of the social conservative woman resides in her role as a traditional woman. Amid the perceived moral chaos of the 1960s, the social conservative woman was provoked to action. Feminism symbolized a threat to traditional ways, the devaluation of motherhood. Feminism was perceived as encouraging women to abandon their husbands and children, to pursue their own self-interest. The social conservative woman was drawn into the political arena "to clean up America," to retain her sense of self-worth, and to protect against the total masculinization of the world. Like feminists, the social conservative woman protests male values, but she does so on totally different grounds. The social conservative woman fears that a gender-free society will mean a world devoid of qualities such as nurturance, altruism, and self-sacrifice associated with the female role. If women become more like men, she reasons, there will be no one left to instill moral values in the young, to ensure that passions are controlled, to guard against a world besieged by self-interest.

Put in different terms, the social conservative response can be interpreted as a reaction to an increasingly technological society, an organized effort to preserve traditional authority in an ever more bureaucratized world. Against the trend toward specialization and professionalization, the traditional female role represents the last pocket of common humanity, of the private and personal in an impersonal, mechanized world.[28] Connected to this is the specific distaste with which the social conservative woman views the encroachment of the economic sphere on all other realms of society and particularly the monetarization of the final pocket of privacy, the romantic realm. The social conservative woman reacts vehemently against the proposition that marriage is, after all, only an economic partnership. She holds out against this final disenchantment of the world and acts to preserve the last remnant of mystery, the final haven remaining in the modern world.

Acting out of her role as moral gatekeeper, there is an affinity between the traditional female role and the adoption of an ideology that rejects narcissism and self-interest for the "higher" values of self-sacrifice, faith, devotion, and compliance with authority. Yet because of this affinity between the traditional female role and social conservative belief, the future activism of social conservative women remains open. For despite ideological commitment, the possibility of women living a traditional lifestyle as full-time homemakers is diminishing. Between 1970 and 1987 women's labor force participation rate increased from 43.3 to 55.6 percent.[29] Moreover, research shows that employed women are more likely to believe in equality between the sexes than are full-time homemakers.[30] Thus, as women become paid laborers and face the realities of the job market, there may be an inevitable decline in female social conservatism.

Another possibility is that the very act of being politically involved may transform the social conservative woman. The "rough and tumble" political world which involves competition, aggression, power, independence, and rational decision-making may pose contradictions for the traditional female ideals of docility, passivity, dependence, and irrationality.[31] While we have seen how social conservative ideology expands to incorporate new roles for traditional women, there may be a point at which the social conservative woman crosses over the boundaries of traditional gender roles to enter the "nontraditional" domain. Indicative of the changes political activism can bring, one anti-ERA activist mentioned several friends who had gotten divorced after becoming involved in politics. Unfortunately, it was not possible to interview these women. Another social conservative activist commented: "Well, it would be a little difficult to go and organize Brownie parties after this [political involvement]. I mean it doesn't make sense. Can you imagine Howard Phillips picking up his job and deciding he was going to run a PTA?"

Anita Bryant stands as an example of a woman transformed. In 1977 she became a national leader of the social conservative cause, heading the Florida crusade against homosexual rights. Three years later she announced she was divorcing her husband of twenty years, saying that "everything may be gone, but now I can stand up and be counted for what I am—not for what someone else wants me to be."[32] She also remarked: "There are some valid reasons why militant feminists are doing what they're doing. Having experienced a form of male chauvinism among Christians that was devastating, I can see how women are controlled in a very ungodly, un-Christ-like way." Renouncing her former campaign, she now professes that people should "live and let live."[33]

In short, there may be latent effects to the social conservative woman's activism which undermine her own beliefs. However, given the deep-rooted nature of world views and the resiliency of ideology to incorporate new behavior, a mass exodus among social conservative women is unlikely. Even so, the social conservative woman certainly exists as a crucial role model to a generation of daughters. Mothers who are outspoken, self-confident leaders in the community pose as nontraditional images in the socialization of girls. Whether daughters of social conservative women will follow in traditional ways or whether their mothers' vocal and active roles in the political world will provoke their own departure from tradition remains to be seen.

What about the motivation of the laissez-faire conservative woman's activism? Unlike her social conservative counterpart, the laissez-faire conservative woman is not motivated by religious belief. She acts out of a secular desire to return America to supremacy as the land of liberty. Some laissez-faire conservatives are drawn to politics in reaction to the ever-expanding growth of the welfare state and the subsequent increase in taxation. Other laissez-faire conservatives act to defend American status in the wake of Soviet ascendancy. Nor does the laissez-faire woman act as an extension of the female role. She is not motivated out of an altruistic need to protect her children or as the moral guardian of society. She does not act in defense of the status of women.

Yet given the mutual views of laissez-faire women and feminists concerning gender and discrimination, can laissez-faire women be transformed from women in themselves to women for themselves? While feminist groups to date have not appealed to a constituency of conservative women, the coincidence of interest between the two groups indicates the possibility for coalition. Given the conservative direction of the Supreme Court, in the event of simply protecting a constitutional right to abortion, laissez-faire women may be an untapped constituency of support. However, while an alliance may be possible around specific single issues, any hope for an enduring coalition would be on shaky grounds. First of all, the laissez-faire opposition to government involvement restricts the possibility of any broad agreement on the issues. Laissez-faire women, for example, might be persuaded to rally in support of abortion or appeal to a company to set up day care facilities, but they would not support government aid to poor women to ensure the right to abortion nor would they endorse public support for day care. This alone limits the possibility for any long-term alliance.

A second limitation to an alliance between laissez-faire women and feminists concerns priorities. The laissez-faire woman's support for issues related to the economy and defense supersedes her concern about women's issues. Indicative of this, in a May 1984 meeting of the Republican National Committee's National Women's Coalition, a group of seventy business and professional women conceded that while they disagreed with Reagan on a number of women's issues, they agreed that the state of the economy overrode these concerns. In their view, only when inflation and interest rates were down and employment was on the rise would both men and women prosper.[34] These differences in agenda make the possibility of a lasting coalition unlikely.

At the same time, the laissez-faire conservative stance against government involvement poses potential conflict for the New Right. Although social and laissez-faire conservatives united to "get government off our backs" in electing and reelecting Ronald Reagan, in fact the two worlds hold diametrically opposed positions regarding the role of the state. While both social and laissez-faire conservatives criticize the existing state, essentially they call for its replacement by different kinds of state. Social conservatives wish to replace the values and interests now embodied in public institutions with their own set of beliefs and values. Rejecting any notion of moral neutrality, they seek to use the state to achieve righteous ends, calling for the insertion of traditional values based on Biblical principles. Laissez-faire conservatives, on the other hand, do not want to replace the values embedded in public institutions with some other set of values; rather, they wish to cut back or eliminate the public sector altogether.

In particular, the two worlds are in fundamental disagreement over the role of the state in the private realm. Social conservatives look toward the state to legislate morality. Social conservative women ardently oppose day care, abortion, and gay rights, all seen as eroding traditional gender roles and weakening the family. They do not really want less state; rather they want a different kind of state. Laissez-faire women, on the other hand, firmly reject any government role in legislating morality. They are pro-choice and support day care, as long as it remains in private hands. They reject any effort to introduce public authority into the private realm, vehemently opposing government as Big Brother. For laissez-faire conservatives the state itself is inherently evil, a threat to individual rights.

Signs of strain between the two worlds over the role of government are already evident. Social conservatives have expressed dismay over Reagan's neglect to use state power to endorse traditional values. They charge Reagan with being preoccupied with economic and defense issues, ignoring the social issues that helped get him elected. In July 1982 the *Conservative Digest* ran an entire issue entitled "Has Reagan Deserted the Conservatives?" Marshner's answer was an emphatic "yes":

> Since taking office the White House has expressed precious little concern about anything but economic problems. . . . By ignoring the social agenda or relegating it to a place at the bottom of the heap the people who run the Reagan administration are losing the 1982 election *and* their own chances to achieve economic reform, as well as the country's best chance for moral and social reclamation.[35]

Social conservatives continuously criticize Reagan for giving only rhetorical support to such issues as abortion, busing, and school prayer. They claim, for instance, that while Reagan made an all-out effort to muster support for the MX missiles or for sale of the AWACs to Saudi Arabia, no major lobbying effort was undertaken in support of a constitutional amendment banning abortion.[36]

Should this strain lead to conflict, what is the likely outcome? Laissez-faire conservatives seem to be in the stronger position. Contrary to the claims of social conservatives, analyses of the 1980 election conclude that Reagan's election did *not* represent a triumph of social conservatives.[37] Abortion and the ERA, for example, were *not* very important issues during the election; in fact, those people supporting abortion actually voted for Reagan nearly as frequently as those who opposed abortion.[38] While the media played up the social issues, they were not stressed in Reagan's campaign nor were they mentioned prominently in exit polls of voters during the election.[39] Further, Gallup polls indicate that the social issues have declined in general import among the mass public since the early 1970s.[40]

Additionally, while there seems to be a conservative trend among the college-age generation, with 58 percent of young voters (aged 18–29) supporting Reagan in 1984,[41] it is not the social issues that they support. One Reagan campaign official acknowledged that in October when television ads castigated Republicans as the party of the Moral Majority, Reagan support among 18-to-24-year-old voters plummeted twenty points in five days.[42] Similarly, Edward Rollins, the director of Reagan's 1984 reelection campaign, reported that most of the young voters whom Republicans had success with in 1984 were libertarian in orientation.[43] As Martin Franks, executive director of the Democratic Congressional Campaign Committee, put it, "If there is anything that puts a shudder into young voters, it's the right wing's social agenda."[44] The baby boom generation also rejects social conservatism. Predicted to be the single biggest bloc of voters in 1988 by election forecaster Patrick Caddell, the baby boomers tend to be economically conservative but liberal on the social issues.[45]

These factors indicate that should conflict erupt within the New Right, laissez-faire conservatives, who have a greater degree of support among the mass population, are likely to be the victors. Yet in assessing the future of the New Right the judiciary offers another avenue for social conservative victory. Although social conservatives have been relatively unsuccessful in promoting their social agenda through legislative means, judicial appointments are made for life and are only removable for "treason, bribery, or other high crimes and misdemeanors." Thus, they have more long-term impact than do elected officials. In fact, President Reagan made more lower court appointments than any of his recent predecessors. By October 1985, 30 percent of all U.S. District Court judges and 27 percent of all U.S. Court of Appeals judges were Reagan appointees.[46] In terms of the Supreme Court, while social conservatives were angry about the appointment of Sandra Day O'Connor because of her mixed voting record on abortion, the recent appointment of Judge Antonin Scalia and the promotion of Justice William H. Rehnquist to Chief Justice show more promise for social conservatives.

In terms of issues, while the Supreme Court recently upheld the *Roe*

v. *Wade* decision, preserving a woman's right to abortion, the vote shifted from the original 7-2 vote in support of the decision to a 5-4 vote by the Court. Although disappointed by the decision, social conservatives were encouraged by the possibility of overturning abortion during the Rehnquist court. Further, the recent decision upholding Georgia's law which outlaws homosexual sodomy signifies a triumph for the social conservative view of the state's role in legislating morality.

In short, while the two worlds of the New Right will continue to share a common opposition to the size of government and continue to favor dismantling the welfare state, tax cutbacks, re-arming America, and a foreign policy based on anti-Communism, disputes over the *priorities* of the political agenda are bound to escalate in the coming years. In particular, the issue of state involvement in the private realm could become the battleground of the New Right. Because the debate over morality raises issues concerning the family, sexual freedom, and reproductive rights, women will continue to have a central stake in this battle. Women of the New Right no doubt will play a key role in determining the course of America's new wave of conservatism.

Notes

1. Lipset and Raab (1970).
2. See, for example, Hunter (1981) and Rusher (1982).
3. It is not entirely clear whether the lack of attention to women in the Old Right is due to the small number of female participants in the movement or to the male bias of the researchers.
4. See, for example, Arrington and Kyle (1978); Brady and Tedin (1976); Conover and Gray (1983); Dworkin (1983); Eisenstein (1981); Luker (1984); Merton (1981); Mueller (1976, 1981); and Petchesky (1984).
5. Right-to-life activists were excluded both because abortion is a complex issue, drawing in many single-issue activists who are motivated by strong religious convictions but who do not align themselves with the conservative movement as a whole, and because of the abundance of data available.
6. Several points of entry were used to acquire names of activists. In the fall of 1981 Howard Phillips, a leading figure of the New Right, offered a study group at Harvard University. Through him and through other guest speakers, names of female leaders were gathered. These became part of a subsample of national leaders of the right, constituting approximately one quarter of the total sample. Local activists were located through a variety of sources including inquiries of national organizations requesting names of local activists; use of newspaper articles to locate names of local conservative

activists; names obtained through the producer of a local radio program on right-wing women in Massachusetts. Once initial contact was made, the snowball technique was used to gather additional names. However, references from any one person were limited so as not to bias the sample. Because of limited funding, all interviews with local activists took place in Massachusetts.

The final sample includes organizational affiliations with the following groups: American Legislative Exchange Council, College Republicans, Conservative Caucus, Eagle Forum, Family Forum, Free Congress Foundation, Libertarian party, Moral Majority, Morality in the Media, Pro-Family Forum, Republican National Committee, Republican party, Women for Constitutional Government, Women's Republican Club, and local anti-busing, anti-tax, and anti-gun-control organizations.

7. See, for example, Hofstadter (1952); Lipset and Raab (1970); Pheneger (1966); Wallerstein (1954); Wolfinger et al. (1969).

8. Conferences attended include Phyllis Schlafly's Over the Rainbow Celebration of the defeat of the ERA (July 1, 1982, Washington, D.C.); Family Forum II: Traditional Values Work, co-sponsored by the Moral Majority and the Free Congress Foundation (July 27–29, 1982, Washington, D.C.); the Conservative Political Action Conference, co-sponsored by the American Conservative Union and Young Americans for Freedom (February 17–20, 1983, Washington, D.C.); and local meetings of the Libertarian party and the South Shore Pro-Family Forum.

9. Included are publications from the Alabama Christian Educational Association, American Conservative Union, Christian Voice, Center for Family Studies, Citizens for Educational Freedom, Coalition for Decency, College Republican National Committee, Conservative Caucus, Eagle Forum, Free Congress Research and Education Foundation, Free the Eagle, Freemen Institute, Home Education Resource Center, Intercessors for America, John Birch Society, Libertarian party, Moral Majority, National Federation of Parents for Drug Free Youth, Pro-Family Forum, Republican National Committee, United Families of America, Utah Association of Women, and Young Americans for Freedom.

10. See, for example, Hunter (1981); Himmelstein (1983); and Wilson (1980).

11. For further discussion of the methodology and the ethical issues involved in carrying out this research, see Klatch (1988).

12. Whether the founders of classical liberalism would associate themselves with laissez-faire conservatism is another question. In fact, Adam Smith (1966) expressed much skepticism about the morals of businessmen. His view of the self-interested nature of individuals was also accompanied by belief in a natural sympathy toward others.

13. Jerry Falwell, quoted in Fitzgerald (1981), p. 110.

14. Marshner (1982b).

15. Schlafly (1977), pp. 45–56.

16. See McGraw (1980).

17. McGraw (1980), p. 1.

18. Marshner (1982b).

19. Schlafly (1977), p. 100.

20. Schlafly (1977), pp. 72–73.

21. Schlafly (1977), p. 177.

22. Marshner (1982b).

23. See Kirkpatrick (1974).

24. Radl (1983), p. 177.

25. Dworkin (1983), p. 17. A notable exception to this assumption of the "false consciousness" of the antifeminist woman is found in Luker (1984).

26. I am indebted to Kristin Luker for making use of this distinction drawn from Marx. Marx discusses a class in itself and a class for itself in discussing how capital creates a mass of people in a common situation who share common interests. See Marx (1978), p. 218.

27. Luker (1984), p. 200.

28. Similarly, Marshall (1984) argues that the antisuffrage movement was a reaction to industrialization, in which the home was seen as an oasis of noncommercial values in the midst of an acquisitive society.

29. See U.S. Department of Labor (1980, 1987).

30. See Sapiro (1983), p. 182.

31. Sapiro (1983), pp. 30, 87.

32. Bryant, quoted in Brothers (1980), pp. 106–111.

33. Bryant, quoted in Jahr (1980), p. 68.

34. Sandra Salmans, "Women's Panel Using Economy to Back Reagan," *New York Times*, May 22, 1984.

35. Marshner (1982a), p. 18.

36. See Curtis Wilkie, "Reagan's Inaction on Busing, Abortion Frustrates Far Right," *Boston Globe*, August 21, 1983.

37. See Lipset and Raab (1982); Himmelstein and McRae (1984).

38. See Conover and Gray (1983).

39. See Himmelstein and McRae (1984).

40. Himmelstein and McRae (1984).

41. *New York Times*/CBS Poll, in the *New York Times*, November 8, 1984.

42. From Kevin Phillips, "Hubris on the Right," *New York Times Magazine*, May 12, 1985. Also see Himmelstein and McRae (1984).

43. Phil Gailey, "Evangelism and a Fight with Peril to Both Sides," *New York Times*, March 17, 1986.

44. Quoted in Gailey.

45. Sara Rimer, "Experts Study the Habits of Genus Baby Boomer," *New York Times*, April 21, 1986. Also see Steven Roberts, "Making Mark on Politics, 'Baby Boomers' Appear to Rally Around Reagan," *New York Times*, November 5, 1984; and David Boaz, "In '88, Who'll Win the Baby Boomers?" *New York Times*, November 7, 1985.

46. "Reagan Justice," in *Newsweek*, June 30, 1986; and *Facts on File: World News Digest*, October 25, 1985, p. 803.

PART VI
Afterword

23

Women in American Politics

Sidney Verba

The chapters in this volume are about the changing role of women in American politics in the twentieth century. The subject matter is rich and complex and the chapters reflect that richness. They cover various aspects of the subject, using varied methods and quite different intellectual perspectives. They look outward as well as inward: outward to the real world of politics to see how the political participation of women has changed and how that change has affected American politics, and inward to the social science disciplines that try to make sense of that change. The dual perspective is appropriate and important. The changing reality of politics affects, as it must, our attempts at social science understanding. And, in turn, the concepts and theories that are chosen to explain the role of women in politics have implications in the real world of politics.

The evolving role of women in American politics poses a challenge to the theory and practice of politics. The American polity is an ongoing system of institutions, patterns of behavior, and mutually accepted understandings. When a group previously excluded from some or all aspects of political life attempts to enter the political system, one of three things may happen. (1) The new participating group—such as women—may be rejected and barred from an expanded voice in the polity. (2) If the new group finds its way into the ongoing system, it may be integrated, assimilated, absorbed, or coopted into the existing system (it all may be the same thing, the word chosen depending on whether one likes it or not). (3) Or the new group may transform the established ways of doing things in the polity.

In American politics what has (or should have) happened is a matter of debate. Women have certainly expanded their role in politics as interested and participant citizens, as activists in parties and organizations, and as holders of governmental office. In that sense they have not been barred from access. The chapters in this volume contain ample evidence of this. And the space on the political agenda occupied by issues relating to gender has also expanded dramatically. Full equality with men in these matters? In some respects yes; in many others no. But substantial change, without a doubt.

Does this increased presence of women and of gender issues constitute the incorporation of a new group into the political system, leaving it essentially as it was? Or has there been a fundamental change in the American political process? Or, if not yet a fundamental change, does it promise a fundamental change in the future as more women enter the political process? The answers to these questions are far from unambiguous. Much of the new activity of women is within the traditional American political modes such as voting, partisan activity, organized interest groups, officeholding, and traditional institutions. Women have engaged in protest activity, but that is not new in American politics. Yet it is not merely more of the same. The scope of concern and the arena of activities of women participants differ from that of American men. And perhaps the style of political activity differs as well. The female-male differences are real. Could they be differences that transform the political process?

The greater involvement of women has certainly had consequences for American politics. Governmental programs and priorities change as a group becomes more involved and active in politics, and as the members or leaders of the group develop a consciousness of their joint interests and articulate those joint interests as demands for governmental response. Political activity by a group is neither a necessary condition nor a sufficient one for government attention. Some politically inactive groups receive much government support while other active groups receive little. But activity helps. Similarly, a group that is active need not be self-conscious about its joint interests and need not articulate them for there to be governmental response. Government officials anticipate the needs and demands of groups and are likely to be sensitive to activists no matter how fully they articulate group demands. But awareness and explicit articulation of group concerns also help.

The increased activity and the increased consciousness of women have brought issues affecting women onto the political agenda and affected public policy. However, what I have in mind as a transformation of American politics goes beyond the increased attention to women's interests that might accompany a greater female role in politics. I refer to the possibility that the increased involvement of women in politics will transform the way in which politics is carried out in America—make politics perhaps less conflictual, less self-interested, more communitarian and humane. Such changes are what one might expect from some of the literature on female-male differences in attitude and behavior. The terms are imprecise but far from meaningless. And since I am not designing a precise research project but asking an interesting question, we can leave the terms imprecise as we look for traces of such changes or speculate about the future. To take the question one step further into a hypothetical, but not impossible or implausible, future: What would American politics look like if the battle for full gender equality in politics were won? If at some time in the future women reach parity with men in political life, will American politics be transformed in some fundamental way?

One cannot extrapolate from the current activity of women; there may be a threshold in terms of numbers of women in the upper ranks of politics that would have to be reached before their presence would change the nature of political life. But some speculation, based on what we know from this volume and other works about women in politics, might be useful in helping to understand whether or not women in politics are "just another group."

One can distinguish between the increasing role of women in politics and the increasing role of women with feminist beliefs.[1] Having more women in American political life will not transform American politics if it means merely a new set of participants with somewhat different preferences. Feminists and the theories and approaches they bring into politics, in contrast, challenge customary ways of conducting politics. Insofar as the increasing role of women in the polity entails an increasing presence of women with feminist beliefs, the application of those beliefs in political life might change the nature of American politics. One might argue, however, that it is artificial to distinguish the possible impact of women in politics from the impact of more women with feminist orientations; that women share a women's voice in politics—a more cooperative and less conflictual approach, for instance—that transcends particular social and political belief systems such as feminism. If this is the case, the involvement of more women in politics might transform the nature of politics, no matter what the particular ideologies held by women.[2]

In this concluding chapter, I would like to explore the distinctiveness of women as participants in politics in the context of American politics more generally, in relation to other groups that seek full incorporation into the political process, and in a comparative perspective. "Distinctive" is used here in two senses: first, in the sense that women are unique compared with all other political actors; second, in the sense that the intergroup relation of men and women is distinctive compared with other intergroup relations.

Women in Politics: How Distinctive?

As the chapters in this volume illustrate, a good deal of the expansion of the role of women in American politics fits neatly into the ongoing processes of American politics. Yet, as they also show, there are distinctive features about women as a group, about women as individuals, and about "women's issues."

A Special Kind of Group?

Political scientists have defined the qualities that differentiate one political group from others: characteristic patterns of attitude or behavior, self-consciousness about membership in the group, political consciousness (realization that there are special policy needs for the group), organization, and leadership. On any of these criteria, women are clearly a distinctive group. This is not to say that women are homogeneous: that they all share the same attitudes, all behave in the same distinctive ways, are all members of the same organizations. As with other American groups they are quite diverse. But the distribution of many politically relevant characteristics differs as between women and men. The existence of these differences is also reflected in the recognition of the special subject matter of women and politics in this volume and the immense recent literature on the subject.[3]

The issue, however, is not whether women differ from the rest of the population—men—in ways that are relevant to politics. The issue is, rather, whether the differences between the genders are such that women represent a unique category among those who have been incorporated into American civic life. Are there special features of "women" as a group that make their movement toward fuller political participation different from that of other categories of people such as "blacks" or "Catholics"? Blacks differ from people of other races and Catholics differ from people of other religions in many politically relevant ways—in the distribution of socioeconomic attributes, in attitudes, in historical experi-

ences. Women also differ from men in these ways. But is there something more; something that makes the study of gender and politics different from the study of other social divisions in relation to politics?[4]
What are some of the possible special features?

NUMBERS   Unlike most groups that have sought political equality in America, women are not a minority. Does the process of accommodation differ if the group is a majority of the public? The number of women, for instance, makes the gender gap in voting more significant than would a similar difference in voting behavior between a small group of the population and the citizenry as a whole. Yet the male-female difference in voting preferences may have less significance than rhetoric sometimes gives it. Although usually described as a distinctive pattern of voting among women, it is in fact a gap between women and men in which their equally distinctive patterns are balanced. (Indeed, it is unclear why the gender gap is always described in female terms—it is equally male.) Furthermore, women are not the only disadvantaged majority in American history. Blacks in a number of the southern states had this status at one time.

HETEROGENEITY   The size of the group has, however, a significant implication: It affects the extent to which women are a heterogeneous category. American society is characterized by a multiplicity of groups divided by shallow cleavages that crisscross each other. There are few categorizations that divide the society into closed segments; individuals can be members of or attached to many categories of people at once. To be Catholic is to belong to a particular religion, but it does not necessarily imply that one has a particular occupation, or party, or lives in a particular place. To be black predicts more in terms of occupation, party, and place of residence, though the prediction is far from perfect and is a lot less strong than it once was. To be a woman does give some information about likely occupation or income, but it implies very little about class, residence, or religion.

Women as a group differ from other significant groups that are politically disadvantaged—from blacks or Hispanics, for instance—in that the characteristics that distinguish women from men are less likely to be those that become the subject of political controversy. The female-male division separates the populations into two relatively homogeneous groups in terms of family matters such as who has prime responsibility for childcare—matters that are not usually the subject of political controversy (at least as that term is commonly understood). Women, on the other hand, are divided among themselves on the basis of class, race, region, religion, ideology, and most other characteristics that are likely to be politically significant. Various chapters in this volume highlight the divisions among women that are based on characteristics such as race or ethnicity.[5] This leads as well to differences in political views. As various of these chapters indicate, one can find among women both the strongest proponents and the strongest opponents of certain feminist positions.[6] Other disadvantaged groups are internally divided, but few are as thoroughly diverse as women. The internal division probably reduces the extent to which women form a distinctive political group. We will return to this when we look at women as political actors. The fact that the clearest difference between men and women is found in the private sphere leads feminist scholars to stress the need to consider the political implications of the family and other "private" patterns.[7]

DISPERSION   In addition to their size as a group, women differ from other social categories in their dispersion throughout the society. At least in terms of residential and family patterns, women and men are intermixed. In this respect, it is *the absence of* special location that is the distinguishing feature of women as a group. In no other case do members of the disadvantaged group live in as close relationship with the more advantaged portion of the population. This characteristic, as much as any, helps explain some of the complexities of gender as a politically relevant variable. The main patterns of female-male relationship emerge and are manifest within the family. The impact of this fact on the political role of women is great, and it calls into question the usual distinction between private and public spheres.

THE SPECIAL RELATIONSHIP TO HUMAN REPRODUCTION   Although the extent to which the biological differences between men and women in relation to reproduction do or should determine patterns of social, economic, and political activity is a matter of debate, the biological basis of differences between the sexes is greater and less mutable than are other biological differences with the possible exception of age. This distinction is surely unique to gender.

Women's Beliefs and Values

Several features of the political beliefs and values of a group increase the likelihood that the group will form a distinctive political bloc and have a distinctive political impact: if the group is internally consensual in attitude while being different from other groups, if the group members identify as members of the group and that identification is significant for political attitudes and behavior, and if the group attends to an agenda different from that of other groups. The evidence on women as a bloc is mixed. They differ from men in a variety of ways, but those differences are differences of central tendency and often mask wide divergences among women. Indeed, there is more compelling evidence for divisions among women than for unity. As Sears and Huddy point out, women's attitudes on some issues, usually associated with war or violence rather than "women's" issues per se, differ from men's attitudes. But even in such areas, women themselves are not necessarily united internally. The "gender gap" discussed above is an average difference between men and women. It does not mean that women are necessarily more united than men. Furthermore, the extent to which women are politically conscious as a group is ambiguous. Almost all women identify as women, but such identification has little or no political implication.[8] It is unrelated to their political attitudes or their vote or their support for the President. A much smaller group of women identify themselves with feminism—and that identification has a major effect on their attitudes. Feminism, however, is a divisive identity for women since not all women so identify.

In general, there is abundant evidence that on all of the issues in which there has been strong political activity on the part of women—for women's suffrage, for prohibition, for humane legislation, for the ERA, for a feminist agenda—there has consistently been strong opposition by women on the other side.

Of particular relevance is the disparity between the views of feminist leaders and the views of women more generally, a disparity not found among American blacks. Leaders of the major black civil rights organizations tend to be somewhat more radical than the black rank and file on issues associated with race, but supported by those for whom they purport to speak. Leaders of feminist organizations are also to the left of their public—American women in general—but they are not similarly supported.[9] Women do not deviate much from the population as a whole in the direction of the feminist leaders—and in some cases women do not deviate from the population norm at all.

Although women are not united in political belief, it is important to note the areas of attitude that produce the clearest female-male divisions. While there are variations from place to place, among different groups, and over time, the general pattern reappears with convincing regularity: women's positions on matters of public policy, in contrast to those of men, are more likely to be compassionate than "tough," communitarian than individualistic, public-interested than self-interested.[10] Whether the issue is arms control or capital punishment or welfare and social service programs, women differ systematically from men in their political views.[11] It is interesting, in fact, that it is not "women's issues"—that is, the issues that have a differential impact on men and women such as abortion and the ERA—but issues associated with violence that most consistently divide men and women.[12] That such is the case supports the position that there may be something special about women's role in the political process compared with that of other groups. One expects a group to have a position on issues directly related to the welfare of the group. There are few blacks—even many of those who are so "deviant" from the norm as to be Republican—who do not share the belief that the government ought to have an interventionist agenda for the benefit of their group. Similarly one expects automobile workers to be concerned about protection from imports and farmers to be concerned about farm subsidies. If women were focused in that way, one might more easily argue that they are "just another group" with a set of views connected to their particular situation. That they have positions outside the realm of attitudes that might reflect group self-interest is what may be most distinctive about them.[13] It suggests a generalized orientation to politics that transcends particular issue positions.

Women as Political Participants

Women's activity in American politics has been most often within the traditional modes of American political participation, but it has had a distinctive cast to it.

WOMEN IN THE SYSTEM   Women have largely followed traditional routes into the political system. As the role of women has expanded in American politics, it has been manifested in their increased participation as voters, as party and organizational activists, as officeholders, and as participants in other traditional ways. In general, women in the United States are somewhat less active than men, the gap growing as one moves up the scale of political activities from voting, where there is little difference between men and women, to those activities that imply important leadership roles where the gap is more substantial. There are good data on voting turnout and on officeholding, but relatively little data on the levels of other kinds of political participation. Fortunately, the National Opinion Research Center's General Social Survey replicated a series of items on political activity that originally appeared in Verba and Nie.[14] Thus one can see how the participation differences between men and women have changed over the past two decades.

Table 23.1 shows the proportions of women and men who report being active on fourteen measures of participation. As one can see, there

**Table 23.1   Women and Men Engaging in Fourteen Acts of Participation,
1967 and 1987**

Specific Activity	Total		Women		Men	
	1967	1987	1967	1987	1967	1987
Regularly vote in presidential elections	66%	58%	64%	59%	66%	56%
Always vote in local elections	47	34	44	33	51	35
Persuade others how to vote	28	32	25	28	31	37
Actively work for party or candidate	26	26	23	24	28	29
Attend political meeting or rally	19	20	18	17	20	23
Contribute money to party or candidate	13	22	12	19	15	25
Belong to political club	8	4	8	4	9	4
Work with others on local problem	31	33	30	32	33	35
Actively work in community problem-solving organization	32	33	31	30	33	37
Form group to help solve local problem	14	17	13	17	16	18
Contact local official: issue-based	14	23	12	22	17	24
Contact state or national official: issue-based	11	20	9	19	14	22
Contact local official: particularized	7	10	6	9	8	11
Contact state or national official: particularized	6	7	6	6	7	9

is some difference between the genders in 1967 and little change in the
gap between them over the twenty-year period. In 1967 women engaged
in, on average, 1.89 political acts (beyond voting) while men engaged in
2.23 acts. In 1987 the respective figures were 2.33 and 2.80; the gap is not
striking, but it is at least as large now as it was earlier.

However, it is equally significant that the difference in political participation between men and women in the United States was relatively
small compared with most other places—a finding that has been
confirmed by several studies.[15] It is also significant that women and men
are similar in terms of the pattern of change over the twenty years. As
the data in Table 23.1 illustrate, there have been some important
changes in the nature of the participatory system in the United States
over the past two decades: the decline in voting and in membership in
political clubs, the rise of "checkbook" participation through contributions, and a substantial increase in direct contacts to officials on issues of

public policy. These changes reflect some well-known trends in American political life: the decline of the significance of parties, the increase in the use of mass mailings to elicit individual contributions to campaigns and causes, the increased role of the member of Congress in responding to the individual needs of constituents, and, perhaps, the greater individuation of American political life. For our purposes, what is striking is that women and men appear to respond in a similar manner to these changes. In that sense, women's participation remains in the mainstream.

Women have narrowed the gap in participation with men on the more elite levels of elected local, state, and national office. However, though there have been substantial gains for women in recent years, the participation gap between men and women is still significantly greater at the higher governmental levels. Women remain a small proportion of the membership of local boards and councils, of state legislatures, and of Congress. In the 100th Congress (1986–1988), women were 5 percent of the membership of the House of Representatives—putting the United States in a position similar to France (6 percent) and Britain (4 percent) but well below the proportions in Scandinavia (Sweden, 28 percent; Norway, 35 percent; and Denmark, 24 percent).[16] The continuing gap appears to have its source in the nomination process. Women do as well as men once nominated; they lag in getting the party support for nomination.[17]

Women's activities are within the mainstream of political life in other ways. Many of their opportunities to take part in political life are constrained by the ongoing institutions of the American political system. Women's partisan activities are channeled within the existing party system; their voting choices are constrained by the same set of choices that faces all Americans.[18] The women's movement of the last two decades has been one of the most important social movements in American history in terms of its impact on how Americans think and act in relation to gender. Interest groups devoted to women's issues or having a large female membership have increased dramatically in their number and in their political influence. Yet they pursue tactics similar to those of male-dominated organizations with which they now share the interest group arena.[19] Even protest by women calls upon the repertory of protest activities pursued by other groups. From this perspective, the expansion of the role of women in politics represents just that: an expansion but not a transformation.

WOMEN AND VOLUNTARISM   The chapters in this volume also document the tendency for women activists to be active in distinctive ways: in particular, to be active in voluntary associations dealing with matters such as social services, reform, and culture. Jennings' data on delegates to the national party conventions show that women and men are about as active in voluntary associations, but that women's activity is heavier in women's groups, abortion-related groups, and education-related groups.[20] The tradition of women as activists in such associations dates back to the early nineteenth century and has continued until the present time.[21] The participants were largely middle-class women. There are no precise data on whether women or men were more active in this way, but the impression one has from the accounts is that this was a realm particularly populated by women. And it was a form of activity with great importance for the development of the American welfare state. If historical interpretations are correct, these organizations paved the way for the welfare state—illustrating a transformation of American society that derived from the special activity of women.

Another Voice? Another Style

There is, however, another, more fundamental change in American politics that might derive from a fuller role by women, a change in the *style* of American politics. If women were to obtain equal—or close to equal—political influence with men, would this have a fundamental effect on American politics? The question may be unrealistic in the short to middle run: The number of women in positions of significant influence remains small. But it is growing. And even if political equality is unlikely in the foreseeable future, the hypothetical question is intriguing for what it allows us to ask about politics and about the role of women in politics.

When more women become active and, more important, influential in politics, will that lead to a transformation of political life? The full answer to that question will come only when women hold a substantial (one third? one half? the larger part?) proportion of the senior decision-making roles.[22] But speculation is possible.

The transformation might be of several kinds. One might expect a change in the agenda of politics and in the policies produced by a government. Over time, women in legislative positions have become more and more the advocates of women's issues such as childcare and spouse abuse.[23] Or one might expect a more humane and communitarian agenda.

More fundamentally, one can ask whether the style of the conduct of politics might change—in the direction of a political life that would be less conflictual, less self-interested, more oriented to communitarian ideals. If Lasswell's political personality valued power over others above all,[24] women would bring a different personality into politics—one that valued compromise and conciliation rather than domination. Some advocates of women's participation—from the time of the suffrage debates on—have argued that women would affect political life in that way. For this to happen, though, women would have to have a "different voice"; they would have to continue to use that voice in politics; and American politics would have to be congenial to use of that style.

WOMEN'S VOICE   Is there a special women's voice? We have already cited evidence of systematic differences between men and women in their support for aggressive actions and policies. The data are consistent across time, across places, and across specific issues and questions. One has to accept the fact that such differences are not contingent on particular issues or samples but represent fundamental differences between the genders. Whether they are the result of nature or nurture is not at issue here. Whichever they are, they would seem to be the kind of deeply ingrained orientation that women would carry into political office. Parallel to these differences are those stressed by writers such as Gilligan: that women have a "different voice" in social interactions—a voice that stresses cooperation rather than conflict, maintaining relationships rather than achieving abstract justice. The evidence is far from conclusive on this subject. These differences are hard to measure precisely and they are, in any case, tendencies rather than dichotomies. Yet the difference does seem to exist.

WOMEN IN POWER   If one looks for evidence of a different style among women in office, however, it is mixed. Women in the same political settings as men behave somewhat differently, but not radically so. Consider the question of whether party or gender is more important for political attitudes. If gender were the predominant determinant of political attitudes, gender differences would override party; if gender were of no significance for political positions, party would be everything. It is clear from Jennings' data reported in this volume that both gender and party are significant.[25] On many issues female-male differences exist within the parties. This is especially the case with issues of national defense as well as, interestingly enough, the issue of the competence of women in politics. Despite these differences between men and women, multivariate analysis shows that the ". . . vast interparty dissimilarities in ideology tend to swamp what modest differences are provided by gender."[26] It is interesting further that the extent to which gender is an independent determinant of attitudes among political elites with differing partisan affiliations appears to depend on the nature of the party system. In the United States, with relatively weak and heterogeneous parties, gender plays more of a role in political attitudes on a variety of issues than it does in Sweden, where the stronger political parties encompass gender issues more fully in their programs and provide a clearer set of alternatives. The result is that political party affiliation affects attitudes on issues more than does gender or feminist ideology.[27]

Women, in general, have taken part in American political life in ways that fit the traditional pattern of activity for American men. In Schlozman's phrase, they "act like the boys."[28] This is not to say that they do not have their own policy concerns and preferences. Kirkpatrick found in her study of state legislators in the 1970s that women legislators were more antiviolence and moralistic than their male counterparts.[29] Evidence about women legislators in Congress and state legislatures, as well as in local government, shows that women are more likely to support feminist causes and to be somewhat more liberal.[30] On the other hand, their behavior within the legislatures does not appear to differ systematically from male legislators'. They are, as Kirkpatrick points out, highly professional.[31]

There are several possible reasons for this absence of a different voice.[32]

One explanation might be that, in fact, women do not approach politics any differently than do men. Women are educated in the same school system, read the same history, are exposed to the same media as men, and, therefore, share a political culture that defines the norms of political behavior. They may receive messages during the socialization process that discourage them from entering politics; they may, because of socialization or genetic makeup, be less inclined to aggressive actions. But they learn about the same politics that men learn about and receive no message that, if they do enter politics, they ought to act differently from men. Indeed, if this is the case, one would expect that, over time, their similarity to men will increase in the political realm—as expectations increase that women can have an active professional career in politics similar to that of men. As Jennings notes about female convention delegates, more and more of them have come to express an interest in higher elective office over the past twelve years—though they still lag behind men in political ambition.[33]

Another explanation might be that the selection process brings into politics those women who are most accepting of the current way of doing things. This implies that women who run for office are nearest to the "political personality." Or if one prefers a less personality-oriented explanation, it may be that those who are recruited into politics are simply those who are most interested in ongoing party politics and, therefore, know how to and are willing to play by the rules that exist.[34]

This suggests that it may be more significant that *feminist* women move into positions of influence than women per se. In that case, an explicit commitment to an alternative political style will supplement commitments that derive from socialization or any innate tendencies that might exist.

A third explanation might be that the structure of American political life is so firmly in place that one can succeed in politics only by playing the game as it is currently played. That is certainly implied by Schlozman's analysis of the tactics used by women lobbyists. It is also part of the story told by Mansbridge on the failure of the pro-ERA forces. An important part of the women's movement, as described by Mansbridge, did not play by male rules. These women eschewed organizational hierarchies in good part because they were committed to communitarian organization and rejected masculine politics. The result was failure in the masculine world of state legislatures.[35]

Note that this does not argue that women who engage in political activity will play by male rules. Clearly, many of those active in the women's movement have played by other rules. The suggestion is that success in mainstream American politics—the world of partisan electoral politics; of local, state, and national legislative, executive, and bureaucratic policymaking; of interest group lobbying; and of bureaucratic implementation—may be impeded by a style of politics that is principled rather than pragmatic, communal rather than individualistic. Principled communal politics flourishes in social movements outside mainstream politics—and, indeed, that is where the women's movement has grown and where it has had a major impact on the policy process. But mainstream politics may demand another style.

If the argument above is true about contemporary American politics, it is not inevitably true. The issue turns on what is the inherent nature of politics. Is politics inevitably an activity in which success depends on toughness and pragmatism? Or does it appear that way because it has long been the domain of men who have given it a style that is congenial to them but not necessarily a part of the enterprise? The answer is by no means clear. Certain activities or occupations may by their very nature require particular approaches for successful performance. A linebacker in the National Football League—whether male or female—must be aggressive to succeed. A mathematician—male or female—has to use abstract logic to succeed; sensitivity to human relations is not of much use. But a parent who is aggressive vis-à-vis his or her children and responds to them only in terms of abstract principles of justice is unlikely to be a very successful parent. (Note that Kirkpatrick's female state legislators did not think of themselves as acting "masculine" by adopting the dominant behavior of their male counterparts in the legislature. They thought of it as "professional" behavior, behavior appropriate to the role.)[36]

Is the formula for success in politics due to the inherent nature of political life or might different standards be possible? The question is intriguing; the answer uncertain. Perhaps there could be an alternative style in politics and women participants might provide it. But the opportunity to test the possibility has not existed. As long as women remain a minority in the upper ranks they may have to play the male game to succeed. If there were enough of them to set the terms of political discourse, perhaps there would be a new style of political activity. On the other hand, by the time the numbers are right, the process of incorporation into politics may have been going on for so long that women will have long since abandoned any distinctive style or approach they once had—as the behavior of many female state legislators or lobbyists seems to suggest. Perhaps there is little option given the nature of politics. But a radical change in the nature of politics cannot be ruled out.

It is a subject well worth watching, a good research topic as the political presence of women grows. In studying the subject, close attention will have to be paid to the selection process into politics. If the selection process favors those who already value the traditional ways of politics (either because they select themselves or are favored by those already in positions of political influence), there will be one outcome. If the process favors those who share feminist beliefs about politics (because the road into politics is through the women's movement and feminist organizations), the outcome will be quite different. Sorting out that which is inherent in politics from that which is a contingent characteristic of politics in contemporary America and sorting out that which is inherent in women's approach to politics from the selection process will be difficult, but a research challenge well worth pursuing.

In sum, women as participants in American politics today are a distinctive group in political orientation and in mode of political activity. But they are also a heterogeneous group whose range of views and modes of activity overlap with their male counterparts'. If sufficient women take positions of power, they may move the American political process in new directions. Whether this will happen is at the present time uncertain.

Notes

1. The term "feminism" has many meanings. I refer here to a belief that women are a disadvantaged and oppressed group—an analytical stance that makes gender a central concept in social analysis and a sociopolitical commitment to change in the role of women.

2. From this perspective, the crucial group may be nonfeminist political activists whose role in politics is also significant. (See Klatch, this volume.) They also have an ideology as to the nature of politics and the role of women, but an ideology that is more traditional and defensive. If one found among them evidence of a "women's voice," it would be intriguing evidence of a political style that transcends ideology.

3. If one looks at the number of articles listed in the *Social Science Citation Index* having the words "sex" or "women" or "gender" and words such as "politics" or "political" in the title, one finds a substantial growth from 16 in 1972 to 66 in 1978 to 144 in 1985.

4. This question is not unique to women as a group. It has been raised about the black experience in America: Can they be seen as just another ethnic minority trying to make it in the majority world, or are there special features of the black experience that make them different from other groups? And as for American blacks, the issue for women is a political one: For a variety of reasons it is preferable to be a distinct group rather than a mere addition to all the other groups in America. From the point of view of the impact of women's increasing participation on American politics, the question is a significant one.

5. See Jones, Brooks, Fernández-Kelly and García, and Hewitt, this volume.

6. See Mansbridge, Klatch, and Sears and Huddy, this volume.

7. The study of power and authority relationships in what is usually considered the private sphere and the relationship between the private and the political is a crucial subject for study. I do not believe, however, that we gain much by expanding the definition of the political to cover all human relationships involving power or influence of dominance over some by others. Concepts can be made less useful if their scope is increased so much that they do not allow for distinctions. If everything is political, then the term is not useful for analytical purposes—much as it may sensitize us to aspects of a relationship that would otherwise not be noticed. We need a concept that refers to government activity in making authoritative allocations for a society, that is, that focuses on public policy. Otherwise we cannot meaningfully talk of something moving into the public arena—for instance, child abuse from a family issue to a political issue. We also, of course, need a language that can encourage and reflect a sensitivity to the contingent nature of power relations in the family.

8. See Sears and Huddy, this volume.

9. For data on the relationship between the views of black leaders and feminist

leaders and their respective population bases, see Verba and Orren (1985), chap. 6.

10. The explanations for this persistent difference are many and varied, ranging from the biological/psychological impact of the nurturant mother role to differential socialization experiences in the family to situational role differentials in adult life that place women in the communitarian setting of the family and men in the individualistic and conflictual settings of the economy.

11. On this subject, see Sears and Huddy and Jennings, this volume, as well as Shapiro and Mahajan (1986) and Githens (1977).

12. Jennings, this volume.

13. One can argue and many have that women have a special stake in the policy domains where they have distinctive positions. Women—so the argument goes—suffer most from inadequate welfare programs because of the special responsibility they have had historically for family welfare, benefit more from communitarian policies, and are more likely to be the true victims of war. Such a position can certainly be argued plausibly for many issues, though it may stretch things a bit to argue for a difference in the potential danger to the two genders of nuclear war (where female-male differences in attitude are most persistent). But even if one can explain the wide-ranging and consistent gender differences in this way, the fact that the differences are so consistent and cover such a broad range of issues would make women a distinctive social category.

14. Verba and Nie (1972).

15. See Verba, Nie, and Kim (1978); and Jennings and Farah (1980).

16. Randall (1987), pp. 97–101.

17. See Uhlaner and Schlozman (1986).

18. This illustrates the difference between activity by women that transforms the system and activity that is within the ongoing system. If the greater involvement of women in party politics led to a new party system—for example, a change from a two-party system or a realignment of the parties— one would certainly describe the change as transformational. If it merely involves more voters choosing from the same two parties, it represents an expansion of the ongoing system. Thus far the involvement of women in party and electoral politics appears to be closer to the latter. However, the "gender gap," if it remains persistent, might represent a more significant change in the party coalitions.

19. Schlozman, this volume.

20. Jennings, this volume.

21. Gittell and Shtob (1980) find that there is a good deal of activity by women in the voluntary associations involved in urban reform. Cott, this volume. See also Baker (1984).

22. On this point, see Kanter (1977).

23. See Gertzog (1984), chap. 9.

24. Lasswell (1948), p. 57

25. Jennings, this volume.

26. Jennings, this volume.

27. See Verba et al. (1987), chap. 10.

28. Schlozman, this volume.

29. Kirkpatrick (1974).

30. See Darcy, Welch, and Clark (1987), pp. 153–154.

31. Kirkpatrick (1974).

32. In the absence of an ability to experiment with the political system, it may be impossible to tell which is the correct explanation. Probably there is some truth in each.

33. Jennings, this volume.

34. Certainly, this selection argument is used to explain some of the tough-minded national leaders—Golda Meir, Indira Gandhi, or Margaret Thatcher—of recent decades.

35. Schlozman and Mansbridge, this volume.

36. Kirkpatrick (1974), pp. 132–134.

Bibliography

Aba-Mecha, Barbara Woods. 1978. "Black Woman Activist in Twentieth Century South Carolina: Modjeska Monteith Simkins." Unpublished doctoral dissertation, Emory University.

Abbott, Edith, and Sophonisba P. Breckinridge. 1921. *The Administration of the Aid-to-Mothers Law in Illinois*. Washington, DC: U.S. Department of Labor, Children's Bureau, Legal Series no. 7, Bureau Publication no. 82.

Abramson, Paul. 1974. "Generational Change in American Electoral Behavior." *American Political Science Review* 68:469–478.

———. 1976. "Generational Change and the Decline of Party Identification in America, 1952–1974." *American Political Science Review* 70:469–478.

Adams, Larry T. 1985. "Changing Employment Patterns of Organized Workers." *Monthly Labor Review* 108:25–31.

Adams, Mildred, 1967. *The Right to Be People*. Philadelphia: Lippincott.

Addams, Jane. 1907. *Newer Ideals of Peace*. New York: Macmillan.

———. 1910. *Twenty Years at Hull-House*. New York: Macmillan.

———. 1912. *A New Conscience and an Ancient Evil*. New York: Macmillan.

———. 1930. *The Second Twenty Years at Hull-House, September 1909 to September 1929*. New York: Macmillan.

———. 1964. *Democracy and Social Ethics*. Edited by Ann Firor Scott. Cambridge, MA: Harvard University Press.

Akey, Denise, ed. 1983. *Encyclopedia of Associations*, 18th ed. Detroit: Gale Research.

Aldrich, Mark, and Randy Albeda. 1980. "Determinants of Working Women's Wages During the Progressive Era." *Explorations in Economic History* 17:323–341.

573

Allen, Florence E. 1930. "The First Ten Years." *Woman's Journal* August: 5–7, 30–32.

———. 1965. *To Do Justly.* Cleveland: Western Reserve.

Almy, Frederic. 1915. "Public Pensions to Widows: Experiences and Observations Which Lead Me to Oppose Such a Law." In Edna Bullock, ed., *Selected Articles on Mothers' Pensions.* White Plains and New York: Wilson.

Alpern, Sara, and Dale Baum. 1985. "Female Ballots: The Impact of the Nineteenth Amendment." *Journal of Interdisciplinary History* 16:43–67.

American Civil Liberties Union. 1985. "Obscenity and Censorship." Public statement, April.

American Women: The Report of the President's Commission on the Status of Women and Other Publications of the Commission. 1965. New York: Scribner.

Amici Curiae Brief of Feminist Anti-Censorship Task Force et al. 1985. Filed in U.S. Court of Appeals, 7th Cir., no. 84-3147, *American Booksellers Association, Inc. et al. v. William Hudnut III et al.*, April 8.

Aminzade, Ronald. 1981. *Class, Politics and Early Industrial Capitalism.* Albany: State University of New York Press.

Andersen, Kristi. 1979. *The Creation of a Democratic Majority, 1928–1932.* Chicago: University of Chicago Press.

Anderson, George. 1929. "Women in Congress." *Commonweal* 9:532–534.

Anderson, Mary, as told to Mary W. Winslow. 1951. *Woman at Work.* Minneapolis: University of Minnesota Press.

Aptheker, Bettina. 1982. "Woman Suffrage and the Crusade Against Lynching." In Bettina Aptheker, *Woman's Legacy: Essays on Race, Sex, and Class in American History.* Amherst: University of Massachusetts Press.

Arneson, Ben A. 1925. "Non-Voting in a Typical Ohio Community." *American Political Science Review* 19:816–825.

Arrington, Theodore S., and Patricia A. Kyle. 1978. "Equal Rights Amendment Activists in North Carolina." *Signs: Journal of Women in Culture and Society* 3:666–680.

Asher, Robert. 1973. "Radicalism and Reform: State Insurance of Workmen's Compensation in Minnesota, 1910–1933." *Labor History* 14:19–41.

———. 1983. "Failure and Fulfillment: Agitation for Employers' Liability Legislation and the Origins of Workmen's Compensation in New York State." *Labor History* 24:198–222.

Bach, Robert L. 1986. "Immigration: Issues of Ethnicity, Class and Public Policy in the United States." *Annals of the American Academy of Political and Social Sciences* 485:139–151.

Baden, Naomi. 1986. "Developing an Agenda: Expanding the Role of Women in Unions." *Labor Studies Journal* 10:229–249.

Baer, Judith A. 1978. *The Chains of Protection: The Judicial Response to Women's Labor Legislation.* Westport, CT: Greenwood Press.

Baker, Elizabeth. 1964. *Technology and Women's Work.* New York: Columbia University Press.

Baker, Paula. 1984. "The Domestication of Politics: Women and American Political Society, 1780–1920." *American Historical Review* 89:620–647.

————. 1987. "The Moral Framework of Public Life: Gender and Politics in Rural New York, 1870–1930." Unpublished doctoral dissertation, Rutgers University.

Bancroft, Gertrude. 1958. *The American Labor Force: Its Growth and Changing Composition*. New York: Wiley.

Banner, Lois. 1974. *Women in Modern America: A Brief History*. New York: Harcourt Brace Jovanovich.

Barker, Eirlys. 1986. " 'The Sneaky, Cowardly Enemy': The Tampa Yellow Fever Epidemic of 1887." *Tampa Bay History* 8:4–21.

Barnard, Eunice Fuller. 1928a. "The Woman Voter Gains Power." *New York Times Magazine*, August 12, 1–3, 20.

————. 1928b. "Women in the Campaign." *Woman's Journal*, December, 7–9, 44–45.

Barnett, Ida B. Wells. 1970. *Crusade for Justice: The Autobiography of Ida B. Wells*. Alfreda M. Duster, ed. Chicago: University of Chicago Press.

————. 1969 [1892]. *On Lynchings: Southern Horrors. A Red Record. Mob Rule in New Orleans*. New York: Arno Press.

Bart, Pauline B.; Linda Freeman; and Peter Kimball. 1985. "The Different Worlds of Women and Men: Attitudes Toward Pornography and Responses to NOT A LOVE STORY, a Film about Pornography." *Women's Studies International Forum* 8:307–322.

Bauer, Raymond A.; Ithiel de Sola Pool; and Lewis Anthony Dexter. 1963. *American Business and Public Policy*. Chicago: Aldine.

Baxter, Sandra, and Marjorie Lansing. 1983. *Women and Politics: The Visible Majority*, 2nd ed. Ann Arbor: University of Michigan Press.

Bean, Frank D., and Marta Tienda. 1987. *The Hispanic Population of the United States*. New York: Russell Sage Foundation.

Beard, Mary Ritter. 1915. *Woman's Work in Municipalities*. New York: Appleton.

Beck, Paul Allen. 1976. "A Socialization Theory of Partisan Realignment." In Richard Niemi and Herbert Weisberg, eds., *Controversies in American Voting Behavior*. San Francisco: Freeman.

Becker, Penny A. Edgell. 1986. *An Analysis of Receptivity to Women in Leadership Roles in Liberal and Conservative Protestant Churches*. Unpublished senior thesis, Department of Sociology, Princeton University.

Becker, Susan D. 1981. *The Origins of the Equal Rights Amendment: American Feminism Between the Wars*. Westport, CT: Greenwood.

Beecher, John. 1934. "The Share Croppers' Union in Alabama." *Journal of Social Forces* 13:124–132.

Beechey, Veronica. 1979a. "On Patriarchy." *Feminist Review* 3:66–82.

————. 1979b. "Reproduction, Production and the Sexual Division of Labor." *Cambridge Journal of Economics* 3:203–225.

Bell, Deborah E. 1985. "Unionized Women in State and Local Government." In Ruth Milkman, ed., *Women, Work and Protest: A Century of U.S. Women's Labor History*. London: Routledge & Kegan Paul.

Benería, Lourdes, and Martha Roldán. 1987. *The Crossroads of Class and Gender*. Chicago: University of Chicago Press.

Benson, Susan Porter. 1978. "Business Heads and Sympathizing Hearts: Women of the Providence Employment Society, 1837–1858." *Journal of Social History* 12:302–312.

———. 1986. *Counter Cultures: Saleswomen, Managers, and Customers in American Department Stores, 1890–1940.* Urbana: University of Illinois Press.

Bentley, Arthur F. 1908. *The Process of Government.* Chicago: University of Chicago Press.

Bequaert, Lucia H. 1976. *Single Women: Alone and Together.* Boston: Beacon Press.

Berelson, Bernard R.; Paul F. Lazarsfeld; and William N. McPhee. 1954. *Voting: A Study of Opinion Formation in a Presidential Campaign.* Chicago: University of Chicago Press.

Berger, Caruthers Gholson. 1971. "Equal Pay, Equal Employment Opportunity and Equal Enforcement of the Law for Women." *Valparaiso Law Review* 5:331.

Berkeley, Kathleen C. 1985. " 'Colored Ladies Also Contributed': Black Women's Activities from Benevolence to Social Welfare, 1866–1896." In Walter J. Fraser, Jr., R. Frank Saunders, Jr., and Jon L. Wakelyn, eds., *The Web of Southern Social Relations: Women, Family, and Education.* Athens: University of Georgia Press.

Berkowitz, Edward, and Kim McQuaid. 1978. "Businessman and Bureaucrat: The Evolution of the American Social Welfare System, 1900–1940." *Journal of Economic History* 38:120–142.

———. 1980. *Creating the Welfare State: The Political Economy of Twentieth Century Reform.* New York: Praeger.

Berry, Jeffrey M. 1977. *Lobbying for the People: The Political Behavior of Public Interest Groups.* Princeton, NJ: Princeton University Press.

———. 1984. *The Interest Group Society.* Boston: Little, Brown.

Blair, Emily Newell. 1929. "Women in the Political Parties." *Annals of the American Academy of Political Science* 143:217–229.

———. 1931. "Why I Am Discouraged About Women in Politics." *Woman's Journal,* January: 20–22.

Blair, Karen J. 1980. *The Clubwoman as Feminist: True Womanhood Redefined, 1868–1914.* New York: Holmes & Meier.

Blakely, Mary Kay. 1985. "Is One Woman's Sexuality Another Woman's Pornography?" *Ms.,* April, 37–47, 120–123.

Bland, Sidney Roderick. 1972. "Techniques of Persuasion: The National Woman's Party and Woman Suffrage, 1913–1919." Unpublished doctoral dissertation, George Washington University.

Blassingame, John W. 1973. "Before the Ghetto: The Making of the Black Community in Savannah, Georgia, 1865–1880." *Journal of Social History* 6:463–487.

Boeckel, Florence Brewer. 1929. "Women in International Affairs." *Annals of the American Academy of Political Science* 143:231–232.

Boles, Janet. 1979. *The Politics of the Equal Rights Amendment.* New York: Longman.

———. 1982. "Building Support for the ERA: A Case of Too Much, Too Late." *PS* 15:572–577.

Boneparth, Ellen. 1984. "Resources and Constraints on Women in the Policymaking Process: State and Local Arenas." In Janet L. Flammang, ed., *Political Women: Current Roles in State and Local Arenas.* Beverly Hills, CA: Sage.

Bordin, Ruth. 1981. *Woman and Temperance: The Quest for Power and Liberty, 1873–1900.* Philadelphia: Temple University Press.

———. 1986. *Frances Willard: A Biography.* Chapel Hill: University of North Carolina Press.

Borjas, George J., and Marta Tienda, eds. 1985. *Hispanics in the U.S. Economy.* New York: Academic Press.

Bourque, Susan C., and Jean Grossholtz. 1974. "Politics an Unnatural Practice: Political Science Looks at Female Participation." *Politics and Society* 4:225–266.

Bowie, Walter Russell. 1942. *Sunrise in the South: The Life of Mary-Cooke Branch Munford.* Richmond, VA: William Byrd Press.

Boylan, Anne M. 1984. "Women in Groups: An Analysis of Women's Benevolent Organizations in New York and Boston, 1797–1840." *Journal of American History* 71:497–523.

Braden, Anne. 1981. "A View from the Fringes." *Southern Exposure* 9:68–74.

Brady, David W., and Kent L. Tedin. 1976. "Ladies in Pink: Religion and Political Ideology in the Anti-ERA Movement." *Social Science Quarterly* 56:564–575.

Brauer, Carl M. 1983. "Women Activists, Southern Conservatives, and the Prohibition of Sex Discrimination in Title VII of the 1964 Civil Rights Act." *Journal of Southern History* 49:37–56.

Breckinridge, Sophonisba P. 1933. *Women in the Twentieth Century: A Study of Theory in Political, Social, and Economic Activities.* New York: McGraw-Hill.

Brill, Alida. 1978. "How Far Out/How Far Away: An Examination of Far Left and Right Criterion Groups." Unpublished paper, University of California, Berkeley.

Brooks, Evelyn. 1988. "Religion, Politics, and Gender: The Leadership of Nannie Helen Burroughs." *Journal of Religious Thought* 44:7–22.

Brothers, Joyce. 1980. "The Surprising Breakup of Anita Bryant's Twenty-Year Marriage to Bob Green." *Good Housekeeping,* 106–111, 191.

Brownmiller, Susan. 1975. *Against Our Will: Men, Women and Rape.* New York: Simon & Schuster.

Brudney, Jeffrey L., and Jean G. McDonald. 1986. "Issue Constellations in 1980." In Ronald B. Rapoport, Alan I. Abramowitz, and John McGlennon, eds., *The Life of the Parties.* Lexington: University of Kentucky Press.

Buechler, Steven M. 1986. *The Transformation of the Woman Suffrage Movement: The Case of Illinois, 1850–1920.* New Brunswick, NJ: Rutgers University Press.

Buenker, John D. 1970–1971. "The Urban Political Machine and Woman Suffrage." *Historian* 33:264–279.

———. 1973. *Urban Liberalism and Progressive Reform.* New York: Scribners.

Buhle, Mari Jo. 1970. "Women and the Socialist Party." *Radical America* 2:36–55.

———. 1981. *Women and American Socialism, 1870–1920.* Urbana: University of Illinois Press.

———, and Paul Buhle, eds. 1978. *The Concise History of Woman Suffrage: Selections from the Classic Work of Stanton, Anthony, Gage, and Harper.* Urbana: University of Illinois Press.

Burawoy, Michael. 1985. *The Politics of Production*. London: New Left Books.

Burner, David. 1967. *The Politics of Provincialism: The Democratic Party in Transition, 1918–1932*. New York: Norton.

Burnham, Walter Dean. 1965. "The Changing Shape of the American Political Universe." *American Political Science Review* 59:7–28.

———. 1974. "Theory and Voting Research: Some Reflections on Converse's 'Change in the American Electorate.'" *American Political Science Review* 68:1002–1023.

Burstyn, Varda, ed. 1985. *Women Against Censorship*. Vancouver and Toronto: McIntyre.

Butler, Sarah Schuyler. 1924. "Women Who Do Not Vote." *Scribner's Magazine*, 76,529–533.

———. 1929. "After Ten Years." *Woman's Journal*, April, 10–11.

California Assembly, Interim Committee on the Judiciary. 1964. Transcript of Proceedings on Domestic Relations, January 8–9.

———. 1965. *Final Report of the Assembly Interim Committee on the Judiciary Relating to Domestic Relations*, January 11.

Cameron, Ardis. 1985. "Bread and Roses Revisited: Women's Culture and Working-Class Activism in the Lawrence Strike of 1912." In Ruth Milkman, ed., *Women, Work and Protest: A Century of Women's Labor History*. Boston: Routledge & Kegan Paul.

Campbell, Angus; Philip E. Converse; Warren E. Miller; and Donald E. Stokes. 1960. *The American Voter*. New York: Wiley.

Campbell, Beatrix. 1984. *Wigan Pier Revisited: Poverty and Politics in the Eighties*. London: Virago.

Campbell, D'Ann. 1978. "Women's Life in Utopia: The Shaker Experiment in Sexual Equality Reappraised—1810 to 1860." *New England Quarterly* 51:23–38.

Carroll, Mary. 1930. "Wanted—a New Feminism: An Interview with Emily Newell Blair." *Independent Woman* 9:499, 544.

Carroll, Susan J. 1984. "Women's Autonomy and the Gender Gap." Paper presented at the American Psychological Association meeting, Toronto, Canada.

Carson, Clayborne. 1981. *In Struggle: SNCC and the Black Awakening of the 1960s*. Cambridge, MA: Harvard University Press.

Carter, Paul. 1977. *Another Part of the Twenties*. New York: Columbia University Press.

Cassetty, Judith. 1978. *Child Support and Public Policy*. Lexington, MA: Lexington Books.

Castles, Francis G. 1978. *The Social Democratic Image of Society*. London: Routledge & Kegan Paul.

Cavanaugh, Michael A. 1986. "Secularization and the Politics of Traditionalism: The Case of the Right-to-Life Movement." *Sociological Forum* 1:251–283.

Center for the American Woman in Politics. 1983. *Women in Public Office: A Biographical Directory and Statistical Analysis*, 3rd ed. Metuchen, NJ: Scarecrow Press.

Chafe, William H. 1972. *The American Woman: Her Changing Social, Economic, and Political Roles, 1920–1970*. New York: Oxford University Press.

———. 1978. *Women and Equality*. New York: Oxford University Press.

———. 1982. "The Civil Rights Revolution, 1945–1960: The Gods Bring Threads to Webs Begun." In Robert H. Bremner and Gary W. Reichard, eds., *Reshaping America: Society and Institutions, 1945–1960*. Columbus: Ohio State University Press.

Chambers, Clarke A. 1963. *Seedtime of Reform*. Minneapolis: University of Minnesota Press.

Chambers, John Whiteclay, II. 1980. *The Tyranny of Change: America in the Progressive Era, 1900–1917*. New York: St. Martin's Press.

Chandler, Alfred D. 1977. *The Visible Hand: The Managerial Revolution in American Business*. Cambridge, MA: Belknap.

Chatfield, Charles. 1971. *For Peace and Justice: Pacifism in America, 1914–1941*. Knoxville: University of Tennessee Press.

Cheadle, Elizabeth A. 1981. "The Development of Sharing Principles in Common Law Marital Property States." *UCLA Law Review* 28:1269–313.

Chemerinsky, Erwin, and Paul J. McGeady. 1985. "Outlawing Pornography: What We Gain, What We Lose." *Human Rights* 12:24–27, 46–48.

Chesson, Michael B. 1984. "Harlots or Heroines? A New Look at the Richmond Bread Riot." *Virginia Magazine of History and Biography* 92:131–175.

Chodorow, Nancy. 1978. *The Reproduction of Mothering: Psychoanalysis and the Sociology of Gender*. Berkeley: University of California Press.

Chubb, John. 1983. *Interest Groups and the Bureaucracy*. Palo Alto, CA: Stanford University Press.

Citizens' Advisory Council on the Status of Women. 1964. *Progress Report on the Status of Women, October 11, 1963 through October 10, 1964*. Washington, DC: Interdepartmental Committee and Citizens' Advisory Council on the Status of Women.

———. 1968. Report of the Task Force on Family Law and Policy. Washington, DC: Citizens' Advisory Council on the Status of Women.

Citrin, Jack, and Donald P. Green. 1988. "The Self-Interest Motive in American Public Opinion." In S. Long, ed., *Research in Micropolitics*, vol. 5. New York: Greenwood Press.

Claggett, William. 1980. "The Life Cycle and Generational Models of the Development of Partisanship: A Test Based on the Delayed Enfranchisement of Women." *Social Science Quarterly* 60:643–650.

Clark, Peter B., and James Q. Wilson. 1961. "Incentive Systems: A Theory of Organizations." *Administrative Science Quarterly* 6:129–166.

Close, Arthur C., ed. 1981. *Washington Representatives—1981*. Washington, DC: Columbia Books.

———. 1984. *Washington Representatives—1984*. Washington, DC: Columbia Books.

Cockburn, Cynthia. 1983. *Brothers: Male Dominance and Technological Change*. London: Pluto Press.

Cohn, Samuel. 1985. *The Process of Occupational Sex-Typing: The Feminization of Clerical Labor in Great Britain*. Philadelphia: Temple University Press.

Commission on California State Government, Organization and Economy. 1985.

Review of Selected Taxing and Enforcing Agencies' Programs to Control the Underground Economy. Los Angeles: Commission on California State Government.

Commission on the Status of Women. 1968. *1968: Time for Action: Highlights of the Fourth National Conference of Commissions on the Status of Women.* Washington, June 20–22.

Congressional Quarterly Almanac, 1950. 1950. Washington, DC: Congressional Quarterly News Features.

Congressional Quarterly Almanac, 1953. 1953. Washington, DC: Congressional Quarterly News Features.

Congressional Quarterly Almanac, 1984. 1985. Washington, DC: Congressional Quarterly.

Conover, Pamela Johnston, and Virginia Gray. 1983. *Feminism and the New Right: Conflict over the American Family.* New York: Praeger.

Converse, Philip E. 1969. "Of Time and Partisan Stability." *Comparative Political Studies* 2:139–171.

———. 1976. *The Dynamics of Party Support: Cohort Analyzing Party Identification.* Beverly Hills, CA: Sage.

———, and Greg B. Markus. 1979. "Plus ça change. . . : The New Election Study Panel." *American Political Science Review* 73:32–49.

Conway, Jill K.; Susan C. Bourque; and Joan W. Scott. 1987. "Introduction: The Concept of Gender." *Daedalus* 116:xxi–xxix.

Cook, Beverly B. 1984. "Women on the State Bench: Correlates of Access." In Janet A. Flammang, ed., *Political Women: Current Roles in State and Local Government.* Beverly Hills, CA: Sage.

Cook, Blanche Wiesen. 1979. "Female Support Networks and Political Activism: Lillian Wald, Crystal Eastman, Emma Goldman." In Nancy A. Cott and Elizabeth H. Pleck, eds., *A Heritage of Her Own: Toward a New Social History of American Women.* New York: Simon & Schuster.

Corcoran, Mary; Greg J. Duncan; Gerald Gurin; and Patricia Gurin. 1985. "Myth and Reality: The Causes and Persistence of Poverty." *Journal of Policy Analysis and Management* 4:516–536.

Costain, Anne N. 1978. "The Role of Individuals and Interest Groups in Changing and/or Maintaining Existing Policies." *Policy Studies Journal* 7:185–195.

———. 1980. "The Struggle for a National Women's Lobby: Organizing a Diffuse Interest." *Western Political Quarterly* 33:476–491.

———. 1981. "Representing Women: The Transition from Social Movement to Interest Group." *Western Political Quarterly* 34:100–113.

———. 1982. "Representing Women." In Ellen Boneparth, ed., *Women, Power, and Policy.* New York: Pergamon.

Costantini, Edmond, and Julie David Bell. 1984. "Women in Political Parties: Gender Differences in Motives Among California Party Activists." In Janet A. Flammang, ed., *Political Women: Current Roles in State and Local Government.* Beverly Hills, CA: Sage.

———, and Kenneth Craik. 1972. "Women as Politicians: The Social Background, Personality, and Political Careers of Female Party Leaders." *Journal of Social Issues* 28:217–236.

Costello, Cynthia B. 1985. " 'WEA're Worth It!' Work Culture and Conflict at the Wisconsin Education Association Insurance Trust." *Feminist Studies* 11:497–518.

Costin, Lela B. 1983. *Two Sisters for Social Justice: A Biography of Grace and Edith Abbott.* Urbana: University of Illinois Press.

Cott, Nancy F. 1977. *The Bonds of Womanhood: 'Woman's Sphere' in New England, 1780–1835.* New Haven: Yale University Press.

———. 1984. "Feminist Politics in the 1920s: The National Woman's Party." *Journal of American History* 71:43–68.

———. 1986. "Feminist Theory and Feminist Movements: The Past Before Us." In Juliet Mitchell and Ann Oakley, eds., *What Is Feminism?* New York: Pantheon Books.

———. 1987. *The Grounding of Modern Feminism.* New Haven: Yale University Press.

Cotter, Cornelius P.; James L. Gibson; John F. Bibby; and Robert J. Huckshorn. 1984. *Party Organization in American Politics.* New York: Praeger.

Council of State Governments. 1986. *Book of the States.* Lexington: Council of State Governments.

Countryman, Edward. 1981. *A People in Revolution: The American Revolution and Political Society in New York, 1760–1790.* Baltimore: Johns Hopkins University Press.

Cowper, Mary O. 1924. "The North Carolina League of Women Voters." *Journal of Social Forces* 2:424.

Crosby, F. J. 1982. *Relative Deprivation and Working Women.* New York: Oxford University Press.

Dahl, Robert A. 1956. *A Preface to Democratic Theory.* Chicago: University of Chicago Press.

———. 1982. *Dilemmas of Pluralist Democracy.* New Haven: Yale University Press.

Dahlerup, Drude. 1987. "Introduction." In Drude Dahlerup, ed., *The New Women's Movement.* Beverly Hills, CA: Sage.

Daniel, Pete. 1981. "The Transformation of the Rural South: From 1930 to the Present." *Agricultural History* 55:231–248.

———. 1985. *Breaking the Land: The Transformation of Cotton, Tobacco, and Rice Cultures since 1880.* Urbana: University of Illinois Press.

Daniels, Doris. 1979. "Building a Winning Coalition: The Suffrage Fight in New York State." *New York History* 60:58–80.

Daniels, Mark R.; Robert Darcy; and Joseph W. Westphal. 1982. "The ERA Won—At Least in the Opinion Polls." *PS* 4:578–584.

Darcy, Robert; Susan Welch; and Janet Clark. 1987. *Women, Elections and Representation.* New York: Longman.

David, Paul T.; Ralph M. Goldman; and Richard C. Bain. 1960. *The Politics of National Party Conventions.* Washington, DC: Brookings Institution.

Davis, Allen F. 1967a. *Spearheads for Reform: The Social Settlements and the Progressive Movement, 1890–1914.* New York: Oxford University Press.

———. 1967b. "Welfare, Reform and World War I." *American Quarterly* 19:516–533.

Davis, Natalie Zemon. 1980. "Gender and Genre: Women as Historical Writers,

1400–1820." In Patricia H. Labalme, ed., *Beyond Their Sex: Learned Women of the European Past*. New York: New York University Press.

De Benedetti, Charles. 1978. *Origins of the Modern American Peace Movement, 1915–1929*. Millwood, NY: KTO Press.

Degler, Carl N. 1980. *At Odds: Women and the Family in America from the Revolution to the Present*. New York: Oxford University Press.

Del Boca, Francis K., and Richard D. Ashmore. 1984. "The Self and Attitudes Toward Gender-Related Public Policy." Paper presented at the American Psychological Association meeting, Toronto.

Del Rio, Emilio. 1972. *Yo Fui Uno de Los Fundadores de Ybor City*. Tampa: author.

Deutchman, Iva Ellen. 1986. "Gender and Power Anxiety: Concept, Relevance, and Political Relevance." Paper presented at the American Political Science Association annual meeting, August.

Diamond, Irene. 1977. *Sex Roles in the State House*. New Haven: Yale University Press.

———. 1982. "Pornography and Repression: A Reconsideration." In Barbara Raffel Price and Natalie J. Sokoloff, eds., *The Criminal Justice System and Women*. New York: Clark Boardman.

———, ed. 1983. *Families, Politics and Public Policy*. New York: Longman.

Dickerson, Mary. 1982. *Democracy in Trade Unions: Studies in Membership, Participation and Control*. St. Lucia: University of Queensboro Press.

Dietrickson, Mary Watkins. 1926. "The Minimum Wage Situation in Minnesota." *Minnesota Woman Voter* 26:9.

Dietz, Mary G. 1985. "Citizenship with a Feminist Face: The Problem with Maternal Thinking." *Political Theory* 13:19–37.

———. 1987. "Feminism and Theories of Citizenship." *Daedalus* 116:1–24.

Dixon, John. 1984. "Defending the Indefensible." *Rights and Freedoms* 53:1–9.

Dobbs, Farrell. 1973. *Teamster Power*. New York: Monad Press.

Dobyns, Winifred Starr. 1927. "The Lady and the Tiger." *Woman Citizen*, January, 20–21, 44–45.

Douglas, Paul. 1936. *Social Security in the United States*. New York: Whittlesey House.

Douglass, H. Paul, and Edmund deS. Brunner. 1935. *The Protestant Church as a Social Institution*. New York: Russell & Russell.

Drake, St. Clair, and Horace R. Cayton. 1945. *Black Metropolis*. New York: Harper & Row.

Dresher, Nuala McGann. 1970. "The Workmen's Compensation and Pension Proposal in the Brewing Industry, 1910–1912: A Case Study in Conflicting Self-Interest." *Industrial Labor Relations Review* 24:32–46.

DuBois, Ellen Carol. 1978. *Feminism and Suffrage: The Emergence of an Independent Women's Movement in America, 1848–1869*. Ithaca: Cornell University Press.

———. 1986. "Working Women, Class Relations, and Suffrage Militance: Harriot Stanton Blatch and the New York Woman Suffrage Movement, 1894–1909." *Journal of American History* 74:34–58.

Duerst-Lahti, Georgia. 1985. "Building an Infrastructure for the Women's Movement: Intergovernmental Structures and Dynamics, 1963 to 1969." Typescript in the files of Herbert Jacob.

Duncan, Greg J., and James N. Morgan. 1980. "The Incidence and Some Consequences of Major Life Events." In University of Michigan Survey Research Center, *Five Thousand American Families—Patterns of Economic Progress*. Ann Arbor: Institute for Social Research.

Dworkin, Andrea. 1979. *Pornography: Men Possessing Women*. New York: Putnam.

———. 1983. *Right-Wing Women*. New York: Perigee Books.

———. 1987. *Intercourse*. New York: Free Press.

Dworkin, Ronald. 1985. "Do We Have Right to Pornography?" In Ronald Dworkin, ed., *A Matter of Principle*. Cambridge, MA: Harvard University Press.

Dye, Nancy Schrom. 1975. "Creating a Feminist Alliance: Sisterhood and Class Conflict in the New York Women's Trade Union League." *Feminist Studies*, 2:24–38.

———. 1980. *As Equals and as Sisters: Feminism, Unionism, and the Women's Trade Union League of New York*. Columbia: University of Missouri Press.

Eakins, David W. 1972. "The Origins of Corporate Liberal Policy Research, 1916–1922: The Political Economic Expert and the Decline of Public Debate." In Jerry Israel, ed., *Building the Organizational Society: Essays on Associational Activities in Modern America*. New York: Free Press.

Earhart, Mary. 1944. *Frances Willard: From Prayers to Politics*. Chicago: University of Chicago Press.

East, Catherine. 1983. *American Women 1969, 1983, 2003*. Washington, DC: National Federation of Business and Professional Women's Clubs.

Easton, David. 1971. *The Political System: An Inquiry into the State of Political Science*, 2nd ed. New York: Knopf.

Echols, Alice. 1986. "The Radical Feminist Movement in the United States, 1967–1975." Unpublished doctoral dissertation, University of Michigan.

Eckstein, Harry. 1975. "Case Study and Theory in Political Science." In Fred I. Greenstein and Nelson W. Polsby, eds., *Strategies of Inquiry*. Handbook of Political Science, vol. 7. Reading, MA: Addison-Wesley.

Edelman, Murray. 1964. *The Symbolic Uses of Politics*. Urbana: University of Illinois Press.

———. 1977. *Political Language: Words That Succeed and Policies That Fail*. New York: Academic Press.

Edmonds, T. J., and Maurice P. Hexter. 1915. "State Pensions to Mothers in Hamilton County, Ohio." In Edna Bullock, ed., *Selected Articles on Mothers' Pensions*. White Plains and New York: Wilson.

Eisenstein, Hester, and Alice Jardine, eds. 1980. *The Future of Difference*. New Brunswick, NJ: Rutgers University Press.

Eisenstein, Zillah. 1981. *The Radical Future of Liberal Feminism*. New York: Longman.

———. 1984. *Feminism and Sexual Equality: Crisis in Liberal America*. New York: Monthly Review Press.

Elshtain, Jean Bethke. 1982. "Feminist Discourse and Its Discontents: Language, Power and Meaning." *Signs: Journal of Women in Culture and Society* 3:342–367.

———. 1983. "Antigone's Daughters: Reflections on Female Identity and the State." In Irene Diamond, ed., *Families, Politics, and Public Policy: A Feminist Dialogue on Women and the State*. New York: Longman.

———. 1984. "The New Porn Wars." *New Republic* 190, 25:15–20.

Epstein, Cynthia. 1988. *Deceptive Distinctions: Sex, Gender and the Social Order*. New Haven: Yale University Press.

Epstein, Leon D. 1983. "The Scholarly Commitment to Parties." In Ada W. Finifter, ed., *Political Science: The State of the Discipline*. Washington, DC: American Political Science Association.

Erickson, Hermann. 1971. "WPA Strikes and Trials of 1939." *Minnesota History* 42:202–214.

Erskine, Hazel Gaudet. 1965. "The Polls: Personal Religion." *Public Opinion Quarterly* 29:145–157.

———. 1971. "The Polls: Government Information Policy." *Public Opinion Quarterly* 35:636–652.

Evans, Peter; Theda Skocpol; and Dietrich Rueschemeyer, eds. 1985. *Bringing the State Back In*. New York: Cambridge University Press.

Farmer-Labor Women's Clubs of Minnesota. 1932. *Report of the Sixth State Convention*. St. Paul: Farmer-Labor Women's Clubs of Minnesota.

Farmer-Labor Women's Federation. 1936a. *Farmer-Labor Women's Federation Annual, 1935–1936*. St. Paul: Farmer-Labor Women's Federation.

———. 1936b. *Women's Political Primer*. St. Paul: Farmer-Labor Women's Federation.

———. 1938. *A Call to the Women of Minnesota*. Minneapolis: Farmer-Labor Women's Federation.

Faue, Elizabeth Victoria. 1987. "Women, Work and Community in Minneapolis, 1929–1946." Unpublished doctoral dissertation, University of Minnesota.

Federal Writers Project. 1939. *These Are Our Lives*. Chapel Hill: University of North Carolina Press.

Ferguson, Ann; Illene Philipson; Irene Diamond; Lee Quinby; Carole S. Vance; and Ann Barr Snitow. 1984. "Signs Forum: The Feminist Sexuality Debates." *Signs: Journal of Women in Culture and Society* 10:106–135.

Fernández-Kelly, M. Patricia, and Anna M. García. 1989. "Informalization at the Core: Hispanic Women, Homework and the Advanced Capitalist State." In Alejandro Portes, Manuel Castells, and Lauren Benton, eds., *The Informal Economy: Comparative Studies in Advanced and Third World Societies*. Baltimore: Johns Hopkins University Press.

Festinger, Leon. 1957. *A Theory of Cognitive Dissonance*. Evanston, IL: Row, Peterson.

Fields, Mamie Garvin, with Karen Fields. 1983. *Lemon Swamp and Other Places: A Carolina Memoir*. New York: Free Press.

Filene, Peter G. 1970. "An Obituary for 'The Progressive Movement,' " *American Quarterly* 22:20–34.

Fineman, Martha L. 1983. "Implementing Equality: Ideology, Contradiction and

Social Change—A Study of the Rhetoric and Results in the Regulation of the Consequences of Divorce." *Wisconsin Law Review:* 789–886.

Fiorina, Morris. 1981. *Retrospective Voting in American National Elections.* New Haven: Yale University Press.

Fireman, Bruce, and William A. Gamson. 1979. "Utilitarian Logic in the Resource Mobilization Perspective." In Mayer N. Zald and John D. McCarthy, eds., *The Dynamics of Social Movements: Resource Mobilization, Social Control and Tactics.* Cambridge, MA: Winthrop.

Fisher, Marguerite J. 1947. "Women in the Political Parties." *Annals of the American Academy of Political Science* 251:87–93.

———, and Betty Whitehead. 1944. "Women and National Party Organization." *American Political Science Review* 38:895–903.

Fitzgerald, Frances. 1981. "A Reporter at Large—A Disciplined, Charging Army." *New Yorker,* May 18.

Fleming, Jeanne J. 1986. "Women Against Men? Gender as a Base of Support for Change in Women's Rights and Roles." In Gwen Moore and Glenna Spitze, eds., *Research in Politics and Society: A Research Annual.* Greenwich, CT: JAI Press.

Flexner, Eleanor. 1968 [1959]. *Century of Struggle: The Woman's Rights Movement in the United States.* New York: Atheneum.

Flexner, Helen Thomas. 1909. "Introduction." In Helen L. Sumner, ed., *Equal Suffrage.* New York: Harper.

Folberg, Jay, ed. 1984. *Joint Custody and Shared Parenting.* Washington, DC: Bureau of National Affairs and the Association of Family and Conciliation Courts.

Foner, Philip S. 1979. *Woman and the American Labor Movement: From Colonial Times to the Eve of World War I.* New York: Free Press.

———. 1982. *Women and the American Labor Movement: From the First Trade Unions to the Present.* New York: Free Press.

Fonow, Mary Margaret. 1977. "Women in Steel: A Case Study of the Participation of Women in a Trade Union." Unpublished doctoral dissertation, Ohio State University.

Foster-Hayes, Carrie. 1984. "The Women and the Warriors: Dorothy Detzer and the WILPF." Unpublished doctoral dissertation, University of Denver.

Fowler, Robert Booth. 1986. *Carrie Catt: Feminist Politician.* Boston: Northeastern University Press.

Frank, Dana. 1985. "Housewives, Socialists, and the Politics of Food: The 1917 New York Cost of Living Protests." *Feminist Studies* 11:255–285.

Frankovic, Kathleen A. 1982. "Sex and Politics—New Alignments, Old Issues." *Political Science* 4:439–448.

———. 1985. "The Election of 1984: The Irrelevance of the Campaign." *PS* 18:39–47.

———. 1987. "The Ferraro Factor: The Women's Movement, the Polls, and the Press." In Carol McClurg Mueller, ed., *The Politics of the Gender Gap: The Social Construction of Political Influence.* Beverly Hills, CA: Sage.

Fraser, Antonia. 1984. *The Weaker Vessel.* New York: Random House.

Fraser, Arvonne, and Sue E. Holbert. 1977. "Women in the Minnesota Legislature." In Barbara Stuhler and Gretchen Kreuter, eds., *Women of Minnesota: Selected Biographical Essays*. St. Paul: Minnesota Historical Society Press.

Frederickson, Mary. 1977. "The Southern Summer School for Women Workers." *Southern Exposure* 4:70–75.

———. 1981. " 'A Place to Speak Our Minds': The Southern Summer School for Women Workers." Unpublished doctoral dissertation, University of North Carolina.

———. 1982. "Four Decades of Change: Black Workers in Southern Textiles, 1941–1981." *Radical America* 16:27–44.

———. 1985. " 'I Know Which Side I'm On': Southern Women in the Labor Movement in the Twentieth Century." In Ruth Milkman, ed., *Women, Work, and Protest: A Century of U.S. Women's History*. Boston: Routledge & Kegan Paul.

Freedman, Estelle B. 1974. "The New Woman: Changing Views of Women in the 1920s." *Journal of American History* 61:372–384.

———. 1979. "Separatism as Strategy: Female Institution Building and American Feminism, 1870–1930." *Feminist Studies* 5:512–529.

———. 1981. *Their Sisters' Keepers: Women's Prison Reform in America, 1830–1930*. Ann Arbor: University of Michigan Press.

Freeman, Jo. 1975. *The Politics of the Women's Liberation Movement*. New York: McKay.

———. 1979. "Resource Mobilization and Strategy: A Model for Analyzing Social Movement Organization Actions." In Mayer N. Zald and John D. McCarthy, eds., *The Dynamics of Social Movements: Resource Mobilization Social Control and Tactics*. Cambridge, MA: Winthrop.

———. 1984. "Women, Law, and Public Policy." In Jo Freeman, ed., *Women: A Feminist Perspective*, 3rd ed. Palo Alto, CA: Mayfield.

Freeman, Richard B., and James L. Medoff. 1984. *What Do Unions Do?* New York: Basic Books.

Friedan, Betty. 1961. "If One Generation Can Ever Tell Another." *Smith Alumnae Quarterly* 52:68–70.

———. 1963. *The Feminine Mystique*. New York: Dell.

———. 1976. *It Changed My Life*. New York: Dell.

———. 1985. "How to Get the Women's Movement Moving Again." *New York Times Magazine*, November 30.

Friedman, Jean E. 1983. "Women's History and the Revision of Southern History." In Joanne V. Hawks and Sheila Skemp, eds., *Sex, Race, and the Role of Women in the South*. Jackson: University Press of Mississippi.

Friedman, Lawrence M., and Jack Ladinsky. 1978. "Social Change and the Law of Industrial Accidents." In Lawrence M. Friedman and Harry N. Scheiber, eds., *American Law and the Constitutional Order: Historical Perspectives*. Cambridge, MA: Harvard University Press.

Furlow, John W. 1976. "Cornelia Bryce Pinchot: Feminism in the Post-Suffrage Era." *Pennsylvania History* 95:329–346.

Gabin, Nancy. 1985. "Women and the United Automobile Workers' Union in the 1950s." In Ruth Milkman, ed., *Women, Work and Protest: A Century of U.S. Women's Labor History*. Boston: Routledge & Kegan Paul.

Gallup, George, Jr. 1982. *Religion in America: 1982*. Princeton, NJ: Princeton Religion Research Center.

———. 1985. *Religion in America: Fifty Years, 1935–1985*. Princeton, NJ: Princeton Religion Research Center.

Gallup, George H. 1971. *The Gallup Poll*. New York: Random House.

———. 1972. *Gallup Poll: Public Opinion, 1935–1971*. New York: Random House.

Galvez, Wen. 1897. *Tampa: Impresiones de Emigrado*. Havana: Tipográfico de Cuba.

Gamson, William A. 1975. *The Strategy of Social Protest*. Homewood, IL: Dorsey.

———; Bruce Fireman; and Steve Rytina. 1982. *Encounters with Unjust Authority*. Homewood, IL: Dorsey.

Gardner, Tom, and Cynthia Stakes Brown. 1981. "The Montgomery Bus Boycott: Interviews with Rosa Parks, E. D. Nixon, Johnny Carr, and Virginia Durr." *Southern Exposure* 9:12–22.

Gelb, Joyce. 1986. "Feminism in Britain: Politics without Power?" In Drude Dahlerup, ed., *The New Women's Movement*. Beverly Hills, CA: Sage.

———, and Marian Lief Palley. 1979. "Women and Interest Group Politics." *Journal of Politics* 41:362–392.

———. 1987. *Women and Public Policies*, rev. ed. Princeton, NJ: Princeton University Press.

Gerlach, Luther P., and Virginia H. Hine. 1970. *People, Power, Change: Movements of Social Transformation*. Indianapolis: Bobbs-Merrill.

Gerould, Katherine F. 1925. "Some American Women and the Vote." *Scribner's*, 77:449–452.

Gerson, Kathleen. 1985. *Hard Choices: How Women Decide about Work, Career, and Motherhood*. Berkeley: University of California Press.

Gertzog, Irwin N. 1984. *Congressional Women: Their Recruitment, Treatment and Behavior*. New York: Praeger.

Giddings, Paula. 1984. *When and Where I Enter: The Impact of Black Women on Race and Sex in America*. New York: Morrow.

Gieske, Millard. 1979. *Minnesota Farmer Laborism: The Third Party Alternative*. Minneapolis: University of Minnesota Press.

Gilkes, Cheryl Townsend. 1985. " 'Together and in Harness': Women's Traditions in the Sanctified Church." *Signs: Journal of Women in Culture and Society* 5:678–699.

Gilligan, Carol. 1982. *In a Different Voice: Psychological Theory and Women's Development*. Cambridge, MA: Harvard University Press.

Gilman, Charlotte Perkins Stetson. 1979. *Herland*. New York: Pantheon Books.

Ginzberg, Lori D. 1985. "Women and the Work of Benevolence: Morality and Politics in the Northeastern United States, 1820–1885." Unpublished doctoral dissertation, Yale University.

———. 1986. " 'Moral Suasion Is Moral Balderdash': Women, Politics, and Social Activism in the 1850s." *Journal of American History* 73:601–622.

Githens, Marianne. 1977. "Spectators, Agitators, or Lawmakers: Women in

State Legislatures." In Marianne Githens and Jewel L. Prestage, eds., *A Portrait of Marginality: The Political Behavior of American Women.* New York: McKay.

Gittell, Marilyn, and Teresa Shtob. 1980. "Changing Women's Roles in Political Voluntarism and Reform of the City." *Signs: Journal of Women in Culture and Society* 5 (supplement):S67–S78.

Glaser, Barney G., and Anselm L. Strauss. 1967. *The Discovery of Grounded Theories: Strategies for Qualitative Research.* Chicago: Aldine.

Glassman, Carol. 1970. "Women and the Welfare System." In Robin Morgan, ed., *Sisterhood Is Powerful.* New York: Vintage.

Glenn, Norval C. 1972. "Sources of the Shift to Political Independence: Some Evidence from a Cohort Analysis." *Social Science Quarterly* 37:1–20.

Glock, Charles Y.; Benjamin Ringer; and Earl R. Babbie. 1967. *To Comfort and to Challenge.* Berkeley and Los Angeles: University of California Press.

Goldstein, Joel H. 1973. "The Effects of the Adoption of Women Suffrage: Sex Differences in Voting Behavior—Illinois, 1914–1921." Unpublished doctoral dissertation, University of Chicago.

Goldstein, Leslie. 1979. *The Constitutional Rights of Women.* New York: Longman.

———. 1984. "The ERA and American Public Policy." Paper presented at the American Political Science Association meeting, Washington.

Golembiewski, Robert T. 1960. " 'The Group Basis of Politics': Notes on Analysis and Development." *American Political Science Review* 54:962–971.

Goodwin, Joanne L. 1986. "Gender and Early Social Welfare Policy: The Case of Mothers' Pensions in the U.S." Social Science History Association Conference, St. Louis.

Goodwyn, Lawrence. 1976. *Democratic Promise: The Populist Moment in America.* New York: Oxford University Press.

Goot, Murray, and Elizabeth Reid. 1975. *Women and Voting Studies: Mindless Matrons or Sexist Scientism?* Beverly Hills, CA: Sage.

Gordon, Felice D. 1982. *After Winning: The New Jersey Suffragists, 1910–1947.* Unpublished doctoral dissertation, Rutgers University.

———. 1986. *After Winning: The Legacy of the New Jersey Suffragists, 1920–1947.* New Brunswick: Rutgers University Press.

Gordon, Linda. 1976. *Woman's Body, Woman's Right: A Social History of Birth Control in America.* New York: Grossman.

———. 1985. "Single Mothers and Child Neglect, 1880–1920." *American Quarterly* 37:173–192.

Gosnell, Harold F. 1935. *Negro Politicians.* Chicago: University of Chicago Press.

———. 1941. "The Negro Vote in Northern Cities." *National Municipal Review* 30:264–267, 268.

———. 1968. *Machine Politics: Chicago Model.* Chicago: University of Chicago Press.

Granberg, Donald E. 1981. "The Abortion Activists." *Family Planning Perspectives* 14:157–163.

Gratton, Brian. 1986. *Urban Elders: Family, Work, and Welfare Among Boston's Aged, 1890–1950.* Philadelphia: Temple University Press.

Greeley, Andrew M., and Mary G. Durkin. 1984. *Angry Catholic Women.* Chicago: Thomas More Press.

Green, Donald P. 1988. "Self-Interest, Public Opinion, and Mass Political Behavior." Unpublished doctoral dissertation, University of California, Berkeley.

Green, Elizabeth. 1925. "I Resign from Female Politics," *New Republic* 42:234–235.

Greenbaum, Susan. 1986. *Afro-Cubans in Ybor City: A Centennial History.* Tampa: Tampa Printing.

Griffin, Susan. 1981. *Pornography and Silence: Culture's Revenge Against Nature.* New York: Harper & Row.

Griffith, Elisabeth. 1984. *In Her Own Right: The Life of Elizabeth Cady Stanton.* New York: Oxford University Press.

Grismer, Karl. 1950. *Tampa: A History of the City of Tampa.* D.B. McKay, ed. *St. Petersburg Times.*

Grubbs, Donald H. 1971. *Cry from the Cotton: The Southern Tenant Farmers' Union and the New Deal.* Chapel Hill: University of North Carolina Press.

Gruberg, Martin. 1968. *Women in American Politics: An Assessment and Sourcebook.* Oshkosh, WI: Academia Press.

Gullett, Gayle. 1984. "City Mothers, City Daughters, and the Dance Hall Girls: The Limits of Female Political Power in San Francisco, 1913." In Barbara J. Harris and JoAnn K. McNamara, eds., *Women and the Structure of Society.* Durham, NC: Duke University Press.

Gurin, Patricia. 1985. "Women's Gender Consciousness." *Public Opinion Quarterly* 49:143–163.

Hagner, Paul R.; Kathleen Knight; and Carolyn V. Lewis. 1986. "Not Ready for a Woman?: Assessing Citizen Perceptions of Geraldine Ferraro." Paper presented at the Midwest Political Science Association meeting, Chicago.

Halbert, Leroy Allen. 1915. "The Widows' Allowance Act in Kansas City." In Edna Bullock, ed., *Selected Articles on Mothers' Pensions.* White Plains and New York: Wilson.

Hall, Jacquelyn Dowd. 1979. *Revolt Against Chivalry: Jessie Daniel Ames and the Women's Campaign Against Lynching.* New York: Columbia University Press.

———; Robert Korstad; and James Leloudis. 1986. "Cotton Mill People: Work, Community, and Protest in the Textile South, 1880–1940." *American Historical Review* 91:245–286.

Hamilton, Tullia Kay Brown. 1978. "The National Association of Colored Women." Unpublished doctoral dissertation, Emory University.

Hammond, John L. 1979. *The Politics of Benevolence: Revival Religion and American Voting Behavior.* New York: Ablex.

Handlin, Oscar, and Mary Handlin. 1961. *The Dimensions of Liberty.* Cambridge, MA: Harvard University Press.

Harbaugh, William M. 1963. "The Republican Party, 1893–1932." In Arthur M. Schlesinger, Jr., ed., *History of U.S. Political Parties,* vol. 3. New York: Chelsea House.

Hard, William. 1915. "Financing Motherhood." In Edna Bullock, ed., *Selected Articles on Mothers' Pensions.* White Plains and New York: Wilson.

Hardin, Russell. 1982. *Collective Action.* Baltimore: Johns Hopkins University Press.

Harding, Vincent. 1981. *There Is a River: The Black Struggle for Freedom in America*. New York: Harcourt Brace Jovanovich.

Harlan, Louis. 1958. *Separate and Unequal: Public School Campaigns and Racism in the Southern Seaboard States, 1901–1915*. Chapel Hill: University of North Carolina Press.

Harley, Sharon, and Rosalyn Terborg-Penn. 1978. *The Afro-American Woman: Struggles and Images*. Port Washington, NY: Kennikat Press.

Harper, Samuel A. 1920. *The Law of Workmen's Compensation*, 2nd ed. Chicago: Callaghan.

Harrison, Cynthia Ellen. 1982. "Prelude to Feminism: Women's Organizations, the Federal Government, and the Rise of the Women's Movement, 1942–1968." Unpublished doctoral dissertation, Columbia University.

———. 1988. *On Account of Sex: The Politics of Women's Issues, 1945–1968*. Berkeley: University of California Press.

Hartmann, Heidi. 1976. "Capitalism, Patriarchy, and Job Segregation by Sex." In Martha Blaxall and Barbara Reagan, eds., *Women and the Work-Place: The Implications of Occupational Segregation*. Chicago: University of Chicago Press.

———. 1981. "The Family as the Locus of Gender, Class and Political Struggle: The Example of Housework." *Signs: Journal of Women in Culture and Society* 6:366–394.

Hauss, Charles S., and L. Sandy Maisel. 1986. "Extremist Delegates: Myth and Reality." In Ronald B. Rapoport, Alan I. Abramowitz, and John McGlennon, eds., *The Life of the Parties*. Lexington: University of Kentucky Press.

Hawley, Ellis. 1979. *The Great War and the Search for a Modern Order*. New York: St. Martin's Press.

———, ed. 1981. *Herbert Hoover as Secretary of Commerce: Studies in New Era Thought*. Iowa City: University of Iowa Press.

Hayes, Michael T. 1981. *Lobbyists and Legislators*. New Brunswick, NJ: Rutgers University Press.

Haynes, John. 1984. *Dubious Alliance: The Making of Minnesota's DFL Party*. Minneapolis: University of Minnesota Press.

Hays, Samuel P. 1964. "The Politics of Reform in Municipal Government in the Progressive Era." *Pacific Northwest Quarterly* 55:157–169.

———. 1975. "Political Parties and the Community-Society Continuum." In William Nesbitt Chambers and Walter Dean Burnham, eds., *The American Party Systems: Stages of Development*, 2nd ed. New York: Oxford University Press.

Heilbroner, Robert L., in collaboration with Aaron Singer. 1977. *The Economic Transformation of America*. New York: Harcourt Brace Jovanovich.

Held, David; James Anderson; Bram Gieben; Stuart Hall; Laurence Harris; Paul Lewis; Noel Parker; and Ben Turok, eds. 1983. *States and Society*. New York: New York University Press.

Heller, Rita R. 1981. "The Bryn Mawr Workers' Summer School, 1921–1922: A Surprising Alliance." *History of Higher Education* (annual), 110–131.

———. 1986. "The Women of Summer: The Bryn Mawr Summer School for Women Workers, 1921–1934." Unpublished doctoral dissertation, Rutgers University.

Henri, Florette. 1975. *Black Migration*. Garden City, NY: Anchor Press.

Heresies. 1981. Special Edition—Sex Issues, 3 (4). Brooklyn: Faculty Press.

Hero, Alfred O., Jr. 1966. "The American Public and the U.N., 1954–1966." *Journal of Conflict Resolution* 10:436–475.

Herring, Neill, and Sue Thrasher. 1980. "UAW Sit-down Strike: Atlanta, 1936." In Marc S. Miller, ed., *Working Lives: The Southern Exposure History of Labor in the South*. New York: Pantheon Books.

Herring, Pendleton. 1929. *Group Representation Before Congress*. Baltimore: Johns Hopkins University Press.

Hewitt, Nancy A. 1984. *Women's Activism and Social Change: Rochester, New York, 1822–1872*. Ithaca: Cornell University Press.

———. 1986. "Feminist Friends: Agrarian Quakers and the Emergence of Woman's Rights in America." *Feminist Studies* 12:27–49.

Hewlett, Sylvia Ann. 1986. *A Lesser Life*. New York: Warner Books.

Himmelstein, Jerome L. 1983. "The New Right." In Robert C. Liebman and Robert Wuthnow, eds., *The New Christian Right*. New York: Aldine.

———, and James A. McRae, Jr. 1984. "Social Conservatism, New Republicans, and the 1980 Election." *Public Opinion Quarterly* 48:592–605.

Hoffman, Eric. 1985. "Feminism, Pornography and the Law." *University of Pennsylvania Law Review* 133:497–534.

Hofstadter, Richard. 1952. *The Paranoid Style in American Politics*. Chicago: University of Chicago Press.

Hole, Judith, and Ellen Levine. 1971. *Rebirth of Feminism*. New York: Quadrangle Books.

Howard, Donald S. 1943. *The Works Progress Administration and Federal Relief Policy*. New York: Russell Sage Foundation.

Howe, Frederic C., and Marie Jenney Howe. 1915. "Pensioning the Widow and the Fatherless." In Edna D. Bullock, ed., *Selected Articles on Mothers' Pension*. White Plains and New York: Wilson.

Huckshorn, Robert J., and John F. Bibby. 1983. "National Party Rules and Delegate Selection in the Republican Party." *Political Science* 16:656–666.

Huddy, Leonie, and David O. Sears. 1986. "Social Identities and Political Disunity Among Women." Paper presented at the Western Psychological Association meeting, Seattle.

Hunter, Allen. 1981. "In the Wings: New Right Ideology and Organization." *Radical America* 15:112–128.

Hunter, Nan D., and Sylvia A. Law. 1985. Brief: Amici Curiae of Feminist Anti-Censorship Task Force, in the U.S. Court of Appeals, 7th Cir., no. 84-3147, April 8.

Hyman, Paula E. 1980. "Immigrant Women and Consumer Protest: The New York City Kosher Meat Boycott of 1902." *American Jewish History* 70:91–105.

Igra, Anna R. 1986. "Motherhood, Culture, and Class in the New York City Jewish Women's Consumer Protests of 1917." Unpublished master's thesis, Sarah Lawrence College.

Ingalls, Robert P. 1987. "Lynching and Establishment Violence in Tampa, Florida, 1858–1935." *Journal of Southern History* 53:613–644.

Irwin, Inez Haynes. 1921. *The Story of the Woman's Party*. New York: Harcourt.

————. 1934. *Angels and Amazons*. Garden City, NY: Doubleday.

Jablonsky, Thomas J. 1978. "Duty, Nature and Stability: The Female Anti-Suffragists in the United States, 1894–1920." Unpublished doctoral dissertation, University of California at Los Angeles.

Jackson, John S., III. 1975. "Some Correlates of Minority Representation in the National Conventions, 1964–1972." *American Politics Quarterly* 3:171–188.

Jacoby, Robin Miller. 1975. "The Women's Trade Union League and American Feminism." *Feminist Studies* 3:126–140.

Jaggar, Allison M. 1983. *Feminist Politics and Human Nature*. Totowa, NJ: Rowman & Allenheld.

Jahr, Cliff. 1980. "Anita Bryant's Startling Reversal." *Ladies' Home Journal* 97:68.

Janeway, Elizabeth. 1980. "Who Is Sylvia? On the Loss of Several Paradigms." *Signs: Journal of Women in Culture and Society* 4:573–589.

Janiewski, Dolores E. 1983. "Sisters Under Their Skins: Southern Working Women, 1880–1950." In Joanne V. Hawks and Sheila Skemp, eds., *Sex, Race and the Rôle of Women in the South*. Jackson: University Press of Mississippi.

————. 1985. *Sisterhood Denied: Race, Gender, and Class in a New South Community*. Philadelphia: Temple University Press.

Jennergren, L. Peter. 1981. "Decentralization in Organizations." In Paul C. Nystrom and William H. Starbuck, eds., *Handbook of Organizational Design*, vol. 2. New York: Oxford University Press.

Jennings, M. Kent, and Barbara G. Farah. 1980. "Ideology, Gender, and Political Action: A Cross National Survey." *British Journal of Political Science* 10, no. 2.

————. 1981. "Social Roles and Political Resources: An over-Time Study of Men and Women in Party Elites." *American Journal of Political Science* 25:462–482.

Jennings, M. Kent, and Greg B. Markus. 1984. "Partisan Orientations over the Long Haul: Results from the Three-Wave Political Socialization Panel Study." *American Political Science Review* 78:1000–1018.

Jennings, M. Kent, and Richard G. Niemi. 1981. *Generations and Politics*. Princeton, NJ: Princeton University Press.

Jennings, M. Kent, and Norman Thomas. 1968. "Men and Women in Party Elites." *Midwest Journal of Political Science* 7:469–492.

Jensen, Joan M. 1981a. "The Evolution of Margaret Sanger's *Family Limitation* Pamphlet, 1914–1921." *Signs: Journal of Women in Culture and Society* 6:548–567.

————. 1981b. *With These Hands: Women Working on the Land*. Old Westbury, NY: Feminist Press.

————. 1983. "All Pink Sisters: The War Department and the Feminist Movement in the 1920s." In Lois Scharf and Joan Jensen, eds., *Decades of Discontent*. Westport, CT: Greenwood.

Jensen, Richard J. 1971. *The Winning of the Midwest: Social and Political Conflict, 1888–1896*. Chicago: University of Chicago Press.

Johnson, Charles S.; Edwin R. Embree; and W. W. Alexander. 1935. *The Collapse of Cotton Tenancy: Summary of Field Studies and Statistical Surveys, 1933–35*. Chapel Hill: University of North Carolina Press.

————. 1943. *To Stem This Tide: A Survey of Racial Tension Areas in the United States*. Boston: Pilgrim Press.

Johnson, Donald Bruce, comp. 1978. *National Party Platforms.* 2 vols. Urbana: University of Illinois Press.

Johnson, Dorothy. 1972. "Organized Women as Lobbyists in the 1920s." *Capitol Studies* 1:41–58.

Jones, Jacqueline. 1985. *Labor of Love, Labor of Sorrow: Black Women, Work, and the Family from Slavery to the Present.* New York: Basic Books.

———. 1986. "Perspectives on the Work of Black and Poor White Women in the Rural South, 1865–1940." Paper presented at the University of California, Irvine, Conference on Social History and Theory.

Kaledin, Eugenia. 1984. *Mothers and More: American Women in the 1950s.* Boston: Twayne.

Kalven, Harry, Jr. 1960. "The Metaphysics of the Law of Obscenity." *Supreme Court Review* 1:1–45.

Kanter, Rosabeth Moss. 1977. *Men and Women of the Corporation.* New York: Basic Books.

Kaplan, Temma. 1982. "Female Consciousness and Collective Action: The Case of Barcelona, 1910–1918." *Signs: Journal of Women in Culture and Society* 7:545–566.

Kaplan, Thomas J. 1986. "The Narrative Structure of Policy Analysis." *Journal of Policy Analysis and Management* 5:761–778.

Katz, Michael B. 1983. *Poverty and Policy in American History.* New York: Academic Press.

Katzenstein, Mary Fainsod. 1987. "Comparing the Feminist Movements of the United States and Western Europe: An Overview." In Mary Fainsod Katzenstein and Carol McClurg Mueller, eds., *The Women's Movements of the United States and Western Europe.* Philadelphia: Temple University Press.

Katzman, David M. 1978. *Seven Days a Week: Women and Domestic Service in Industrializing America.* New York: Oxford University Press.

Katznelson, Ira. 1976. *Black Men, White Cities.* Chicago: University of Chicago Press.

———. 1985. "Working Class Formation and the State: Nineteenth Century England in American Perspective." In Peter Evans, Theda Skocpol, and Dietrich Rueschemeyer, eds., *Bringing the State Back In.* New York: Cambridge University Press.

Keenleyside, Hugh L. 1925. "The American Political Revolution of 1924." *Current History* 21:833–840.

Kellor, Frances. 1923. "Women in British and American Politics." *Current History* 17:831–835.

Kelly, Joan. 1984. "The Doubled Vision of Feminist Theory." In *The Essays of Joan Kelly: Women, History, and Theory.* Chicago: University of Chicago Press.

Kelly, Rita Mae, and Jayne Burgess. 1986. "Using Subjective Group Analysis to Assess Subjective Political Culture and Party Ideology." Paper presented at the Western Political Science Association meeting, Eugene, Oregon.

Kelman, Steven. 1984. "Party Strength and System Governability in the Face of New Demands: The Case of Feminism." Unpublished paper, John F. Kennedy School of Government, Harvard University.

Kemp, Kathryn W. 1983. "Jean and Kate Gordon: New Orleans Social Reformers, 1893–1933." *Louisiana History* 24:389–401.

Kendrick, Walter. 1985. "Exorcising Pornography." *Boston Review*, November 9–10.

———. 1987. *The Secret Museum: Pornography in Modern Culture*. New York: Viking.

Kennedy, David M. 1970. *Birth Control in America: The Career of Margaret Sanger*. New Haven: Yale University Press.

Kent, Frank. 1928. *Political Behavior*. New York: Morrow.

Keohane, Nannerl O. 1981. "Speaking from Silence: Women and the Science of Politics." In Elizabeth Langland and Walter Gove, eds., *A Feminist Perspective in the Academy: The Difference It Makes*. Chicago: University of Chicago Press.

Kessler-Harris, Alice. 1975a. "Stratifying by Sex: Understanding the History of Working Women." In Richard D. Edwards, Michael Reich, and David M. Gordon, eds., *Labor Market Segmentation*. Lexington, MA: Heath.

———. 1975b. "'Where Are the Organized Women Workers?'" *Feminist Studies* 3:92–110.

———. 1982. *Out to Work: A History of Wage-Earning Women in the United States*. New York: Oxford University Press.

———. 1985a. "The Debate over Equality for Women in the Work Place: Recognizing Differences." In Laurie Larwood, Ann H. Stromberg, and Barbara A. Gutek, eds., *Women and Work: An Annual Review*. Beverly Hills, CA: Sage.

———. 1985b. "Problems of Coalition-Building: Women and Trade Unions in the 1920s." In Ruth Milkman, ed., *Women, Work and Protest: A Century of U.S. Women's Labor History*. Boston: Routledge & Kegan Paul.

Kett, Joseph F. 1985. "Women and the Progressive Impulse in Southern Education." In Walter J. Fraser et al., *The Web of Southern Social Relations: Women, Family, and Education*. Athens: University of Georgia Press.

Key, V. O. 1949. *Southern Politics in State and Nation*. New York: Vintage Books.

———. 1956. *American State Politics: An Introduction*. New York: Knopf.

Keyssar, Alexander. 1986. *Out of Work: The First Century of Unemployment in Massachusetts*. New York and Cambridge: Cambridge University Press.

Kilpatrick, Franklin P.; Milton C. Cummings, Jr.; and M. Kent Jennings. 1964. *The Image of the Federal Service*. Washington, DC: Brookings Institution.

Kilson, Martin. 1971. "Political Change in the Negro Ghetto, 1900–1940." In Nathan Huggins, Martin Kilson, and Daniel M. Fox, eds., *Key Issues in the Afro-American Experience*. New York: Harcourt Brace Jovanovich.

Kinder, Donald R., and D. Roderick Kiewit. 1979. "Economic Discontent and Political Behavior: The Role of Personal Grievances and Collective Economic Judgments in Congressional Voting." *American Journal of Political Science* 23:495–527.

Kinder, Donald R.; Stephen J. Rosenstone; and John M. Hansen. 1983. "Group Economic Well-Being and Political Choice." Unpublished manuscript, Institute for Social Research, University of Michigan.

Kirby, Jack Temple. 1984. "Black and White in the Rural South, 1915–1954." *Agricultural History* 58:411–422.

Kirkpatrick, Jeane J. 1974. *Political Woman*. New York: Basic Books.

———. 1976. *The New Presidential Elite*. New York: Russell Sage Foundation.

Klatch, Rebecca E. 1988. "The Methodological Problems of Studying a Politically Sensitive Community." In Robert G. Burgess, ed., *Studies in Qualitative Methodology*, vol. 1. Greenwich, CT: JAI Press.

Klein, Ethel. 1984. *Gender Politics: From Consciousness to Mass Politics*. Cambridge, MA: Harvard University Press.

Kleppner, Paul. 1970. *The Cross of Culture: A Social Analysis of Midwestern Politics, 1850–1900*, 2nd ed. New York: Free Press.

———. 1982. "Were Women to Blame? Female Suffrage and Voter Turnout." *Journal of Interdisciplinary History* 12:621–643.

Knoke, David. 1981. "Commitment and Detachment in Voluntary Associations." *American Sociological Review* 46:141–158.

———. 1982. "Political Mobilization by Voluntary Associations." *Journal of Political and Military Sociology* 10:171–182.

———. 1986. "Associations and Interest Groups." *Annual Review of Sociology* 12:1–21.

———. 1987. "Resource Acquisition and Allocation in U.S. National Associations." In Bert Klandermans, ed., *Organizing for Change: Social Movement Organization Across Cultures*. Greenwich, CT: JAI Press.

———. 1988. "Incentives in Collective Action Organizations." *American Sociological Review* 53:311–329.

———, and Richard E. Adams. 1987. "The Incentive Systems of Associations." *Research in the Sociology of Organizations* 5:285–309.

Knoke, David, and David Prensky. 1984. "What Relevance Do Organization Theories Have for Voluntary Associations?" *Social Science Quarterly* 65:3–20.

Knoke, David, and James R. Wood. 1981. *Organized for Action: Commitment in Voluntary Associations*. New Brunswick, NJ: Rutgers University Press.

Knoke, David, and Christine Wright-Isak. 1982. "Individual Motives and Organizational Incentive Systems." *Research in the Sociology of Organizations* 1:209–254.

Koch, Raymond L. 1967. "The Development of Public Welfare Relief Programs in Minnesota, 1929–1941." Unpublished doctoral dissertation, University of Minnesota.

———. 1968. "Politics and Relief in Minneapolis During the 1930s." *Minnesota History* 41:153–170.

Kochan, Thomas A. 1979. "How American Workers View Labor Unions." *Monthly Labor Review* 102:22–31.

Kocol, Cleo; Lester Kirkendall; Annie Laurie Gaylor; Sol Gordon; and Gina Allen. 1985. "Pornography: A Humanist Issue." *Humanist* 45:23–31, 44.

Koedt, Anne; Ellen Levine; and Anita Rapone, eds. 1973. *Radical Feminism*. New York: Quadrangle, New York Times Books.

Komarovsky, Mirra. 1962. *Blue Collar Marriage*. New York: Vintage.

Korstad, Bob. 1980. "Those Who Were Not Afraid: Winston-Salem, 1943." In Marc S. Miller, ed., *Working Lives: The Southern Exposure History of Labor in the South*. New York: Bantam Books.

Kousser, J. Morgan. 1974. *The Shaping of Southern Politics: Suffrage Restriction and the Establishment of the One-Party South, 1880–1910.* New Haven: Yale University Press.

————. 1980. "Progressivism—For Middle-Class Whites Only: North Carolina Education, 1880–1910." *Journal of Southern History* 46:189–194.

Kraditor, Aileen S. 1965. *The Ideas of the Woman Suffrage Movement, 1890–1920.* New York: Columbia University Press.

————. 1966. "Tactical Problems of the Woman-Suffrage Movement in the South." *Louisiana Studies* 5:289–307.

————. 1971. *The Ideas of the Woman Suffrage Movement, 1890–1920.* Garden City, NY: Anchor/Doubleday.

————. 1981. *The Ideas of the Woman Suffrage Movement, 1890–1920.* New York: Norton.

Krasner, Stephen D. 1984. "Approaches to the State: Alternative Conceptions and Historical Dynamics." *Comparative Politics* 16:223–246.

Kremer, Gary B., and Linda Rea Gibbens. 1983. "The Missouri Home for Negro Girls: The 1930s." *American Studies* 24:77–93.

Kyvig, David. 1976. "Women Against Prohibition." *American Quarterly* 28:465–482.

————. 1979. *Repealing National Prohibition.* Chicago: University of Chicago Press.

Ladd-Taylor, Molly. 1985. "Women Workers and the Yale Strike." *Feminist Studies* 11:465–489.

La Follette, Suzanne. 1926. *Concerning Women.* New York: Boni.

Lane, R.E. 1979. *Political Life.* Glencoe, IL.: Free Press.

Lapham, Lewis H.; Al Goldstein; Midge Decter; Erica Jong; Susan Brownmiller; Jean B. Elshtain; and Aryeh Neier. 1984. "Harper's Forum: The Place of Pornography." *Harper's,* November, 31–39, 42–45.

Lasswell, Harold D. 1948. *Power and Personality.* New York: Norton.

Latham, Earl. 1952. *The Group Basis of Politics.* Ithaca, NY: Cornell University Press.

Laumann, Edward O., and David Knoke. 1987. *The Organizational State.* Madison: University of Wisconsin Press.

Leach, William. 1980. *True Love and Perfect Union: The Feminist Reform of Sex and Society.* New York: Basic Books.

League of Women Voters of the United States. 1956–1958. *Reports I, II, III, IV, V.* Ann Arbor: Survey Research Center, Institute for Social Research, University of Michigan.

————. 1960. *Forty Years of a Great Idea.* Washington, DC: League of Women Voters.

Lebsock, Suzanne. 1984. *The Free Women of Petersburg: Status and Culture in a Southern Town, 1784–1860.* New York: Norton.

————. 1984b. *"A Share of Honour": Virginia Women, 1600–1945.* Richmond: Virginia Women's Cultural History Project.

————. 1985. "Woman Suffrage and White Supremacy: A Virginia Case Study." Paper presented at the Woodrow Wilson International Center for Scholars, Washington, July 18.

Lederer, Laura, ed. 1980. *Take Back the Night.* New York: Morrow.

Lee, Marcia Manning. 1976. "Toward Understanding Why Few Women Hold Public Office." *Political Science Quarterly* 91:297–314.

Leff, Mark H. 1973. "Consensus for Reform: The Mothers'-Pension Movement in the Progressive Era." *Social Service Review* 47:397–429.

Lehmbruch, Gerhard, and Philippe C. Schmitter, eds. 1982. *Patterns of Corporatist Policymaking.* Beverly Hills, CA: Sage.

Leloudis, James L., II. 1983. "School Reform in the New South: The Woman's Association for the Betterment of Public School Houses in North Carolina, 1902–1919." *Journal of American History* 69:886–909.

Lemley, Brad. 1985. "Eleanor Smeal, Giving 'Em Hell." *Washington Post Weekly Edition,* December 9:6–8.

Lemons, J. Stanley. 1973. *The Woman Citizen: Social Feminism in the 1920s.* Urbana: University of Illinois Press.

Lerner, Gerda, ed. 1972. *Black Women in White America: A Documentary History.* New York: Vintage Books.

———. 1977. *The Female Experience: An American Documentary.* Indianapolis: Bobbs-Merrill.

———. 1979. *The Majority Finds Its Past: Placing Women in History.* New York: Oxford University Press.

Lester, Richard A. 1958. *As Unions Mature.* Princeton, NJ: Princeton University Press.

Le Sueur, Meridel. 1955. *Crusaders.* New York: Blue Heron Press.

Levine, Susan. 1983. "Labor's True Woman: Domesticity and Equal Rights in the Knights of Labor." *Journal of American History* 70:323–339.

———. 1984. *Labor's True Woman: Carpet Weavers, Industrialization, and Labor Reform in the Gilded Age.* Philadelphia: Temple University Press.

Lewinson, Paul. 1932. *Race, Class, and Party: A History of Negro Suffrage and White Politics in the South.* New York: Oxford University Press.

Likert, Jane. 1958. *Leadership for Effective Leagues.* Washington, DC: League of Women Voters.

Likert, Rensis. 1960. "Voluntary Organizations." Typescript draft, League of Women Voters papers, Library of Congress.

Link, Arthur S. 1959. "What Happened to the Progressive Movement in the 1920s." *American Historical Review* 64:833–851.

———, and Richard L. McCormick. 1983. *Progressivism.* Arlington Heights, IL: Harlan Davidson.

Linz, Daniel; Steven Penrod; and Edward Donnerstein. 1986. "Issues Bearing on the Legal Regulation of Violent and Sexually Violent Media." *Journal of Social Issues* 42:171–193.

Lipset, Seymour Martin. 1960. *Political Man: The Social Bases of Politics.* Garden City, NY: Doubleday.

———. 1964. "The Sources of the Radical Right." In Daniel Bell, ed., *The Radical Right.* Garden City, NY: Anchor Books.

———, and Earl Raab. 1970. *The Politics of Unreason: Right-Wing Extremism in America, 1790–1970.* New York: Harper & Row.

———. 1982. "The Election and the Evangelicals." In Herbert F. Vetter, ed., *Speakout Against the New Right*. Boston: Beacon Press.

Lipsky, Michael. 1970. *Protest in City Politics*. Chicago: Rand McNally.

———. 1980. *Street-Level Bureaucracy*. New York: Russell Sage Foundation.

Logan, Edward B. 1929. "Lobbying." *Annals of the American Academy of Political Science* 144 (supplement):32–33.

Long, Durward. 1965. "La Résistencia: Tampa's Immigrant Labor Union." *Labor History* 6:193–213.

Longino, Helen E. 1980. "Pornography, Oppression and Freedom: A Closer Look." In Laura Lederer, ed., *Take Back the Night*. New York: Morrow.

Lowi, Theodore. 1969. *The End of Liberalism*. New York: Norton.

Lowry, Tom. 1980. "Little David Blues." In Marc S. Miller, ed., *Working Lives: The Southern Exposure History of Labor in the South*. New York: Pantheon Books.

Lubbell, Samuel. 1951. *The Future of American Politics*. New York: Harper.

Lubove, Roy. 1965. *The Professional Altruist: The Emergence of Social Work as a Career, 1880–1930*. Cambridge, MA: Harvard University Press.

———. 1968. *The Struggle for Social Security, 1900–1935*. Cambridge, MA: Harvard University Press.

Luepnitz, Deborah A. 1982. *Child Custody*. Lexington, MA: Lexington Books.

Luker, Kristin. 1984. *Abortion and the Politics of Motherhood*. Berkeley and Los Angeles: University of California Press.

Lunardini, Christine A. 1986. *From Equal Suffrage to Equal Rights: Alice Paul and the National Woman's Party, 1913–1928*. New York: New York University Press.

Lutz, Alma. 1974. *Created Equal: A Biography of Elizabeth Cady Stanton*. New York: Octagon Books.

Lynn, Naomi B. 1984. "Women and Politics: The Real Majority." In Jo Freeman, ed., *Women: A Feminist Perspective*, 3rd ed. Palo Alto, CA: Mayfield.

Maag, Marilyn J. 1985. "The Indianapolis Pornography Ordinance: Does the Right to Free Speech Outweigh Pornography's Harm to Women?" *University of Cincinnati Law Review* 54:249–271.

McAdam, Doug. 1982. *Political Process and the Development of Black Insurgency, 1930–1970*. Chicago: University of Chicago Press.

McCarthy, Kathleen D. 1982. *Noblesse Oblige: Charity and Cultural Philanthropy in Chicago, 1849–1929*. Chicago: University of Chicago Press.

McClosky, Herbert, and Alida Brill. 1983. *Dimensions of Tolerance*. New York: Russell Sage Foundation.

McClosky, Herbert; Paul J. Hoffman; and Rosemary O'Hara. 1960. "Issue Conflict and Consensus Among Party Leaders and Followers." *American Political Science Review* 54:406–427.

McConnell, Grant. 1966. *Private Power and American Democracy*. New York: Knopf.

McCormick, Anne O'Hare. 1928. "Enter Women, the New Boss of Politics." *New York Times Magazine*, October 21:3, 22.

McCormick, Richard L. 1979. "The Party Period and Public Policy: An Exploratory Hypothesis." *Journal of American History* 66:279–298.

————. 1981. *From Realignment to Reform: Political Change in New York State, 1893–1910.* Ithaca: Cornell University Press.

McDonagh, Eileen, and H. Douglas Price. 1985. "Woman Suffrage in the Progressive Era: Patterns of Opposition and Support in Referendum Voting, 1910–1918." *American Political Science Review* 79:415–435.

McDonald, Forest, and Grady McWhiney. 1980. "The South from Self-Sufficiency to Peonage: An Overview." *American Historical Review* 85:1095–1118.

McDowell, John Patrick, III. 1979. "A Social Gospel in the South: The Woman's Home Mission Movement in the Methodist Episcopal Church, South, 1886–1939." Unpublished doctoral dissertation, Duke University.

————. 1982. *The Social Gospel in the South: The Woman's House Mission Movement in the Methodist Episcopal Church, South, 1886–1939.* Baton Rouge: Louisiana State University Press.

McFarland, Andrew. 1984. *Common Cause: Lobbying in the Public Interest.* Chatham, NJ: Chatham House.

McGerr, Michael E. 1986. *The Decline of Popular Politics: The American North, 1865–1928.* New York: Oxford University Press.

McGlen, Nancy E., and Karen O'Connor. 1983. *Women's Rights: The Struggle for Equality in the Nineteenth and Twentieth Centuries.* New York: Praeger.

McGraw, Onalee. 1980. *The Family, Feminism and the Therapeutic State.* Washington, DC: Heritage Foundation.

McIntosh, Mary. 1978. "The State and the Oppression of Women." In Annette Kuhn and AnnMarie Wolpe, eds., *Feminism and Materialism.* London: Routledge & Kegan Paul.

MacKinnon, Catharine A. 1982. "Feminism, Marxism, Method and the State: An Agenda for Theory." *Signs: Journal of Women in Culture and Society* 7:515–544.

————. 1983. "Feminism, Marxism, Method and the State: Toward Feminist Jurisprudence." *Signs: Journal of Women in Culture and Society* 8:635–658.

————. 1985. "Pornography, Civil Rights and Speech." *Harvard Civil Rights Civil Liberties Law Review* 20:1–70.

————. 1986. "Pornography: Not a Moral Issue." *Women's Studies International Forum* 9:63–78.

McLaurin, Melton Alonzo. 1971. *Paternalism and Protest: Southern Cotton Mill Workers and Organized Labor, 1875–1905.* Westport, CT: Greenwood Press.

Magdol, Edward. 1977. *A Right to the Land: Essays on the Freedman's Community.* Westport, CT: Greenwood Press.

Mahoney, Joseph F. 1969. "Woman Suffrage and the Urban Masses." *New Jersey History* 87:151–172.

Malamuth, Neil M., and James V. P. Check. 1985. "The Effects of Aggression Pornography on Beliefs in Rape Myth: Individual Differences." *Journal of Research in Personality* 19:299–320.

Malamuth, Neil M., and Edward Donnerstein, eds. 1984. *Pornography and Sexual Aggression.* New York: Academic Press.

Mandel, Ruth B. 1981. *In the Running: The New Woman Candidate.* Boston: Beacon Press.

Mansbridge, Jane J. 1980. *Beyond Adversarial Democracy*. New York: Basic Books.
———. 1985. "Myth and Reality: The ERA and the Gender Gap in the 1980 Election." *Public Opinion Quarterly* 49:164–178.
———. 1986. *Why We Lost the ERA*. Chicago: University of Chicago Press.
Marcus, Robert D. 1971. *Grand Old Party*. New York: Oxford University Press.
Marcus, Steven. 1964. *The Other Victorians: A Study of Sexuality and Pornography in Mid-Nineteenth Century England*. New York: Basic Books.
Marmon, Sharon, and Howard A. Palley. 1986. "The Decade After Roe v. Wade: Ideology, Political Cleavage, and the Policy Process." In Gwen Moore and Glenna Spitze, eds., *Research in Politics and Society: A Research Annual*. Greenwich, CT: JAI Press.
Marshall, Susan. 1984. "In Defense of Separate Spheres: Class and Status Politics in the Anti-Suffrage Movement." Paper presented at the American Sociological Association meeting, San Antonio, August.
Marshino, Ora, and Lawrence J. O'Malley. 1937. "Wage and Hour Legislation in the Courts." *George Washington Law Review* 5:865–878.
Marshner, Connie. 1982a. "Conservatives Speak Out." *Conservative Digest* 8:18.
———. 1982b. "Who Is the New Traditional Woman?" Paper presented at Family Forum II, Washington, July 29.
Martin, Anne. 1922. "Woman's Vote and Woman's Chains." *Sunset* 14:12–14.
———. 1925. "Feminists and Future Political Action." *Nation* 115:185–186.
Marwell, Gerald, and Ruth E. Ames. 1979. "Experiments on the Provision of Public Goods. I. Resources, Interest, Group Size, and the Free Rider Problem." *American Journal of Sociology* 84:1335–360.
Marx, Karl. 1978. "The Poverty of Philosophy." In Robert C. Tucker, ed., *The Marx-Engels Reader*, 2nd ed. New York: Norton.
Mayer, George H. 1951. *The Political Career of Floyd B. Olson*. Minneapolis: University of Minnesota Press.
Meister, Albert. 1984. *Participation, Associations, Development, and Change*. New Brunswick: Transaction Books.
Merriam, Charles Edward, and Harold Foote Gosnell. 1924. *Non-Voting: Causes and Methods of Control*. Chicago: University of Chicago Press.
Merton, Andrew H. 1981. *Enemies of Choice: The Right-to-Life Movement and Its Threat to Abortion*. Boston: Beacon Press.
Michels, Robert. 1949 [1915]. *Political Parties: A Sociological Study of the Oligarchical Tendencies of Modern Democracy*. Glencoe, IL: Free Press.
Milbrath, Lester. 1959. *The Washington Lobbyists*. Chicago: Rand McNally.
Milkman, Ruth. 1987. *Gender at Work: The Dynamics of Job Segregation by Sex during World War II*. Urbana: University of Illinois Press.
Miller, Kelly. 1980. "The City Negro: Industrial Status." In Philip S. Foner and Ronald L. Lewis, eds., *The Black Worker from 1900–1919*. The Black Worker: A Documentary History from Colonial Times to the Present, vol. 5. Philadelphia: Temple University Press.
Miller, Stephen, and David O. Sears. 1986. "Stability and Change in Social Tolerance: A Test of the Persistence Hypothesis." *American Journal of Political Science* 30:214–236.
Miller, Warren E., and M. Kent Jennings. 1986. *Parties in Transition: A Lon-

gitudinal Study of Party Elites and Party Supporters. New York: Russell Sage Foundation.

Minnesota Emergency Relief Administration. 1935a. *Analysis and Report on Old Age Pension and Mothers' Allowance by Counties.* St. Paul: State of Minnesota.

————. 1935b. *Women's Work in Minnesota Under the Civil Works Administration and the Emergency Relief Administration.* St. Paul: State of Minnesota.

Minnesota Minimum Wage Commission. 1922. *Second Biennial Report.* St. Paul: State of Minnesota.

Minnesota State Council of Social Work. 1935. *A Study of Mothers' Pensions in Minnesota.* St. Paul: State of Minnesota.

Minnesota State Legislature. 1929–1941. *House and Senate Journals.* St. Paul: State of Minnesota.

Mitchell, Harry Leland. 1979. *Mean Things Happening in the Land: The Life and Times of H. L. Mitchell, Co-Founder of the Southern Tenant Farmers Union.* Montclair, NJ: Allanheld, Osmun.

Mitchell, Margaret. 1985. "The Effects of Unemployment on the Social Condition of Women and Children in the 1930s." *History Workshop* 19:105–127.

"The Modern Woman: How Far Has She Come?" 1979. *Public Opinion,* January-February,35–39.

Moe, Terry M. 1980. *The Organization of Interests.* Chicago: University of Chicago Press.

Morantz-Sanchez, Regina Markell. 1985. *Sympathy and Science: Women Physicians in American Medicine.* New York: Oxford University Press.

Morgan, Edmund S. 1975. *American Slavery, American Freedom: The Ordeal of Colonial Virginia.* New York: Norton.

Morgan, Robin, ed. 1970. "SCUM Manifesto." In *Sisterhood is Powerful.* New York: Vintage.

Mormino, Gary, and George Pozzetta. 1987. *The Immigrant World of Ybor City: Italians and Their Latin Neighbors.* Urbana: University of Illinois Press.

Morrison, Glenda Eileen. 1978. *Women's Participation in the 1928 Presidential Campaign.* Unpublished doctoral dissertation, University of Kansas.

Moskowitz, Belle L. 1930. "Junior Politics and Politicians." *Saturday Evening Post* 203:6–7.

Moyer-Wing, Alice C. 1928. "The Vote: Our First Comeback." *Scribner's,* 84,259–264.

Mueller, Carol McClurg. 1976. "Rancorous Conflict and Opposition to the ERA." Paper presented at the American Sociological Association meeting, New York, August.

————. 1981. "Women's Issues and the Search for a New Religious Right: A Belief Systems Analysis, 1972–1980." Paper presented at the American Political Science Association meeting, New York, September.

————. 1986. "Nurturance and Mastery: Competing Qualifications for Women's Access to High Public Office?" In Gwen Moore and Glenna Spitze, eds., *Research in Politics and Society: A Research Annual.* Greenwich, CT: JAI Press.

————. 1987. "The Empowerment of Women: Polling and the Women's Voting Bloc." In Carol McClurg Mueller, ed., *The Politics of the Gender Gap: The Social Construction of Political Influence.* Beverly Hills, CA: Sage.

Muñiz, José. 1969. *The Ybor City Story*. Tampa: Tampa Tribune Press.

Myres, Sandra L. 1982. *Westering Women and the Frontier Experience, 1800–1915*. Albuquerque: University of New Mexico Press.

Nagi, Saad Z. 1969. *Disability and Rehabilitation: Legal, Clinical, and Self-Concepts and Measurement*. Columbus: Ohio State University Press.

National Conference of Commissioners on Uniform State Laws. 1970. *Handbook of the National Conference of Commissioners on Uniform State Laws and Proceedings of the Annual Conference Meeting*. Chicago: National Conference of Commissioners on Uniform State Laws.

Nelson, Barbara J. 1979. "Clients and Bureaucracies: Applicant Evaluations of Public Human Service and Benefit Programs." Paper presented at the American Political Science Association meeting, New York.

———. 1981. "Client Evaluations of Social Programs." In Charles T. Goodsell, ed., *The Public Encounter: Where State and Citizen Meet*. Bloomington: Indiana University Press.

———. 1984. "Women's Poverty and Women's Citizenship: Some Political Consequences of Economic Marginality." *Signs: Journal of Women in Culture and Society* 10:209–231.

———. 1985. "Family Politics and Policy in the United States and Western Europe." *Comparative Politics* 17:351–371.

Nelson, Candace, and Marta Tienda. 1985. "The Structuring of Hispanic Ethnicity: Historical and Contemporary Perspectives." *Ethnic and Racial Studies* 8:49–74.

Nesbitt, Florence. 1923. *Standards of Public Aid to Children in Their Own Homes*. Washington, DC: U.S. Department of Labor, Children's Bureau, Bureau Publication no. 118.

Neverdon-Morton, Cynthia. 1978. "The Black Woman's Struggle for Equality in the South, 1895–1925." In Sharon Harley and Rosalyn Terborg-Penn, eds. *The Afro-American Woman: Struggles and Images*. Port Washington, NY: Kennikat Press.

———. 1989. *Afro-American Women of the South and the Advancement of the Race*. Knoxville: University of Tennessee Press.

New York Joint Legislative Committee on Matrimonial and Family Law. 1965. Transcript of Public Hearings, October–December.

New York Red Book, 1966–1967. Albany: Williams Press.

Newell, Margaretta. 1930. "Must Women Fight in Politics?" *Woman's Journal*, January:10–11, 34–35.

Nichols, Carole. 1983. *Votes and More for Women: Suffrage and After in Connecticut*. New York: Haworth Press.

Nimmons, Julius F. 1981. "Social Reform and Moral Uplift in the Black Community, 1890–1910: Social Settlements, Temperance and Social Purity." Unpublished doctoral dissertation, Harvard University.

Nordlinger, Eric. 1981. *On the Autonomy of the Democratic State*. Cambridge, MA: Harvard University Press.

Nuez Gonzalez, Ada de la. 1978. *Mujeres en Revolucion*. Havana: Editorial de Ciéncias Sociales.

O'Connor, Karen. 1980. *Women's Organizations' Use of the Courts.* Lexington, MA: Heath.

Odegard, Peter. 1928. *Pressure Politics: The Story of the Anti-Saloon League.* New York: Columbia University Press.

Offe, Claus. 1984. "Social Policy and the Theory of the State." In John Keane, ed., *Claus Offe: Contradictions of the Welfare State.* Cambridge, MA: MIT Press.

Ogburn, William F., and Inez Goltra. 1919. "How Women Vote: A Study of an Election in Portland, Oregon." *Political Science Quarterly* 34:413–433.

Olsen, Marvin E. 1972. "Social Participation and Voting Turnout: A Multivariate Analysis." *American Sociological Review* 37:317–332.

———. 1982. *Participatory Pluralism: Political Participation and Influence in the United States and Sweden.* Chicago: Nelson-Hall.

Olson, Floyd B. 1934. *A Primer on Unemployment Insurance.* St. Paul: Minnesota Historical Society.

Olson, Mancur. 1971 [1965]. *The Logic of Collective Action.* Cambridge, MA: Harvard University Press.

O'Neill, William L. 1969. *Everyone Was Brave: The History of Feminism in America.* Chicago: Quadrangle Books.

———. 1975. *The Progressive Years: America Comes of Age.* New York: Dodd, Mead.

Orloff, Ann Shola, and Theda Skocpol. 1984. "Why Not Equal Protection? Explaining the Politics of Public Social Spending in Britain, 1900–1911, and in the United States, 1880s–1920." *American Sociological Review* 49:726–750.

Painter, Nell Irvin. 1987. *Standing at Armageddon: The United States, 1877–1919.* New York: Norton.

Palley, Marian Lief. 1987. "The Women's Movement in Recent American Politics." In Sara E. Rix, ed., *The American Woman—1987–88.* New York: Norton.

Palys, T. S. 1986. "Testing the Common Wisdom: The Social Content of Video Pornography." *Canadian Psychology/Psychologie Canadienne* 27:22–35.

Papachristou, Judith. 1985. *Bibliography in the History of Women in the Progressive Era.* Bronxville, NY: Sarah Lawrence College.

Pardo, Thomas C. 1979. *The NWP Papers, 1913–1974: A Guide to the Microfilm Edition.* Stanford: Microfilm Corporation of America.

Park, Maud Wood. 1960. *Front Door Lobby.* Edna Stantial, ed. Boston: Beacon Press.

Parrilla Cruz, Carmen E. 1984. "Coming into Being Among Cuban Women." Unpublished master's thesis, New School for Social Research.

Pateman, Carol. 1970. *Participation and Democratic Theory.* Cambridge and New York: Cambridge University Press.

Patterson, James T. 1969. *The New Deal and the States: Federalism in Transition.* Princeton, NJ: Princeton University Press.

Paul, Alice. 1972–1973. "Conversations: Woman Suffrage and the ERA." Oral history interviews with Amelia R. Fry. Berkeley: Bancroft Library, University of California.

Peattie, Lisa, and Martin Rein. 1983. *Women's Claims: A Study in Political Economy.* New York: Oxford University Press.

Pérez, Louis A., Jr. 1983. *Cuba Between Empires, 1878–1902*. Pittsburgh: University of Pittsburgh Press.

Perkins, Jerry. 1986. "Political Ambition Among Black and White Women: An Intragender Test of the Socialization Model." *Women and Politics* 6:27–40.

Petchesky, Rosalind Pollack. 1984. *Abortion and Woman's Choice: The State, Sexuality, and Reproductive Freedom*. Boston: Northeastern University Press.

Peterson, Mark A., and Jack L. Walker. 1985. "The Impact of the First Reagan Administration on the National Interest Group System." Paper presented at the American Political Science Association annual meeting.

Pheneger, Grace A. 1966. "The Correlation Between Religious Fundamentalism and Political Ultra-Conservatism." Unpublished master's thesis, Bowling Green State University.

Piven, Frances Fox, and Richard Cloward. 1977. *Poor People's Movements: Why They Succeed, How They Fail*. New York: Vintage Books.

Poole, K. T., and L. H. Zeigler. 1981. "The Diffusion of Feminist Ideology." *Political Behavior* 3:229–256.

———. 1985. *Women, Public Opinion, and Politics: The Changing Political Attitudes of American Women*. New York: Longman.

Portes, Alejandro. 1987. *Sociological Perspectives* 30:340–372.

———, and Robert L. Bach. 1985. *Latin Journey: Cuban and Mexican Immigrants in the United States*. Berkeley: University of California Press.

Pratt, Norma Fain. 1978. "Transitions in Judaism: The Jewish American Woman Through the 1930s." In Janet James, ed., *Women in American Religion*. Philadelphia: University of Pennsylvania Press.

President's Commission on the Status of Women. 1963. *American Women: Report of the President's Commission on the Status of Women*. Washington, DC: U.S. Government Printing Office.

President's Committee on Social Trends. 1934. *Recent Social Trends*. New York: McGraw-Hill.

Price, David E. 1984. *Bringing Back the Parties*. Washington, DC: Congressional Quarterly.

Proceedings of the Conference on the Care of Dependent Children. 1909. S. doc. 721, Washington, DC: U.S. Government Printing Office.

Przeworski, Adam. 1980. "Maternal Interests, Class Compromise and the Transition to Socialism." *Politics and Society* 10:125–153.

Purcell, Edward A., Jr. 1973. *The Crisis of Democratic Theory*. Lexington: University Press of Kentucky.

Quadagno, Jill. 1984. "Welfare Capitalism and the Social Security Act of 1935." *American Sociological Review* 49:632–647.

Radl, Shirley Rogers. 1983. *The Invisible Woman: Target of the Religious New Right*. New York: Delacorte Press.

Raines, Howell. 1977. *My Soul Is Rested: Movement Days in the Deep South Remembered*. New York: Putnam.

Randall, Vicky. 1987. *Women and Politics: An International Perspective*. Chicago: University of Chicago Press.

Ransom, Roger L., and Richard Sutch. 1977. *One Kind of Freedom: The Economic Consequences of Emancipation.* Cambridge and New York: Cambridge University Press.

Rapp, Rayna. 1982. "Family and Class in Contemporary America: Notes Toward an Understanding of Ideology." In Barrie Thorne and Marilyn Yalom, eds., *Rethinking the Family.* New York: Longman.

Rawalt, Marguerite. 1983. "The Equal Rights Amendment." In Irene Tinker, ed., *Women in Washington: Advocates for Public Policy.* Beverly Hills, CA: Sage.

Reagon, Bernice Johnson. 1982. "My Black Mothers and Sisters, or On Beginning a Cultural Autobiography." *Feminist Studies* 8:81–96.

Reed, James. 1984 [1978]. *The Birth Control Movement and American Society: From Private Vice to Public Virtue.* Princeton, NJ: Princeton University Press.

Reed, Ruth. 1920. "The Negro Women of Gainesville, Georgia." Phelps-Stokes Fellowship Fund Study, no. 6. Athens: University of Georgia.

Reuter, Peter. 1986. "The Social Costs of the Demand for Quantification." *Journal of Policy Analysis and Management* 5:807–812.

Rice, Stuart D., and Malcolm M. Willey. 1924a. "American Women's Ineffective Use of the Vote." *Current History* 20:641–647.

———. 1924b. "A Sex Cleavage in the Presidential Election of 1920." *Journal of the American Statistical Association* 19:519–520.

Robbe-Grillet, Alain. 1985. "Les dernières nouvelles du sexe: mefions-nous de l'amour." *Le Nouvel Observateur,* June 27,44–45.

Roberson, Nellie. 1922–1923. "The Organized Work of Women in One State." *Journal of Social Forces* 1:50–55, 173–177, 613–615.

Robinson, Ernest L. 1928. *History of Hillsborough County, Florida.* St. Augustine: Record Company Printers.

Rodgers, Daniel T. 1977. "Tradition, Modernity, and the American Industrial Worker: Reflections and Critique." *Journal of Interdisciplinary History* 7:655–682.

———. 1982. "In Search of Progressivism." *Reviews in American History* 10:113–132.

Rokkan, Stein. 1970. "The Mobilization of the Periphery: Data on Turnout, Party Membership and Candidate Recruitment in Norway." In Stein Rokkan, *Citizens, Elections, Parties.* New York: McKay.

Rosaldo, Michelle. 1980. "The Use and Abuse of Anthropology: Reflections on Feminism and Cross-Cultural Understanding." *Signs: Journal of Women in Culture and Society* 5:389–417.

Rosenberg, Rosalind. 1982. *Beyond Separate Spheres: Intellectual Roots of Modern Feminism.* New Haven: Yale University Press.

Rosengarten, Theodore. 1974. *All God's Dangers: The Life of Nate Shaw.* New York: Random House.

Rosenthal, Naomi, et al. 1985. "Social Movements and Network Analysis: A Case Study of Nineteenth-Century Women's Reform in New York State." *American Journal of Sociology* 90:1022–1054.

Ross, Ellen. 1983. "Survival Networks: Women's Neighborhood Sharing in London Before World War I." *History Workshop Journal* 15:4–27.

Rothman, Sheila M. 1978. *Woman's Proper Place*. New York: Basic Books.

Rothschild, Mary Aiken. 1982. *A Case of Black and White: Northern Volunteers and the Southern Freedom Summers, 1964–65*. Westport, CT: Greenwood Press.

Rouse, Jacqueline Anne. 1983. "Lugenia D. Burns Hope: A Black Female Reformer in the South, 1871–1947." Unpublished doctoral dissertation, Emory University.

Rowbotham, Sheila. 1980. *Hidden from History*. London: Penguin.

————. 1982. "The Trouble with 'Patriarchy.' " In Mary Evans, ed., *The Woman Question: Readings on the Subordination of Women*. Oxford: Fontana.

Roydhouse, Marion W. 1980. "The Universal Sisterhood of Women: Women and Labor Reform in North Carolina, 1900–1932." Unpublished doctoral dissertation, Duke University.

Rubinow, I. M. 1913. *Social Insurance: With Special Reference to American Conditions*. New York: Holt.

Ruddick, Sara. 1980. "Maternal Thinking." *Feminist Studies* 6:342–367.

Ruggie, Mary. 1984. *The State and Working Women: A Comparative Study of Britain and Sweden*. Princeton, NJ: Princeton University Press.

Rupp, Leila. 1982. "The Survival of American Feminism: The Women's Movement in the Postwar Period." In Robert Bremner and Gary Reichard, eds., *Reshaping America: Society and Institutions, 1945–1960*. Columbus: Ohio State University Press.

————, and Verta Taylor. 1987. *Survival in the Doldrums: The American Women's Rights Movement, 1945 to the 1960s*. New York: Oxford University Press.

Rusher, William A. 1982. "The New Right: Past and Prospects." In Robert W. Whitaker, ed., *The New Right Papers*. New York: St. Martin's Press.

Russ, Joanna. 1985. *Magic Mommas, Trembling Sisters, Puritans and Perverts*. New York: Crossing Press.

Russell, Charles Edward. 1924. "Is Woman Suffrage a Failure?" *Century Magazine* 35:730.

Russell, Diana E. H. 1980. "Pornography and Violence: What Does the New Research Say?" In Laura Lederer, ed., *Take Back the Night*. New York: Morrow.

Ryan, Mary P. 1979. "The Power of Women's Networks: A Case Study of Female Moral Reform in Antebellum America." *Feminist Studies* 5:66–85.

————. 1981. *Cradle of the Middle Class: The Family in Oneida County, New York, 1790–1865*. Cambridge and New York: Cambridge University Press.

Sacks, Karen. 1985. "How Women Organized." Paper presented at the Society for the Study of Social Problems annual meeting, Washington.

————. 1987. *Caring by the Hour: Women, Work and Organizing at Duke Medical Center*. Urbana: University of Illinois Press.

St. Julien, Milly. 1986. " 'We Are Our Neighbors' Keepers': The Role of Women in Tampa's Benevolent Organizations, 1895–1915." Unpublished paper in possession of Nancy Hewitt.

Salisbury, Robert H. 1984. "Interest Representation: The Dominance of Institutions." *American Political Science Review* 78:64–76.

Sapiro, Virginia. 1979. "Women's Studies and Political Conflict." In Julia Sherman and Evelyn Beck, eds., *The Prism of Sex: Essays in the Sociology of Knowledge*. Madison: University of Wisconsin Press.

———. 1983. *The Political Integration of Women: Roles, Socialization, and Politics*. Urbana: University of Illinois Press.

———. 1984. "Women, Citizenship, and Nationality: Immigration and Naturalization Policies in the United States." *Politics and Society* 13:1–26.

———. 1986. "The Gender Basis of American Social Policy." *Political Science Quarterly* 101:221–238.

Sayles, Leonard R., and George Strauss. 1967. *The Local Union*. New York: Harcourt, Brace & World.

Schaffer, Ronald. 1962. "The New York City Woman Suffrage Party, 1910–1919." *New York History* 43:269–287.

Scharf, Lois. 1980. *To Work and to Wed: Female Employment, Feminism and the Great Depression*. Westport, CT: Greenwood Press.

———, and Joan M. Jensen, eds. 1983. *Decades of Discontent*. Westport, CT: Greenwood Press.

Schattschneider, E. E. 1960. *The Semisovereign People*. New York: Holt, Rinehart & Winston.

———. 1969. *Two Hundred Million Americans in Search of Government*. New York: Holt, Rinehart & Winston.

Schirmer, Jennifer. 1982. *The Limits of Reform: Women, Capital and Welfare*. Cambridge, MA: Schenkman.

Schlafly, Phyllis. 1977. *The Power of the Positive Woman*. New York: Jove.

Schlesinger, Arthur M., and E. M. Eriksson. 1924. "The Vanishing Voter." *New Republic* 60:162–167.

Schlozman, Kay Lehman, and John T. Tierney. 1983. "More of the Same: Washington Pressure Group Activity in a Decade of Change." *Journal of Politics* 45:351–377.

———. 1986. *Organized Interests and American Democracy*. New York: Harper & Row.

Schmidt, Alvin J. 1973. *Oligarchy in Fraternal Organizations*. Detroit: Gale Research.

Schmitter, Philippe C., and Gerhard Lehmbruch, eds. 1979. *Trends Towards Corporatist Intermediation*. Beverly Hills, CA: Sage.

Schriftgiesser, Karl. 1951. *The Lobbyists*. Boston: Little, Brown.

Schulman, Joanne, and Valerie Pitt. 1982. "Second Thoughts on Joint Child Custody: Analysis of Legislation and Its Implications for Women and Children." *Golden Gate University Law Review* 12:538–577.

Schuman, Howard; Charlotte Steeh; and Lawrence Bobo. 1985. *Racial Attitudes in America: Trends and Interpretations*. Cambridge, MA: Harvard University Press.

Schwartz, Bonnie Fox. 1984. *The Civil Works Administration, 1933–1934; The Business of Emergency Employment in the New Deal*. Princeton, NJ: Princeton University Press.

Scime, Joy A. 1983. "Section 213 of the 1932 Economy Act: Government Policy,

Working Women, and Feminism." Paper presented at the American Society for Legal History annual convention, Baltimore.

Scott, Anne Firor. 1970. *The Southern Lady: From Pedestal to Politics, 1830–1930*. Chicago: University of Chicago Press.

———. 1984a. "On Seeing and Not Seeing: A Case of Historical Invisibility." *Journal of American History* 71:7–21.

———. 1984b. *Making the Invisible Woman Visible*. Urbana: University of Illinois Press.

———, and Andrew MacKay Scott. 1982. *One Half the People: The Fight for Woman Suffrage*. Urbana: University of Illinois Press.

Scott, Joan W. 1986. "Gender: A Useful Category of Historical Analysis." *American Historical Review* 91:1053–1075.

Scott, William G.; Terence R. Mitchell; and Newman S. Perry. 1981. "Organizational Governance." In Paul C. Nystrom and William H. Starbuck, eds., *Handbook of Organizational Design*. New York: Oxford University Press.

Sears, David O. 1969. "Political Behavior." In Gardner Lindzey and E. Aronson, eds., *Handbook of Social Psychology*, Second ed., vol. 5. Reading, MA: Addison-Wesley.

———. 1983. "The Persistence of Early Political Predispositions: The Roles of Attitude Object and Life Stage." In Ladd Wheeler and Phillip Shaver, eds., *Review of Personality and Social Psychology*, vol. 4. Beverly Hills, CA: Sage.

———. 1986. "Some Uses and Abuses of Structural Variables in Social Psychology." Paper presented at the American Sociological Association meeting, New York.

———, and Jack Citrin. 1985. *Tax Revolt: Something for Nothing in California*. Cambridge, MA: Harvard University Press.

———, and Richard Kosterman. 1985. "The White Response to Jesse Jackson in 1984." Paper presented at the American Psychological Association meeting, Los Angeles, and the American Political Science Association meeting, New Orleans.

Sears, David O., and Carolyn L. Funk. 1990. "Self-Interest in Americans' Political Opinions." In Jane Mansbridge, ed. *Beyond Self-Interest*. Chicago: University of Chicago Press.

Sears, David O.; Leonie Huddy; and Lynitta Schaffer. 1986. "A Schematic Variant of Symbolic Politics Theory, As Applied to Racial and Gender Equality." In R. R. Lau and David O. Sears, eds., *Political Cognition: The 19th Annual Carnegie Symposium on Cognition*. Hillsdale, NJ: Erlbaum.

Sears, David O.; Tom Jessor; and Martin T. Gahart. 1984. "Group Consciousness Among Women: Contrasting Structural and Symbolic Approaches." Paper presented at the Western Psychological Association meeting, Los Angeles.

Sears, David O., and Donald R. Kinder. 1985. "Whites' Opposition to Busing: On Conceptualizing and Operationalizing Group Conflict." *Journal of Personality and Social Psychology* 48:1141–1147.

Sears, David O.; Richard R. Lau; Tom R. Tyler; and Harris M. Allen, Jr. 1980. "Self-Interest vs. Symbolic Politics in Policy Attitudes and Presidential Voting." *American Political Science Review* 74:670–684.

Segner, Paul. 1937. *Minneapolis Unemployed: A Description and Analysis of the Resident Relief Population in the City of Minneapolis, 1900–1937*. Minneapolis: Works Progress Administration.

Seymour, Helen. 1937. *When Clients Organize*. Chicago: Public Welfare Association.

Shafer, Byron E. 1983. *Quiet Revolution*. New York: Russell Sage Foundation.

Shaffer, Robert. 1980. "Women and the Communist Party, U.S.A., 1930–1940." *Socialism Review* 45:73–118.

Shaffer, Stephen D. 1985. "The Evolution of Gender Differences." Paper presented at the American Political Science Association annual meeting, New Orleans.

Shalev, Michael. 1983. "The Social Democratic Model and Beyond: Two 'Generations' of Comparative Research on the Welfare State." In Richard F. Tomasson, ed., *Comparative Social Research: The Welfare State, 1883–1983*, vol. 6. Greenwich, CT: JAI Press.

Shankman, Arnold. 1981. "Dorothy Tilly and the Fellowship of the Concerned." In Walter J. Fraser, Jr., and Winifred B. Moore, eds., *From the Old South to the New: Essays on the Transitional South*. Westport, CT: Greenwood Press.

Shapiro, Robert Y., and Harprett Mahajan. 1986. "Gender Differences in Policy Preferences: A Summary of Trends from the 1960s to the 1980s." *Public Opinion Quarterly* 50:42–61.

Sheffield, Ada E. 1915. "Administration of the Mothers' Aid Law in Massachusetts." In Edna Bullock, ed., *Selected Articles on Mothers' Pensions*. White Plains and New York: Wilson.

Sheinfeld, Lois P. 1984. "Banning Porn: The New Censorship." *Nation*, September 8,174–175.

Shepher, Joseph, and Judith Reisman. 1985. "Pornography: A Sociobiological Attempt at Understanding." *Ethology and Sociobiology* 6:103–114.

Silva, Ruth C. 1962. *Rum, Religion and Votes: 1928 Re-Examined*. University Park: Pennsylvania State University Press.

Sims, Anastatia. 1982. "Sisterhoods of Service: Women's Clubs and Methodist Women's Missionary Societies in North Carolina, 1890–1930." In Rosemary Skinner Keller, Louise L. Queen, and Hilah F. Thomas, eds., *Women in New Worlds: Historical Perspectives on the Wesleyan Tradition*. Nashville: Abingdon.

Sitkoff, Harvard. 1981. *The Struggle for Black Equality, 1954–1980*. New York: Hill & Wang.

Sklar, Kathryn Kish. 1985. "Hull House in the 1890s: A Community of Women Reformers." *Signs: Journal of Women in Culture and Society* 10:658–677.

Skocpol, Theda. 1980. "Political Response to Capitalist Crisis: Neo-Marxist Theories of the State and the Case of the New Deal." *Politics and Society* 10:155–202.

———, and Margaret Somers. 1980. "The Uses of Comparative History in Macrosocial Inquiry." *Comparative Studies in Society and History* 22:174–197.

Skocpol, Theda, and Kenneth Finegold. 1982. "State Capacity and Economic Intervention in the Early New Deal." *Political Science Quarterly* 97:255–278.

Skocpol, Theda, and John Ikenberry. 1983. "The Political Formation of the American Welfare State in Historical and Comparative Perspective." In Richard F. Tomasson, ed., *Comparative Social Research: The Welfare State, 1883–1983*, vol. 6. Greenwich, CT: JAI Press.

———. 1985. "Bringing the State Back In: Strategies of Analysis in Current Research." In Peter B. Evans, Dietrich Rueschmeyer, and Theda Skocpol, eds., *Bringing the State Back In*. Cambridge: Cambridge University Press.

Skowronek, Stephen. 1982. *Building a New American State: The Expansion of National Administrative Capacities, 1877–1920s*. Cambridge and New York: Cambridge University Press.

Smith, Adam. 1966. *The Theory of Moral Sentiments*. New York: Kelley.

Smith, Bonnie G. 1984. "The Contribution of Women to Modern Historiography in Great Britain, France, and the United States." *American Historical Review* 89:709–732.

Smith, Judith E. 1985. *Family Connections: A History of Italian and Jewish Immigrant Lives in Providence, Rhode Island, 1900–1940*. Albany: State University of New York Press.

Smith, Lillian. 1949. *Killers of the Dream*. New York: Norton.

Smith, Richard E. 1984. "Advocacy, Interpretation, and Influence in the U.S. Congress." *American Political Science Review* 78:44–63.

Smith, Tom W. 1984. "The Polls: Gender and Attitudes Toward Violence." *Public Opinion Quarterly* 48:384–396.

Smith-Rosenberg, Carroll. 1971a. *Religion and the Rise of the City: The New York City Mission Movement, 1812–1870*. Ithaca: Cornell University Press.

———. 1971b. "Beauty, the Beast, and the Militant Woman: A Case Study in Sex Roles and Social Stress in Jacksonian America." *American Quarterly* 23:562–584.

Snitow, Ann. 1985. "Retrenchment versus Transformation: The Politics of the Antipornography Movement." In Varda Burstyn, ed., *Women Against Censorship*. Vancouver and Toronto: McIntyre.

———; Christine Stansell; and Sharon Thompson, eds. 1983. *Powers of Desire: The Politics of Sexuality*. New York: Monthly Review Press.

Sochen, June. 1981. *Consecrate Each Day: The Public Lives of Jewish American Women, 1880–1980*. Albany: State University of New York Press.

Solomon, Barbara Miller. 1985. *In the Company of Educated Women: A History of Women and Higher Education in America*. New Haven: Yale University Press.

Soule, John W., and Wilma E. McGrath. 1977. "A Comparative Study of Male-Female Attitudes at Citizen and Elite Levels." In Marianne Githens and Jewell L. Prestage, eds., *A Portrait of Marginality*. New York: Longman.

Sourcebook for the 12th Annual Conference on Women and the Law. 1981. "Penis as Weapon."

South Carolina Code of Laws. 1985. Rochester, NY: Lawyers Co-Operative.

Spretnak, Charlene. 1982. "The Politics of Women's Spirituality." In Charlene Spretnak, ed., *The Politics of Women's Spirituality: Essays in the Rise of Spiritual Power Within the Feminist Movement*. Garden City, NY: Anchor.

Stacey, Judith. 1983. "The New Conservative Feminism." *Feminist Studies* 9:559–583.

Stageberg, Susie W. 1938. "As a Woman Sees It." *Minnesota Leader,* March 12.

———. 1940. "The Contribution of Women to the Farmer-Labor Party." Manuscript, September 1. Susie Stageberg Papers, box 2, Minnesota Historical Society.

Stanton, Elizabeth Cady, and Susan B. Anthony. 1981. *Correspondence, Writings, Speeches.* Ellen Carol Du Bois, ed. New York: Schocken Books.

Starr, Karen. 1983. "Fighting for the Future: Farm Women of the Nonpartisan League." *Minnesota History* 48:255–262.

Steffy, Joan Marie. 1975. "The Cuban Immigrants of Tampa, Florida, 1886–1898." Unpublished master's thesis, University of South Florida, Tampa.

Steiner, Gilbert. 1976. *The Children's Cause.* Washington, DC: Brookings Institution.

———. 1985. *Constitutional Inequality.* Washington, DC: Brookings Institution.

Steinson, Barbara J. 1982. *American Women's Activism in World War I.* New York: Garland.

Stevens, Doris. 1920. *Jailed for Freedom.* New York: Liveright.

Stevenson, Louise L. 1979. "Women Anti-Suffragists in the 1915 Massachusetts Campaign." *New England Quarterly* 52:80–93.

Stinchcombe, Arthur L. 1965. "Social Structure and Organizations." In James G. March, ed., *Handbook of Organizations.* Chicago: Rand McNally.

Stokes, Allen H., Jr. 1977. "Black and White Labor and the Development of the Southern Textile Industry, 1800–1920." Unpublished doctoral dissertation, University of South Carolina.

Strom, Sharon Hartman. 1975. "Leadership and Tactics in the American Woman Suffrage Movement: A New Perspective from Massachusetts." *Journal of American History* 62:296–315.

———. 1983. "Challenging 'Women's Place': Feminism, the Left, and Industrial Unionism in the 1930s." *Feminist Studies* 9:359–386.

Sumner, Helen L. 1909. *Equal Suffrage.* New York: Harper.

Swain, Martha H. 1983. "The Public Role of Southern Women." In Joanne V. Hawks and Sheila Skemp, eds., *Sex, Race, and the Role of Women in the South.* Jackson: University Press of Mississippi.

Szasz, Ferenc Morton. 1982. *The Divided Mind of Protestant America, 1880–1920.* Tuscaloosa: University of Alabama Press.

Taggard, Genevieve, ed. 1925. *May Days: An Anthology of Verse from Masses—Liberator.* New York: Boni & Liveright.

Tampa, City of. 1893. *The Gate-to-the-Gulf (Tampa) City Directory and Hillsborough County Guide.* Tampa: Clarke.

Tannebaum, Arnold. 1960. "Control Structures and Effectiveness in a Voluntary Organization." Typescript draft, League of Women Voters papers, Library of Congress.

———. 1968. *Control in Organizations.* New York: McGraw-Hill.

Task Force on Family Law and Policy. 1968. *Report.* Washington, DC: Citizen's Advisory Council on the Status of Women.

Taylor, A. Elizabeth. 1961. "The Woman Suffrage Movement in North Carolina." *North Carolina Historical Review* 38:45–62, 173–189.

Taylor, Paul Craig. 1966. *The Entrance of Women into Party Politics: The 1920s.*
Unpublished doctoral dissertation, Harvard University.

Taylor, Paul S. 1980. "Mexican Women in Los Angeles Industry in 1928." *Aztlan:
International Journal of Chicano Studies Research* 11:99–129.

Tax, Meredith. 1980. *The Rising of the Women: Feminist Solidarity and Class Conflict,
1880–1917.* New York: Monthly Review Press.

Tedin, Kent L.; David W. Brady; Mary E. Buxton; Barbara M. Gorman; and Judy
L. Thompson. 1977. "Social Background and Political Differences Between
Pro- and Anti-ERA Activists." *American Politics Quarterly* 5:395–408.

Tedrow, Lucky, and E. R. Mahoney. 1979. "Trends in Attitudes Toward Abortion: 1972–1976." *Public Opinion Quarterly* 43:181–189.

Tentler, Leslie Woodcock. 1979. *Wage-Earning Women: Industrial Work and Family
Life in the United States, 1900–1930.* New York: Oxford University Press.

Terborg-Penn, Rosalyn M. 1977. "Afro-Americans in the Struggle for Woman
Suffrage." Unpublished doctoral dissertation, Howard University.

———. 1978. "Discrimination against Afro-American Women in the Women's
Movement, 1830–1920." In Sharon Harley and Rosalyn Terborg-Penn, eds.,
The Afro-American Woman: Struggles and Images. Port Washington, NY: Ken-
nikat Press.

———. 1983. "Discontented Black Feminists: Prelude and Postscript to the Passage of the Nineteenth Amendment." In Lois Scharf and Joan M. Jensen, eds.,
Decades of Discontent: The Women's Movement, 1920–1940. Westport, CT: Greenwood Press.

———. 1985. "Survival Strategies Among African-American Women Workers: A
Continuing Process." Ruth Milkman, ed., *Women, Work, and Protest: A Century
of Women's Labor History.* Boston: Routledge & Kegan Paul.

Terrell, Mary Church. 1968. *A Colored Woman in a White World.* Washington, DC:
National Association of Colored Women's Clubs.

Terrill, Tom E., and Jerrald Hirsch. 1978. *Such as Us: Southern Voices of the Thirties.*
New York: Norton.

Thelen, David P. 1969. "Social Tensions and the Origins of Progressivism."
Journal of American History 56:323–341.

Thompson, Laura A. 1919. See U.S. Department of Labor, Children's
Bureau.

Thorne, Barrie, and Marilyn Yalom, eds. 1982. *Rethinking the Family, Some Feminist Questions.* New York: Longman.

Thornton, Arland; Duane F. Alwin; and D. Camburn. 1983. "Causes and Consequences of Sex-Role Attitudes and Attitude Change." *American Sociological
Review* 48:211–217.

Thornton, Arland, and Deborah Freedman. 1979. "Changes in the Sex-Role
Attitudes of Women, 1962–77: Evidence from a Panel Study." *American
Sociological Review* 44:831–842.

Tilly, Charles, ed. 1975. *The Formation of National States in Western Europe.* Princeton, NJ: Princeton University Press.

————. 1981. "Introduction." In Louise A. Tilly and Charles Tilly, eds. *Class Conflict and Collective Action*. Beverly Hills, CA: Sage.

————. 1984. *Big Structures, Large Processes, Huge Comparisons*. New York: Russell Sage Foundation.

————. 1986. "European Violence and Collective Action since 1700." *Social Research* 53:159–184.

Tilly, Louise A. 1986. "Paths of Proletarianization: Organization of Production, Sexual Division of Labor, and Women's Collective Action." In Eleanor Leacock and Helen I. Safa, eds., *Women's Work*. South Hadley, MA: Bergin & Garvey.

————, and Joan W. Scott. 1978. *Women, Work, and Family*. New York: Holt, Rinehart & Winston.

Tingsten, Herbert. 1937. *Political Behavior: Studies in Election Statistics*. London: King.

Tinker, Irene, ed. 1983. *Women in Washington*. Beverly Hills, CA: Sage.

Tishler, Hace Sorel. 1971. *Self-Reliance and Social Security, 1870–1917*. Port Washington, NY: Kennikat Press.

Tocqueville, Alexis de. 1947 [1835–1840]. *Democracy in America*, abridged ed. New York and London: Oxford University Press.

Tomasson, Richard F., ed. 1983. *Comparative Social Research: The Welfare State, 1883–1983*. Greenwich, CT: JAI Press.

Tormey, Judith. 1976. "Exploitation, Oppression, and Self-Sacrifice." In Carol C. Gould and Marx W. Wartofsky, eds., *Women and Philosophy: Toward a Theory of Liberation*. New York: Putnam.

Trattner, Walter I. 1974. *From Poor Law to Welfare State*. New York: Free Press.

Tribe, Laurence H. 1978. *American Constitutional Law*. Mineola, NY: Foundation Press.

Trow, Martin A. 1957. "Right-Wing Radicalism and Political Intolerance: A Study of Support of McCarthy in a New England Town." Unpublished doctoral dissertation, Columbia University.

Truman, David B. 1952. *The Governmental Process*. New York: Knopf.

Tselos, George. 1970. "The Labor Movement in Minneapolis in the 1930s." Unpublished doctoral dissertation, University of Minnesota.

Turley, Donna. 1986. "The Feminist Debate on Pornography: An Unorthodox Interpretation." *Socialist Review* 16:81–96.

Uhlaner, Carole, and Kay L. Schlozman. 1986. "Candidate Gender and Congressional Campaign Receipts." *Journal of Politics* 48:30–50.

U.S. Bureau of the Census. 1923. *Statistical Abstract of the United States, 1922*. Washington, DC: U.S. Government Printing Office.

————. 1970. *Historical Statistics of the United States: Colonial Times to 1970*. Washington, DC: U.S. Government Printing Office.

————. 1980. *Census of Population*.

————. 1985. *Statistical Abstract of the United States, 1985*. Washington, DC: U.S. Government Printing Office.

————. 1986a. *Child Support and Alimony: 1983*. Current Population Reports, Special Studies, series P-23, no. 148.

———. 1986b. *Statistical Abstract of the United States, 1986*. Washington, DC: U.S. Government Printing Office.

U.S. Department of Commerce. 1923. *Statistical Abstract of the U.S.: 1922*. Washington, DC: U.S. Government Printing Office.

U.S. Department of Commerce and Labor. 1910. *Statistical Abstract of the United States, 1909*. Washington, DC: U.S. Government Printing Office.

U.S. Department of Labor. 1910. *Report on Condition of Women and Child Wage Earners in the United States in Cotton Textile Industry*. Washington, DC: U.S. Government Printing Office.

———. 1980. *Employment in Perspective: Working Women*. Washington, DC: U.S. Government Printing Office.

———. 1987. *Employment in Perspective: Women in the Labor Force*. Washington, DC: U.S. Government Printing Office.

———, Bureau of Labor Statistics. 1917. *Proceedings of the Third Annual Meeting of the International Association of Industrial Accident Boards and Commissions*. Washington, DC: U.S. Government Printing Office.

———. 1979. *Employment and Earnings, United States, 1909–1978*. Washington, DC: U.S. Government Printing Office.

———. 1984. *Supplement to Employment and Earnings, United States, 1909–1978*. Washington, DC: U.S. Government Printing Office.

U.S. Department of Labor, Children's Bureau. 1919. *Laws Relating to "Mothers' Pensions" in the United States, Canada, Denmark, and New Zealand*. Washington, DC: U.S. Government Printing Office.

———. 1933. *Mothers' Aid, 1931*. Washington, DC: U.S. Government Printing Office.

U.S. Department of Labor, Women's Bureau. 1928. *The Effects of Labor Legislation upon the Employment Opportunities of Women*. Washington, DC: U.S. Government Printing Office.

———. 1935. *Chronological Development of Labor Legislation for Women in the United States*. Bulletin no. 66-II. Washington, DC: U.S. Government Printing Office.

———. 1983. *The 1983 Handbook on Women Workers*. Washington, DC: U.S. Government Printing Office.

U.S. Federal Emergency Relief Administration. 1934. *Unemployment Relief Census, October 1933*. Washington, DC: U.S. Government Printing Office.

U.S. House of Representatives. 1940. *Investigation and Study of the Works Progress Administration, Hearings Before a Subcommittee*. 75th Cong., 3rd sess. Washington, DC: U.S. Government Printing Office.

U.S. Senate. 1909. *Proceedings of the Conference on the Care of Dependent Children*. Senate Document no. 721. Washington, DC: U.S. Government Printing Office.

———. 1938. *Hearings on the Works Progress Administration*. Washington, DC: U.S. Government Printing Office.

Valelly, Richard Martin. 1984. "State-Level Radicalism and the Nationalization of American Politics: The Case of the Minnesota Farmer Labor Party." Unpublished doctoral dissertation, Harvard University.

Vance, Carole S. 1982. *Diary of a Conference on Sexuality: The Scholar and the*

Feminist, Toward a Politics of Sexuality. New York: Barnard Women's Center and Faculty Press.

———. 1984. *Pleasure and Danger: Exploring Female Sexuality.* Boston: Routledge & Kegan Paul.

Vandepol, Ann. 1982. "Dependent Children, Child Custody, and Mothers' Pensions." *Social Problems* 29:221–235.

Van Kleeck, Mary. 1934. "The Workers' Unemployment and Pension Bill." *New Republic,* December 12,121–124.

Verba, Sidney; Richard A. Brody; Edward B. Parker; Norman H. Nie; Nelson W. Polsby; Paul Ekman; and Gordon S. Black. 1967. "Public Opinion and the War in Vietnam." *American Political Science Review* 61:317–333.

Verba, Sidney, and Norman H. Nie. 1987. *Participation in America: Political Democracy and Social Equality.* New York: Harper & Row.

———; and Jae-on Kim. 1978. *Participation and Political Equality: A Seven-Nation Study.* New York: Cambridge University Press.

Verba, Sidney, and Gary Orren. 1985. *Equality in America: The View from the Top.* Cambridge, MA: Harvard University Press.

Vines, Kenneth, and Henry Robert Glick. 1967. "The Impact of Universal Suffrage: A Comparison of Popular and Property Suffrage." *American Political Science Review* 61:1078–1087.

Wagner, Mary Jo. 1986. "Farms, Families, and Reform: Women in the Farmers' Alliance and Populist Party." Unpublished doctoral dissertation, University of Oregon.

Walker, Jack L. 1983. "The Origins and Maintenance of Interest Groups in America." *American Political Science Review* 77:390–406.

Walkowitz, Daniel J. 1978. *Worker City, Company Town: Iron and Cotton Worker Protest in Troy and Cohoes, New York, 1855–1884.* Urbana: University of Illinois Press.

Wall Street Journal. 1986. "Labor Letter," March 25.

Wallerstein, Immanuel. 1954. "McCarthyism and the Conservative." Unpublished master's thesis, Columbia University.

Walton, Hanes. 1975. *Black Republicans: The Politics of the Black and Tans.* Metuchen, NJ: Scarecrow Press.

———. 1985. *Invisible Politics: Black Political Behavior.* Albany: State University of New York Press.

Ware, Susan. 1981. *Beyond Suffrage: Women in the New Deal.* Cambridge, MA: Harvard University Press.

———. 1982. *Holding Their Own: American Women in the 1930s.* Boston: Twayne.

———. 1985. "General Introduction." *Papers of the League of Women Voters, 1918–1974.* Frederick, MD: University Publications of America.

Wedel, Janet Marie. 1975. *The Origins of State Patriarchy During the Progressive Era: A Sociological Study of the Mothers' Aid Movement.* Unpublished doctoral dissertation, Washington University.

Weiner, Lynn. 1985. *From Working Girl to Working Mother: The Female Labor Force in the United States, 1820–1980.* Chapel Hill: University of North Carolina Press.

Weinstein, James. 1968. *The Corporate Ideal in the Liberal State, 1900–1918*. Boston: Beacon Press.

Weiss, Nancy J. 1983. *Farewell to the Party of Lincoln: Black Politics in the Age of FDR*. Princeton, NJ: Princeton University Press.

Weitzman, Lenore J. 1985. *The Divorce Revolution: The Unexpected Social and Economic Consequences for Women and Children in America*. New York: Free Press.

Welch, Susan, and Philip Secret. 1981. "Sex, Race and Political Participation." *Western Political Quarterly* 34:5–16.

Wells, Marguerite M. 1929. "Some Effect of Women Suffrage." *Annals of the American Academy of Political Science* 143:207–216.

———. 1938. "A Portrait of the League of Women Voters at the Age of Eighteen." Washington, DC: League of Women Voters.

Welter, Barbara. 1976. "The Cult of True Womanhood: 1800–1860." In Barbara Welter, ed., *Dimity Convictions*. Athens: Ohio University Press.

Werner, Emmy E. 1968. "Women in State Legislatures." *Western Political Quarterly* 21:42.

Wertheimer, Barbara Meyer. 1977. *We Were There: The Story of Working Women in America*. New York: Pantheon Books.

———, and Anne Nelson. 1975. *Trade Union Women: A Study of Their Participation in New York City Locals*. New York: Praeger.

Wesley, Charles H. 1984. *The History of the National Association of Colored Women's Clubs, Inc.: A Legacy of Service*. Washington, DC: National Association of Colored Women's Clubs.

Westwood, Sallie. 1984. *All Day, Every Day: Factory and Family in the Making of Women's Lives*. Urbana: University of Illinois Press.

Wheaton, Anne Williams. 1929. "The Woman Voter." *The Woman's Journal*, February:28.

Wiebe, Robert H. 1967. *The Search for Order: 1877–1920*. New York: Hill & Wang.

Wiener, Jonathan. 1978. *Social Origins of the New South: Alabama, 1860–1885*. Baton Rouge: Louisiana State University Press.

Wilensky, Harold L. 1975. *The Welfare State and Equality: Structural and Ideological Roots of Public Expenditures*. Berkeley: University of California Press.

Williamson, Joel. 1984. *The Crucible of Race: Black-White Relations in the American South Since Emancipation*. New York: Oxford University Press.

Wilson, Elizabeth. 1977. *Women and the Welfare State*. London: Tavistock.

Wilson, Graham. 1981. *Interest Groups in the United States*. Oxford: Oxford University Press.

Wilson, James Q. 1960. *Negro Politics*. New York: Free Press.

———. 1973. *Political Organizations*. New York: Basic Books.

———. 1980. "Reagan and the Republican Revival." *Commentary*, 70,25–32.

Wilson, Joan Hoff. 1975. *Herbert Hoover, Forgotten Progressive*. Boston: Little, Brown.

Wilson, K., and T. Orum. 1976. "Mobilizing People for Collective Political Action." *Journal of Political and Military Sociology* 4:187–202.

Wilson, Margaret Gibbons. 1979. *The American Woman in Transition: The Urban Influence, 1879–1920*. Westport, CT: Greenwood Press.

Wise, Leah, and Sue Thrasher. 1980. "The Southern Tenant Farmers' Union." In Marc S. Miller, ed., *Working Lives: The Southern Exposure History of Labor in the South.* New York: Pantheon Books.

Wolfe, Allis Rosenberg. 1975. "Women, Consumerism, and the National Consumers' League in the Progressive Era, 1900–1923." *Labor History* 16:378–392.

Wolfinger, Raymond et al. 1969. "America's Radical Right: Politics and Ideology." In Robert A. Schoenberger, ed., *The American Right Wing: Readings in Political Behavior.* New York: Holt, Rinehart & Winston.

Wolfson, Theresa. 1929. "Trade Union Activities of Women." *Annals of the American Academy of Political Science* 143:130–131.

Wolman, Leo. 1924. *Growth of American Trade Unions, 1880–1923.* New York: National Bureau of Economic Research.

Woloch, Nancy. 1984. *Women and the American Experience.* New York: Knopf.

"Women and Men: Is a Realignment Under Way?" 1982. *Public Opinion,* April-May:21–37.

Wood, James R. 1981. *Legitimate Leadership in Voluntary Organizations.* New Brunswick, NJ: Rutgers University Press.

Wood, Katherine D. 1936. *Urban Workers on Relief, Part 2.* Washington, DC: Works Progress Administration.

Woodward, C. Vann. 1974. *The Strange Career of Jim Crow,* 3rd ed. New York: Oxford University Press.

Wright, Erik O. 1985. *Classes.* London: New Left Books.

Wright, Gavin. 1986. *Old South, New South: Revolutions in the Southern Economy Since the Civil War.* New York: Basic Books.

Wuthnow, Robert. 1973. Religious Commitment and Conservatism: In Quest of an Elusive Relationship." In Charles Y. Glock, ed., *Religion in Sociological Perspective.* Belmont, CA: Wadsworth.

———. 1976. *The Consciousness Reformation.* Berkeley and Los Angeles: University of California Press.

———. 1978. *Experimentation in American Religion.* Berkeley and Los Angeles: University of California Press.

———. 1983. "The Political Rebirth of American Evangelicals." In Robert C. Liebman and Robert Wuthnow, eds., *The New Christian Right.* New York: Aldine.

———. 1987. "American Democracy and the Democratization of American Religion." *Politics and Society* 14:176–185.

———. 1988. *The Restructuring of American Religion: Society and Faith Since World War II.* Princeton, NJ: Princeton University Press.

Young, Iris. 1980. "Socialist Feminism and the Limits of Dual Systems Theory." *Socialist Review* 10:169–188.

Young, Louise M. 1950. *Understanding Politics: A Practical Guide for Women.* New York: Pellegrini & Cudahy.

———. 1976. "Women's Place in American Politics: The Historical Perspective." *Journal of Politics* 38:295–335.

Zaretsky, Eli. 1976. *Capitalism, the Family and Personal Life.* New York: Harper & Row.

————. 1982. "The Place of the Family in the Origins of the Welfare State." In Barrie Thorne and Marilyn Yalom, eds., *Rethinking the Family: Some Feminist Questions.* New York: Longman.

Zelman, Patricia G. 1982. *Women, Work and National Policy: The Kennedy-Johnson Years.* Ann Arbor: UMI Research Press.

Zimmerman, Loretta Ellen. 1964. "Alice Paul and the National Woman's Party, 1912–1920." Unpublished doctoral dissertation, Tulane University.

Zipp, John F., and Eric Plutzer. 1985. "Gender Difference in Voting for Female Candidates: Evidence from the 1982 Election." *Public Opinion Quarterly* 49:179–197.

Name Index

Boldface numbers refer to figures and tables.

Subject Index

Boldface numbers refer to figures and tables.